THE COLOR ENCYCLOPEDIA OF CAPE BULBS

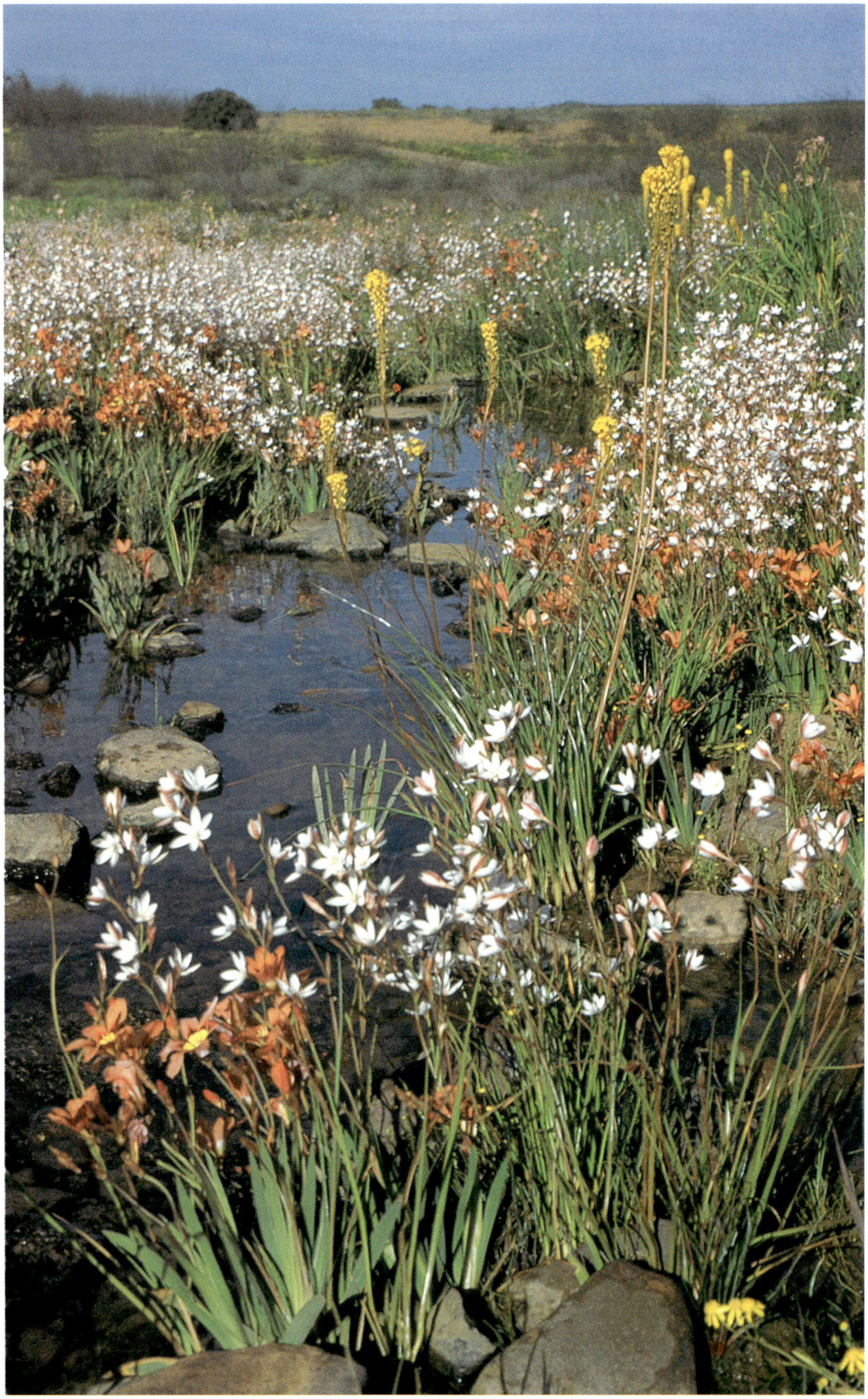

THE COLOR ENCYCLOPEDIA OF CAPE BULBS

JOHN MANNING
PETER GOLDBLATT
DEE SNIJMAN

TIMBER PRESS
Portland · Cambridge

TO ANDRIES DE VILLIERS

All photographs by John Manning and Peter Goldblatt unless otherwise indicated; half-title page, *Watsonia tabularis* with male and female orange-breasted sunbirds; frontispiece, *Bulbinella nutans* subsp. *nutans*, *Sparaxis tricolor*, and *Hesperantha rivulicola* along a stream near Nieuwoudtville. Maps by Don Mayne, Gecko Design, Cape Town.

Copyright © 2002 by John Manning, Peter Goldblatt, and Dee Snijman. All rights reserved

Published in 2002 by

Timber Press, Inc.
The Haseltine Building
133 S.W. Second Avenue, Suite 450
Portland, Oregon 97204, U.S.A.

Timber Press
2 Station Road
Swavesey
Cambridge CB4 4QJ, U.K.

Printed in Singapore

Library of Congress Cataloging-in-Publication Data

Manning, John
 The color encyclopedia of cape bulbs / John Manning, Peter Goldblatt & Dee Snijman.
   p. cm.
  Includes bibliographical references (p.).
  ISBN 0-88192-547-0
  1. Cape bulbs—Encyclopedias. 2. Cape bulbs—Pictorial works.
I. Goldblatt, Peter. II. Snijman, Dee. III. Title.

SB425 .M335 2002
635.9'4—dc21

2002020455

CONTENTS

Preface 7

Bulbs at the Cape 9
  Exploration of the Cape
    Flora 11
  Vegetation of the Cape
    17
  Climate, Geology, and
    Soils of the Cape 19
  Biogeography of the
    Cape 23

Bulbs in the Garden 31
  Bulb Structure 33
  Bulb Cultivation 35

Families of Cape Bulbs 41
  Agapanthaceae 43
  Alliaceae 43
  Amaryllidaceae 44
  Araceae 45
  Asphodelaceae 45
  Colchicaceae 46
  Haemodoraceae 46
  Hyacinthaceae 47
  Hypoxidaceae 48
  Iridaceae 49

Lanariaceae 51
Ruscaceae 52
Tecophilaeaceae 52

Bulbs of the Cape 53
  Agapanthus 53
  Albuca 55
  Allium 61
  Amaryllis 62
  Ammocharis 63
  Androcymbium 64
  Apodolirion 68
  Aristea 70
  Babiana 77
  Baeometra 90
  Bobartia 91
  Boophone 94
  Bowiea 95
  Brunsvigia 96
  Bulbinella 100
  Chasmanthe 107
  Clivia 108
  Crinum 110
  Crossyne 111
  Cyanella 113
  Cybistetes 115
  Cyrtanthus 116

Daubenya 124
Devia 127
Dierama 128
Dietes 129
Dilatris 130
Dipcadi 133
Drimia 134
Empodium 142
Eriospermum 145
Eucomis 154
Ferraria 155
Freesia 158
Geissorhiza 162
Gethyllis 180
Gladiolus 186
Haemanthus 217
Hesperantha 222
Hessea 231
Hypoxis 234
Ixia 236
Kniphofia 248
Lachenalia 251
Lanaria 264
Lapeirousia 266
Ledebouria 272
Massonia 274
Melasphaerula 276

Micranthus 277
Moraea 279
Neodregea 310
Neopatersonia 310
Nerine 311
Onixotis 313
Ornithogalum 315
Ornithoglossum 325
Pauridia 327
Pillansia 328
Polyxena 329
Romulea 332
Scadoxus 352
Scilla 353
Sparaxis 354
Spiloxene 361
Strumaria 367
Syringodea 372
Thereianthus 374
Tritonia 377
Tritoniopsis 382
Tulbaghia 392
Veltheimia 394
Wachendorfia 395
Walleria 397
Watsonia 399
Whiteheadia 408

Wurmbea 409
Xenoscapa 412
Zantedeschia 413

Keys to Species 417
Agapanthus 417
Albuca 417
Androcymbium 418
Apodolirion 419
Aristea 419
Babiana 421
Bobartia 423
Boophone 423
Brunsvigia 423
Bulbinella 424
Chasmanthe 424
Crinum 424
Crossyne 424
Cyanella 424

Cyrtanthus 425
Daubenya 426
Dilatris 426
Dipcadi 426
Drimia 426
Empodium 427
Eriospermum 427
Eucomis 429
Ferraria 430
Freesia 430
Geissorhiza 430
Gethyllis 434
Gladiolus 435
Haemanthus 441
Hesperantha 442
Hessea 443
Hypoxis 443
Ixia 444

Kniphofia 446
Lachenalia 446
Lapeirousia 449
Ledebouria 450
Massonia 450
Micranthus 450
Moraea 450
Nerine 456
Onixotis 456
Ornithogalum 456
Ornithoglossum 458
Pauridia 458
Polyxena 458
Romulea 459
Scadoxus 461
Sparaxis 462
Spiloxene 462
Strumaria 463

Syringodea 464
Thereianthus 464
Tritonia 464
Tritoniopsis 465
Tulbaghia 466
Veltheimia 466
Wachendorfia 466
Watsonia 466
Wurmbea 468
Zantedeschia 468

Conversion Table 469
Specialist Suppliers 470
Glossary 471
References 475
Index of Synonyms 481
Index of Common Names 485

PREFACE

PLANTS WITH BULBS and similar subterranean storage organs such as rhizomes, tubers, and corms are an important and fascinating part of gardening as well as the horticultural market and cut flower trade. Their almost magical ability to produce a display of flowers from a dormant ball buried in a garden or pot has lost none of its appeal over the centuries. This singular feature of bulbous plants, combined with their often relatively large, long-lasting, and striking flowers, has ensured their continuing popularity, from the ancient civilizations of Egypt and Greece through the Dutch tulip mania of the 18th century to today's booming trade in bulbs for the vase and garden.

Although bulbous plants occur widely in the floras of the world, the southern African bulb flora easily ranks among the richest. The southern tip of the subcontinent in particular, known to biologists as the Cape Floral Region, is prodigious in its wealth of bulbous plants. It is home to 60% of the southern African bulb species, most of which grow nowhere else. Bulbous plants from the Cape of Good Hope were first introduced into horticulture in Europe in the early 17th century. Rather sporadic importation into Europe over the following decades was vastly supplemented by expeditions mounted specifically to collect species for botanical gardens and for the hothouses of the gentry and nobility of Europe. This culminated in a great passion for Cape bulbs that peaked over the decades at the end of the 18th century.

Most of today's cultivated bulbous plants are hybrids or selected cultivars produced by plant breeders from wild stocks first collected in their native habitat in the 17th, 18th, and 19th centuries, and Cape bulbs are no exception. All the most famous Cape bulbs—gladiolus, freesia, amaryllis, sparaxis, and chincherinchee—are known in horticulture mainly from the cultivated strains bred primarily or entirely from Cape stock. Wild species, however, are vastly more variable than the cultivars, and only a fraction of them have been involved in the production of the plethora of cultivars available commercially. There are, in fact, thousands of wild bulbous plant species in the world, many with horticultural potential and the vast majority of more than passing interest. Despite this, the majority are almost unknown to the horticultural world. It is one of the main aims of *The Color Encyclopedia of Cape Bulbs* to expose this wonderful variety. More importantly, however, it will help anybody to identify and name the species of Cape bulbs that they encounter. This includes gardeners, ecologists, conservationists, hikers, and anybody with an interest in these important and often beautiful plants.

The literature on Cape bulbs, although vast, is either scattered in scientific journals or presented incompletely in the more accessible publications. It is thus not easy for people to identify many species with any certainty of success. *The Color Encyclopedia of Cape Bulbs* aims to correct this. It is an encyclopedic account of Cape bulbs, including all species in those families regarded by tradition as bulbs. It offers, for the first time, an accurate guide to the identification of all Cape bulbs, using keys, descriptions, and photographs. To achieve this we have assembled all available knowledge from the scientific literature, studied the extensive collections of dried plants housed in the world's major botanical institutions, and examined the plants in their natural habitats. Genera that have not been critically studied recently were carefully reviewed. In addition, we have included some newly discovered and still unnamed species in our keys and descriptions in an effort to make this account as comprehensive as possible. Since the main appeal of bulbs lies in their flowers, we have made every effort to illustrate them. Every genus and more than half the species have been photographed in the wild, many for the first time. We hope that *The Color Encyclopedia of Cape Bulbs* will stimulate more research, more field exploration, and lead to a deeper understanding of the flora. More than that, we hope that by making information about Cape bulbs widely accessible, the unique flora of the Cape will become better appreciated and, in consequence, better conserved. We are confident that *The Color Encyclopedia of Cape Bulbs* will serve as the basic reference work on the identification of Cape bulbs for many years.

Thanks are due to several people who have helped us with this work, in particular Andries de Villiers, who is not only unfailing in his enthusiasm of all things bulbous but who prodded us intellectually with many provocative questions over the years; Colin Paterson-Jones for his companionship and encouragement on several field expeditions, for allowing us to use many of his photographs, and for his critical comments on the manuscript; Graham Duncan for his advice on cultivation of bulbs and for information used in the treatment of *Lachenalia*; and Clifford Dorse and Robin Jangle for their valuable assistance with *Gethyllis*. We acknowledge with gratitude a grant from the Stanley Smith Horticultural Trust, which contributed substantially toward the publication of this book, and also the contributions from the Mia Karsten Bequest and the Indigenous Bulb Association of South Africa. Lastly, we thank our respective institutions, the National Botanical Institute of South Africa and the Missouri Botanical Garden, for their continued support.

BULBS AT THE CAPE

DEFINED LARGELY on the basis of its peculiar plants and nutrient-poor soils, the Cape Floral Region occupies the southwestern corner of the African continent between latitudes 31° and 34°30′ south of the equator (Figure 1). From the Cape Peninsula and the city of Cape Town it extends northward for some 400 km (250 miles) along the Atlantic coast to the mouth of the Olifants River and eastward along the Indian Ocean coast as far as Port Elizabeth, some 650 km (400 miles) from Cape Town. Its inland limits are defined by the mountain ranges of the Cape Fold Belt. Among the more important of these are the Cedarberg and Bokkeveld Mountains in the northwest, the Witteberg and Swartberg Mountains in the center, and the Great Winterhoek and Baviaanskloof Mountains in the east. Covering some 90,000 km² (35,000 square miles), the Cape Floral Region encompasses a large part of southern Africa with winter rainfall and a Mediterranean climate.

The Cape Floral Region is a botanical anomaly. Not only does it have more plant species than would be anticipated given its latitude and climate, it is also home to far more bulbous plants than anywhere else in the world. Its flora is in fact so singular in many respects that the region is classified as one of the world's six floral kingdoms. This is truly remarkable given the unusually small area occupied by the Cape Floral Region, only 0.04% of the earth's land surface. The other floral kingdoms, in comparison, occupy all or most of one or more continents: Holarctic (c. 42% of earth's land surface), Paleotropical (35%), Neotropical (14%), Australian (8%), Holantarctic (southern South America and subantarctic islands, 1%).

Elsewhere in the world the number of plant species per unit area increases from temperate to tropical latitudes and from arid or semiarid habitats to well-watered ones. The Cape Floral Region defies these trends. Although it lies well within the temperate zone and most of it experiences a semiarid climate of low annual rainfall and summer drought, it is nevertheless home to about 9000 plant species in an area of only 90,000 km² (35,000 square miles). This is more species than in the species-rich, wet tropics of Panama, which covers a comparable area, and only slightly fewer than in Costa Rica, another tropical area of comparable size. Comparisons between the floras of regions with a Mediterranean climate, which characterizes much of the Cape Floral Region, only emphasize the remarkable richness of the Cape flora. California, for instance, which is recognized as having a rich and diverse flora, actually only supports about 5000 species (just over half the number found in the Cape flora) in an area more than three times larger than the Cape Floral Region. Another peculiarity of the Cape flora is its remarkably high level of endemism. Almost 70% of the species in the Cape flora are found nowhere else on earth. This level of endemism is characteristic of isolated oceanic islands and is unique for a continental flora.

Geophytes, plants that have their renewal buds buried underground, are widespread around the world in many habitats but are typically most diverse and abundant in regions with a Mediterranean climate. The Cape stands out among these regions in the extraordinary richness of its geophyte flora. Of a flora of 9000 species, some 1500 are geophytes, 17% of the total flora. This proportion is three to seven times that found in other areas with a Mediterranean climate.

Geophytes occur widely among the flowering plants, in families as diverse as the daisies (Asteraceae) and grasses (Poaceae). Among this diversity, however, few species actually form true bulbs, and "bulb" has been rather loosely used for any geophyte that is more or less horticulturally interesting, with the consequence that the boundaries of the group are rather loosely and often idiosyncratically drawn. The core families in this group are those that develop either true bulbs, such as the amaryllis, onion, lily, and hyacinth families (Amaryllidaceae, Alliaceae, Liliaceae, and Hyacinthaceae), or those that develop corms, mainly the iris and colchicum families (Iridaceae and Colchicaceae). All bear more or less showy, lily-like flowers. Traditionally, many bulbous species were included in a rather broadly defined lily family but it is now clear that they actually belong in several families, and the lily family, in its more strictly defined sense, is not represented outside the Northern Hemisphere.

The families treated in *The Color Encyclopedia of Cape Bulbs* include all the lily-like geophytes except for the Anthericaceae, whose Cape representatives are seldom grown. In addition, two genera of the asphodel family (Asphodelaceae), *Bulbine* and *Trachyandra*, although predominantly geophytic, have been excluded because they are more usually treated by gardeners as succulents.

Figure 1. The location of the Cape Floral Region

This modified concept of bulbous plants, although excluding several families with geophytic members, still includes the majority of Cape geophytes—1183 species, close to 15% of the total flora. This represents the richest concentration of bulbous plants anywhere in the world. Although southern Africa as a whole, well known for the richness of its bulb flora, boasts some 2000 species of bulbous plants, these comprise just about 11% of its total flora. It is not surprising, then, that the Cape is the center of diversity of several of the larger bulbous families, including the iris, hyacinth, colchicum, and star grass families (Iridaceae, Hyacinthaceae, Colchicaceae, and Hypoxidaceae), and both the amaryllis and lily-of-the-valley families (Amaryllidaceae and Ruscaceae) are particularly well represented in the region.

Exploration of the Cape Flora

DISCOVERY & EARLY EXPLORATION

The remarkable flora at the Cape has been known to European botanists and horticulturists for nearly four centuries. Between 1600 and 1850 no fewer than 180 European explorers had collected plants in southern Africa, the vast majority of them mainly or entirely in the Cape region. Cape Town, at the southern tip of Africa, was established by the Dutch East India Company in 1652 as a way station for ships plying the trade in spices, tea, cloth, and ceramics with the East. It continued to be a major port of call for the East India trade until the opening of the Suez Canal in 1869. Cape bulbs, however, had impressed European growers even before the establishment of a

Sparaxis pillansii in a dolerite outcrop near Nieuwoudtville

Onixotis stricta and other aquatics in a seasonal pool near Hopefield

port at Cape Town. Among the very first Cape plants to reach Europe were bulbs of *Haemanthus coccineus* that had been dug up at the Cape by Gouarus de Keyser in the first years of the 17th Century. They flowered in Belgium in 1603 and were illustrated in 1605. A few years later, in 1612, the Dutch nurseryman Emanuel Sweert produced an illustrated catalog or florilegium of the plants for sale at the Frankfurt Fair that included *Boophone haemanthoides, Drimia capensis,* and a gladiolus that may be *Gladiolus carneus.* Although the gladiolus was almost certainly collected at Cape Town itself, the boophone at least was without doubt gathered around Saldanha Bay to the north. This sheltered anchorage was well known to seafarers at the time, and both the boophone and the drimia grow there today.

The first European to record observations on Cape plants in their native habitat was the Dutch missionary Justus Heurnius, who stopped at Cape Town briefly in the autumn of 1624. He prepared sketches of a few local plants, among them *Haemanthus coccineus* and *Kniphofia uvaria,* which were subsequently published in Amsterdam in 1644.

The Dutch maintained a keen interest in exotic plants throughout the 17th and 18th centuries, and ship captains and travelers were prevailed upon by plant enthusiasts, amateur and professional, to bring back plants from the Cape. They complied whenever they could, carrying seeds and the eminently portable bulbs of many species back to Holland. If this movement was at first a trickle, it soon began to swell. The effect of the settlement of Cape Town on European botany was soon felt. In 1685, Simon van der Stel, then governor of the tiny colony, mounted an expedition into the Cape interior to explore its resources with an eye, of course, on commercial development. Accompanying the expedition was the artist Claudius, who recorded the plants and animals they en-

Kniphofia sarmentosa and *Bulbinella nutans* subsp. *nutans* along a stream on the Verlatekloof Pass between Sutherland and Matjiesfontein

countered. Claudius kept copious notes and drawings that were copied repeatedly in Europe. Though not published until the 20th century, these drawings were known to scientists of the 18th century and included the first important accounts of Cape bulbs. Among the species illustrated by Claudius are species of *Gladiolus, Lapeirousia, Lachenalia, Albuca, Wurmbea,* and *Veltheimia.*

Simon van der Stel and his son, Willem, governors of the Cape Colony, 1679–1699 and 1699–1706, respectively, were responsible for shipping numerous consignments of bulbs to Holland from the Cape, most of them collected by the gardeners Heinrich Oldenland and Jan Hartog. These plants were received with delight by prominent Dutch citizens and gardeners, and Cape plants soon became one of the principal interests in European nurseries.

Members of the amaryllis family (Amaryllidaceae) featured prominently among the early Cape bulbs grown in Europe because these autumn-flowering plants were conspicuous at the very time that the Dutch and British ships were returning from the Indies to Europe on the southeastern trade winds. The wealth of spring-flowering bulbs that would have been in bloom on the outbound trip would not only have failed to survive the trip to the East and back but are not easily found when dormant in autumn.

Another attractive autumn-flowering amaryllid from near Cape Town that made its appearance in Europe early in the 17th century was the lovely *Nerine sarniensis*. First illustrated in 1635, as *Narcissus japonicus rutilo flore* (reddish orange-flowered narcissus of Japan) from a plant that was flowered by the French grower Jean Morin the previous year, its epithet *(japonicus)* bears eloquent, if mistaken, testimony to the land of embarkation. Morin had presumably confused his nerine with the startlingly similar *Lycoris radiata,* a native of Japan. Keeping accurate records of the various bulbs that were stowed, probably in any convenient spot in a crowded hold or cabin, was clearly a difficult job. The confusion regarding the provenance of *Nerine sarniensis* did not, however, end there, and its introduction to England some 20 years later was attended by further misunderstanding. A popular and rather poetic version originated with the Oxford don, Robert Morison. By his account, a Dutch ship returning from Japan in about 1655 with bulbs in her cargo, at least some of which must have been taken on board in Cape Town, ran aground on the island of Guernsey in the English Channel. Some of the bulbs floated ashore and, a few years later, flowered upon the strand in a glorious floral tribute to the wreck. Hence the genus received the name *Nerine,* in classical mythology the name of a sea nymph, whereas the specific epithet commemorates Sarnia, the Latin name for Guernsey. In a development of this account, some of these plants were subsequently sent to Major-General John Lambert, a noted bulb fancier of the day, who flowered them in his garden at Wimbledon in 1659. The truth is that Lambert almost certainly obtained his plants from the Continent, possibly from the original stock grown by Morin. Lambert, a Parliamentarian, was exiled to Guernsey in 1662 after the Restoration and took his bulbs with him. Finding the climate very much to their liking, the plants flourished to the extent that by the end of the 18th century, Guernsey had become the major supplier of its eponymous lily to the English horticultural trade. Although it has been established that *N. sarniensis* was adventive on the island, the error of its supposed Asian origin persisted in the literature for some time longer. The names of several other Cape bulbs described in the 17th century make wildly inaccurate allusions to their purported places of origin, among them *Albuca canadensis* (= *A. flaccida*), *Brunsvigia orientalis,* and the Malgas (Madagascar) lily, *Cybistetes longifolia.*

The time of European expansion and exploration coincided with the Enlightenment and the conviction that it was a worthy task to document and catalog the plants and animals of the world. Foremost among the group of people that we would now call scientists was the Swedish physician Carl Linnaeus, who developed the binomial system of naming all organisms. Also known as the father of the science of botany, Linnaeus traveled to Holland early in his career, in 1735. During the course of his visit he became aware of the unusual and diverse Cape plants that were being grown there or that were preserved as dry, pressed specimens in the collections of the wealthy. Linnaeus was not content to write about the plant and animal life of Europe only; he actively sought information from other parts of the world. He made further acquaintance with Cape plants through Anders Sparrman, a Swede who visited the Cape in the 1770s. Sparrman corresponded with Linnaeus and, more importantly, sent specimens to him that were subsequently described as species. In 1772, Linnaeus sent a promising student, Carl Peter Thunberg, to the Cape to study the flora. By that time the authority of the Dutch administration at the Cape was weakening, and exploration of the region by other nations was easier. Thunberg made the most of the 3 years that he spent at the Cape, managing to travel into the remotest parts of the colony and amass a huge collection of dried plants. He was accompanied on several of his expeditions by the indefatigable Scottish plant collector Francis Masson, sent to the Cape independently to collect for Kew Gardens by Sir Joseph Banks, who was at that time virtually the director of the Royal Gardens at Kew. Masson visited South Africa twice, the first time from 1772 to 1775, and the second from 1786 to 1795.

Austrian interest in Cape plants at this time was equally fervent. By 1763, the Imperial Gardens at Schönbrunn, under the direction of Nikolaus von Jacquin, had become among the most celebrated of their day. A severe frost in 1780, however, decimated the collections, and in an effort to obtain new plants several expeditions were mounted. Two gardeners, Franz Boos and Georg Scholl, were dispatched to the Cape, where they arrived in 1786. They made several short trips with Masson that year and other, longer trips during the next 9 months, at least one into Namaqualand and another into the eastern Cape. Although Boos returned to Vienna in 1788, Scholl remained in the Cape for 12 years, during which time he sent frequent consignments of bulbs and seeds to Vienna. These account for the immense number of Cape plants figured in Jacquin's publications, culminating in his great work on the plants cultivated at Schönbrunn, the *Plantarum Rariorum Horti Caesarei Schoenbrunnensis Descriptiones et Icones*, which appeared in parts from 1797 to 1804.

Botanists visiting the Cape at this time were made particularly welcome by the commander of the garrison in Cape Town, Colonel Robert Gordon, himself a respected explorer with a keen interest in natural history. Gordon had accompanied Thunberg and Masson on an excursion around the Cape Peninsula in 1773, shortly after their arrival in Cape Town, and later almost certainly guided Masson and Scholl on several other expeditions. Scholl and Boos had also availed themselves of Gordon's interest by using his garden to grow many of their botanical accessions before dispatching them to Austria.

Masson, after whom the bulbous genus *Massonia* was named, was primarily a plant collector, whereas Thunberg was a scientist and had less immediately practical aims. Their influence, although equally profound, was thus in the complementary disciplines of horticulture and systematic botany. Masson's collections had a tremendous influence on British horticulture. Grown first at Kew, they were later dispersed to gardens elsewhere in Britain and then to Europe. Thunberg, as far as we know, grew no plants, but on his return to Sweden he and Linnaeus's son, Carl, who had succeeded his father, described and named most of those that he had collected at the Cape. Thunberg acceded to the post of professor of botany at Uppsala University in 1784 after the younger Linnaeus's death, where he proceeded to consolidate his position as the father of African botany. A preliminary account of Cape plants, *Prodromus Plantarum Capensium*, appeared in the 1790s, followed by the first detailed account of the flora, *Flora Capensis*, 1807–1820. Although much of the Cape flora remained to be discovered, Thunberg's and Masson's scientific and horticultural achievements had revealed its broad outlines, most particularly the extraordinary wealth of its bulbous plants.

THE CAPE PERIOD

The torrent of Cape plants pouring into Europe toward the end of the 18th century through the activities of Francis Masson, Franz Boos, and Georg Scholl launched a new horticultural fashion. Over the 30 or so years spanning the end of the 18th and the early decades of the 19th centuries, Cape plants enjoyed an unprecedented period of vogue, although by then some had been grown in Europe nearly 200 years. At the height of the fashion, Cape plants, including shrubs, perennials, and annuals as well as bulbs, were eagerly sought by the wealthy of Europe. The ruling houses of France and Austria supported both extensive living collections as well as expensive publications to showcase original paintings of new or unusual Cape plants. The sumptuously illustrated volumes by Nikolaus von Jacquin and Pierre-Joseph Redouté, now treasured in library collections, tell us more eloquently than in words the value placed at the time on the maintenance of exotic plant collections.

In Britain at this time, a similar craze for Cape plants had taken hold, despite the fact that royal patronage directly subsidized neither botanical exploration nor the production of illustrated books about rare plants. Instead, the aristocracy and the wealthy vied with one another to develop collections of rare and exotic flora. Botany, in fact, had become a popular recreation. Magazine-like publications produced by public subscription that dealt with ornamental plants enjoyed great popularity. The most famous of these, William Curtis's *Botanical Magazine*, Henry Andrews's *Botanist's Repository*, and Sydenham Edwards's *Botanical Register*, were devoted entirely to paintings and descriptions of unusual or newly discovered plants that were grown in Britain. *Curtis's Botanical Magazine* is still published, a vivid testimony to the continuing depth of British interest in wild plants. Volumes of these works that appeared in the later 18th century all have a far greater representation of Cape plants than one might expect and reflect what has been called the Cape Period or *Kapzeit* in horticulture. Bulbous plants, with their particular interest and ease of cultivation, featured conspicuously in all these volumes. Almost 500 species of Cape bulbs were grown in Europe and illustrated in these publications over the roughly 30 years encompassed by the Cape Period.

The Cape, conveniently situated along the sea route to the East, was an obvious area for European botanical activity, and the Cape Period was a direct result of this strategic location combined with nascent British imperialism. The origin and duration of the Cape Period are well illustrated by developments at the Royal Botanic Gardens, Kew, at the time. Kew during the 1760s and 1770s was well on the way to becoming one of the richest repositories of the world's flora. Seeds and plants were acquired from abroad, and local nurseries scoured for new introductions. Following his return from the Pacific in 1771—he had been on James Cook's Australian expedition—Sir Joseph Banks associated himself with Kew. Enthusiastic about the results of his discoveries, Banks, a man of broad vision and independent means, saw the promise that plant exploration held for expanding Britain's foreign interests. By means of Banks's endeavors, Kew became one of the great gardens in the world. He directed his energies toward replacing the random acquisition policy that had prevailed at Kew with a more active policy of purposeful collecting in selected regions of the world. Together with His Majesty's Gardener, William Aiton, he effected a swift conversion of Kew from a grand repository of plants into a dynamic botanic garden, its glasshouses filled with the discoveries of its collectors. Francis Masson, first of Kew's plant collectors, was sent to the Cape in 1772 to initiate Banks's program in southern Africa. Returning to London in 1775 with a bounty of plants unknown in Europe at that time, Masson was in great measure responsible for propelling Kew to its position of prominence among the gardens of Europe. Proteas, crassulas, mesembryanthemums, ericas, pelargoniums, and bulbs such as ixias and gladioli formed the bulk of Masson's consignments. The Cape Period had been launched and would last into the first decades of the 19th century.

The effects of Banks's policy were soon felt. The number of species in cultivation at Kew rose from 3400 in 1768 to 5600 in 1789, and reached 11,000 by 1813, with Masson's contribution from the Cape numbering almost 1000. Although attention at Kew had begun to turn elsewhere, particularly toward Australia, South America, and China, in the belief that the South African flora was relatively well sampled, a steady influx of plants from the Cape continued as ships passed by on their way home from the East. A special Cape House had been first constructed at Kew in 1792 for small Cape and Australian plants, but it was replaced in 1803 by a second structure when the original building was pressed into service to house a consignment of Guianan plants captured from the French. By 1824, the Cape House had glazed frames or bulb borders along its length, filled primarily with the collections of Masson and James Bowie, who was Masson's replacement in South Africa from 1817 until 1823, when he was recalled by the economies of the Treasury.

The death of Banks in 1820 signaled not only the end of Kew's golden age of exploration but also the end of the Cape Period. By 1844, the shift in botanical interest away from the Cape was evident in the addition of wings to the Cape House for the accommodation of plants from Australia and New Zealand. Other developments of a more technical nature at the time also conspired to shift the focus of horticulturists away from Cape bulbs. Improvements in hothouse technology were one. Stove heating had been used in hothouses in Europe until about 1800 with a resulting dry heat, suitable for bulbs, succulents, and in fact most Cape plants. Steam heat was first introduced in 1790, with the result that hothouses could become moist and humid, conditions inimical to most Cape plants but favoring leafy tropical plants, ferns, and orchids. The importation of tender tropical plants was also facilitated by the adoption in 1833 of the Wardian case. This was an almost airtight glass case that could sustain plants for long periods of time on board ship by protecting them from the effects of salt spray and drought. Until this development, the losses suffered by plants while on board were tremendous, and it was only hardy, drought-resistant plants, or bulbs, that had any guarantee of arriving in Europe alive.

These innovations combined with the almost feverish quest for novelties that had caught the scientific imagination. The tropics of Africa and South America, still botanically very much unknown, beckoned the inquisitive minds of the age particularly strongly with their wealth of exotic orchids and foliage plants, which were becoming popular in Victorian England. Control of the Cape Colony passed from the Dutch to the British at the beginning of the 19th century and although enthusiasm for plant exploration was by no means dimmed, the focus shifted to the north, first into the interior of southern Africa, then to tropical Africa. Nevertheless, Cape plants were actively collected during the first half of the 19th century by a number of famous plant explorers motivated by a variety of reasons ranging from romantic disappointment to commercial enterprise. Among these were William Burchell, Johann Franz Drège, Christian Friedrich Ecklon, and Carl Ludwig Zeyher. Burchell ventured deep into the subcontinent, returning along a novel southern route, and was among the earliest explorers with an interest in botany to climb the heights of the Langeberg Mountains in the southern Cape, bringing back the first records of many of the endemic plants of the range. Zeyher explored the western Cape and Namaqualand and, like Drège and Ecklon, also collected throughout the southern Cape Floral Region and into the eastern Cape. With the shift of scientific interest away from the Cape to the tropics in the mid-19th century, there was little botanical activity at the Cape until the end of the century, when collecting activity revived. This was no doubt a result of the great British projects to produce and publish accounts of the floras of the parts of the world under their dominion. Thus was borne a new and more ambitious *Flora Capensis,* a floristic account not only of the Cape Floral Region but of all temperate southern Africa. Begun in the mid-19th century, the last volume of *Flora Capensis* was published in 1932. The main volume treating the families of bulbous plants was published in 1896 and with it, one might have hoped, a satisfactory account of Cape bulbs. Regrettably, this was not so.

THE MODERN PERIOD

Paradoxically, the very richness of the Cape bulb flora was at first an impediment to a more thorough study, for so large a flora is not easy to document and understand from so great a distance as Europe. Plant collections made by local botanists after 1890 quickly revealed how inadequately the Cape flora was actually known. Botanists like Harry Bolus, Peter MacOwan, Rudolf Schlechter, and somewhat later, Rudolf Marloth, H. M. L. (Louisa) Bolus, and Robert H. Compton discovered hundreds of previously unknown species across the Cape Floral Region well into the 1930s. It became evident that much more needed to be known before the flora even of so small an area as the Cape Floral Region could become adequately documented, let alone understood. After the 1930s, South African botanists began the task of synthesizing the available knowledge and producing monographic accounts of Cape bulbs. The preeminent position that the Compton Herbarium at Kirstenbosch botanical garden occupies today in the study of Cape bulbs owes much to the careful collections assembled by Winsome

F. Barker during her tenure there, 1933–1972. Two other contemporary Cape botanists, Gwendoline J. Lewis and Miriam P. de Vos, were responsible for the first modern treatments of many genera of the Iridaceae.

Any study of Cape bulbs, although as complete as possible at the time of its publication, has invariably been rendered obsolete within a short time by new discoveries. For example, *Gladiolus in Southern Africa*, published in 1998, was on the shelves for no more than 6 months before one new Cape species and another from eastern southern Africa came to light. Despite past achievements, it is abundantly clear that the study of the Cape flora is an ongoing process. Since 1990, we have named no fewer than 33 previously undescribed species of Cape bulbs, and several more await publication. (Some of these, temporarily designated with numbers only, are listed at the end of the alphabetically arranged species descriptions for the genera *Androcymbium*, *Aristea*, *Cyrtanthus*, *Drimia*, *Ledebouria*, *Ornithogalum*, *Spiloxene*, and *Thereianthus*.) Still others remain to be discovered and it will be many years before the bounty of the Cape flora is fully explored.

Vegetation of the Cape

The boundaries of the Cape Floral Region are based largely on the distribution of its dominant vegetation type, the fynbos (fine-leaved bush), which is in turn determined by the coincidence of moderate to high amounts of rain and acidic, nutrient-poor sandstone soils. This combination of climate and geology occurs sporadically in subtropical and tropical Africa, where it supports a similar African fynbos, but true Cape fynbos is restricted to those parts of temperate southern Africa that receive moderate to high amounts of winter rain. The extreme western Karoo along the margin of the Roggeveld Plateau, although technically falling outside the Cape Floral Region, has a bulb flora so closely allied to that of the Cape that we include it here. (*Roggeveld* means rye shrub-

Watsonia stokoei flowering in the spring after a summer burn in a seep in the Grootwinterhoek Mountains

Amaryllis belladonna flowering in the autumn after a summer fire on the granite slopes of Lion's Head in Cape Town

Haemanthus canaliculatus flowering soon after a summer burn in a coastal seep near Betty's Bay

land, the name derived from the Afrikaans or Dutch *rog* in reference to the only southern African species of rye, *Secale africanum*.)

Fynbos is a heathy shrubland dominated by small to large evergreen shrubs with tough leaves. It is characterized by the presence of members of the protea, erica, and citrus families (Proteaceae, Ericaceae, and Rutaceae). The leaves of Cape fynbos shrubs are typically small and hard, but in most proteas they are larger and leathery. Another characteristic component of Cape fynbos are the grass-like restios (Restionaceae), which largely replace the true grasses that are common in other temperate vegetation types. Although fynbos species account for more than 80% of all species in the Cape Floral Region, fynbos vegetation itself covers something less than half the area. Another vegetation type known as renosterveld is the dominant vegetation of the richer clay soils of the Cape lowlands. Renosterveld is dominated by fine-leaved members of the daisy family (Asteraceae), especially the so-called renosterbos *(Elytropappus rhinocerotis)*, the source of the name renosterveld (rhinoceros shrubland), but renosterveld supports a wealth of bulbous species. In areas of low rainfall the renosterveld gives way to succulent karoo (a word in Khoekhoen, meaning arid, dry, hard ground), a sparse vegetation dominated by dwarf shrubs, most of which have succulent leaves. Broad-leaved woody vegetation has a restricted distribution in the Cape Floral Region. The coastal belt supports subtropical thicket, which lacks typical fynbos elements, and true forest is restricted to the wetter gorges and southern mountain slopes. Extensive forests did, however, occur in historical times around George and Knysna on the southern coast.

Fire is a critical factor in the long-term survival of fynbos and, to a lesser extent, renosterveld. In both vegetation types it serves to clear the canopy and provide open areas in which herbaceous and bulbous species find a temporary habitat suitable for growth. In fynbos, however, it plays a vital role in nutrient cycling. The sandstone soils on which fynbos grows are deficient in several nutrients essential for plant growth, especially nitrogen and phosphorus. These are rapidly depleted and after several years the vegetation becomes moribund, and flowering is poor. A fire at this time rejuvenates the vegetation by releasing the nutrients locked up in plant matter back into the soil. The importance of periodic fires for fynbos plants is evident in the tremendous flushes of new growth and flowering, particularly among bulbous species, in the year or two after a fire has cleared and fertilized the sandstone soil. Species of *Cyrtanthus* and *Haemanthus* in particular respond rapidly, sending up their flowers within 2 weeks of a burn.

Climate, Geology, and Soils of the Cape

Rainfall patterns vary considerably across the Cape Floral Region and divide it into two climatic zones depending on the seasonality of the rainfall. The exact boundary between these two zones is blurred, but the transition between the two lies between Caledon and Swellendam. The western part of the region experiences a true Mediterranean climate in which most precipitation falls in winter, April to September. Complete summer drought is characteristic of the western half of the Cape Floral Region, and in most years there is little precipitation between November and March. At that time of the year the vegetation suffers an extreme moisture deficit as a result of increased evaporation and transpiration. This summer aridity is ameliorated over the windward coastal mountains in the southwest by orographic clouds that reduce evaporation and provide local precipitation. Rainfall is highest in the southwest, especially along the Hottentots Holland Mountains, and in the mountains above Stellenbosch reaches 3000 mm (120 inches) a year, but 380–760 mm (15–30 inches) a year is usual in the lowlands. North of these mountains the total rainfall drops gradually to about 250 mm (10 inches) a year but is considerably less than that in the interior mountain valleys, on parts of the Bokkeveld-Roggeveld Escarpment complex, and in the Tanqua Basin. Although relatively low, the rainfall is concentrated in the cooler months when it

Moraea tripetala on clay flats near Nieuwoudtville

Sparaxis bulbifera and *Geissorhiza radians* on damp granite flats near Darling

Moraea tulbaghensis in a patch of renosterveld on clay slopes near Piketberg

more than compensates for moisture lost through evaporation and transpiration.

Rainfall is much less seasonal in the eastern half of the Cape Floral Region, where summer rain is normal. Although seldom ample, it is sufficient for the development of a distinct late summer bulbous flora. Summer precipitation is produced as light drizzle or fog driven against the east–west trending coastal ranges by the southeastern trade winds and is most effective on the southern slopes and foothills of these ranges. The proportion of summer rainfall increases toward the east and predominates east of Port Elizabeth, which marks the eastern extent of the Cape Floral Region.

Throughout the Cape Floral Region, winters are relatively mild with temperatures seldom dropping below 4°C (40°F) along the coastal lowlands. Winter temperatures in the interior are cooler, and frost is normal. In the mountains, even near the coast, snowfalls are usual although seldom long-lasting.

These generalizations are often confounded by the complexity of local geology and the fractured nature of the terrain, which foster a diversity of microclimates. In this way, plants adapted to desert habitats can be found in the drier inland valleys that fall in the rain shadow of a mountain range, and less tolerant species are assured of niches on damper southern slopes or at higher elevations. Despite these variations, midsummer is the period of greatest stress for plants across the entire Cape Floral Region, and the hot, windy conditions during summer are extremely desiccating, even on the cooler upper slopes. In consequence, the majority of Cape bulbs are winter growing.

A Mediterranean climate has only been established at the Cape for the last 4–5 million years. The gradual onset of aridity that began to take place also resulted in the increasing importance of fire as an ecological factor that has played a crucial role in the evolution of much of the Cape vegetation. Flowering in many Cape bulbs, especially those that occur on sandstones, is stimulated by fire, and the year after a burn the landscape can be transformed into a carpet of flowering bulbs. During the following seasons, the shrubby undergrowth rapidly reestablishes itself, cutting off light to the surface and depleting the soil of its nutrients. Flowering of understory species, including bulbous plants, is inhibited until the canopy is cleared by another fire and nutrients from the ashes of burned plants are released into the soil.

Each of the main rock types present in the Cape Floral Region erodes or weathers to produce a distinctive soil type, differing in physical characteristics such as particle size and water retention, and in chemical characteristics such as nutrient status and pH. Each soil supports a characteristic vegetation type. Fynbos dominates the sandy substrates and limestones; renosterveld and succulent karoo occur on the clays. Each vegetation type includes a component of bulbous species, and although Cape bulbs often exhibit a marked soil preference in the wild, this is seldom critical in cultivation. The sandstones of the Cape geological system weather to form shallow, coarse-grained, acidic sands that are heavily leached and low in nutrients, particularly phosphates. In cracks or fissures where humus can accumulate, the soil is more loamy, and localized differences in soil depth, moisture, and nutrient status provide a variety of niches. The coastal sands, although deeper, are equally poor in nutrients. In marked contrast, the shales of the Malmesbury and Bokkeveld formations, and to some extent the granites, weather into fine-grained clays that are richer in nutrients than the sands and not as acidic. The coastal limestones are calcium-rich and alkaline. Although found in all habitats and on all types of soil, Cape bulbs are most common on richer soils derived from granite, shale, or dolerite. Relatively few genera of Cape bulbs are more or less restricted to the acidic, nutrient-poor sandstone soils that support the characteristic fynbos of the Cape Floral Region. Among them are *Dilatris* and *Wachendorfia* (Haemodoraceae), *Lanaria* (Lanariaceae), and *Micranthus, Thereianthus,* and *Tritoniopsis* (Iridaceae).

The geological formations that comprise the Cape Floral Region are the result of several cycles of deposition and erosion stretching over millions of years. The oldest

Ixia maculata on granite flats near Darling

rocks in the region were deposited along the edges of a large inland basin 950–650 million years ago. They are mostly fine-grained shales of the Malmesbury formation, visible now in the rolling landscape of the western forelands, but including the Kango limestones near Oudtshoorn. These sedimentary rocks were deformed by folding 600–500 million years ago, at which time they were intruded by granites from within the earth's mantle. These granites are now exposed along the western coast and at Paarl. A cycle of erosion followed that lasted some 50 million years, during which this ancient mountainous landscape was reduced to a low, rather featureless plain. About 450 million years ago a new cycle of deposition was initiated by subsidence of the ancient landscape. Over a period of 110 million years, several distinct layers of sediment were deposited, starting with the mainly coarse-grained Table Mountain group, followed by the fine-grained mudstones and shales of the Bokkeveld group, and ending with another series of mainly sandy deposits intercalated with fine-grained shales, which constitute the Witteberg group. Together this great geological sandwich constitutes the Cape supergroup. This relatively stable cycle of deposition ended 280–215 million years ago with a massive uplift of the land, during which the rocks of the Cape supergroup were buckled and thrust upward in great folds, forming the ranges of the Cape Fold Mountains. The contorted layering visible in many Cape mountains is striking evidence of the violence of this folding. Another result of this uplift was the formation of a great inland basin over the present Karoo, which gradually began to fill with fine-grained sediments. As they were elevated, the Cape mountains became a southerly source of sediments to the Karoo Basin.

About 140 million years ago the great southern supercontinent of Gondwana began to fracture as the continental plates that made it up started to drift apart. In the Cape this fragmentation led to faulting and the formation of several large basins, among them the Worcester Basin and Little Karoo. Subsequent erosion of the Cape mountains is responsible for the accumulation in these basins of pebble-rich conglomerates, mudstones, and soft sandstones. Severe climatic fluctuations were a feature of the following 100 million years, resulting in dramatic changes in sea level. Sea levels 65 million years ago were much higher than they are today, and the shoreline of the Cape Floral Region was located near the base of the present mountain ranges, with much of the coastal plain inundated.

The vegetation covering the Cape region 65 million years ago was mainly evergreen forest, but typical fynbos elements were also present, including members of the protea, erica and restio families. These ancestors of today's fynbos were probably already adapted to nutrient-poor, sandy soils, much like their modern counterparts on the sandstones and quartzites in subtropical Africa. During the subsequent drier phase, the sea level retreated and a drier woodland vegetation predominated, the forests retreating to riversides and sheltered gorges.

Romulea sabulosa and the smaller, pale yellow *R. hirta* with pink *Hesperantha pauciflora* in renosterveld near Nieuwoudtville

Under the influence of this drier climate, the early fynbos vegetation probably also expanded. A return of warmer, wetter conditions about 20 million years ago was accompanied by a rise in sea level, resulting in the deposition of much of the present coastal limestones. Several rises and falls in sea level over the last 10 million years, coinciding with the ice ages that swept the Northern Hemisphere, initiated the most recent cycles of erosion and deposition. During these climatic fluctuations, large bodies of sand and limestone deposited off the coast were reworked into the extensive dunes that characterize the southern and western coasts today. The present landscape is a clear record of these long cycles of erosion and deposition.

The last 16 million years have seen a gradual drying in the world's climates, interspersed with occasional wetter periods. By 5 million years ago the subtropical forests of the Cape region had given way to an open shrubland, which included many important fynbos elements. Forests became confined to the coast, river valleys, and damper mountain slopes. With the development of a Mediterranean climate from 5 to 2 million years ago, the fynbos elements underwent a massive burst of speciation, resulting in the astonishing diversity that characterizes the Cape Floral Region today.

Biogeography of the Cape

Local variation in rainfall patterns within the Cape Floral Region has led to the development of distinctive local floras, each characterized by particular suites of species. These local floras are known as phytogeographic centers; six are recognized within the Cape Floral Region (Figure 2). Because of the clear affinities between the bulbous flora of the Cape Floral Region and that of the Roggeveld Escarpment, between Calvinia and Sutherland, we include the Roggeveld as the seventh phytogeographic center in *The Color Encyclopedia of Cape Bulbs*. Each center is well

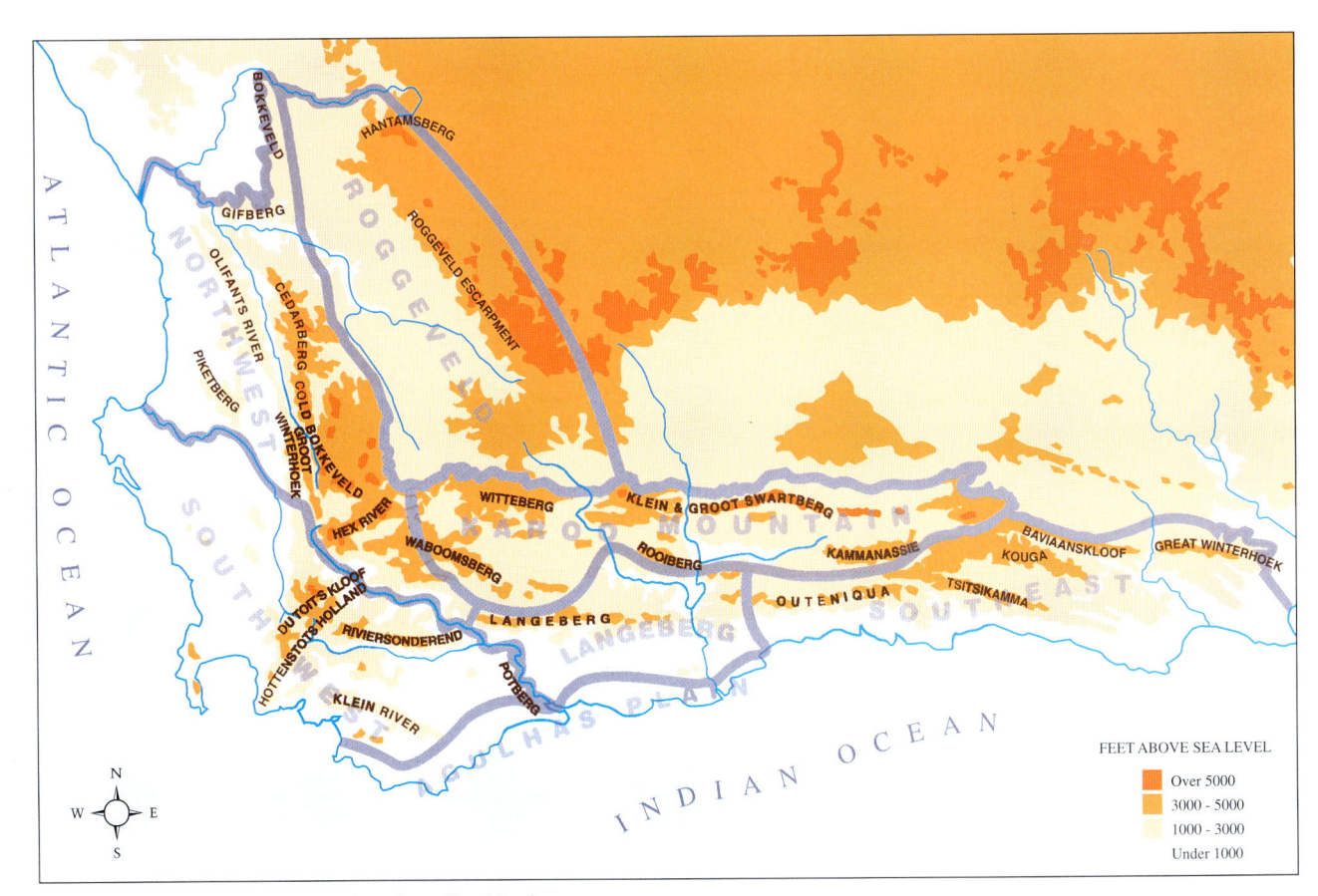

Figure 2. Phytogeographic centers of the Cape Floral Region

Daubenya aurea is restricted to a few small ridges of dolerite on the Roggeveld Escarpment

Romulea sabulosa is endemic to renosterveld around Nieuwoudtville

circumscribed geographically and climatically, and each has a distinct complement of endemic bulbous species.

ROGGEVELD CENTER (RV)

Bordering the Central or Great Karoo, the Roggeveld Center skirts the arid interior plateau, extending from the Hantamsberg at Calvinia southward along the Roggeveld Escarpment to the foothills of the Witteberg at Matjiesfontein. It is largely arid, and effective rainfall is restricted to the winter months. Rainfall over most of the area is 125–250 mm (5–10 inches) a year but along the escarpment itself may amount to more than 250 mm (10 inches) a year. The topography of the western Karoo is dominated by the Roggeveld Escarpment, rising abruptly from the extremely arid Tanqua Basin, which lies in the rain shadow of the Cedarberg Mountains. The Roggeveld is a fairly flat, rocky plain lying at 900–1200 m (3000–4000 feet) but dotted with isolated, steep-sided mountains that reach 1500–1800 m (5000–6000 feet). The most prominent of these flat-topped mountains is the Hantamsberg at Calvinia. This steep-sided mountain rises some 460 m (1500 feet) above the western Karoo plain and supports an interesting endemic flora on its summit. Winter temperatures at the higher elevations are low, and frost and snow are usual. The richest and most interesting bulb flora in the center occurs along the edges of the main Roggeveld Escarpment and the Hantamsberg, which receive the most rain. The soils are fine-grained and derived from shale or dolerite. In the wet season, the doleritic clays may become particularly glutinous when waterlogged.

Many of the cold-tolerant dwarf bulbs from the Roggeveld Center make excellent and exciting pot subjects. Foremost among them are several species of *Romulea*, the Southern Hemisphere equivalent of the crocus. Particularly noteworthy are the exquisite, fiery-flowered *R. monadelpha* and *R. unifolia*, and the early-blooming *R. tortuosa* and *R. hallii*. Perhaps the most famous of the Roggeveld bulbs is *Daubenya aurea* but other beauties include *Gladiolus marlothii*, a lovely bluebell gladiolus, and *Hesperantha vaginata*, both of which deserve horticultural attention. Probably the least appreciated species, *Moraea speciosa*, well merits its epithet, which means beautiful, for the tall plants bear huge, cup-shaped, blue, vanilla-scented flowers. Rare in the wild, it is seldom seen in its habitat, the very driest and most inaccessible parts of the western Karoo.

NORTHWEST CENTER (NW)

The rugged Northwest Center stretches from the northern limit of the Cape Floral Region, which extends as a finger along the escarpment of the Bokkeveld Mountains near Nieuwoudtville, to Piketberg and Worcester in the south. It supports a very large bulb flora of 654 known species. The topography is dominated by the Cedarberg mountain complex, which is situated near the center of a mountainous backbone, the peaks of which rise to more than 1800 m (6000 feet). Extending southward from the Cedarberg Mountains are the Cold Bokkeveld, Grootwinterhoek, and Piketberg Mountains; to the north lie the Pakhuis, Nardouw, Gifberg, and Bokkeveld Mountains. The landscape is much dissected by narrow valleys, including the Botterkloof, Olifants River, and Tulbagh Valleys. Rainfall is highest in the mountains, reaching more than 1250 mm (50 inches) a year in some mountain ravines, but is mostly 250–750 mm (10–30 inches) a year. The forelands and coastal plain west of the Olifants River and Piketberg Mountains are fairly dry with an annual rainfall of 50–250 mm (2–10 inches). The soils of the mountain ranges are mostly derived from sandstone interspersed with pockets of shale that give rise to rich, clay soils. Lying between the mountains and the coastal sands is a broad belt of shale. The renosterveld that grew here is

Orange *Bulbinella latifolia* subsp. *doleritica* and yellow *B. nutans* subsp. *nutans* in the background, pale yellow *Moraea fragrans* and lilac *Ixia rapunculoides* in the center, and the boldly marked brown and yellow *Hesperantha vaginata* in the foreground are among the numerous bulbs that occur on the dolerite flats near Nieuwoudtville

now much diminished in extent through agriculture, but its dark cast gave rise to the local term for the region, the swartland or black land.

The bulb flora of the Northwest Center is the most diverse in the Cape Floral Region; the shale and doleritic soils of the Bokkeveld Escarpment near Nieuwoudtville are especially rich in endemic bulbs. Several spectacular species of *Romulea* are restricted to seasonal seeps along the wetter margins of this high plateau (page 24). A genus that comes to mind immediately for its contribution to horticulture is *Sparaxis,* and the escarpment around Nieuwoudtville is home to both *S. tricolor* and *S. elegans,* the parents of the *Sparaxis* hybrids available commercially. Other characteristic plants of the area are the bulbinellas, of which at least 11 species occur in the center, several shared with the Roggeveld Center. Not yet well known in cultivation, these resilient plants deserve to be widely cultivated in gardens, and their long-lasting, columnar racemes, often consisting of hundreds of flowers, have great potential as cut flowers (page 25). Many of the Northwest Center's more showy species are components of renosterveld vegetation, and as this has disappeared under the plow, many bulbs have become rare and threatened. Among the more striking plants facing extinction are the several species of the group known as peacock moraeas from their iridescent markings. The autumnal flowering of the amaryllids ranks high among the floral highlights of the Northwest Center. In good years, the large, pink inflorescences of *Brunsvigia bosmaniae* coalesce in lakes of color across the dun landscape. One of the most extraordinary finds in more recent years is the discovery of a species of *Clivia* in a remote valley in the Bokkeveld Mountains. This small genus is otherwise restricted to coastal and mist belt forests along the eastern seaboard of southern Africa; *C. mirabilis* has seemingly been isolated in the Bokkeveld Mountains for millions of years, a relict from a time when the climate there was much wetter.

Brunsvigia bosmaniae on the flats at the foot of the Gifberg near Vanrhynsdorp

SOUTHWEST CENTER (SW)

Lying at the geographic heart of the Cape Floral Region, the Southwest Center extends from St. Helena Bay on the western coast across the coastal plain to the Breede River at Cape Infanta on the south coast. The Southwest Center is decidedly the botanical center of the Cape Floral Region; more than 4650 species are recorded here. With not quite 600 bulbous species, however, it is slightly poorer in bulbs than the Northwest Center. The topography is rugged with peaks of the Du Toit's Kloof and Hottentots Holland Mountains reaching more than 1500 m (5000 feet), some more than 1800 m (6000 feet), and often mantled with snow after winter storms. The annual rainfall in these mountains is well over 1000 mm (40 inches) and even the coastal plain receives more than 500 mm (20 inches) a year. The mountains are sandstone with a leached, sandy soil, but the more fertile valleys have heavy soils derived from shales or granites. The flat coastal plain is very heavily farmed and its once rich bulbous flora is reduced to small pockets on nonarable land or to the few small nature reserves that dot the wheatlands. The West Coast National Park preserves the distinctive coastal flora, which is rich in annuals along with some fine bulbous species, and the Kogelberg Biosphere Reserve is a haven for many fynbos species. Unfortunately, much of the renosterveld vegetation that occurred naturally on the clay lowlands has disappeared under agriculture, pushing many beautiful bulbous species close to extinction.

Among the more prominent bulbous species of the Southwest Center are *Nerine sarniensis* and the New Year lily, *Gladiolus cardinalis*, both red-flowered and blooming in the summer and early autumn. There are, in fact, more than 60 different *Gladiolus* species in this tiny corner of the world, smaller than the island of Sicily. Several extraordinary suites of species occur in the center. Among these, the wine cups, particularly *Babiana rubrocyanea*, *Geissorhiza radians*, and *G. mathewsii*, are quite remarkable for their violet flowers with a bright scarlet cup. The area also boasts the greatest concentration of brilliantly colored ixias, notably several orange-flowered species like *Ixia maculata* and the startling, turquoise-flowered *I. viridiflora*. The Southwest Center is also home to the belladonna lily, *Amaryllis belladonna*, a plant that often flowers poorly in the wild but blooms well in cultivation. Its huge, lily-like flowers, pushing through the dry soil at the end of summer, are a welcome sight as harbingers of cool weather and the coming winter rains. Two *Agapanthus* species, *A. africanus* and *A. walshii*, grow on the upper mountain slopes in the Southwest Center, but both flower well only after fire in the wild and have not been successfully domesticated.

AGULHAS PLAIN (AP)

Smallest of the Cape phytogeographic centers, the Agulhas Plain stretches in a narrow band along the southern Cape coast from Gansbaai to Mossel Bay. This ancient seabed is dotted with low ridges, none reaching much more than 300 m (1000 feet). The annual rainfall is mostly 250–380 mm (10–15 inches) but the coastal ranges may receive slightly more. The distinctive flora of the center is largely a result of a limestone substrate, a rock rare elsewhere in the Cape Floral Region. The sandy or limestone soils are porous and well drained, so the flora is drought resistant.

Many distinctive races of more widespread plants occur on the limestone flats and calcareous sands. The soil is not exclusively limestone and is locally interspersed with clay and sandstone beds. Particularly fine species of the Agulhas Plain are *Freesia leichtlinii*, *Gladiolus variegatus*, and the inappropriately named *Tritonia squalida*. This latter, easily grown species has lovely pale to deep pink flowers that would grace any garden. Although often restricted to limestone substrates in the wild, the bulbs of the Agulhas Plain grow well in cultivation in ordinary soil mixes.

KAROO MOUNTAIN CENTER (KM)

The largely arid Karoo Mountain Center includes the dry Little Karoo, an extended valley lying between the Langeberg and Swartberg Mountains. The north side of the Little Karoo is dominated by the jagged Swartberg Mountains, rising steeply out of the plain. These mountains include several of the highest peaks in the Cape Floral Region, a few reaching more than 2100 m (7000 feet). Annual rainfall is mostly 250–500 mm (10–20 inches) but the southern slopes of the mountains receive rather more and the northern slopes and valleys are much drier. As elsewhere in the Cape Floral Region, the mountains consist of sandstones and the valleys largely of clay soils.

The Karoo Mountain Center has a bulb flora that is decidedly modest by the standards of the Cape flora. Several tritonias are native here, among which the creamy-flowered *Tritonia pallida* and orange-flowered *T. watermeyeri* make particularly valuable additions to the horticultural palette, the latter unfortunately difficult to grow well. Another species that is conspicuous on sheltered rocky slopes around Montagu is *Veltheimia capensis*. Endemic bulbs include two lovely *Syringodea* species and the handsome purple-flowered *Moraea regalis*. Two pink-flowered *Gladiolus* species, *G. aquamontanus* and *G. nigromontanus*, are known from only a few sites in the Swartberg Mountains.

LANGEBERG CENTER (LB)

Comprising the high Langeberg Mountains and the coastal plain to the south, the Langeberg Center extends from the Cogman's Kloof gap near Montagu in the west to Robinson's Pass in the east. The Langeberg Mountains dominate the landscape, their steep sandstone slopes rising to more than 1200 m (4000 feet) with peaks reaching more than 1500 m (5000 feet). The southern slopes are well watered, with an annual rainfall of more than 750 mm (30 inches). The wetter slopes are densely cloaked in fynbos vegetation, but the northern slopes are rocky and rather arid. The much gentler landscape of the coastal plain to the south of the Langeberg is also drier with 250–500 mm (10–20 inches) of rain a year, and the softer shales are weathered into rolling hills of heavy clay soil.

The bulb flora of the Langeberg Center is interesting and includes two striking tritonias, *Tritonia crocata* and *T. deusta*, both with bright orange to scarlet flowers, and several species of *Cyrtanthus* and *Gladiolus*. Some of these, like *G. permeabilis* and *G. stellatus*, are admittedly small flowered but deserve attention because of their strong violet-like fragrance. The area is also the center of the ranges of the two lovely dwarf watsonias, *W. aletroides* and *W. laccata*, although both species also grow in the adjacent centers.

SOUTHEAST CENTER (SE)

Although part of the Cape Floral Region, the Southeast Center is not a region of exclusively winter rainfall; at least half the annual rainfall occurs over the summer months. The center extends from Robinson's Pass and George in the west to Port Elizabeth in the east. The topography is very broken, with the Outeniqua and Tsitsikamma Mountains rising abruptly from a narrow coastal plain, and the Kouga, Baviaanskloof, and Great Winterhoek Mountains forming its interior border. The narrow Long Kloof, a valley extending half the length of the center, lies between the coastal and interior mountains. The Southeast Center has one of the smallest bulb floras of the Cape phytogeographic centers for its size. This is a direct result of the fairly high, rather nonseasonal rainfall, mainly 500–760 mm (20–30 inches) a year, which favors a dense vegetation with a mix of fynbos and evergreen forest, leaving little room for bulbs.

Among the more striking bulbs of the center are several watsonias, which make fine displays in the wild. Perhaps the most famous of the bulbs of the area is the plant known in Britain as the Scarborough lily, *Cyrtanthus elatus*, which has huge, bright scarlet flowers and is a worthy subject for any bulb garden. Other notable species are *Gladiolus sempervirens* and, particularly, *Agapanthus praecox*, which extends eastward into the summer-rainfall part of southern Africa. This latter species is cultivated all over the world and is undoubtedly the area's most important contribution to horticulture. Unlike its Western Cape relatives, *A. praecox* is easy to grow and produces huge umbels of blue flowers in even the most neglected corners of the garden. It seems equally at home in summer-rainfall gardens as in winter-rainfall ones and tolerates more winter cold than its wild habitat might suggest. In fact, many of the plants from this region take readily to cultivation, most probably because they are adapted to a relatively nonseasonal rainfall.

IN ALL, SOME 1183 species of bulbous plants are known from the Cape Floral Region and Roggeveld (excluding the 11 or so species of *Chlorophytum* known from the area), more than 70% of which are endemic. The iris family is by far the most important in number of species and alone contributes more than half the total number of bulbous species in the region. Together, the amaryllis and hyacinth families contribute a further 316 species to the total.

The importance of a true Mediterranean climate in favoring the bulbous species is evident even at the local level within the Cape Floral Region, where the richest concentration of bulbs is found in the west, which experiences a pronounced summer drought. The Northwest Center has the richest bulb flora with 632 species, followed by the Southwest Center with 594 species. Together the two centers account for nearly 70% of all Cape bulbs. The triangle formed by these two centers, with Nieuwoudtville, Cape Town, and Bredasdorp at it corners, is home to almost 800 species of bulbs. The arid Roggeveld Center has fewer bulbous species, not surprising given its relatively modest flora. Most of the Cape bulbous families are best represented in the Northwest Center, but the Iridaceae seem to favor slightly wetter habitats and are most diverse in the Southwest Center.

Among the more important reasons for the wealth of the Cape bulb flora may be the relatively mild winter temperatures and predictable rains that characterize the climate. Moderate winter temperatures allow for an early initiation of growth while minimizing the risk that the plant will not complete its growth cycle, during which the bulb must replenish its reserves. Southern Africa, unlike other regions of the world, has enjoyed the additional advantage of a seasonal but fairly mild, predictable climate for millions of years. Combined with an open vegetation that allows space for bulbs, this climatic stability has favored the accumulation of geophytes over a long period, among them the ancestors of today's Cape bulbs. With the establishment of a highly seasonal winter-rainfall regime over the past 5 million years, the stage was set for the extraordinary speciation that has resulted in the huge numbers of geophytes in the Cape.

Apart from stimulating the evolution of a distinctive, spring-flowering bulb flora, the climatic characteristics of the Cape Floral Region have also stimulated the evolution of several autumn-flowering bulbs, particularly among the Amaryllidaceae. The majority of Cape amaryllids produce large, juicy seeds unable to withstand desiccation but ideally suited for rapid germination and establishment of seedlings as the rainy season begins. Although able to flower in the dry months by drawing upon moisture and nutrient reserves in the bulb, these plants must wait until the rainy season before producing leaves. The separation of leafing and flowering phases is a strategy that has been adopted by several other Cape bulbs, including some *Gladiolus* species and almost all species of *Drimia* and *Eriospermum*. A great advantage to those species of the winter-rainfall region that produce their flowers in summer, at a time when relatively few other plants are in bloom, is the enhanced opportunities provided for pollination and, thus, seed set.

One of the most striking aspects of many Cape species of Amaryllidaceae is their ball-like seed heads, like tumbleweeds adapted to seed dispersal by wind. Semidesert areas are known for the prevalence of tumbleweeds, probably because of the low height of the vegetation; the drier northwestern part of the Cape Floral Region is no exception. The large infructescences of *Boophone, Brunsvigia, Crossyne,* and *Cybistetes,* with a diameter of 15–50 cm, are especially conspicuous, often piling up against fences or bushes. Although most evident in the Cape members of the Amaryllidaceae, the tumbling strategy of seed dis-

Species of bulbous plants in the phytogeographic centers of the Cape

FAMILY	TOTAL	RV	NW	SW	AP	KM	LB	SE
Agapanthaceae	3	0	0	2	1	0	1	1
Alliaceae	5	3	3	3	1	1	2	4
Amaryllidaceae	103	22	48	39	22	17	18	32
Araceae	2	1	1	1	1	1	1	1
Asphodelaceae	19	6	14	11	2	5	5	5
Colchicaceae	35	12	23	16	6	13	10	8
Haemodoraceae	8	0	7	8	3	1	5	3
Hyacinthaceae	213	59	125	95	39	63	35	55
Hypoxidaceae	30	5	15	16	9	3	10	10
Iridaceae	708	94	359	383	98	113	146	121
Lanariaceae	1	0	0	1	1	0	1	1
Ruscaceae	52	15	32	17	7	20	11	16
Tecophilaeaceae	6	3	5	2	1	3	2	1
	1183	220	632	594	191	240	247	258

* RV, Roggeveld; NW, Northwest; SW, Southwest; AP, Agulhas Plain; KM, Karoo Mountain; LB, Langeberg; SE, Southeast. Rows do not add to the total because most species are not endemic to a single center

persal is also developed in *Daubenya*, *Massonia* (Hyacinthaceae), and some species of *Trachyandra* (Asphodelaceae).

The Cape bulb flora is distinguished by some striking and highly unusual growth forms. Nowhere else, for instance, are bulbous plants found with their leaf or leaves pressed to the ground, as occurs in many species of *Brunsvigia* and *Crossyne* (Amaryllidaceae) and *Massonia* and *Lachenalia* (Hyacinthaceae). Similarly, the tightly coiled leaves of some species of *Albuca*, *Dipcadi*, and *Ornithogalum* (Hyacinthaceae), *Gethyllis* (Amaryllidaceae), and *Moraea* (Iridaceae) are virtually unique to the Cape bulb flora. Climate and latitude are thought to be responsible for these leaf modifications, which are most likely adaptations that allow the plants to maximize the use of sunlight at a low angle during winter when they grow actively. Another strategy that has been developed among diverse Cape bulbs is the production of a long-lived inflorescence axis that assumes the dominant role in photosynthesis, whereas the leaves are reduced or soon wither. Intriguingly, the inflorescence axis is wiry and often coiled at the base like a spring. This curious habit is found in species of *Bulbine* (Asphodelaceae), *Drimia* (Hyacinthaceae), *Eriospermum* (Ruscaceae), and *Strumaria* (Amaryllidaceae) among others.

FURTHER READING. Cowling and Richardson (1995) provided a well-illustrated, highly readable introduction to the ecology and flora of the Cape region. More technical accounts appeared in the book edited by Cowling (1992). Detailed characteristics of the flora and a complete account of the species have been provided by Goldblatt and Manning (2000a). The origin and evolution of seed dispersal strategies in amaryllids was discussed by Snijman and Linder (1996), and Esler et al. (1999) documented the occurrence and discussed the adaptive value of the prostrate leaves characteristic of several genera of Cape bulbs.

BULBS IN THE GARDEN

CAPE BULBS, with the exception of various hybrids and cultivars of *Freesia, Ixia,* and *Sparaxis* (Iridaceae), are poorly known outside specialist collections. Several factors have militated against their popularity in general garden cultivation, including the inability of several species to withstand garden irrigation during the dormancy period, the extremely short flowering period of some, and the delicate or fragile nature of many species. This is a pity, for many species are worth growing and several of the larger species are exceptionally rewarding even in large gardens. While it is true that the majority of the species are too small to feature in mixed plantings, much of their charm lies in their curiously shaped, delicately marked, and often deliciously fragrant flowers. These features are best appreciated if the plants are grown in rock gardens where they can be admired to advantage. Rock gardens have the additional advantages of better drainage and allowing greater control over watering plus the provision of numerous microhabitats.

Cape bulbs, with few exceptions, will not tolerate more than light frost and are therefore not hardy across most of North America and Eurasia. They are more safely grown under glass in cool temperate zones. In warm temperate climates, however, many species are grown to advantage in the garden in both the Southern and Northern Hemispheres. Naturally, they are much easier to grow under conditions comparable to those in their area of origin and thrive in regions with a Mediterranean climate. Several of the larger species of *Watsonia,* for instance, are important plants in the open garden and as a component of roadside plantings in and around Cape Town itself. There are also some wonderful garden plantings of Cape bulbs in California. Conditions in southwestern and southeastern Australia, which experience a Mediterranean climate, are apparently ideal, and a number of Cape bulbs have become naturalized there. These include *Gladiolus caryophyllaceus,* which is positively luxuriant in parts of Perth although difficult to cultivate in the Cape, and *G. undulatus,* which is a weed of roadside ditches. Other Cape bulbs that have thrived after emigration include species of Amaryllidaceae, Hyacinthaceae, and several other Iridaceae. All these species have proliferated through vegetative propagation, and it is quite certain that many others will grow successfully if introduced.

The ease and success with which Cape bulbs can be grown in the open in regions that do not experience a true Mediterranean climate depend largely on their provenance in the Cape region itself. Species from the Northwest and Southwest Centers are adapted to true summer drought and often tolerate moisture poorly during their dormant period, whereas those from the Southeast Center are often more or less evergreen and depend on some moisture throughout the year. The latter are correspondingly easier to grow in the garden, where individual watering regimes are not easily imposed. Cape bulbs prefer open ground in neutral to acidic soil, and healthy plants are best left undisturbed in the ground for years. This may not be possible in areas that cannot be left dry and empty for the summer, and in that case the bulbs should be lifted in early summer and stored dry until the following autumn. Good drainage will also go a long way toward alleviating the influence of summer moisture. Our experience is that many species suffer little, if at all, from modest summer moisture in the fairly mild summers of the southern African interior plateau as long as the ground is well drained. Rock gardens are consequently an ideal place in which to grow many of these species.

Bulbs resting in situ are also at some risk from a range of predators, including insect grubs, herbivorous mammals, and wildfowl. In the Cape region itself the main predators of bulbs are mole rats and porcupines, but baboons can also be destructive locally. Some wildfowl, particularly guinea fowl and the partridge-like francolins, wreak havoc among seedlings. Although bulbous plants are potentially long-lived, perhaps able to live hundreds of years, it is doubtful whether many species survive the depredations of these predators in nature for many years.

Among the species particularly recommended for the garden and rockery are all the chasmanthes, cyanellas, freesias, and ixias, many of the gladioli, moraeas, and sparaxis, and several of the babianas, bulbinellas, and larger-flowered lachenalias. Summer drought is not essential for those species that grow along streams or in seasonally wet places, and *Gladiolus angustus*, for instance, can endure even heavy watering during the summer. Two of the most worthwhile Cape bulbs for garden use, the calla lily (*Zantedeschia aethiopica*) and golden scepter (*Wachendorfia thyrsiflora*), are plants of seasonal wetlands. Indeed, in some places they even grow together in the wild, where their differently shaped leaves and colored flowers complement one another beautifully. The golden scepter, in

Wachendorfia thyrsiflora and *Zantedeschia aethiopica* in a marsh in the sandstone mountains near Grabouw

particular, cannot be recommended highly enough for pond-side plantings. Its tall, long-lasting spires of chrome yellow flowers are a great asset. Another wetland species, the greater water phlox *(Onixotis stricta),* is much more delicate, but its cherry blossom-like flowers are most attractive.

Bulb Structure

Specialized underground organs for the storage of food reserves have been developed many times in the plant kingdom as a strategy for surviving seasonal conditions unfavorable for growth, be they cold, aridity, or competition from other plants. Plants that have adopted this strategy produce seasonal flushes of aboveground parts that last through the growing season but die back completely to the subterranean perennating parts during periods unfavorable for growth. Although these underground organs may seem dormant for much of the dry season, in many instances all sorts of physiological processes take place at this time, including the initiation of leaves and inflorescences in anticipation of rapid development once the environmental conditions that stimulate growth occur.

Plants with underground storage organs are found throughout the world in a variety of seasonal habitats, but in all cases the advantages of this habit lie in the rapidity with which the plants can respond to more favorable growing conditions. Bulbs, for instance, are a conspicuous element of the spring flora of alpine and arctic regions because their underground storage organs, overwintering in subterranean safety, enable the plants to respond rapidly to the spring thaw and complete their life cycle of growth and reproduction over the short summer period. The value of such a rapid growth cycle is also evident in plants on the floor of temperate deciduous woodlands. There, the underground reserves of bulbous plants enable them to establish their foliage quickly enough in spring to take advantage of the available light before the tree canopy can develop. By early summer, when the forest floor is heavily shaded and the surface layers of the soil have dried out because of the high rates of transpiration of the woody plants, most of the bulbs have set seed and died back to their underground reserves. Bulbs are a particularly conspicuous part of the flora of regions with a Mediterranean climate in which mild wet winters suitable for growth alternate with hot dry summers, sometimes accompanied by desiccating winds. In those regions, the production of underground storage organs is not only a crucial strategy that enables plants to survive the dry summers, it has the additional advantage that plants may separate their leafing and flowering phases. Plants that have adopted this strategy are able to produce flowers during summer and autumn when they can take advantage of reduced competition for pollinators as well as shed their seeds immediately before the growing season, thereby reducing the period during which seeds lie vulnerable to predation.

Bulbous plants, more correctly known as geophytes, are a heterogeneous assemblage belonging to many genera and a number of different plant families. General horticultural tradition groups the lily-like monocotyledonous plant families with underground storage organs and a seasonal habit together as bulbs regardless of the actual nature of their underground storage organs. (Monocots are flowering plants whose embryo has only one cotyledon; the group includes palms, lilies, orchids, and grasses among other plants.) The underground organs are actually very diverse in structure, and technically, many are not bulbs at all. The storage organs of geophytes in the Cape Floral Region include rhizomes, corms, tubers, and, of course, true bulbs. All serve the same purpose, and the distinction between them is structural rather than functional, with the storage reserves concentrated in different organs, typically the stems, leaves, or roots.

RHIZOMES REPRESENT the least specialized type of storage organ and may be thought of as more or less horizontal stems that are fleshy, filled with stored food, often starch, and produce roots from the underside. The rhizome is usually elongated and bears the scars of leaves of past seasons at joints or nodes, giving the organ a segmented appearance. A bud primordium is located in the axil of the leaf scar at each node, giving the rhizome a great capacity for branching and spreading. As the rhizome grows, the older parts become more or less exhausted and atrophy, and in this way the growing points can migrate through the soil. This wandering habit contrasts with the more or less sedentary nature of other types of storage organ. At each growing point on the rhizome is an apical bud, consisting of leaf primordia enclosing a tiny shoot apex. Although rhizomes are typically more or less horizontal they may be quite short, and even more or less vertical, and sometimes are not readily visible on the growing plant. Cape Asphodelaceae and Haemodoraceae have rhizomes as do all Agapanthaceae, some Hypoxidaceae, and some Iridaceae, notably *Aristea*, *Bobartia*, and *Dietes*. The distinctive red pigment produced by the bloodroot family, Haemodoraceae, often colors their rhizomes a characteristic bright red.

Corms are modified, shortened rhizomes of relatively few nodes, comprising a fairly dry, starchy nugget of stem tissue topped by a small, fleshy apical bud. The apical bud of the corm consists of a microscopic shoot apex surrounded by leaf primordia. Roots are usually produced from the lower part of the corm but in two genera of Iridaceae, *Ferraria* and *Moraea*, they issue from the base of the current year's shoot. Corms are usually enclosed in special layers, usually called corm tunics, derived either from the bases of ordinary foliage leaves or from special sheathing leaves called cataphylls. They are often papery or fibrous but may be truly woody in some genera. In Iridaceae, the appearance of the corm tunics is often important for purposes of identification at the generic and sometimes even at the species level. Most Cape Colchicaceae, Hypoxidaceae, Iridaceae, and Tecophilaeaceae have corms.

Tubers are also swollen storage stems but are typically not covered by tunics and have their initiation buds scattered over the surface and not confined to the nodes. They often develop from the tips of rhizomes and are not as discrete as corms nor as upright.

Tuberous roots are swollen roots and are hence unable to produce adventitious buds except where they attach to the short stem or rhizome and form the crown. New tuberous roots are formed each growth cycle, although those from the previous season may persist as dry, withered remnants. The tuberous swelling can be restricted to parts of the roots, often near the tips, or the entire root may be thickened. Tuberous roots are relatively rare in Cape bulbs but characterize most species of Asphodelaceae, sometimes in conjunction with well-developed storage rhizomes.

True bulbs are highly specialized storage structures in which the storage function has been transferred from the stem to the leaves. The stem is reduced to a small disk of tissue bearing apical and axillary buds, all closely wrapped by enlarged, persistent leaves or leaf bases that comprise the main storage tissues. These storage bases can be distinguished either as tunics if they wrap entirely around the shoot in a continuous collar or as scales if they are narrower and incompletely sheathing. The roots, which may persist for several seasons, are produced from the central core of stem tissue, often called a basal disk or plate. The basal plate may be relatively large, as in species of *Haemanthus*, or hardly visible from the outside. With time, the outer leaf bases gradually dry out so that bulbs become enveloped in dry layers called bulb coats. These often decay in a characteristic manner, becoming fibrous, papery, or somewhat woody. Cape species of the families Alliaceae, Amaryllidaceae, and Hyacinthaceae all have true bulbs. Species of *Tulbaghia* (Alliaceae) typically produce clumps of small bulbs attached to an elongated rhizomatous base plate.

Bulbs, corms, and rhizomes are similar then in their basic organization but vary considerably in the proportional contribution that the different organs make to the storage tissues. Corms are also distinctive in that they are replaced completely each growing season, whereas rhizomes and bulbs are only partially replaced each season. The distinction between these three types of organ is not always absolute; in some species, some storage may take place in both the stem and the leaves. Less easy to define are the tuber-like storage structures of *Eriospermum* (Ruscaceae). These stem tubers are fleshy, or dry and starchy, and lack obvious nodes and leaf scars yet produce roots from the underside and have a shoot apex that produces leaves and a stem in the growing season.

An understanding of the structure and true nature of underground storage organs is not an idle academic distinction but is sometimes necessary for successful cultivation. It is important to distinguish true bulbs from corms and rhizomes for several reasons, of which one of the most important concerns the periodic formation of the future flower shoots. In true bulbs, flower shoots are formed during the dormant period preceding growth, whereas in corms and rhizomes they generally develop after sprouting has commenced for the current season. The conditions under which resting bulbs are stored are therefore far more critical to subsequent flowering than they are for corms. Also, it is useful to appreciate the significance of the basal disk in bulbs. If this tissue is badly damaged or lost when cleaning or collecting a bulb, then the bulb immediately loses its ability to form roots and is rendered unable to grow and flower ever again. The necessity of ensuring that a portion of the basal disk remains attached to each leaf scale removed for vegetative propagation also becomes evident, for shoots and roots rarely arise from the leaf alone (some species of *Lachenalia* excepted) but usually from axillary and adventitious buds on the stem.

Bulb Cultivation

The majority of Cape bulbs are adapted to a Mediterranean climate with winter rains and summer drought. The exceptions are those species that enter the region from the adjacent summer-rainfall parts of the country in the extreme east. There, the rainfall is not highly seasonal, and many of the bulbs are more or less evergreen or have a short dormant phase immediately after fruiting. An extended or pronounced dry resting period is therefore not as critical for the survival of those species and they are correspondingly easier to cultivate, both in pots and in the garden. Typically, however, the growth cycle of Cape bulbs is characterized by a period of dormancy during the hot dry summer; dormancy is broken by the production of new vegetative growth in autumn as soon as temperatures begin to fall. This initiates a period of rapid vegetative growth during the mild wet winters, followed by flowering in the spring as the weather warms and periods of daylight lengthen. Seed production and dispersal are completed by early summer, and the bulb then enters its summer dormancy.

Most plants, and Cape bulbs are no exception, respond best in cultivation if their natural growth requirements are duplicated as closely as possible. Although we can offer some generalizations, the multitude of species and corresponding diversity of habitats make it essential that each species be considered independently. Much useful information can be gleaned by determining the natural ecology and distribution of each species from the accounts of the species in *The Color Encyclopedia of Cape Bulbs*, then referring to the climatic descriptions provided for the relevant phytogeographic centers. Species that are widespread, especially those that occur across several centers of diversity, can be expected to be more tolerant of a range of environmental conditions and thus easier to cultivate. Particular recommendations for cultivation are given for each genus.

The great rarity of many of the Cape bulbs provides an additional stimulus to their cultivation. It is an unfortunate fact that agriculture, mining, and urban sprawl are exerting increasing pressure on the survival of many species in the wild. While cultivation can be a boon to conservation, this is only true if it does not increase the demand for wild-collected plants. We therefore urge that species be grown only from seed or from cultivated rootstocks that have themselves been grown from seed. There is seldom justification for collecting mature plants in the wild, and plants grown from seed often adapt to cultivation better than mature individuals that have been stripped from their native habitat.

TEMPERATURE & LIGHT

In general, Cape bulbs are best grown under long-day conditions at moderate temperatures, 12–17°C (54–62°F). Alternating day/night temperatures of 22/17°C (72/62°F) have been found to be optimal for growth and flowering in *Ornithogalum dubium*, for instance. Similarly, flowering in hybrid gladiolus derived from Cape parents occurs when the plants are grown under temperature regimes of 15/12°C (59/54°F) or 20/17°C (68/62°F) but not at a warmer temperature of 25°C (77°F). Watering should begin once the bulb has sprouted but should be gradually withheld after flowering to allow the bulbs to dry off. Dry bulbs are best stored, either in the pots or paper bags, until planting time in autumn. Optimal storage temperature varies but is generally 18–22°C (64–72°F); although it may be as high as 25°C (77°F) for some species, it should not exceed this. Moving dormant bulbs of *O. dubium* to a lower temperature, 10–15°C (50–59°F), for 3 weeks before planting enhances the quality of flowering, but a similar treatment merely accelerates flowering in some Cape species of *Gladiolus*. Although the dormant period in cormous and rhizomatous species is truly a period of quiescence, such is not the case in those species with true bulbs. For true bulbs, the dormant period is in fact the most important phase in their development, particularly amaryllis and hyacinth families (Amaryllidaceae and Hyacinthaceae). It is during this period that leaves and inflorescence are formed within the bulb, and storage conditions are therefore critical for successful flowering the following season. This contrasts sharply with the situation in cormous species such as most members of the iris family (Iridaceae) in which flower buds are initiated in late autumn or early winter after the first leaf has sprouted. Particular attention should therefore be paid to the storage temperatures of true bulbs.

In the Northern Hemisphere, most Cape bulbs are hardy enough to be grown outdoors in milder climates or in a cool glasshouse that provides frost protection at night. They should be given as much light and ventilation as possible to prevent etiolation. In hotter climates, however, it is essential that pots not overheat; a general rule is cool roots, warm shoots. This applies also to dormant bulbs, which should not be stored in too hot or sunny a location. Although the period of vegetative growth invariably falls during winter months, there is substantial variation between species in the flowering period. Several of the smaller members of the hyacinth family—*Massonia, Polyxena,* and some species of *Daubenya,* for example—flower in late autumn or early winter, almost before vegetative growth is completed. Others, including several species of *Ornithogalum* (Hyacinthaceae) and most *Tritoniopsis* (Iridaceae), flower in summer when the leaves are drying off. This temporal separation between the production of leaves and the production of flowers is particularly marked in the majority of amaryllids (Amaryllidaceae). In these plants, flowering is delayed until summer or autumn, long after vegetative growth has been terminated and by which time the leaves have completely withered or blown away.

SOIL

As a rule, Cape bulbs need well-drained soil because the fleshy organs are prone to rotting when waterlogged, especially when in the dormant state. Species that grow on more fine-grained soils derived from shales in the wild do well in a medium consisting of two parts medium- or coarse-grained sand, one part loam, and one part compost. Another formula comprises two parts coarse river sand and one part fine potting medium. Planting the bulbs in a layer of pure sand on top of the medium is a good way of reducing the risk of rotting. In some species it may be necessary to reduce the amount of compost or dispense with it entirely. An alternative medium that is used with success at the Royal Botanic Gardens, Kew, comprises John Innes no. 2 compost (basically a loam-based potting soil with intermediate amounts of fertilizer added), with or without added sharp sand to improve drainage. Species that are restricted to the acidic, nutrient-poor sands of the Cape mountains should be tried in a much coarser mixture of three to five parts sand and one part compost or loam, or even in pure sand.

Our experience is that most bulbs respond well to kinder treatment than they often receive in the wild, and that although they favor particular soils in nature, they do not necessarily require those soils for optimal growth. Plants may be found on rock outcrops only because their nutritious underground parts are readily reached by predators when they grow in open ground. Similarly, some species typically found on clay soils may grow there because those soils hold water longer than well-drained sands rather than because the clays have some other intrinsic advantage. For most species it is safe to plant the bulbs in a moderately rich soil but not a heavy one. Ensure good drainage, and avoid standing water at all times, except in wetland species such as the wine cup geissorhizas (Iridaceae) and *Onixotis* (Colchicaceae), which flourish in saucers filled with water during the winter growing season. Apart from such exceptions, it is seldom advisable to try to re-create in a pot the soil type that a plant favors in nature, and it is better to err toward a coarser mix.

PLANTING

Planting should be done in the autumn, optimally in late March or April in the Southern Hemisphere, October in the Northern Hemisphere, for those species that flower in the spring. Early-flowering species should be planted a month or two earlier. The latter group includes species of *Daubenya, Massonia,* and *Polyxena* (Hyacinthaceae), which flower in early winter (May or June in the Southern Hemisphere). It is usually not necessary to lift the dormant bulbs each season unless the species is prone to extensive vegetative reproduction, especially through fragmentation of the bulb, producing bulblets, or the production of stolons. If they are not lifted and separated, the bulblets will compete for space and nutrients. Members of the amaryllis family, which all have perennial fleshy roots, should not be disturbed once they have become established. If it is necessary to transplant them, that should be done immediately after new leaves appear while the bulbs are in active growth.

Bulb coats and corm tunics protect the living inner tissue from mechanical damage, help keep the soft tissue from drying out, and possibly also help protect bulbs and corms from predators. It is therefore advisable to remove only the older, outer tunics when cleaning bulbs or corms. Removing the inner tunics exposes the delicate apical buds, and the damage to the surface can provide a point of entry for bacteria that often cause the internal tissue to rot.

It is also helpful to look at corms and bulbs before planting. The position of old roots indicates the bottom of the organ; although it is usually simple to establish the orientation of the organ, this is not always easy in those species of *Eriospermum* (Ruscaceae) in which the shoot tissues from near the base of the stem tuber. Corms and bulbs planted upside down or on their side have a harder time germinating and sprouting; although this does not necessarily mean they will fail, it does not promote good growth.

Although most bulbs are subterranean, the depth at which they grow varies tremendously. As a general rule, rhizomes should be planted at or just below the surface and corms at a depth that is about three times the height of the corm, although most cormous plants can survive at shallower depths. Exceptions are *Androcymbium* (Colchicaceae), *Babiana* (Iridaceae), and *Cyanella* (Tecophilaeaceae), which may be planted somewhat deeper. For true bulbs, however, planting depth varies tremendously among the genera. Most Hyacinthaceae are best planted below the surface, generally at a depth 1.5 times the height of the bulb, whereas *Eucomis,* along with many Amaryllidaceae, should be planted at much shallower depths with the top of the bulb level with the surface. Other species of Amaryllidaceae and Hyacinthaceae, often those with relatively large bulbs, like *Boophone, Crinum, Cyrtanthus,* and *Veltheimia,* should be planted with at least two-thirds of the bulb exposed above the soil. Finally, those like *Albuca batteniana, Bowiea,* and *Ornithogalum longibracteatum,* which are all more or less evergreen, must be planted completely above the soil with just the roots buried. All geophytes start their lives as seeds that germinate close to the soil surface. As they grow, they are able to retract their bulb or corm to the depth they prefer. A bulb or corm planted too near the surface will take care of the problem by itself in the next season if not the one in which it was planted. Planting too deep, however, will retard growth and weaken the plant; it is thus better to err on the shallow side.

Both plastic and terra-cotta pots may be used. Although the former have a price advantage, they suffer from the tendency to overheat in warm climates if exposed to direct sunlight, unlike terra-cotta pots, which cool by evaporation from the sides. In warmer, drier climates, however, terra-cotta pots tend to dry out too rapidly, and larger pots that retain moisture are preferable. The problem of overheating can be avoided by shading the pots, either by screening them or by plunging them into larger pots, filling the space between the two with gravel. Good drainage is essential; this can be ensured by drilling or cutting extra holes in the sides of plastic pots near the base.

Many of the smaller species can be crowded in a single pot to give a good display. Species of *Cyrtanthus* (Amaryllidaceae) in particular actually prefer this and may be shy to flower if given room. Although most species can be repotted each year, this is not recommended for the larger amaryllids such as *Boophone, Brunsvigia,* and *Crinum,* which prefer to remain undisturbed and should not be repotted until necessary, certainly not more frequently than every 5–6 years.

WATERING

Once planted, pots should be watered well and then not again until leaf shoots appear, after which a good soaking every week or two is recommended, as opposed to light applications at irregular intervals. It is particularly important under glass to keep water away from the crown of the plant to avoid rotting in still, damp weather. Overwatering of container-grown plants will soon lead to rotting; it is preferable for the growing medium to be slightly dry rather than too wet. This is particularly important for species of Amaryllidaceae, some of which require watering only once a month. Exceptions are those aquatic or wetland species like *Onixotis* (Colchicaceae) and the wine cup geissorhizas (Iridaceae), which should be kept moist throughout the growing period. Water must be completely withheld after the flowers fade or as soon as the foliage begins to yellow. This is usually toward the end of spring but may be later in some species; it is best to continue watering until leaves begin to yellow. After the leaves have withered and seed has been harvested, the containers can be moved into a moderately cool, dry place for storage until the following autumn when new shoots emerge.

FERTILIZING

One of the main reasons for repotting bulbs is to replenish soil that has been depleted of nutrients or become compacted. If repotted into fresh soil every year or every alternate year, most Cape bulbs can be grown successfully without supplementary feeding because of their low nutritional requirements, and repotting is not recommended at all for the larger Amaryllidaceae. For those and other species that are left in the same pot for years, however, some feeding is recommended for continued vigorous growth. Most liquid fertilizers are adequate but should be low in nitrogen. Fertilize once or twice in the growing season only.

PESTS

Like most bulbs in cultivation, Cape bulbs are susceptible to infestations by mealybugs. These pests will transmit viral infections between plants, and immediate treatment is essential. The most effective is to drench the entire pot with an organophosphate, chlorpyrifos, available under the trade name Chlorpirifos. Snails and slugs will also carry viruses and should be controlled. Members of the amaryllis family are almost certain to suffer from attack by the lily borer moth, also known as amaryllis caterpillar. Blackening of the foliage followed by collapse of the plant indicates infestation by this pest. Repeated foliar sprays with carbaryl, available under the trade names Carbaryl or Karbaspray, are recommended. Members of the iris family, particularly the genus *Babiana,* are often infested with red spider mites, which form a fine web on the leaves, particularly the undersurface. Spraying with chlorpyrifos is an effective treatment. This is also useful against aphids, which attack the leaves and flower buds of a wide range of Cape bulbs. Less toxic alternatives are recommended; ladybugs are natural predators of aphids.

SEEDS

Generally, the seeds of Cape bulbs germinate readily. Seeds should be sown in autumn in deep seed trays or pots. A good general medium is equal parts sand and fine compost or loam. The flat, black seeds of *Cyrtanthus* (Amaryllidaceae) can also be germinated in glass containers filled with water that should be replaced every week. Once they have produced a few leaves, seedlings can then be transferred to pots or trays. Seeds should be sown thinly and covered with a thin layer of sand. Exceptions are the large fleshy seeds of many members of the amaryllis family, which are simply pressed into the medium slightly. Seedlings should remain in the seed tray or pot at least one full season, and in some species two or three, before being planted out into permanent containers or into the garden. The seeds of large amaryllids, such as *Boophone, Brunsvigia,* and *Haemanthus,* should be given ample room in which to form their bulbs and long, fleshy roots, and are best planted singly in large pots where they can remain undisturbed 5–6 years. Under such conditions the plants will reach flowering size much more rapidly than if started in smaller containers.

Seedling pots should be kept in a lighted place, but out of direct sunlight, under the same temperature conditions recommended for growing adult plants. Although seedlings of certain species, including *Albuca clanwilliamigloria*, *Gladiolus carneus*, and *Lachenalia bulbifera*, have a first growing period of 18 months and can therefore be kept moist throughout the first dormant period, most seedlings should be allowed to enter dormancy in early summer. Seedling pots that show no germination in the first year should be held over until the following season because it is common for the germination to be staggered over a few seasons. This is particularly true of species of *Lapeirousia*.

Flowering in Cape bulbs can generally be expected to occur the first time in the third year after sowing, but this depends very much on the genera concerned, and smaller species can be expected to flower sooner than larger ones. Most smaller species of the amaryllis, hyacinth, and iris families will flower the first time in 2–3 years, but the larger amaryllids, particularly, take much longer to reach flowering size. We know of one example, *Boophone haemanthoides*, that took 12 years from seed to reach flowering size.

The seeds of most Cape bulbs are not very long-lived and generally lose viability within a few years. Seed longevity is generally lowest in those species with soft, flat seeds and highest in those that produce rounded seeds with a hard, smooth coat. Seeds of Iridaceae usually remain viable 3 years after shedding but their viability drops after this. In hard-seeded genera such as *Dierama*, however, seeds have germinated well after 10 years. Among members of the Hyacinthaceae, the flat seeds of genera such as *Ornithogalum* are generally good only 6–12 months, whereas the hard, round seeds of *Lachenalia* and *Massonia* and their allies remain good 2–3 years or more. In Asphodelaceae, seeds of *Kniphofia* also remain viable more than 2 years, but those of *Bulbinella* are only good 1 year, with viability falling off rapidly thereafter and no germination after 2 years. Seeds of *Agapanthus* (Agapanthaceae) are particularly short-lived, probably less than 6 months, and should be sown immediately after harvesting. Seed longevity in Cape amaryllids is almost universally low. The flat, black seeds of *Cyrtanthus* are good as long as 12 months but for other genera, seed viability is measured in weeks. The highly specialized fleshy seeds produced by most Cape amaryllids are adapted for immediate germination, even upon the parent plant if not disturbed, drawing upon the nutrients stored in the copious endosperm. Such seeds are known as recalcitrant and, in essence, the embryo grows continuously after fertilization without entering a resting phase as in most seeds. These recalcitrant seeds cannot withstand desiccation and should be sown immediately.

Although the seeds of several nonbulbous Cape plants are deeply dormant and require a fire or treatment with smoke to break dormancy, this strategy is rare in Cape bulbs. It may, however, be present in *Lanaria* (Lanariaceae), and possibly *Hypoxis* (Hypoxidaceae).

FURTHER READING. General information on the cultivation and propagation of bulbs was summarized by Bryan and Griffiths (1995) and Mathew (1998). Knippels (1999) provided a wealth of specific recommendations based on his wide experience with pot culture in the Netherlands. These sources are particularly useful for growers in the Northern Hemisphere. More specific information on growing southern African bulbs, including Cape species, has been provided by Du Plessis and Duncan (1989), and Duncan (2000).

FAMILIES OF CAPE BULBS

Species with bulbs, corms, or similar underground storage organs are widespread among plants. They are rarely, however, the predominant life form in entire families except among the large group known as monocots. Consequently, monocots account for the vast majority of what are popularly known as bulbs. The 1183 species of bulbous plants treated in *The Color Encyclopedia of Cape Bulbs* are distributed among 13 monocot families, of which just three, the amaryllis, hyacinth, and iris families (Amaryllidaceae, Hyacinthaceae, and Iridaceae), account for nearly 90% of the species. It is these families that constitute Cape bulbs in the minds of most gardeners. Some of the smaller families may be less familiar yet they contain a wealth of distinctive and interesting genera and species. The circumscription of some plant families has been controversial in the past, but modern research in DNA sequencing is producing a consensus among botanists. The family names and circumscriptions used in this book reflect the most modern understanding of plant classification. Most Cape bulbs can be readily assigned to their appropriate family once the characteristics of these families are known. The accompanying Key to Families of Cape Bulbs will facilitate this.

Within a family it is often more difficult to identify the genera. Again, this is eased by understanding the features important in characterizing each genus. Each family description is accompanied by a key to the genera in that family, when there is more than one genus. These keys are essential in understanding the circumscriptions currently used for genera. They are the only unambiguous method for finding the genus in which an unfamiliar species is placed. The nomenclature of Cape bulbs, like that of all plants, is at times confusing and may even appear whimsical as the application of names changes with the discovery of new information. Some of the genera used here will be novel to most readers, but they represent the latest in botanical understanding. To facilitate cross-referencing to other sources, we provide an Index of Scientific Names, which lists more recently used synonyms.

About three-quarters of the 79 genera in *The Color Encyclopedia of Cape Bulbs* include descriptions of more than one species. The species in those genera may be identified by using the Keys to Species, provided as an appendix. In the keys, variability in some characteristics is accounted for by using the following convention. For example, (6)8(–10) means that whereas 8 is the usual number, sometimes it is only 6 (and not 7), sometimes 9 or 10. In keys and descriptions, measurements given in the form of, for example, 5–7 × 2 mm, describe length × width. Equivalents for metric measurements are provided in the appendix, Conversion Table.

FAMILIES OF CAPE BULBS

AGAPANTHACEAE
   Agapanthus 3 spp.
ALLIACEAE
   Allium 1 sp.
   Tulbaghia 4 spp.
AMARYLLIDACEAE
   Amaryllis 1 sp.
   Ammocharis 1 sp.
   Apodolirion 3 spp.
   Boophone 2 spp.
   Brunsvigia 9 spp.
   Clivia 1 sp.
   Crinum 2 spp.
   Crossyne 2 spp.
   Cybistetes 1 sp.
   Cyrtanthus 22 spp.
   Gethyllis 19 spp.
   Haemanthus 11 spp.
   Hessea 8 spp.
   Nerine 4 spp.
   Scadoxus 2 spp.
   Strumaria 15 spp.
ARACEAE
   Zantedeschia 2 spp.
ASPHODELACEAE
   Bulbinella 14 spp.
   Kniphofia 5 spp.
COLCHICACEAE
   Androcymbium 13 spp.
   Baeometra 1 sp.
   Neodregea 1 sp.
   Onixotis 2 spp.
   Ornithoglossum 5 spp.
   Wurmbea 13 spp.
HAEMODORACEAE
   Dilatris 4 spp.
   Wachendorfia 4 spp.
HYACINTHACEAE
   Albuca 28 spp.
   Bowiea 1 sp.
   Daubenya 6 spp.
   Dipcadi 4 spp.
   Drimia 29 spp.
   Eucomis 3 spp.
   Lachenalia 80 spp.
   Ledebouria 5 spp.
   Massonia 4 spp.
   Neopatersonia 1 sp.
   Ornithogalum 43 spp.
   Polyxena 5 spp.
   Scilla 1 sp.
   Veltheimia 2 spp.
   Whiteheadia 1 sp.
HYPOXIDACEAE
   Empodium 5 spp.
   Hypoxis 7 spp.
   Pauridia 2 spp.
   Spiloxene 16 spp.
IRIDACEAE
   Aristea 32 spp.
   Babiana 49 spp.
   Bobartia 14 spp.
   Chasmanthe 3 spp.
   Devia 1 sp.
   Dierama 1 sp.
   Dietes 1 sp.
   Ferraria 7 spp.
   Freesia 12 spp.
   Geissorhiza 83 spp.
   Gladiolus 110 spp.
   Hesperantha 34 spp.
   Ixia 50 spp.
   Lapeirousia 15 spp.
   Melasphaerula 1 sp.
   Micranthus 3 spp.
   Moraea 123 spp.
   Pillansia 1 sp.
   Romulea 64 spp.
   Sparaxis 15 spp.
   Syringodea 4 spp.
   Thereianthus 8 spp.
   Tritonia 18 spp.
   Tritoniopsis 24 spp.
   Watsonia 33 spp.
   Xenoscapa 1 sp.
LANARIACEAE
   Lanaria 1 sp.
RUSCACEAE
   Eriospermum 52 spp.
TECOPHILAEACEAE
   Cyanella 5 spp.
   Walleria 1 sp.

KEY TO FAMILIES OF CAPE BULBS

1 Flowers unisexual, sessile and without subtending bracts, clustered in a fleshy spike subtended by a large, often showy bract or spathe; tepals absent or reduced to inconspicuous scales .... ARACEAE
1' Flowers bisexual, sessile or pedicellate but always with subtending bracts, never clustered in a fleshy spike; tepals always present and conspicuous 2
2 Ovary more or less inferior, rarely superior but then stamens 3 and leaves pleated and unifacial; stamens 3 or 6 3
2' Ovary superior; stamens 6 7
3 Stamens 3, opposite the outer tepals; rootstock a corm or rhizome .... IRIDACEAE
3' Stamens 6 or 3 but then opposite the inner tepals 4
4 Flowers solitary or numerous, apparently in umbels or racemes, borne on naked scapes with terminal bracts; ovules usually several per locule 5
4' Flowers numerous, in helicoid cymes on stems bearing scattered bracts; ovules 1–2 per locule 6
5 Rootstock a bulb or rhizome; leaves 2-ranked or appearing as if in a rosette; flowers with nectaries; seeds variously shaped but never with a prominent funicle .... AMARYLLIDACEAE
5' Rootstock a corm or rhizome; leaves 3-ranked; flowers without nectaries; seeds globose to ellipsoidal with a prominent pointed funicle ... HYPOXIDACEAE
6 Stamens 6; hairs mainly plumose; leaves bifacial, channeled; fruit 1-seeded, papery, and enclosed in the persistent perianth, indehiscent and fragmenting irregularly .... LANARIACEAE
6' Stamens 3; hairs all simple; leaves unifacial, sword-shaped; rhizome bright red; fruit 3-seeded, firm, dehiscent .... HAEMODORACEAE
7 Anthers dehiscing by an apical pore, often unequal; filaments short, inserted at the mouth of the perianth tube; stems leafy; rootstock a corm or tuber ....
.... TECOPHILAEACEAE
7' Anthers dehiscing by longitudinal slits or rarely by apical pores but then scapes leafless; rootstock a rhizome, bulb or tuber 8

8 Flowers apparently in umbels subtended by spathe-like bracts 9
8' Flowers in spikes or racemes, sometimes condensed 10
9 Flowers perfectly actinomorphic with stamens spreading or anthers sessile; capsules ovoid; plants usually smelling of onion or garlic; rootstock a bulb or rhizome .... ALLIACEAE
9' Flowers slightly zygomorphic with stamens declinate and the tips curved upward; capsules 3-angled or 3-winged, deflexed; plants never smelling of onion or garlic; rootstock a rhizome ...... AGAPANTHACEAE
10 Seeds woolly; flowering stems leafless except for a clasping basal leafy bract; leaves absent at flowering, petiolate; rootstock a stem tuber .... RUSCACEAE
10' Seeds hairless; flowering stems leafy or leafless but then without a basal bract; rootstock a bulb, corm or rhizome 11
11 Rootstock a bulb, rarely with loose scales; flowers borne on naked peduncles .... HYACINTHACEAE
11' Rootstock a corm or rhizome 12
12 Rootstock a corm; flowers usually apparently opposite the bracts; nectaries perigonal, situated at the base of the tepal limbs and often conspicuous in color or shape; seeds brown, subglobose ...... COLCHICACEAE
12' Rootstock a rhizome; flowers evidently in the axils of the bracts; nectaries septal, inconspicuous; seeds black, angular or flattened .... ASPHODELACEAE

AGAPANTHACEAE

COMMON NAME agapanthus family. Deciduous or evergreen perennials, containing saponins responsible for the characteristic slimy sap, and calcium oxalate crystals. ROOTSTOCK a rhizome, often exposed, giving rise to copious fleshy roots. LEAVES basal, in two ranks, numerous, strap-like, slightly fleshy or leathery, lightly channeled, the bases somewhat swollen and bulb-like in the deciduous species. INFLORESCENCE an umbel-like cluster (functionally an umbel), subtended by two deciduous, membranous sheathing bracts united along the margins in bud; floral bracts numerous, thread-like, the scape solid. FLOWERS several to many, weakly zygomorphic, blue or white, unscented, tepals six, subequal, united below into a short tube. STAMENS six, inserted on the tepals at the top of the tube, declinate, unequal, introrse; POLLEN monosulcate and reticulate. OVARY superior, three-locular, ovules numerous, axile; nectaries septal; STYLE one, slender, declinate. FRUIT a three-angled loculicidal capsule, sharply deflexed. SEEDS several per locule, flat and winged, black, with phytomelan in the testa. Temperate and subtropical southern Africa; 1 genus (*Agapanthus*), 10 spp., 3 in the Cape.

ALLIACEAE

COMMON NAME onion family. Perennial herbs, containing allylic sulfides responsible for the characteristic onion smell, and calcium oxalate crystals. ROOTSTOCK a bulb with membranous or fibrous outer tunics, or rarely a short rhizome. LEAVES basal, spirally inserted, strap-like to terete or tubular, sheathing below, rarely pseudopetiolate. INFLORESCENCE an umbel-like cluster (functionally an umbel), subtended by two membranous sheathing bracts; floral bracts small, membranous, the scape solid or hollow, sometimes angular. FLOWERS one to many, usually actinomorphic, white to blue or violet, green, or yellow, tepals six, almost free or united below in a cup-shaped or tubular perianth, sometimes bearing a corona at the throat. STAMENS six, rarely some reduced to staminodes, inserted at the base of the tepals or on the perianth tube, the filaments more or less flattened and the inner sometimes trifid, free or united, introrse; POLLEN monosulcate and reticulate. OVARY superior, three-locular, ovules few to several per locule, axile or basal; nectaries septal; STYLE one. FRUIT a loculicidal capsule. SEEDS wedge-shaped or ovoid to subglobose, usually black, with phytomelan in the testa. Widespread but mainly South America; 13 genera, 2 in the Cape, c. 600 spp., 5 in the Cape.

Genera of Alliaceae
1 Flowers cup-shaped, the tepals united only at the base and without a corona; stamens with the inner filaments tricuspidate .... *Allium*
1' Flowers narrowly trumpet-shaped, the tepals united more than half their length into a tube and with a toothed or ring-like corona at the mouth; stamens with the anthers sessile .... *Tulbaghia*

AMARYLLIDACEAE

COMMON NAME amaryllis family. Deciduous or evergreen, terrestrial or occasionally aquatic or epiphytic perennials, rich in family-specific alkaloids. ROOTSTOCK a bulb, rarely rhizomatous, the roots contractile and perennial or short-lived and fibrous. LEAVES basal, in two ranks or rarely spirally arranged, linear to oval or with a petiole-like base and lanceolate to elliptical blade, sometimes sheathing basally and forming an aerial pseudostem, occasionally hairy. INFLORESCENCE an umbel-like cluster (functionally an umbel) on a naked scape, enclosed by two or more sheathing bracts, the outer bract overlapping the inner at the base, usually free, sometimes united basally or on one side, the scape solid or hollow, terete or compressed, sometimes subterranean. FLOWERS one to many, sessile or pedicellate, actinomorphic or zygomorphic, tubular, star-, funnel-, or salver-shaped, various colors but rarely blue, tepals six, free or united below in a short or long tube, sometimes with a one-sided swelling, persistent or deciduous, sometimes bearing a conspicuous corona or an inconspicuous ring of scales or fimbriae at the throat. STAMENS 6, rarely 5, 18, or more, subequal or varying in length, inserted at or below the perianth throat, sometimes shortly decurrent on the tepals, filaments sometimes united, occasionally with appendages, rarely joined to the style, anthers dorsifixed, rarely centrifixed or basifixed, dehiscing longitudinally or rarely from a terminal pore; POLLEN monosulcate and semitectate-columellate or bisulculate and spinulose. OVARY inferior, three-locular, rarely one-locular, ovules axile or basal; nectaries septal; STYLE filiform, rarely swollen toward the base, stigma capitate to deeply trifid. FRUIT a loculicidal capsule, sometimes indehiscent with dry or rarely fleshy walls. SEEDS flattened and winged, usually with a black or brown outer layer, sometimes with an oily appendage, otherwise globose to subglobose, fleshy to hard and pink, cream, or green. Widespread but mainly in southern Africa, South America, and the Mediterranean; 59 genera, 16 in the Cape, c. 850 spp., 103 in the Cape.

Tribes of Amaryllidaceae

1 Leaves and bulb coats with extensible fibers when torn; scape solid; pollen bisulculate .... tribe Amaryllideae
1' Leaves and bulb coats, or rarely rhizomes, without extensible fibers when torn; scape hollow or solid; pollen monosulcate 2
2 Scape hollow except occasionally solid at the base; mature fruit a dry capsule .... tribe Cyrtantheae: *Cyrtanthus*
2' Scape solid throughout; mature fruit pulpy and berry-like .... tribe Haemantheae

Amaryllidaceae Tribe Amaryllideae

1 Leaf margins smooth, softly hairy or raised, reddened, and fringed with long bristles or short, branched, minute hairs; pedicels rarely shorter than flowers at anthesis; filaments more or less united at the base, if free then joined to the style base; fruits dehiscent 2
1' Leaf margins hyaline, more or less fringed with short, branched, minute hairs; pedicels usually shorter than flowers at anthesis; filaments free to base; fruits indehiscent 7
2 Leaves with a prominent midrib; flowers usually much longer than pedicels .... *Amaryllis*
2' Leaves without a midrib; flowers approximately as long as or much shorter than pedicels 3
3 Flowers zygomorphic (sometimes only by the deflexed style) 4
3' Flowers actinomorphic 6
4 Leaves narrow, usually less than 25 mm wide, and subsucculent; pedicels slender, rarely longer than flowers; tepal margins more or less undulate ...... *Nerine*
4' Leaves broad, usually more than 25 mm wide, and leathery; pedicels stout, usually much longer than flowers; tepal margins usually smooth, rarely crisped 5
5 Leaves immaculate; margins smooth or fringed with short, branched, minute hairs; pedicels obscurely 3-angled in cross section; filaments tightly clustered .... *Brunsvigia*
5' Leaves speckled with red; margins fringed with long bristles; pedicels sharply triangular in cross section; filaments more or less spreading .... *Crossyne*
6 Leaves 2(3), smooth or rarely minutely hairy; flowers remaining outspread after anthesis; filaments united into a short to long tube, free from the style; anthers centrifixed to subcentrifixed .... *Hessea*

6' Leaves 2–6, smooth or hairy; flowers withering and closing after anthesis; filaments free or sometimes united into a tube; one or both filament whorls joined to the style base; anthers subcentrifixed to dorsifixed .... *Strumaria*

7 Leaves annual, closely abutting each other to form an erect outspread fan; all leaf tips subacute to obtuse; fruiting head detaching from scape apex; fruit 3-angled, prominently 3-ribbed .... *Boophone*

7' Leaves perennial, suberect or prostrate; tips of all but the youngest leaves usually truncate; fruiting head not detaching from the scape apex; fruit irregularly shaped, smooth or 6-ribbed 8

8 Pedicels elongating and radiating after anthesis, dry and stout in fruit; fruiting head detaching at ground level; fruit papery, 6-ribbed .... *Cybistetes*

8' Pedicels remaining unchanged in fruit; fruiting head persisting and drooping; fruit membranous or rarely fleshy, smooth 9

9 Leaves spreading evenly or in a vertical 2-ranked pattern, suberect to recurved, often sheathing to form a false stem; flowers zygomorphic, sometimes only by the deflexed style; perianth tube mostly curved, occasionally straight .... *Crinum*

9' Leaves arching or spreading on the ground in 2 fans; flowers actinomorphic; perianth tube straight .... *Ammocharis*

Amaryllidaceae Tribe Haemantheae

1 Flowers solitary, held at ground level 2
1' Flowers many, held well above ground level 3
2 Leaves few to many, smooth or hairy, often with conspicuous basal sheaths around the foliage leaves; stamens uniseriate; anthers 6 to many .... *Gethyllis*
2' Leaves one or few, smooth, basal sheaths not conspicuous; stamens biseriate; anthers 6 .... *Apodolirion*
3 Plants with large, fleshy bulbs; leaves sword- to tongue-shaped, without a midrib, succulent and often hairy .... *Haemanthus*
3' Plants rhizomatous 4
4 Leaves elliptical with a petiole-like base and prominent midrib, thin textured; scape elliptical in section .... *Scadoxus*
4' Leaves narrowly sword-shaped, leathery; scape strongly flattened and sharp-edged in section ..... *Clivia*

ARACEAE

COMMON NAME arum family. Deciduous or evergreen perennials, occasionally with aerial stems or floating, often with latex or resin ducts, sometimes containing calcium oxalate crystals and steroidal saponins. ROOTSTOCK usually a rhizome or tuber. LEAVES several, usually petiolate with a sheathing base, the blades simple or divided, rarely the leaves linear, sword-shaped or broad and sessile, sometimes spotted with white, the main venation pinnate. INFLORESCENCE a spike subtended by a more or less petaloid spathe, rarely more than one, sometimes scented. FLOWERS minute, crowded on a slender axis (spadix), the upper part sometimes forming a sterile appendix, bisexual, unisexual, or neuter, tepals present or lacking, free. STAMENS six or four, free or united, dehiscing by slits or pores; POLLEN one-, two-, or three-sulcate, zonisulcate, two- or four-foraminate, trichotomosulcate or inaperturate. OVARY one- or three-locular, ovules several per locule; STYLE one, short, sometimes producing nectar from the stigma. FRUIT usually a fleshy berry. SEEDS one or few per chamber, dry or fleshy. Worldwide; c. 110 genera, one in the Cape (*Zantedeschia*), c. 2450 spp., 2 in the Cape.

ASPHODELACEAE

COMMON NAME asphodel family. Herbaceous or woody perennials, sometimes functionally annual, often succulent, containing calcium oxalate crystals and, often, anthraquinones, responsible for the yellow sap, but lacking steroidal saponins. ROOTSTOCK a rhizome with cylindrical or apically swollen roots, or not evident. LEAVES basal or apical in the woody forms, spirally inserted although sometimes becoming two-ranked later, strap-shaped to elliptical or terete, sheathing at the base, the margins sometimes serrate or toothed. INFLORESCENCE a simple or compound raceme or spike, the peduncle often nearly leafless or sparsely bracteate, solid. FLOWERS usually actinomorphic, greenish, white or yellow to red, tepals six, free or united below to form a tubular perianth. STAMENS six, inserted at the base of the ovary, the filaments more or less terete, rarely scabrid or hairy, introrse; POLLEN monosulcate and reticulate or perforate. OVARY superior, three-locular, ovules usually arillate, two to many per locule, axile; nectaries septal; STYLE one. FRUIT a loculicidal capsule, rarely leathery. SEEDS ovoid and more or less flattened or wedge-shaped, with phytomelan in the testa but covered with a membranous aril and thus apparently dull gray although actually black. Old World and particularly southern Africa; c. 15 genera, 8 in the Cape, c. 750 spp., 19 bulb spp. in the Cape.

Genera of Asphodelaceae
1 Flowers cup- or star-shaped, not nodding; tepals free or shortly united at the base; stamens equal .... *Bulbinella*
1' Flowers usually tubular, nodding; tepals united most of their length; stamens of different lengths ..... *Kniphofia*

COLCHICACEAE

COMMON NAME colchicum family. Perennial herbs, sometimes twining, containing chelidonic acid and the alkaloid colchicine or related compounds, and often calcium oxalate as crystal sand, but lacking saponins. ROOTSTOCK usually a corm, often with papery or fibrous tunics but sometimes more or less naked and tuber-like, sometimes stoloniferous. LEAVES basal or scattered, spirally inserted, strap-like or lanceolate, often attenuate and sometimes ending in a tendril, sheathing below, rarely pseudopetiolate, rarely hysteranthus. INFLORESCENCE a leafy raceme or contracted scorpioid cymes and appearing racemose or spicate or single-flowered. FLOWERS actinomorphic or weakly zygomorphic, white or green to yellow or red, often bicolored, tepals 6, rarely 7–12, often somewhat clawed, free or united below in a cup-shaped or tubular perianth; nectaries perigonal, often on the tepal claws. STAMENS six, inserted at the base of the tepals or on the claw, the filaments often somewhat swollen, usually extrorse but rarely latrorse or almost introrse; POLLEN monosulcate and reticulate or two- to four-aperturate. OVARY superior, three-locular, the locules often separated above, ovules few to many, axile; STYLE divided mostly or completely into three separate stylules. FRUIT a septicidal or loculicidal capsule. SEEDS globose or ovoid, brown and with phlobaphene in the testa, sometimes strophiolate or arillate. Africa, Eurasia, North America, and Australia, mostly southern Africa; 19 genera, 6 in the Cape, c. 225 spp., 35 in the Cape.

Genera of Colchicaceae
1 Bracts well developed and more or less leaf-like, subtending all the flowers, never narrow and thread-like ... 2
1' Bracts absent or reduced and subtending only the lower flowers, if present then narrow and thread-like 3
2 Flowers few, erect on short pedicels, usually in a head overtopped by green or petaloid bracts; styles more or less erect .... *Androcymbium*
2' Flowers several in a raceme, nodding on long pedicels; styles slender and spreading .... *Ornithoglossum*
3 Flowers pedicellate, the lower subtended by a slender bract; anthers 2–4 mm long; flowers orange or yellow ... . *Baeometra*
3' Flowers sessile, without bracts or the lower apparently subtended by a large leafy bract; anthers to 1.5 mm long; flowers yellow, white, cream, or pink to maroon 4
4 Tepals united at the base, not conspicuously eared .... *Wurmbea*
4' Tepals free, conspicuously eared above the claw 5
5 Styles short and hooked, arising laterally on truncate ovary lobes; tepals attenuate .... *Neodregea*
5' Styles slender, arising terminally on the ovary; tepals obovate .... *Onixotis*

HAEMODORACEAE

COMMON NAME bloodroot family. Perennial herbs, mostly evergreen and often coarse, containing calcium oxalate crystals and chelidonic acid. ROOTSTOCK a short rhizome, stem tuber, or bulb, sometimes containing the bright orange-red pigment hemocorin. LEAVES basal or scattered, in two ranks, unifacial, strap-like or lanceolate, or sometimes triangular or pleated. INFLORESCENCE a paniculate or subumbellate thyrse or raceme, sometimes single-flowered, the axis usually roughly hairy with the hairs simple or branched. FLOWERS weakly to strongly zygomorphic, sometimes left- or right-handed, violet to red, orange, yellow, or partially green or black, tepals six, free or united below to form a tubular perianth, usually hairy on the outer surface. STAMENS three or six, inserted at the base of the tepals or often on the tepals, introrse; POLLEN monosulcate and verrucate or foveolate, or two-to eight-aperturate and rugulose. OVARY superior, inferior, or half-inferior, three-locular, ovules one to many per locule, axile; nectaries septal; STYLE slender. FRUIT a loculicidal or septicidal capsule, rarely tardily septifragal. SEEDS angled to ovoid or depressed and discoid, pale or brown to black, without phytomelan in the testa. Mainly Southern Hemisphere; 14 genera, 2 in the Cape, c. 100 spp., 8 in the Cape.

Genera of Haemodoraceae

1 Leaves flat or ribbed; perianth actinomorphic, long-lasting, persistent and papery in fruit; stamens dimorphic, one shorter with a larger anther; ovary inferior .... *Dilatris*

1′ Leaves pleated; perianth zygomorphic, lasting a day and deliquescing; stamens similar; ovary superior .... *Wachendorfia*

HYACINTHACEAE

COMMON NAME hyacinth family. Perennial, usually deciduous herbs, containing steroidal saponins, forming a characteristic slimy sap, calcium oxalate crystals, and chelidonic acid. ROOTSTOCK a bulb with membranous outer tunics or scales, or rarely a short rhizome, the roots sometimes thick and usually contractile. LEAVES basal, spirally inserted, strap-like to terete or ovate and sheathing below, rarely the blade lacking. INFLORESCENCE a raceme or spike, sometimes very short and contracted, rarely much branched, the upper flowers often sterile; bracts small or large, usually membranous but sometimes green or fleshy, sometimes spurred, the scape solid. FLOWERS actinomorphic, rarely zygomorphic, white to blue or violet, green, or yellow to red or brown, tepals six, free or united below to form a cup-shaped or tubular perianth. STAMENS six, rarely the outer sterile, free or united below, inserted at the base of the tepals or on the perianth tube, sometimes inserted obliquely on the perianth or in two series at different levels, the filaments often more or less flattened and the inner in particular sometimes lobed below, introrse; POLLEN monosulcate and reticulate. OVARY superior, three-locular, ovules two to several per locule, axile; nectaries septal; STYLE one, the stigma small or subglobose or trilobed. FRUIT a loculicidal capsule. SEEDS wedge-shaped to ellipsoidal or subglobose, black, with phytomelan in the testa. Widespread but mostly southern Africa and Eurasia; 35 genera, 14 in the Cape, c. 900 spp., 213 in the Cape.

Genera of Hyacinthaceae

1 Bracts (at least the lower) spurred; leaves often dry at flowering; seed coat brittle, loose; bulb of more or less overlapping scales, often pinkish 2

1′ Bracts not spurred; leaves mostly green at flowering; seed coat tightly adhering; bulb of sheathing tunics or overlapping scales 3

2 Flowers long-lived, tepals persistent in fruit, free; inflorescence branched and twining, somewhat fleshy .... *Bowiea*

2′ Flowers short-lived, tepals caducous, cohering above when faded, circumscissile below, often united below; inflorescence simple or rarely branched but then wiry .... *Drimia*

3 Ovary stalked, abruptly expanded above base and mushroom-shaped; ovules 2 in each locule, apparently basal; leaves often spotted; inflorescences often several and apparently axillary .... *Ledebouria*

3′ Ovary usually sessile, subglobose or ovoid; ovules 2 to several in each locule, axillary; inflorescence solitary and obviously central 4

4 Filaments either inserted in 2 series at different levels or inserted obliquely in perianth, never united below; bracts often reduced 5

4′ Filaments inserted in one series at the same level, rarely obliquely in the lower flowers only, which are then very zygomorphic; bracts always well developed 7

5 Plants robust with several lanceolate leaves; perianth tube long, more than 6 times as long as the tepals; stamens inserted near the middle of the tube; ovules 2 per locule .... *Veltheimia*

5′ Plants various; perianth tube short or long but less than 5 times as long as the tepals; stamens inserted near the top of the tube; ovules several to many per locule 6

6 Perianth tube less than a third the length of the tepals, the outer tepals often shorter than the inner; stamens usually declinate .... *Lachenalia*

6′ Perianth tube longer than a third the length of the tepals, the tepals subequal; stamens spreading ... *Polyxena*

7 Leaves 2, spreading or prostrate; inflorescence not distinctly peduncled; tepals united below into a cup or tube 8

7' Leaves several, usually ascending; inflorescence distinctly peduncled; tepals more or less free or united below 10
8 Leaves firm, glossy with impressed longitudinal striations; flowers partially or entirely yellow or red, rarely white but then filaments united into a narrow tube about half their length; bracts shorter or longer than flowers .... *Daubenya*
8' Leaves soft, leathery, or somewhat succulent, matte, and smooth, pustulate, or setose; flowers white to pink, filaments at most shortly united; bracts always longer than flowers 9
9 Inflorescence spicate and erect above leaves; bracts all green and fleshy .... *Whiteheadia*
9' Inflorescence corymbose or capitate and sessile at ground level between leaves; bracts mostly membranous .... *Massonia*
10 Inflorescence topped by a crown of leafy bracts longer than flowers .... *Eucomis*
10' Inflorescence not topped by a crown of leafy bracts 11
11 Inflorescence usually a secund, inclined raceme; tepals united below into an elongate tube at least half as long as lobes; stamens included, filaments closely appressed to inner tepals and anthers appearing sessile .... *Dipcadi*
11' Inflorescence never secund; tepals free or united at base; stamens more or less exserted and free from tepals above 12
12 Flowers blue; tepals recurved above .... *Scilla*
12' Flowers white, yellow, orange, or green; tepals erect or spreading 13
13 Inner tepals erect, cucullate, enclosing stamens and ovary; inner whorl of filaments at least pinched below, outer whorl sometimes sterile; ovary ornamented with paired, diverging septal crests; style usually prismatic and papillate .... *Albuca*
13' Tepals all spreading, subequal; filaments sometimes expanded below but never pinched; ovary never crested; style terete and smooth 14
14 Stigma bluntly 3-lobed; seeds angular to discoid .... *Ornithogalum*
14' Stigma with 3 divergent branches; seeds pear-shaped or subglobose .... *Neopatersonia*

HYPOXIDACEAE

Common name star grass family. Deciduous or rarely evergreen, terrestrial or occasionally aquatic perennials. Rootstock a somewhat tuberous rhizome or corm. Leaves basal, three-ranked, sessile or pseudopetiolate, linear to lanceolate, sometimes pleated, smooth or with simple or compound hairs. Inflorescence a spike, raceme, or corymb, or sometimes reduced to a single flower, on a smooth or hairy scape, often several per plant, the scape usually terminated by one or more small or leaf-like bracts. Flowers usually pedicellate, sometimes sessile, actinomorphic, yellow, orange, pink, or white, tepals six or four, persistent or deciduous, free or united into a sometimes long narrow tube. Stamens usually six, sometimes as few as two, free, the filaments short, inserted in the throat or at the tepal base, the anthers long, basifixed or dorsifixed low down, dehiscing longitudinally, sometimes with apical appendages; pollen monosulcate or rarely bisulcate, and reticulate. Ovary inferior, three- or one-locular, ovules few to many, axile or parietal; nectaries absent; style short or rarely elongate, with three, sometimes two, dry stigma lobes. Fruit a circumscissile or loculicidal capsule, sometimes more or less fleshy, indehiscent and beaked. Seeds subglobose to J-shaped, black or sometimes brown, glossy or dull, smooth to papillate or rarely hairy with a prominent funicle, the embryo small. Warm temperate to tropical regions of the Americas, Africa, Asia, and Australia, mainly in the Southern Hemisphere; 9 genera, 4 in the Cape, c. 130 spp., 30 in the Cape.

Genera of Hypoxidaceae

1 Plants hairy, at least on the back of the tepals; hairs usually long, varying from irregularly branched to star-like .... *Hypoxis*
1' Plants smooth or if with a few, short, recurved hairs then the tepals always smooth 2
2 Leaves usually pleated; scape and spathe bracts absent; pedicel flattened on one side, long or often hidden by leaf sheaths; ovary 1-locular, placentation parietal .... *Empodium*
2' Leaves terete, channeled, or V-shaped; scape long to short; spathe bracts one or more; pedicel if present terete; ovary 3-locular at least in the lower half, placentation axile 3
3 Tepals united into a hollow tube at the base; stamens 3 with 3 staminodes joined to the base of the style; stigma trifid, lobes slender .... *Pauridia*

3′ Tepals free or united into a solid neck at the base; stamens 6, rarely 5, 4, or 2; style without staminodes; stigma trifid, rarely bifid, lobes usually broad, sometimes diverging into papillate tails at the base .... *Spiloxene*

IRIDACEAE

COMMON NAME iris family. Deciduous or evergreen perennials, rarely shrubs with anomalous secondary growth or annuals, usually containing styloid crystals. ROOTSTOCK a rhizome or corm (or a bulb in New World and Eurasian species), or when shrubs a woody caudex. LEAVES mostly unifacial and oriented edgewise to the stem, sometimes bifacial with the upper surface facing the stem, with or without a distinct central vein, mostly in two ranks, usually green at flowering, rarely produced later; when unifacial, the blades mostly plane, sometimes ribbed, pleated, terete, or with winged margins; when bifacial the blades channeled to flat and usually without a median vein; margins plane or sometimes undulate to crisped, sometimes thickened and fibrotic or raised into wings; the lower one to three leaves without blades and entirely sheathing, reaching shortly above ground (thus cataphylls). INFLORESCENCE either an umbel (i.e., rhipidium) enclosed in opposed leafy to dry bracts (spathes) with flowers usually pedicellate, the rhipidia often arranged in a compound structure; or flowers sessile, subtended by a pair of opposed bracts and in a spike or solitary, the axis usually aerial, rarely subterranean, simple or branched, terete or flattened and angled or winged. FLOWERS actinomorphic or zygomorphic, variously colored, often with contrasting markings, tepals six, subequal or unequal, free or united into a short or long perianth tube. STAMENS three (two in the Australian *Diplarrhena*), inserted at the base of the outer tepals or in the tube, symmetrically disposed or unilateral and arched or declinate, the filaments free or partly to fully joined, the anthers usually extrorse and dehiscing longitudinally; POLLEN mostly monosulcate, or bisulcate, zonisulcate, dizonisulculate, trisulcate, polyaperturate, or inaperturate, reticulate, perforate, or intectate. OVARY inferior (superior in the Tasmanian *Isophysis*), three-locular, ovules few to many, axile; nectaries septal, perigonal, or lacking; STYLE filiform, usually three-branched, rarely simple or three-lobed, style branches either filiform to distally expanded, sometimes divided above, stigmatic toward the apices, or the branches thickened or flattened and petaloid, stigma then abaxial below the branch apex. FRUIT a loculicidal capsule, rarely indehiscent, firm to cartilaginous, occasionally woody. SEEDS globose to angular or discoid, sometimes broadly winged, rarely seed coat fleshy or an aril present, shiny or matte. Nearly worldwide but rare in tropical lowlands and at high latitudes, best represented in southern Africa; c. 65 genera, 27 in the Cape, c. 1800 spp., 708 in the Cape.

Subfamilies of Iridaceae

1 Inflorescence a spike or, by reduction, flowers solitary on branches, always sessile and subtended by a pair of opposed bracts; tepals always united in a tube; flowers lasting at least 2 days; style dividing into filiform branches, rarely simple; rootstock a corm producing roots from the base; nectaries septal; pollen grains usually with exine perforate-scabrate, rarely reticulate; pollen grain apertures usually with a banded operculum .... subfamily Crocoideae (synonym, Ixioideae)

1′ Flowers in tight umbellate clusters (rhipidia) enclosed by a pair of opposed leafy bracts (spathes), rarely solitary on the peduncles or plants stemless but then style either dividing below the anthers into tangentially compressed, petal-like branches or dividing below or above the base of the anthers and obscurely 3-lobed apically, the lobes entire or fringed, individual flowers mostly pedicellate, sometimes sessile; rootstock a woody caudex, rhizome, corm rooting from the apical bud, bulb, or not evident; flowers with the tepals free to basally united, or united in an extended tube; lasting 1–2 days or more 2

2 At least the terminal rhipidia united in pairs (binate); style notched or divided apically into 3 lobes, occasionally forming filiform branches; nectaries when present mostly septal ... subfamily Nivenioideae

2′ Rhipidia never united in pairs; style dividing below the level of the anthers into 3 branches, these either filiform, extending between the stamens, or thickened or flattened and lying opposite the stamens, usually each terminating in paired appendages (style crests); nectaries (or oil glands) when present perigonal .... subfamily Iridoideae

Iridaceae Subfamilies Nivenioideae and Iridoideae

1. Style eccentric, apically notched or divided into 3 lobes, the lobes sometimes fringed; flowers usually deep blue, occasionally lilac, white, or pale blue; tepals shortly united basally .... *Aristea*
1'. Style central, usually dividing near the base of the anthers into distinct branches, these either extending between the anthers or appressed to them, sometimes the style exceeding the anthers; flowers variously colored; tepals free, united basally or into a tube 2
2. Plants evergreen, with a creeping or erect rhizome; pedicels hairy above; filaments usually free 3
2'. Plants deciduous, with a corm; pedicels smooth or lacking (flowers sessile); filaments usually partly to fully united 4
3. Tepals with well-defined ascending claws and spreading limbs, outer tepals larger than the inner; style branches broad and petal-like, compressed tangentially, terminating in paired erect crests; anthers appressed to the abaxial side of the style branches .... *Dietes*
3'. Tepals not clawed, the inner and outer whorls subequal; style branches filiform, spreading nearly horizontally; anthers ascending, alternating with the style branches .... *Bobartia*
4. Leaves unifacial, oriented edgewise to the stem; old corms persisting for some years, evidently without tunics; tepals with crisped edges; style branches terminating in a fringed, feathery tuft .... *Ferraria*
4'. Leaves bifacial or terete; corm usually completely replaced annually, with obvious fibrous to woody tunics; tepals with plane or wavy edges; style branches usually terminating in paired crests or evidently without appendages (feathery tufts present in 1 sp.) .... *Moraea*

Iridaceae Subfamily Crocoideae

1. Outer and inner bracts membranous to scarious, usually translucent to transparent with the veins often darkly colored, occasionally the outer solid below but then the margins lacerate 2
1'. Outer and inner bracts firm to soft textured, green or leathery and dry, never lacerate, sometimes the inner bracts with broad membranous to scarious margins 7
2. Plants stemless; leaves mostly entirely bifacial, usually channeled or grooved above, sometimes terete but then never grooved; bracts tubular below; corm tunics woody; flowers blue to purple .... *Syringodea*
2'. Plants stemless or with aerial stems; leaves unifacial, rarely bifacial, plane, or terete but then grooved; bracts with the margins free to the base or united below; corm tunics woody or papery to fibrous; flowers variously colored 3
3. Bracts pale, dry, papery and crinkled, or solid, irregularly streaked with dark flecks or veins 4
3'. Bracts pale or rust colored, membranous or dry but not papery and crinkled, sometimes streaked with dark flecks or veins 5
4. Flowers nodding, borne on wiry stems; leaves linear, narrow, tough, and fibrotic .... *Dierama*
4'. Flowers upright or facing to the side, borne on firm, somewhat fleshy stems; leaves lanceolate, relatively succulent, and without fibers .... *Sparaxis*
5. Leaves oval in cross section with 4 major and 4 minor longitudinal grooves; flowers dusty pink, actinomorphic with the stamens twisted anticlockwise ..... *Devia*
5'. Leaves flat or rounded in cross section and then mostly with 4 longitudinal grooves; flowers variously colored, actinomorphic or zygomorphic but the stamens never twisted anticlockwise 6
6. Perianth zygomorphic with the stamens unilateral, rarely the perianth actinomorphic but then the stamens irregularly spreading and the style eccentric or the tepals orange with conspicuous brown veining; stems firm and relatively thick, never wiry ...... *Tritonia*
6'. Perianth actinomorphic with the stamens either symmetrically disposed around a central style or unilateral with the anthers drooping and dehiscing partially from the base; stems often more or less wiry .... *Ixia*
7. Style branches dividing at apex of perianth tube or within tube, the branches long and ascending to laxly spreading .... *Hesperantha*
7'. Style branches usually dividing well above mouth of perianth tube, the branches relatively short and recurved, to laxly spreading, sometimes each deeply divided 8
8. Corms bell-shaped, with a flat base; leaves plane or ridged 9
8'. Corms globose to obconical, round or pointed at the base, rarely bell-shaped 10
9. Ovary globose; style branches usually divided more or less half their length, rarely undivided or apically notched; leaves often corrugate, sometimes plane but then usually leathery in texture .... *Lapeirousia*
9'. Ovary deeply 3-lobed above; style branches undivided; leaves plane and soft textured .... *Melasphaerula*

10 Style branches deeply divided, usually once, occasionally multifid 11
10′ Style branches undivided or at most notched at the tips 16
11 Leaves round to oval in cross section with narrow longitudinal grooves, or 4-winged; corm tunics composed of brittle woody concentric layers; flowers actinomorphic, solitary on branches, not arranged in spikes or stems subterranean ..... *Romulea*
11′ Leaves usually with plane blades or round in cross section but without longitudinal grooves; corm tunics of leathery to fibrous layers; flowers zygomorphic or if actinomorphic arranged in spikes, never stemless 12
12 Flowers solitary on branches; leaves prostrate, thin textured, and with broadly rounded tips ..... *Xenoscapa*
12′ Flowers arranged in erect or inclined spikes; leaves usually erect, occasionally prostrate 13
13 Spikes inclined to horizontal, flowers borne on upper side; bracts green or dry above, then often dark brown at the tips .... *Freesia*
13′ Spikes erect, flowers 2-ranked or spirally arranged; bracts green or partly to entirely dry but then never dark brown at the tips 14
14 Flowers small, less than 12 mm long, crowded on dense, 2-ranked spikes; bracts solid below with broad membranous margins .... *Micranthus*
14′ Flowers medium to large, mostly at least 15 mm long (measured when closed), in 2-ranked or spiral spikes; bracts without obviously membranous margins 15
15 Flowers mostly red, pink, or orange; spikes 2-ranked; leaf blades plane, relatively broad, margins moderately to strongly thickened; perianth tube always curved, flowers usually facing to side ... *Watsonia*
15′ Flowers shades of blue to violet or white; spikes spiral; leaf blades rounded in cross section or plane but then narrow and without thickened margins; perianth tube more or less straight, flowers mostly facing upward .... *Thereianthus*
16 Plants evergreen, with leathery, fibrotic leaves without a midrib; inflorescence a rounded panicle, individual flowers mostly with a short peduncle below the bracts; flowers actinomorphic, bright orange .... *Pillansia*
16′ Plants mostly deciduous and leaves with an obvious midrib unless multiridged; inflorescence a simple or branched spike, flowers sessile (spike rarely with a single flower); flowers actinomorphic or zygomorphic, variously colored 17

17 Floral bracts fairly short, leathery and often partly to entirely dry at flowering time, the inner bract always longer than outer; leaves mostly with more than one prominent vein unless very narrow, thus without a single midrib, sometimes with a long pseudopetiole .... *Tritoniopsis*
17′ Characters not combined as above 18
18 Leaves several in a 2-ranked fan, blades plane, hairless; flowers shades of orange to scarlet; floral bracts short, more or less twice as long as the ovary, leathery, green or dry, nearly equal .... *Chasmanthe*
18′ Characters not combined as above 19
19 Leaf blades usually pleated, sometimes more or less linear and striate; stems and or leaves or bracts usually pubescent to pilose .... *Babiana*
19′ Leaf blades plane, ridged, or rounded in cross section with or without 4 longitudinal grooves; stems and or leaves occasionally hairy or scabrid 20
20 Corm tunics mostly woody, rarely fibrous; flowers actinomorphic with an eccentric style or the stamens and style unilateral and declinate; seeds rounded to angular .... *Geissorhiza*
20′ Corm tunics varied, papery to firm or fibrous, the fibers soft or wiry to woody but tunics rarely forming solid woody layers; flowers mostly zygomorphic with the stamens and style unilateral and arcuate, when actinomorphic the style central; seeds with a broad circumferential wing .... *Gladiolus*

LANARIACEAE

COMMON NAME kapok lily family. Evergreen perennial herb, containing calcium oxalate crystals. ROOTSTOCK a short vertical rhizome with hard thick roots. LEAVES basal, in two ranks, strap-like, channeled, fibrotic, sheathing at the base, the sheaths of the inner leaves appressed-villous below with simple or slightly feathery hairs. INFLORESCENCE a panicle of scorpioid cymes, the axis densely white woolly with feathery hairs. FLOWERS actinomorphic, pinkish, tepals six, united half their length into a tubular perianth, densely woolly on the outer surface with feathery hairs. STAMENS six, the three inner somewhat shorter, inserted on the tepals at the mouth of the tube, introrse; POLLEN monosulcate and foveolate. OVARY inferior, three-locular, ovules two per locule, axile; nectaries septal; STYLE slender with small three-lobed stigma. FRUIT indehiscent, thin-walled, tightly enclosed by the persistent perianth, fragmenting with age. SEED one per capsule, obovoid to globose, glossy black, with phytomelan in the testa. South Africa; 1 genus (*Lanaria*), 1 sp.

RUSCACEAE

COMMON NAME lily-of-the-valley family. Evergreen or deciduous perennials or shrubs with or without aerial stems, containing steroidal saponins and calcium oxalate crystals. ROOTSTOCK usually a rhizome with fibrous or tuberous roots, sometimes a tuber. LEAVES one to many, often with a distinct petiole-like base, the blade linear to rounded, hairless or variously hairy, sometimes with simple or complex appendages or outgrowths produced from the upper surface. INFLORESCENCE a spike, raceme, or panicle; bracts minute or vestigial. FLOWERS actinomorphic or weakly zygomorphic, white, pinkish or greenish or yellow, tepals six, subequal or markedly unequal, free or united below into a cup-shaped or tubular perianth. STAMENS (4)6(8, 10, 12), free or united, inserted on the tepals within the tube or at its throat, introrse or latrorse; POLLEN monosulcate and reticulate or perforate, or rarely inaperturate. OVARY usually superior, three-locular, ovules two to several per locule, axile; nectaries septal; STYLE one, short or long, usually with a small three-lobed stigma. FRUIT a berry or loculicidal capsule. SEEDS ovoid or comma-shaped, light brown, densely covered with woolly hairs in *Eriospermum*, with phlobaphene in the testa. Widespread, especially the Old World; 19 genera, one in the Cape (*Eriospermum*), c. 330 spp., 52 in the Cape.

TECOPHILAEACEAE

COMMON NAME cyanella family. Perennial herbs, rarely twining, containing calcium oxalate crystals. ROOTSTOCK a corm with fibrous tunics or naked. LEAVES basal or scattered, lanceolate, sometimes scabrid on the midrib beneath. INFLORESCENCE usually a simple or branched thyrse or raceme, or flowers solitary. FLOWERS actinomorphic or weakly zygomorphic, often nodding, rarely enantiostylous (style directed to the left or right), blue or violet, yellow or white, tepals six, almost free or united below into a tubular perianth; nectaries septal or absent. STAMENS six, inserted on the tepals near the base, with short filaments inserted at the base of the often large anthers, sometimes unequal with some stamens, usually the upper, reduced or transformed into staminodes, dehiscing apically by pores or short introrse longitudinal slits; POLLEN monosulcate and foveolate, usually operculate. OVARY more or less half-inferior, three-locular, ovules two to several per locule, axile or basal; STYLE slender. FRUIT an apically loculicidal capsule. SEEDS ovoid, often wrinkled, black, with phytomelan in the testa (except in *Walleria*). Mainly Southern Hemisphere; 8 genera, 2 in the Cape, c. 25 spp., 6 in the Cape.

Genera of Tecophilaeaceae
1 Corm with fibrous tunic; stems erect with leaves basal, usually in a rosette; flowers in a raceme or solitary, weakly zygomorphic; anthers unequal .... *Cyanella*
1' Corm naked; stems erect or twining, sometimes prickly, leaves scattered along the length; flowers axillary, actinomorphic; anthers equal .... *Walleria*

BULBS OF THE CAPE

Agapanthus

COMMON NAMES agapanthus, blue lily, FAMILY Agapanthaceae. Deciduous or evergreen perennials. ROOTSTOCK a rhizome, often exposed, giving rise to copious fleshy roots. LEAVES basal, in two ranks, strap-like, slightly fleshy or leathery, lightly channeled, the bases somewhat swollen and bulb-like in the deciduous species. INFLORESCENCE an umbel on a naked peduncle, the umbel subtended by two large membranous bracts united along the margins in bud. FLOWERS funnel-shaped or tubular, the tepals united below into a short tube, blue or white, unscented. STAMENS inserted on the tepals at the top of the tube, declinate, unequal. OVARY ovoid or oblong; STYLE slender, declinate. FRUIT a three-angled loculicidal capsule. SEEDS several per chamber, flat and winged, black. Basic chromosome number $x = 15$, also 16. Temperate and subtropical southern Africa; 10 spp., 3 in the Cape.

Agapanthus was traditionally included in the family Alliaceae along with *Tulbaghia*, another South African genus, but Alliaceae are well defined by the presence of various sulfur compounds responsible for the characteristic onion or garlic smell of its members. These compounds are conspicuously lacking in *Agapanthus*, which DNA sequencing indicates is more closely related to the Amaryllidaceae. *Agapanthus* is most appropriately treated as in a family of its own, close to the Amaryllidaceae but not included in it.

Characteristic of rocky grasslands, species of *Agapanthus* are found along the southern and eastern fringes of southern Africa but are absent from the arid interior. The four evergreen species are restricted to the southern parts of the subcontinent, where the rain falls either predominantly in winter or intermittently more or less throughout the year. Farther north, where there is a pronounced winter drought, the species are all deciduous, a reversal in the trend usual in South African geophytes. The two species with drooping tubular flowers, *A. inapertus* Beauverd from the Mpumalanga Drakensberg and *A. walshii*, are visited by sunbirds whereas the remaining species with more open flowers are mostly visited by large bees, particularly carpenter bees (Apidae: Xylocopinae).

Agapanthus praecox, the largest of the evergreen species, is one of the most commonly grown ornamentals in the world, and its ease of cultivation and rapid multiplication have made it a firm feature of street plantings, large parks, and gardens. Forms or hybrids of this species have been erroneously known among Northern Hemisphere horticulturists under the name *A. africanus*, but *A. africanus* is a quite different plant, little known in cultivation. *Agapanthus praecox* does well in even the poorest soil but must receive some moisture in the summer and requires full sun for good flowering. Because of its large size, it is best grown in the garden or in large pots or urns. The species will survive light frost but in colder climates must be brought indoors during the winter where it should be

Agapanthus africanus

Agapanthus walshii

stored in a cool glasshouse. The remaining two evergreen species, A. *africanus* and A. *walshii*, are not suited to cultivation, which is unfortunate because the flowers of A. *africanus* are a particularly deep, almost navy blue, and the lovely nodding, rather tubular flowers of A. *walshii* are unusual in the genus and approached in form only by those of A. *inapertus*. Neither of these two species flowers well in nature unless burned and in the wild can only be seen in good bloom the season following one of the periodic fires that sweep across the Cape mountains. Unlike A. *praecox*, which requires summer moisture but will tolerate some moisture throughout the year, A. *africanus* and A. *walshii* must be kept dry in the summer and are best tried in the rock garden or in large terra-cotta pots in a well-drained, acidic, sandy soil. Like all agapanthuses, the rhizomes should be planted just below the surface, and a mulch of gravel or stone chips will assist in keeping the crown of the plants free of excess moisture.

FURTHER READING. *Agapanthus* was revised by Leighton (1965). Although Leighton's remains the most comprehensive taxonomic work on the genus, Duncan (1998a) provided a well-illustrated guide to the species that also covers their cultivation and propagation.

Agapanthus africanus (Linnaeus) Hoffmannsegg

Plants evergreen, 25–70 cm high. Leaves strap-shaped, channeled. Flowers spreading on pedicels 1.5–5 cm long, broadly funnel-shaped, tepals thick in texture, deep blue, 25–40 mm long, united below for 9–14 mm, stamens shorter than the tepals. Flowering December–April, mainly after fire. Rocky sandstone slopes, mostly montane, SW, AP, LB (Cape Peninsula to Swellendam).

Agapanthus praecox Willdenow

Plants evergreen, 50–100 cm high. Leaves strap-shaped, channeled. Flowers spreading on pedicels 4–12 cm long, broadly funnel-shaped, tepals thin in texture, white to medium blue, 30–70 mm long, united below for 7–26 mm, stamens mostly as long as the tepals. Flowering December–February. Stony slopes, SE (Knysna to Eastern Cape).

Agapanthus walshii L. Bolus

Plants evergreen, 60–70 cm high. Leaves strap-shaped, channeled. Flowers nodding on pedicels 0.5–2.5 cm long, tubular, tepals thick in texture, pale to deep blue, 30–55 mm long, united below for 15–40 mm, stamens finally as long as the tepals. Flowering January–February, mainly after fire. Rocky sandstone slopes, montane, SW (Steenbras Mountains).

Albuca

COMMON NAME slime lily, FAMILY Hyacinthaceae. Deciduous or rarely evergreen perennials. ROOTSTOCK a globose, often large bulb, subterranean or partially exposed, the tunics sometimes only loosely overlapping, rarely fragmenting into triangular segments, the flesh sometimes pink or reddish. LEAVES few to several, rarely one, rarely dry at flowering, linear to oblong or terete, hairless or rarely hairy, glandular hairy or margins minutely hairy, suberect, the sheaths sometimes persistent and forming a papery or weakly or strongly fibrous, sometimes horizontally barred sheath around the base of the stem. INFLORESCENCE a several- to many-flowered raceme, sometimes subcorymbose with shortened axis, hairless or hairy in the lower part; bracts usually membranous or leafy. FLOWERS suberect, closing at night, often scented, erect or nodding on conspicuous pedicels but always erect in fruit, cup-shaped but rarely weakly zygomorphic, the tepals dimorphic, more or less free, white to yellowish green with broad green keels, the outer tepals suberect or spreading, the inner tepals erect and more or less connivent around the stamens and style and cupped or hooded and papillate at the tips and sometimes developing a fleshy apical knob or flap that can be conspicuously hinged. STAMENS with filaments joined to the base of the tepals, narrowly oblong to linear-lanceolate, the inner or both whorls pinched and more or less expanded below, the outer anthers usually smaller or vestigial or absent. OVARY ovoid to ellipsoidal with more or less conspicuous, often crested paraseptal ridges around the nectaries, with many ovules per locule; STYLE subcylindrical or more or less trigonous or prismatic, sometimes strongly papillate, about as long as the perianth, stigma three-angled and pyramidal or horned, papillate and sometimes fringed with longer papillae. FRUIT an ovoid capsule, more or less three-angled. SEEDS many per chamber, discoid and stacked tightly one on top of another, black. Basic chromosome number $x = 9$. Africa and Arabia, mainly winter-rainfall southern Africa; c. 60 spp., 28 in the Cape.

Largely African, *Albuca* is richest and most diverse in the more arid winter-rainfall part of southern Africa where the two most specialized subgenera, *Albuca* and *Mitropetalum*, are concentrated. The less specialized subgenera, *Falconera* and *Pallastema*, are found chiefly in the summer-rainfall part of the subcontinent. The ornamentation of the inner tepals and style in *Albuca* are critical features in assigning the species to one of the four subgenera, but within the subgenera the differences between species are almost entirely vegetative.

Albuca is closely related to *Ornithogalum*, especially the species of *Ornithogalum* placed in subgenus *Osmyne*, but the two genera can usually be separated easily enough by the shape and arrangement of the tepals. In *Ornithogalum*, the two series of six tepals are similar in form and orientation and are disposed in a more or less open cup or star, whereas in *Albuca* the inner tepals remain erect and conceal the stamens and ovary. Other differences between the genera are found in the ovary and stamens. In all species of *Albuca*, at least the inner filaments are pinched near the base and the ovary is provided with V-shaped crests on each of the septa, but these characters are usually lacking in *Ornithogalum*.

Little is known about the pollination biology of *Albuca* but it is clear that several of the florally more specialized species use the ornamented style for secondary pollen transfer. In this strategy the pollen, rather than being deposited directly onto a visiting insect, is shed onto the style, where it is held by the crests and papillae that ornament it, and is later transferred from there to the body of the pollinator. The dull but relatively large and usually scented flowers are visited by several larger species of solitary bees of the families Apidae (Anthophorinae) and Megachilidae, and these are likely to be the primary pollinators.

Although a few of the larger, evergreen species of

Albuca, especially *A. batteniana* and *A. nelsonii* N. E. Brown of coastal eastern South Africa, are cultivated in specialist collections, some of the deciduous species are also recommended for the garden. Both *A. fragrans* and *A. maxima* are robust plants that produce attractive inflorescences of nodding, lantern-like flowers in the spring. The true giant of the genus, however, is *A. clanwilliamigloria*, a relatively recent discovery from deep sandy soils along the coastal plain and adjacent lower reaches of the Olifants River Valley. The slender inflorescences tower more than 2 m and bear numerous, narrow, golden yellow flowers. In the wild, this species is one of the most dramatic in the genus and flowers later in the season than many.

FURTHER READING. The taxonomy of *Albuca* is poorly understood and no complete account of the genus exists. The partial treatments of the South African species by U. Müller-Doblies (1994, 1995) are very incomplete. The attractive Cape species *A. clanwilliamigloria* was illustrated separately with cultivation notes by Manning et al. (1999a).

Albuca acuminata Baker
Plants 20–30 cm high; bulb scales becoming fibrous above. Leaves two to six, channeled, slender, clasping below. Flowers nodding, yellow to green with green keels, 15–25 mm long, inner tepals hinged above, outer stamens sterile. Flowering September–October. Deep sands, NW, SW, KM, LB (Namaqualand to Mossel Bay).

Albuca aurea Jacquin
Plants to 50 cm high; bulbs often bluish. Leaves two to six, lanceolate, channeled, clasping below. Inflorescence often subsecund with an inclined peduncle, flowers erect, whitish or yellow with green keels, 15–25 mm long, inner tepals cowled and yellowish above, outer anthers smaller. Flowering mostly September–December. Stony clay slopes, NW, SW, KM (Clanwilliam to Worcester and Little Karoo).

Albuca batteniana Hilliard & B. L. Burtt
Plants to 60 cm high, evergreen; bulb borne above ground, green, scales firm, truncate and fibrous above. Leaves 6–12, lanceolate, firm. Inflorescence subsecund with an inclined peduncle, flowers erect on long pedicels, white with pale greenish keels, 25–40 mm long, outer tepals spreading-recurved, inner tepals cowled above, outer anthers smaller. Flowering July–October. Coastal cliffs, SE (Knysna and Kei Mouth).

Albuca ciliaris U. Müller-Doblies
Plants to 20 cm high; bulb depressed-globose. Leaves 5–20, short, not clasping, flat, narrowly oblong, often twisted, margins minutely hairy. Flowers few, nodding, dull greenish, 15–25 mm long, inner tepals hinged above, outer stamens sterile. Flowering September–October. Rocky sandstone slopes, NW (Namaqualand to Clanwilliam).

Albuca clanwilliamigloria

Albuca clanwilliamigloria U. Müller-Doblies

Plants to 2 m; bulb depressed-globose, sometimes producing bulblets. Leaves three or four, narrow, channeled, fleshy, dry at flowering. Flowers nodding in slender, elongate racemes, scarcely flaring, dull yellow with dark yellow or green keels, 25–35 mm long, inner tepals cupped above, outer anthers slightly smaller; stylar cells fusiform. Flowering October–November. Deep sandy soils in fynbos dominated by Restionaceae, NW (Olifants River Valley to Elands Bay).

Albuca cooperi Baker

Plants 35–60 cm high; bulb tunics fibrous above. Leaves two or three, slender, channeled, conspicuously clasping and warty basally. Flowers nodding, yellow with green keels, 15–25 mm long, inner tepals hinged above, outer stamens sterile. Flowering September–November. Stony, mostly sandy slopes and flats, rarely limestone, RV, NW, SW, AP, KM, LB, SE (Richtersveld and western Karoo to Cape Peninsula to Willowmore).

Albuca cremnophila Van Jaarsveld & van Wyk

Plants to 2 m long, pendent, evergreen; bulb usually epigeal, grayish green, scales firm, truncate above. Leaves 6–12, lanceolate, firm. Flowers erect on long pedicels, subsecund on a pendent peduncle, white with pale greenish keels, 10–20 mm long, outer tepals suberect, inner tepals cowled above, outer anthers smaller. Flowering December–February. Cliffs, SE (Baviaanskloof Mountains).

Albuca decipiens U. Müller-Doblies

Plants to 80 cm high. Leaves four to six, channeled, clasping below. Flowers erect, white with green keels, 15–25 mm long, inner tepals cupped above, outer stamens sterile. Flowering August–September. Rocky slopes, NW (Namaqualand to Olifants River Valley).

Albuca echinosperma U. Müller-Doblies

Like A. flaccida but more delicate with one to three leaves and distinctly papillate seeds. Flowering August–October. Rocky sandstone slopes, NW, SW (Piketberg to Hermanus).

Albuca exuviata Baker

Plants to 30 cm high; bulb tunics coarsely fibrous above, forming a thick neck with conspicuous, woody rings. Leaves two to four, linear-filiform, not clasping. Flowers erect, subcorymbose, white to yellow with green keels, 15–25 mm long, inner tepals cowled above, all stamens fertile. Flowering mostly August–September. Clay soils, KM, SE (Little Karoo to Eastern Cape).

Albuca flaccida Jacquin

Plants 40–100 cm high; bulb tunics membranous. Leaves three to five, channeled, fleshy, clasping below. Flowers nodding, mostly yellow, sometimes with green keels, lightly fragrant, 15–25 mm long, inner tepals hinged above, outer stamens sterile. Flowering August–October.

Albuca cooperi

Albuca flaccida

Mostly coastal in deep sandy soils, NW, SW, AP (southern Namaqualand to Still Bay).

Albuca foetida U. Müller-Doblies

Plants 20–40 cm high. Leaves two to four, channeled, clasping below, glandular hairy, peduncle also glandular hairy. Flowers nodding, yellow with green keels, 12–20 mm long, inner tepals cupped above, outer stamens sterile. Flowering September–October. Stony slopes, RV, NW, SW, KM (Namaqualand and western Karoo to Tulbagh, Oudtshoorn).

Albuca fragrans Jacquin

Plants to 1 m; bulb sometimes forming bulblets. Leaves two to four, channeled, shortly clasping below, drying at flowering. Flowers nodding in drooping racemes, yellow with green keels, 15–25 mm long, outer anthers slightly smaller, fragrant; stylar cells fusiform. Flowering September–October. Sandy slopes and flats, often coastal, NW, SW (Bokkeveld Mountains to Hermanus).

Albuca glandulosa Baker

Plants to 35 cm high, glandular hairy; bulb tunics membranous with rings around the neck. Leaves one to four, narrow, channeled, clasping below. Flowers erect, yellow with greenish keels, 15–25 mm long, inner tepals cowled above, outer stamens sterile. Flowering August–September. Dry, stony, shale slopes, KM (Namaqualand and western Karoo to Little Karoo).

Albuca goswinii U. Müller-Doblies

Plants 15–60 cm high. Leaves two or three, linear, channeled, clasping below. Flowers nodding in drooping racemes, yellow with green keels, 15–25 mm long, outer stamens sterile. Flowering September–October. Stony slopes, SW, LB (Houwhoek to Riversdale).

Albuca hallii U. Müller-Doblies

Plants 10–15 cm high. Leaves three to six, linear, glandular, corkscrewed above, obtuse. Flowers nodding, yellow with green keels, 12–15 mm long, inner tepals hinged above, outer stamens sterile. Flowering March–May. Stony slopes, NW, KM (southern Namibia to Little Karoo).

Albuca juncifolia Baker
Plants 15–30 cm high. Leaves 4–10, slender and stiff, channeled below but usually terete above, not clasping below. Flowers nodding in drooping racemes, yellow with green keels, 15–25 mm long, inner tepals hinged above, outer stamens sterile. Flowering September–October. Sandy and calcareous flats, NW, SW, AP, LB (Ceres to Cape Peninsula to Mossel Bay).

Albuca longipes Baker
Plants to 30 cm high; outer bulb tunics often dry and wrinkled above. Leaves two to six, linear, channeled, not clasping below, dry at flowering. Flowers often corymbose, erect on long pedicels, white with green keels, 15–20 mm long, inner tepals cowled and bright yellow at the tips, outer anthers smaller. Flowering September–November. Clay or lime slopes, RV, NW, SW, AP, LB, SE (Richtersveld and western Karoo to Cape Peninsula to Willowmore).

Albuca massonii Baker
Plants 20–30 cm high; bulb scales becoming fibrous above. Leaves two or three, channeled, slender, clasping below. Flowers nodding, yellow to green with green keels, 8–10 mm long, inner tepals hinged above, outer stamens sterile, style about half as long as the ovary. Flowering September–October. Sandstone slopes, NW (Bokkeveld to Pakhuis Mountains).

Albuca maxima Burman fil.
Plants 40–150 cm high; bulb tunics slightly fibrous above. Leaves four to six, lanceolate, channeled, fleshy, clasping below. Flowers nodding, white with green keels, 15–25 mm long, inner tepals hinged above, outer stamens sterile, filaments oblanceolate. Flowering August–November. Rocky sandstone or granitic soils, RV, NW, SW, KM, LB (Namaqualand to Riversdale).

Albuca namaquensis Baker
Plants to 30 cm high; bulb tunics membranous. Leaves 4–20, channeled or rolled, usually coiled above, not clasping below, scabrid or hairy. Flowers nodding, yellow with green keels, 15–25 mm long, inner tepals hinged

Albuca longipes

Albuca maxima

Albuca namaquensis

above, outer stamens sterile. Flowering September–October. Stony sandstone slopes, RV, NW, SW, KM, SE (Namibia to Eastern Cape).

Albuca navicula U. Müller-Doblies
Plants to 20 cm high; bulb depressed-globose. Leaves four to eight, short, oblong, margins densely minutely hairy, clasping below, longitudinally folded and boat-shaped above. Flowers few, nodding, dull greenish, 12–20 mm long, inner tepals hinged above, outer stamens sterile. Flowering September–October. Red sandy flats, NW (Namaqualand to Clanwilliam).

Albuca papyracea J. C. Manning & Goldblatt
Plants 50–80 cm high; bulb tunics papery and fibrous above. Leaves two to four, linear, clasping, rarely warty below. Flowers nodding in drooping racemes, yellow with green keels, 15–20 mm long, outer anthers slightly smaller. Flowering September–November. Stony shale slopes, KM (Little Karoo).

Albuca paradoxa Dinter
Plants 40–100 cm high; bulb conspicuously depressed and fragmenting into segments, tunics membranous. Leaves four to six, channeled, fleshy, clasping below. Flowers nodding, mostly yellow, sometimes with green keels, lightly fragrant, 15–25 mm long, inner tepals hinged above, outer stamens sterile. Flowering July–August. Red sandy flats, NW (southern Namibia to Clanwilliam).

Albuca schoenlandii Baker
Plants to 30 cm high; outer bulb tunics dry and firm. Leaves four to seven, oblong, flat, margins hyaline. Flowers erect on long pedicels, subcorymbose, white and green, 15–25 mm long, inner tepals cowled above, outer anthers smaller. Flowering September–November. Dry sandstone slopes, KM, SE (Oudtshoorn to Eastern Cape).

Albuca setosa Jacquin
Plants 15–60 cm high; bulb large, basal sheaths fibrous. Leaves two to six, narrow, fleshy, not clasping below, margins hyaline and often ciliolate. Flowers erect on long

Albuca namaquensis

Albuca setosa

pedicels, yellow with green keels, 15–25 mm long, inner tepals cowled above, outer anthers slightly smaller. Flowering October–November. Rocky clay flats and slopes, RV, NW, SW, KM, SE (southern Namaqualand to Swaziland).

Albuca spiralis Linnaeus fil.
Plants 20–40 cm high. Leaves 3–10, linear, channeled or rolled, often spirally twisted above, clasping below, glandular hairy and peduncle also glandular hairy below. Flowers nodding, green, outer tepals with cream to yellow margins, sweetly fragrant, 15–25 mm long, inner tepals hinged above, outer stamens sterile. Flowering August–October. Sandy and stony slopes, NW, SW (Namaqualand to Cape Peninsula).

Albuca viscosa

Albuca viscosa Linnaeus fil.
Plants 20–40 cm high; bulbs ovoid, often pink, tunics dry and wrinkled above. Leaves 4–20, semiterete, often spirally twisted above, glandular hairy, not clasping below, peduncle base also glandular hairy. Flowers nodding, yellow with green keels, fragrant, 15–25 mm long, inner tepals cupped above, outer anthers smaller. Flowering August–October. Rocky flats, RV, NW, SW, AP, KM, LB (Namibia and Karoo to Riversdale).

Allium

COMMON NAME wild onion, FAMILY Alliaceae. Deciduous perennials, usually with an onion smell when bruised. ROOTSTOCK a bulb, rarely a short rhizome. LEAVES several, clustered at the base or scattered up the stem, straplike or terete and hollow. INFLORESCENCE an umbel on a naked peduncle, the umbel subtended by one or two large bracts united along the margins in bud, sometimes producing bulblets. FLOWERS star- or cup-shaped, the tepals free or shortly united, white to pinkish or purplish or yellow, sometime scented. STAMENS with filaments sometimes flattened or toothed above, usually broadened below and shortly united together and joined to the base of the tepals. OVARY ovoid; STYLE slender, arising from near the base of the ovary. FRUIT a globose capsule. SEEDS one to four per locule, wedge-shaped, black. Basic chromosome number $x = 8$ or 7. Mainly Northern Hemisphere but 1 sp. in sub-Saharan Africa; c. 550 spp.

Well represented in seasonally dry areas, especially in the Mediterranean and Middle East, the genus *Allium* includes several important culinary species, including garlic (*A. sativum*) and its milder relatives the onion (*A. cepa*), chives (*A. schoenoprasum*), leek (*A. porrum*), and shallot (*A. ascalonicum*). The whole family is characterized by the presence of various sulfur compounds, often mildly antiseptic, which are responsible for the typical onion smell released when the plants are bruised. There is some doubt as to whether the single sub-Saharan species is in fact native at all, but there are some small differences between it and closely related European species, in particular *A. ampeloprasum*, which suggest that it might be. The single southern African species is probably visited by a variety of insects for pollen or nectar.

FURTHER READING. The African species of *Allium* were revised by Dewilde-Duyfjes (1976).

Allium dregeanum Kunth

Plants 35–80 cm high, strongly aromatic; outer tunics papery, brown. Leaves dry at flowering, two to four along the stem, linear, keeled or flat. Flowers in a compact spherical head 2.5–6 cm diam., pedicels 7–25 mm long, tepals white to pink, 5–7 mm long, filaments c. 5 mm long, inner tricuspidate with outer cusps longest. Flowering October–December. Dry stony slopes and flats, often along roadsides or in old cornfields, RV, NW, LB, SE (Namaqualand, western Karoo, Clanwilliam to Long Kloof, dry areas throughout southern Africa).

Allium dregeanum

Amaryllis

COMMON NAME belladonna lily, FAMILY Amaryllidaceae. Large deciduous perennials. ROOTSTOCK a bulb. LEAVES 5–11 in an evenly spreading or suberect basal cluster, dry at flowering, narrowly strap-shaped or broad and tapering toward each end, midrib prominent, sometimes forming a short sheathing neck, smooth or sparsely hairy. INFLORESCENCE a spreading umbel on a tall, stout, erect scape; spathe bracts two, rapidly withering. FLOWERS trumpet-shaped, the pedicels shorter than the perianth but elongated in fruit, the tepals free, broad and overlapping in the lower half, spreading and reflexed toward the tip, white to pink, faintly narcissus scented. STAMENS inserted at the tepal base, very shortly united together basally, clustered together against the lower tepal, straight but upturned toward the tip, the inner somewhat longer than the outer but both whorls shorter than the tepals, the anthers dorsifixed, curved, cream. OVARY with four to eight ovules per locule; STYLE protruding beyond the stamens, upturned toward the tip, the stigma minutely to distinctly trifid. FRUIT a large, rounded, papery capsule, splitting open regularly. SEEDS fleshy, more or less globose, c. 15 mm diam., glossy, white to pink, the embryo green. Basic chromosome number $x = 11$. Winter-rainfall South Africa; 2 spp., 1 in the Cape.

For two centuries or more, the Cape genus *Amaryllis* was believed to have just one species, the much celebrated *A. belladonna*. In 1997, however, an expedition to the extremely arid Richtersveld, north of the Cape Floral Region, led to the surprising discovery of a second, equally beautiful species, *A. paradisicola* Snijman. In the wild, both species flower opportunistically, *A. paradisicola* after good autumn showers, and *A. belladonna* most prolifically after hot summers and fire.

The pale pink, trumpet-shaped flowers of *Amaryllis belladonna* are especially heavily scented in the evening, when they are visited by noctuid moths. Day visitors are large carpenter bees, but these are active on relatively few plants in a population. When mature, the heavy seeds are shaken free of the dry capsules, close to the parent plants. The pearly pink seeds germinate immediately, and seedlings are rapidly established. Over time, this leads to highly localized, dense concentrations of plants. The stately pink inflorescences of *A. belladonna* are produced reliably in cultivation, provided the plants are given sufficient warmth. The species has proven so popular that plants are now naturalized in Mediterranean climates throughout the world. This success is not yet shared by its sister species, which most often fails to flower in cultivation.

FURTHER READING. A well-illustrated account of *Amaryllis belladonna* was published by Dyer (1955), and notes on the reproductive biology were reported by Johnson and Snijman (1996). Tjaden (1989) dealt with the difficulties of flowering amaryllis in cool climates. The more recently discovered *A. paradisicola* was formally described by Snijman and Williamson (1998).

Amaryllis belladonna Linnaeus
Plants to 90 cm high; bulb c. 10 cm diam. Leaves 5–11, dry at flowering, spreading to suberect, lanceolate, 15–75 mm wide, channeled, smooth, the midrib distinct. Flowers usually 6–12, occasionally more, turned to one side or evenly spreading, trumpet-shaped, fragrant, white to pink, usually pale lemon at the base, the veins often dark pink, tepals 8–10 cm long, slightly longer than stamens and style. Flowering February–April. Loamy soils in seasonally moist sites, NW, SW, AP, LB, SE (Olifants River Valley to Knysna).

Ammocharis

COMMON NAME ammocharis, FAMILY Amaryllidaceae. Large to small deciduous perennials. ROOTSTOCK a bulb covered by tough leathery tunics. LEAVES perennial, as many as 15, usually green at flowering, narrowly to broadly strap-shaped, in two opposite, spreading fans with a very short hyaline fringe, the mature leaves ending abruptly as if cut. INFLORESCENCE a slightly spreading umbel on a slightly reclining, compressed scape; spathe bracts two, rapidly withering. FLOWERS actinomorphic, salver- to narrowly trumpet-shaped, the pedicels shorter or about as long as the perianth, hardly elongated at fruiting, the perianth tube short to long cylindrical, the tepals narrow, shorter to slightly longer than the tube, spreading to recurved, white to pink, usually sweetly scented. STAMENS inserted in or slightly below the perianth throat, free to the base, evenly spreading, slightly to much shorter than the tepals, the anthers dorsifixed, curved, cream. OVARY with 4–30 ovules per locule; STYLE straight, exserted or included in the perianth tube, the stigma undivided. FRUIT subglobose, membranous, bluntly beaked, disintegrating irregularly. SEEDS fleshy, subglobose, 7–15 mm diam., greenish with a thin, pale, corky covering, the embryo green. Basic chromosome number $x = 11$. Sub-Saharan Africa; 5 spp., 1 in the Cape.

Because of their ability to resprout, the mature leaves of *Ammocharis* always appear to be cut off at their tips. This characteristic originates when the mature blades die back at the beginning of each dry season, subsequently growing out again when favorable conditions return. The seeds of *Ammocharis* are usually dropped close to the parent plants after the fruiting head collapses to the ground and disintegrates. As a result of this dispersal method,

Amaryllis belladonna (Colin Paterson-Jones); see also page 18

many populations are highly localized, often occurring in seasonally wet depressions. In southern Africa, the Swazi and southern Sotho peoples use a paste made from the cooked bulbs of *A. coranica* to mend clay pots and to shape small ornaments. The pale color and sweet fragrance of the flowers suggest that they attract butterflies and moths but this has yet to be confirmed.

FURTHER READING. *Ammocharis* was last revised by Milne-Redhead and Schweickerdt (1939). Pole Evans (1938) included ethnobotanical notes in his illustrated account of *A. coranica*.

Ammocharis coranica (Ker Gawler) Herbert

Compact summer-growing plants to 35 cm high; bulb c. 16 cm diam. Leaves c. 15, flat, often curved sideways, strap-shaped, 0.5–7.5 cm wide, shortly fringed. Flowers 3–56 in an evenly spreading umbel 15–20 cm wide, trumpet-shaped, pale to deep pink, sweetly scented, pedicels not elongating in fruit, perianth tube 0.8–2.5 cm long, tepals 2.8–5.5 cm long, stamens straight, evenly spreading, exserted from tube by 3.5–5.5 cm, about as long as the style. Flowering November–February. Seasonally damp flats, KM, SE (Oudtshoorn to southern Angola and Zimbabwe).

Androcymbium

COMMON NAMES cup-and-saucer, men-in-a-boat, FAMILY Colchicaceae. Short-stemmed or stemless deciduous perennials. ROOTSTOCK an asymmetric ovoid corm with a pronounced, fan-like, basal fold, covered with dark leathery to woody tunics. LEAVES few to several, scattered along the stem or in the stemless species congested and often prostrate, ovate to linear-lanceolate, clasping below, soft or leathery, the margins sometimes crisped and smooth or ciliolate or bristly. INFLORESCENCE a single- to few-flowered, bracteate, usually congested raceme, in the stemless species sessile and subumbellate; bracts leaf-like or more usually broader and often colored or patterned, the inner successively smaller. FLOWERS erect, usually on short stout pedicels or subsessile, usually unscented or unpleasantly scented, the tepals scarcely spreading, free, narrowed and clawed below with a nectary at the base of the filaments, the limb expanded below and often eared with the lobes curving inward to form a cup at the base, persistent in fruit, whitish or greenish, the base of the filaments sometimes dark purple. STAMENS arising from the top of the claws, sometimes swollen at the base. OVARY cylindrical, deeply lobed with many ovules per locule; STYLES three, subterminal on the ovary lobes. FRUIT an ovoid septicidal capsule. SEEDS many per locule, globose or subglobose, brown. Basic chromosome number $x = 9$ or 8. Africa and Mediterranean, mostly southern Africa; c. 40 spp., 13 in the Cape.

Unlike the Mediterranean and Eurasian genus *Colchicum* to which it is allied on the basis of its unusual, two- to four-aperturate pollen and often stemless growth form, *Androcymbium* finds its greatest expression in the winter-rainfall zone of southern Africa. The few Mediterranean species most resemble the genus *Colchicum* and have well-developed stems, narrow, leaf-like bracts, and

Ammocharis coranica (Colin Paterson-Jones)

more or less flat tepal limbs. In contrast, most of the Cape species have curious, cupped tepal limbs, which hold the nectar, and often, broad, colorful floral bracts that resemble large petals, which envelop the small flowers. The genus is most common in the more arid parts of the southern African winter-rainfall zone, and most species occur in the western Karoo and Namaqualand, which lies to the north of the Cape Floral Region.

The curious appearance of the species suggests equally interesting pollination systems. The location of the nectaries on the tepals does not favor the development of a floral tube and thus co-evolution with long-tongued floral visitors to effect pollination. To compensate, it seems that various genera of the family Colchicaceae, including *Androcymbium*, have exploited a diversity of less well studied pollinators such as small flies and wasps, beetles, butterflies, and in several Cape androcymbiums, possibly even rodents.

Androcymbium is of limited horticultural appeal but some species are true curiosities. The more colorful ones, such as the Namaqualand *A. ciliolatum* Schlechter & Krause and *A. latifolium*, are a charming sight as the late afternoon light slants though their pale or reddish sail-like bracts. *Androcymbium* is long-lived, reaching at least 20–25 years of age in European species. After that, the corm usually produces a stolon or dropper root, at the tip of which a new corm develops some distance from the mother corm, which is subsequently completely resorbed into the daughter. In this way, the plants migrate slowly over decades. The plants reach flowering, on average, 4 years from seed. Because of their deep-seated corms, they are best grown in pots that have the bottoms removed and are then sunk into beds.

FURTHER READING. The taxonomy of *Androcymbium* is poorly understood and no complete account of the species exists. The partial treatments of the South African species by U. and D. Müller-Doblies (1984, 1998) are very inadequate.

Androcymbium burchellii Baker

Plants stemless. Leaves prostrate, ovate-lanceolate, margins sometimes minutely hairy, leathery, 3–8 cm long; bracts broadly ovate to rounded, green above with white markings below or entirely white. Flowers one or two, tepal claws c. 13 mm long, limbs eared and cupped below, 4–6 mm long, filaments 8–9 mm long, styles as long as the ovary. Flowering June–August. Stony clay flats, RV, NW, KM (western Karoo and Bokkeveld Mountains to Little Karoo).

Androcymbium capense (Linnaeus) Krause

Plants stemless. Leaves spreading or prostrate, ovate-lanceolate to lanceolate, margins often minutely hairy, leathery, 4–15 cm long; bracts broadly ovate, green above but marked with white below or mostly white. Flowers two to five, sometimes single, tepal claws 8–10 mm long, limbs eared and deeply cupped or tubular below, 6–8 mm long, filaments 5–7 mm long, styles as long as or slightly longer than the ovary. Flowering May–August. Clay or loam flats, RV, NW, SW, LB (Namaqualand and western Karoo to Swellendam).

Androcymbium capense

Androcymbium crispum Schinz

Plants stemless. Leaves spreading, narrowly lanceolate, the margins crisped and bristly, leathery, 4–6 cm long; bracts broadly ovate, green above with white windows below or entirely white. Flowers one to three, honey scented, tepal claws 6–7 mm long, limbs eared and deeply cupped or almost tubular below, 5–6 mm long, filaments 7–8 mm long, styles longer than the ovary. Flowering July–August. Gravelly clay flats, RV (Hantamsberg at Calvinia).

Androcymbium cuspidatum Baker

Plants stemless. Leaves in three ranks, prostrate, ovate-lanceolate, striate, 1.5–5 cm long; bracts leaf-like, smaller than the flowers and spreading. Flowers one or two, sometimes three, exposed, acridly scented, tepal claws 5–8 mm long, limbs cupped below, 6–8 mm long, filaments 4–5 mm long, styles as long as or slightly longer than the ovary. Flowering July–August. Stony flats, RV, NW, KM, SE (western Karoo and Cedarberg to Uniondale).

Androcymbium crispum

Androcymbium dregei C. Presl

Plants slender, with a short stem, mostly 2–4 cm high. Leaves spreading or suberect, linear-attenuate, channeled, 2–10 cm long; bracts like the leaves, spreading. Flowers one or two, exposed, tepal claws 2–3 mm long, blades plane, ovate-attenuate, 5–7 mm long, filaments 0.5–1 mm long with a black, cushion-like base, styles half as long as the ovary. Flowering June–August. Sheltered rock outcrops, NW, KM (Namaqualand to Montagu).

Androcymbium eucomoides (Jacquin) Willdenow

Plants stemless. Leaves lanceolate to lanceolate-attenuate, spreading, 6–40 cm long; bracts ovate, green or whitish. Flowers two to seven, sour or fermented smelling, tepal claws 5–8 mm long, limbs eared and cupped below, 7–10 mm long, filaments 5–8 mm long, styles about as long as or longer than the ovary. Flowering July–August. Clay flats, NW, SW, AP, KM, LB, SE (Namaqualand to Eastern Cape).

Androcymbium hughocymbion U. & D. Müller-Doblies

Plants stemless. Leaves in three ranks, prostrate, lanceolate-attenuate, aristate, 2–7 cm long; bracts leaf-like but acute, smaller than the flowers and spreading. Flowers one to three, sometimes as many as seven, exposed, tepal claws 3–5 mm long, limbs cupped below, 5–7 mm long, filaments 3–4 mm long, styles about as long as the ovary. Flowering June–July. Stony flats and slopes, NW, SW (Worcester to Potberg).

Androcymbium latifolium Schinz

Plants stemless. Leaves prostrate, ovate-lanceolate, margins sometimes minutely hairy, leathery, 4–15 cm long; bracts broadly ovate to rounded, wine red with green markings below. Flowers two or three, tepal claws c. 12 mm long, limbs eared and cupped below, 4–6 mm long, filaments 10–12 mm long, styles longer than the ovary. Flowering July–August. Dolerite and clay flats, RV, NW (western Karoo and Bokkeveld Plateau).

Androcymbium longipes Baker

Plants stemless. Leaves spreading, narrowly lanceolate, channeled, 10–20 cm long; bracts leaf-like, green. Flow-

Androcymbium cuspidatum

Androcymbium dregei

Androcymbium eucomoides

Androcymbium latifolium

ers one to three, sometimes as many as nine, tepal claws 10–35 mm long, blades eared and cupped below, 9–15 mm long, filaments 5–6 mm long, styles about as long as the ovary. Flowering mainly April–August. Moist slopes and stony grasslands, KM, SE (Ladismith to Eastern Cape).

Androcymbium melanthioides Willdenow
Plants caulescent, 10–20 cm high. Leaves suberect, lanceolate to linear-lanceolate, channeled, 10–30 cm long; bracts ovate-lanceolate, creamy white with conspicuous green veins. Flowers three to seven, conspicuously pedicellate, tepal claws 4–5 mm long, limbs eared and deeply cupped or tubular below, 7–8 mm long, filaments 8–10 mm long, styles about as long as the ovary, slender. Flowering mainly May–August. Stony flats and slopes, RV (western and Great Karoo to tropical Africa).

Androcymbium orienticapense U. & D. Müller-Doblies
Plants usually caulescent, 10–20 cm high. Leaves suberect, lanceolate to linear-lanceolate, channeled, 10–30 cm long; bracts ovate-lanceolate, creamy white with conspicuous green veins. Flowers three to seven, conspicuously pedicellate, tepal claws 4–5 mm long, limbs eared and channeled below, linear and channeled above, 8–9 mm long, filaments 4–5 mm long, styles about as long as the ovary, slender. Flowering May–August. Grassland, SE (Knysna to tropical Africa).

Androcymbium volutare Burchell
Plants stemless or short-stemmed. Leaves suberect, linear-lanceolate, channeled, often coiled at the tips, 5–12 cm long; bracts large, ovate, pale green. Flowers two or three, tepal claws c. 6 mm long, limbs eared and cupped below, c. 7 mm long, filaments c. 8 mm long, anthers large, 4–6 mm long, styles shorter than the ovary, slender. Flowering August–September. Clay soils, RV, NW, KM (western Karoo to Little Karoo).

Androcymbium sp. 1
Plants stemless. Leaves prostrate, lanceolate, leathery, 6–12 cm long; bracts erect, oblong, green tinged red or purple below. Flowers two or three, tepal claws 8–14 mm long, limbs eared below, c. 10 mm long, filaments 6–8 mm long, styles longer than the ovary, slender. Flowering August. Clay flats, RV (western Karoo).

Apodolirion
COMMON NAME ground lily, FAMILY Amaryllidaceae. Small deciduous perennials. ROOTSTOCK a bulb. LEAVES one to four, usually dry at flowering, smooth, sometimes spiraled. INFLORESCENCE a single flower held close to the ground on a short scape; spathe bracts united into a membranous sheath with a bifid apex, hidden in the bulb neck. FLOWER actinomorphic, salver- to funnel-shaped, fugacious, white, delicate pink or dull red, fragrant, the pedicel a few millimeters long, the perianth tube long, cylindrical and narrow, the tepals ascending to recurved, shorter than the tube. STAMENS free, evenly spreading, much shorter than the tepals, both whorls inserted at or slightly below the perianth throat or the inner whorl inserted higher up on the tepals, the anthers dimorphic, the inner basifixed, the outer more or less medifixed, opening by curling backward from the apex, cream-yellow. OVARY subterranean with many ovules per locule;

Androcymbium volutare

STYLE exserted, often deflexed, the stigma broad, obscurely three-lobed. FRUIT a long, fleshy and club-shaped berry or thin-walled and oval, rupturing irregularly. SEEDS subglobose, 2.5–4 mm diam., translucent, the embryo green. Basic chromosome number $x = 6$. Southern Africa; c. 6 spp., 3 in the Cape.

Apodolirion is distinguished from *Gethyllis* by a difference in the attachment of the anthers. Anthers are uniformly basifixed in *Gethyllis* whereas the inner anthers of *Apodolirion* are basifixed and the outer are somewhat medifixed. The subtlety of this difference is arguably insufficient to separate genera, but we have chosen to maintain both *Gethyllis* and *Apodolirion* until the relationships between their species are more fully understood.

Plants of *Apodolirion* are notoriously difficult to locate in the wild, particularly in the Cape Floral Region, where the appearance of the delicate, short-lived flowers coincides with the summer drought. Moreover, the flowering, fruiting, and leafing periods rarely overlap. Like its closest ally, *Gethyllis*, the flowers of *Apodolirion* usually have a subterranean ovary. This specialized feature is thought to provide protection for the ovary during the summer heat while its many seeds develop and mature in time for the autumn rains. The seeds do not go through a period of dormancy and germinate readily, usually in close proximity to the parent plant. Fascinating as they are, our understanding of these plants, particularly their distribution and reproductive biology, remains poor.

FURTHER READING. The field studies of Hilliard and Burtt (1973) provide the most comprehensive account of *Apodolirion*. More recently, D. Müller-Doblies (1986) recognized two additional species. Burtt (1970) has considered the evolution and taxonomic significance of the subterranean ovary in *Apodolirion* and other monocotyledons.

Apodolirion cedarbergense D. Müller-Doblies
Plants to 3 cm high; bulb c. 15 mm diam. Leaves two or three, dry at flowering, recurved, linear, c. 2 mm wide, channeled, smooth. Flowers solitary, white to delicate pink, fragrant, tepals 2.5–3.5 cm long, both stamen whorls about equally long, less than half as long as the tepals, inserted at the throat. Berry purplish, texture unknown. Flowering January. Sandy flats and slopes, NW (northern Cedarberg Mountains).

Apodolirion lanceolatum (Thunberg) Baker
Plants to 3 cm high; bulb c. 30 mm diam. Leaf single, dry at flowering, almost flat on the ground, lanceolate, 4–10 mm wide, smooth. Flowers solitary, pure white, fragrant, tepals 2.5–4.5 cm long, stamens inserted at the throat with the inner filaments decurrent on the lower third of the tepals, less than half as long as the tepals. Berry succulent, yellow. Flowering December–February. South-facing slopes among rocks, AP, KM, LB (Ladismith, Oudtshoorn, Still Bay, Swellendam).

Apodolirion macowanii Baker
Plants to 7 cm high; bulb c. 25 mm diam. Leaves two to four, sometimes green at flowering, suberect, strap-shaped, c. 5 mm wide, firm, twisted, the margins slightly raised and rough. Flowers solitary, pure white, fragrant, tepals c. 3.5 cm long, stamens inserted at the throat, the inner stamens reaching c. 7.5 mm beyond the outer stamens, less than half as long as tepals. Berry succulent,

Apodolirion cedarbergense (Colin Paterson-Jones)

orange-yellow. Flowering December–April. Sandy flats, SE (Uitenhage to Eastern Cape).

Aristea

COMMON NAME aristea, FAMILY Iridaceae. Evergreen perennials. ROOTSTOCK a rhizome, short to long. LEAVES sword-shaped to linear or terete, in two ranks, crowded basally; stems rounded to compressed and two-sided or strongly winged, simple or branched, bearing reduced leaves below or leafless except for a subterminal leaflet. INFLORESCENCES binate rhipidia (flower clusters in two series unless reduced to one or two flowers); binate rhipidia one to many, either terminal on main and secondary axes or axillary, then stalked or sessile; spathes green or partly to entirely membranous or scarious, margins entire, irregularly torn, or fringed; floral bracts (within spathes) membranous or scarious, entire, irregularly torn, or fringed. FLOWERS fugacious, often sessile, actinomorphic, usually dark blue, occasionally pale blue, white, or mauve, occasionally with contrasting markings, each lasting a day, perianth twisting spirally on fading, scentless, nectar produced in 1 sp. from perigonal nectaries; tepals basally united 0.5–2 mm, usually subequal, in a few species the outer tepals smaller than the inner, lanceolate to ovate, usually spreading horizontally or sometimes ascending. STAMENS erect, free; anthers oblong to linear. STYLE filiform, eccentric, the tip either minutely three-notched or divided into three short stigmatic lobes, the lobes entire or fringed. FRUIT an ovoid to oblong or cylindrical capsule, rounded in cross section or shallowly to deeply three-lobed, or broadly three-winged, subsessile or stalked, remains of perianth usually persisting on the capsule. SEEDS rounded to angular, shortly cylindrical, compressed, or depressed, many per locule or only one or two. Basic chromosome number $x = 16$. Sub-Saharan Africa and Madagascar, especially winter-rainfall southern Africa; c. 50 spp., 32 in the Cape.

Most diverse in southern Africa, *Aristea* extends from the Western Cape to Senegal and Ethiopia in the north and has seven species in Madagascar. In summer-rainfall tropical and eastern southern Africa, species are most frequent in moist highlands in grassland, on rocky outcrops, or in marshes; in winter-rainfall South Africa, species are often montane and mostly grow in rocky sandstone habitats, often flowering in mass after fires.

Pollen grains, capsules, and seeds of the genus are unusually variable for the family Iridaceae. Flowers of most species open early in the morning and fade at midday or early in the afternoon and are pollinated by bees foraging for pollen. A few southwestern Cape species have flowers that are darkly marked and last an entire day and are pollinated by monkey beetles (Scarabaeidae: Hopliini). One species, *Aristea spiralis*, produces nectar and is pollinated by long-proboscid flies (*Philoliche*, of the Tabanidae).

Despite their handsome, deep blue flowers and, in many cases, elegant foliage, aristeas are barely known in cultivation. One reason may be that the flowers are short-lived, opening early in the morning and fading in the early afternoon. Plants do not transplant well, either, so the would-be grower must obtain seeds and wait as long as 3 years for the plants to reach flowering size. Nevertheless, several species are worth the wait. Plantings at Kirstenbosch botanical garden have for many years boasted glorious displays of the blue scepter, *Aristea capitata*, which is native there and flowers wild among the bush in October–November. More recently, plants have been raised from seed and planted out for display within the cultivated part of the garden, and *A. capitata* is also beginning to appear in street plantings in Western Cape cities and towns. The plants bear sturdy flowering stems that reach 1.2–1.8 m and dense clusters of large, deep blue flowers. A pale pink form is also available. Each plant produces hundreds of flowers, so there are daily displays of blooms throughout its 4- to 6-week flowering season. Plants can be easily grown from seeds, and some nurseries also sell seedlings and young plants. *Aristea capitata* grows naturally on clay and granite slopes as well as the sandstone soils of the Cape mountains and will thrive in any garden situation as long as the roots are not disturbed. In a few years, each individual will form a dense tuft of handsome, sword-shaped leaves and will produce numerous flowering stems.

Another species generally available in South African nurseries is *Aristea ecklonii*. It does well in light shade and is grown for its attractive, pale green foliage as well as its flowers. The dwarf *A. africana* is also tolerant of a range of conditions in the wild and may occasionally be seen in gardens where the bright blue flowers are a cheerful sight. No other aristeas have to our knowledge ever been tried in gardens. It seems likely that the tall, multiflowered *A. bakeri* (also widely known as *A. confusa*) and *A. inaequalis* will do well in garden situations. In the wild, both species favor sandstone soils and flower best after fire. That pattern is often easily overcome in gardens by the application of fertilizer, and the effect of fire need not be duplicated.

The most notable species of *Aristea* are undoubtedly *A. lugens,* which has pale blue or white inner tepals and black outer tepals, and its relative, *A. biflora,* which bears large, poppy-like, pale bluish flowers with the tepals having transparent windows at their lower edges. Both species grow in tufts and make extraordinary displays in the wild. Unfortunately, they do not respond well in cultivation. They do need fire to stimulate flowering and usually flower well only in the spring following a fire the previous summer or autumn. In the wild, they grow on well-drained granite or clay slopes that bake hard and dry all summer long. Both species were flowered in Britain in the late 18th and early 19th centuries, but wild plants rescued from development projects in the Western Cape have not responded kindly to attempts to grow them in a variety of ways. Although they do not die, they rarely flower.

FURTHER READING. The taxonomic revision of *Aristea* by Weimarck (1940) is very outdated but no complete modern treatment exists. Several new species were described by Goldblatt and Manning (1997a, b), and the classification and evolution of the genus have been studied by Goldblatt and Le Thomas (1997).

Aristea abyssinica Pax

Plants evergreen, rhizomatous, 10–15 cm high, stem compressed and two-winged, consisting of one long internode with a short subterminal leaf. Leaves linear, narrow, 1.6–3 mm wide. Flowers blue, tepals c. 10 mm long, style three-lobed, spathes green with dry margins; bracts dry-membranous, torn with age. Capsules ovoid. Flowering November–January. Coastal grassland and forest margins, SE (Humansdorp to Ethiopia and Cameroon).

Aristea africana (Linnaeus) Hoffmannsegg

Plants evergreen, rhizomatous, mostly 10–15 cm high, stem compressed, subdichotomously branched, sometimes simple. Leaves linear, 1.5–4 mm wide. Flowers blue, tepals mostly 8–12 mm long, style with three fringed lobes, spathes and bracts green with wide translucent margins closely and deeply fringed and curled, sometimes rusty above. Capsules short, three-winged. Flowering mainly October–January. Sandy flats and mountain slopes, NW, SW, AP, LB (Gifberg to Bredasdorp and Riversdale).

Aristea africana

Aristea anceps Ecklon ex Klatt

Plants evergreen, rhizomatous, 10–30 cm high, stem flattened and two-winged, consisting of one long internode with a short subterminal leaf. Leaves linear to sword-shaped, mostly 3–4 mm wide. Flowers blue, tepals 10–14 mm long, style three-lobed, spathes green to dry and rusty; bracts dry, rusty, torn with age. Capsules oblong. Flowering September–January. Mainly sandy coastal slopes and flats, SE (Humansdorp to Transkei).

Aristea bakeri Klatt

Plants evergreen, rhizomatous, to 1 m high, stems rounded, usually much branched. Leaves linear to sword-shaped, 6–20 mm wide, fibrotic. Flowers blue, tepals 14–20 mm long, style minutely three-notched, spathes ovate, often minutely hairy below, rust brown with transparent margins; bracts similar. Capsules oblong, three-winged. Flowering mainly October–December, mostly after fire. Stony sandstone slopes, NW, SW, LB, SE (Piketberg to Port Elizabeth and Eastern Cape).

Aristea bakeri

Aristea biflora Weimarck

Plants evergreen, rhizomatous, 20–40 cm high, forming tufts, stems unbranched, lateral flower clusters sessile or lacking. Leaves linear, narrow, mostly 3–5 mm wide. Flowers large, lilac to purple, tepals 25–30 mm long, the inner tepals with transparent to translucent bronze windows on the lower margins, spathes green, style three-lobed. Capsules elongate. Flowering August–October. Loamy clay in renosterveld, SW (Caledon to Drayton).

Aristea bracteata Persoon

Plants evergreen, rhizomatous, to 1.3 m high, stem subterete, often much branched, branches short, upper flower clusters sessile. Leaves linear to sword-shaped, often broad, 3–6 mm wide, fibrotic. Flowers blue, tepals 16–20 mm long, style minutely three-notched, spathes and bracts large, dry-membranous, rusty, translucent on the edges, sparsely hairy or scabrid. Capsules short, three-winged. Flowering August–October. Sandstone slopes, 300–1000 m, NW, SW (Cedarberg Mountains to Du Toit's Kloof).

Aristea biflora

Aristea cantharophila Goldblatt & J. C. Manning
Plants evergreen, rhizomatous, 20–40 cm high, forming tufts, stems unbranched, lateral flower clusters sessile. Leaves linear, narrow, 2–3 mm wide. Flowers lilac to cream with a dark center, tepals 22–26 mm long, style three-lobed, spathes greenish. Capsules elongate. Flowering August–September. Clay and granite slopes in fynbos or renosterveld, SW (Kuils River to Bot River).

Aristea capitata (Linnaeus) Ker Gawler
Plants evergreen, rhizomatous, to 1.5 m high, stems rounded with crowded, short branches above, flower clusters overlapping. Leaves linear, strap-like, mostly 10–16 mm wide, fibrotic. Flowers blue, tepals 12–16 mm long, style minutely three-notched, spathes and bracts lanceolate, dry-membranous, translucent with dark keels. Capsules short, three-winged. Flowering October–December. Mountain slopes, 100–900 m, NW, SW, LB, SE (Piketberg to George).

Aristea dichotoma (Thunberg) Ker Gawler
Plants evergreen, rhizomatous, 15–30 cm high, forming obvious cushions, stems flattened below, dichotomously three- to five-branched. Leaves narrow, 1.5–3 mm wide, glaucous. Flowers blue, tepals c. 15 mm long, style with three fringed lobes, spathes and bracts translucent with broad dark keels. Capsules short, three-winged. Flowering December–March. Sandy flats and lower slopes, NW, SW (Namaqualand to Cape Peninsula).

Aristea ecklonii Baker
Plants evergreen, rhizomatous, to 50 cm high, stem two-winged, usually much branched. Leaves broad, sword-shaped, mostly 8–12 mm wide, soft. Flowers deep blue, tepals mostly 8–10 mm long, style three-lobed, spathes green with dry margins; bracts papery, brownish. Capsules oblong, three-lobed. Flowering September–December. Coastal and montane, mostly forest margins, SE (Humansdorp to Uganda and Cameroon).

Aristea ensifolia Muir
Plants evergreen, rhizomatous, to 50 cm high, stem compressed and two-winged, few- to many-branched. Leaves

Aristea capitata

Aristea dichotoma

sword-shaped, 6–12 mm wide, soft. Flowers blue, tepals c. 15 mm long, style three-lobed, spathes greenish; bracts dry-membranous. Capsules elongate, cylindrical and three-lobed, indehiscent, decaying with age. Flowering September–November. Coastal forests, shade or clearings, LB, SE (Riversdale to Uitenhage).

Aristea fimbriata Goldblatt & J. C. Manning

Plants evergreen, rhizomatous, 20–30 cm high, forming cushions, stems rounded. Leaves linear to sword-shaped, narrow, 3–4 mm wide, firm. Flowers blue, tepals c. 14 mm long, style minutely three-notched, spathes and bracts translucent, margins closely fringed and rust brown. Capsules oblong, three-winged. Flowering December–January. Rocky sandstone slopes in fynbos, 500–800 m, NW (Piketberg).

Aristea glauca Klatt

Plants evergreen, rhizomatous, 10–15 cm high, forming diffuse low cushions, spreading by stolons, stems strongly compressed and two-winged, dichotomously branched or simple. Leaves linear, narrow, 1–3 mm wide, glaucous. Flowers blue, tepals c. 18 mm long, style with three fringed lobes, spathes and bracts green to brown with wide translucent margins. Capsules short, three-winged. Flowering October–December. Coastal and lower slopes, NW, SW, AP, LB (Ceres and Cape Peninsula to Riversdale).

Aristea inaequalis Goldblatt & J. C. Manning

Plants evergreen, rhizomatous, to 1.5 m high, stems rounded with long, spreading branches, lateral flower clusters sessile, widely spaced. Leaves linear, narrow, gray with reddish margins, 4–5 mm wide, fibrotic. Inflorescence secund, flowers blue, tepals 14–16 mm long, stamens unequal, style minutely three-notched, spathes dry-membranous, translucent with dark keels. Capsules short, three-winged. Flowering October–November. Sandstone rocks, 500–900 m, NW (Bokkeveld Mountains to Pakhuis Pass).

Aristea juncifolia Baker

Plants evergreen, rhizomatous, 12–30 cm high with rounded stems, usually unbranched, lateral flower clus-

Aristea fimbriata

Aristea glauca

ters sessile and subtended by prominently keeled bracts. Leaves almost round to elliptical in cross section, mostly 1.5–2 mm wide, tough and fibrotic. Flowers blue, tepals 16–20 mm long, style minutely three-notched, spathes and bracts rust brown, transparent on the edges. Capsules oblong, three-winged. Flowering November–December. Coastal and lower mountain slopes, SW (Cape Peninsula to Klein River Mountains).

Aristea latifolia G.J. Lewis
Plants evergreen, rhizomatous, to 1 m high, stem lightly compressed, usually much branched above. Leaves sword-shaped, 15–25 mm wide, fairly soft. Flowers deep blue, tepals c. 12 mm long, style three-lobed, spathes pale, papery and becoming torn. Capsules ovoid with three shallow, rounded lobes. Flowering November–January. Shady kloofs and gullies, 500–1500 m, SW (Bain's Kloof to Hottentots Holland Mountains).

Aristea lugens (Linnaeus fil.) Steudel
Plants evergreen, rhizomatous, 30–40 cm high, stem compressed below, unbranched, lateral flower clusters sessile. Leaves short, falcate, 3–6 mm wide. Flowers pale blue to whitish, outer tepals suberect, dark blue-black, 16–20 mm long, the inner larger, spreading, 28–35 mm long, style three-lobed, spathes greenish. Capsules elongate. Flowering September–October. Low granitic hills in renosterveld, SW (Riebeek Kasteel to Stellenbosch).

Aristea oligocephala Baker
Plants evergreen, rhizomatous, 15–25 cm high, stems compressed, dichotomously branched. Leaves linear, 1.5–3 mm wide, rigid, elliptical in cross section. Flowers blue, 18–22 mm long, style with three fringed lobes, spathes and bracts silvery translucent with narrow dark keels. Capsules short, three-winged. Flowering November–January. Sandstone slopes, SW, AP (Hottentots Holland Mountains to Bredasdorp).

Aristea palustris Schlechter
Plants evergreen, rhizomatous, to 1 m high, stem rounded, subdichotomously branched. Leaves linear to sword-shaped, 4–9 mm wide, soft. Flowers blue, tepals 12–14 mm long, style with three fringed lobes, spathes and bracts silvery translucent with narrow dark keels. Capsules short, three-winged. Flowering November–January. Coastal and lower slopes in wet sites, SW, AP (Bredasdorp).

Aristea pauciflora Wolley Dod
Plants evergreen, rhizomatous, 20–40 cm high, forming tufts, stems elliptical in cross section, unbranched, lateral flower clusters sessile. Leaves linear, 2–4 mm wide. Flowers deep blue, tepals 15–20 mm long, style three-lobed, spathes greenish. Capsules elongate, locules acute. Flowering October–December. Mainly clay and granite slopes, SW (Cape Peninsula).

Aristea pusilla (Thunberg) Ker Gawler
Plants evergreen, rhizomatous, to 20 cm high, stem flattened and two-winged, lateral flower clusters few and sessile or lacking. Leaves linear to sword-shaped, 2–5 mm wide, fairly soft. Flowers blue, tepals 8–14 mm long, style three-lobed, spathes green with hyaline or rusty margins. Capsules cylindrical and three-lobed, elongate. Flowering September–November. Mainly clay flats and lower slopes in renosterveld, AP, KM, LB, SE (Swartberg Mountains and Swellendam to Eastern Cape).

Aristea racemosa Baker
Plants evergreen, rhizomatous, to 40 cm high, stems rounded, usually unbranched, lateral flower clusters ses-

Aristea lugens

sile, the lower ones each often subtended by a large inflated bract. Leaves subterete, 1.5–3 mm wide, fibrotic. Flowers blue, tepals 12–16 mm long, style minutely three-notched, spathes and bracts dry-membranous, rusty, translucent on the edges. Capsules oblong, three-winged. Flowering October–December. Rocky sandstone slopes, 200–1000 m, SW, AP, KM, LB, SE (Paarl to George, Swartberg Mountains).

Aristea recisa Weimarck
Plants evergreen, rhizomatous, 15–35 cm high, forming small tufts, stems subdichotomously branched, flattened, slender. Leaves sword-shaped, 3–5 mm wide, soft. Flowers blue, tepals c. 12 mm long, style with three fringed lobes, spathes green with broad translucent margins closely and shallowly fringed, rusty at the edges. Capsules short, three-winged. Flowering mainly September–October. Sandstone slopes in wet sandy places, 600–1200 m, SW, LB (Hottentots Holland Mountains to Hermanus and Swellendam).

Aristea spiralis

Aristea rigidifolia G. J. Lewis
Plants evergreen, rhizomatous, to 1.5 m high, stems rounded with short branches or lateral flower clusters sessile. Leaves elliptical in cross section, 2–5 mm wide, fibrotic. Flowers blue, 18–24 mm wide, style minutely three-notched, spathes and bracts ovate, rusty, becoming lacerate. Capsules oblong, three-winged. Flowering October–November. Sandy flats, SW (Cape Peninsula to Hermanus Mountains).

Aristea rupicola Goldblatt & J. C. Manning
Plants evergreen, rhizomatous, to 40 cm high, stems rounded, divaricately branched. Leaves linear, 3–4 mm wide, fibrotic. Flowers light blue, tepals 8–14 mm long, style minutely three-notched, spathes and bracts ovate, rusty, margins translucent flecked with brown, hairy to scabrid on the inside. Capsules short, three-winged. Flowering December–March. Sandstone outcrops, c. 1000 m, NW (northern Cedarberg Mountains).

Aristea schizolaena Harvey ex Baker
Plants evergreen, rhizomatous, to 80 cm high, stem elliptical in cross section, sometimes with a few branches and with sessile lateral flower clusters. Leaves linear to sword-shaped, 4–8 mm wide. Flowers blue, tepals c. 12 mm long, style three-lobed, spathes dry, rust brown, becoming torn with age. Capsules ovoid. Flowering December–June. Mainly coastal grassland, SE (Plettenberg Bay to Mpumalanga).

Aristea simplex Weimarck
Plants evergreen, rhizomatous, to 50 cm high, forming tufts, stems elliptical in cross section, unbranched, lateral flower clusters sessile. Leaves linear, narrow, 2–3 mm wide. Flowers facing to the side, pale blue, tepals 15–20 mm long, style three-lobed, spathes green. Capsules elongate. Flowering September–October. Clay flats and lower slopes in renosterveld, SW, KM, LB, SE (Stellenbosch to George, and Swartberg Mountains).

Aristea singularis Weimarck
Plants evergreen, rhizomatous, to 40 cm high, forming diffuse tufts, stems slightly flattened, dichotomously

branched and rooting at the nodes. Leaves sword-shaped, 3–6 mm wide, fairly soft. Flowers blue, nodding, tepals 12–15 mm long, style obscurely three-lobed, spathes greenish translucent, lightly lacerate. Capsules short, three-lobed. Flowering July–August. Sandstone slopes near streams and in shade, NW (Pakhuis Mountains).

Aristea spiralis (Linnaeus fil.) Ker Gawler

Plants evergreen, rhizomatous, 20–50 cm high, often in small tufts, stems flattened and two-winged, usually unbranched, lateral flower clusters sessile. Leaves 4–7 mm wide, soft. Flowers facing to the side, white or pale blue, tepals 30–35 mm long, stamens and style often fairly long, style three-lobed, spathes green with hyaline margins. Capsules elongate. Flowering mainly September–November. Rocky sandstone and granite slopes to 600 m, SW, AP, LB, SE (Cape Peninsula to Knysna).

Aristea teretifolia Goldblatt & J. C. Manning

Plants evergreen, rhizomatous, 20–40 cm high, stem rounded, unbranched, lateral flower clusters sessile. Leaves linear, often terete, 1–2 mm wide. Flowers large, lilac to cream, tepals unequal, the outer c. 22 mm long, the inner 24–28 mm long, with a large dark mark toward the base, style three-lobed, spathes green. Capsules elongate. Flowering August–September. Low clay hills in renosterveld, SW (Shaw's Pass to Napier and Elim).

Aristea zeyheri Baker

Plants evergreen, rhizomatous, 15–30 cm high, stem terete, slender, unbranched with one or two sessile lateral flower clusters. Leaves terete, filiform, c. 1 mm wide. Flowers blue, tepals 12–16 mm wide, style obscurely three-lobed, spathes and bracts greenish with hyaline margins. Capsules elongate, three-winged. Flowering November–December. Sandstone slopes, usually damp sites, SW (Cape Peninsula to Hermanus Mountains).

Aristea sp. 1

Synonym, *A. cuspidata* in the sense of Weimarck, not Schinz. Plants evergreen, rhizomatous, 20–60 cm high, stems lightly compressed. Leaves linear, fairly narrow, 3–6 mm wide. Flowers blue, tepals c. 12 mm long, style minutely notched, spathes and bracts rust brown, transparent on the margins. Capsules three-winged. Flowering October–December. Sandstone slopes, SW, KM, LB, SE (Cape Peninsula to Knysna, and Swartberg Mountains).

Babiana

COMMON NAME babiana, FAMILY Iridaceae. Deciduous perennials, the stem either well developed or short and subterranean. ROOTSTOCK a globose, usually deep-seated corm with tough and fibrous tunics, often forming a long neck. LEAVES several, unifacial without a definite midrib, the blades often oblique, ovate to narrowly lanceolate or terete, sometimes abruptly truncate, pleated and usually hairy. INFLORESCENCE a simple or branched spike, usually hairy; bracts green with more or less dry brown apices, rarely entirely dry, often hairy, the inner bracts usually shorter, forked or deeply divided to the base. FLOWERS actinomorphic or zygomorphic, cup-shaped, salverform or two-lipped, the tepals united below into a short or long funnel-shaped or slender tube, usually blue to mauve or white but also yellow or red, often marked, scented or unscented. STAMENS inserted in the mouth of the tube, erect and symmetrical or arching. STYLE slender, three-branched apically, the branches sometimes broad, channeled. FRUIT globose to oblong. SEEDS several per locule, subglobose with a prominent swollen funicle. Basic chromosome number $x = 7$. Most diverse in western southern Africa, especially Namaqualand and the Western Cape, with 1 sp. in southern tropical Africa, 1 in Socotra doubtfully this genus; c. 80 spp., 49 in the Cape.

The very distinctive genus *Babiana* is easily recognized by the deep-seated corms, usually with a very tough, fibrous neck, the pleated, usually hairy leaves, and medium to large, mainly blue to violet flowers. It is almost restricted to the winter-rainfall region of southern Africa, with a single species in grasslands of eastern South Africa, Zimbabwe, and Zambia to the north and another extraordinary disjunct (which may not belong in the genus) on the island of Socotra off the coast of Somalia at the entrance to the Gulf of Aden. Most of the species are restricted in distribution, sometimes to very small areas. Although several species are limited to sandy soils, either montane or coastal, most are characteristic of more stony, fine-grained clay soils derived from shales. Because these fairly rich soils are now largely under cultivation, many species are rare and endangered in their wild habitats. The differences between some of the species are rather subtle, and several of the species, especially in the *Disticha* and *Villosula* groups, are neither well defined nor always easy to tell apart.

The majority of species have bright blue to violet flowers, sometimes heavily scented of violets or less attractively with a more acrid, chemical smell. The scented species typically have relatively short perianth tubes and are pollinated by large solitary bees of the family Apidae. Most of the long-tubed species are unscented and are adapted to pollination by long-proboscid flies of the family Nemestrinidae. Several of the actinomorphically flowered species are visited by pollen-collecting bees, especially honeybees, whereas those with contrasting, boldly colored centers are adapted for pollination by monkey beetles (Scarabaeidae: Hopliini). The two red-flowered species, long segregated in the genus *Antholyza*, are highly specialized for pollination by sunbirds.

The long-lasting, brightly colored flowers of many of the species make them very attractive subjects for cultivation. The actinomorphically flowered species in particular are often brilliantly and unusually colored. Species like *Babiana rubrocyanea* and *B. villosa* have large, open flowers intensely colored blue, purple, or red, sometimes in vibrant combination, and the species with the largest flowers in the genus, *B. pygmaea*, has poppy-sized creamy yellow flowers with a purple-brown center. Another attraction of several of the species is the strong fragrance they produce. The scents of *B. nana*, *B. odorata*, *B. patersoniae*, and *B. sambucina* are especially fine. All except *B. patersoniae* are low-growing but their scent makes them horticulturally desirable. Although often at home in loamy soils, some of the species are found in deep, sandy soils; among these we recommend *B. thunbergii* highly for coastal gardens. This plant, once placed in *Anaclanthe* or *Antholyza*, may grow to a height of 2 m and makes a very interesting garden accent. Because it is a strand plant, it will thrive in coastal gardens but it has been grown with equal success inland in rich soil where it withstands light frost. The related *B. ringens* (long known as *Antholyza ringens*) has larger, more striking, bright red flowers borne shortly above the ground. The main branch of the stem is sterile and forms a sturdy perch for visiting sunbirds.

In a genus of about 75 species, all with large, attractive flowers, it is difficult to choose the most desirable. We recommend growing any species that can be obtained. Corms will flower within a year but seeds may take 2 years, even 3, to reach flowering size. Species are especially drought tolerant and will thrive in desert gardens if kept dry most of the summer and given only minimal amounts of water in the winter. Plants grown in sunny situations will tolerate slightly warmer temperatures than other Cape bulbs. Many babianas offered in the trade are hybrids of unknown parentage and are not particularly distinctive.

FURTHER READING. The detailed taxonomic revision of *Babiana* by Lewis (1959a), although comprehensive at the time, is somewhat outdated.

Babiana ambigua (Roemer & Schultes) G. J. Lewis

Plants 5–8 cm high, stem underground; corm tunics netted. Leaves linear-lanceolate, longer than the stem, pleated, hairy. Flowers zygomorphic, blue to mauve with white to cream markings, fragrant, tube funnel-shaped, 10–19 mm long, lower tepals shortly joined below, filaments arched, 13–16 mm long, anthers 6–8 mm long, ovary hairless or shortly hairy on the ribs above; bracts 15–30 mm long, usually entirely green, inner bracts divided to the base. Flowering August–September. Sandy flats and lower slopes, NW, SW, AP, LB (Gifberg to Riversdale).

Babiana angustifolia Sweet

Plants 10–20 cm high, stem inclined. Leaves lanceolate, pleated, hairy. Flowers zygomorphic, inverted, dark blue to violet, lower tepals with black or red markings, perianth tube curved, narrowly funnel-shaped, 11–17 mm long, filaments arched, 8–12 mm long, anthers 5–6 mm long, ovary hairy; bracts 10–20 mm long, inner bracts divided to the base. Flowering August–September. Damp clay flats and lower slopes, renosterveld, NW, SW (Piketberg to Somerset West).

Babiana auriculata G. J. Lewis

Plants 4–10 cm high, stem short. Leaves lanceolate, pleated, hairy. Flowers zygomorphic, facing the stem apex, mauve and yellow, tube funnel-shaped, 15–20 mm long, lower tepals shortly united below, the outer conspicuously eared at the base, filaments arched, 15–18 mm long, anthers 4–6 mm long, ovary hairy on the angles above; bracts dry and brown above, 13–25 mm long, inner bracts forked to halfway. Flowering September. Sandstone crevices, NW (Pakhuis Mountains).

Babiana blanda (L. Bolus) G. J. Lewis.

Plants to 15 cm high. Leaves lanceolate, pleated, hairy. Flowers actinomorphic, rosy pink, tepals obovate or rounded, perianth tube slender, 20–27 mm long, filaments erect, 5–8 mm long, anthers 7–9 mm long, ovary hairy above; bracts 25–45 mm long, inner bracts divided to the base. Flowering August–September. Sandy flats, SW (Darling to Paarl).

Babiana cedarbergensis G. J. Lewis

Plants 4–6 cm high, stem very short. Leaves lanceolate, rigid, almost pungent, pleated, velvety hairy. Flowers zygomorphic, mauve with yellow markings, tube funnel-shaped, 16–18 mm long, lower tepals shortly united below, filaments arched, c. 13 mm long, anthers 7–9 mm long, ovary hairy above; bracts 20–25 mm long, inner bracts forked to halfway. Flowering September. Rocky sandstone soils, NW (Cedarberg Mountains).

Babiana crispa G. J. Lewis

Plants to 13 cm high, stem mostly underground. Leaves lanceolate, crisped and undulate, scarcely pleated, hairy. Flowers zygomorphic, mauve with yellow markings, acridly scented, perianth tube funnel-shaped, 14–20 mm long, filaments arched, 15 mm long, anthers 6–7 mm long, ovary hairless; bracts 28–30 mm long, inner bracts shortly forked. Flowering July. Hard clay and shale, RV, NW (Namaqualand and western Karoo, Botterkloof to Biedouw Valley).

Babiana ambigua

Babiana angustifolia

Babiana cuneifolia J. C. Manning & Goldblatt
Plants to 12 cm high, stem short or underground. Leaves cuneate, truncate, pleated, hairless or finely velvety. Flowers zygomorphic, mauve marked with white, tube 40–55 mm long, cylindrical, straight, filaments arched, 15–18 mm long, anthers 6–8 mm long, ovary hairless; bracts 25–50 mm long, inner bracts forked above. Flowering July–August. Arid fynbos on sandstone, NW (Bokkeveld Mountains to Cold Bokkeveld).

Babiana disticha Ker Gawler
Plants 7–20 cm high. Leaves lanceolate, pleated, hairy. Flowers zygomorphic, pale yellow or medium to pale blue marked with yellow, fragrant, perianth tube narrowly funnel-shaped, 18–25 mm long, filaments arched, 10–13 mm long, anthers 6–7 mm long, ovary hairy; bracts 12–25 mm long, inner bracts divided to the base. Flowering July–September. Sandstone slopes, NW, SW (Porterville to Cape Peninsula).

Babiana ecklonii Klatt
Plants 10–30 cm high, stem erect and often well developed and branched. Leaves lanceolate, soft and weakly pleated, hairy. Flowers zygomorphic, violet with dark blue and cream markings, perianth tube cylindrical, sharply curved at the top, 35–45 mm long, lower tepals joined below, filaments arcuate, 13–15 mm long, anthers 5–6 mm long, ovary hairy above; bracts 14–40 mm long, inner bracts divided to the base. Flowering August–September. Sandstone crevices, mountain slopes and flats, 200–500 m, NW (Gifberg to Elandskloof and Piketberg).

Babiana fimbriata (Klatt) Baker
Plants 15–20 cm high, stem usually branched. Leaves linear, spirally coiled above, hairless or hairy on the margins and veins. Flowers zygomorphic, blue or mauve with yellow markings, tepals clawed, the upper arched, the lower three shortly united, perianth tube funnel-shaped, 8–10 mm long, filaments arched, c. 15 mm long, anthers 4 mm long, ovary hairless; bracts 8–10 mm long, inner bracts forked to halfway. Flowering August–September. Sandy flats and slopes, NW (Namaqualand to Klawer).

Babiana flabellifolia Harvey ex Klatt
Plants 5–15 cm high, stem very short. Leaves oblong-cuneate, pleated, hairy. Flowers weakly zygomorphic, violet with cream markings, perianth tube 40–60 mm long, cylindrical, straight, tepals subequal, filaments suberect, 6–7 mm long, anthers 6 mm long, ovary hairless; bracts 25–50 mm long, inner bracts forked above. Flowering June–July. Dolerite outcrops in rock cracks, RV (Hantamsberg to Laingsburg).

Babiana foliosa G. J. Lewis
Plants to 10 cm high. Leaves lanceolate, pleated, hairy. Flowers actinomorphic, mauve with cream markings, tube slender, c. 20 mm long, filaments erect, c. 10 mm long, anthers 5–6 mm long, ovary hairy; bracts entirely green, 20–30 mm long, inner bracts divided to the base. Flowering August. Habitat unknown, SW (Riviersonderend).

Babiana fourcadei G. J. Lewis
Plants 7–15 cm high. Leaves lanceolate, pleated, hairy. Flowers zygomorphic, mauve with yellow and violet markings, carnation scented, tube narrowly funnel-shaped, curved above, 25–30 mm long, lower tepals shortly joined below, filaments arched, c. 17 mm long, anthers 5–7 mm long, ovary hairless; bracts 14–20 mm long, inner bracts divided to the base. Flowering September–October. Mountain slopes, LB, SE (Riversdale to George).

Babiana framesii L. Bolus
Plants to 10 cm high, stem mostly underground. Leaves lanceolate, pleated, hairy. Flowers zygomorphic, dark blue to purple with white markings, perianth tube 60–70 mm long, cylindrical, curved above, filaments arched, 10–12 mm long, anthers 7–9 mm long, ovary hairless; inner bracts forked at the tips. Flowering August–September. Rock outcrops in karroid scrub, RV, NW (Namaqualand to Bokkeveld Escarpment).

Babiana geniculata G. J. Lewis
Plants 2–6 cm high, stem very short. Leaves lanceolate, pleated, hairy. Flowers zygomorphic, purple with white

Babiana disticha

Babiana ecklonii

Babiana flabellifolia

Babiana framesii

markings, tube 35–45 mm long, cylindrical, sharply bent at the top, tepals unequal, lower shortly joined below, filaments arched and slightly spreading, 13–15 mm long, anthers 7 mm long, ovary hairy above, style branching at the throat, branches 11–13 mm long; inner bracts forked at the tips. Flowering August. Rocky sandstone in dry fynbos, NW (Pakhuis Mountains).

Babiana klaverensis G. J. Lewis

Plants 6–10 cm high, stem mostly underground. Leaves rigid, lanceolate, scarcely pleated, hairy, with thickened margins. Flowers zygomorphic, blue to mauve, tube narrowly funnel-shaped, c. 10 mm long, lower tepals united below, filaments arched, c. 13 mm long, anthers 6 mm long, ovary hairy; bracts 11–15 mm long, inner bracts divided to the base. Flowering June–July. Rocky sandstone slopes, NW (Bokkeveld Mountains to Gifberg).

Babiana leipoldtii G. J. Lewis

Plants 6–15 cm high, stem erect and branched. Leaves lanceolate, pleated, hairy. Flowers actinomorphic, blue-violet with a dark center, lightly violet scented, tube slender, 15–20 mm long, filaments erect, 8–10 mm long, anthers 6–8 mm long, ovary hairy above; bracts 20–35 mm long, inner bracts divided to the base. Flowering August–September. Damp sandy flats, SW (Darling to Klipheuwel).

Babiana lineolata Klatt

Plants 13–25 cm high, stem often branched. Leaves lanceolate, pleated, hairy. Flowers zygomorphic, pale blue to mauve with yellow markings, rose scented, tube narrowly funnel-shaped, 8–10 mm long, lower tepals joined below, filaments arched, 11–14 mm long, anthers 4.5–6 mm long, ovary hairy; bracts 7–12 mm long, inner bracts divided to the base. Flowering September. Sandy flats, NW (Piketberg to Cold Bokkeveld).

Babiana melanops Goldblatt & J. C. Manning

Plants 10–30 cm high, stem branched. Leaves lanceolate, pleated, hairy. Flowers actinomorphic, dark blue or purple, darker in the center, scented or unscented, perianth tube slender to filiform, 17–36 mm long, filaments erect, symmetrical, 8–15 mm long, anthers arrow-shaped with a broad connective, blackish, or turquoise on the back, 7–9 mm long, ovary hairy; bracts 16–28 mm long with dry brown tips, inner bracts divided to the base. Flowering August–September. Sandy, granitic gravel flats and slopes in renosterveld, SW (Mamre to Malmesbury).

Babiana minuta G. J. Lewis

Plants 7–13 cm high, stem short. Leaves lanceolate, pleated at the base, hairy. Flowers zygomorphic, pale reddish mauve with yellow markings, fragrant, lower tepals shortly united, tube funnel-shaped, 20–22 mm long, filaments arched, 15–17 mm long, anthers 5–6 mm long, ovary hairless; bracts 20–32 mm long, inner bracts forked at the tips. Flowering July–September. Shale and rocky sandstone soils, RV, NW (southern Namaqualand to Karoopoort and western Karoo).

Babiana montana G. J. Lewis

Plants 6–7 cm high. Leaves lanceolate, pleated, hairy. Flowers zygomorphic, mauve with yellow and purple

Babiana minuta

markings, perianth tube narrowly funnel-shaped, 17–20 mm long, filaments unequal, the median one longer, 7–10 mm, anthers 7 mm long, ovary hairless, stigmas flattened and rounded; bracts 28–38 mm long, inner bracts divided to the base. Flowering June–August. Sandstone and limestone slopes, SW, AP (Caledon to Bredasdorp).

Babiana mucronata (Jacquin) Ker Gawler
Plants 5–15 cm high. Leaves lanceolate, pleated, hairy. Flowers zygomorphic, pale blue with yellow lower tepals, lightly acridly scented, perianth tube narrowly funnel-shaped, 15–20 mm long, lower tepals united below, filaments arched, 13–16 mm long, anthers 5–7 mm long, ovary hairy; bracts 15–25 mm long, inner bracts divided to the base. Flowering July–September. Rocky sandstone slopes and flats, NW (Bokkeveld Mountains to Tulbagh).

Babiana nana (Andrews) Sprengel
Plants 3–10 cm high, stem mostly underground. Leaves obliquely ovate to lanceolate, not or weakly pleated, hairy. Flowers zygomorphic, blue or purple with white markings, rose-violet scented, tube funnel-shaped, 12–17 mm long, filaments arched, 12–15 mm long, anthers 5–6 mm long, ovary hairless or shortly hairy on the ribs; bracts 16–30 mm long, inner bracts forked at the tips. Flowering August–September. Sandy coastal flats and dunes, NW, SW, AP, LB (Lambert's Bay to Mossel Bay).

Babiana noctiflora J. C. Manning & Goldblatt
Plants 20–30 cm high, stem usually branched. Leaves lanceolate, pleated, hairy. Flowers zygomorphic, creamy yellow, violet scented, perianth tube 32–38 mm long, widening in the upper half, curved, filaments arched, 28 mm long, anthers 6–7 mm long, ovary hairy; bracts 12–15 mm long, inner bracts divided to the base. Flowering September–October. Granite outcrops, SW (Paardeberg).

Babiana obliqua E. Phillips
Plants to 16 cm high, stem erect. Leaves very obliquely lanceolate, not pleated, hairy. Flowers zygomorphic, lilac with yellow markings, lower tepals shortly united, tube

Babiana mucronata

Babiana nana

funnel-shaped, 18–20 mm long, filaments arched, 15 mm long, anthers 7–8 mm long, ovary hairless; bracts 30–40 mm long, inner bracts divided to the base. Flowering July. Sandy coastal soils, NW, SW (Lambert's Bay to Mamre).

Babiana odorata
Babiana purpurea 

Babiana odorata L. Bolus
Plants 5–15 cm high. Leaves lanceolate, pleated, hairy. Flowers zygomorphic, yellow to creamy yellow, violet scented, perianth tube narrowly funnel-shaped, 10–14 mm long, lower tepals united below, filaments arched, 14–17 mm long, anthers 5–6 mm long, ovary hairy; bracts 15–25 mm long, inner bracts divided to the base. Flowering July–September. Clay soils in renosterveld, NW, SW (Porterville to Tygerberg).

Babiana papyracea Goldblatt & J. C. Manning
Plants 30 cm high, stem short or subterranean, closely few-branched. Leaves linear, pleated, velvety. Flowers actinomorphic, blue, perianth tube 35–45 mm long, filiform, straight, filaments erect, symmetrical, c. 7 mm long, anthers c. 8 mm long, ovary hairless; bracts papery, pale with brown flecks, cuspidate, 30–35 mm long, inner bracts divided to below the middle. Flowering October. Hard, stony clay in renosterveld, RV (Bokkeveld Escarpment near Nieuwoudtville).

Babiana patersoniae L. Bolus
Plants 15–25 cm high. Leaves lanceolate, pleated, hairy. Flowers zygomorphic, white to pale blue to mauve with yellow markings, fragrant, perianth tube narrowly funnel-shaped, 20–30 mm long, filaments arched, 8–12 mm long, anthers 4–5 mm long, ovary hairy; bracts 12–30 mm long, inner bracts divided to the base. Flowering August–October. Clay slopes in renosterveld, SW, LB, SE (Caledon to Eastern Cape).

Babiana patula N. E. Brown
Plants 2–8 cm high, stem usually very short. Leaves lanceolate, pleated, hairy. Flowers zygomorphic, mauve to blue with yellow markings or entirely dull yellow, intensely fragrant, perianth tube narrowly funnel-shaped, 10–14 mm long, lower tepals united below, filaments arched, 12–14 mm long, anthers 6 mm long, ovary hairless or shortly hairy on the ribs; bracts 10–20 mm long, inner bracts divided to the base. Flowering August–September. Clay flats and lower slopes, SW, AP, LB (Tulbagh to Albertinia).

Babiana pauciflora G.J. Lewis.
Plants to 10 cm high, stem short. Leaves obliquely oblong-lanceolate, pleated at the base, hairy on the veins. Flowers zygomorphic, violet with yellow markings, fragrant, tube cylindrical below, 35–45 mm long, filaments arched, 15 mm long, anthers 8 mm long, ovary hairless; bracts 35–55 mm long, inner bracts forked at the tips. Flowering June. Rocky flats, NW (Bokkeveld Escarpment).

Babiana purpurea (Jacquin) Ker Gawler
Plants 10–15 cm high, slender. Leaves lanceolate, pleated, hairy. Flowers weakly zygomorphic, pink to purple, fragrant, perianth tube narrowly funnel-shaped, 18–28 mm long, filaments arched, 10–14 mm long, anthers arrow-shaped, 6–8 mm long, ovary hairy; bracts 15–25 mm long, inner bracts divided to the base. Flowering August–September. Clay flats and slopes in renosterveld, SW (Robertson to Bredasdorp).

Babiana pygmaea (Burman fil.) N.E. Brown
Plants to 10 cm high. Leaves lanceolate, pleated, hairy. Flowers actinomorphic, yellow with dark purplish or brown center, tepals obovate, tube cylindrical, 15–25 mm long, filaments almost included, erect, 3–6 mm long, anthers 8–10 mm long, ovary hairy above or on the ribs; bracts 30–36 mm long, inner bracts shortly forked or divided halfway. Flowering August–September. Gravelly flats, SW (Hopefield to Darling).

Babiana regia (G.J. Lewis) Goldblatt & J.C. Manning
Plants 5–12 cm high, stem inclined. Leaves narrowly lanceolate, pleated, shortly hairy. Flowers actinomorphic, deep blue with red cup, tube narrowly funnel-shaped, 10–12 mm long, filaments 8 mm long, anthers 5 mm long, ovary densely hairy; bracts 12–22 mm long, inner divided to the base. Flowering September–October. Sandy and gravelly flats, SW (Malmesbury to Stellenbosch).

Babiana ringens (Linnaeus) Ker Gawler
Plants 15–40 cm high, main spike axis sterile. Leaves linear-lanceolate or almost terete, stiff, pungent, pleated, hairless. Flowers on a side branch near ground level, very

Babiana pygmaea

Babiana ringens

Babiana rubrocyanea

Babiana sambucina

zygomorphic, red with yellow throat, upper tepal tubular below and enclosing filaments and style, 25–50 mm long, lower tepals shortly united, tube narrowly funnel-shaped, expanded in the upper third, curved upward, 30–45 mm long, filaments straight, 35–60 mm long, anthers 5–6 mm long, ovary hairless; bracts 20–50 mm long, inner bracts forked to halfway. Flowering August–October. Sandy flats in fynbos, 30–500 m, NW, SW, AP (Bokkeveld Mountains to Bredasdorp).

Babiana rubrocyanea (Jacquin) Ker Gawler

Plants 5–15 cm high. Leaves lanceolate, pleated, hairy. Flowers actinomorphic, deep blue with red center, unscented, tube narrowly funnel-shaped, 15–20 mm long, tepals broadly clawed, filaments arched or suberect, 10–13 mm long, anthers 6–7 mm long, ovary hairy, stigmas large and flattened; bracts 18–30 mm long, inner bracts divided to the base. Flowering August–September. Granitic sands in renosterveld, SW (Darling to Mamre).

Babiana sambucina (Jacquin) Ker Gawler

Plants 5–15 cm high, stem mostly underground. Leaves linear to lanceolate, pleated, hairy. Flowers zygomorphic, mauve to violet with white and sometimes red markings, fragrant, tube 30–50 mm long, gradually flaring, straight, filaments arched, 10–15 mm long, anthers 7–10 mm long, ovary hairless; bracts mostly 25–40 mm long, inner bracts forked at the tips. Flowering July–September. Sandstone slopes and flats in fynbos and renosterveld, NW, SW, AP, KM, LB, SE (Bokkeveld Mountains to Port Elizabeth, Karoo, Eastern Cape).

Babiana scabrifolia Brehmer ex Klatt

Plants 5–15 cm high. Leaves lanceolate, scarcely pleated, minutely and sparsely hairy or almost hairless, narrow and twisted when young. Flowers zygomorphic, blue to lilac with yellow and purple markings, narcissus scented, perianth tube narrowly funnel-shaped, 12–18 mm long, lower tepals joined below, filaments arched, 13–18 mm long, anthers 6–8 mm long, ovary thinly hairy above or on the ribs; bracts 20–32 mm long, inner bracts divided to the base. Flowering June–August. Sandy soils in dry fynbos, NW (Olifants River Valley).

Babiana scariosa G.J. Lewis
Plants 10–40 cm high, stem erect, branched. Leaves linear-lanceolate, pleated, velvety. Flowers zygomorphic, mauve with pale yellow markings, the lower tepals clawed and shortly united, perianth tube narrowly funnel-shaped, c. 20 mm long, filaments arched, 12–14 mm long, anthers 5–7 mm long, ovary hairless; bracts papery, pale brown or colorless with brown flecks, cuspidate, 20–24 mm long, inner bracts divided nearly to the base. Flowering August–September. Dry sandstone or clay, in fynbos or karroid scrub, NW, KM (Bokkeveld Mountains and western Little Karoo).

Babiana secunda (Thunberg) Ker Gawler
Plants 15–35 cm high, stem flexed horizontally, many-flowered and often widely branched. Leaves lanceolate, pleated, hairy. Flowers zygomorphic, inverted, blue with yellow or white markings, perianth tube narrowly funnel-shaped, 6–8 mm long, lower tepals shortly joined below, filaments arched, 12–14 mm long, anthers yellow, 6 mm long, ovary hairless; bracts tricuspidate with a long central awn, hairless and often dry at flowering, 10–13 mm long, inner bracts divided to the base. Flowering October–November. Clay flats and lower slopes in renosterveld, SW (Hopefield to Paarl).

Babiana sinuata G.J. Lewis
Plants 10–25 cm high, stem erect, much branched. Leaves narrow, undulate and twisted, margins crisped and long-hairy, striate, woolly at the base. Flowers zygomorphic, blue with yellow markings, tepals clawed, the upper arched, the lower three shortly joined, tube funnel-shaped, 8–9 mm long, filaments arched, 20 mm long, anthers cohering, 7 mm long, ovary hairless; bracts 8–10 mm long, inner bracts forked to halfway. Flowering August–September. Rocky shale slopes, NW (Namaqualand to Clanwilliam).

Babiana spathacea (Linnaeus fil.) Ker Gawler
Plants 10–60 cm high, stem erect, branched. Leaves linear-lanceolate, pleated, velvety. Flowers zygomorphic, cream or flushed lilac with small red markings, perianth tube cylindrical, sharply curved above, 35–45 mm long,

Babiana scariosa

Babiana spathacea

filaments weakly arched, c. 10 mm long, anthers 4–5 mm long, ovary hairless; bracts papery, pale brown or colorless with brown flecks, cuspidate, 25–50 mm long, inner bracts divided to the base. Flowering September–October. Doleritic clay in karroid scrub, RV (western Karoo).

Babiana stricta (Aiton) Ker Gawler

Plants 10–20 cm high, slender. Leaves lanceolate, pleated, hairy. Flowers weakly zygomorphic, purple to blue, white or yellow, unscented or violet scented, perianth tube narrowly funnel-shaped, 10–16 mm long, filaments weakly arched, 8–13 mm long, anthers arrow-shaped with a broad connective, 4–7 mm long, ovary hairy; bracts 8–25 mm long, inner bracts divided to the base. Flowering August–October. Clay soils in renosterveld, NW, SW, LB (Piketberg to Swellendam).

Babiana thunbergii Ker Gawler

Plants 40–70 cm high, stem erect with short horizontal branches. Leaves lanceolate, stiff, pleated, finely velvety. Flowers zygomorphic, recurved such that the upper tepal and stamens appear to be lowermost, red with lower tepals yellowish marked with black, upper tepal clawed, 15–20 mm long, lower tepals united below, tube narrowly funnel-shaped, expanded in the upper half, curved upward, 30–40 mm long, filaments straight, c. 40 mm long, anthers 5–6 mm long, ovary hairless; bracts brown tipped, 15–30 mm long, inner bracts forked to halfway. Flowering July–October. Sandy flats and dunes, coastal, NW, SW (Orange River mouth to Saldanha).

Babiana tubulosa (Burman fil.) Ker Gawler

Plants 7–15 cm high, stem mostly underground. Leaves linear to lanceolate, pleated, hairy. Flowers zygomorphic, white to cream, sometimes with red markings, perianth tube (45–)55–85 mm long, cylindrical, tepals somewhat clawed, filaments arched, 20 mm long, anthers 5–7 mm long, ovary 65–90 mm long; bracts 20–40 mm long, inner bracts forked at the tips. Flowering September–October. Sandy flats and lower slopes, NW, SW, AP, LB (Elands Bay to Riversdale).

Babiana stricta

Babiana thunbergii

Babiana unguiculata G.J. Lewis
Plants 10–20 cm high, stem erect, sometimes branched. Leaves linear, sometimes twisted, pleated, hairless or shortly hairy. Flowers zygomorphic, yellow, perianth tube 8–10 mm long, tepals clawed, the upper arched, lower three united below, filaments arched, 13–15 mm long, anthers 5–6 mm long, ovary hairy; bracts brown at the tips, 6–8 mm long, inner bracts forked to halfway or slightly more. Flowering August–September. Lower mountain slopes, NW (Nardouw Mountains).

Babiana vanzyliae L. Bolus
Plants 4–12 cm high, stem rarely branched. Leaves lanceolate, pleated, velvety hairy. Flowers zygomorphic, yellow to mauve, fragrant, lower tepals shortly united, perianth tube narrowly funnel-shaped, 25–35(–50) mm long, filaments arched, 15–17 mm long, anthers 7–8 mm long, ovary hairless or shortly hairy on the ribs; bracts 25–40 mm long, dry at the tips, inner bracts shortly forked. Flowering August–September. Rocky sandstone soils in fynbos, NW (Bokkeveld Mountains).

Babiana villosa (Aiton) Ker Gawler
Plants 10–20 cm high. Leaves lanceolate, pleated, hairy. Flowers actinomorphic, mauve or pink to dark red, unscented, perianth tube slender, 12–20 mm long, filaments erect, symmetrical, 7–10 mm long, anthers arrow-shaped with a broad connective, often blackish, 7–9 mm long, ovary hairy; bracts 13–18 mm long with dry brown tips, inner bracts divided to the base. Flowering August–September. Clay flats and slopes in renosterveld, NW, SW (Tulbagh to Malmesbury). Page 90.

Babiana villosula (Gmelin) Ker Gawler ex Steudel
Plants 3–15 cm high. Leaves lanceolate, pleated, hairy. Flowers actinomorphic, pale blue to mauve with white center, lightly acridly or violet scented, tube slender, 18–25(–30) mm long, filaments erect, 4–6 mm long, anthers 5–6 mm long, ovary hairy above; bracts 20–40 mm long, inner bracts divided to the base. Flowering mainly May–July. Sandy flats and lower slopes in fynbos, SW (Malmesbury to Gordon's Bay).

Babiana tubulosa

Babiana vanzyliae

Babiana virginea Goldblatt

Plants 5–15 cm high, stem short or subterranean. Leaves lanceolate, pleated, hairy. Flowers zygomorphic, white or tinged mauve with pale yellow markings, fragrant, perianth tube 60–65 mm long, gradually flaring, straight, filaments arched, 15 mm long, anthers 9–11 mm long, ovary hairless; bracts 25–80 mm long, inner bracts forked above. Flowering September. Rock outcrops, RV (Roggeveld Escarpment at Middelpos).

Baeometra

COMMON NAME beetle lily, FAMILY Colchicaceae. Deciduous perennial. ROOTSTOCK an asymmetric ovoid corm covered with dark leathery or cartilaginous tunics. LEAVES few to several, scattered along the stem, linear-lanceolate, clasping below. INFLORESCENCE a bracteate, racemose, or spike-like scorpioid cyme; bracts linear-oblanceolate or thread-like, successively smaller and absent from the upper flowers. FLOWERS erect, usually on short stout pedicels expanded and scalloped above or ses-

Babiana villosa

Babiana virginea

Baeometra uniflora

sile, the tepals scarcely spreading, free, narrowed and clawed below but without a nectary, deciduous, orange with the claw black and the reverse reddish, unscented. STAMENS arising from the top of the claws. OVARY cylindrical with many ovules per locule; STYLES three, very short and hook-like. FRUIT a long, cylindrical, septicidal capsule. SEEDS many per locule, subglobose but angled by pressure, brown. Basic chromosome number $x = 11$. South Africa; 1 sp.

Restricted to the Cape Floral Region, *Baeometra*, with a single species, occupies a tribe by itself but is clearly closely related to the three genera in Colchicaceae tribe Anguillarieae from the Western Cape. It shares the rather short, hooked styles, arising more or less laterally on truncate ovary lobes, with *Neodregea* and *Wurmbea*, but it has the deciduous perianth of *Onixotis*. The relatively large, orange flowers with dark centers are adapted to pollination by flower-visiting monkey beetles (Scarabaeidae: Hopliini). These beetles do not feed on nectar, and the loss of nectaries in the genus, as well as the short styles, are adaptations to this pollination strategy. Although small in stature, *Baeometra* is sometimes cultivated for its unusually colored flowers.

FURTHER READING. *Baeometra* was last treated in any detail by Adamson (1950).

Baeometra uniflora (Jacquin) G. J. Lewis

Plants to 25 cm high. Leaves five to eight, lanceolate. Flowers one to five, tepals ascending, orange with reddish reverse and black claw, 15–28 mm long, narrowed below into a claw 3–12 mm long, filaments c. 3 mm long, anthers 2–4 mm long, styles c. 0.5 mm long. Flowering August–October. Mainly rocky sandstone and granite slopes, SW, AP, LB (Malmesbury to Riversdale).

Bobartia

COMMON NAME rush iris, FAMILY Iridaceae. Evergreen perennials, often growing in large tufts. ROOTSTOCK a creeping or erect rhizome. LEAVES unifacial and linear and flat to elliptical or round in cross section, then usually with narrow grooves alternating with veins, usually crowded together basally, tough and fibrotic, when unifacial without a distinct midrib; stems usually round in cross section, elliptical in cross section in 2 spp., branched or more often consisting of a long internode terminating in few to many flower clusters crowded together, these subtended by a subterminal leaf. INFLORESCENCES rhipidia, these occasionally single and terminal on branches or more often few to many crowded apically; spathes green and firm to leathery or more or less dry, brown to gray, the inner exceeding the outer; floral bracts membranous. FLOWERS fugacious, one to several per cluster, borne serially on elongating pedicels pubescent to villous above, actinomorphic, usually yellow, blue in 1 sp., probably unscented and without nectar, the tepals free or united in a tube in 1 sp., not clawed, subequal, the inner slightly smaller. STAMENS with filaments free, erect, often contiguous below; anthers erect, twisting when dry. OVARY sometimes tuberculate, usually exserted, occasionally included in the spathes; STYLE slender and short, dividing into three filiform, apically stigmatic style arms extending between stamens. FRUIT a woody capsules, ovoid-truncate, smooth or tuberculate. SEEDS angular, rough. Basic chromosome number $x = 10$. Western and Eastern Cape Provinces, mostly montane in rocky sandstone soils and often conspicuous after fires; 14 spp.

Bobartia was traditionally placed among New World and Australasian genera of Iridaceae tribe Sisyrinchieae, with which it shares close floral similarity but is now regarded as a member of the Old World tribe Irideae and closely related to *Dietes*. Species favor rocky, well-drained sandstone soils, which are low in nutrients. Plants are also unpalatable and avoided by sheep and cattle. In overgrazed fields, *Bobartia* species can become dominant; although they make an attractive display, they indicate poorly managed land of little or no agricultural value. The flowers are short-lived, lasting less than a day, and appear to be adapted for pollination by bees foraging for pollen.

We know of no attempts to cultivate *Bobartia* species, and there is no information on growth requirements. They are probably slow-growing and will clearly thrive in poor, acidic soils. Several species are attractive when in bloom, and the flowering season is often extended. *Bobartia robusta* flowers virtually year-round with flowering peaks when there has been ample rain. Because of their drought tolerance and general hardiness, bobartias may, like *Dietes*, have value as a street planting, especially in exposed, windswept, or dry situations with poor soils.

FURTHER READING. A detailed taxonomic treatment of *Bobartia* was provided by Strid (1974).

Bobartia aphylla (Linnaeus fil.) Ker Gawler
Plants evergreen, rhizomatous, slender, 30–60 cm high. Leaves terete. Flowers enclosed by green spathes arranged in a small head of mostly 5–10 cymes, yellow, tepals 18–26 mm long; ovary and capsules tuberculate. Flowering mainly November–March. Grassy, mainly coastal slopes, LB, SE (Mossel Bay to Plettenberg Bay).

Bobartia fasciculata J. B. Gillett ex Strid
Plants evergreen, rhizomatous, 80–150 cm high. Leaves terete. Flowers enclosed by fibrous, straw-colored spathes arranged in distinct, somewhat flattened clusters in a loose head of mostly 20–60 rhipidia, yellow, tepals 16–23 mm long. Flowering August–November. Mountain slopes, NW, SW (Porterville and Olifants River Mountains).

Bobartia filiformis (Linnaeus fil.) Ker Gawler
Plants evergreen, rhizomatous, 15–55 cm high. Leaves subterete to linear. Flowers enclosed by green spathes with individual clusters one to few at the branch tips, yellow, tepals 17–26 mm long. Flowering September–December, mostly after fire. Sandy lower to middle slopes in fynbos, SW, AP (Malmesbury Paardeberg to Michell's Pass to Agulhas).

Bobartia gladiata (Linnaeus fil.) Ker Gawler
Plants evergreen, rhizomatous, 20–80 cm high, stems usually flat. Leaves linear, elliptical in cross section. Flowers enclosed by green spathes arranged in a head of mostly 8–12 flattened individual clusters, yellow, tepals 22–34 mm long. Flowering September–December. Mountain slopes and coastal flats, in fynbos, SW (Cape Peninsula and Bain's Kloof to Hermanus).

Bobartia indica Linnaeus
Plants evergreen, rhizomatous, 50–100 cm high. Leaves terete, longer than stems and trailing. Flowers enclosed by green spathes arranged in a dense head of mostly 20–40 rhipidia, yellow, tepals 19–28 mm long. Flowering mainly October–March. Sandy flats and slopes, SW, AP (Mamre to Caledon).

Bobartia lilacina G. J. Lewis
Plants evergreen, rhizomatous, 30–70 cm high, stem laxly branched and sticky below the nodes. Leaves plane, narrowly sword-shaped. Flowers in solitary flower clusters, violet, tepals 14–18 mm long. Flowering January–March. Mountain slopes on shale, 600–1500 m, SW (Bain's Kloof to Franschhoek).

Bobartia longicyma J. B. Gillett
Plants evergreen, rhizomatous, to 1.8 m high. Leaves terete. Flowers enclosed by green to purple spathes, arranged in a small head of 2–20 relatively long individual

Bobartia filiformis

clusters, yellow, tepals 16–38 mm long. Capsules obovoid, 10–20 mm long. Flowering August–December. Sandy flats and lower slopes, SW, AP (Kuils River to Potberg).

Bobartia macrocarpa Strid

Plants evergreen, rhizomatous, to 1 m high. Leaves terete. Flowers enclosed by dull green to brownish spathes, arranged in a small head of two to six individual clusters, yellow, tepals 18–24 mm long. Capsules obovoid to oblong. Flowering August–February. Grassy slopes, SE (Humansdorp to Eastern Cape).

Bobartia macrospatha Baker

Plants evergreen, rhizomatous, 50–110 cm high. Leaves terete to linear. Flowers enclosed by fibrous, slightly inflated spathes arranged in a dense head of mostly 10–30 individual clusters, yellow, tepals 18–32 mm long, the tepals united below in a short tube. Flowering mainly August–November. Mountain slopes in fynbos, AP, LB, SE (Swellendam to Humansdorp).

Bobartia orientalis J. B. Gillett

Plants evergreen, rhizomatous, 40–130 cm high. Leaves terete, long and trailing above. Flowers enclosed by green spathes arranged in a dense head of mostly 40–100 fairly short individual clusters, yellow, tepals 11–22 mm long. Capsules subglobose, 4–8 mm diam. Flowering mainly August–November. Mainly dry, stony, sandstone slopes, NW, SW, LB, SE (Piketberg and Riviersonderend Mountains to Transkei).

Bobartia paniculata G. J. Lewis

Plants evergreen, rhizomatous, 40–100 cm high, stem branched above and sticky below nodes. Leaves more or less flat, linear. Flowers in solitary flower clusters loosely arranged near the top of the stem, yellow, tepals 12–16 mm long. Flowering January–February. Middle to upper slopes in dry fynbos, KM (Kammanassie Mountains).

Bobartia parva J. B. Gillett

Plants evergreen, rhizomatous, 15–40 cm high. Leaves terete. Flowers enclosed by fibrous, somewhat inflated spathes arranged in a small head of three to seven individual clusters, yellow, tepals 14–18 mm long. Flowering November–February. Moist mountain slopes, LB (Langeberg Mountains from Swellendam to Lemoenshoek).

Bobartia robusta Baker

Plants evergreen, rhizomatous, 70–210 cm high. Leaves terete. Flowers enclosed by fibrous, dry, brownish spathes arranged in a dense head of 8–40 individual clusters, yellow, tepals 22–32 mm long; ovary and capsules tuberculate. Flowering mainly August–October. Coastal and lower mountain slopes, LB, SE (Riversdale to George).

Bobartia rufa Strid

Plants evergreen, rhizomatous, 50–90 cm high. Leaves terete. Flowers enclosed by fibrous, dry, reddish brown spathes arranged in a compact rounded head composed of c. 50 individual clusters, yellow, tepals 15–19 mm long. Flowering September–November. Mountain fynbos, NW (Cedarberg to Hex River Mountains).

Bobartia indica

Boophone disticha (Colin Paterson-Jones)

Boophone haemanthoides

Boophone

COMMON NAME oxbane, FAMILY Amaryllidaceae. Large deciduous perennials. ROOTSTOCK a bulb, densely covered by grayish parchment-like tunics, more or less exposed. LEAVES 12–20, usually green after flowering, spreading into an erect fan, narrowly lanceolate, smooth, often gray-green, sometimes undulate, the margins hyaline. INFLORESCENCE a dense globose umbel with as many as 100 flowers or more, on a compressed, erect scape; spathe bracts two, erect or reflexed. FLOWERS actinomorphic, funnel-shaped, pale to deep pink, red, or cream, the pedicels spreading, usually as long as the perianth, radiating and lengthening considerably in fruit, the perianth tube short, narrow and funnel-shaped, the tepals spreading, often recurved toward the apex, narrowly lanceolate. STAMENS inserted in the throat, free, more or less spreading, longer than tepals, the anthers dorsifixed, cream. OVARY with one or two ovules per locule; STYLE straight or slightly curved, filiform, the stigma undivided. FRUIT three-angled, shortly beaked and three-shouldered, tapering basally, the three angles prominently ribbed, the walls papery, disintegrating irregularly. SEEDS fleshy, subglobose, 8–11 mm diam., pale green with a thin corky covering, the embryo green. Basic chromosome number $x = 11$. Widespread throughout sub-Saharan Africa; 2 spp.

Of Africa's many bulbous plants, *Boophone* is possibly the most widely known for its poisonous and medicinal properties. Its uses range from providing ingredients for arrow poison to skin dressings for cuts, sores, boils, and burns. Most common names refer to its toxic properties, but the Xhosa name *incwadi*, book, refers more poetically to the striking appearance of the foliage, which spreads open like a fan or book. Like many of its allies in Amaryllidaceae tribe Amaryllideae, the fruiting heads break loose and tumble in the wind, but *Boophone* is unique in that the dry spherical head detaches from the top rather than the bottom of the scape. In this way, the tumbler sometimes breaks into smaller units, rather than consistently remaining intact as in other wind-dispersed species of *Brunsvigia, Crossyne, Cybistetes, Hessea,* and *Strumaria.* Much confusion has surrounded the spelling of the genus, but *Boophone* has been formally proposed as the correct form.

FURTHER READING. Useful accounts of *Boophone* are Dyer's (1953) brief history and illustrated description of *B. disticha* and Leighton's (1947) original description of *B. haemanthoides*. Archer et al. (2001) have motivated for the name *Boophone* to be conserved against the alternative spellings, *Boophane*, *Buphane*, and *Buphone*.

Boophone disticha (Linnaeus fil.) Herbert

Plants to c. 50 cm high; bulb 5–18 cm diam. Leaves 12–20, usually dry at flowering, in an upright fan, lanceolate, 1–4 cm wide, deeply channeled, gray-green, the edges usually undulate with acute tips. Flowers 50–100 or more in a dense, spreading cluster, pink to red, fragrant, perianth tube 5–10 mm long, tepals 2–3 cm long, reflexed, pedicels elongating considerably in fruit. Flowering September–March. Rocky slopes and flats, SW, AP, LB, SE (Worcester, Robertson, and Bredasdorp to tropical East Africa).

Boophone haemanthoides F. M. Leighton

Plants 30–40 cm high; bulb to 18 cm diam. Leaves c. 20, dry at flowering, in an upright fan, lanceolate, 2.5–8.0 cm wide, channeled, gray-green, the margins undulate with obtuse tips. Flowers 100 or more in a compact, brush-like cluster, surrounded by two large, mostly upright spathe bracts, cream, turning pink when old, fragrant, perianth tube 5 mm long, tepals 2–3 cm long, spreading, pedicels elongating considerably in fruit. Flowering mainly November–February. In sand or dolerite outcrops on coastal flats or upland slopes, RV, NW, SW (Namaqualand to Saldanha, and Bokkeveld Plateau).

Bowiea

COMMON NAME climbing onion, FAMILY Hyacinthaceae. Deciduous perennial. ROOTSTOCK a large globose bulb, exposed, the scales truncate and overlapping, green. LEAVES ephemeral and soon withering, small, linear, channeled, suberect. INFLORESCENCE a many-flowered twining raceme, intricately branched above, the branches reflexed-spreading, fleshy and bright green, the pedicels long and spreading, the lower often erect and sterile; bracts small, green, spurred. FLOWERS star-shaped, the tepals lightly to strongly reflexed, free, persistent, green or white, lightly scented. STAMENS with filaments suberect or slightly spreading, joined to the base of the tepals, filiform from a cuneate base. OVARY rather squat, depressed-globose with several ovules per locule; STYLE one, short. FRUIT an ovoid capsule. SEEDS few per chamber, ellipsoidal with a peripheral wing, black. Basic chromosome number $x = 10$. Southern and tropical Africa; 1 sp.

The unusual *Bowiea* is no less curious today than when it was first introduced to science in 1867. The leaves are reduced and short-lived, and the role of photosynthesis is assumed by the intricately branched, rather fleshy inflorescences. Readily mistaken for stems, the inflorescences sprawl over rocks and twine among bushes, remaining green most of the year before withering. Al-

Boophone haemanthoides foliage (rear), *Brunsvigia bosmaniae* (front)

though *Bowiea* was long thought to be related to the genus *Schizobasis* (here included in *Drimia*) on account of its long-lasting, branched inflorescence, this alliance appears to be mistaken, representing ecological convergence rather than a close evolutionary relationship. Among the group of species of Hyacinthaceae segregated either as the tribe Caudibracteatae or subfamily Urgineoideae on the basis of the unusual characteristic of spurred bracts, *Bowiea* is the only member in which the flower is long-lasting and the perianth persistent, remaining attached to the base of the capsule during ripening. In the remaining species, the flower lasts less than a day, often only a few hours, and the perianth abscises from below and twists above the ovary to form a withered cap on top of the developing fruit. This specialized condition separates these species (including *Drimia* group *Schizobasis*, represented in the Cape Floral Region by *D. intricata*) from *Bowiea*, which retains the more primitive condition of a persistent perianth. The bulb is widely used in traditional medicine but all parts of the plant are extremely poisonous and potentially lethal if ingested, and several cardiotoxic glycosides have been isolated from it. The small, green, open flowers with their unpleasant smell are adapted for pollination by a variety of carrion flies and houseflies (Tachinidae and Muscidae) and wasps.

Its unique, climbing inflorescence and prominent, exposed bulb have made *Bowiea* a curiosity among specialist collectors, predominantly those interested in succulents. It is best grown in a glasshouse, where its twining habit can be exploited by leading the inflorescence up nearby supports.

FURTHER READING. An illustrated account of *Bowiea volubilis* was provided by Dyer (1941) and the genus was revised by Jessop (1977). A second species, *B. gariepensis*, described and illustrated more recently (Van Jaarsveld 1983, D. and U. Müller-Doblies 1991), is best regarded as no more than a subspecies (Bruyns and Vosa 1987).

Bowiea volubilis Harvey ex Hooker fil.

Plants with trailing stems to 3 m long; bulb exposed, green. Leaves dry at flowering, linear channeled, 2–4 cm long. Flowers in a twining or trailing, fleshy, diffusely branched raceme, yellowish green, scented of fish, pedicels 20–50 mm long, tepals lightly reflexed, triangular-lanceolate, 5–7 × 2 mm, stamens 2–3 mm long, anthers c. 1 mm long, ovary globose-conical, style 2–2.5 mm long. Capsule ovoid-conical, c. 13 mm long; seeds ellipsoidal, 7–8 mm long. Flowering January–February. Rock outcrops and bush margins, SE (southern Namibia and northern Namaqualand, Baviaanskloof Mountains to tropical Africa).

Brunsvigia

COMMON NAME candelabra lily, FAMILY Amaryllidaceae. Large to small deciduous perennials. ROOTSTOCK a bulb, usually covered with tan, brittle tunics. LEAVES 2–20 but mostly 4–6, green or dry at flowering, suberect or pressed to the ground, oblong to tongue-shaped, the upper surface smooth to papillate or bristly, the margins

Bowiea volubilis

usually raised, often minutely fringed. INFLORESCENCE a widely spreading hemispherical to globose umbel, as many as 80-flowered, on a compressed, erect scape; spathe bracts two, rapidly withering. FLOWERS zygomorphic, rarely almost actinomorphic, widely flared to somewhat funnel-shaped, pink, red, or rarely white, the pedicels radiating, usually much longer than the perianth, the perianth tube short, the tepals recurved, usually flat. STAMENS shortly united basally, attached to tepals near the base, tightly clustered, upturned toward the tip, sometimes with lateral appendages near the base, the anthers dorsifixed, wine red. OVARY with 3–10 ovules per locule; STYLE filiform, protruding beyond the stamens, upturned toward the tip, the stigma three-lobed. FRUIT a papery capsule, round, elongated or three-angled and tapering basally, three-ribbed with transverse veining. SEEDS fleshy, ovoid, 5–10 mm diam., reddish green; embryo green. Basic chromosome number $x = 11$. Southern Africa, particularly in semiarid areas; c. 20 spp., 9 in the Cape.

Brunsvigia is widespread in southern Africa, where it is best developed in the winter-rainfall region in Namaqualand and the Western Cape. There, the plants flower in the autumn at the end of the dry season, at which time the leaves, which only appear in the winter, are dry and withered. In favorable years, several of these species may flower en masse, turning large areas of the veld pink or red for brief periods in autumn. A second center of species diversity is the Drakensberg Mountains in KwaZulu-Natal. In summer-rainfall southern Africa, brunsvigias produce the flower heads together with their leaves in late summer.

Species of *Brunsvigia* vary in the color and form of their flowers, reflecting a variety of pollination strategies. The widely flared, pink flowers of *B. bosmaniae* are pollinated by noctuid moths whereas the brilliant red, tightly clustered flowers of *B. marginata* are pollinated by the large satyrid butterfly, *Aeropetes tulbaghia*, commonly known as the pride of Table Mountain. In contrast, the large, red, somewhat tubular flowers of *B. josephinae*, *B. litoralis*, and *B. orientalis* are pollinated by species of sunbirds. Brunsvigias are easy to propagate from seed, but large plants like *B. josephinae* can take 14 years or more to mature. Furthermore, they flower erratically out of their natural habitats.

The fruiting heads are dispersed by tumbling across the ground in the wind, and *Brunsvigia bosmaniae* and *B. orientalis* have enlarged, triangular capsules particularly well suited to this strategy. Individual species are often widespread and variable, particularly with respect to size and coloring. The eastern Cape species, in particular, are poorly understood and still require careful study.

FURTHER READING. *Brunsvigia* was last reviewed by Dyer (1950–1951), who recognized 17 species. Since then, 5 additional species have been described by Barker (1963), Goldblatt (1972a), D. and U. Müller-Doblies (1994), and Snijman (2001a).

Brunsvigia bosmaniae F. M. Leighton

Plants variable in size, to c. 40 cm high; bulb 5–10 cm diam., the tunics brittle. Leaves five or six, dry at flower-

Brunsvigia bosmaniae; see also pages 26, 95

ing, pressed to the ground, oblong, 5–12 cm wide, the upper surface dark green with red margins. Flowers c. 20 to c. 70 in a dense rounded umbel, scented of narcissus, tepals 20–40 mm long, almost free to the base, broadly oblong, pale to deep pink, glistening, often with a greenish yellow center, five- to seven-veined, the tips obtuse, the outer stamens shorter than the inner, sometimes only half as long, filaments often basally toothed. Capsule 30–60 mm long, sharply three-angled, the angles strongly ribbed, more or less flat-topped, tapering gradually to the pedicel. Flowering March–May. Open flats, coastal sand, loam, or granite soils, RV, NW, SW (Namaqualand to Tygerberg, Bokkeveld Plateau to Roggeveld).

Brunsvigia comptonii W. F. Barker

Plants to 12 cm high; bulb 2.5–4.0 cm diam., often compressed, the tunics brittle. Leaves usually 3(–5), dry at flowering, elliptical to strap-shaped, 1.5–4 cm wide, pressed to the ground, the upper surface minutely papillate. Flowers 5–19, widely spreading, tepals 20–25 mm long, almost free to the base, all flared upward or often one remaining basal, recurved in the upper half, pale to deep pink with dark veins, yellowish at the base. Capsule 10–20 mm long, rounded, tapering basally, soft-walled, scarcely ribbed. Flowering February–March. Gravel flats and slopes, often between slate chips, RV (Tanqua Karoo and western Karoo).

Brunsvigia elandsmontana Snijman

Compact plants to 20 cm high; bulb c. 4 cm diam., the tunics brittle. Leaves four to six, dry at flowering, pressed to the ground, elliptical, 2.5–7 cm wide, the upper surface dark green with pink cartilaginous margins. Flowers 6–18, in a compact spherical umbel, bright pink, pedicels elongating in fruit, perianth tube to 5 mm long, tepals 15–20 mm long, outspread, stamens slightly spreading, shorter than or as long as the tepals. Capsule 10–25 mm long, three-angled, thinly ribbed, rounded apically, tapering basally. Flowering March–May. Lowlands in pebbly soils, SW (Elandsberg near Wellington).

Brunsvigia gregaria R. A. Dyer

Plants to 40 cm high; bulb 3–6 cm diam., the tunics brittle. Leaves four to eight, appearing soon after flowering, pressed to the ground, tongue-shaped, to 6–10 cm wide, the upper surface rough, the margin red or pale, scabrous. Flowers 30–50, spreading, perianth tube 4–5 mm long, tepals 25–40 mm long, more or less evenly spreading or the upper curved upward, 5- to 10-veined, pink to red. Capsule 25–35 mm long, three-angled, prominently ribbed, heart-shaped. Flowering January–April. Sandstone or clay flats or slopes, SE (Jeffreys Bay and Baviaanskloof to Eastern Cape).

Brunsvigia josephinae (Redouté) Ker Gawler

Plants to 65 cm high; bulbs usually exposed, c. 20 cm diam., the tunics parchment-like. Leaves 8–20, dry at flowering, recurved, oblong, to 20 cm wide, grayish, smooth. Flowers 30–40, in an open, widely spreading umbel, dark red, orange-yellow toward the base, perianth

Brunsvigia josephinae

tube to 15 mm long, tepals 45–80 mm long, overlapping before recurving strongly, pedicels stout, curved in flower, straight when fruiting, the filaments stout. Capsule 30–50 mm long, more or less cylindrical, ribs at most moderately thickened. Flowering February–April. Rocky slopes and clay flats, renosterveld, RV, NW, SW, AP, KM (western Karoo, Worcester, Malgas to Willowmore).

Brunsvigia litoralis R. A. Dyer
Plants to 60 cm high; bulb 10–13 cm diam., deep-seated, the tunics parchment-like. Leaves c. 18, dry at flowering, upright, to 7.5 cm wide, with a half-twist toward the apex, grayish, smooth. Flowers c. 20, sometimes as many as c. 40, widely spreading, red, streaked with yellow, similar in shape to those of *B. josephinae* but with the perianth tube 15–25 mm long. Capsule c. 30 mm long, more or less cylindrical. Flowering February–April. Coastal sands, SE (Knysna to Port Elizabeth).

Brunsvigia marginata (Jacquin) Aiton
Compact plants to 20 cm high; bulb c. 6 cm diam., the tunics brittle. Leaves four, dry at flowering, pressed to the ground, elliptical, 4–10 cm wide, leathery. Flowers more or less actinomorphic, 10–20 in a compact, hemispherical umbel, brilliant scarlet, pedicels elongating in fruit, perianth tube 5–10 mm long, tepals 20–30 mm long, outspread to slightly recurved, stamens tightly clustered, well exserted, very slightly curved. Capsule 20–25 mm long, three-angled, thinly ribbed, tapering basally. Flowering March–June. Rocky slopes in shale bands, NW, SW (Citrusdal to Du Toit's Kloof).

Brunsvigia orientalis (Linnaeus) Aiton ex Ecklon
Plants 40–50 cm high; bulb 10–15 cm diam., the tunics brittle. Leaves four to eight, dry at flowering, flat on the ground, oblong, 7–19 cm wide, the upper surface usually velvety. Flowers 20–40, rarely more, in a large spherical umbel, bright to light red, perianth tube to 5 mm long, tepals 40–60 mm long, overlapping then rolled back, pedicels stout, curved at flowering, straight at fruiting. Capsule 30–70 mm long, three-angled, the angles strongly ribbed, flat-topped, tapering basally. Flowering Febru-

Brunsvigia litoralis

Brunsvigia marginata (Colin Paterson-Jones)

ary–April. Usually on coastal forelands in sand, rarely clay, NW, SW, AP, SE (southern Namaqualand to Worcester, Cape Peninsula to Knysna).

Brunsvigia striata (Jacquin) Aiton

Plants variable in size, 15–35 cm high; bulb 4–7 cm diam. Leaves four to six, dry at flowering, pressed to the ground, elliptical, 3–7 cm wide, leathery, the upper surface dark green, minutely papillate, rarely with a few scattered scale-like hairs, the margin red, cartilaginous, often undulate. Flowers 8–30, widely spreading, perianth tube to 4 mm long, tepals 20–30 mm long, usually flared upward with the lower remaining basal, mostly three- to five-veined, pale to reddish pink, the inner surface often pale with a dark central stripe, stamens usually as long as the tepals. Capsule 15–25 mm long, rounded apically, thinly ribbed, tapering basally. Flowering March–April. Heavy, often stony soils, NW, AP, KM, LB (Bokkeveld Mountains to Cape Infanta, Montagu, and Oudtshoorn).

Bulbinella

COMMON NAME bulbinella, FAMILY Asphodelaceae. Tufted deciduous perennials, solitary or forming clumps. ROOTSTOCK a compact rhizome surrounded by membranous cataphylls and often fibrous leaf bases, roots somewhat fleshy. LEAVES few to several, spirally arranged, somewhat fleshy, round or triangular in cross section or strap-shaped and keeled, the margins smooth or minutely toothed. INFLORESCENCE a more or less dense raceme; bracts small and papery. FLOWERS star- or cup-shaped, the tepals free or united at the base only, white, cream, yellow, or orange, usually unscented but sometimes with a musty smell. STAMENS inserted below the ovary and joined to the base of the tepals. OVARY ovoid with two ovules per locule; STYLE slender. FRUIT a globose or ovoid capsule. SEEDS one or two per locule, depressed-ovate and shield-shaped with a peripheral wing, black. Basic chromosome number $x = 7$. Southern Hemisphere, mostly South Africa; c. 23 spp., 14 in the Cape.

Bulbinella has an interesting and unusual, highly disjunct distribution. Although most of the species are restricted to winter-rainfall South Africa, six occur naturally in New Zealand. Only the antipodean species enjoy any cultivation outside of botanical gardens, but they are all rather coarse in appearance and monotonously similar. The Cape species, in contrast, are highly diverse in color and stature but are little known in cultivation. Those South African species that occur naturally on the

Brunsvigia orientalis

Brunsvigia striata

well-drained, nutrient-poor sands of the Cape series are not easy to cultivate, but they are in the minority; a dry summer or at least good drainage over that time will allow ready cultivation of many of the others. Species of *Bulbinella* are characterized by a dense raceme of small flowers, often bright yellow but also lemon, cream, white, or even orange. Unlike those of the related genera *Bulbine* and *Trachyandra*, *Bulbinella* flowers last more than a day, and the result is a tightly massed spire of blooms more like that seen in *Kniphofia*. Although superficially similar to some species of *Bulbine*, the smooth filaments of *Bulbinella* are quite unlike the hairy filaments characteristic of *Bulbine*, and the leaves are rather fibrous and not at all soft or succulent. Most species are probably pollinated by a variety of pollen-collecting insects. *Bulbinella* and *Bulbine* are unique in the family Asphodelaceae in lacking nectaries; pollen is the only reward for visiting insects.

Resembling the European genera *Eremurus* and *Asphodeline*, or smaller species of *Kniphofia*, the elegant and often brightly colored inflorescences of *Bulbinella* make them very desirable subjects for either the pot or garden. The larger species, such as *B. elata*, *B. latifolia*, and *B. nutans*, are best grown in borders or beds. The latter two are highly communal in the wild and favor seasonal pools or streamsides on mountains or plateaus where they can occur in the thousands. The unusual orange-flowered form of *B. latifolia* is restricted in the wild to fine-grained dolerite-derived clays near Nieuwoudtville and in a good season can set swaths of land ablaze with color. Colorful and long-lasting in the vase, all the species are recommended as cut flowers. Plants should be grown in large pots or in the open ground to allow room for the storage roots to develop. Care should be taken not to damage these roots when plants are divided or when digging around the plants. Bulbinellas should not be lifted for storage because of the sensitivity of their storage roots to damage and desiccation. For the latter reason, it is also important to water plants lightly during the dormant season.

FURTHER READING. Detailed, fully illustrated accounts of the African species of *Bulbinella*, including notes on cultivation, have been provided by Perry (1987, 1999).

Bulbinella barkerae P. L. Perry
Plants to 60 cm high; roots spindle-shaped, white. Leaves 6–13, the inner smaller, linear channeled, margins densely and shortly hairy. Flowers in a narrow cylindrical raceme 20 mm diam., white, to 9 mm diam., with a musty odor. Flowering September–October. Shale flats in renosterveld, SW, AP, LB (Bot River to Riversdale).

Bulbinella caudafelis (Linnaeus fil.) Durand & Schinz
Plants to 80 cm high, sheathing fibers coarse and bristle-like or tightly netted; roots spindle-shaped, white. Leaves 5–11, the inner smaller, linear channeled, margins smooth or finely toothed. Flowers in a narrowly conical raceme 30 mm diam., white with pink keels, to 13 mm diam., unscented. Flowering August–December. Sandstone, granite, or clay, RV, NW, SW, AP, KM, LB, SE (Namaqualand and western Karoo to Avontuur).

Bulbinella caudafelis

Bulbinella chartacea P. L. Perry
Plants to 40 cm high, sheathing fibers flat and papery; roots spindle-shaped, white. Leaves scarcely developed at flowering, three to five, linear channeled, margins smooth. Flowers in a narrowly conical raceme to 16 mm diam., yellow, c. 9 mm diam. Flowering February–April. Sandstone slopes in fynbos, NW, SW (Olifants River Mountains to Riviersonderend Mountains).

Bulbinella divaginata P. L. Perry
Plants to 45 cm high, sheathing fibers fine, bristle-like, shorter than the membranous cataphylls; roots spindle-shaped, white. Leaves scarcely developed at flowering, 4–10, filiform, margins smooth. Flowers in a narrowly cylindrical raceme to 20 mm diam., yellow, 7–9 mm diam., sour smelling or unscented. Flowering March–June. Mainly clay soils in renosterveld, NW, SW (Namaqualand to False Bay).

Bulbinella eburniflora P. L. Perry
Plants to 75 cm high, sheathing fibers fine and somewhat netted; roots spindle-shaped, white. Leaves three to seven, the inner smaller, linear channeled, margins finely toothed. Flowers in a cylindrical raceme to 35 mm diam., ivory colored or pale straw, 9–10 mm diam., with a musty odor. Flowering August–September. Clay and sand, NW (Bokkeveld Escarpment).

Bulbinella elata P. L. Perry
Plants to 1 m high, sheathing fibers thin, loose; roots cylindrical, tapering, orange. Leaves six to eight, the inner smaller, linear, flat, margins smooth, bright green. Flowers in a long, slender raceme 30 mm diam., cream, 10 mm diam., faintly scented. Flowering July–August. Clay and granite soils, NW, SW (Pakhuis Mountains to Mamre).

Bulbinella elegans Schlechter ex P. L. Perry
Plants to 60 cm high, sheathing fibers tough and netted; roots spindle-shaped, white. Leaves 3–25, linear, margins finely and irregularly toothed. Flowers in a compact cylindrical raceme to 25 mm diam., yellow to white with pink tinge, 7–8 mm diam., unscented. Flowering mainly August–September. Various soils, RV, NW, KM (Bokkeveld Escarpment and western Karoo to Witteberg).

Bulbinella graminifolia P. L. Perry
Plants to 65 cm high, sheathing fibers soft, somewhat netted; roots spindle-shaped, white. Leaves four to nine, the inner smaller, linear channeled, margins finely toothed. Flowers in a narrowly cylindrical raceme to 15 mm diam., white, to 8 mm diam. Flowering July–August. Clay in renosterveld, NW (Namaqualand to Citrudsal).

Bulbinella latifolia Kunth
Plants to 1 m high, sheathing fibers fine to medium, straight or partly netted; roots cylindrical, yellow. Leaves 5–10, the inner smaller, linear to lanceolate, shallowly channeled, margins smooth or minutely toothed, bright green, to 65 mm wide. Flowers in a conical raceme to 40 mm diam., cream, yellow, or orange, 9–10 mm diam., unscented. Flowering August–October. Seasonally damp sandstone or granite, rarely dolerite, RV, NW (Namaqualand and western Karoo to Cold Bokkeveld).

Four subspecies are recognized: subspecies *denticulata* P. L. Perry with smooth or minutely toothed leaf margins, lemon yellow flowers, flowering September–October, clay flats in mountain renosterveld or karroid scrub, NW (Cold Bokkeveld to Hex River Pass), subspecies *doleritica* (P. L. Perry) P. L. Perry with smooth leaf margins, orange flowers, flowering August–September, doleritic clay, RV (Bokkeveld Escarpment), subspecies *latifolia* with smooth or minutely toothed leaf margins, bright yellow flowers, flowering August–October, seeps on granite or sandstone, NW (Springbok to Cedarberg), and subspecies *toximontana* P. L. Perry with smooth leaf margins, cream flowers, flowering July–August, peaty seeps on sandstone, NW (Gifberg). Pages 104, 105.

Bulbinella nutans (Thunberg) Durand & Schinz
Plants to 1 m high, sheathing fibers fine to medium, straight or partly netted; roots cylindrical, yellow. Leaves 5–13, the inner smaller, linear channeled, margins smooth or finely toothed, bright green, to 25 mm wide. Flowers in a conical raceme to 55 mm diam., yellow or

Bulbinella divaginata

Bulbinella eburniflora

Bulbinella elegans

Bulbinella graminifolia

Bulbinella latifolia subsp. *doleritica*; see also page 25

Bulbinella latifolia subsp. *latifolia*

Bulbinella nutans subsp. *nutans*

Bulbinella latifolia subsp. *toximontana*

Bulbinella nutans subsp. *turfosicola*

cream, 10–12 mm diam., unscented. Flowering July–October. Damp peaty soils, RV, NW, SW, LB (Loeriesfontein to Swellendam).

Two subspecies are recognized: subspecies *nutans* with leaves to 16 mm wide, margins smooth, flowers yellow or cream, flowering July–October, mainly seasonally damp clay, RV, NW, SW, LB (Loeriesfontein to Swellendam), and subspecies *turfosicola* (P. L. Perry) P. L. Perry with leaves to 25 mm wide, margins smooth or finely toothed, flowers cream, flowering October–December, mountain seeps, NW, SW (Cedarberg Mountains to Table Mountain).

Bulbinella potbergensis P. L. Perry

Plants to 60 cm high, sheathing fibers netted; roots spindle-shaped, white. Leaf single, rarely two, semiterete, leathery. Flowers in a narrowly conical raceme 9–15 mm diam., yellow with faint green keels, 6.5–7 mm diam. Flowering September. Silcrete, SW (Potberg).

Bulbinella punctulata A. Zahlbruckner

Plants to 1 m high, sheathing fibers closely netted; roots spindle-shaped, white. Leaves two, sometimes three or four, the inner smaller, linear channeled, margins smooth. Flowers in a cylindrical raceme to 20 mm diam., yellow with green keels, c. 9 mm diam. Flowering August–October. Rocky sandstone, often in wet places, NW (Gifberg to Porterville Mountains).

Bulbinella trinervis (Baker) P. L. Perry

Plants to 40 cm high, sheathing fibers fine, straight or somewhat netted; roots spindle-shaped, white. Leaves scarcely developed at flowering, five to seven, semiterete, margins sparsely and minutely toothed. Flowers in a narrowly cylindrical raceme to c. 20 mm diam., white to pinkish, 6–7 mm diam., unscented. Flowering mostly March–April. Rocky sandstone slopes, SW, KM, LB, SE (Malmesbury to Baviaanskloof Mountains).

Bulbinella triquetra (Linnaeus fil.) Kunth

Plants to 35 cm high, sheathing fibers fine to medium, bristle-like; roots spindle-shaped, white. Leaves 10–40, filiform-trigonous, margins finely toothed. Flowers in a subcorymbose to narrowly conical raceme 20–24 mm

Bulbinella trinervis

Bulbinella triquetra

diam., yellow, 8–9 m diam., unscented. Flowering mainly September–November. Damp sand and granite, RV, NW, SW (Bokkeveld Mountains and western Karoo to Bredasdorp).

Chasmanthe

COMMON NAME cobra lily, FAMILY Iridaceae. Deciduous perennials. ROOTSTOCK a depressed-globose corm rooting from below, basal in origin, with firm-papery tunics, often becoming coarsely fibrous. LEAVES several, the lower two or three forming cataphylls, foliage leaves unifacial with a definite midrib, mostly basal and forming a two-ranked fan, blades lanceolate to sword-shaped, plane, cauline leaves few and reduced; stem terete, simple or branched. INFLORESCENCE a two-ranked or secund spike, usually many-flowered and crowded; bracts small, green, becoming dry at the tips, firm textured, the inner as long as or shorter than outer and notched apically. FLOWERS zygomorphic, orange, the lower tepals without contrasting markings or green, unscented, with nectar from septal nectaries; perianth tube elongate, cylindrical below and sometimes spirally twisted, expanded abruptly and tubular and horizontal above; tepals unequal, the dorsal largest, extended horizontally and concave, the remaining tepals much smaller, directed forward or recurved. STAMENS unilateral and arcuate, the lowermost (central) slightly longer than the other two; anthers parallel, subversatile. STYLE long-exserted, horizontal, the branches filiform. FRUIT a globose capsule, leathery. SEEDS globose, usually two per locule, raphal vascular trace excluded, orange, shiny and smooth when fresh, coat sometimes fleshy, then becoming wrinkled on drying. Basic chromosome number $x = 10$. Restricted to South Africa, Western Cape to Transkei, usually in bush, or forest margins; 3 spp.

Chasmanthe is evidently closely related to *Crocosmia*, and the two genera differ mainly in seed features and basic chromosome number ($x = 11$ in *Crocosmia*, which has small, dry, dark seeds). The bright orange seeds of *Chasmanthe* are thought to be adapted for bird dispersal. The seeds of *C. aethiopica* have a watery or fleshy outer layer, which is consumed by birds, but in the other species the seeds are quite dry and do not provide any reward. The flowers are pollinated by sunbirds. Their red to orange color, exserted anthers, long perianth tube, extended upper tepal, and reduced lower tepals are all features that occur in bird-pollinated flowers in several other genera of Iridaceae and other families of the African flora.

All the species of *Chasmanthe* are worth horticultural attention. The largest and most striking, *C. floribunda*, has tall stems that may exceed a meter. The numerous orange to scarlet flowers are borne in two opposed ranks and lend the plants a very elegant appearance, even after flowering. The yellow-flowered cultivar, 'Duckittiae', makes an excellent display and is much favored in Cape gardens. *Chasmanthe bicolor* is slightly smaller and bears orange flowers with green-tipped tepals. In its own way, it is as attractive as *C. floribunda*. It is something of a mystery plant for there is no confirmed locality in the wild today, and early records are vague about its source; the species was named from plants grown in Europe in the 18th century. The early flowering *C. aethiopica* is a smaller plant than its two relatives and bears its curved and unbranched spike early in the season, flowering at the Cape in April or May. Its early flowering habit makes it especially useful in the garden, for it blooms at a time when few other Cape bulbs do. All *Chasmanthe* species are easy to grow and ideal for the garden. They thrive on a variety of soils but do best on rich loamy substrates. They also respond well to feeding and added water, for in the wild they are most common in wetter situations. The large corms grow quickly; plants grown from seeds may reach flowering size in 2 years. All species make excellent cut flowers, and *C. floribunda* has entered the cut flower trade as a specialty item.

FURTHER READING. Taxonomic accounts of *Chasmanthe* were provided by De Vos (1985, 1999c).

Chasmanthe aethiopica (Linnaeus) N. E. Brown

Plants 40–65 high, stem unbranched; corm depressed-globose with papery to fibrous tunics. Leaves sword-shaped to lanceolate, fairly soft textured. Flowers in a secund, inclined to horizontal spike, orange, perianth tube abruptly expanded and almost pouched at the base of the upper part, dorsal tepal arising 4–7 mm beyond the lower, lateral tepals 10–18 mm long, lightly recurved, stamens extending under the dorsal tepal, the anthers not reaching the tepal apex. Seeds globose, bright orange with a fleshy coat when fresh. Flowering April–July. Hills and flats on granite, sandstone, or shale, mainly coastal, in bush or forest margins, SW, AP, LB, SE (Darling to Eastern Cape).

Chasmanthe bicolor (Gasparrini ex Tenore) N. E. Brown
Plants 70–90 cm high, stem erect and usually branched; corm large, depressed-globose with papery to fibrous tunics. Leaves sword-shaped, relatively soft textured. Flowers in a secund, erect spike, orange-red with green markings, perianth tube flaring gradually into the wider upper part, 30–33 mm long, dorsal tepal arising at the same level as the lower, 30–40 mm long, upper lateral tepals directed forward, 5–8 mm long, stamens extending under the dorsal tepal, the anthers slightly exceeding the tepal apex. Seeds subglobose, orange, the coat dry. Flowering July–August. Sheltered ravines, probably on shale, SW (Robertson district?).

Chasmanthe floribunda (Salisbury) N. E. Brown
Plants 45–100 cm high, stem erect, usually branched; corm large, depressed, with firm-papery tunics, becoming fibrous with age. Flowers in a two-ranked erect spike, orange-red, rarely yellow, perianth tube flaring gradually into the wider upper half, 25–40 mm long, dorsal tepal arising 3–5 mm beyond the lower, 30–35 mm long, lateral tepals 12–20 mm long, lightly recurved, stamens extending under the dorsal tepal, the anthers not reaching the tepal apex. Seeds subglobose to weakly angular, bright orange with a smooth, dry coat. Flowering July–September. Coastal and montane on sandstone and granite, RV, NW, SW (Bokkeveld Mountains and western Karoo to Hermanus).

Clivia

COMMON NAME clivia, FAMILY Amaryllidaceae. Large evergreen plants. ROOTSTOCK a rhizome. LEAVES 5–20 in a basal or cauline cluster, suberect or recurved, strap-shaped with a tapering or broad, sometimes notched

Chasmanthe aethiopica

Chasmanthe floribunda

apex, longer than the inflorescence, midrib sometimes pale, smooth or the margin minutely serrated. INFLORESCENCE a spreading or lax umbel on a fleshy, erect, compressed scape; spathe bracts four or more, soon withering. FLOWERS actinomorphic or slightly zygomorphic, narrowly to widely funnel-shaped, nodding to spreading, red, orange, and yellow, the pedicels shorter than or as long as the perianth, the perianth tube short, the tepals overlapping throughout or spreading in the upper half and reflexed toward the tip. STAMENS inserted in the throat, free, evenly spreading, as long as or slightly longer than the tepals, the anthers dorsifixed, yellow. OVARY with five to nine ovules per locule; STYLE straight or slightly curved, as long as the perianth or exserted, the stigma minutely trifid. FRUIT indehiscent, subglobose to irregularly spindle-shaped, red with yellow flesh. SEEDS turgid, more or less globose, ivory colored, the embryo green. Basic chromosome number $x = 11$. Northwestern Cape and eastern southern Africa; c. 5 spp., 1 in the Cape.

The genus *Clivia* was until more recently known only from summer-rainfall southern Africa, where the species occur in coastal and inland forests along the eastern seaboard. An astonishing discovery, made in late 2001, revealed a new species, *C. mirabilis*, at the northern tip of the Cape winter-rainfall region, more than 320 km (200 miles) from its relatives to the southeast. This extraordinary species appears to have been isolated in a single deep gorge as the climate of the region became drier and more seasonal.

The species of *Clivia* have traditionally been grouped according to floral form. The bird-pollinated species, including *C. mirabilis*, have nodding, somewhat narrow, cylindrical flowers, whereas *C. miniata*, which is butterfly pollinated, has trumpet-shaped flowers that radiate outward on straight pedicels.

Clivias are long-lived plants with well-developed perennial roots and are remarkably drought tolerant. The fleshy fruits, which hold as many as 25 turgid seeds, are most often slow to mature, particularly in *Clivia miniata*, in which seeds take as long as a year to ripen. The Cape species, *C. mirabilis*, is exceptional in having fruits that mature in less than 6 months, allowing germination to coincide with the first winter rains.

Clivias are among the easiest Amaryllidaceae to grow. Plants were first introduced into England in the mid-18th century, since when many hybrids and cultivars have been raised. The renewed demand for clivias, as horticultural subjects in the East and for traditional medicine in southern Africa, has resulted in large-scale poaching from the wild, raising deep concern for the conservation of natural populations.

FURTHER READING. Duncan (1999) published a well-illustrated guide to the species, cultivation, and propagation of *Clivia*. A key to the summer-rainfall species was provided by Vorster and Smith (1994; whose account of *C. nobilis* erroneously included a color plate of *C. gardenii*), and the winter-rainfall species was described by Rourke (2002).

Clivia mirabilis Rourke

Plants to 80 cm high; rhizome compact with many thick roots. Leaves 5–12 in a suberect basal cluster, strap-shaped, 3–4 cm wide, smooth, dark green, often with a

Clivia mirabilis

central whitish stripe down the upper surface. Flowers 20–35, tubular, scarlet with green to yellow tips, on lax reddish pedicels c. 25 mm long, tepals united into a slightly flared tube c. 1 cm long, free for c. 3 cm, stamens as long as the tepals, style slightly exserted. Fruit scarlet, irregularly spindle-shaped. Flowering October–November. Loamy soil among rocks in light shade, NW (Bokkeveld Mountains).

Crinum

COMMON NAME marsh lily, FAMILY Amaryllidaceae. Large to small evergreen perennials, often forming clumps. ROOTSTOCK a bulb. LEAVES perennial, four to many, green at flowering, with or without a prominent midrib, the sheathing bases often forming a false stem, the margins more or less shortly fringed, the apex of mature leaves often ending abruptly as if cut. INFLORESCENCE a 1- to 25-flowered umbel on a short to tall, somewhat compressed scape; spathe bracts two, soon withering. FLOWERS trumpet-shaped or with a slender straight tube and spreading tepals, white to deep pink, often with deep pink keels, usually heavily scented, the pedicels shorter than the perianth, the perianth tube long and narrow, often curved, the tepals narrow to broad, reflexed or spreading and recurved toward the apex. STAMENS inserted in the perianth throat, curved and spreading regularly or bent downward with upturned tips, the anthers dorsifixed, curved, cream or wine red. OVARY with c. 12 ovules per locule; STYLE bent laterally or curved downward with an upturned apex, the stigma obscurely three-lobed. FRUIT subglobose, membranous to fleshy, sometimes beaked, opening irregularly. SEEDS water-rich, 2–3 cm diam., with a thin corky covering, sometimes papillate, outer layers green, the embryo green. Basic chromosome number $x = 11$. Pantropical but mostly in sub-Saharan Africa; c. 65 spp., 2 in the Cape.

Crinum gives its name to the subtribe Crininae of Amaryllidaceae tribe Amaryllideae, which also includes *Ammocharis* and *Cybistetes*. Unlike those small genera, which are restricted to sub-Saharan Africa, *Crinum* is rich in species and represented worldwide. Most species of *Crinum* with a basic chromosome number $x = 11$ will intercross, and hybrids with the Eastern Cape and KwaZulu-Natal *C. moorei* Hooker fil. are much favored in cultivation. Although cultivated crinums are typically large plants of more forested habitats and esteemed for garden landscaping, there are several species of diminutive proportions and ephemeral habit from the arid areas of southern Africa that are suited to pot culture.

The water-rich seeds of *Crinum* are among the most specialized of all the Amaryllidaceae; whereas most monocotyledonous seeds have two integuments, those of *Crinum* have only one. The entire seed is covered by a thin corky layer, serving to insulate it and making it waterproof. This feature appears to have been important in enabling the genus to occupy a wide range of habitats, varying from salt pans in the arid regions of southwestern Africa to the edges of permanent water bodies in the tropics. Seeds of the Asiatic *C. asiaticum* var. *japonicum* Baker are so durable that they germinate successfully even after 2 years in salt water.

Crinum variabile

FURTHER READING. *Crinum* was revised in southern Africa by Verdoorn (1973), in tropical East Africa by Nordal (1982), in central Africa by Geerinck (1973), and in tropical West Africa by Hepper (1968). Notes on the cultivation of the African species were published by Lehmiller (1996) and Pettit (1999). Fennell et al. (2001) studied the micropropagation of *C. variabile*. Seed morphology and germination in *Crinum* were examined by Koshimizu (1930). *Crinum* has been studied by several botanists working independently in various parts of Africa but a global study of the genus is long overdue.

Crinum lineare Linnaeus fil.

Plants to 70 cm high; bulbs 6–9 cm diam., forming clumps. Leaves about eight, arching from the base, linear, 0.5–2.5 cm wide, channeled, firm, grass green. Flowers 4–14, spreading, white to pale pink with a deep pink keel, perianth tube 3–10 cm long, shorter or longer than the tepals, tepals overlapping to form a funnel with the upper third recurved, stamens bent downward, white or turning red toward the apex, anthers black. Flowering January–March. Coastal sands, SE (Port Elizabeth to Eastern Cape).

Crinum variabile (Jacquin) Herbert

Plants 40–60 cm high; bulbs 5–9 cm diam., forming clumps. Leaves c. 10, recurved near the ground, lanceolate to linear, 0.4–5 cm wide, narrow toward the center, increasing in size outward, channeled. Flowers 6–12, white to pale pink, with deeper pink or green keels, heavily scented, perianth tube 2–4 cm long, shorter than the tepals, tepals overlapping to form a funnel with the upper third recurved, stamens bent downward, white or pink, anthers cream. Flowering January–May. Rocky or sandy streambeds, RV, NW (Namaqualand, Bokkeveld Escarpment, Biedouw River, and western Karoo).

Crossyne

COMMON NAME parasol lily, FAMILY Amaryllidaceae. Large plants. ROOTSTOCK a bulb with brittle, tan tunics, the neck bristly, transversally ridged. LEAVES annual, usually four to six, dry at flowering, broadly strap-shaped, prostrate, in two opposite, spreading clusters, the margins with a long bristly fringe. INFLORESCENCE a large, spherical, umbel on an erect, strongly compressed scape; spathe bracts two, reflexed. FLOWERS small, strongly to weakly zygomorphic, blackish maroon, dusky pink or pale yellow, much shorter than the pedicels, the perianth tube short, the tepals narrow, reflexed. STAMENS inserted in the perianth throat, declinate or spreading, the filaments swollen and shortly united at the base, the anthers dorsifixed. OVARY with two to four ovules per locule; STYLE bent downward, the stigma minutely trifid. FRUIT an ovoid papery capsule. SEEDS fleshy, ovoid c. 5 mm diam., reddish green, the embryo green. Basic chromosome number $x = 11$. Winter-rainfall South Africa; 2 spp.

The name *Crossyne* came into popular use as recently as 1994. Previously, *C. guttata* and *C. flava* were placed in *Boophone* under the misconception that they were closely allied to *B. disticha*. *Crossyne* differs from *Boophone* in several respects, particularly the capsules and seeds. The capsules of *Crossyne* are dehiscent and the seed coat is covered with stomata, whereas the fruits of *Boophone* are indehiscent and the seed coat is corky. In *Crossyne*, as in *Boophone*, each inflorescence bears 100 flowers or more but the flowers are much smaller. Nevertheless, their density and coloring, augmented by the pigmented pedicels, create a striking impression even at a distance. The fruiting heads of *Crossyne* break loose when dry, and their perfectly spherical form allows them to tumble easily in the wind, releasing seeds in clearly defined tracks or up against fences. Studies show that *C. flava* cannot set seed without cross-fertilization; it is visited by short-proboscid flies, small butterflies, wasps, and honeybees. *Crossyne guttata* is also pollinated by the same suite of insects. The flowers mature sequentially, so the attractiveness of the umbel is prolonged.

FURTHER READING. *Crossyne* was reviewed by D. and U. Müller-Doblies (1994).

Crossyne flava (W. F. Barker ex Snijman) D. & U. Müller-Doblies

Plants to 50 cm high; bulb 10–13 cm diam. Leaves mostly four to six, dry at flowering, broadly strap-shaped, 5–11 cm wide, usually prostrate, fringed with long, white or

Crossyne flava

Crossyne guttata

Crossyne guttata (Colin Paterson-Jones)

Cyanella alba

straw-colored bristles, with small, angular, red speckles beneath. Flowers as many as c. 200, small, pale yellow, radiating on rigid, pale lemon to dull pink pedicels, perianth tube short, tepals 9–14 mm long, narrow, strongly reflexed, stamens bulbous toward the base, united together and inserted in the perianth throat, declinate, dull yellow, turning pink toward the tip, style slightly curved. Flowering March–May. Shale flats and rocky slopes, NW (Namaqualand to Cedarberg Mountains).

Crossyne guttata (Linnaeus) D. & U. Müller-Doblies
Bulb and leaves like those of *C. flava*. Flowers as many as c. 200, small, maroon or dusky pink, on rigid, radiating pedicels, perianth tube short, tepals c. 5 mm long, narrow, slightly recurved, stamens swollen toward the base, united together in the perianth throat, evenly spreading, white basally, dark apically, style curved slightly to the side. Shale and granite flats and lower slopes, NW, SW, AP, LB (Piketberg to Mossel Bay).

Cyanella

COMMON NAME lady's-hand, FAMILY Tecophilaeaceae. Deciduous perennials. ROOTSTOCK a deep-seated corm with fibrous tunics. LEAVES several in a basal tuft or rosette, filiform or linear to ovate-lanceolate, rarely shortly hairy. INFLORESCENCE a simple or branched raceme or thyrse, or rarely flowers solitary; bracts green and leaf-like, inner bracts inserted about two-thirds up the pedicels. FLOWERS zygomorphic, facing outward or slightly downward on slender spreading or suberect pedicels, the tepals spreading or slightly reflexed, free, blue to pink, white, or yellow, often distinctly veined or patterned, usually scented. STAMENS inserted at the base of the tepals, in two groups, dimorphic, either three upper and three lower or five upper and one lower, filaments slender or swollen, free or partly united, dehiscing by an apical pore. OVARY almost superior, ovoid, with many ovules per locule; STYLE slender, sometimes weakly directed toward the left or right. FRUIT a three-lobed, globose to ovoid, apically loculicidal capsule. SEEDS several per locule, ovoid, wrinkled, black. Basic chromosome number $x = 12$. Southern Africa; 7 spp., 5 in the Cape.

Largely characteristic of the more arid parts of the southern African winter-rainfall region, *Cyanella* is thought to have originated in southern Namibia and northern Namaqualand. Most species prefer heavy clay soils, with *C. aquatica* an extreme case, restricted to seasonally wet, glutinous clays at the foot of dolerite outcrops. The brightly colored flowers are pleasantly scented and long-lasting. Enantiomorphy is more or less developed in the species with a single lower stamen, but only *C. alba* is conspicuously enantiostylous with the style and lower stamen alternately flexed either to the right or to the left on different plants, a condition common in the family Haemodoraceae.

The flowers of all species are buzz pollinated by large solitary bees (Apidae: Anthophorinae). This is a highly specialized pollination system in which the pollen is not released passively through longitudinal slits in the anthers, as in most plants, but is retained within the anthers and only released through small apical pores when the anthers are vibrated or manipulated by the pollinator, invariably a type of bee. Associated with this strategy are widely spreading tepals, prominent, protruding, often tightly clustered anthers with poricidal dehiscence, and dry pollen.

All the species of *Cyanella* are recommended for pot culture. Their idiosyncratically shaped flowers, delicate colors, and lovely fragrances are all very attractive. The deeply seated corms render the plants drought resistant, and they are admirable garden plants in drier climates. Cyanellas should be planted in deep pots in a coarse, well-drained medium and grow best in full sunlight.

FURTHER READING. An illustrated taxonomic account of *Cyanella* by Scott (1991) is an excellent source of information about the genus.

Cyanella alba Linnaeus fil.
Plants 12–25 cm high. Leaves filiform, terete. Flowers one or two on long pedicels, white to pink, or yellow, tepals 12–20 × 6–10 mm, enantiostylous, magnolia scented, with five upper stamens and one larger lower, filaments free but anthers cohering and sometimes spotted, with sterile spathulate tips, upper filaments 4 mm long, lower 2 mm long. Flowering August–October. Stony clay and

Cyanella aquatica

Cyanella hyacinthoides

Cyanella lutea

Cyanella orchidiformis

sandstone soils, RV, NW (western Karoo and Bokkeveld Plateau to Ceres).

Cyanella aquatica Obermeyer ex G. Scott
Plants to 40 cm high. Leaves linear-lanceolate. Flowers in a sparsely branched, lax raceme on spreading pedicels, orange, tepals 8–10 × 3–5 mm long, weakly enantiostylous, lightly scented, with five upper stamens and one larger lower, filaments united, 0.5 mm long. Flowering October–November. Seasonally waterlogged dolerite outcrops, RV (Bokkeveld Plateau).

Cyanella hyacinthoides Linnaeus
Plants 25–40 cm high. Leaves linear-lanceolate, hairless to finely hairy. Flowers in a branched raceme on spreading pedicels, blue to mauve, rarely white, tepals 8–10 × 3–4 mm, weakly enantiostylous, violet scented, with five upper stamens and one larger lower, filaments united, upper 0.5 mm long, lower 1 mm long. Flowering August–November. Mostly clay and granite slopes, often in renosterveld, NW, SW, KM, LB (Namaqualand to Riversdale).

Cyanella lutea Linnaeus fil.
Plants 12–25 cm high. Leaves linear-lanceolate to oblong. Flowers in a branched raceme on suberect pedicels, yellow, rarely pink, tepals 12–18 × 2–4 mm, weakly enantiostylous, violet scented, with five upper stamens and one larger lower, filaments free, 2.5 mm long. Flowering September–October. Mostly clay, or limestone flats, RV, NW, SW, AP, KM, LB, SE (southern Namibia to Lesotho, Botswana).

Cyanella orchidiformis Jacquin
Plants 30–40 cm high. Leaves lanceolate, often undulate. Flowers in a branched raceme on suberect pedicels, mauve with darker center, tepals 8–10 × 2–5 mm, carnation scented, with three upper and three larger lower stamens, filaments 1–2 mm. Flowering July–September. Rocky flats and lower slopes, often wet sites, NW (southern Namibia to Clanwilliam).

Cybistetes

COMMON NAME Malgas lily, FAMILY Amaryllidaceae. Large perennial. ROOTSTOCK a bulb with tough leathery tunics. LEAVES perennial, green or dry at flowering, strap-shaped, in two opposite, spreading clusters with a short cartilaginous fringe, the tips of mature leaves appearing to be cut off. INFLORESCENCE a spreading to somewhat compact umbel on a somewhat compressed scape; spathe bracts two, rapidly withering. FLOWERS widely funnel-shaped, ivory to deep pink, sweetly scented, the pedicels spreading, lengthening considerably at fruiting, the perianth tube subcylindrical, the tepals broad, spreading, longer than the tube. STAMENS inserted below the perianth throat, free, spreading, slightly declinate, the anthers dorsifixed. OVARY with 1–19 ovules per locule; STYLE exserted, slightly declinate, the stigma undivided. FRUIT more or less spindle-shaped, prominently six-ribbed, with papery walls, disintegrating irregularly. SEEDS fleshy, subglobose, 5–30 mm diam., greenish with a thin pale corky covering, the embryo green. Basic chromosome number $x = 11$. Southern Namibia, Namaqualand, and Western Cape; 1 sp.

Cybistetes, with a single species, is most closely related to *Ammocharis* and it is questionable whether *Cybistetes* warrants status as a separate genus. Both genera have spreading leaves that exhibit the characteristic cutoff appearance when mature. Unlike *Ammocharis*, *Cybistetes* has a specialized fruiting head in which the pedicels elongate, spread apart, stiffen, and ultimately radiate outward in all directions. Together, these highly integrated features enable the dry heads to tumble in the wind, breaking open the indehiscent capsules as they roll over the veld. Southern populations of *Cybistetes* have many-seeded fruits whereas plants from the southern Knersvlakte and Namaqualand bear fewer, large seeds. The fragrant, lily-like flowers are almost certainly pollinated by moths. The perianth is white to ivory when the flowers first open but soon flushes a deep pink.

FURTHER READING. Snijman and Williamson (1994) reassessed the taxonomy of *Cybistetes*, which was first described by Milne-Redhead and Schweickerdt (1939). *Cybistetes* was illustrated by Dyer (1946).

Cybistetes longifolia (Colin Paterson-Jones)

Cybistetes longifolia (Linnaeus) Milne-Redhead & Schweickerdt
Plants to 50 cm high; bulb 10–15 cm diam. with a neck to 6 cm long. Leaves 9–14, green or dry at flowering, spreading, curved sideways, variable in length and width, 13–55 mm wide, the innermost narrower than the outermost, the apex of mature leaves truncate. Flowers 13–90, ivory to deep pink, frangipani scented, perianth tube 0.8–1.5 cm long, tepals 4–6.5 cm, gradually spreading, stamens exserted from the perianth tube, filaments upturned near the tips. Flowering December–April. Sandy or gravelly flats, NW, SW (southern Namibia to Cape Peninsula and Montagu).

Cyrtanthus

COMMON NAME fire lily, FAMILY Amaryllidaceae. Large to small, deciduous or evergreen perennials. ROOTSTOCK a bulb, often producing many bulblets. LEAVES few to many, linear to strap-shaped, erect to spreading, sometimes twisted or spiraled, often with a prominent midrib. INFLORESCENCE single- to many-flowered in a tight umbel on an erect, mostly hollow scape; spathe bracts two, often indistinguishable from the many bracteoles. FLOWERS actinomorphic or zygomorphic, tubular to widely trumpet-shaped, erect or nodding, pink, red, orange, yellow, or white, sometimes sweetly scented, the perianth tube usually curved, the tepals mostly shorter than the tube. STAMENS inserted in the perianth throat or tube, free, rarely with the bases expanded, spreading, arcuate or declinate, the anthers dorsifixed. OVARY with 10–30 ovules per locule; STYLE straight or curved, exserted or rarely included, the stigma three-branched or undivided. FRUIT an ellipsoidal capsule, the valves reflexing when dry. SEEDS black, flattened, somewhat winged. Basic chromosome number $x = 8$. East Africa to southern Africa; c. 57 spp., 22 in the Cape.

The species-rich genus *Cyrtanthus* is concentrated in the moister eastern portion of southern Africa. Only six species extend into the summer-dry southwestern Cape, and only two occur in East Africa to the north. The evergreen *C. herrei* (Leighton) R. A. Dyer, a remarkable endemic of the extremely arid Richtersveld north of the Cape Floral Region, is probably a relict of a once widespread ancestral species from a cooler climatic period in the past.

Cyrtanthus varies considerably in the form, color, and orientation of the flowers. A few species have actinomorphic flowers, but the majority deviate from this arrangement by the curvature of the perianth tube, a feature usually associated with their nodding habit. Floral asymmetry, however, is most developed in the few species with a bilabiate perianth.

The genus exploits a variety of pollinators. The summer- and autumn-flowering species with red flowers are visited by the large satyrid butterfly known as the pride of Table Mountain, *Aeropetes tulbaghia,* irrespective of their form; those with tubular red flowers are visited by sunbirds; and those with narrowly tubular, scented flowers are probably visited by moths.

Flowering in several species is most prolific after summer fires. In some species, small numbers of individuals may flower in the years between fires, but in others the flowers only appear immediately after fire. This fascinating but ephemeral behavior dictates the slow progress of studying *Cyrtanthus* in the wild. The more ornamental representatives are highly favored horticultural subjects. In general, the evergreen species are easier to cultivate than the deciduous ones. Most are suited to container cultivation rather than general garden culture. One of the easiest to grow and most floriferous is *C. sanguineus,* whereas the striking C. *elatus* tends to flower erratically in cultivation if not lifted and replanted regularly. Several *Cyrtanthus* species from the dry areas of the Cape are difficult to grow and easily succumb to overwatering. Many commercially available cyrtanthuses are of hybrid origin.

FURTHER READING. Nordal (1979) researched the East African species of *Cyrtanthus*, and Reid and Dyer (1984) published a brief review of the southern African species. More recently, Snijman and van Jaarsveld (1995) and Snijman (1999a, 2001b) described four further species from the Cape. Duncan (1990a, b) dealt with the general cultivation of *Cyrtanthus* and listed the most rewarding species for propagation. Holford (1998) contributed notes on cultivating *Cyrtanthus* for cut flowers. Hybridization has been well covered by Duncan (1990c), Holford (1989), Ising (1997), and Koopowitz (1986). McAlister et al. (1998) examined the micropropagation of some cyrtanthuses.

Cyrtanthus angustifolius (Colin Paterson-Jones)

Cyrtanthus angustifolius (Linnaeus fil.) Aiton

Plants variable in size, to 60 cm high; bulbs often in clumps. Leaves two to four, dry or green at flowering, suberect, strap-shaped, 7–15 mm wide, channeled, somewhat fleshy. Flowers 4–10, nodding, red with orange inside, 3–7 cm long, tubular, firm with slightly spreading, narrow tepals, stamens inserted in the slightly widened throat, evenly spreading, half as long as the tepals, style longer than the perianth, stigma three-branched. Flowering mostly October–February, occasionally in winter or spring after fire. Mountain slopes and flats in seasonal streams and marshes, NW, SW, AP, KM, LB, SE (Cedarberg to Port Elizabeth).

Cyrtanthus carneus Lindley

Robust plants to 75 cm high; bulbs in clumps. Leaves as many as 10, usually green at flowering, suberect, strap-shaped, 2–6 cm wide, twisted, somewhat leathery. Flowers 15–25, nodding, red or pink, 5.5–7 cm long, tubular with slightly spreading narrow tepals, stamens inserted in the slightly widened throat, evenly spreading, about half as long as the tepals, filaments with dilated bases, style slightly shorter than the perianth, stigma undivided.

Cyrtanthus carneus (Colin Paterson-Jones)

Flowering December–February. Coastal sand and gravel, SW, AP (Caledon to Mossel Bay).

Cyrtanthus collinus Ker Gawler

Plants to 35 cm high; bulbs in clumps. Leaves usually two, dry or green at flowering, spreading, narrowly strap-shaped, 3–5 mm wide, slightly channeled, grayish green. Flowers 4–11, spreading, bright red, 3.5–4.5 cm long, tubular to narrowly funnel-shaped with spreading, narrow tepals, tube sometimes dilated toward the throat, stamens inserted in or slightly below the throat, the outer slightly lower than the inner, style slightly shorter than the perianth, arched against the upper tepal, stigma three-branched. Flowering December–May. Rocky sandstone slopes, SW, KM, SE (Greyton to Eastern Cape).

Cyrtanthus debilis Snijman

Plants to 15 cm high. Leaves usually three, dry at flowering, suberect, linear, c. 1 mm wide. Flowers solitary, sometimes as many as three, suberect, pale to bright pink, backed with dark pink central stripes, 5–6 cm long, narrowly trumpet-shaped with slightly spreading tepals, tube widening evenly from the base to the throat, slightly longer than the tepals, stamens inserted about midway down the tube, tightly clustered against the lowest tepal, style longer than the stamens, curved against the lowest tepal, stigma three-branched. Flowering November–April, after fire. Gravelly soil on rocky slopes, SE (Outeniqua Mountains).

Cyrtanthus elatus (Jacquin) Traub

Striking plants to 60 cm high. Leaves about five, green at flowering, suberect, strap-shaped, 1–2.5 cm wide, slightly channeled. Flowers two to nine, suberect to spreading, bright red, rarely pink or white, 7–10 cm long, widely funnel-shaped with broad, spreading tepals, stamens inserted in the wide, open throat, almost as long as the tepals, style as long as or longer than the perianth, slightly curved, stigma subcapitate. Flowering November–March, often after fire. Forest margins and moist mountain slopes, SE (George to Humansdorp).

Cyrtanthus fergusoniae L. Bolus

Plants to 35 cm high. Leaves one to three, dry or green at flowering, suberect, linear, 2–4 mm wide, as thick as wide, channeled, striate below, with prominent midrib, the veins minutely papillate. Flowers three to eight, horizontal to nodding, bright red, 5.5–8.5 cm long, tubular with bilabiate tepals, tepals about half as long as the tube, three upper tepals overlapping and projecting forward, two lateral tepals spreading, the lowest curved downward, five upper stamens arched against the upper lip, lowermost stamen deflexed against the lower tepal, the outer inserted in the slightly widened throat, the inner attached midway up the tepals, style as long as the perianth, arched close to the upper lip, stigma capitate. Flowering December–January. Loam or sand, usually on limestone ridges, AP (Bredasdorp to Stilbaai).

Cyrtanthus flammosus Snijman & van Jaarsveld

Striking plants to 25 cm high; bulbs partially exposed. Leaves two to four, green at flowering, recurved, lanceolate, 1.5–2 cm wide, thick, grayish green, shading to maroon at the narrow base. Flowers solitary, sometimes two, erect, on a short stout pedicel, scarlet with a green tube, 8–10 cm long, widely funnel-shaped with broad, spreading tepals, stamens inserted in the wide, open throat, somewhat incurved, slightly shorter than the tepals, style as long as the perianth, curved against the lower tepals, stigma three-branched. Flowering March. Shaded rock crevices on cliffs, SE (Baviaanskloof Mountains).

Cyrtanthus guthrieae L. Bolus

Plants c. 15 cm high. Leaves two or three, usually dry at flowering, spreading, linear, c. 2 mm wide. Flowers solitary, sometimes two, erect, on a very short pedicel, bright red, 6–8.5 cm long, widely funnel-shaped with broad, spreading tepals more or less as long as the tube, stamens suberect, inserted in the wide, open throat, slightly shorter than the tepals, style erect, as long as the perianth, stigma capitate. Flowering March–April, after fire. Lower sandstone slopes, SW (Bredasdorp).

Cyrtanthus elatus (Colin Paterson-Jones)

Cyrtanthus fergusoniae

Cyrtanthus flammosus (Colin Paterson-Jones)

Cyrtanthus guthrieae (Colin Paterson-Jones)

Cyrtanthus labiatus (Colin Paterson-Jones)

Cyrtanthus leptosiphon (Colin Paterson-Jones)

Cyrtanthus inaequalis O'Brien

Plants to 30 cm high. Leaves two or three, green at flowering, suberect, linear, 3–5 mm wide, channeled, midrib slightly thickened. Flowers four to nine, suberect to spreading, bright coral red, 5–8.5 cm long with bilabiate tepals, tube expanding evenly from the base, tepals a third as long as the tube, the three upper hooded, the two lateral spreading and the lower decurved, three upper stamens arched against the upper lip, the three lower spreading, style slightly shorter than the perianth, arched against the upper lip, stigma minutely tricuspidate. Flowering January. Rocky slopes in gravelly soil, KM, LB, SE (Barrydale, Ladismith, George).

Cyrtanthus labiatus R. A. Dyer

Plants to 30 cm high, forming bulblets. Leaves four to seven, green at flowering, spreading, strap-shaped, 1–2 cm wide, almost plane, without a prominent midrib, grayish green. Flowers about eight, suberect, coral red, often with a greenish tube, 5.5–6 cm long, tubular with distinctly bilabiate, strongly ribbed tepals, tube widening slightly toward the throat, distinctly longer than the tepals, four upper tepals overlapping and forming a hood, the two lower spreading downward, stamens inserted in the throat, the four upper arcuate, the two lower spreading-deflexed, style arched against the upper tepals, then strongly decurved toward the lower tepal, stigma subcapitate. Sandstone cliff faces, SE (Kouga and Baviaanskloof Mountains).

Cyrtanthus leptosiphon Snijman

Plants 20–30 cm high; bulbs clumped. Leaves one to five, usually dry at flowering, suberect, linear, c. 2 mm wide, twisted once or twice, shallowly channeled. Flowers solitary, sometimes as many as four, erect, cream with pink to peach on the tube and tepal keels, 6–9 cm long, tubular with weakly bilabiate tepals, tube widening gradually to the throat, spreading into three upper and three lower tepals, stamens incurved, the outer inserted in the throat, the inner on the tepals, style slightly shorter than the perianth, arched against the uppermost tepal, stigma minutely three-lobed. Flowering February–March. Gravelly loamy soils, LB (Swellendam).

Cyrtanthus leucanthus Schlechter

Plants to 30 cm high. Leaves one or two, usually dry at flowering, erect, linear, 1–2 mm wide. Flowers one to four, suberect, cream to white, sweetly scented, 5–7 cm long, tubular with broad, spreading tepals, stamens short, the outer inserted in the narrow throat, the inner on the tepals, style somewhat shorter than the perianth, slightly curved, stigma three-branched. Flowering January–March. Sandstone or limestone slopes or flats, SW, AP (Betty's Bay to Potberg).

Cyrtanthus loddigesianus (Herbert) R. A. Dyer

Plants 8–30 cm high. Leaves one to three, sometimes dry at flowering, spreading, narrowly strap-shaped, 2–8 mm wide. Flowers one to five, suberect, cream with yellow to green or rarely reddish midribs, 3.5–7 cm long, funnel-shaped with widely spreading tepals, stamens inserted in the flared upper part of tube, the outer lower than the inner, short and incurved, style slightly longer than the tube, curved against the lower tepal, stigma three-branched. Flowering October–March, after rain. Grassy fynbos or grassland in coastal sands, SE (Humansdorp to Eastern Cape).

Cyrtanthus montanus R. A. Dyer

Plants to 25 cm high, producing bulblets. Leaves three to five, green at flowering, recurved, strap-shaped, 1–2 cm wide. Flowers 5–10, erect, coral red, 5–6 cm long, widely funnel-shaped with widely spreading tepals, tube slightly shorter than the tepals, stamens prominent and spreading, the outer inserted in the wide, open throat, the inner on the tepals, style straight, exceeding the stamens, stigma subcapitate. Flowering January–March. In rock crevices on upper slopes, SE (Baviaanskloof Mountains).

Cyrtanthus obliquus (Linnaeus fil.) Aiton

Robust plants to 35 cm high; bulbs clumped. Leaves about six, green at flowering, suberect, strap-shaped, 3–6 cm broad, twisted toward the apex, pale green. Flowers 6–12, nodding, fleshy, yellow to orange with green tips, 7–8.5 cm long, narrowly funnel-shaped with a relatively wide throat and slightly spreading, overlapping tepals, tube longer than the tepals, stamens inserted about half-

Cyrtanthus leucanthus (Colin Paterson-Jones)

Cyrtanthus loddigesianus (Colin Paterson-Jones)

Cyrtanthus obliquus (Dee Snijman)

Cyrtanthus odorus (Colin Paterson-Jones)

way down the tube, curved slightly to one side, style and stamens slightly shorter than the perianth, stigma minutely trifid. Flowering August–February. Grassland and grassy fynbos, SE (Knysna to KwaZulu-Natal).

Cyrtanthus ochroleucus (Herbert) Burchell ex Steudel
Plants to 35 cm high. Leaves dry at flowering, linear, 1–2 mm wide. Flowers two to four, suberect, cream to yellow, tinged with pink or green, with a dull, bittersweet scent, 4–5.5 cm long, tubular with narrow, spreading tepals, the outer stamens short, inserted slightly below the throat, the inner longer, inserted in the narrow throat, style slightly shorter than the perianth, curved against the upper tepals, stigma shortly trifid. Flowering November–February. Dry, sandy or stony middle slopes or flats, AP, LB (Albertinia coastal plain and Langeberg Mountains).

Cyrtanthus odorus Ker Gawler
Plants to 30 cm high. Leaves two or three, dry or green at flowering, suberect, linear, 2.5–3.5 mm wide, slightly channeled. Flowers one to five, suberect, dark red, narcissus scented, 5–6 cm long, tubular with narrow, spreading tepals, stamens short, the outer inserted just below the throat, the inner slightly longer and inserted in the narrow throat, style somewhat shorter than the perianth, stigma three-branched. Flowering February–April, after fire. Lower to middle slopes, LB (Langeberg Mountains near Swellendam).

Cyrtanthus spiralis Burchell ex Ker Gawler
Plants to 30 cm high. Leaves two or three, usually dry at flowering, suberect, strap-shaped, c. 1 cm wide, spirally twisted, firm, grayish green. Flowers three to seven, nodding, firm, flame red, flecked with gold, 4–7 cm long, narrowly trumpet-shaped with widely spreading tepals, tube dilated from near the base, the tepal sinuses thickened, stamens short, the outer inserted slightly below the throat, the inner inserted in the relatively wide throat, style about as long as the perianth, stigma three-branched. Flowering December–February. Flats and lower slopes in semiarid habitats, SE (Uitenhage to Port Elizabeth).

Cyrtanthus staadensis Schönland

Plants to 40 cm high. Leaves two to five, green at flowering, spreading, linear, c. 2 mm wide, slightly channeled. Flowers two to six, spreading to nodding, bright to medium red, 3.5–5 cm long, narrowly trumpet-shaped with slightly spreading, oblong tepals, tube narrow and curved at the base, becoming inflated and urn-shaped above, stamens short, incurved, inserted just below the relatively wide throat, style slightly exserted from the throat, stigma three-branched. Flowering February–March. Grassy fynbos on moist slopes, SE (Port Elizabeth to Eastern Cape).

Cyrtanthus ventricosus (Jacquin) Willdenow

Plants 10–25 cm high. Leaves one to five, dry at flowering, spreading, linear, 2–7 mm wide, channeled, without a keel. Flowers 2–10, nodding, bright shiny red, often with shell pink tepals, 4–5 cm long, tubular to narrowly trumpet-shaped with spreading tepals, stamens long, inserted in the lower third of the tube, arched downward from the uppermost tepal, style arched downward from the upper tepal, exceeding the stamens, stigma undivided. Flowering December–May, after fire. South-facing sandstone slopes in fynbos, SW, AP, SE (Cape Peninsula to Baviaanskloof Mountains).

Cyrtanthus ventricosus (Colin Paterson-Jones)

Cyrtanthus wellandii Snijman

Plants 20–40 cm high. Leaves two or three, green or dry at flowering, suberect, linear, c. 3 mm wide. Flowers four to seven, small, spreading, light to bright red, 3.5–4 cm long, funnel-shaped with outspread tepals, stamens short, incurved, inserted about halfway up the flared part of the tube, the outer slightly lower than the inner, style included in the tube below the stamens, stigma broadly three-lobed. Flowering February. Stony slopes in grassy renosterveld, SE (Humansdorp).

***Cyrtanthus* sp. 1**

Plants to 50 cm high. Leaf single, sometimes two, usually dry at flowering, suberect, c. 7 mm wide, V-shaped and keeled. Flowers two or three, spreading, peach to salmon with scarlet nectar guides leading into tube from the tepal sinuses, c. 7.5 cm long, widely funnel-shaped with

Cyrtanthus wellandii (Colin Paterson-Jones)

slightly spreading tepals, stamens shorter than the tepals, inserted in the throat, slightly declinate, style exceeding the stamens, curved against the lower tepal, stigma three-branched. Flowering March. Rocky south-facing slopes in fynbos, SE (Baviaanskloof Mountains, Humansdorp).

Daubenya

COMMON NAME pincushion lily, FAMILY Hyacinthaceae. Deciduous perennials. ROOTSTOCK a globose bulb with dark brown, leathery outer tunics extended as a neck of narrow, papery strips. LEAVES two, prostrate, oblong to broadly elliptical, leathery, the veins depressed, hairless. INFLORESCENCE a condensed or corymbose raceme; bracts small or the lower large, green or membranous. FLOWERS tubular, the tepals united at the base into a long, often delicate tube, usually suberect, the lower or outer flowers sometimes more or less zygomorphic, white, yellow, or red, scented or unscented. STAMENS with firm filaments, free or united into a shallow cup or elongate tube inserted at the mouth of the perianth tube, rarely the mouth of the staminal tube occluded by a disk. OVARY ovoid or obtriangular with several ovules per locule; STYLE much longer than the ovary, slender, the stigma minute. FRUIT a papery capsule, ovoid, loculicidal or tardily dehiscent, style sometimes persistent. SEEDS several per locule, subglobose, black, smooth or finely wrinkled. Basic chromosome numbers x = 17, 16. Almost restricted to the winter-rainfall region of South Africa, Northern and Western Cape Provinces; 8 spp., 6 in the Cape.

Originally described to accommodate a single species, *Daubenya aurea*, the genus *Daubenya* is now considered as comprising eight species of plants with two spreading leaves and white to yellow or red tubular flowers borne in a condensed or subcorymbose raceme and producing papery capsules containing globose, smooth, glossy seeds. These species were previously accommodated in several genera, often with a single species, described specifically to accommodate their rather bizarre flowers. DNA sequence studies have revealed that they are, in fact, closely related to one another. Their floral differences are now understood as representing specializations for different pollinators. Typically occurring on stony clay or dolerite flats, most of the species are restricted in distribution, sometimes severely so. Species such as *D. stylosa* have a poor seed dispersal mechanism in which the ovoid capsules remain at or just below ground level with little active dispersal of the seeds. This is in sharp contrast to *D. capensis*, which, like the species of *Massonia* is beautifully adapted for wind dispersal of its seeds. The peduncles and pedicels elongate during fruiting to lift the winged fruits and their sail-like bracts above the ground, effectively exposing the balloon-like infructescence to the wind.

The pollination biology of the species is diverse. Some species are generalists and their pleasantly fragrant flowers are visited by honeybees, also butterflies. Two unscented species, however, show striking adaptations for very different pollinators. *Daubenya zeyheri* is visited by sunbirds attracted to the copious nectar held in the purple cup formed at the base of the orange filaments, which causes the nectar to glisten blackish purple. *Daubenya aurea* attracts monkey beetles (Scarabaeidae: Hopliini), which are typically drawn to the flat platforms of daisies, by imitating the ray florets of the daisies most convincingly through an enlargement of the outer tepals in the peripheral flowers.

With their brightly colored and sometimes flamboyantly shaped flowers, all species of *Daubenya* are worth cultivating. Already grown in England by 1835, *Daubenya aurea* is undoubtedly the best known, but both *D. capensis* and *D. zeyheri* deserve equal attention. Like *Massonia*, the species are easily cultivated in pots. Several of the species flower in the winter and should be potted somewhat earlier than usual for Cape bulbs, in August or September in the northern Hemisphere.

FURTHER READING. The circumscription of *Daubenya* was radically altered by Goldblatt and Manning (2000a) to include several other species and monotypic genera. The earlier revisions of *Daubenya* and allied genera by Jessop (1976) and U. and D. Müller-Doblies (1997), especially the latter, are still useful at the species level, notwithstanding their outdated concepts of genera. Fully illustrated accounts of some of the species are available separately (Phillips 1922a, b, Brandham 1989, 1990), the latter two with detailed notes on cultivation in the Northern Hemisphere.

Daubenya alba A. M. van der Merwe
Plants to 5 cm high. Leaves striate, to 10 × 5 cm. Flowers white with lilac stamens, the mouth of the staminal tube sometimes pale yellow, tube 10–15 × 1.5 mm, tepals linear, 6–13 mm long, filaments 10–20 mm long, united below into a tube 7–10 mm long, style 20–27 mm long; bracts membranous, lanceolate, the lower 3–4 mm long. Flowering May. Doleritic clay, RV (western Karoo).

Daubenya aurea Lindley
Plants to 5 cm high. Leaves striate, the margins sometimes crisped, 5–14 × 2–6 cm. Flowers red or yellow, unscented, the lower zygomorphic with the lower tepals much enlarged and oblanceolate, tube 20–30 × 1.5–2 mm, tepals mostly 3–6 mm long and oblong but the lower flowers with the lower tepals 20–30 mm long, filaments 3–10 mm long, united below as much as 3 mm or the outer free in the lower flowers, style c. 25 mm long; bracts oblong to obovate, membranous, the lower 15–30 mm long. Capsule ovoid. Flowering September. Dolerite clay flats, RV (western Karoo near Middelpos).

Daubenya capensis (Schlechter) A. M. van der Merwe & J. C. Manning
Plants to 5 cm high. Leaves striate, sometimes spotted darker green, to 15 × 9 cm. Flowers yellow with the disk at the mouth of the staminal tube red, yeast scented, tube 6–11 × 1.5–2 mm, tepals narrowly oblong, 11–13 mm long, filaments 25 mm long, united below into a tube 11 mm long with a disk at the mouth, style 20–25 mm long; bracts membranous, lanceolate, the lower 25–30 mm long. Capsule obtriangular, three-winged. Flowering June–September. Doleritic clay, NW (Bokkeveld Escarpment near Nieuwoudtville). Page 126.

Daubenya marginata (Willdenow ex Kunth) J. C. Manning & A. M. van der Merwe
Plants to 8 cm high. Leaves striate, the margins sometimes finely crisped, 4–8 × 1.5–4 cm. Flowers yellow with yellow to orange filaments, unscented, tube 10–20

Daubenya aurea; see also page 24

Daubenya aurea

Daubenya capensis

× 2–3 mm, tepals ovate-oblong, 6–8 mm long, filaments 10–20 mm long, united below as much as 2 mm, style 11–20 mm long; bracts membranous, triangular to ovate, the lower 2–5 mm long, the uppermost forming a conspicuous coma above the flowers. Capsule ovoid and shortly beaked. Flowering May–August. Clay flats, RV, NW (Knersvlakte and western Karoo).

Daubenya stylosa (W. F. Barker) A. M. van der Merwe & J. C. Manning

Plants to 5 cm high. Leaves striate, 8–20 × 1.5–4 cm. Flowers subsessile, greenish yellow, honey scented, tube 3–10 × 1.5–2 mm, tepals united into a narrow tube 10–20 mm long with lobes c. 2 mm long, filaments c. 25 mm long, united below into a tube 11–15 mm long, style 20–30 mm long; bracts membranous, to 10 mm long. Capsule compressed-ovoid, attenuate-beaked, tardily dehiscent from below. Flowering May–June. Clay soils, NW (Bokkeveld Escarpment near Nieuwoudtville).

Daubenya stylosa

Daubenya zeyheri

Daubenya zeyheri (Kunth) J. C. Manning & A. M. van der Merwe

Plants to 10 cm high. Leaves striate, the margins sometimes finely crisped, 4–15 × 1.5–6 cm. Flowers whitish with reddish filaments that are purple at the base, unscented, tube of lower flowers 15–20 × 1.5–2 mm, tepals ovate-oblong, 5–9 mm long, filaments 12–19 mm long, united below as much as 1 mm, style 15–30 mm long; bracts membranous, triangular to ovate, the lower 2–5 mm long. Capsule ovoid and shortly beaked. Flowering May–June. Calcareous coastal sands, SW (Paternoster to Saldanha).

Devia

COMMON NAME devia, FAMILY Iridaceae. More or less evergreen perennial. ROOTSTOCK a depressed-globose corm, rooting from the base, basal in origin, with tunics of coarse fibers accumulating in a dense mass around the stem base. LEAVES several, the lower two or three forming cataphylls, foliage leaves unifacial with a definite midrib, mostly basal, linear, oval in cross section, midrib and a second pair of veins on either side heavily thickened, leaves thus with two narrow longitudinal grooves on each surface, margins unthickened, edged by narrow grooves, dry or becoming dry at flowering time, cauline leaves few and reduced; stem branched, sheathed below by a thick, coarsely fibrous neck. INFLORESCENCE a secund spike; bracts leathery, dry at flowering, the inner about as long as outer and notched apically. FLOWERS actinomorphic with nectar from septal nectaries; perianth tube narrowly funnel-shaped; tepals subequal. STAMENS symmetrically disposed, rotated counterclockwise; anthers lying opposite the inner tepals in the open flower, facing inward. STYLE eccentric, the branches short, notched apically. FRUIT a globose cartilaginous capsule, lightly warty above. SEEDS globose, flattened at the chalazal end, hard and shiny, one or two per locule, smooth, with an excluded raphal vascular trace. Basic chromosome number $x = 10$. A narrow endemic of the Roggeveld Escarpment in the western Karoo and found on stony clay soils in mountain renosterveld, and unusual in flowering in early summer in this area of low, predominantly winter rainfall; 1 sp.

Devia is distinctive in its longitudinally grooved, narrow leaves, pink perianth, and rotated stamens. It is perhaps most closely allied to *Crocosmia*, and its internal leaf anatomy and capsule and seed characteristics are consistent with that genus and its allies: *Chasmanthe*, *Sparaxis*, and *Tritonia*. The inconspicuous flowers are visited and presumably pollinated by various long-proboscid flies of the family Bombyliidae and long-tongued solitary bees of the family Apidae (Anthophorinae).

Devia is no more than a curiosity in horticulture, a plant for the dedicated bulb enthusiast. It does not seem to thrive in cultivation. Plants grow moderately well in pots or raised beds, but flower poorly if at all. Perhaps this is a case in which one should try to mimic the natural conditions, namely, a stony clay soil, bitterly cold winters, and searing, dry summers.

FURTHER READING. Fully illustrated accounts of *Devia* have been provided by Goldblatt and Manning (1990) and Goldblatt (1999).

Devia xeromorpha Goldblatt & J. C. Manning

Plants 50–70 cm high; corms globose with tunics of coarsely netted fibers forming a neck around the base. Leaves linear, oval in cross section with eight fine longi-

Devia xeromorpha

tudinal grooves, tough and fibrotic. Flowers in short spikes, dusty pink, perianth tube narrowly funnel-shaped, c. 9 mm long, tepals c. 6 mm long., stamens twisted and rotated counterclockwise, lying opposite the inner tepals in the open flower. Flowering November–December. Rocky slopes in mountain renosterveld, RV (Roggeveld Escarpment).

Dierama

COMMON NAME hairbell, FAMILY Iridaceae. Evergreen perennials, sometimes growing in clumps. ROOTSTOCK a depressed-globose corm rooting from below, those of past seasons often not fully resorbed, basal in origin, with coarsely fibrous tunics, often accumulating in a dense mass. LEAVES several, the lower two or three forming cataphylls, these often dry and becoming fibrous, foliage leaves unifacial, often without a definite midrib in mature plants, plane, linear, leathery and fibrotic; stem terete, thin and wiry, usually with several branches, often drooping above, sometimes erect, subtending bracts dry and thread-like. INFLORESCENCE a spike, the axes wiry to thread-like, usually drooping, occasionally erect; bracts dry, usually papery, crinkled, and translucent, occasionally solid, becoming lacerate above and usually streaked or flecked with brown, sometimes caudate, inner bracts smaller than the outer and forked apically. FLOWERS actinomorphic and bell-shaped, usually nodding, often shades of pink to mauve, also red, purple, yellow, or white, usually with small markings near the tepal bases, unscented, with nectar from septal nectaries; perianth tube funnel-shaped, fairly short; tepals subequal, cupped and often enclosing the stamens and style. STAMENS symmetrically disposed and central; anthers exserted from the tube, sometimes barely so. STYLE exserted from the tube, seldom from the perianth, branches short, slender, slightly expanded above and recurved. CAPSULES globose, cartilaginous. SEEDS globose or lightly angled, flattened at the chalazal end, smooth, hard, often shiny, surface smooth with the raphal vascular trace excluded. Basic chromosome number $x = 10$. Sub-Saharan Africa, extending from Knysna in the southern Cape to Ethiopia, centered in eastern southern Africa, and there summer growing and both coastal and montane; 44 spp., 1 in the Cape.

Dierama is mainly a genus of the southern African summer-rainfall region with only a single species extending into the Cape Floral Region. It is closely allied to the genus *Ixia*, which is restricted to the winter-rainfall region of South Africa. *Dierama* is recognizable by the wiry, usually drooping spikes, pendent actinomorphic flowers, and dry, either solid or scarious floral bracts, generally pale with brown streaks and veins. The fairly large flowers are usually bell-shaped and have a very graceful appearance. The flowers are pollinated by bees.

All the species of *Dierama* are worth cultivating. Most are summer growing; *D. pendulum* is the only winter-growing species. This pink-flowered species has stems as long as c. 1 m and the large, bell-like flowers for which the genus is known. In the wild, it grows on stony lower slopes on loamy clay soils and does well in cultivation. It

Dierama pendulum

was the first species of *Dierama* to be discovered and named. Because of the difficulties in distinguishing the species, the name *D. pendulum* has been applied indiscriminately to most species until relatively recently. There is thus every chance that plants sold as *D. pendulum* may not be that species. Only when plants flower will any errors in identification become evident.

FURTHER READING. A detailed, beautifully illustrated monograph of *Dierama* has been provided by Hilliard et al. (1991).

Dierama pendulum (Linnaeus fil.) Baker

Plants 70–110 cm high; corm depressed-globose, enclosed in a mass of fibrous tunics, stem slender and wiry, laxly branched. Leaves linear, fibrotic, mostly 4–6 mm wide. Flowers nodding in drooping spikes, pink, perianth tube 8–12 mm long, tepals mostly 24–30 mm long. Flowering mainly October–December. Rocky, loamy clay or sandstone slopes and flats, SE (Knysna to Grahamstown).

Dietes

COMMON NAMES dietes, wood iris, FAMILY Iridaceae. Evergreen perennials. ROOTSTOCK a thick, creeping rhizome, persisting for several years. LEAVES several, unifacial, sword-shaped to lanceolate, in two ranks, leathery, without a midrib, veins along the leaf center sometimes crowded together; stem usually erect, bearing leaves at the lower nodes, persisting for more than one season, with sheathing leaves at the upper nodes; branching irregularly in the upper half or forming a divaricately branched pseudopanicle. INFLORESCENCE a rhipidium; spathes leathery, tightly sheathing, outer spathe smaller than the inner. FLOWERS usually fugacious or lasting as long as 3 days in 1 sp., several per rhipidium, pedicellate, the pedicels pubescent above; actinomorphic, *Iris*-like, shades of white to yellow, style branches sometimes violet, limbs of outer tepals bearing contrasting markings near their bases, unscented, without nectar; tepals free, broadly clawed, the claws ascending, limbs spreading, outer tepals larger than the inner, with pubescent claws. STAMENS usually free, flattened and broader below, the filaments occasionally united below in 1 sp.; anthers linear, appressed to the style branches. STYLE dividing shortly above the base into three broad petaloid branches opposed to the outer tepals, each branch terminating in a pair of erect petaloid appendages (crests); stigmas transverse, abaxial, below the base of the crests. FRUIT an oblong to broadly ovoid or nearly hemispherical capsule, apex truncate, cartilaginous to woody, irregularly rugose or smooth, tardily dehiscent or indehiscent. SEEDS irregularly angled, fairly large, with a chalazal crest. Basic chromosome number $x = 10$. Southern and East Africa, and Lord Howe Island, Australasia; 6 spp., 1 in the winter-rainfall zone of South Africa, in forest and scrub.

Dietes is closely related to the Northern Hemisphere *Iris* and differs from it largely in having flowers without a perianth tube and with the inner tepal limbs spreading rather than erect. The geographic disjunction in the genus between Africa and Lord Howe Island, in the Pacific Ocean northeast of Sydney, Australia, is remarkable. The Lord Howe Island species, *D. robinsoniana* (F. Mueller) Klatt, is closely allied to *D. bicolor* from the Eastern Cape, South Africa, which is probably the most primitive in the genus. All the species grow in partly shaded habitats, often in forest margins or on the forest floor. *Dietes bicolor* is most often found on the banks of perennial streams or rivers.

The flowers of *Dietes* are probably pollinated mainly by bees. In most species they are short-lived and last less than a day, but they last 3 days in *D. grandiflora* N. E. Brown from the Eastern Cape. *Dietes iridioides*, the only species to enter into the Cape Floral Region, has the widest range of any in the genus, extending from near the town of Villiersdorp, near Cape Town, to the evergreen forests of East Africa and Ethiopia. Only plants from the Cape flower in late spring and early summer, but there is otherwise little difference in populations from the different ends of the range. Unlike its more glamorous relative, *D. grandiflora*, which has large, long-lasting flowers with brown markings on the tepals and violet style arms, *D. iridioides* is very plain with small, off-white flowers with pale violet style arms that last only a day. The two species are often confused in the literature, and the name *D. vegeta* has been misapplied to both in the past. *Dietes iridioides*

Dietes iridioides (Colin Paterson-Jones)

is best treated as a plant for shady sites and does best when watered both summer and winter. *Dietes grandiflora* is a favorite street planting for it tolerates only occasional watering and persists even when treated poorly. Plantings of that species make a fine display for 3–5 years, after which they become overcrowded and moribund. All species of *Dietes* can be grown from rhizomes. Seeds are often slow to germinate and may not reach flowering size for 3 years.

FURTHER READING. *Dietes* was thoroughly revised by Goldblatt (1981a).

Dietes iridioides (Linnaeus) Sweet ex Klatt

Plants evergreen, to 60 cm high; rhizome thick, creeping, stem irregularly branched. Leaves sword-shaped, in a close fan. Flowers in tight clusters enclosed by leathery spathes, white with violet style arms, lasting only a day. Flowering mainly August–December. Evergreen forest and forest margins, SW, LB, SE (Riviersonderend Mountains to Ethiopia).

Dilatris

COMMON NAME bloodroot, FAMILY Haemodoraceae. Evergreen perennials. ROOTSTOCK a short rhizome with bright red flesh. LEAVES several, unifacial, linear to sword-shaped, rigid, clasping below. INFLORESCENCE a rounded or flat-topped paniculate thyrse, the axis hairy or glandular hairy; bracts more or less dry and membranous, hairy. FLOWERS actinomorphic, star- or cup-shaped, the tepals free, gland-dotted at the tips, hairy or glandular hairy on the outer surface, mauve or yellow to orange, unscented or lightly scented. STAMENS three, inserted at the base of the inner tepals, filaments slender, unequal, one stamen shorter and erect with a larger, yellow anther, the remaining two more or less spreading, with smaller, reddish anthers. OVARY inferior, ovoid, with one ovule per locule, hairy; STYLE slender, bent sideways (left or right in any single flower). FRUIT either a glandular-hairy, three-locular septicidal capsule or a hairy, septifragal capsule with only one locule maturing and topped by the persistent papery perianth. SEEDS one per locule, depressed spherical, shield-shaped. Basic chromosome numbers $x = 21–19$. South Africa; 4 spp.

Dilatris is endemic to the Cape Floral Region with most species restricted to the southwestern portion of the Cape Fold Mountains from near Tulbagh to Kogelberg. Most common on rocky sandstone slopes, the species all flower best after a fire. The genus is dominated by mauve-flowered species that are superficially similar to one another although they are readily distinguished by details of the stamens. In sharp contrast, *D. viscosa* is distinctive in its reddish glandular stems and yellow flowers that nod in bud. It is also unusual in the genus for its fruit. In the mauve-flowered species only one locule, containing a single seed, typically matures, the remaining two locules usually aborting. At maturity, the single-seeded fertile segment breaks free from the remaining locules. The flattened seed is tightly clasped within the locule, which also has the papery perianth attached. This acts as a parachute to aid in wind dispersal. In *D. viscosa*, however, all three locules of the fruit invariably mature, and the capsules, which remain attached to the axis, split septicidally from above to expose one flat, disk-like seed in each ovule. These seeds are free to be shaken out of the capsule and dispersed individually by the wind.

The phenomenon of enantiomorphy, or the presence of left- and right-handed flowers (expressed in *Dilatris* in the direction in which the style is flexed), is typical of all genera of the family Haemodoraceae. In *Dilatris*, however, individual flowers are alternately right- or left-handed along each branch of the inflorescence whereas in other genera all the flowers on a plant are of one type. It is likely that the flowers are visited by pollen-collecting bees, but monkey beetles (Scarabaeidae: Hopliini) have been seen on *D. pillansii*. The dimorphic stamens represent a sophisticated pollination strategy in which the large, yellow anther is clearly offered as a pollen source to the visiting insect and its pollen sacrificed. The inconspicuous smaller anthers, however, escape the visitor's attention and deposit pollen onto its body, from where it is picked up by the style of the next flower to be visited.

Species of *Dilatris* can be grown in large pots but are best suited for the rock garden. All the species are attractive and free-flowering. Plants should be left undisturbed to form large clumps, which will produce numerous inflorescences each season. They thrive on liberal watering throughout the year, provided that they are grown in an acidic, sandy mix, but will tolerate some summer drought.

FURTHER READING. The revision of *Dilatris* by Barker (1940) remains current apart from a single species that is no longer recognized (Goldblatt and Manning 2000a).

Dilatris corymbosa P. J. Bergius

Plants 40–60 cm high, stem whitish hairy. Leaves linear-oblong, 5–6 mm wide. Flowers in a flat-topped cluster, erect in bud, mauve, tepals lanceolate, densely hairy, to 13 × 6 mm, long stamens 12–13 mm long with anthers 1 mm long, short stamen 8–9 mm long with anther 2.5 mm long. Capsule topped with the conspicuous papery perianth, fragmenting to release the fertile locule. Flowering August–January. Damp sandy slopes and flats, NW, SW (Tulbagh to Hottentots Holland Mountains).

Dilatris ixioides Lamarck

Plants 20–40 cm high, stem whitish hairy. Leaves linear-oblong, 2–4 mm wide. Flowers in a flat-topped cluster, erect in bud, mauve, tepals ovate-cucullate, sparsely hairy, 7–10 × 3–4 mm, long stamens 15–16 mm long with anthers 1 mm long, short stamen 10–11 mm long with anther 3–4 mm long. Capsule topped with the conspicuous papery perianth, fragmenting to release the fertile locule. Flowering September–February. Rocky sandstone slopes, NW, SW, LB, SE (Bokkeveld Mountains to George).

Dilatris corymbosa

Dilatris corymbosa

Dilatris ixioides

Dilatris pillansii

Dilatris pillansii W. F. Barker
Plants 20–45 cm high, stem whitish hairy. Leaves linear-oblong, 3–5 mm wide. Flowers in a rounded cluster, erect in bud, mauve, tepals ovate-cucullate, hairy, to 10 × 6 mm, long stamens 5–6 mm long with anthers 1.25 mm long, short stamen 3–4 mm long with anther 2 mm long. Capsule topped with the conspicuous papery perianth, fragmenting to release the fertile locule. Flowering August–January. Rocky sandstone slopes, NW, SW, AP, LB (Cedarberg Mountains to Agulhas).

Dilatris viscosa Linnaeus fil.
Plants 45–60 cm high, stem orange to reddish glandular hairy. Leaves sword-shaped, to 17 mm wide. Flowers in a flat-topped cluster, nodding in bud, dull orange or yellow, tepals linear-oblanceolate, glandular hairy, 10–13 × 2.5 mm, long stamens 12–14 mm long with anthers 1–1.5 mm long, short stamen 8–10 mm long with anther 2–2.5 mm long. Capsule septicidal, topped with scanty perianth remains. Flowering August–December. Marshy places on sandstone slopes and plateaus, NW, SW, LB (Ceres to Cape Peninsula to Langeberg Mountains).

Dilatris viscosa

Dipcadi

COMMON NAME snakeroot, FAMILY Hyacinthaceae. Deciduous perennials. ROOTSTOCK an ovoid bulb with pale, papery or thinly leathery outer tunics lightly barred above and sometimes extending as a short neck. LEAVES rarely dry at flowering, one to several, linear to lanceolate, sometimes spirally twisted, hairless or hairy under, the margins usually straight but rarely undulate or sometimes almost crisped, usually hairless but rarely margins minutely hairy, papillate or thickened. INFLORESCENCE a few- to many-flowered raceme, drooping in bud, often secund, the peduncle rarely papillate, the pedicels elongating more or less in fruit; bracts pale and soft, ovate to attenuate, persistent or caducous. FLOWERS nodding but becoming erect in fruit, tubular or trumpet-shaped, the tepals united below as much as two-thirds but shortly connivent above the tube and then more or less recurved, the outer tepals sometimes with a more or less tail-like apical appendage, the inner tepals usually erect above and recurved only at the tips, the tepals in at least some species recurving more prominently at night, greenish or brownish, scented at night. STAMENS with linear filaments, fragile and membranous, inserted at the top of the tube, short or longer but closely appressed to the tepals and the anthers appearing sessile or subsessile, included, the connective rarely produced into a short appendage above. OVARY ovoid to cylindrical or top-shaped, rarely with three apical knobs, with several ovules per locule; STYLE short to as long as the ovary, sometimes papillate, the stigma three-lobed, shorter than the stamens and included in the flower. FRUIT a three-lobed oblong or top-shaped capsule, truncate or retuse, or rarely umbonate above. SEEDS several per locule, discoid, transversely packed tightly on top of one another, black. Basic chromosome numbers $x = 9, 6, 4$. Africa, Mediterranean, and India; c. 30 spp., 4 in the Cape.

Concentrated in the more arid parts of southern Africa, the relatively unassuming species of *Dipcadi* are widespread across the interior of the subcontinent. The genus is largely adapted to a summer-rainfall climate with only two species confined to the winter-rainfall region of southern Africa. Plants typically occur on dry shales and rocky slopes but some may grow on sand or favor damper sites. Their dull flowers are often difficult to locate against the earth, and their main interest horticulturally lies in their unusual appearance and nocturnal fragrance. Some of the species are known to be more or less toxic, at least at certain times of the year, but others are apparently edible and form part of the traditional diet of country people in Africa and India. The disk-like seeds stacked horizontally in the capsules recall those of *Albuca, Galtonia,* and *Pseudogaltonia*.

The dull-colored, tubular flowers, with included anthers, become fragrant at night and are clearly adapted to pollination by moths. The tepals usually roll back more prominently in the evening. Although the particular scent of most species is unrecorded, in *G. brevifolium* and *G. viride* it is unpleasant and very acrid, rendering an unobtrusive plant almost repellent. The species are seldom cultivated, but the curly leaves of *D. crispum* are not without interest if the plants are grown in pots or rock gardens. Plants are easily propagated by seed.

FURTHER READING. The South African species of *Dipcadi* were revised by Obermeyer (1963).

Dipcadi brevifolium (Thunberg) Fourcade

Plants 20–40 cm high. Leaves dry or present at flowering, two to four, linear to filiform or channeled, straight or coiled. Inflorescence secund, flowers brown, green or

Dipcadi brevifolium

cream, acridly scented at night, 12–20 mm long, tepals united in the lower half, subacute or obtuse, the outer recurved, the inner erect and forming a tube above with the tips recurved. Flowering August–April. Stony flats or slopes, RV, NW, SW, AP, KM, SE (Namaqualand and western Karoo to Eastern Cape).

Dipcadi ciliare (Zeyher ex Harvey) Baker

Plants to 40 cm high. Leaves usually present at flowering, about six, linear and channeled, often coiled, roughly hairy beneath, margins hairy and usually crisped or undulate. Inflorescence secund, flowers brown, green, or cream, 16–28 mm long, tepals united in the lower third, acute to attenuate, recurved. Flowering November–May. Stony flats or slopes, KM, SE (Oudtshoorn to Port Elizabeth, Karoo to northern provinces).

Dipcadi crispum Baker

Plants to 30 cm high. Leaves about four, usually coiled and clasping below, linear to narrowly lanceolate, gray, usually softly hairy beneath, the margins usually crisped and hairy; the peduncle also sometimes hairy. Inflorescence secund, flowers brown to gray-green, 15–20 mm long, tepals united in the lower half, acuminate to attenuate, the outer slightly longer, with short, caudate appendages 1–4 mm long, recurved above, the inner erect and forming a tube above with the tips recurved. Flowering mostly April–June. Stony flats or slopes, RV, NW (southern Namibia, Namaqualand, and western Karoo to Clanwilliam).

Dipcadi viride (Linnaeus) Moench

Plants 15–120 cm high. Leaves usually present at flowering, one to four, long, erect, linear to narrowly lanceolate, channeled. Inflorescence secund, flowers green to brown, 12–15 mm long (excluding appendages), acridly scented at night, tepals united in the lower third, acuminate to aristate, the outer longer, with short to long, filiform appendages 2–30 mm long, which are progressively longer on the upper flowers, recurved above, the inner erect and forming a tube above with the tips recurved. Flowering September–February. Stony grassland, KM, LB, SE (Ladismith and Riversdale to Port Elizabeth, widespread in eastern southern Africa and northern Namibia to Ethiopia).

Drimia

COMMON NAMES poison squill, tallboy, FAMILY Hyacinthaceae. Deciduous perennials. ROOTSTOCK a globose, often large bulb, subterranean or partially exposed, the scales often relatively small, sometimes only loosely overlapping, the flesh sometimes pink or reddish. LEAVES one to several, often dry at flowering, linear to oblanceolate or terete, hairless or rarely hairy or the margins hairy, erect to prostrate, the sheaths sometimes persistent and forming a papery or fibrous, sometimes horizontally barred, sheath around the base of the scape. INFLORES-

Dipcadi crispum

CENCE a single- to many-flowered raceme, sometimes subcorymbose with shortened axis, rarely branched, often wiry, hairless or minutely roughly hairy in the lower part, the hairs often in longitudinal rows; bracts usually small, membranous, at least the lower spurred. FLOWERS suberect, erect or nodding but erect in fruit, rarely the pedicel deflexed at the base and erect apically, usually star- or cup-shaped, the tepals erect, spreading or recurved to reflexed, more or less free or united below into a deep cup or short tube, white to yellowish green or brown, often with darker keels, short-lived, usually lasting less than a day, rarely 2 days, unscented or rarely scented, perianth abscising below and twisting above, forming a cap over the developing capsule. STAMENS with filaments joined to the base of the tepals, linear-lanceolate to ovate or vestigial, ascending to erect and connivent around the style at anthesis or inflexed over the ovary; the anthers dehiscing longitudinally or by apical pores or slits, sometimes shortly apiculate or barbed below. OVARY ovoid with several ovules per locule; STYLE cylindrical, erect or slightly declinate, shorter than to about as long as the perianth, stigma three-grooved or slightly excavated. FRUIT an ovoid or ellipsoidal capsule, sometimes three-lobed or three-winged. SEEDS several per chamber, angular to elliptical with a peripheral wing, black. Basic chromosome number x = 10 or 9. Africa, Mediterranean, and Asia; c. 100 spp., 29 in the Cape.

Traditionally divided with varying success into several smaller genera, *Drimia* is more rationally considered to include all the species with spurred bracts and short-lived flowers. The smaller groups of related species that have been identified as genera in the past, including *Drimia* in the narrow sense and *Litanthus, Rhadamanthus, Schizobasis,* and *Tenicroa,* appear to be derived from various ancestors in a poorly defined *Urginea.* In a broader and more natural circumscription, *Drimia* is well defined by the short-lived flowers in which the perianth abscises below and twists above to form a cap on top of the developing fruit. The peduncle is often wiry and minutely roughly hairy or scabrid below, and the tepals are free or more or less united at the base, sometimes for some distance. The flowers in most species last no more than a few hours with one to three blooms opening each day. In the larger species, many more flowers may open simultaneously and last for most of a day or, in some species of *Drimia* group *Drimia,* even 2 days.

Species of *Drimia* are typically found in seasonally dry or even semiarid regions, and many flower in the late spring or summer regardless of the rainfall pattern. In the species from the winter-rainfall zone of southern Africa, the leaves are usually produced during the wet winter season and are often dry and withered at flowering. Species diversity is highest in the semiarid parts of the winter-rainfall zone, and most of the highly specialized species, those traditionally segregated into several smaller genera (some with but a single species), occur along the edge of the Karoo and Namaqualand. The bulbs of some species contain cardiotoxic glycosides and are highly poisonous if ingested; they may even cause irritation to the skin through surface contact.

Most species with more open, white or silvery flowers are visited by long-tongued bees of the family Apidae (Anthophorinae) in search of pollen or nectar or both. The flowers are typically unscented, but species in the *Tenicroa* group are wonderfully fragrant and occasional species in the *Rhadamanthus* and *Urginea* groups are also scented, sometimes less pleasantly. Species that have anthers with poricidal dehiscence are buzz pollinated (described under *Cyanella*) by solitary bees, whereas a few night-flowering species such as *D. revoluta* are probably pollinated by moths.

Mainly a genus of horticultural curiosity, only the larger species of *Drimia,* in particular *D. capensis,* are of any real garden merit. Its tall, spike-like inflorescences are an extraordinary sight in summer as they tower to 2 m high in the scrub, and *D. capensis* is well worth growing in rock gardens. The small stature and dull, short-lived flowers of most other species limit their value to the gardener considerably, although the violet-like scent of species in the *Tenicroa* group is a great recommendation. Because of the often loose bulb scales, which are easily dislodged, it is best not to repot species of *Drimia* too frequently. Growing bulbs should be watered sparingly, and watering should be stopped at the beginning of the dormant period to force the plants into dormancy; otherwise the leaves will continue to grow.

Further Reading. The circumscription of the genus *Drimia* has been greatly expanded (Jessop 1977, Goldblatt and Manning 2000a) to include several smaller genera previously regarded as distinct. Although adequate revisions of some of the segregates exist (Nordenstam 1970, Obermeyer 1980a, b), the treatment of the majority of the genus (Jessop 1977) is flawed by its excessively broad species concepts. An additional species was described by Snijman et al. (1999).

Drimia albiflora (B. Nordenstam) J. C. Manning & Goldblatt
Plants 12–24 cm high, scape minutely hairy below. Leaves unknown. Flowers on wiry pedicels 3–9 mm long, bowl-shaped, nodding, white with brown keels, tepals c. 5.5 mm long, united below as much as 1.5 mm, filaments 0.3–0.5 mm long, anthers dehiscing longitudinally, c. 2.5 mm long, style c. 1.8 mm long. Flowering December. Mountain slopes, SW (Stormsvlei east of Caledon).

Drimia arenicola (B. Nordenstam) J. C. Manning & Goldblatt
Plants 10–15 cm high, scape smooth; bulb scales loosely overlapping. Leaves several, suberect, linear, c. 1 mm wide, with a barred sheath below. Flowers on pedicels 4–10 mm long, urn-shaped, nodding, whitish or light brown with brown keels, tepals 3.5–4 mm long, united below for c. 2 mm, filaments c. 1 mm long, anthers dehiscing apically, apiculate below, c. 1 mm long, style to 0.5 mm long. Capsule ovoid, 4–5 mm long; seeds oblong, c. 4 mm long. Flowering October–November. Sandy habitats, RV, NW (Namaqualand and western Karoo to Clanwilliam).

Drimia capensis (Burman fil.) Wijnands
Plants 1–2 m high; bulb large, subterranean or partially exposed. Leaves dry at flowering, suberect, oblong to lanceolate, slightly undulate, often grayish, 30–50 × 10 cm. Flowers irregularly clustered in an elongate raceme on

Drimia capensis in karroid scrub in the Hex River Valley

pedicels 2–5 mm long, white to yellowish with green keels, tepals 12–20 mm long, united below for 2–4 mm, filaments 8–12 mm long, anthers green, 3–8 mm long, style 8–12 mm long. Capsules oblong, three-lobed, 12–15 mm long; seeds ovate, 8–10 mm long. Flowering November–March. Mostly clay but also limestone or deep red sands, NW, SW, AP, KM, LB, SE (southern Namaqualand to Port Elizabeth).

Drimia ciliata (Linnaeus fil.) Baker

Plants 7–15 cm high, scape scabrid below. Leaves dry at flowering, three to five in a rosette, spreading, elliptical to oblanceolate, to 35 × 12 mm, leathery, margins hyaline-hairy. Flowers in lax racemes on wiry, spreading pedicels 10–20 mm long, nodding in bud, white, stellate, sweetly scented, opening late afternoon, tepals ovate, 4–6 mm long, united below for 0.5 mm, filaments c. 2 mm long, ascending, anthers c. 1 mm long, style c. 1.5 mm long. Capsules subglobose, c. 5 mm long; seeds angular, c. 2 mm long. Flowering December–February. Rock outcrops, AP, KM, LB, SE (De Hoop to Grahamstown).

Drimia convallarioides (Linnaeus fil.) J. C. Manning & Goldblatt

Plants 5–30 cm high, scape minutely hairy below. Leaves 3–25, suberect, subterete, 2–3 mm diam., often with a barred sheath below. Flowers on pedicels 2–20 mm long, urn-shaped, nodding, sometimes somewhat unilateral, pinkish to brownish, tepals 5–8 mm long, united below for 1–3 mm, filaments 1–2 mm long, anthers dehiscing apically, 1–2 mm long, style 1–2.5 mm long. Capsule subglobose, 4–7 mm long; seeds elliptical to obovate, 2–4 mm long. Flowering October–February. Sandy, seasonally moist rock pavement, RV, NW, SW, KM (Namaqualand and western Karoo to Jonkershoek Mountains and Little Karoo). Page 138.

Drimia dregei (Baker) J. C. Manning & Goldblatt

Plants 15–30 cm high. Leaf dry at flowering, solitary, erect, terete. Flowers crowded in slender racemes on pedicels to 5 mm long, mostly white with dark keels, opening during the day, tepals c. 4 mm long, united below for c. 1 mm, filaments c. 2 mm long, anthers c. 1 mm long,

Drimia capensis

Drimia ciliata

Drimia convallarioides

Drimia dregei

Drimia elata

Drimia exuviata

style c. 1.5 mm long. Capsules ovoid to ellipsoidal, 6–7 mm long; seeds oblong-fusiform, c. 3 mm long. Flowering November–March. Damp sandy flats and slopes, SW, LB (Cape Peninsula to Swellendam).

Drimia elata Jacquin ex Willdenow

Plants 30–100 cm high. Leaves 5–10, dry at flowering, erect to spreading, linear-lanceolate, often undulate, c. 25 × 1.5 cm, sometimes hairy, the margins softly hairy. Flowers in a narrow, crowded raceme on pedicels 6–8 mm long, silvery white, green, or purple, tepals 10–15 mm long, united below for 3–7 mm, filaments 6–8 mm long, anthers dark blue or purple, c. 2 mm long, style 8–13 mm long. Capsule oblong, three-lobed, 10–15 mm long; seeds ovate, c. 7 mm long. Flowering mainly December–April. Sandy and clay soils, NW, SW, AP, KM, LB, SE (southern Namaqualand to Cape Peninsula to East Africa).

Drimia exuviata (Jacquin) Jessop

Plants 20–80 cm high. Leaves one to four, sometimes as many as five, erect, semiterete, leathery, grayish, (2–)3–4 mm diam., about as long as the raceme, enclosed below in a strongly barred, often coarsely fibrous sheath. Flowers on pedicels 8–10 mm long, white with green keels, often flushed purple, usually fragrant, tepals 10–15 mm long, almost free, filaments 4–7 mm long, anthers c. 3 mm long, style 5–9 mm long. Capsule ovoid to ellipsoidal, 10–25 mm long; seeds ovate, 5–8 mm long. Flowering September–October. Rocky slopes and flats, often clay or granite, NW, SW, KM, SE (Namaqualand to Tygerberg to Grahamstown).

Drimia filifolia (Jacquin) J. C. Manning & Goldblatt

Plants 10–30 cm high. Leaves one to many, erect, terete, leathery, 0.5–2 mm wide, about as long as the raceme, enclosed below in a conspicuously barred, lightly fibrous sheath. Flowers and fruit as in *D. exuviata*. Flowering September–December. Sandy slopes and flats, often moist, NW, SW, AP, KM, LB (Namaqualand to Swellendam).

Drimia fragrans (Jacquin) J. C. Manning & Goldblatt

Plants 30–80 cm high. Leaves usually 15–30, terete, lightly flexuous, subsucculent, 10–35 × c. 1 mm, about half as long as the raceme, enclosed below by a papery neck, often long and smooth below, lightly barred above. Flowers in an elongate raceme with narrowly elliptical tepals, otherwise flowers and fruit as in *D. exuviata*. Flowering September–November. Sandy flats, NW (Bokkeveld Mountains to Hex River Valley).

Drimia haworthioides Baker

Plants 20–40 cm high; bulb exposed, with loose scales. Leaves 5–10, dry at flowering, spreading, lanceolate, the margins usually softly hairy. Flowers in a short cylindrical raceme on pedicels 5–6 mm long, greenish brown, tepals 10–15 mm long, united below for 2–4 mm, filaments 5–6 mm long, anthers mauve, c. 1 mm long. Capsules oblong, three-lobed, 8–10 mm long. Flowering November–February. Dry karroid areas, NW, KM, SE (Worcester to Eastern Cape and Karoo).

Drimia intricata (Baker) J. C. Manning & Goldblatt

Wire onion. Plants 10–50 cm high, scape more or less intricately branched, minutely hairy below. Leaf linear, 4–6 cm long. Flowers on spreading or deflexed pedicels to 50 mm long, star-shaped, white, pale yellow, or pink, tepals c. 3 mm long, united below for c. 1 mm, filaments 1–1.5 mm long, anthers c. 0.8 mm long, style 1–1.5 mm long. Capsule ovoid, 3–5 mm long; seeds angular-obovoid, c. 2 mm long. Flowering January–March. Rock outcrops, NW, KM, SE (Botterkloof to Port Elizabeth, dry areas of southern and tropical Africa).

Drimia involuta (J. C. Manning & Snijman) J. C. Manning & Goldblatt

Plants 10–15 cm high, scape minutely hairy below. Leaves two to six, suberect, linear, c. 1 mm wide. Flowers on pedicels 3–4 mm long, cup-shaped, facing outward, white with green basal markings, outer tepals spreading above, inner tepals longitudinally rolled, c. 4 mm long, united below for c. 1 mm, filaments 0.5 mm long, anthers dehiscing longitudinally, 1.5 mm long, style 1.5 mm long. Capsule ovoid, c. 3 mm long; seeds elliptical to oblong, c. 2 mm long. Flowering November–December. Loamy soil on exposed sandstone pavement, NW (Bokkeveld Mountains).

Drimia karooica (Obermeyer) J. C. Manning & Goldblatt
Plants to 20 cm high, scape smooth; bulb scales loose. Leaves four to six, suberect or spreading, oblong-oblanceolate, usually 7–9 mm wide. Flowers on pedicels 3–8 mm long, urn-shaped, nodding, pale lilac to green, tepals 6–8 mm long, united below for 1–2 mm, filaments 2–2.5 mm long, anthers dehiscing longitudinally, c. 1 mm long, style c. 2 mm long. Capsule ovoid, c. 8 mm long; seeds elliptical to obovate, c. 4 mm long. Flowering January–February. Rock outcrops, RV, KM (western and Little Karoo).

Drimia marginata (Thunberg) Jessop
Plants to 20 cm high. Leaves dry at flowering, two or three, prostrate, leathery, shiny, oblong, broadly obtuse, 60 × 8 mm, margins thickened, cartilaginous. Flowers in a subumbellate head-like raceme on pedicels 5–9 mm long, white to pale brown or pink, opening in the evening, tepals c. 4 mm long, united below for c. 1.5 mm, filaments ascending, c. 2 mm long, anthers c. 1.5 mm long, style c. 2 mm long. Flowering October–January. Sandy or stony slopes, RV, NW (western Karoo to Hex River Mountains).

Drimia media Jacquin ex Willdenow
Plants 30–55 cm high. Leaves mostly 10–20, emergent or present at flowering, erect, semiterete, rigid, to 30 × 0.3 cm. Flowers in a lax cylindrical raceme on pedicels 5–7 mm long, silvery purple-brown, tepals 10–15 mm long, united below for 3–5 mm, filaments 6–8 mm long, anthers purple, 1–2 mm long, style 6–8 mm long. Capsule oblong, three-lobed, c. 10 mm long; seeds ovate, c. 7 mm long. Flowering January–March. Sandy coastal flats and slopes, SW, AP, LB, SE (Saldanha to Knysna).

Drimia minor (A. V. Duthie) Jessop
Plants 5–20 cm high. Leaves dry at flowering, mostly 4–8, sometimes as many as 15, erect, terete, 1–2 mm diam. Flowers few in a head-like corymbose raceme on pedicels 4–10(–15) mm long, white to brownish, opening in the morning, tepals 3–4 mm long, united below for c. 1 mm, filaments ascending, c. 2 mm long, anthers c. 1 mm long, style 1–2 mm. Capsules globose, 5–7 mm long; seeds elliptical, 3–5 mm long. Flowering mostly November–March. Sandy flats, NW, SW, KM, LB (Bokkeveld and Swartberg Mountains to De Hoop).

Drimia multifolia (G. J. Lewis) Jessop
Plants to 15(–30) cm high. Leaves usually 30–50, filiform, coiled, subsucculent, 5–15 × c. 0.5 mm, less than half as long as the raceme, enclosed below by a papery or membranous, lightly barred sheath. Flowers and fruit as in *D. exuviata*. Flowering September–October. Rock pavement, RV, NW, SW (southern Namibia, Namaqualand, and western Karoo to Breede River Valley).

Drimia physodes (Jacquin) Jessop
Plants to 10 cm high, scape irregularly puberulous below; bulb large. Leaves dry at flowering, three to seven, erect, twisted, lanceolate, to 15 × 3 cm, margins often sparsely ciliolate. Flowers in a subcorymbose raceme on long, spreading pedicels mostly 15–25 mm long, white, opening in the afternoon, tepals 4–5 mm long, united below

Drimia multifolia

for c. 0.5 mm, filaments ascending, 2–3 mm long, anthers c. 1 mm long, style c. 2 mm. Capsules globose, c. 9 mm long; seeds discoid, c. 6 mm long. Flowering October–April. Stony and clay flats, RV, NW, KM (Namaqualand and western Karoo to Worcester and Little Karoo).

Drimia platyphylla (B. Nordenstam) J. C. Manning & Goldblatt
Plants 3–15 cm high, scape minutely hairy throughout. Leaves usually two, elliptical to broadly ovate, velvety above, prostrate, 6–25 mm wide. Flowers on pedicels 3–10 mm long, urn-shaped, nodding, reddish brown to creamy pink, tepals 3.5–6 mm long, united below for 1–3 mm, filaments papillate-hairy, 1–1.5 mm long, anthers dehiscing apically, 1–1.8 mm long, the thecae diverging and barbed below, style c. 1 mm long. Capsule ovoid to subglobose, 5–7 mm long; seeds elliptical to oblong, 3–4 mm long. Flowering November–January. Rock flushes, RV, NW, SW, AP, KM, SE (Namibia, Namaqualand, and Karoo to Bredasdorp, Uniondale).

Drimia pusilla Jacquin
Plants 6–15 cm high. Leaves few, dry at flowering, erect to spreading, oblanceolate, often undulate, the margins softly hairy, to 7 × 1 cm. Flowers in a short cylindrical raceme on pedicels 5–6 mm long, silvery white, green, or purple, tepals 9–10 mm long, united below for 2–3 mm, filaments 5–6 mm long, anthers dark blue or purple, 1 mm long. Capsule depressed-oblong, three-winged, 10–12 mm long; seeds discoid, c. 7 mm long. Flowering mainly December–April. Sandy and clay soils, NW, SW (southern Namaqualand to Cape Peninsula).

Drimia revoluta (A. V. Duthie) J. C. Manning & Goldblatt
Plants 15–30 cm high, scape scabrid below. Leaves dry at flowering, solitary, rarely two, terete, firm, erect, c. 1.5 mm diam. Flowers in flexuous racemes on pedicels 9–10 mm long, brown, lightly fruit scented, opening at night, tepals reflexed from near the base, narrowly oblong, 8 mm long, almost free; stamens connivent, filaments 6 mm long, anthers c. 1 mm long, style 5 mm long. Capsules globose, 6–8 mm long; seeds angular, c. 2 mm long. Flowering January–February, mostly after fire. Rocky sandstone or limestone slopes and flats, SW, AP (Bain's Kloof to De Hoop).

Drimia salteri (Compton) J. C. Manning & Goldblatt
Plants to 25 cm high. Leaves emergent or present at flowering, two to several, erect or falcate, subterete, fleshy, 1–2 mm diam. Flowers crowded in a slender raceme on pedicels to 5 mm long, whitish to brown or maroon, opening at night, tepals 4 mm long, united below for c. 1–1.5 mm, filaments 1.5–2 mm, anthers c. 1 mm, style c. 2 mm long. Capsules ovoid, c. 5 mm long. Flowering October–February. Sandy or stony soils, SW (Bain's Kloof to Hermanus).

Drimia sclerophylla J. C. Manning & Goldblatt
Plants 10–30 cm high, scape scabrid below. Leaves dry at flowering, two or three, terete, fibrous and striate, erect, c. 1.5 mm diam. Flowers in lax racemes on wiry, spreading pedicels 10–15 mm long, nodding in bud, white, stel-

Drimia revoluta

late, sweetly scented, opening in late afternoon, tepals 4–6 mm long, ovate, united below for 0.5 mm, filaments c. 2 mm long, ascending, anthers c. 2 mm long, style c. 1.5 mm long. Capsules ovoid, c. 7 mm long; seeds ovate, elliptical, c. 4 mm long. Flowering December–January. Rocky slopes, KM, SE (Little Karoo to Graaf Reinet).

Drimia uniflora J. C. Manning & Goldblatt
Fairy snowdrop. Plants 2–8 cm high at flowering, scape minutely hairy below. Leaves two to four, usually dry at flowering, spreading, linear, c. 40 × 1 mm. Flowers solitary, rarely two, on pedicels 1–1.5 mm long, white to pale pink with green keels, tepals 4–8 mm long, united most of their length into a tubular perianth, the free parts triangular, 0.75–1 mm long, filaments c. 0.5 mm long, anthers 1–1.5 mm long, style 2–4 mm long. Capsule ovoid to narrowly ellipsoidal, 3–6 mm long; seeds wedge-shaped, c. 0.8 mm long. Flowering December–March. Rocky outcrops and rock flushes, NW, KM, SE (Namaqualand to Zimbabwe).

Drimia uranthera (R. A. Dyer) J. C. Manning & Goldblatt
Plants 12–20 cm high, scape minutely hairy throughout. Leaves two to eight, suberect, linear, c. 0.5 mm wide. Flowers on pedicels 3–12 mm long, urn-shaped, nodding, light brown, tepals c. 4 mm long, united below for c. 1 mm, filaments c. 1 mm long, anthers dehiscing apically, c. 1.5 mm long, tailed below, ovary minutely hairy, style not evident. Flowering March–April. Stony slopes, KM (Oudtshoorn).

Drimia virens Schlechter
Plants to 20 cm high. Leaves dry at flowering, one or two, falcate, fleshy, to 8 × 0.3 mm, margins often sparsely and minutely hairy. Flowers in a subcorymbose raceme on long, spreading pedicels mostly 6–15 mm long, white, opening in the afternoon, tepals 4–5 mm long, united below for c. 1 mm, filaments ascending, 2 mm long, anthers c. 1 mm long, style c. 1.5 mm long. Capsules globose, c. 9 mm long; seeds discoid, c. 6 mm long. Flowering September–February. Stony flats, RV, NW, AP, KM, LB (western Karoo to Cedarberg, Little Karoo to Still Bay).

Drimia sp. 1
Plants to 20 cm high, scape finely hairy below. Leaves about five, elliptical, softly hairy, to 30 × 6 mm. Flowers in a corymbose head-like raceme on pedicels 5–6 mm long, white to pale brown or pink, tepals c. 3 mm long, united below for c. 1 mm, filaments ascending, c. 1.5 mm long, anthers c. 0.5 mm long, style c. 1 mm long. Flowering October–December. Shale slopes, NW (Piketberg).

Drimia sp. 2
Plants to 50 cm high, scape scabrid below, with banded, papery cataphylls. Leaves usually dry at flowering, single, terete, firm, erect, c. 3 mm diam. Flowers in a narrow raceme, buds crowded, pedicels spreading-ascending, whitish, tepals lightly reflexed, elliptical, 4–5 mm long, united below for c. 1 mm, filaments ascending, c. 2 mm long, anthers c. 1 mm long, style c. 2 mm long. Flowering November–December. Stony slopes, SE (Baviaanskloof and southern Karoo).

Empodium

COMMON NAME autumn star, FAMILY Hypoxidaceae. Deciduous perennials, sometimes forming clumps. ROOTSTOCK a corm; roots thin or contractile. LEAVES as many as seven, dry or green at flowering, linear to lanceolate, more or less pleated, in a basal cluster, hairless or with short recurved hairs on the margins and ribs. INFLORESCENCE single-flowered on a long pedicel but several per corm, the pedicel three-angled in cross section and often sparsely ciliate, sometimes hidden in the leaf sheaths. FLOWER star- to salver-shaped, yellow, sometimes scented, the six tepals united into a short to long, solid, sometimes ciliate neck, lobes narrowly ovate, spreading to reflexed, green-backed. STAMENS six, inserted at the tepal base, erect to spreading, about half as long as the tepals, filaments attached near base of anther, anthers sometimes with a prominent apical appendage. OVARY one-locular with many ovules borne on three parietal placentas, exserted from or enclosed by the leaf sheaths; STYLE with three long stigmatic lobes. FRUIT indehiscent, bearing a short or long beak, thin-walled to subsucculent. SEEDS shiny black, often with a swollen white funicle. Basic chromosome number $x = 7$. Southern Africa; c. 7 spp., 5 in the Cape.

Because of its autumn-flowering habit with flowers often appearing in advance of the leaves, *Empodium* has frequently been overlooked by plant explorers. As a result, the distribution information on several species is poorly recorded. As in various other genera with subterranean ovaries, *Empodium* has either berry-like fruits with fleshy walls or capsule-like fruits with thin walls. Flowering in *Empodium* seems not to be strictly rhythmical, unlike the situation common in other genera with a subterranean ovary, including *Gethyllis* in the Southern Hemisphere and *Crocus* and *Colchicum* in the Northern Hemisphere. Determining the influence of immediate local conditions on the display of the flowers relative to the leaves still requires careful study.

The flowers of most species are usually unscented, but in some populations the flowers are quite fragrant. All the species are visited by pollen-collecting bees. An interesting feature of *Empodium flexile* and the summer-flowering *E. monophyllum* (Nel) B. L. Burtt of eastern southern Africa is the presence of stout appendages on the tips of the anthers. Studies have yet to determine whether these act as a lure to pollinators, either as food or scent.

FURTHER READING. Hilliard and Burtt (1973) provided the most comprehensive information so far available on *Empodium*.

Empodium flexile (Nel) M. F. Thompson ex Snijman
Plants c. 10 cm high. Leaves three, usually dry at flowering, narrowly lanceolate, c. 5 mm wide, softly pleated with ciliate ribs, basal sheaths papery or fibrous. Flowers yellow, scented, tepals 15–30 × 3–5 mm, recurved from a neck 1–3 cm long, stamens spreading, bearing short to long, usually orange apical appendages, ovary subterranean to shortly exserted. Fruit semisucculent. Flowering February–June. Clay or sand on stony flats, RV, NW, KM (Namaqualand to Oudtshoorn).

Empodium gloriosum (Nel) B. L. Burtt
Plants 4–20 cm high, solitary. Leaves as many as eight, tufted, lanceolate, longer than the inflorescence, 2–10 mm wide with long, narrow tips, softly pleated, hairless

Empodium flexile

Empodium gloriosum

Empodium namaquensis

Empodium plicatum

Empodium veratrifolium

or the ribs occasionally hispid when young, basal sheaths light brown. Flowers yellow, sometimes lemon scented, tepals 10–25 × 3–5 mm, outspread from a smooth neck 2–8 cm long, stamens suberect, ovary subterranean. Fruit shortly exserted. Flowering March–June. Sandy or loamy soil on lower slopes and flats, AP, KM, LB, SE (Montagu, Bredasdorp to Eastern Cape).

Empodium namaquensis (Baker) M. F. Thompson
Plants 15–30 cm high, in clumps. Leaves one to five, ovate-lanceolate, longer than the inflorescence, 15–60 mm wide, with tapered recurved tips, softly pleated, the margin and ribs ciliate, basal sheaths membranous, pale with dark tips. Flowers yellow, sometimes scented, tepals 20–30 × 3–6 mm, outspread from a sparsely hispid neck c. 2 cm long, stamens spreading, ovary narrow, exserted from the ground 2–5 cm. Fruit fleshy, aromatic. Flowering April–May. Seasonally moist sites in sand or loam on granite or sandstone outcrops, NW (Namaqualand to Clanwilliam).

Empodium plicatum (Thunberg) Garside
Plants 10–30 cm high, solitary or clumped. Leaves one to four, lanceolate, dry or emerging at flowering, initially shorter than the inflorescence but c. 30 cm long and 5–10 mm wide when mature, with deeply pleated blades and hispid ribs, basal sheaths pale and membranous. Flowers yellow, rarely scented, tepals 13–30 × 3–5 mm, outspread from a somewhat hispid neck 5–10 cm long, stamens suberect, ovary subterranean. Fruit exserted from the ground less than 3 cm. Flowering April–June. Clay and loamy flats or lower slopes, in seasonally damp sites, RV, NW, SW, AP (Namaqualand, Bokkeveld and Roggeveld Escarpments to Cape Peninsula and Breede River mouth).

Empodium veratrifolium (Willdenow) M. F. Thompson
Plants 10–30 cm high, forming large clumps. Leaves three to six, tufted, lanceolate, often longer than the inflorescence, 10–20 mm wide, softly pleated, with sparsely ciliate ribs, basal sheaths long, dark brown and papery. Flowers yellow, unscented, tepals 15–40 × 5–8 mm, outspread from a neck c. 1 cm long, stamens spreading, ovary narrow, exserted from the ground 10 cm or more. Fruit

fleshy, aromatic. Flowering May–June. Granite rocks along the coast, NW, SW (Lambert's Bay to Saldanha Bay).

Eriospermum

COMMON NAME cottonseed, FAMILY Ruscaceae. Small deciduous perennials. ROOTSTOCK a globose or irregularly shaped stem tuber, sometimes producing rhizomes or stolons, the flesh white, yellow, or pink, with the growing point apical, lateral, or basal, and protected by a fibrous neck. LEAVES mostly solitary and produced before the flowers, less commonly several or present at flowering, erect to prostrate, with a distinct petiole-like base, the blade narrow to almost round, hairless or variously hairy, sometimes with simple or complex appendages or outgrowths produced from the upper surface. INFLORESCENCE a raceme, elongate or corymbose, the petioles short or long, sometimes persistent and remaining green after fruiting, the scape erect or flexuous, sometimes hairy below, subtended at the base by a single clasping peduncular bract; bracts minute, membranous. FLOWERS small, star- or cup-shaped, the tepals almost free, more or less spreading or dimorphic with the inner erect, broader, and folded at the tips, white to pinkish or greenish, or yellow, usually unscented. STAMENS with filaments often flattened and broader below, joined to the base of the tepals, rarely united at the base. OVARY ovoid with two to several ovules per locule; STYLE usually shorter to as long as the ovary. FRUIT a top-shaped or subglobose capsule, three-lobed and retuse above, the valves spreading or reflexed at dehiscence. SEEDS two to four per locule, ovoid or comma-shaped, light brown and containing phlobaphene, densely covered with woolly hairs. Basic chromosome number $x = 7$. Sub-Saharan Africa; c. 100 spp. or more, 52 in the Cape.

A large genus without close allies, *Eriospermum* occurs throughout the drier parts of sub-Saharan Africa with a concentration of species in the winter-rainfall zone of southern Africa. This curious genus is distinctive in its rounded tuber and woolly seeds, and in the frequently solitary leaf with a narrowed, petiole-like base. Long placed alone in the family Eriospermaceae, the genus had been regarded as rather an isolated one whose relationships were obscure. Molecular studies, however, indicate an intimate although unexpected alliance with the genera previously placed in the family Ruscaceae (synonym, Convallariaceae), which includes the African genera *Dracaena* and *Sansevieria* and the Eurasian and North American *Convallaria* (lily-of-the-valley).

Eriospermums are seldom conspicuous, typically flowering in the hot summer months, by which time the leaf has withered and blown away. The small and usually dun-colored flowers are rarely of much help in identifying individual species but are important in indicating relationships among species. In about half the species, the flowers are cup-shaped with all the tepals similar, but in the other half the inner tepals are broader, erect, and folded around the stamens and ovary whereas the outer tepals are spreading. The color of the tuber flesh and the position of the growing bud on the tuber itself, whether apical, lateral, or basal, are also valuable characters in assessing relationships. If the variation in the flowers is modest in scale, however, then that found in the leaves is positively extravagant; several species are worth cultivating for their bizarre foliage. In those species, the leaf blade itself is rather reduced but bears on its upper surface more or less elaborate outgrowths, also called enations. These vary in shape from simple cylindrical or blade-like structures to complex, highly branched growths resembling antlers, twigs, or even miniature fir trees. The small flowers are visited by a variety of insects, especially various Hymenoptera (both bees and wasps), and also syrphid flies.

The species are best grown in pots where their particular attractions can best be appreciated. Those that produce complex outgrowths on the leaves are probably most interesting, and *Eriospermum paradoxum*, which produces an enation exactly resembling a miniature fir tree, is almost capable of arousing a mild sensation. The distinctive woolly seeds are wind dispersed and are conspicuous when ripe, especially when the capsules are borne on long peduncles. The seeds are shed toward the beginning of the rainy season and appear to lose viability rapidly. Plants are sensitive to rotting.

FURTHER READING. A well-illustrated monograph of *Eriospermum* was provided by Perry (1994).

Eriospermum aequilibre Poellnitz
Plants to 45 cm high; tuber irregularly shaped, flesh white, growing point basal. Leaf dry at flowering, erect, narrowly lanceolate, rugose with prominent veins, to 180 × 18 mm. Flowers in a narrowly cylindrical raceme on a slender peduncle, star-shaped, light green, 9–10 mm diam., pedicels to 6 mm long. Flowering March–April. Rocky ground in succulent Karoo, KM (De Rust to Kammanassie Mountains).

Eriospermum alcicorne Baker
Plants to 8 cm high; tuber pear-shaped to irregular, sometimes stoloniferous, flesh whitish to pale pink, growing point basal to lateral. Leaf dry at flowering, erect, ovate, rarely hairy, to 20 × 15 mm, often with several flattened outgrowths. Flowers crowded in a conical raceme on a short peduncle, inner tepals suberect, white, scented, to 14 mm diam., pedicels to 7 mm long. Flowering January–April. Clay and sandstone soils, RV, NW, KM (Namaqualand to Willowmore).

Eriospermum aphyllum Marloth
Plants to 8 cm high; tuber subglobose, flesh white, becoming yellowish, growing point apical. Leaf dry at flowering, erect, filiform and terete, to 30 × 1–3 mm. Flowers in a broadly cylindrical to subcorymbose raceme on a short peduncle, broadly bell-shaped, whitish to pink, to 14 mm diam., pedicels mostly 18–25 mm long, pedicels and peduncle persistent and remaining green. Flowering March–April. Hard, stony clay, RV, NW (Namaqualand and western Karoo to Nardouw Mountains).

Eriospermum arenosum P. L. Perry
Plants to 20 cm high; tuber subglobose, flesh white, growing point apical. Leaf dry at flowering, suberect, heart-shaped, to 30 × 18 mm. Flowers in a lax raceme on a wiry peduncle, more or less star-shaped, white, 7 mm diam., pedicels wiry, to 55 mm long. Flowering March–April. Coastal sands, NW (Namaqualand to Aurora).

Eriospermum bayeri P. L. Perry
Plants to 45 cm high; tuber pear-shaped, becoming irregularly knobby, flesh white, growing point basal. Leaf dry at flowering, erect, lanceolate, margin lightly wavy, to 100 × 25 mm. Flowers in a narrow spike-like raceme on a slender peduncle, star-shaped, pale greenish, 12 mm diam., pedicels 2–7 mm long. Flowering March–May. Shale slopes in renosterveld, RV, NW, SW (western Karoo to Robertson Karoo).

Eriospermum bifidum R. A. Dyer
Plants to 30 cm high; tuber pear-shaped to irregularly cylindrical, flesh white, growing point basal. Leaf dry at flowering, erect, narrowly lanceolate to heart-shaped, leathery, to 120 × 63 mm. Flowers in a subcorymbose to broadly cylindrical raceme on a slender peduncle, star-shaped, yellowish green, to 11 mm diam., filaments oblong, bifid above and overtopping the anthers, pedicels to 40 mm long. Flowering January–April. Shale flats, RV, KM, SE (Namaqualand and western Karoo to Grahamstown).

Eriospermum bowieanum Baker
Plants to 80 cm high; tuber oblong, flesh pink to red, growing point basal to lateral. Leaf dry at flowering, suberect, blade reduced, ovate to heart-shaped, margin rolled under, to 10 × 10 mm, with simple or branched, almost club-shaped, terete outgrowths. Flowers crowded in a spike-like raceme on a short peduncle, inner tepals suberect, white, to 7 mm diam., pedicels to 1.5 mm long. Flowering February–March. Clay soils, NW (Montagu to Ashton and Riviersonderend).

Eriospermum brevipes Baker
Plants to 30 cm high; tuber irregularly shaped, flesh white, growing point lateral. Leaf dry at flowering, spreading, heart-shaped, sparsely or densely hairy, to 90 × 90 mm. Flowers in a spike-like raceme on a slender peduncle, cup-shaped, white, fragrant, 8–9 mm diam., pedicels to 12 mm long. Flowering January–March. Sandstone slopes, grassland or fynbos, SE (Plettenberg Bay to Transkei).

Eriospermum breviscapum Marloth ex P. L. Perry
Plants to 12 cm high; tuber pear-shaped, flesh white, growing point basal to lateral. Leaf dry at flowering, pros-

trate, round to heart-shaped, fleshy, to 60×80 mm. Flowers crowded in a narrowly conical raceme on a short peduncle, star-shaped, white, fragrant, 7–8 mm diam., pedicels 3–6 mm long. Flowering February–March. Shale slopes in renosterveld and succulent Karoo, SW, AP (Robertson to Still Bay).

Eriospermum bruynsii P. L. Perry
Plants to 25 cm high; tuber irregularly shaped, flesh white, growing point basal. Leaf dry at flowering, erect, lanceolate, petiole hairy, to 42×25 mm. Flowers in a narrow spike-like raceme on a slender peduncle, star-shaped, pale green, 6.5 mm diam., pedicels to 3 mm long. Flowering March–April. Stony slopes, KM (Calitzdorp).

Eriospermum capense (Linnaeus) Thunberg
Plants to 50 cm high, sometimes clumped; tuber pear-shaped to irregular, rarely stoloniferous, flesh maroon, growing point basal to lateral. Leaf dry at flowering, heart-shaped, suberect or spreading, often with red ridges, hairless or sparsely hairy, to 75×60 mm. Flowers in a lax raceme on a slender peduncle, inner tepals erect, yellowish, to 12 mm diam., pedicels wiry, 30–60 mm long. Flowering November–March. Mainly clay soils, RV, NW, SW, AP, KM, LB, SE (Namaqualand to Grahamstown).

Two subspecies are recognized: subspecies *capense* with leaf suberect, ovate, hairless, grayish green, flowering November–February, RV, NW, SW, AP, KM, LB, SE (Namaqualand to Grahamstown), and subspecies *stoloniferum* (Marloth) P. L. Perry with leaf prostrate, round, sparsely hairy, bright green, flowering November–April, SW (Malmesbury to Caledon).

Eriospermum cernuum Baker
Plants to 35 cm high; tuber pear-shaped or subglobose, flesh white, growing point lateral. Leaf dry at flowering, erect, lanceolate to heart-shaped, leathery, margin sometimes red, to 90×23 mm. Flowers in a slender, often subsecund, spike-like raceme on a slender peduncle, cup-shaped, white, lightly scented, 8–9 mm diam., pedicels 2–3 mm long. Flowering February–April. Damp sites on sandstone soils, NW, SW, KM (Clanwilliam to Bredasdorp).

Eriospermum cervicorne Marloth
Plants to 12 cm high; tuber pear-shaped to irregular, flesh pink, becoming red, growing point basal to lateral. Leaf dry at flowering, spreading, ovate to heart-shaped, to 20×15 mm, with a few branched, terete outgrowths, sparsely to densely woolly. Flowers crowded in a conical raceme on a short peduncle, inner tepals erect, white, to 14 mm diam., pedicels to 10 mm long. Flowering March–April. Granite outcrops, RV (Namaqualand to Tanqua Karoo).

Eriospermum ciliatum P. L. Perry
Plants to 24 cm high; tuber narrowly pear-shaped, flesh white, becoming pink, growing point basal. Leaf dry at flowering, prostrate, broadly ovate to heart-shaped, margin minutely hairy, 12×13 mm. Flowers few on a wiry peduncle minutely hairy at the base, cup- or star-shaped, bright yellow, 12 mm diam., pedicels to 8 mm long. Flowering February–April. Sandstone slopes, fynbos or grassland, SE (Humansdorp to Port Elizabeth).

Eriospermum capense subsp. *stoloniferum*; see also page 152

Eriospermum cordiforme

Eriospermum cordiforme

Eriospermum cordiforme T. M. Salter
Plants to 40 cm high; tuber irregularly shaped and warty, flesh pink, growing point basal to lateral. Leaf dry at flowering, spreading, heart-shaped, surface wrinkled. Flowers in a spike-like, secund raceme, inner tepals erect, cream, to 14 mm diam., pedicels wiry, to 9 mm long. Flowering January–February. Sandstone and granite soils, SW, LB, SE (Darling to Alexandria).

Eriospermum crispum P. L. Perry
Plants to 35 cm high; tuber irregularly knobby, flesh white, growing point basal. Leaf dry at flowering, erect, sword-shaped, leathery, margin crisped, to 80 × 32 mm. Flowers in a subcorymbose or broadly conical raceme on a slender peduncle, star-shaped, white, 21 mm diam., pedicels to 18 mm long. Flowering March–April. Stony slopes, KM (Calitzdorp).

Eriospermum dielsianum Schlechter ex Poellnitz
Plants to 25 cm high, sometimes clumped; tuber simple or multiple, pear-shaped to subglobose, flesh white or pink, growing point lateral. Leaf dry at flowering, erect, lanceolate to heart-shaped, petiole and blade usually hairy, to 100 × 60 mm. Flowers in a cylindrical raceme on a slender peduncle, cup- or star-shaped, white, to 14 mm diam., pedicels to 20 mm long. Flowering January–April. Mostly sandstone soils, RV, NW, SW, AP, KM, LB, SE (western Karoo and Cold Bokkeveld to Port Elizabeth).

Two subspecies are recognized: subspecies *dielsianum* with white tuber flesh, leaf sheath and blade hairless or hairy, tepals about 6 mm long, flowering January–March, mostly sandstone soils, RV, NW, SW, AP, KM, LB (western Karoo and Cold Bokkeveld to Swellendam), and subspecies *molle* Marloth ex P. L. Perry with pink tuber flesh, leaf sheath and blade densely hairy, tepals 8–10 mm long, flowering January–April, coastal fynbos in damp peaty soil, AP, SE (Albertinia to Port Elizabeth).

Eriospermum dissitiflorum Schlechter
Plants to 40 cm high; tuber becoming irregularly cylindrical, flesh deep pink, growing point basal or lateral. Leaf dry at flowering, erect, elliptical to lanceolate, to 100 × 65 mm. Flowers in a lax raceme on a slender peduncle, inner

Eriospermum dielsianum subsp. *dielsianum*

tepals erect, white, to 10 mm diam., pedicels wiry, to 40 mm long. Flowering January–April. Clay and sandstone soils, fynbos and renosterveld, LB, SE (Riversdale to Transkei).

Eriospermum dregei Schönland
Plants to 14 cm high; tuber pear-shaped to irregular, warty, flesh pink to maroon, growing point basal. Leaf dry at flowering, blade ovate to heart-shaped, to 18 × 22 mm, with simple or branched, terete outgrowths forming a mop-like structure, covered with stellate clusters of curly hairs. Flowers in a dense raceme, inner tepals erect, white, to 10 mm diam., pedicels to 8 mm long. Flowering March. Grassland, KM, SE (Montagu to Grahamstown).

Eriospermum erinum P. L. Perry
Plants to 20 cm high; tuber pear-shaped, flesh white, growing point basal. Leaf dry at flowering, suberect, ovate to heart-shaped, to 25 × 25 mm, with short cylindrical outgrowths each with an apical tuft of hairs. Flowers in a lax raceme on a wiry peduncle, inner tepals erect, whitish, c. 10 mm diam., pedicels wiry, to 30 mm long. Flowering February–April. Tillite flats in renosterveld, NW (Bokkeveld Mountains).

Eriospermum exigium P. L. Perry
Plants to 15 cm high; tuber pear-shaped, flesh pale pink, growing point basal. Leaf dry at flowering, erect, oblong-linear, to 45 × 2.5 mm, petiole wiry. Flowers in a cylindrical raceme on a wiry peduncle, inner tepals suberect and attenuate, white, 8–9 mm diam., pedicels to 8 mm long. Flowering March. Sandstone pavement, NW (Bokkeveld Mountains to Gifberg).

Eriospermum exile P. L. Perry
Plants to 30 cm high; tuber pear-shaped, rarely stoloniferous, flesh white, growing point basal. Leaf dry at flowering, erect, linear-lanceolate, to 125 × 8 mm, petiole wiry. Flowers in a spike-like raceme on a wiry peduncle, inner tepals erect, white to pale yellow, 8–9 mm diam., pedicels to 4 mm long. Flowering January–March. Quartzite and shale in shade, NW, KM (Worcester to De Rust).

Eriospermum flabellatum P. L. Perry
Plants to 80 cm high; tuber irregularly shaped, flesh red, growing point basal. Leaf dry at flowering, blade reduced, heart-shaped, to 6 mm diam., with branched, terete outgrowths. Flowers crowded in a spike-like raceme on a short peduncle, inner tepals erect, white, c. 7 mm diam., pedicels to 2.5 mm long. Flowering March–April. Shale slopes, RV, KM (Montagu to Barrydale and western Karoo).

Eriospermum flavum P. L. Perry
Plants to 6 cm high; tuber subglobose, flesh pale pink, growing point apical. Leaf dry at flowering, erect, filiform and terete, to 40 × 0.5 mm. Flowers in a lax, flexuous raceme on a wiry, coiled peduncle, cup-shaped, bright yellow, c. 6 mm diam., pedicels very wiry, to 45 mm long, persistent. Flowering May–June. Damp sandstone pavement and flats, NW, SW (Nardouw Mountains to Cold Bokkeveld and Elandsberg).

Eriospermum glaciale P. L. Perry
Plants to 5 cm high; tuber irregularly shaped, flesh pink, growing point basal to lateral. Leaf dry at flowering, erect, elliptical to lanceolate, white woolly beneath, to 45 × 20 mm. Flowers crowded in a compact spike-like raceme on a short peduncle, inner tepals erect, white, 8–9 mm diam., pedicels 5 mm long. Flowering April. Clay flats in renosterveld scrub, NW (Bokkeveld Escarpment).

Eriospermum graminifolium A. V. Duthie
Plants to 30 cm high; tuber pear-shaped to irregular, rarely stoloniferous, flesh pink, growing point basal to lateral. Leaf dry at flowering, linear-lanceolate, leathery, margin often rolled upward and shortly hairy, to 100 × 9 mm. Flowers in a lax raceme on a slender peduncle, inner tepals erect, white, to 12 mm diam., pedicels wiry, to 45 mm long. Flowering February–April. Sand and clay, NW, SW, AP, KM, LB, SE (Bokkeveld Mountains to George).

Eriospermum inconspicuum P. L. Perry
Plants to 8 cm high; tuber irregularly shaped, flesh white, growing point apical. Leaf dry at flowering, erect, broadly elliptical to ovate, rugose, with prominent veins, to 16 ×

Eriospermum lanceifolium

Eriospermum lanceifolium foliage

14 mm. Flowers in a lax raceme on a slender peduncle, star-shaped, white, 8 mm diam., pedicels wiry, to 18 mm long. Flowering April. Sandstone soils in fynbos, SW, LB, SE (Caledon to Outeniqua Mountains).

Eriospermum lanceifolium Jacquin
Plants to 40 cm high; tuber irregularly shaped, warty, rarely stoloniferous, flesh pink, growing point basal to lateral. Leaf erect, lanceolate, leathery, bluish, margin wavy, sometimes hairy, to 160 × 48 mm. Flowers in a lax or subspicate raceme on a slender peduncle, inner tepals erect, white, to 12 mm diam., pedicels to 30 mm long. Flowering March–April. Sandstone or granite soil, NW, SW, KM, LB (Olifants River Mountains to Albertinia).

Eriospermum lanimarginatum Marloth ex P. L. Perry
Plants to 25 cm high; tuber pear-shaped to irregular, flesh white, growing point basal to lateral. Leaf dry at flowering, prostrate or pressed to the ground, heart-shaped, somewhat fleshy, curly hairy on the margin. Flowers in a lax raceme on a slender peduncle, shortly tubular, inner tepals erect-recurved, c. 10 mm diam., pedicels wiry, to 28 mm long. Flowering March. Clay flats in karroid scrub, RV (western and Great Karoo).

Eriospermum lanuginosum Jacquin
Plants to 38 cm high; tuber becoming irregularly shaped, flesh maroon-red, growing point basal to lateral. Leaf dry at flowering, spreading, heart-shaped, glabrous to sparsely hairy above but white woolly beneath, to 130 × 130 mm. Flowers in a lax raceme on a slender peduncle, inner tepals erect, cream, to 12 mm diam., filaments narrowly triangular, pedicels to 40 mm long. Flowering February–March. Sandstone slopes in fynbos, NW, SW (Bokkeveld Mountains to Gouda).

Eriospermum laxiracemosum P. L. Perry
Plants to 30 cm high; tuber pear-shaped to irregular, flesh pink, growing point basal to lateral. Leaf dry at flowering, erect, lanceolate, to 160 × 25 mm. Flowers in a lax raceme on a slender peduncle, inner tepals erect, white, 13–14 mm diam., pedicels to 90 mm long. Flowering Febru-

ary–April. Sandstone rocks, NW (Gifberg to Pakhuis Mountains).

Eriospermum macgregorianum P. L. Perry
Plants to 11.5 cm high, clumped; tubers ovoid, forming chains, flesh white, growing point apical or lateral. Leaf dry at flowering, erect, elliptical to ovate, to 60 × 17 mm. Flowers in a subcorymbose raceme on a slender peduncle, star-shaped, bright yellow, 12 mm diam., pedicels to 18 mm long. Flowering February–March. Clay and dolerite flats, RV, NW (Nieuwoudtville to Calvinia).

Eriospermum marginatum Marloth ex P. L. Perry
Plants to 25 cm high, solitary or clumped; tuber irregularly shaped, rarely tuberculate and stoloniferous, flesh maroon, growing point basal to lateral. Leaves dry at flowering, prostrate, heart-shaped, leathery, margin minutely hairy, to 80 × 80 mm. Flowers in a lax raceme on a slender peduncle, inner tepals erect, white, c. 10 mm diam., pedicels to 50 mm long. Stony slopes in karroid scrub, RV, NW, KM (Namaqualand and western Karoo to Barrydale).

Eriospermum minutipustulatum P. L. Perry
Plants to 12 cm high, solitary or clumped; tuber small, irregularly shaped, stoloniferous, flesh white, growing point lateral. Leaf dry at flowering, prostrate, heart-shaped, pustulate-hairy, to 20 × 16 mm. Flowers in a lax raceme on a wiry peduncle, inner tepals erect, white, 8 mm diam., pedicels wiry, to 17 mm long. Flowering March. Clay flats, NW (Kobee Pass).

Eriospermum nanum Marloth
Plants to 30 cm high; tuber irregularly shaped, rarely stoloniferous, flesh pink, growing point basal to lateral. Leaf dry at flowering, suberect, heart-shaped, to 45 × 55 mm. Flowers in a lax raceme on a slender peduncle, inner tepals erect, cream, to 8 mm diam., filaments narrowly triangular, pedicels wiry, to 30 mm long. Flowering February–May. Sandstone soils, NW, SW, AP (Pakhuis Mountains to De Hoop).

Eriospermum orthophyllum P. L. Perry
Plants to 40 cm high; tuber pear-shaped or irregularly cylindrical, flesh pink, growing point basal to lateral. Leaf dry at flowering, erect, lanceolate to elliptical, leathery, margin yellow or purple, to 60 × 30 mm. Flowers in a lax raceme on a slender peduncle, inner tepals erect, white, to 8 mm diam., pedicels wiry, to 40 mm long. Flowering January–February. Sandy soils, SE (Port Elizabeth to Transkei).

Eriospermum paradoxum (Jacquin) Ker Gawler
Plants to 10 cm high; tuber oblong or irregular, flesh pink, becoming red, growing point basal to lateral. Leaf dry at flowering, small, ovate to heart-shaped, to 7 × 6 mm, bearing a much branched or plumose, woolly outgrowth to 110 × 30 mm. Flowers crowded in a cylindrical raceme on a short, usually hairy peduncle, star-shaped, white, fragrant, to 17 mm diam., pedicels to 6 mm long. Flowering April–May. Sandy and clay soils, RV, NW, SW, AP, KM, LB, SE (Namaqualand to Grahamstown). Page 152.

Eriospermum parvifolium Jacquin
Plants to 30 cm high; tuber subglobose, flesh white, growing point apical. Leaf dry at flowering, erect, elliptical to ovate, leathery, pale or reddish beneath, to 80 × 40 mm.

Eriospermum paradoxum

Flowers in a narrowly cylindrical raceme on a slender peduncle, star-shaped, white, c. 6 mm diam., pedicels to 14 mm long. Flowering March–April. Stony clay soils, NW (Namaqualand to Bokkeveld Escarpment).

Eriospermum patentiflorum Schlechter

Plants to 40 cm high; tuber pear-shaped, flesh white, growing point basal. Leaf dry at flowering, erect, ovate to lanceolate to heart-shaped, minutely white hairy, to 80 × 35 mm, petiole abruptly inflated, persisting around the base of the plant as loosely sheathing collars. Flowers in a lax raceme on a slender peduncle, star-shaped, white, c. 10 mm diam., pedicels spreading, wiry, to 32 mm long. Flowering March. Rocky slopes in arid fynbos, NW (southern Namaqualand to Olifants River Valley).

Eriospermum porphyrium Archibald

Plants to 70 cm high; tuber cylindrical to irregular, simple or stoloniferous, flesh white, growing point lateral. Leaf dry at flowering, prostrate, ovate to heart-shaped, to 120 × 90 mm. Flowers in a dense, narrowly cylindrical raceme on a long peduncle, star-shaped, cream to greenish, fragrant, c. 13 mm diam., pedicels to 14 mm long. Flowering December–May. Clay soils in grassland, SE (Kouga Mountains to Northern Province).

Eriospermum proliferum Baker

Plants to 30 cm high, sometimes clumped; tuber pear-shaped to irregular, stoloniferous, flesh pink, growing point basal to lateral. Leaf dry at flowering, spreading, ovate to heart-shaped, to 60 × 35 mm, small, often with thread-like outgrowths, almost hairless or hairy. Flowers few in a lax raceme on a slender peduncle, inner tepals erect, white, to 12 mm diam., pedicels wiry, c. 25 mm long. Flowering February–March. Clay and sand, RV, NW, SW, AP, KM, SE (Namaqualand to Baviaanskloof Mountains).

Eriospermum pubescens Jacquin

Plants to 30 cm high, sometimes clumped; tuber irregularly shaped, flesh maroon, growing point basal to lateral. Leaf dry at flowering, prostrate, heart-shaped, almost hairless or with straight hairs pressed to the surface, especially beneath, to 60 × 70 mm. Flowers in a lax raceme on a slender peduncle, inner tepals erect, white, to 12 mm diam., pedicels wiry, to 65 mm long. Flowering February–April. Mainly clay soil in renosterveld, NW, SW, KM, LB, SE (Ceres to Somerset West to Knysna).

Eriospermum pumilum T. M. Salter

Plants to 25 cm high; tuber depressed-globose or irregular, flesh white, growing point apical. Leaf dry at flowering, erect, oblong-lanceolate to elliptical, margin red, to 47 × 8 mm. Flowers in a narrow raceme on a wiry peduncle, star-shaped, white, to 6 mm diam., pedicels 4–12 mm long. Flowering March–April. Sandy slopes, RV, NW, SW (Namaqualand and western Karoo to False Bay).

Eriospermum pustulatum Marloth ex A. V. Duthie

Plants to 40 cm high; tuber irregularly shaped, flesh pinkish, growing point basal or lateral. Leaf dry at flowering, prostrate, heart-shaped, silvery white, pustulate and

Foliage of *Eriospermum paradoxum* (left) and *E. capense* subsp. *stoloniferum* (right)

golden hairy, margin minutely hairy, to 70 × 115. Flowers in a lax raceme on a slender peduncle, inner tepals erect, white, c. 8 mm diam., pedicels wiry, to 32 mm long. Flowering November–December. Clay in succulent karoo, RV, NW (Nardouw Mountains to Karoo).

Eriospermum rhizomatum P. L. Perry
Plants to 50 cm high, rhizomatous and clumped; tuber small and irregularly shaped, flesh white, growing point lateral and terminal. Leaf usually dry at flowering, spreading, heart-shaped, leathery, to 70 × 66 mm. Flowers in a spike-like raceme on a slender peduncle, cup-shaped, white, c. 8 mm diam., pedicels to 3 mm long. Flowering February–March. Sandstone slopes in shade, KM (Calitzdorp to Oudtshoorn).

Eriospermum schlechteri Baker
Plants to 23 cm high; tuber subglobose, sometimes multiple, flesh deep pink, growing points several, apical. Leaf dry at flowering, erect, elliptical, ribbed, to 45 × 20 mm. Flowers in a lax raceme on a wiry peduncle, star-shaped, bright yellow, to 12 mm diam., pedicels wiry, c. 20 mm long. Flowering March–April. Sandstone slopes in fynbos, SW (Kogelberg to Shaw's Mountain, Caledon).

Eriospermum spirale C. H. Bergius ex Schultes
Plants to 6 cm high; tuber subglobose, flesh white, growing point apical. Leaf dry at flowering, terete, to 25 × 1.5 mm. Flowers in a corymbose raceme with thickened axis on a wiry, coiled peduncle, star-shaped, white to yellow, to 6 mm diam., fragrant, pedicels to 25 mm long, persistent and remaining green. Flowering April–June. Sandstone flats and granite outcrops, NW (Gifberg to False Bay).

Eriospermum subincanum P. L. Perry
Plants to 25 cm high; tuber pear-shaped, flesh white, becoming red, growing point basal. Leaf dry at flowering, prostrate, heart-shaped, shiny green above, densely white woolly beneath, margin undulate and red. Flowers in a lax raceme on a slender peduncle, inner tepals erect, yellowish green, to 7 mm diam., pedicels wiry, 9–15 mm long. Flowering February–March. Rocky outcrops, NW (Gifberg to Biedouw).

Eriospermum subtile P. L. Perry
Plants to 20 cm high; tuber subglobose, flesh white, growing point basal to lateral. Leaf dry at flowering, erect, ovate, to 46 × 30 mm. Flowers in a lax raceme on a slender peduncle, somewhat urn-shaped, inner tepals erect and attenuate, white, to 6 mm diam., pedicels wiry, to 25 mm long. Flowering March–April. Shale in renosterveld, NW, KM (Bokkeveld Mountains to Koo).

Eriospermum vermiforme Marloth ex P. L. Perry
Plants to 15 cm high, clumped; tubers irregularly shaped, stoloniferous, flesh pink, growing points terminal. Leaf dry at flowering, spreading, heart-shaped, margin minutely hairy, to 23 × 22 mm. Flowers in a conical raceme, inner tepals erect, white, 12 mm diam., pedicels to 15 mm long. Flowering February–March. Sandstone flats, LB (Mossel Bay).

Eriospermum villosum Baker
Plants to 20 cm high; tuber irregularly shaped, flesh pink, growing point basal to lateral. Leaf dry at flowering, erect,

Eriospermum spirale

lanceolate, gray, densely hairy, to 180 × 10 mm. Flowers in a lax raceme on a slender peduncle, inner tepals erect, white, to 10 mm diam., pedicels to 25 mm long. Flowering December–February. Granite and shale, NW, SW (Namaqualand to Elandskloof Mountains).

Eriospermum zeyheri R. A. Dyer

Plants to 50 cm high; tuber pear-shaped, flesh white, growing point basal. Leaf dry at flowering, prostrate, round to heart-shaped, to 65 × 100 mm. Flowers in a narrowly cylindrical raceme on a long peduncle, star-shaped, cream to greenish, fragrant, to 12 mm diam., filaments oblong, pedicels to 8 mm long. Flowering December–March. Clay soils in renosterveld, SW, KM, LB, SE (MacGregor to Grahamstown).

Eucomis

COMMON NAME pineapple lily, FAMILY Hyacinthaceae. Deciduous perennials. ROOTSTOCK a pear-shaped or globose bulb, often large, usually with dark brown or black, papery outer tunics lightly barred above. LEAVES few to several, linear to lanceolate or broadly oblanceolate, suberect or prostrate. INFLORESCENCE a many-flowered raceme, the upper bracts sterile and enlarged to form a leafy crown; bracts green, the lower smaller and broader. FLOWERS spreading or more or less nodding, cup- or bowl-shaped, the tepals spreading or suberect, united below into a shallow cup, white to greenish, often flushed or spotted purple, sometimes scented. STAMENS with filaments narrowly triangular, broadened and united below to one another and to the base of the tepals. OVARY subglobose with several ovules per locule; STYLE tapering, about as long as the ovary. FRUIT an ovoid capsule, sometimes inflated and papery. SEEDS several per locule, subglobose or ovoid, glossy black. Basic chromosome number $x = 10$. South Africa to southern tropical Africa; 10 spp., 3 in the Cape.

Characteristic of moist montane and subalpine grasslands in the summer-rainfall region of southeastern Africa, the species of *Eucomis* are rather similar in floral morphology, differing mostly in stature and the development of purple markings or blotches on the leaves, peduncle, and flowers. Flower color varies somewhat between white and green with a greater or lesser degree of purple shading or speckling, rarely uniformly purple. The single species endemic to the winter-rainfall region of southern Africa, *E. regia*, is closely allied to the montane summer-rainfall species *E. schijfii* Reyneke. Both have conspicuously striate, obovate leaves, spreading flat on the ground, and inflated capsules, but *E. schijfii* is distinctive in its uniformly purple flowers. The form and color of the flowers suggest that they are pollinated by wasps and flies.

Although not brightly colored, the taller-flowered species of *Eucomis* make fascinating and long-lasting subjects for the garden. Also attractive in fruit, the inflorescences provide interest for several months and are excellent as cut flowers. The bulbs are usually large, and the genus is particularly recommended for rock gardens. Although they grow best in sun, they will also grow near the roots of trees, which give partial shade, provided they are well watered during the growing season. The montane species are quite hardy. Plants can be placed outdoors when the temperature is above 10°C (50°F). The summer-growing

Eucomis regia

species must be kept damp during the growing and flowering period, and the leaves are prone to sunburn.

FURTHER READING. The only relatively complete treatment of *Eucomis* is the unpublished thesis by Reyneke (1972).

Eucomis autumnalis (Miller) Chittenden
Plants 6–30 cm high. Leaves suberect, ovate to lanceolate, uniformly green, margins undulate or crisped. Flowers congested on pedicels 3–9 mm long, white to greenish, tepals 6–13 × 4–7 mm; terminal bracts suberect to spreading, mostly shorter than the inflorescence axis. Capsule papery, pale. Flowering December–February. Rocky, grassy slopes, SE (Knysna northward throughout eastern southern Africa).

Eucomis comosa (Houttuyn) H. R. Wehrhahn
Plants 17–100 cm high. Leaves suberect, oblong-lanceolate, speckled with purple beneath, margins undulate or crisped. Flowers on pedicels 15–30 mm long, greenish with purplish ovary, tepals 8–13 × 3–7 mm; terminal bracts suberect, much shorter than the inflorescence axis. Capsule firm, purple. Flowering December–February. Grassland and marshes, SE (Port Elizabeth to KwaZulu-Natal).

Eucomis regia (Linnaeus) L'Héritier
Plants 8–15 cm high. Leaves usually prostrate, broadly oblanceolate, uniformly green, striate. Flowers congested on pedicels to 2 mm long, cream to greenish, tepals 10–15 × 4–5 mm; terminal bracts deflexed, slightly shorter than the inflorescence axis. Capsule inflated, papery, pale. Flowering July–September. Mostly cooler south-facing clay slopes, RV, NW, SW, AP, KM (Namaqualand and western Karoo to Bredasdorp, Little Karoo).

Ferraria

COMMON NAME spider iris, FAMILY Iridaceae. Deciduous perennials. ROOTSTOCK a persistent, depressed-globose, apically rooting corm, new corms produced from the base of the flowering stem, older corms not resorbed and accumulating below the current corm, the tunics membranous, soon disintegrating. LEAVES unifacial, sword-shaped to linear or falcate, thick and leathery to somewhat succulent, usually glaucous, usually without a central vein; stem erect, often covered by overlapping leaf sheaths, sticky below the nodes in one tropical sp., usually branched, branches usually crowded in the upper half. INFLORESCENCE a rhipidium, single and terminal on long branches or several crowded on short branches; spathes somewhat fleshy, resembling leaves in texture and color, the inner exceeding outer. FLOWERS fugacious or lasting as long as 3 days, two to six per rhipidium, often dull colored, shades of brown to yellow, occasionally blue, usually mottled with darker color, tepal margins lighter or darker, often unpleasantly scented, or sweetly vanilla scented; tepals free, subequal or the outer slightly larger than the inner, clawed, the claws forming a wide cup, limbs usually attenuate, spreading horizontally or somewhat below the horizontal, margins crisped. STAMENS with the filaments united below in a column around the style, diverging above; anthers appressed to the style branches, anther lobes parallel or diverging. OVARY ovoid-truncate to narrowly oblong, tapering above, extending upward in a sterile tubular beak in some species; STYLE filiform, dividing above the filament column, the branches short, deeply divided into two flattened lobes, these each with an abaxial stigma lobe and divided terminally into fringed crests. CAPSULES oblong to ellipsoidal, with a short to long acute apex. SEEDS globose or angled by pressure, more or less rugose. Basic chromosome number $x = 10$. Southern tropical Africa to the southern Cape, centered along the western coast of southern Africa, mostly in sandy soils; 11 spp., 7 in the Cape.

Ferraria is characterized by tough, long-lived corms lacking visible tunics and accumulating from year to year in a chain. The flowers are usually dull-colored and have crinkled tepal margins and fringed style crests. The genus is centered in the winter-rainfall region of southern Africa, with a single species, *F. glutinosa* (Baker) Rendle, in summer-rainfall western, southern, and tropical Africa. The species typically favor drier areas, mostly on sand, but some grow on shale or stony substrates. The flowers of some species are short-lived, lasting only a day, but others may last as long as 3 days.

At least some species are known to be pollinated by a variety of flies, including carrion flies and houseflies (Calliphoridae and Muscidae), attracted to the nectar in the flowers by the moldy or somewhat spicy scent and dull, often mottled coloring. The often sweetly scented and pale flowers of *Ferraria ferrariola* are pollinated by honeybees.

Because of their unusual and fascinating flowers, all the species of *Ferraria* are worth horticultural attention. Although the flowers of some species last only a day, individual plants will produce numerous blooms over a 2- to 3-week flowering period. Most species have a fairly compact growth form and are perhaps best grown as pot plants, but *F. crispa* and *F. foliosa* can be robust and reach 0.6–0.8 m in height. They are ideal subjects for the rock garden. The flowers of all ferrarias have tepals with crinkled edges and are usually dull-colored and speckled, but some forms of *F. crispa* have flowers of a glorious deep chocolate color, fringed with golden yellow, and *F. uncinata* can have deep blue to violet flowers. Ferrarias are best raised from corms if these can be obtained, but it is probably more practical to purchase seeds, which germinate quickly. These should be sown in autumn and fertilized generously. Plants may produce their first flowers in their second growing season.

FURTHER READING. A complete, illustrated revision of *Ferraria* was provided by De Vos (1979).

Ferraria crispa Burman

Plants 40–100 cm high, leafy and much branched, the stem covered by leaf sheaths. Leaves sword-shaped, in two ranks, with a thickened zone in the middle and a strong midrib, mostly 8–12 mm wide. Flowers brown and speckled, or uniformly dark brown with light brown edges, 22–30 mm long, anther lobes parallel, ovary spindle-shaped, without a beak. Flowering August–October. Mainly coastal, sandstone or granite rocks, NW, SW, AP, KM, LB (Lambert's Bay to Mossel Bay and Little Karoo).

Ferraria densepunctulata M. P. de Vos

Plants 12–35 cm high with a slender habit. Lower leaves linear, compressed-cylindrical, to 5 mm wide. Flowers pale greenish to gray, with maroon or purple spots, lightly scented, 25–30 mm long, anther lobes parallel, ovary spindle-shaped, without a beak. Flowering May–July. Rocky sites, mostly coastal, NW, SW (Lambert's Bay to Langebaan).

Ferraria divaricata Sweet

Plants 6–20 cm high, often much branched, the stem covered by leaf sheaths. Leaves sword-shaped, crowded basally, in two ranks, to 20 mm wide, the margins thickened. Flowers yellowish to blue with dark spots and margins, 27–45 mm long, anther lobes at first parallel, becoming divergent toward the base, ovary elongate with a beak 10–12 mm long. Flowering August–November. Sandy and shale flats and rock outcrops, NW, SW, AP, KM (southern Namibia to Clanwilliam and western Karoo to Oudtshoorn).

Ferraria ferrariola (Jacquin) Willdenow

Plants 15–60 cm high, slender in habit with stems partly exposed, red to purple below, spotted with white. Lower leaves linear, to 4 mm wide. Flowers greenish, blue, or yellow, often sweetly almond or aniseed scented, 30–40 mm long, anther lobes divergent, ovary elongate with a beak 8–20 mm long. Flowering June–August. Granite and sandstone slopes, NW (northern Namaqualand to Clanwilliam).

Ferraria foliosa G. J. Lewis

Plants 40–100 cm high, leafy and much branched, the stem covered by leaf sheaths. Leaves sword-shaped, spirally two-ranked, shorter than the sheaths, the blades with numerous fine veins, 6–8 mm wide. Flowers brown and speckled, tepals maroon, purple, or dark brown, 30–35 mm long, anther lobes parallel, ovary spindle-shaped, without a beak. Flowering August–October. Deep sand, western coast, NW (Namaqualand to Elands Bay). Page 158.

Ferraria kamiesbergensis M. P. de Vos

Plants mostly 5–20 cm high with branches crowded in the upper half of the stem. Leaves with overlapping sheaths, blades linear to sword-shaped. Flowers cream to pale yellow or greenish, often with darker spots on the te-

Ferraria crispa

Ferraria densepunctulata

Ferraria divaricata

Ferraria ferrariola

Ferraria foliosa

Ferraria uncinata

pal claws, lightly sweetly scented, tepals attenuate, the tips coiled, anther lobes divergent, ovary with a long, sterile beak. Flowering August–October. Sandy flats, RV (Namaqualand to Calvinia).

Ferraria uncinata Sweet

Plants 10–40 cm high, the stem covered by leaf bases. Leaves lanceolate, obtuse, in a tight fan, blades mostly 5–12 mm wide, margins thickened and crisped. Flowers dull yellow, or blue to purple, honey scented, tepal tips attenuate and coiled, 25–40 mm long, anther lobes divergent, ovary with a beak 5–20 mm long. Flowering August–October. Rock outcrops and dry slopes, NW, SW (Namaqualand to Tulbagh and Malmesbury).

Freesia

COMMON NAME freesia, FAMILY Iridaceae. Deciduous perennials. ROOTSTOCK a conical corm, rooting from below, basal in origin, with finely to coarsely fibrous tunics. LEAVES several, the lower two or three forming cataphylls, foliage leaves unifacial with a distinct midrib, in a two-ranked fan, blades plane, firm or soft textured, sometimes prostrate; stem erect, or prostrate below, simple or branched, sometimes compressed and angled. INFLORESCENCE a secund spike, flexed at the base and inclined to horizontal, with flowers borne on the upper side; bracts green and leathery or soft textured, then often brown at the apices. FLOWERS zygomorphic, narrowly to widely funnel-shaped to tubular, mostly white to yellow, or pink to red, rarely greenish to dull purple, sometimes with contrasting darker markings on the lower three tepals, often strongly and sweetly scented, nectar when produced from septal nectaries; perianth tube either slender and cylindrical throughout or narrow below, widened into a narrowly or broadly flared upper part; tepals subequal or the dorsal larger and erect. STAMENS unilateral and arcuate. STYLE filiform, the branches deeply divided and recurved. FRUIT a more or less globose capsule, leathery, usually lightly warty or rough. SEEDS globose, hard and shiny, smooth or wrinkled, the raphe inflated, flattened, or concave at the chalazal end.

Basic chromosome number $x = 11$. Mainly in the southern African winter-rainfall region, 2 spp. in eastern southern Africa and tropical Africa, 1 sp. extending to Sudan; 14 spp., 12 in the Cape.

In its older, narrow delimitation, *Freesia* included only those species with scented, funnel-shaped flowers, mostly colored white or cream with yellow markings. Several species of a second genus, *Anomatheca*, have all the taxonomically critical features of *Freesia*, including a flexed to horizontal spike and smooth, rounded seeds that are swollen along one side, and the two genera have been united under the name *Freesia*. This redefinition brought two red-flowered species from eastern southern and tropical Africa into the genus as well as two other Cape species with narrow floral tubes, one of which, *F. verrucosa*, also has a sweetly scented flower. Although freesias are most common in clay soils in renosterveld or karroid scrub, the two species of the summer-rainfall region occur in light shade in woodland or forest margins. The genus is most closely related to *Ixia* and *Crocosmia*.

The species with highly scented, funnel-shaped flowers are mostly pollinated by solitary bees, whereas the narrow-tubed, pink or red species are probably visited by butterflies. The curious greenish, narrow-tubed flowers of *Freesia viridis* appear to be adapted to pollination by moths but the species is also prone to self-fertilization.

The freesias of cultivation are without exception hybrids, the result of the work of English gardeners who in the 19th century crossed the few wild species then available to produce a range of plants that were floriferous, easy to grow, and had that delightful freesia perfume. Later hybridization resulted in the production of a greater range of flower colors, including clear yellows, blues, pinks, and pure white. The cultivated freesias are now polyploid and thus more robust and taller than their diploid ancestors, and some semidouble forms have been bred. Scent is often much weaker in the hybrids than in wild species but is rarely completely lost. Some hybrids have an elegance of form that make them highly desirable cut flowers. Their Cape ancestry renders them ideal for mild climates though less suitable for areas of summer rain and cold or dark winters.

Wild species like *Freesia alba* and the autumn- or winter-flowering *F. caryophyllacea* have by far the finest scent, and both make excellent pot plants. They can also be planted in odd corners in the rock garden. Usually yellow flowered, *F. corymbosa* and *F. occidentalis* have flowers with a much milder scent and a pleasing form. The very common *F. refracta* often has rather dull greenish flowers and a spicy vanilla odor or may be scentless. In the older literature, all freesias were called *F. refracta*, but this is certainly not one of the species used to develop the cultivated hybrids. The curious green-flowered *F. viridis* confused botanists so much that it has been placed in several genera, including at one time or another, *Gladiolus*, *Lapeirousia*, and *Tritonia*. It is very easy to cultivate. The plants flower freely and set good seeds by self-pollination. Plants from coastal habitats have soft, plane leaves but those from dry country in the Cape interior or from Namaqualand have somewhat leathery leaves with a waxy bloom and tightly curled leaf margins. An interesting range of hybrids was produced between *F. viridis* and the summer-growing *F. laxa* (Thunberg) Goldblatt & J. C. Manning at the Missouri Botanical Garden. They had dark red flowers and grew even more easily than the parents. Being fairly small plants, most freesias can be raised from seed to flower in 2 years, sometimes even a single year. The wild Cape species also reproduce freely by cormels and a pot will become filled with corms in only 2–3 years.

FURTHER READING. Originally revised by Goldblatt (1982a), *Freesia* was later expanded to include several species previously referred to *Anomatheca* (Goldblatt and Manning 1995c). A further species was described by Manning and Goldblatt (2001a).

Freesia alba (G. L. Meyer) Gumbleton

Plants 12–40 cm high; corm conical with finely netted tunics. Leaves ascending to erect, sword-shaped and acute. Flowers in a horizontal spike, white, often mauve on the outside, strongly sweetly scented, perianth tube broadly funnel-shaped, mostly 20–30 mm long, tepals subequal, 15–18 mm long; bracts green and leathery. Flowering July–October. Sandy or stony soils, mainly coastal, SW, LB, AP, SE (Hermanus to Plettenberg Bay).

Freesia alba

Freesia caryophyllacea

Freesia caryophyllacea (Burman fil.) N. E. Brown
Plants 5–10 cm high; corm conical with tunics of medium-textured fibers. Leaves sword-shaped, obtuse, usually prostrate. Flowers in a horizontal spike, yellow or cream with yellow markings, strongly sweetly scented, perianth tube broadly funnel-shaped, 20–25 mm long, tepals unequal, the dorsal markedly larger, 16–20 mm long; bracts green and leathery. Flowering April–June. Clay soils and limestone, renosterveld and coastal bush, SW, AP, LB (Villiersdorp to Swellendam and Bredasdorp).

Freesia corymbosa (Burman fil.) N. E. Brown
Plants 25–50 cm high; corm conical with tunics of medium to coarse fibers. Leaves sword-shaped, more or less acute, mostly half as long as the stem. Flowers in a horizontal spike, yellow, sometimes pink, usually lightly scented, perianth tube broadly funnel-shaped, c. 20 mm long, tepals 9–12 mm long, the dorsal slightly larger than the lower, the inner tepals heart-shaped at the base; bracts soft textured with dark brown tips. Flowering mostly August–November. Mainly stony sandstone slopes, SE (Long Kloof to Eastern Cape).

Freesia fergusoniae L. Bolus
Plants 10–20 cm high; corm conical with tunics of medium to coarse fibers. Leaves sword-shaped, obtuse, mostly prostrate. Flowers in a horizontal spike, yellow with orange markings, sweetly scented, perianth tube broadly funnel-shaped, 22–26 mm long, tepals 12–14 mm long; bracts green and leathery. Flowering August–September. Clay soils, renosterveld, LB (Heidelberg to Mossel Bay).

Freesia fucata J. C. Manning & Goldblatt
Plants 8–20 cm high; corm conical with tunics of medium-textured netted fibers. Leaves narrowly sword-shaped, inclined or suberect. Flowers in a horizontal or drooping spike, white flushed purple with broad yellow markings, sweetly violet scented, perianth tube broadly funnel-shaped, 20–30 mm long, tepals 10–18 mm long, the dorsal slightly larger than the lower; bracts green and leathery, tricuspidate. Flowering July. Clay slopes in renosterveld, SW (Villiersdorp).

Freesia leichtlinii Klatt
Plants 8–20 cm high; corm conical with tunics of finely netted fibers. Leaves sword-shaped, often inclined, sometimes prostrate. Flowers in a horizontal spike, cream with broad yellow markings, sweetly scented, perianth tube broadly funnel-shaped, 15–25 mm long, tepals 14–18 mm long, the dorsal slightly larger than the lower; bracts green and leathery. Flowering August–September. Deep sands in coastal fynbos, AP, LB (Cape Agulhas to Mossel Bay).

Freesia occidentalis L. Bolus
Plants 9–50 cm high; corm conical with tunics of medium to coarse fibers. Leaves sword-shaped, mostly obtuse, more than half as long as the stem. Flowers in a horizontal spike, creamy white and yellow, lightly scented, perianth tube broadly funnel-shaped, 18–25 mm long, tepals 8–11 mm long, the inner tepals heart-shaped at the base; bracts soft textured, often with brown tips. Flowering July–September. Stony, mainly sandstone soils, RV, NW, KM (Cedarberg Mountains to Touws River and western Karoo).

Freesia sparrmannii (Thunberg) N. E. Brown
Plants 12–18 cm high; corm conical with tunics of finely netted fibers. Leaves sword-shaped, often inclined to prostrate. Flowers in a horizontal spike, white, flushed purple on the outside, faintly scented, perianth tube narrowly funnel-shaped, 20–27 mm long, tepals subequal, 9–11 mm long; bracts green and leathery. Flowering September. Forest margins in loam, LB (Langeberg foothills from Swellendam to Heidelberg).

Freesia speciosa L. Bolus
Plants 8–20 cm high; corm conical with tunics of coarse fibers. Leaves sword-shaped, obtuse, inclined to prostrate. Flowers in a horizontal spike, large, 50–70 mm long, white and deep yellow, sweetly scented, perianth tube funnel-shaped, 35–50 mm long, tepals 13–18 mm long, the dorsal slightly larger than the lower; bracts soft textured with brown tips. Flowering August–September. Stony karroid flats, KM (Montagu to Calitzdorp).

Freesia refracta (Jacquin) Klatt
Plants 18–45 cm high; corm conical with tunics of finely netted fibers. Leaves usually erect or suberect, sword-shaped, acute. Flowers in a horizontal spike, greenish or dull purple with yellow to orange markings, usually strongly spice scented or scentless, perianth tube broadly funnel-shaped, 16–24 mm long, tepals 10–14 mm long, the dorsal larger than the lower tepals, the inner tepals heart-shaped at the base; bracts soft textured, submembranous, sometimes with dark brown tips. Flowering July–September. Dry stony slopes and flats in karroid bush and arid fynbos, SW, KM (Worcester to Oudtshoorn).

Freesia verrucosa (Vogel) Goldblatt & J. C. Manning
Plants 8–20 cm high; corm conical with finely fibrous tunics. Leaves sword-shaped, acute or subobtuse. Flowers in an inclined to horizontal spike, pink, sometimes

Freesia refracta

lightly scented, perianth tube uniformly narrow, 10–15 mm long, tepals spreading, c. 9 mm long, subequal; bracts greenish, soft textured, often with brown tips. Flowering August–October. Clay soils in renosterveld, KM, SE (Oudtshoorn to Humansdorp).

Freesia viridis (Aiton) Goldblatt & J. C. Manning

Plants 10–35 cm high; corm conical with tunics of medium-textured fibers. Leaves sword-shaped, acute, sometimes glaucous, often inclined toward the ground, the margins sometimes crisped. Flowers in an inclined spike, small, green to dull purplish, faintly clove scented or scentless, perianth tube slender and curved, 20–30 mm long, dorsal tepal erect, 12–20 mm long, other tepals smaller, tapering and lightly reflexed; bracts soft textured, more or less membranous. Flowering July–September. Stony clay and limestone or occasionally sandstone slopes, NW, SW (southern Namibia to Mamre).

Freesia viridis

Geissorhiza

COMMON NAMES satinflower, wine cup, FAMILY Iridaceae. Deciduous perennials. ROOTSTOCK a corm, globose to ovoid and asymmetric or bell-shaped, usually with a basal ridge from which the roots emerge, basal in origin, the tunics woody or rarely membranous to fibrous, concentric or overlapping, then notched below. LEAVES few to several, the lower two or three forming cataphylls, foliage leaves unifacial, usually with a definite midrib, two to several, the blades plane to round or H-shaped in cross section, sometimes the margins and or midrib raised and winged, sometimes hairy or sticky; stem aerial, simple or branched, round in cross section, sometimes puberulous or scabrid, drooping in bud. INFLORESCENCE a spike, rarely the flowers solitary on the branches, the flowers usually spirally arranged; bracts green and soft textured to membranous, the inner smaller than the outer and notched apically. FLOWERS rotate to salverform or cup-shaped, variously colored, often shades of blue to violet, also pink, yellow, cream, purple, red, or bicolored, actinomorphic or zygomorphic, unscented, sometimes with nectar, then from septal nectaries; perianth tube short to long, funnel-shaped or cylindrical; tepals subequal, the inner usually shorter than the outer, cupped or spreading from the base. STAMENS symmetrically disposed or unilateral and declinate, sometimes unequal with one filament shorter than the other two. STYLE filiform, central, eccentric or unilateral and arching below the stamens, usually exserted, the branches usually slender and recurved, or broadly expanded above. FRUIT a globose to oblong or cylindrical capsule, membranous to cartilaginous. SEEDS angular to globose, flattened at the chalazal end. Basic chromosome number $x = 13$. Centered in the Western Cape but extending north into Namaqualand, the western Karoo, and east to Grahamstown in the Eastern Cape; 84 spp., 83 in the Cape.

Geissorhiza and the allied genus *Hesperantha* are distinguished in Iridaceae subfamily Crocoideae by their asymmetric corms, which have a basal ridge from which the roots arise and unusual woody corm tunics. They also share the unusual basic chromosome number $x = 13$.

Geissorhiza is the less specialized of the two and difficult to define except in relation to *Hesperantha*. In *Geissorhiza* the flowering stems are typically nodding in bud, and in most species the style is eccentric and divides above the level of the anthers into fairly short, recurved branches. In *Hesperantha* the spikes are erect in bud, and the style divides at the mouth of the narrow perianth tube into long and laxly spreading style branches. The extensive leaf modifications that occur in *Geissorhiza*, including thickening of the margins and veins, development of hairs, or reduction of the leaf area into a terete blade, are never encountered in *Hesperantha*, which almost always has flat, sword-shaped leaves.

There are two subgenera of *Geissorhiza*, distinguished by their corms. Subgenus *Weihea* has corms in which the brownish tunics from successive years overlap one another completely and protrude beneath the outermost only at the base. The tunics tend to fragment above into narrow segments drawn into pointed tips. Subgenus *Geissorhiza* has visibly overlapping, mostly blackish tunics, the older layers riding over the newer ones and characteristically notched below. The layers of overlapping, notched tunics in subgenus *Geissorhiza* recall roof tiles or shingles, the source of the name *Geissorhiza*, meaning tile-root. Evolutionary radiation in *Geissorhiza* is extensive with species adapted to a variety of habitats and the flowers to a range of pollinators. Several species are restricted to cliffs close to or under waterfalls.

The star-shaped flowers of most species are pollinated by a variety of insects, particularly bees. Several pink-flowered, long-tubed species are adapted to pollination by long-proboscid flies of the families Tabanidae and Nemestrinidae, including all the species previously placed in the genus *Engysiphon*. A few species with a dark purplish center are pollinated by monkey beetles (Scarabaeidae: Hopliini).

Although a large genus, *Geissorhiza* has relatively few horticulturally desirable species, for most have small flowers without distinctive form. A few species, however, have relatively large flowers, and some have quite brilliant coloring. The small group of species known as wine cups, including *G. eurystigma* and *G. radians*, have large violet flowers with a deep red center, in the latter species with a white edge separating the two main colors. Both grow in seasonally wet sites in the wild but make striking pot subjects, and *G. radians* makes an eye-catching sight growing massed in a large raised bed at Kirstenbosch botanical garden. Another large-flowered species, *G. tulbaghensis,* also does well in pots where the large white flowers with a dull brown-purple center and gracefully arching, dark brown stamens are shown off to advantage. All these species are small plants and would be lost in the rock garden. Very common in the wild and so given little attention, *G. aspera* often grows in such masses that the small, star-like, deep blue flowers make a substantial splash of color. The species seeds freely and plants have become naturalized on road banks and park grounds in the Western Cape, suggesting a potential for easy domestication. Another species that merits attention is *G. inflexa*. A plant of fairly dry clay banks, it has red, purple, and cream forms. The red form, which also has larger flowers than usual, initially known as *G. erosa* when cultivated in Britain in the late 18th century, is particularly recommended because of the sheer beauty of the flowers. The Bokkeveld pride, *G. splendidissima,* from the Nieuwoudtville area in the north of the Cape region, is another exceptional species. The large, brilliant dark blue flowers with a glossy sheen and large, arching, brown anthers are a striking sight in the wild. It is probably not difficult to grow in cultivation. The majority of the larger-flowered geissorhizas, such as *G. callista*, *G. confusa*, *G. exscapa*, and *G. schinzii*, are plants of sandy mountain slopes and flower well in the wild only after fire. Their white or pale pink flowers then often make a dazzling display. Whether this can be duplicated in the rock garden or planter remains to be determined. Almost all the species of *Geissorhiza* will reward the gardener who takes the trouble to obtain seeds or corms.

FURTHER READING. *Geissorhiza* was monographed by Goldblatt (1981b). Several more species were described by Goldblatt (1989a) and Goldblatt and Manning (1995a).

Geissorhiza alticola Goldblatt

Plants 20–30 cm high; corm globose with softly papery tunics soon decaying. Leaves linear, the margins and midrib heavily thickened and with two grooves on each surface, 2–3 mm wide. Flowers in a three- to five-flowered spike, blue-violet, perianth tube 2–3 mm long, tepals spreading, 11–13 mm long; bracts green, becoming dry at the tips. Flowering December–February. High rocky slopes and peaks, 1500–2000 m, SW (Bain's Kloof to Wemmershoek Mountains).

Geissorhiza arenicola L. Bolus
Plants 12–25 cm high, stem minutely velvety; corm ovoid with woody, overlapping tunics. Leaves linear with thickened and winged margins and midrib, narrowly two-grooved on each surface, c. 2 mm wide. Flowers in a 3- to 10-flowered spike, blue or white, perianth tube c. 2 mm long, tepals spreading, 12–15 mm long, stamens usually with one shorter filament; bracts green, becoming dry above. Flowering August–September. Sandy mountain soils in fynbos, NW (Bokkeveld Mountains to Gifberg).

Geissorhiza aspera Goldblatt
Plants 10–35 cm high, stem roughly scabrid; corm ovoid with woody, overlapping tunics. Leaves sword-shaped to linear, margins and midrib lightly thickened, mostly 2–5 mm wide. Flowers in a three- to seven-flowered spike, blue to violet, sometimes with a darker center, rarely white, perianth tube c. 2 mm long, tepals spreading, 11–15 mm long, stamens usually slightly unequal with one shorter filament; bracts green or drying brown above. Flowering August–September. Mostly sandy soils, flats and slopes, 10–700 m, NW, SW (Gifberg to Bredasdorp).

Geissorhiza barkerae Goldblatt
Plants 10–20 cm high; corm ovoid with woody, overlapping tunics. Leaves linear to sword-shaped, several-ribbed, 2–4 mm wide. Flowers in a 2- to 10-flowered spike, yellow with a purple center, perianth tube c. 7 mm long, tepals cupped, 22–30 mm long, stamens and style unilateral, arching downward, with one shorter filament; bracts green, often reddish and becoming dry above. Flowering September–October. Marshes and seeps at the foot of mountains, NW (Piketberg to Citrusdal).

Geissorhiza bolusii Baker
Plants 3–10 cm high; corm ovoid with softly woody, concentric tunics. Leaves lanceolate to ovate, the lower usually prostrate, 2–4 mm wide. Flowers in a two- to eight-flowered spike, small, white, perianth tube 3–4 mm long, tepals spreading, 7–10 mm long, buds often aborted and replaced by cormels, never producing capsules; bracts green. Flowering October–January. Damp, shady, sandstone slopes in moss, 400–1500 m, NW, SW (Cedarberg to Cape Peninsula and Riviersonderend Mountains).

Geissorhiza bonaspei Goldblatt
Plants 12–20 cm high; corm ovoid with woody, concentric tunics. Leaves linear, the margins raised into wings, thus H-shaped in cross section, sticky and with sand adhering, c. 5 mm wide. Flowers in a one- to five-flowered spike, pale pink, fading darker pink and with dark veins, perianth tube cylindrical, 20–30 mm long, tepals spreading, 24–27 mm long, stamens and style unilateral, arching downward; bracts green, often sticky. Flowering September–November, mainly after fire. Rocky sandstone slopes in fynbos, SW (Cape Peninsula).

Geissorhiza aspera; see also the illustration for *Sparaxis grandiflora* subsp. *grandiflora*

Geissorhiza bracteata Klatt

Plants mostly 6–12 cm high, often with two or three stems from the base; corm ovoid with woody, concentric tunics. Leaves sword-shaped, the margins and midrib hardly thickened, 2–9 mm wide. Flowers mostly one or two per spike, white, perianth tube 3–5 mm long, tepals spreading, 5–12 mm long; bracts green, firm. Flowering September–October. Mostly clay slopes in renosterveld, LB, SE (Albertinia to Grahamstown and Somerset East).

Geissorhiza brehmii Ecklon ex Klatt

Plants 20–30 cm high; corm ovoid with woody, overlapping tunics. Leaves terete with several shallow grooves, c. 1.5 mm diam. Flowers in a two- to six-flowered spike, white to cream, perianth tube 5–8 mm long, tepals spreading, 15–26 mm long; bracts green, becoming dry above. Flowering August–October. Seasonal pools, mainly in stony or sandy flats, SW (Malmesbury and Cape Peninsula to Bredasdorp).

Geissorhiza brevituba (G. J. Lewis) Goldblatt

Plants 12–20 cm high; corm ovoid with woody, concentric tunics. Leaves linear to sword-shaped, sticky and with adhering sand, the margins and midrib heavily thickened and with two narrow grooves on each surface. Flowers in a one- to three-flowered spike, deep pink, darker on the veins, perianth tube c. 8 mm long, tepals cupped, 25–30 mm long, stamens and style unilateral and arching downward; bracts green. Flowering September, mainly after fire. Rocky sandstone slopes, NW (Piketberg).

Geissorhiza bryicola Goldblatt

Plants 15–30 cm high, stem inclined to drooping; corm ovoid with woody, overlapping tunics. Leaves linear, soft and trailing, 1.5–4 mm wide. Flowers in a three- to eight-flowered spike, white, perianth tube c. 2.5 mm long, tepals spreading, 8–10 mm long, stamens with one shorter filament; bracts green. Flowering September–November. Wet rocks, waterfalls, stream edges, SW (Hermanus Mountains).

Geissorhiza barkerae

Geissorhiza bonaspei

Geissorhiza burchellii R. C. Foster

Plants 12–20 cm high; corm ovoid with papery, overlapping tunics. Leaves linear, the margins and midrib moderately thickened, 1.5–3 mm wide. Flowers in a three- to nine-flowered spike nodding at the tip, dark purple, perianth tube 4–6 mm long, tepals spreading to lightly reflexed, 12–22 mm long, stamens unequal and unilateral, arching downward; bracts green. Flowering December–January, mostly after fire. Rocky sandstone slopes, 200–400 m, SW, LB (Bain's Kloof to Langeberg Mountains).

Geissorhiza callista Goldblatt

Plants 15–30 cm high; corm ovoid with entire, papery tunics. Leaves linear, the margins and midrib thickened. Flowers in a nodding, two- to five-flowered spike, bright pink with dark purple center, perianth tube 22–25 mm long, tepals cupped, 24–26 mm long, stamens and style unilateral, filaments unequal; bracts green. Flowering October–November, mainly after fire. Wet rocks and seeps on south-facing sandstone slopes, SW, LB (Riviersonderend and Langeberg Mountains).

Geissorhiza confusa

Geissorhiza cataractarum Goldblatt

Plants 10–30 cm high, stem often drooping; corm ovoid with tunics membranous, not accumulating. Leaves slender, trailing, the margins and midrib moderately thickened and with two grooves on each surface, c. 1.5 mm wide. Flowers in a one- to five-flowered spike, pale blue, perianth tube 4–6 mm long, tepals spreading, 14–20 mm long; bracts green. Flowering November–January. Waterfalls and damp cliffs, SW (Betty's Bay to Hermanus).

Geissorhiza cedarmontana Goldblatt

Plants mostly 15–30 cm high; corm ovoid with softly woody, concentric tunics. Leaves linear, c. 1.5 mm wide, the margins and midrib strongly thickened and with two narrow grooves on each surface. Flowers in a two- to five-flowered spike, pale pink, dark red at the tepal bases, perianth tube cylindrical, 13–15 mm long, tepals spreading, 12–14 mm long, stamens and style included in the lower half of the tube; bracts green. Flowering October–November. Damp south slopes and rock crevices, NW (Cedarberg Mountains).

Geissorhiza ciliatula Goldblatt

Plants 6–12 cm high, stem finely velvety; corm ovoid with woody, overlapping tunics. Leaves linear, soft, with margins and midrib strongly thickened, c. 1 mm wide. Flowers in a one- to four-flowered spike, white fading mauve, perianth tube c. 1.5 mm long, tepals spreading, 6–7 mm long; bracts green below, dry and transparent above. Flowering October–November. Moist rocky sandstone slopes, 600–1000 m, NW (Cedarberg Mountains).

Geissorhiza confusa Goldblatt

Plants 12–30 cm high; corm ovoid with woody, concentric tunics. Leaves more or less linear, the margins and midribs thickened, thus with two longitudinal grooves on each surface, sticky and with sand adhering, 3–7 mm wide. Flowers in a two- to four-, sometimes as many as eight-flowered spike, creamy beige to whitish, fading pink with darker veins, perianth tube cylindrical, 25–40 mm long, tepals spreading, 28–40 mm long, stamens and style unilateral and arching downward; bracts green. Flowering mostly October–November, especially after fire. Rocky sandstone slopes in fynbos, mostly above 350 m, NW, SW (Gifberg to Villiersdorp).

Geissorhiza corrugata Klatt
Plants c. 5 cm high, often with two or three stems from the base; corm ovoid with woody, concentric tunics. Leaves linear, 1–2 mm wide, spirally twisted. Flowers mostly single, sometimes two per stalk, bright yellow, perianth tube c. 3 mm long, tepals cupped, 12–15 mm long, style usually dividing opposite the top of the filaments; bracts green, dry and brown above. Flowering August–September. Shale slopes, RV (southwest of Calvinia).

Geissorhiza darlingensis Goldblatt
Plants 7–15 cm high; corm globose with woody, concentric tunics. Leaves linear, 2–3 mm wide, sticky below, the margins and midrib thickened and raised, minutely hairy on the edges, 2–3 mm wide. Flowers in a two- to five-flowered spike, yellow with a dark brown center, perianth tube 9–11 mm long, tepals cupped, 23–26 mm long; bracts green. Flowering September–October. Damp flats, SW (Darling).

Geissorhiza delicatula Goldblatt
Plants mostly 3–8 cm high; corm ovoid with soft, concentric tunics. Leaves linear to sword-shaped, soft, often prostrate, 1.5–4.5 mm wide. Flowers in a one- to three-flowered spike, pale lilac, perianth tube c. 2.5 mm long, tepals spreading, 2.5–4.5 mm long; bracts green, soft. Flowering August–December. Sandstone outcrops, in sheltered places, KM (Swartberg Mountains).

Geissorhiza divaricata Goldblatt
Plants 20–45 cm high, stems divaricately branched; corm ovoid with woody, overlapping tunics. Leaves linear to sword-shaped, the margins and veins thickened and short-velvety, 2–3 mm wide. Flowers in a three- to five-flowered spike, small, white to pale mauve, dark mauve on the reverse, perianth tube c. 1.5 mm long, tepals spreading, c. 10 mm long; bracts dry, brownish above. Flowering September–October. Sandstone rocks, NW (Bokkeveld Mountains to Gifberg).

Geissorhiza elsiae Goldblatt
Plants 14–25 cm high; corm ovoid with soft, concentric tunics. Leaves sword-shaped to linear, soft, 3–6 mm wide. Flowers in a two- to four-flowered spike, purple to deep pink, perianth tube 6–10 mm long, tepals 15–20 mm long, spreading; bracts green with red margins and veins.

Geissorhiza corrugata

Geissorhiza darlingensis

Geissorhiza eurystigma; see also the illustration for *Ixia curta*

Geissorhiza exscapa

Flowering October–November. Damp south-facing slopes and cliffs, often in moss, KM (Kammanassie Mountains).

Geissorhiza erubescens Goldblatt
Plants 8–15 cm high, stem finely velvety; corm ovoid with woody, overlapping tunics. Leaves narrowly sword-shaped, margins and midrib thickened, thus two-grooved on each surface, 2–3 mm wide. Flowers in a two- to seven-flowered spike, small, cream, bright red on the outside, perianth tube c. 1.5 mm long, tepals spreading, mostly 8–10 mm long. Flowering September. Shale and loam slopes, NW (Pakhuis Mountains).

Geissorhiza esterhuyseniae Goldblatt
Plants 7–15 cm high; corm unknown, probably ovoid with woody, concentric tunics. Leaves linear or falcate, 3–5 mm wide, the margins and midrib moderately thickened. Flowers in a one- to three-flowered spike, white, sweetly scented, perianth tube cylindrical, 10–16 mm long, tepals spreading, 13–15 mm long, stamens and style included in the lower half of the tube; bracts green, pale and membranous to dry above. Flowering October. Rocky, south-facing, sandstone slopes, c. 1200 m, NW (Grootwinterhoek Mountains).

Geissorhiza eurystigma L. Bolus
Plants 8–20 cm high; corm ovoid with woody, overlapping tunics. Leaves sword-shaped to linear, several-ribbed, 3–6 mm wide. Flowers usually in a two- to five-flowered spike, deep blue-violet with a bright red center, tepals widely cupped, style branches broad and villous, held well above the anthers. Flowering September–October. Granitic soils in renosterveld, SW (Darling to Malmesbury).

Geissorhiza exscapa (Thunberg) Goldblatt
Plants 18–30 cm high, stem mostly shorter than the leaves; corm ovoid with woody, concentric tunics. Leaves linear, the margins raised into wings, thus H-shaped in cross section, sticky and with sand adhering, 4–7 mm wide. Flowers usually in a three- to nine-flowered spike, whitish to pink, aging darker pink and often darker on

the veins, perianth tube cylindrical, 40–80 mm long, tepals spreading, 26–35 mm long, stamens and style unilateral, arching downward; bracts green. Flowering October–November. Sandy flats and slopes, mainly along the coast, NW, SW (Namaqualand to Melkbos).

Geissorhiza foliosa Klatt
Plants mostly 10–20 cm high, stems usually with one or more short lateral branches; corm ovoid with woody, concentric tunics. Leaves short, lanceolate, 3–6 mm wide. Flowers in a two- to five-flowered spike, lilac to purple with whitish anthers, perianth tube c. 5 mm long, tepals spreading, 13–17 mm long; bracts green, becoming dry and pale above. Flowering September–November. Clay slopes and flats in renosterveld, LB (Swellendam to Riversdale).

Geissorhiza fourcadei (L. Bolus) G. J. Lewis
Plants 12–30 cm high, stems usually with one or two branches; corm ovoid with firm, papery, concentric tunics tapering to attenuate tips, forming a neck around the stem base. Leaves terete or nearly so with four narrow longitudinal grooves, c. 1.5 mm wide. Flowers always one per branch, large, pink to mauve, perianth tube mostly 15–20 mm long, tepals spreading, 25–30 mm long, stamens and style unilateral, arching downward. Flowering mostly March–May. Seasonally moist sandstone rocks, KM, LB, SE (eastern Langeberg, Swartberg, and Outeniqua Mountains to Baviaanskloof).

Geissorhiza furva Ker Gawler ex Baker
Plants 8–14 cm high; corm ovoid with woody, concentric tunics. Leaves terete with four narrow longitudinal grooves, c. 1.2 mm diam. Flowers in a one- to three-flowered spike, large, golden yellow, perianth tube 3–5 mm long, tepals cupped, 15–28 mm long; bracts green below, dry and brown toward the tips. Flowering September–October. Stony flats and lower slopes, NW, SW (Piketberg to Paarl).

Geissorhiza geminata E. Meyer ex Baker
Plants 12–30 cm high, usually with two nearly equal ascending branches; corm ovoid with woody, concentric tunics. Leaves linear, 2–3 mm wide. Flowers in a one- to three-flowered spike, white to cream, perianth tube 6–8 mm long, tepals cupped, 12–14 mm long; bracts green, often reddish on the margins. Flowering September–November. Marshes and pools, NW (Cold Bokkeveld to Worcester).

Geissorhiza grandiflora Goldblatt
Plants mostly 35–35 cm high; corm ovoid with soft, papery to membranous, overlapping tunics. Leaves linear, the margins and midrib moderately thickened, thus two-grooved on each surface, 2–4 mm wide. Flowers in a three- to eight-flowered spike, large, pink, darker at the mouth of the tube, perianth tube cylindrical, 15–22 mm long, tepals cupped, 22–30 mm long, stamens and style unilateral, arching downward, with one shorter filament. Flowering November–December. Rocky sandstone slopes, NW, SW (Grootwinterhoek Mountains to Villiersdorp).

Geissorhiza foliosa

Geissorhiza hesperanthoides Schlechter

Plants 15–30 cm high; corm ovoid with fibrous tunics. Leaves linear, the margins and midrib heavily thickened, thus with two narrow grooves on each surface, 2–3 mm wide. Flowers in a one- to three-flowered spike, blue to violet, perianth tube 5–10 mm long, tepals spreading, 12–18 mm long; bracts green, often reddish at the tips. Flowering November–January. Damp and marshy mountain slopes, 800–1500 m, SW (Bain's Kloof to Bredasdorp).

Geissorhiza heterostyla L. Bolus

Plants 12–45 cm high, stem finely velvety with a scale-like bract below the spike and often branched in this axil; corm ovoid with woody, overlapping tunics. Leaves linear to sword-shaped, the margins and midribs raised, winged and minutely hairy, 2–5 mm wide. Flowers usually in a three- to seven-flowered spike, blue to purple, sometimes dark in the center, perianth tube c. 1.5 mm long, tepals spreading, mostly 10–18 mm long, stamens with one shorter filament, sometimes the styles of different lengths. Flowering August–October. Mainly stony clay slopes in renosterveld, RV, NW, SW, KM, LB, SE (southern Namaqualand to Port Elizabeth and western Karoo).

Geissorhiza hispidula (R. C. Foster) Goldblatt

Plants 7–25 cm high; corm ovoid with woody, concentric tunics. Leaves linear, c. 2 mm wide, sticky and with adhering sand, the margins and midrib heavily thickened and often hispid, thus with two narrow grooves on each surface, 1–2 mm wide. Flowers in a two- to five-flowered spike, small, cream or white, often flushed red on the outside, perianth tube c. 4 mm long, tepals spreading, 10–15 mm long; bracts green, often with reddish margins, sticky. Flowering August–September, mostly after fire. Sandy flats and mountain slopes, SW, LB (Cape Peninsula to Albertinia).

Geissorhiza humilis (Thunberg) Ker Gawler

Plants 8–14 cm high; corm globose with woody, concentric tunics. Leaves linear, sticky below and often with adhering sand, the margins and midrib heavily thickened, thus two-grooved on each surface, 2–3 mm wide. Flowers in a two- to eight-flowered spike, clear pale yellow, perianth tube c. 6 mm long, tepals lightly cupped, 16–22 mm long; bracts green, sticky. Flowering August–October, mainly after fire. Sandy soils in fynbos, 50–300 m, SW (Cape Peninsula to Paarl).

Geissorhiza imbricata (D. Delaroche) Ker Gawler

Plants 8–30 cm high; corm ovoid with woody, overlapping tunics. Leaves several-ribbed, sword-shaped to linear, mostly 3–7 mm wide. Flowers in a 6- to 9-flowered spike, sometimes as few as 2- or as many as 14-flowered, white to yellow, often reddish on the outside and occasionally darker in the center, perianth tube 3–8 mm long, tepals spreading, mostly 10–15 mm long, occasionally longer; bracts green, often becoming dry above. Flowering August–November. Wet sandy flats, marshes, streamsides, NW, SW (Gifberg to Bredasdorp).

Geissorhiza imbricata

Geissorhiza inaequalis L. Bolus
Plants 8–15 cm high, stem roughly velvety; corm ovoid with woody, overlapping tunics. Leaves sword-shaped, 4–10 mm wide. Flowers in a two- to seven-flowered spike, pale blue-mauve, perianth tube 2–3 mm long, tepals spreading, 20–23 mm long, stamens and style more or less unilateral and horizontal, with one shorter filament. Flowering August–October. Rocky slopes in heavy clay, RV, NW (Bokkeveld Escarpment and western Karoo).

Geissorhiza inconspicua Baker
Plants 10–30 cm high; corm ovoid with woody, concentric tunics. Leaves sword-shaped to linear, 2.5–6 mm wide. Flowers mostly in a four- to seven-flowered spike, white or blue to purple, perianth tube c. 5 mm long, tepals spreading, mostly 8–12 mm long; bracts green often with red edges. Flowering mostly October–November, rarely as late as February. Mountains and flats, LB, SE (Swellendam to Uitenhage).

Geissorhiza inflexa (D. Delaroche) Ker Gawler
Plants 12–35 cm high; corm ovoid with woody, overlapping tunics. Leaves sword-shaped to linear, the margins usually with wings held at right angles to the blade, minutely hairy on veins and margin edges, 2–10 mm wide. Flowers in a two- to six-flowered spike, white to cream, sometimes red or purple, perianth tube c. 2 mm long, tepals mostly 10–15 mm long, rarely as long as 24 mm; bracts dry, rusty above. Flowering August–September. Clay flats and slopes in renosterveld, NW, SW (Piketberg to Bredasdorp).

Geissorhiza intermedia Goldblatt
Plants 5–12 cm high, stem velvety; corm ovoid with woody, concentric tunics. Leaves sword-shaped to falcate, the margins and midrib moderately thickened, thus with two broad longitudinal grooves on each surface, 1.5–3.5 mm wide, sticky below. Flowers in a one- to three-flowered spike, white, perianth tube c. 2.5 mm long, tepals spreading, 8–10 mm long; bracts green, hyaline at the tips. Flowering September–October. Sandstone soils in fynbos, NW, SW (Porterville to Stellenbosch).

Geissorhiza juncea (Link) A. Dietrich
Plants 20–40 cm high; corm ovoid with woody, concentric tunics. Leaves terete with four narrow longitudinal grooves, c. 1.2 mm diam. Flowers mostly in a five- to eight-flowered spike, small, white to pale yellow, perianth tube c. 2.5 mm long, tepals spreading, mostly 8–12 mm long; bracts green below, dry toward the tips. Flowering August–November. Sandy flats and slopes, to 400 m, NW, SW (Cedarberg Mountains to Stanford).

Geissorhiza karooica Goldblatt
Plants 3–6 cm high, stem single or two to four from the base; corm ovoid with woody, concentric tunics. Leaves linear to falcate, 1–2 mm wide. Flowers one per stem, purple, pale yellow in the center edged with darker purple, perianth tube 6–8 mm long, tepals spreading, 12–15 mm long, stamens and style unilateral, more or less horizontal; bracts green below, membranous to dry and pur-

Geissorhiza inflexa

Geissorhiza karooica

plish above. Flowering August–September. Shale slopes, RV (Roggeveld Mountains to Matjiesfontein).

Geissorhiza leipoldtii R. C. Foster

Plants 12–30 cm high, stem thinly velvety; corm ovoid with woody, overlapping tunics. Leaves sword-shaped, shortly hairy on the margins and midrib, 3–5 mm wide. Flowers in a two- to six-flowered spike, white, pink, or mauve, perianth tube c. 2 mm long, tepals spreading, 14–28 mm long, stamens usually with one shorter filament; bracts dry and light brown above. Flowering August–September. Mostly south-facing shale slopes, NW (Pakhuis Mountains to Citrusdal).

Geissorhiza lithicola Goldblatt

Plants 15–30 cm high; corm ovoid with woody, concentric tunics. Leaves linear, the margins and midrib heavily thickened, thus with four narrow longitudinal grooves, c. 1 mm diam. Flowers in a one- to four-flowered spike, violet, perianth tube 7–8 mm long, tepals spreading, 15–20 mm long; bracts green below, drying above. Flowering October. Lower rocky slopes, 50–200 m, SW (Kogel Bay to Rooi Els).

Geissorhiza longifolia (G. J. Lewis) Goldblatt

Plants 12–20 cm high; corm ovoid with woody, concentric tunics. Leaves linear, margins raised into wings, the midrib lightly thickened, sticky and with sand adhering, 6–8 mm wide. Flowers in a four- to nine-flowered spike, white, fading pink with darker veins, perianth tube 14–25 mm long, tepals spreading, 17–27 mm long, stamens and style unilateral and arching downward; bracts green. Flowering September–November. Stony, often shale soils, NW (Gifberg to Piketberg and Ceres).

Geissorhiza louisabolusiae R. C. Foster

Plants 15–20 cm high; corm ovoid with woody, overlapping tunics. Leaves linear and lightly grooved to terete with shallow longitudinal grooves, 1–2 mm wide. Flowers in a three- to seven-flowered spike, pale yellow, perianth tube 4–6 mm long, tepals cupped, 18–28 mm long, stamens usually unequal; bracts green or becoming dry

Geissorhiza leipoldtii

above. Flowering August–September. Wet sandy flats, NW (Olifants River Valley and Cold Bokkeveld).

Geissorhiza malmesburiensis R. C. Foster
Plants 5–8 cm high; corms bell-shaped with a flat base, with woody, concentric tunics toothed along the lower margins. Leaves linear, c. 1 mm wide. Flowers mostly one per spike, pale yellow, perianth tube c. 4 mm long, tepals cupped, 13–25 mm long; bracts green with translucent tips. Flowering September–October. Sandy granitic slopes in renosterveld, SW (Malmesbury).

Geissorhiza minuta Goldblatt
Plants 3–12 cm high; corm ovoid with woody, overlapping tunics. Leaves linear, the margins and midrib moderately thickened, c. 1 mm wide. Flowers in a two- to six-flowered spike, tiny, white, perianth tube c. 1 mm long, tepals spreading, 7–8 mm long. Flowering September–October. Wet stony sites, NW (Pakhuis Mountains and Gifberg).

Geissorhiza mathewsii L. Bolus
Plants 8–18 cm high; corm ovoid with woody, overlapping tunics. Leaves sword-shaped, several-ribbed, 2–4 mm wide. Flowers in a two- to six-flowered spike, violet with a bright red center, perianth tube c. 3 mm long, tepals shallowly cupped, c. 15 mm long, anthers red-brown, arching inward and lying over the broad, hairy style branches; bracts green, becoming dry at the tips. Flowering August–September. Wet sandy flats, SW (only near Darling).

Geissorhiza monanthos Ecklon
Plants 6–20 cm high, stem short-velvety; corm ovoid with woody, overlapping tunics. Leaves sword-shaped to linear, mostly 2.4–4 mm wide, often minutely hairy on the margins. Flowers in a one- to five-flowered spike, glossy dark blue, often pale in the center edged with a broad dark ring, perianth tube c. 2 mm long, tepals widely cupped, 14–18 mm long, stamens and style unilateral, arching downward, usually with one shorter filament; bracts green below, dry and brown above. Flowering August–October. Sandy slopes, granite outcrops, NW, SW (Citrusdal, Saldanha to Somerset West).

Geissorhiza nana Klatt
Plants 5–7 cm high; corm ovoid with woody, concentric tunics. Leaves linear to sword-shaped, 1–2 mm wide. Flowers mostly one per spike, tiny, white, perianth tube c. 2 mm long, tepals spreading, mostly 4–6 mm long; bracts green, firm. Flowering September–October. Clay slopes and flats in renosterveld, SW, LB (Caledon to Riversdale).

Geissorhiza nigromontana Goldblatt
Plants 10–16 cm high; corm ovoid with woody, concentric tunics. Leaves lanceolate-falcate, usually trailing, 4–10 mm wide. Flowers one or two per spike, sometimes three, blue, perianth tube c. 2.5 mm long, tepals spreading, 14–16 mm long; bracts green. Flowering January–February. Along streams, KM (Swartberg Mountains).

Geissorhiza monanthos; see also the illustration for *Ixia curta*

Geissorhiza nubigena

Geissorhiza nubigena Goldblatt
Plants 15–30 cm high; corm globose with fibrous tunics. Leaves linear, the margins and midrib moderately thickened, thus two-grooved on each surface, 2–3 mm wide, often sticky below. Flowers in a two- to five-flowered spike, deep pink to mauve, perianth tube 10–18 mm long, tepals spreading, 17–22 mm long; bracts green, often reddish above. Flowering December–January. High rocky slopes, 1000–1800 m, SW (Victoria Peak to Kogelberg).

Geissorhiza ornithogaloides Klatt
Plants 4–10 cm high; corms bell-shaped with a flat base or ovoid with a rounded base, with woody, concentric tunics. Leaves linear, mostly 1–2 mm wide. Flowers usually one per spike, sometimes two, bright yellow, perianth tube 2–3 mm long, tepals spreading when fully open, 6–12(–18) mm long; bracts firm with red margins. Flowering August–October. Mostly clay or granitic flats and lower slopes, but sometimes in thin, rocky, sandstone soil, NW, SW, LB, SE (Cedarberg Mountains to Humansdorp).

Geissorhiza outeniquensis Goldblatt
Plants 20–50 cm high, stems often trailing; corm ovoid with soft, overlapping tunics. Leaves more or less linear, trailing, 3–6 mm wide. Flowers in a two- to four-flowered spike, pink to mauve, with reddish markings at the base of the lower or all the tepals, perianth tube 10–13 mm long, tepals shallowly cupped, 26–32 mm long, stamens and style unilateral, arching downward. Flowering mostly October–December, occasionally later. Streambanks, waterfalls, and wet rocks in shade, SE (Outeniqua Mountains).

Geissorhiza ovalifolia R. C. Foster
Plants 3–9 cm high, stem often with a cormel in the axils of the lower leaves; corm small, ovoid, with softly woody to papery, concentric tunics. Leaves oblong, often prostrate, 2–5 mm wide. Flowers in a one- to six-flowered spike, white, perianth tube 2–3 mm long, tepals spreading, 6–8 mm long; bracts green, becoming membranous

Geissorhiza nubigena

Geissorhiza ornithogaloides

above. Flowering October–November. Damp places, NW, SW (Cold Bokkeveld to Franschhoek Mountains).

Geissorhiza ovata (Burman fil.) Ascherson & Graebner
Plants 6–15 cm high; corm ovoid with woody, concentric tunics. Leaves lanceolate to ovate, prostrate, 5–12 mm wide. Flowers mostly two to four per spike, white to pale pink, deep pink on the reverse and reddish at the tepal bases, perianth tube cylindrical, 10–18(–30) mm long, tepals spreading, 7–13 mm long; bracts firm, green, often flushed with red. Flowering August–October, especially after fire. Sandstone slopes and flats, NW, SW (Olifants River Mountains to Riversdale).

Geissorhiza pappei Baker
Plants 5–10 cm high; corm ovoid with softly woody to papery, concentric tunics. Leaves linear, the margins and midribs thickened and sticky, 0.5–1.3 mm wide. Flowers in a one- to four-flowered spike, small, white to cream, perianth tube c. 3 mm long, tepals spreading, 6–9 mm long; bracts green, hyaline toward the tips. Flowering September–October. Sandy mountain soils, NW, SW (Ceres to Caledon).

Geissorhiza parva Baker
Plants 4–12 cm high; corm ovoid with woody, concentric tunics. Leaves lanceolate to oblong, leathery, the lower spreading to prostrate, 1.5–4.5 mm wide. Flowers mostly two to four per spike, small, cream to yellow, perianth tube 3–4 mm long, tepals spreading, 6–8 mm long; bracts firm, often red on the margins. Flowering August–November. Sandy soils, mountains and flats, NW, SW, LB (Cedarberg Mountains to Swellendam).

Geissorhiza purpureolutea Baker
Plants 10–15 cm high; corm ovoid with woody, overlapping tunics. Leaves sword-shaped to linear, several-ribbed, 1–2.5 mm wide. Flowers in a one- to four-flowered spike, yellowish, usually with a dark center, perianth tube c. 3 mm long, tepals spreading, 10–18 mm long; bracts green. Flowering August–September. Wet sandy flats, NW, SW (Piketberg to Paarl).

Geissorhiza pseudinaequalis Goldblatt
Plants 9–30 cm high; corm ovoid with papery, overlapping tunics. Leaves linear, 2–4 mm wide, sometimes sparsely hairy on the margins. Flowers in a three- to seven-flowered spike, blue to violet, perianth tube 3–5 mm long, tepals spreading, 12–20 mm long, stamens unequal with one shorter filament. Flowering mainly October–December. Mountain slopes and cliffs, SW (Bain's Kloof to Simonsberg).

Geissorhiza purpurascens Goldblatt
Plants 15–30 cm high; corm ovoid with woody, concentric tunics. Leaves linear to sword-shaped, 3–5 mm wide, the margins raised into wings, the blade thus H-shaped in cross section, sticky below and with sand adhering, the edges of the wings sparsely hairy. Flowers in a 4- to 10-flowered spike, mauve, perianth tube 3–6 mm long, tepals spreading, 10–16 mm long; bracts initially green below, membranous above, becoming pale and dry.

Geissorhiza ovata

Flowering September–October. Sandy flats, NW, SW (Piketberg to Stellenbosch).

Geissorhiza pusilla (Andrews) Klatt
Plants 7–20 cm high; corm ovoid with woody, concentric tunics. Leaves sword-shaped, lightly villous at least below, the margins and midrib minutely hairy. Flowers in a two- to six-flowered spike, blue to mauve, perianth tube c. 2 mm long, tepals spreading, 7–10 mm long; bracts green below, dry and brown above. Flowering August–October. Damp shady places, SW (Cape Peninsula to Paarl).

Geissorhiza radians (Thunberg) Goldblatt
Plants 8–16 cm high; corm ovoid with woody, overlapping tunics. Leaves linear, oval in cross section, the margins and midrib heavily thickened, thus two-grooved on each surface, 0.5–1.5 mm wide. Flowers in a one- to six-flowered spike, deep blue-violet with a bright red center edged with a white ring, tepals cupped, pitted in the lower midline, 15–22 mm long, stamens and style unilateral, arching downward. Flowering September–October. Damp sandy or granitic soils, SW (Malmesbury to Gordon's Bay).

Geissorhiza ramosa Ker Gawler ex Klatt
Plants 20–45 cm high, stem mostly several-branched; corm ovoid with woody, overlapping tunics. Leaves linear, the margins and midrib lightly thickened, 1–2.5 mm wide. Flowers in a 5- to 10-flowered spike, small, blue to purple, perianth tube 2–3 mm long, tepals spreading, 5–8 mm long, stamens unequal with one shorter filament; bracts green or becoming dry above. Flowering October–December. Stony mountain slopes, NW, SW, LB (Tulbagh to Swellendam).

Geissorhiza roseoalba (G. J. Lewis) Goldblatt
Plants 15–20 cm high; corm ovoid with woody, concentric, dark brown tunics. Leaves sword-shaped, the margins and midrib thickened, 4–6 mm wide. Flowers in a one- to three-flowered spike, pale pink with red markings at the tepal bases, pink on the reverse, perianth tube 8–10 mm long, tepals loosely cupped, 22–32 mm long, stamens and style unilateral, arching downward. Flowering August–September, mostly after fire. Sandstone soils on dry, rocky slopes in fynbos, KM, LB, SE (Little Karoo to Uitenhage).

Geissorhiza rupicola Goldblatt & J. C. Manning
Plants 15–20 cm high; corm ovoid with fibrous tunics. Leaves linear, the margins thickened, c. 2 mm wide. Flowers in a two- to six-flowered spike, pale pink, perianth tube cylindrical, 16–23 mm long, tepals loosely cupped, 12–15 mm long; bracts pale green or flushed purple. Flowering November–December. Wet sandstone cliffs, NW (Ceres).

Geissorhiza schinzii (Baker) Goldblatt
Plants 10–20 cm high; corm ovoid with woody, concentric tunics. Leaves linear, the margins and midrib thickened, thus with two narrow grooves on each surface, sticky and with sand adhering, 4–6 mm wide. Flowers in a one- to four-flowered spike, large, pink with darker

Geissorhiza radians; see also page 120

veins, perianth tube 24–32 mm long, tepals spreading, 35–40 mm long, stamens and style unilateral, arching downward; bracts green, sticky. Flowering August–October, especially after fire. Stony sandstone slopes, SW (Riviersonderend and Houw Hoek Mountains to Napier).

Geissorhiza scillaris A. Dietrich

Plants 12–35 cm high, stem bearing a scale-like bract below the spike; corm globose with woody, overlapping tunics. Leaves linear to terete, the margins and midrib heavily thickened, with four narrow longitudinal grooves, the second leaf entirely sheathing. Flowers in a 4- to 10-flowered spike, sometimes as many as 20-flowered, small, white to pale blue or mauve, perianth tube c. 1.5 mm long, tepals spreading, 8–9 mm long; bracts green below, becoming transparent to dry and brown in the upper half. Flowering August–November. Rocky sandstone slopes and flats, NW, SW (Cedarberg Mountains to Shaw's Pass).

Geissorhiza scopulosa Goldblatt

Plants 6–20 cm high, stem usually inclined, finely velvety; corm ovoid with soft, membranous, overlapping tunics. Leaves linear, the margins winged and the midrib lightly thickened, 1–2 mm wide, sticky below and with sand adhering. Flowers in a two- to seven-flowered spike, blue-violet, perianth tube c. 2.5 mm long, tepals spreading, c. 9 mm long, stamens unequal with one shorter filament. Flowering November. Rocky sandstone soils, 500–1500 m, NW (Hex River Mountains).

Geissorhiza setacea (Thunberg) Ker Gawler

Plants 4–8 cm high; corm ovoid with woody, concentric tunics. Leaves linear to sword-shaped, 1–2.5 mm wide. Flowers mostly one per spike, rarely two, white or cream, rarely with a dark center, perianth tube c. 6 mm long, tepals spreading, 8–12 mm long; bracts green, firm. Flowering mostly July–September. Damp, sandy, stony flats, SW (Gouda to Gordon's Bay).

Geissorhiza silenoides Goldblatt & J. C. Manning

Plants 20–30 cm high, stem finely velvety; corm ovoid with woody, overlapping tunics. Leaves linear, the mar-

Geissorhiza schinzii

Geissorhiza setacea

Geissorhiza silenoides

Geissorhiza splendidissima

gins and midrib strongly thickened. Flowers in a four- to seven-flowered spike, pale pink, perianth tube cylindrical, 15–17 mm long, tepals spreading, 12–14 mm long, stamens unequal with one shorter filament; bracts pale green. Flowering September–October. Shale slopes in fynbos, NW (Gydo Mountains, Ceres).

Geissorhiza similis Goldblatt

Plants 12–35 cm high; corm globose with woody, overlapping tunics. Leaves linear, the margins and midrib moderately thickened, 1–2 mm wide. Flowers in a three- to eight-flowered spike, white, often the outer tepals flushed pink outside, perianth tube c. 2.5 mm long, tepals spreading, 9–12 mm long; bracts green, often translucent above. Flowering August–October. Sandy slopes and flats, SW (Bain's Kloof to Cape Peninsula).

Geissorhiza spiralis (Burchell) M. P. de Vos ex Goldblatt

Plants c. 4 cm high, stem single or two or three from the base; corm ovoid with woody, concentric tunics. Leaves linear, 0.5–2 mm wide, loosely twisted spirally. Flowers one per stalk, mauve, darkly marked at the tepal bases, perianth tube c. 4.5 mm long, tepals cupped, 13–15 mm long, style usually dividing opposite the base of the anthers; bracts membranous, dry and purplish above. Flowering August–September. Stony slopes, RV (Roggeveld near Sutherland).

Geissorhiza splendidissima Diels

Plants 8–20 cm high, stem finely velvety; corm ovoid with woody, overlapping tunics. Leaves linear, the margins and midrib raised and thickened, thus two-grooved on each surface, c. 2 mm wide. Flowers usually in a three- to five-flowered, inclined spike, glossy blue-violet, blackish in the center, perianth tube 2–4 mm long, tepals widely cupped, 15–22 mm long, stamens and style unilateral, arching downward, stamens with one shorter filament, anthers red-brown. Flowering August–September. Clay soils in renosterveld, NW (Bokkeveld Plateau).

Geissorhiza stenosiphon Goldblatt

Plants 15–30 cm high; corm ovoid with woody, concentric tunics drawn into bristles above. Leaves terete with four narrow longitudinal grooves, c. 1 mm diam. Flowers in a one- or two-flowered spike, tubular, white, perianth tube and outside of the tepals pink, tube cylindrical, 40–50 mm long, tepals spreading, 12–14 mm long; bracts green below, dry toward the tips. Flowering November–December. Rocky sandstone slopes above 400 m, NW (Cold Bokkeveld Mountains).

Geissorhiza subrigida L. Bolus
Plants 12–30 cm high; corm ovoid with woody, overlapping tunics. Leaves sword-shaped, lightly ridged, velvety, 3–6 mm wide. Flowers in a two- to five-flowered spike, blue-violet, perianth tube c. 2.5 mm long, tepals spreading, 12–17 mm long; bracts dry, rusty above. Flowering August–September. Rocky sandstone soils, NW (Bokkeveld Mountains).

Geissorhiza sulphurascens Schlechter ex R. C. Foster
Plants 12–20 cm high; corm ovoid with woody, overlapping tunics. Leaves linear, few grooved, 1–2 mm wide. Flowers in a 4- to 10-flowered spike, white to cream, small, perianth tube 3–4 mm long, tepals spreading, 13–18 mm long; bracts green, often reddish above. Flowering August–September. Wet sandy flats, NW (Bokkeveld Mountains).

Geissorhiza tabularis Goldblatt
Plants 25–35 cm high; corm ovoid with woody, overlapping tunics. Leaves linear to sword-shaped, the margins and midrib lightly thickened, 2–3 mm wide, the stem often branched. Flowers in a three- to eight-flowered spike, mauve, rarely white, perianth tube c. 2 mm long, tepals spreading, 15–18 mm long, stamens unequal with one shorter filament; bracts green, becoming dry above. Flowering October–December. Cool, damp sandstone slopes, SW (Cape Peninsula).

Geissorhiza tenella Goldblatt
Plants 10–30 cm high; corm ovoid with woody, concentric tunics. Leaves linear, the margins raised into wings, thus H-shaped in cross section, sticky and with sand adhering, c. 5 mm wide. Flowers usually in a two- to five-flowered spike, white to pale pink, often darker with age, perianth tube cylindrical, 20–50 mm long, tepals 14–23 mm long, stamens and style unilateral, arching downward; bracts green. Flowering mostly October–November, especially after fire. Sandy flats and dunes, SW (Darling to Bredasdorp).

Geissorhiza tulbaghensis F. Bolus
Plants 8–15 cm high, stem short-velvety; corm ovoid with woody, overlapping tunics. Leaves linear, the margins lightly thickened, mostly 3–8 mm wide. Flowers in a one- or two-flowered spike, white with a dark brown to purple center, perianth tube c. 4.5 mm long, tepals widely cupped, 18–22 mm long, stamens and style unilateral, arching downward; bracts green below, dry and brown above. Flowering August–September. Clay flats and banks, NW, SW (Porterville to Wellington).

Geissorhiza uliginosa Goldblatt & J. C. Manning
Plants 15–30 cm high, stem usually branched, branches drooping; corm reduced, ovoid, with soft-textured concentric tunics soon disintegrating. Leaves linear with lightly thickened margins and midrib, 2–3 mm wide. Flowers one per stem, dark pink, perianth tube 9–13 mm long, tepals 20–22 mm long, stamens and style unilateral, arching downward; bracts green with reddish margins. Flowering December–January. Waterfalls and wet cliffs, KM (Swartberg and Kammanassie Mountains).

Geissorhiza umbrosa G. J. Lewis
Plants 12–30 cm high; corm ovoid with papery to fibrous tunics. Leaves linear, fleshy, the margins and midrib thickened, thus broadly two-grooved on each surface, 1–2 mm wide. Flowers in a 2- to 10-flowered spike, white to cream, perianth tube 2.5–4 mm long, tepals spreading, 10–13 mm long; bracts green or becoming dry in the upper half. Flowering October–December. Sandstone slopes in damp sites mostly above 400 m, NW, SW (Cedarberg Mountains to Cape Peninsula and Riviersonderend Mountains).

Geissorhiza unifolia Goldblatt
Plants 5–10 cm high; corm ovoid with papery, concentric tunics. Leaves mostly single, linear, the margins and

midrib moderately thickened, 0.5–1.3 mm wide. Flowers in a one- to five-flowered spike, small, white, perianth tube 1.5–2 mm long, tepals 3.5–5 mm long; bracts green below, dry and pale above. Flowering October. Sandstone rocks at high elevation, NW (Cedarberg Mountains).

Gethyllis

COMMON NAME kukumakranka, FAMILY Amaryllidaceae. Deciduous perennials. ROOTSTOCK a bulb, sometimes dividing to form clumps, often with a conspicuous neck. LEAVES few to several, mostly dry at flowering, frequently spiraled, linear to strap-shaped or elliptical, often hairy, rarely undulate, surrounded by one or more often conspicuous basal sheaths. INFLORESCENCE a solitary flower held at ground level on a subterranean scape; spathe bracts two, united into a sheath. FLOWER actinomorphic or weakly so by the deflection of the style, white, cream or pale to deep pink, usually scented, the pedicel short at anthesis, elongating in fruit, the perianth tube long, slender and cylindrical, the tepals spreading, narrowly to broadly lanceolate. STAMENS inserted in the throat, the filaments six or more, and clustered, short, free or partially united, the anthers 6–60, basifixed, rolled backward when mature. OVARY subterranean with many ovules; STYLE short and erect or long and laterally deflexed, the stigma small or broadly three-lobed. FRUIT a club-shaped to cylindrical berry, the walls succulent to membranous, red, yellow, or white, often darkly spotted, usually aromatic, disintegrating irregularly. SEEDS water-rich, subglobose, cream or reddish, the embryo green. Basic chromosome number $x = 6$. Mostly the winter-rainfall region of southern Africa, extending to the Great Karoo and Free State; c. 32 spp., 19 in the Cape.

The flowers of *Gethyllis*, although relatively uniform in structure, have characteristics useful in placing the species into major groupings. In contrast, the leaves are often sufficiently distinctive to identify the species. The large and many-seeded fruits, which have long been valued for their aromatic essences, are probably more variable than the descriptions indicate. Several bulb enthusiasts believe that *Gethyllis* has many undescribed species that warrant recognition. Studies of natural populations, however, show that several species, particularly *G. afra*, form highly variable complexes, making the taxonomic treatment of the genus extremely difficult.

All species of *Gethyllis* are summer flowering, and to survive under dry summer conditions they have several unusual adaptations. Like the other Amaryllidaceae tribe Haemantheae (*Clivia, Cryptostephanus, Haemanthus,* and *Scadoxus*), *Gethyllis* and its close relative, *Apodolirion*, have berry-like fruits but are unique in having solitary flowers with a subterranean ovary. At flowering, the perianth emerges fleetingly for a few days while the many-ovuled ovary remains cool and protected below ground. The fruits mature slowly and finally emerge in autumn, slightly before the main leafing period begins. The seeds germinate immediately, enabling young bulbs to become well established by the time the favorable growing season ends in September.

In some species of *Gethyllis* the flowers lack a style and are male. Preliminary observations indicate that small plants, often in their first season of flowering, are male whereas larger plants are bisexual. This suggests that gender is influenced by the bulb's resource status and that only large plants are able to bear the reproductive costs of producing bisexual flowers. In contrast, the large number of anthers present in the bisexual flowers of species like *G. afra* is probably genetically controlled.

Cultivated plants of a single species often flower synchronously, even if some receive water and others do not. This remarkable response has prompted speculation that the bulbs react to the fluctuations in temperature and pressure that accompany occasional summer showers or passing cold fronts.

The pollination biology of *Gethyllis* has not been studied but the suggestion that the long-tubed, fragrant flowers are pollinated by moths is confounded by the fact that the tubes are in fact completely occluded by the style and do not contain nectar. It is more likely that the species are visited by bees for pollen, especially in view of the fact that in several species the anthers are multiplied in number above the usual six.

FURTHER READING. The most recent taxonomic literature of *Gethyllis* is a synopsis by D. Müller-Doblies

(1986) but a key and complete descriptions of the species are still needed. The significance of the subterranean ovary in *Gethyllis* was reviewed by Burtt (1970). The unusual growth stages were illustrated in color by Liltved (1992). Micropropagation of *Gethyllis* was studied by Drewes and van Staden (1994).

Gethyllis afra Linnaeus

Plants 10–14 cm high. Leaves dry at flowering, 12–30, linear, 1–3 mm wide, erect to spreading, spiraled, usually channeled, occasionally with simple, soft, spreading hairs on one or both surfaces or the margin, the basal sheath single, not prominent. Flower cup-shaped, white with pink keels on reverse, tepals 20–30 mm long, anthers 9–18 in six clusters, filaments in each cluster united at the base for as much as half their length, style straight, as long as the stamens, sometimes absent, stigma small, bifid or trifid. Berry club-shaped, fleshy, yellow to red. Flowering December–January. Lowland flats in fynbos, SW, AP, LB (Clanwilliam to Cape Peninsula and Heidelberg).

Gethyllis barkerae D. Müller-Doblies

Plants small. Leaves one to eight, dry at flowering, prostrate, elliptical, 5–9 mm wide, somewhat narrowed near the base, plane, both surfaces with soft star-like hairs, the basal sheath not prominent. Flower and fruit like those of *G. villosa*. Flowering December. Lowland and upland sandy flats in dry fynbos, NW (southern Namaqualand, Heerenlogement, Nardouw Mountains).

Two subspecies are recognized: subspecies *barkerae* with three to eight leaves, sandy flats (southern Namaqualand), and subspecies *paucifolia* D. Müller-Doblies with one or two leaves, rarely three, sandy flats in dry fynbos (Matsikamma Mountains to Nardouw Mountains).

Gethyllis britteniana Baker

Plants 15–25 cm high; bulbs to 75 mm wide. Leaves 19–45, dry at flowering, narrowly strap-shaped, 1.5–4 mm wide, suberect, spiraled, smooth, somewhat gray-green, the basal sheaths two, prominent, white with maroon spots. Flower widely cup-shaped, ivory to pink, waxy, tepals 30–65 mm long with prominently apiculate tips, anthers 35–60, apparently in more than six clusters, filaments in each cluster united as much as half their length, style straight, as long as the stamens, stigma narrowly trifid. Berry club-shaped, yellow spotted with red. Flowering October–March. Sandveld or rocky slopes, NW (Namaqualand to Nardouw Mountains).

Subspecies *bruynsii* D. Müller-Doblies and *herrei* (L. Bolus) D. Müller-Doblies are poorly known.

Gethyllis campanulata L. Bolus

Plants sometimes clumped, 25–30 cm high. Leaves 9–23, dry at flowering, suberect, wiry, hemiterete, 1–1.5 mm wide, loosely to scarcely twisted, smooth or with short simple reflexed hairs, the basal sheath not prominent. Flower cup-shaped, white to cream, tepals 30–40 mm long, anthers 12 in six pairs with the filaments of each pair united at the base, style erect, as long as the stamens, stigma minutely trilobed. Berry club-shaped, yellow. Flowering November–January. Upland dolerite flats and gravelly lower slopes, NW, SW, KM (Nieuwoudtville, Worcester, Montagu, Matjiesfontein).

Gethyllis campanulata

Gethyllis ciliaris (Thunberg) Thunberg

Plants often forming clumps, 15–30 cm high. Leaves 15–25, dry at flowering, narrowly strap-shaped, 2–3 mm wide, suberect, spiraled, firm, shiny green, the margins fringed with rigid upturned hairs, sometimes undulate, the basal sheath single, mostly subterranean, sometimes as long as the green leaves, pale, spotted with maroon when exposed. Flower cup-shaped, ivory to deep pink, waxy, tepals 30–70 mm long, anthers 23–31 in six clusters, filaments in each cluster broad and hardly divided, style straight and stout, as long as the stamens, stigma narrowly trifid. Berry club-shaped, yellow. Flowering December–February. Mountain slopes and coastal flats in deep sand, NW, SW (southern Namaqualand, Nardouw Mountains to Cape Peninsula).

Two subspecies are recognized: subspecies *ciliaris* with ivory tepals, usually with pink keels on the outer surface, periath tube to 9 cm long, NW, SW (Nardouw Mountains to Cape Peninsula), and subspecies *longituba* (L. Bolus) D. Müller-Doblies, tepals usually rose pink, wine red on the outer surface, perianth tube to 17 cm long, NW (southern Namaqualand).

Gethyllis fimbriatula D. Müller-Doblies

Plant 2–4 cm high. Leaves c. 15, dry at flowering, linear, 1 mm wide, suberect, tightly coiled, both surfaces more or less smooth, the margin densely fringed with pale, stiff, short, spreading, simple hairs, the basal sheath not prominent, not enclosing the first foliage leaf. Flower like that of *G. lanuginosa*. Flowering November? Wedged between rocks on south-facing slopes, RV (Matjiesfontein).

Gethyllis gregoriana D. Müller-Doblies

Plants clumped, 15 cm high. Leaves one or two, dry at flowering, opposite, strap-shaped, 4–8 mm wide, erect, plane, gray, smooth or with long, soft, simple hairs, the basal sheath not prominent. Flower white, tepals 35 mm long, anthers six, each on a widely spreading stout filament, style erect, as long as the stamens, stigma slightly dilated. Flowering December. Uplands on sandy or clay flats, NW (southern Namaqualand, Bokkeveld Mountains to Cedarberg).

Gethyllis kaapensis D. Müller-Doblies

Plants solitary, 10–15 cm high; bulb c. 15 mm diam. Leaves about seven, usually green at flowering, suberect, linear, c. 1 mm wide, weakly spiraled, smooth, the basal sheath not exposed. Flower cup-shaped, white with outer surface pink, the keels usually dark pink, tepals c. 3 cm long, anthers six, each on a tapering, slightly spreading filament, style erect, as long as the stamens, stigma narrowly lobed. Flowering November–December, after fire. Marshy lowlands in coastal fynbos, SW (Cape Peninsula).

Gethyllis lanuginosa Marloth

Plants clumped, 4–10 cm high. Leaves 10–18, dry at flowering, linear, 0.5–2 mm wide, erect, loosely to tightly coiled in the upper half, both surfaces with soft simple hairs, the basal sheath papery. Flower white with a pink blush, tepals 15–25 mm long, anthers six, each on a filiform suberect filament, style longer than the stamens, laterally deflexed, stigma disk-like, three-lobed. Berry club-shaped, yellow with red apex when ripe. Flowering November. Sandy or stony soils on flats or lower slopes, NW, SW (Namaqualand, Nieuwoudtville to Hopefield).

Gethyllis lata L. Bolus

Plants 3–4 cm high. Leaves two to six, dry at flowering, lanceolate to elliptical, prostrate, 5–13 mm wide, smooth, plane, the margin thick and cartilaginous, straw colored to reddish, sometimes minutely crisped, the basal sheath not prominent. Flower white to pale pink, tepals 20–33 mm long, obovate, anthers six, each on a filiform, suberect filament, style longer than the stamens, laterally deflexed, stigma broad, three-lobed. Flowering October–November. Upland and lowland clay flats, RV (southern Namaqualand, Bokkeveld Plateau).

Gethyllis latifolia Baker

Plants 8–25 cm high. Leaves 4–18, dry at flowering, strap-shaped, 8–12 mm wide, erect to horizontal, twisted, slightly channeled, somewhat fleshy, gray-green, occasionally fringed with simple soft hairs, the basal sheath single, long, slender, white, spotted with maroon when exposed. Flower cup-shaped, cream with outer tips tinged pink, tepals 50–80 mm long, anthers c. 30 with c.

Gethyllis ciliaris subsp. *ciliaris*

Gethyllis ciliaris subsp. *longituba* (Colin Paterson-Jones)

Gethyllis kaapensis (Colin Paterson-Jones)

Gethyllis lanuginosa

5 in each cluster, filaments in each cluster united, style straight, as long as the stamens, stigma small, trifid. Flowering December–January. Lowland flats in sandveld, NW, SW (southern Namaqualand to Darling).

Gethyllis linearis L. Bolus
Plants forming compact clumps of 10–20 individuals, 2–5 cm high. Leaves 5–10, dry at flowering, linear, 1–3 mm wide, spreading, tightly coiled, smooth, gray-green, somewhat succulent, basal sheath papery. Flower white, tinged with pink, tepals 20–35 mm long, anthers six, each on a filiform suberect filament, style longer than the stamens, laterally deflexed, stigma disk-like, three-lobed. Flowering October–November. Upland and lowland semiarid flats in sand or gravel, NW (southern Namaqualand, Nieuwoudtville).

Gethyllis pectinata D. Müller-Doblies
Plants small. Leaves four, broadly elliptical, c. 8 mm wide, prostrate, plane, both surfaces smooth, the margin with a straw-colored spreading fringe of distinctly clustered bristles, the basal sheath not prominent. Flower white, tepals narrowly ovate, otherwise like that of *G. lata*. Flowering November? Upland clay flats among dolerite boulders, RV (Nieuwoudtville to Calvinia).

Gethyllis roggeveldensis D. Müller-Doblies
Plants c. 7 cm high. Leaves 5–15, dry at flowering, narrowly to broadly lanceolate, 2–10 mm wide, prostrate, sometimes upturned near the apex, flaccid to subsucculent with a smooth green margin, the basal sheath sometimes absent. Flower white to delicate pink, tepals 20–40 mm long, anthers six, each on a filiform, suberect filament, style longer than the stamens, more or less curved sideways, stigma broadly trilobed. Berry succulent, yellow with reddish tip, aromatic. Flowering November. Stony clays on south-facing slopes, RV (Calvinia to Matjiesfontein).

Gethyllis spiralis (Thunberg) Thunberg
Plants 6–15 cm high. Leaves 6–12, dry at flowering, linear, 1 mm wide, suberect, channeled, spiraled, smooth or rarely ciliate, the basal sheath sometimes not surrounding the first foliage leaf. Flower white with pale pink outer surface, tepals c. 2.0 mm long, anthers six, each on a slightly spreading filament, style longer than the stamens, curved sideways, stigma broadly trilobed. Berry club-shaped, straw colored. Flowering November–January. Stony slopes, SW, KM, SE (Worcester, Little Karoo, Long Kloof).

Gethyllis transkarooica D. Müller-Doblies
Plants 10–15 cm high. Leaves 5–11, dry at flowering, linear, 1–2 mm wide, usually coiled toward the apex, mostly smooth, the basal sheath not prominent. Flower solid rose pink, tepals 15–30 mm long, anthers six, distinctly tailed, each on a filiform, suberect filament, style curved laterally, longer than the stamens, stigma broadly trilobed. Flowering November–December. Slopes or flats in sand or clay, NW, KM, LB (Ceres, Great Karoo, Free State).

Gethyllis verrucosa Marloth
Plants 5–8 cm. Leaves three to seven, dry at flowering, narrowly strap-shaped, 3–7 mm wide, suberect, loosely spiraled toward the apex, covered with silver, scale-like, parallel-armed hairs on a central dark attachment, basal sheath not prominent. Flower white, tepals 25–30 mm long, anthers six, each on a filiform, suberect filament, style longer than the stamens, curved sideways, stigma broadly three-lobed. Flowering October–December. Lower slopes and flats in heavy soils, RV, AP (western Karoo, Bredasdorp).

Gethyllis verticillata R. Brown ex Herbert
Plant 10–30 cm high. Leaves 4–11, dry at flowering, linear to narrowly strap-shaped, 3–7 mm wide, suberect, coiled toward the apex, smooth, the basal sheaths paired, white with maroon blotches and fimbriate at the apex. Flower white, tepals 20–50 mm long, anthers six, each on a filiform, erect filament, style curved sideways, usually long, sometimes absent, stigma broadly three-lobed. Berry yellow spotted red. Flowering November–February. Rock outcrops on middle slopes and well-drained flats, NW, SW (Namaqualand, Bokkeveld Mountains to Darling).

Gethyllis villosa (Thunberg) Thunberg
Plants 3–15 cm high, sometimes clumped. Leaves 4–12, dry at flowering, narrowly lanceolate, 2–5 mm wide,

spreading, loosely spiraled toward the apex, more or less covered with soft, white, star-like hairs, the margin and apex often with nonradiating, firm, compound hairs. Flower white or pink, tepals 20–40 mm long, anthers six, each on a filiform, erect filament, style longer than the stamens, curved sideways, stigma broadly three-lobed. Berry slender, cylindrical, membranous, white with red seeds. Flowering October–December. In sand or clay on flats or south-facing slopes, RV, NW, SW, AP (Namaqualand to Mossel Bay and western Karoo).

Gethyllis verticillata

Gethyllis roggeveldensis foliage (Colin Paterson-Jones)

Gethyllis villosa

Gethyllis transkarooica (Colin Paterson-Jones)

Gethyllis villosa fruit and foliage

Gladiolus

COMMON NAMES Afrikaner, gladiolus, FAMILY Iridaceae. Deciduous perennials, evergreen in 1 sp. ROOTSTOCK a corm rooting from the base, the tunics leathery to papery or membranous to fibrous. LEAVES few to many, foliage leaves unifacial, usually with a definite midrib, two to several, basal or some arising above ground level, sometimes blade reduced or lacking, thus entire leaf partly to entirely sheathing, blades linear to lanceolate, sometimes puberulous or hairy, either plane and margins, midrib, and sometimes other veins not or only lightly thickened and hyaline, or margins or midrib strongly raised, sometimes even winged (thus H- or X-shaped in cross section), or midribs and margins much thickened and blade evidently terete but with four narrow longitudinal grooves, usually contemporary with flowers, occasionally borne earlier or later than flowers and on separate shoots; stem terete or occasionally compressed and angled, often flexuous, occasionally scabrid to minutely hairy. INFLORESCENCE a spike, usually secund, flowers occasionally in two ranks; bracts green, sometimes dry above or almost entirely, usually relatively large, inner usually slightly smaller than outer, notched apically 1–2 mm or entire. FLOWERS mostly zygomorphic, actinomorphic in a few species, often bilabiate, sometimes the tube elongate, lower tepals usually with contrasting markings, stamens unilateral and arcuate, or symmetric in actinomorphic species, frequently closing at night, often fragrant, with nectar from septal nectaries; perianth tube obliquely funnel-shaped to cylindrical, shorter or longer than the bracts; tepals usually unequal, the dorsal broader and arched to hooded over the stamens, the lower three narrower, sometimes clawed below and united for a short distance. STAMENS with filiform filaments, arising at base of upper part of the perianth tube; anthers subbasifixed, occasionally medifixed, rarely with sterile tails, sometimes with an acute to apiculate appendage. STYLE filiform, branches undivided, slender below, expanded gradually or abruptly above and often bilobed apically. FRUIT a usually slightly inflated capsule, often large, ovoid to ellipsoidal. SEEDS usually discoid with a broad circumferential wing, rarely globose to angled, smooth, matte. Basic chromosome number $x = 15$, other numbers 14, 12, 11. Southwestern Cape and Namaqualand through tropical Africa and Madagascar to Europe and the Middle East; c. 260 spp., 165 spp. in southern Africa, 110 in the Cape.

Second largest genus of the family after *Iris*, *Gladiolus* is one of few African genera of Iridaceae that has speciated conspicuously outside the Cape Floral Region. The genus is defined by its specialized winged seeds and an ancestral basic chromosome number $x = 15$. It has no close relatives.

Flower form in *Gladiolus* is extremely diverse. Pollination by long-tongued bees, mainly Apidae (Anthophorinae), is most common. These large solitary bees visit a wide range of flower types in *Gladiolus* and other genera. Several species produce long-tubed red flowers that are pollinated by sunbirds or, in a few instances (e.g., *G. cardinalis*), by the large satyrid butterfly known as the pride of Table Mountain, *Aeropetes tulbaghia*. Long-tubed white- or brown-flowered species, scented throughout the day or only in the evenings, are pollinated by a range of moths whereas long-tubed pink- or white-flowered species with red markings are pollinated by long-proboscid flies, *Moegistorhynchus* and *Prosoeca* (both Nemestrinidae) or *Philoliche* (Tabanidae).

Floral diversity in *Gladiolus* is matched by numerous vegetative adaptations, notably a reduction in leaf number and the development of winged midribs and or margins, or reduction of the entire leaf blade. In some species, flowering occurs before the leaves are produced or after they have dried.

Nearly all species of *Gladiolus* are worth horticultural attention. The taller species may be grown in flower beds or the rock garden; the smaller ones are ideal for pot culture. *Gladiolus tristis* and *G. liliaceus* are old garden favorites, prized both for their tall stems and large flowers that produce a rich, heady perfume at night. They also make fine cut flowers with the added bonus that the fragrance can be enjoyed indoors. Two other scented wild *Gladiolus* species of the Cape, *G. carinatus* and *G. gracilis*, were so favored in the past that bunches were regularly picked from the wild each spring and offered by flower sellers, who found ready buyers. It is a mystery why these two delightful species have not been domesticated by the horticultural trade. Their elegant sky blue flowers and strong scent rival those of freesias and may even exceed them.

The red-flowered *Gladiolus cunonius* and its allies, *G. saccatus* and *G. splendens,* would make particularly fine garden plants. They are easy to grow and once established should persist for they reproduce readily from cormels produced at the base of the main corm as well as from seed. Their branching habit and numerous bright red flowers ensure a good display. The so-called great red gladioli of the Cape, *G. cardinalis, G. sempervirens,* and *G. stefaniae,* are especially worth attention because of their huge, brilliant red flowers marked with white splashes on the lower tepals. Although *G. cardinalis* grows on wet cliffs and under waterfalls, it does perfectly well in the herbaceous border where it can form clumps that each produce several flowering stems. Closely related to these species is the extremely variable *G. carneus,* known as *G. blandus* in the older literature, which has white or pale to deep pink flowers with darker pink to red markings on the lower tepals. It was a favorite among Cape bulbs in 19th century gardens and is a parent of many of the smaller-flowered hybrids, the so-called Colville and nanus strains.

Favorites of residents at the Cape are species of the *Gladiolus alatus* group, known affectionately as *kalkoentjies,* loosely translated as turkey chicks. Most of them have large flowers, colored either scarlet to pink or rather cryptically in green, dull purple, or brown. All the species have a fine perfume, in some exceeding that of the best freesia. The rare *G. watermeyeri* produces perhaps the finest scent; its presence in the wild can always be detected by smell long before the low-growing plants are seen. Taller growing and more floriferous, *G. orchidiflorus* is also desirable, as is the orange-flowered *G. alatus.*

Gladiolus corms do well in a light peaty loam, and we have found them to benefit from regular feeding. They tend to become weak in the stem in dull weather for they thrive in full sun in the wild and are best staked if treated as pot subjects. Seeds usually take 3 years to flower, but with heavy application of fertilizer, *G. carneus* has been successfully flowered in a single season at Kirstenbosch botanical garden, a notable achievement.

FURTHER READING. *Gladiolus* in southern Africa was the subject of a lavishly illustrated and detailed monograph by Goldblatt and Manning (1998). Two further species were described by Manning et al. (1999b).

Gladiolus abbreviatus (Andrews) Goldblatt & M. P. de Vos

Plants 30–65 cm high; corm globose with leathery tunics aging into firm vertical fibers. Leaves linear, X-shaped in cross section, 3–4 mm wide. Flowers in a four- to nine-flowered spike, orange to reddish, often with green or maroon lower tepals, perianth tube cylindrical, wider and horizontal above, 40–52 mm long, dorsal tepal largest, 16–31 mm long, extending horizontally, lower tepals very short. Flowering June–September. Clay soils in renosterveld, SW, LB (Bot River to Riversdale).

Gladiolus acuminatus F. Bolus

Plants 25–50 cm high; corm ovoid with tunics of firm, wiry fibers. Leaves linear, the midribs lightly thickened, 1–1.5 mm wide. Flowers in a 3- to 10-flowered spike, greenish yellow, fragrant, perianth tube narrow, widening at the mouth, 16–30 mm long, tepals attenuate and recurving, the dorsal largest, 15–21 mm long, the lower arching downward. Flowering August–September. Stony clay soils, SW (Caledon to Bredasdorp).

Gladiolus alatus Linnaeus

Plants 8–25 cm high, stem compressed and angled; corm depressed globose with papery tunics, bearing cormels at the base. Leaves linear to falcate, ribbed, 2–6 mm wide. Flowers mostly in a two- to five-flowered spike, bilabiate, orange marked yellow to greenish, fragrant, perianth tube funnel-shaped, 10–14 mm long, dorsal tepal suberect to inclined, 35–50 mm long, lower tepals narrow, arching downward, filaments minutely hairy. Flowering August–September. Flats, slopes, and plateaus, mainly in sand, NW, SW, AP (Bokkeveld Mountains to Bredasdorp).

Gladiolus albens Goldblatt & J. C. Manning

Plants 30–40 cm high; corm globose with tunics of vertical fibers. Leaves linear, the blades often short, leathery, without evident veins, 1–2 mm wide. Flowers in a one- to five-flowered spike, white to cream, fragrant, perianth

Gladiolus alatus

Gladiolus angustus

tube slender, 35–65 mm long, tepals subequal, the dorsal slightly larger, 23–35 mm long, the lower tepals arching outward. Flowering March–May. Grassy slopes, SE (George to Alexandria).

Gladiolus angustus Linnaeus
Plants 60–120 cm high; corm globose with papery to fibrous tunics. Leaves sword-shaped to linear, glaucous, the midrib lightly thickened, 3–10 mm wide. Flowers mostly in a five- to nine-flowered spike, cream to pale pink, with reddish, diamond-shaped markings on the lower tepals, perianth tube cylindrical, mostly 50–100 mm long, dorsal tepal largest, 32–40 mm long, arching to hooded over the stamens, the lower tepals smaller, directed forward. Flowering October–November. Streams and marshes on sandstone soils, NW, SW (Cedarberg Mountains to Cape Peninsula).

Gladiolus aquamontanus Goldblatt
Plants 40–100 cm high, stem inclined to drooping; corm small, rhizome-like, with membranous tunics. Leaves sword-shaped, the margins and midribs usually lightly thickened, 8–15 mm wide. Flowers mostly in a four- to eight-flowered spike, mauve-pink with purple markings on the lower tepals, perianth tube cylindrical, 25–40 mm long, dorsal tepal largest, 30–35 mm long, arching over the stamens, the lower tepals smaller, directed forward. Flowering November–December. Streams and wet cliffs, KM (Swartberg Mountains).

Gladiolus arcuatus Klatt
Plants 12–20 cm high; corm depressed-globose with soft, papery tunics. Leaves linear to sword-shaped and falcate, leathery, hairy on the sheaths and on the margins and midrib above, 5–12 mm wide. Flowers in a four- to seven-flowered, flexuous, horizontal spike, bilabiate, windowed in profile, greenish or dull yellow with purple markings, fragrant, perianth tube funnel-shaped, mostly 10–15 mm long, dorsal tepal largest, 26–32 mm long, arching over the stamens, the lower tepals narrow, arching downward. Flowering June–August. Silty clay slopes, NW (Namaqualand to Klawer).

Gladiolus atropictus Goldblatt & J. C. Manning

Plants to 40 cm high; corm conical with firm, papery tunics aging into vertical fibers. Leaves linear, the margins and midrib lightly thickened, 1.5–2 mm wide. Flowers in a one- or two-flowered spike, bilabiate, blue with reddish streaks on the lower tepals, fragrant, perianth tube funnel-shaped, c. 13 mm long, dorsal tepal largest, arching over the stamens, 30–33 mm long, lower tepals narrow, arching downward. Flowering July–August. Rocky sandstone slopes, SW (Riviersonderend Mountains).

Gladiolus aureus Baker

Plants 30–50 cm high; corm globose with coarsely fibrous tunics. Leaves linear, often very short, lightly hairy, 3–5.5 mm wide. Flowers in a three- to eight-flowered spike, bright yellow, perianth tube filiform below, abruptly expanded near the mouth, 19–24 mm long, tepals subequal, 20–24 mm long, the dorsal inclined over the stamens, the lower directed forward. Flowering August–September. Seeps on rocky sandstone slopes, SW (Cape Peninsula).

Gladiolus aureus

Gladiolus bilineatus G. J. Lewis

Plants 20–40 cm high; corm globose with fibrous tunics. Leaves relatively short, sword-shaped, 6–8 mm wide. Flowers in a one- to three-flowered spike, cream to pink with reddish lines near the base of the lower tepals, perianth tube cylindrical, widening above, 50–70 mm long, dorsal tepal largest, c. 23 mm long, arching over the stamens, the lower tepals directed forward. Flowering March–April. Clay and loamy sand, fynbos, LB (Swellendam to Albertinia).

Gladiolus blommesteinii L. Bolus

Plants 30–60 cm high; corm globose with more or less woody to coarsely fibrous tunics. Leaves linear with thickened margins and midrib, 1–1.5 mm wide. Flowers in a one- to four-flowered, inclined spike, bilabiate, mauve or pink with dark longitudinal streaks on the lower tepals, perianth tube 13–24 mm long, dorsal tepal largest arching over the stamens, 28–44 mm long, the lower tepals arching outward; bracts ridged. Flowering

Gladiolus bilineatus

Gladiolus bonaspei

Gladiolus brevifolius

August–October. Sandstone slopes in fynbos, SW (Du Toit's Kloof to Riviersonderend Mountains).

Gladiolus bonaspei Goldblatt & M. P. de Vos
Plants 30–50 cm high; corm ovoid with coarsely fibrous tunics. Leaves more or less linear, fairly short, lightly hairy, 2–5.5 mm wide. Flowers in a two- to seven-flowered spike, orange or rarely yellow, perianth tube cylindrical, wide and horizontal above, 35–43 mm long, the upper three tepals largest, 18–23 mm long, the dorsal nearly horizontal, the lower slightly smaller, arching outward. Flowering April–August. Sandy flats and slopes to 250 m, SW (Cape Peninsula).

Gladiolus brevifolius Jacquin
Plants mostly 20–50 cm high, flowering stem bearing only sheathing leaves; corm globose with coarsely fibrous tunics. Leaf produced after flowering, solitary, linear to sword-shaped with thickened margins, usually sparsely hairy, 3–6 mm wide. Flowers mostly in an 8- to 12-flowered, erect spike, bilabiate, pink, rarely brownish or gray, with yellow markings on the lower tepals, perianth tube funnel-shaped, 11–13 mm long, dorsal tepal largest, 19–29 mm long, arching over the stamens, the lower tepals narrower, arching toward the ground. Flowering March–May. Sandstone and shale slopes, NW, SW (Clanwilliam to Riviersonderend and Bredasdorp).

Gladiolus brevitubus G. J. Lewis
Plants 12–35 cm high; corm globose with softly fibrous tunics. Leaves linear, margins and midrib lightly thickened, 1–3.5 mm wide. Flowers in a two- to eight-flowered spike, almost actinomorphic, orange with yellow markings at the base of the lower tepals, faintly scented, perianth tube 2.5–4 mm long, tepals subequal, 11–18 mm long, spreading, often held nearly vertical, the stamens and style unilateral. Flowering September–November. Rocky sandstone slopes, SW (Somerset West to Riviersonderend Mountains and Hermanus).

Gladiolus buckerveldii (L. Bolus) Goldblatt
Plants 80–125 cm high, stem inclined to drooping; corm

globose with softly papery tunics. Leaves sword-shaped, the midrib lightly thickened, 25–35 mm wide. Flowers in a 12- to 20-flowered spike, cream with red, diamond-shaped markings on the lower tepals, perianth tube slender, widening above, 45–50 mm long, dorsal tepal largest, 28–32 mm long, inclined over the stamens, the lower tepals much smaller, directed forward. Flowering December–January. Rocky streambanks and waterfalls, NW (Cedarberg Mountains).

Gladiolus bullatus Thunberg ex G. J. Lewis
Plants 50–80 cm high; corm globose with woody or coarsely fibrous tunics. Leaves linear, the blades fairly short, the margins heavily and midrib lightly thickened, c. 2 mm wide. Flowers in a one- or two-flowered spike, bell-like, blue with transverse yellow markings on the lower tepals, perianth tube 10–16 mm long, dorsal tepal largest, hooded over the stamens, 25–35 mm long, the lower tepals narrower, directed forward; bracts ridged. Flowering August–October. Sandstone slopes in fynbos, SW, AP (Kogelberg to Potberg).

Gladiolus caeruleus Goldblatt & J. C. Manning
Plants 40–60 cm high; corm globose with woody tunics. Leaves linear, the margins raised into wings at right angles to the blade, thus H-shaped in cross section, 3–7 mm wide. Flowers mostly in an 8- to 10-flowered spike, bilabiate, blue with darkly speckled lower tepals, fragrant, perianth tube funnel-shaped, c. 15 mm long, dorsal tepal largest, inclined over the stamens, 30–32 mm long, lower tepals narrower, arching outward. Flowering August–September. Limestone outcrops and calcareous sands, SW (Saldanha to Yzerfontein).

Gladiolus cardinalis Curtis
Plants 60–90 cm high, stem inclined to drooping; corm globose with leathery to firm, papery tunics. Leaves sword-shaped, often drooping, the midrib moderately thickened, 11–21 mm wide. Flowers in a 4- to 11-flowered spike, large, red with white splashes on the lower tepals, perianth tube 32–40 mm long, dorsal tepal largest, 45–55 mm long, suberect to weakly inclined, the lower tepals slightly smaller, arching forward. Flowering

Gladiolus bullatus

Gladiolus caeruleus

Gladiolus cardinalis

December–January. Waterfalls and wet cliffs, SW (Bain's Kloof to Riviersonderend Mountains).

Gladiolus carinatus Aiton

Plants 30–60 cm high, stem base purple, mottled with white; corm globose with tunics of fairly soft fibers. Leaves linear, the midrib prominent, the margins lightly thickened, 2–9 mm wide. Flowers in a four- to eight-flowered spike, bilabiate, blue to violet or yellow, rarely pink, often with transverse yellow markings on the lower tepals, fragrant, perianth tube funnel-shaped, 13–16 mm long, dorsal tepal largest, 24–36 mm long, arching over the stamens, lower tepals narrow, arching downward. Flowering August–September. Sandstone slopes or deep coastal sands, NW, SW, AP, LB, SE (Namaqualand to Knysna).

Gladiolus carmineus C. H. Wright

Plants mostly 30–50 cm high; corm globose with papery tunics. Leaves produced after flowering, sword-shaped, glaucous, the midrib lightly thickened, 8–10 mm wide. Flowers in a two- to six-flowered spike, deep pink to carmine, with white markings on the lower tepals, perianth tube narrowly funnel-shaped, 30–35 mm long, outer tepals larger than the inner, the dorsal 35–45 mm long, weakly inclined, the lower tepals spreading. Flowering February–April. Coastal sandstone cliffs and rocks, SW, AP (Cape Hangklip to Cape Infanta).

Gladiolus carneus D. Delaroche

Plants 25–60 cm high; corm globose with papery tunics. Leaves sword-shaped to linear, the margins and midrib lightly thickened, glaucous, mostly 4–12 mm wide. Flowers mostly in a three- to eight-flowered spike, pink or white, often with dark pink markings on the lower tepals, perianth tube almost cylindrical, mostly 25–40 mm long, dorsal tepal largest, 28–45 mm long, suberect or inclined, the lower tepals slightly smaller, arching forward. Flowering mainly October–November. Sandstone slopes, often wet sites, to 500 m, NW, SW, LB, SE (Cold Bokkeveld to Knysna).

Gladiolus caryophyllaceus (Burman fil.) Poiret

Plants 25–110 cm high; corm globose with coarsely fibrous tunics. Leaves sword-shaped to linear, the margins and midribs thickened, hairy, 10–27 mm wide. Flowers in a two- to eight-flowered spike, large, pink to mauve, speckled on the lower tepals, fragrant, perianth tube narrowly funnel-shaped, 30–40 mm long, dorsal tepal largest, 37–45 mm long, arching over the stamens, the lower tepals smaller, arching outward. Flowering August–October. Sandstone flats and slopes, NW, SW, KM (southern Namaqualand to Mamre and Swartberg Mountains).

Gladiolus ceresianus L. Bolus

Plants 8–15 cm high; corm depressed-globose with hard, fibrous to woody tunics. Leaves linear, the sheaths overlapping, terete with four longitudinal grooves, c. 2 mm diam. Flowers in a one- to four-flowered, inclined spike, bilabiate, dull purple to brownish with dark veining, fragrant, perianth tube funnel-shaped, 12–16 mm long, dorsal tepal erect, the margins curved back, 28–45 mm long, the lower tepals narrow, directed downward. Flowering August–October. Stony slopes and flats in clay soil, RV, NW, KM (southern Namaqualand and western Karoo to the Witteberg and Cold Bokkeveld).

Gladiolus carinatus

Gladiolus carmineus

Gladiolus carneus

Gladiolus caryophyllaceus

Gladiolus ceresianus

Gladiolus cunonius

Gladiolus debilis

Gladiolus comptonii G. J. Lewis

Plants 45–60 cm high; corm globose with coarsely fibrous tunics. Leaves linear, the margins and midrib lightly thickened, 1.5–3 mm wide. Flowers in a one- to three-flowered spike, bilabiate, yellow with brown streaks on the lower tepals, perianth tube funnel-shaped, 11–14 mm long, tepals attenuate, the dorsal largest, 40–50 mm long, arching over the stamens, the lower tepals arching downward. Flowering June–July. Rocky sandstone slopes, NW (Heerenlogement Mountain).

Gladiolus crispulatus L. Bolus

Plants 30–40 cm high; corm globose with fibrous tunics. Leaves linear, two-veined on one surface, 1–3 mm wide. Flowers in a two- to four-flowered spike, bilabiate, deep pink, the lower tepals with triangular median streaks and dark spots in the throat, perianth tube funnel-shaped, 20–26 mm long, tepals with crisped margins, the dorsal largest, 28–34 mm long, arching over the stamens, the lower tepals smaller, arching downward. Flowering November–December, especially after fire. Rocky sandstone slopes, LB (Langeberg Mountains from Swellendam to Riversdale).

Gladiolus cunonius (Linnaeus) Gaertner

Plants 20–70 cm high; corm globose with papery tunics, producing cormels on long, slender stolons. Leaves sword-shaped, thickened in the midline, 5–12 mm wide. Flowers mostly in a five- to eight-flowered, strongly inclined spike, bright red, the lower tepals yellow or green, perianth tube slender below, abruptly expanded, 12–15 mm long, dorsal tepal largest, elongate and spoon-shaped, 26–29 mm long, upper lateral tepals held erect, lower tepals small, directed forward, anthers with long, free tails. Flowering September–October. Coastal in sandy soils, SW, AP, SE (Saldanha to Knysna).

Gladiolus cylindraceus G. J. Lewis

Plants 30–50 cm high; corm globose with tunics of coarse fibers. Leaves linear, X-shaped in cross section, 2–3 mm wide. Flowers in a five- to eight-flowered spike, pale pink with dark red marks on the lower tepals, perianth tube cylindrical, mostly 25–50 mm long, dorsal tepal erect,

18–25 mm long, the lower tepals smaller, spreading horizontally. Flowering December–January. Sandstone slopes, NW (Cold Bokkeveld and Tulbagh Mountains).

Gladiolus debilis Ker Gawler

Plants mostly 25–45 cm high; corm globose with coarsely fibrous to woody tunics. Leaves linear, the margins and midrib thickened, 1–1.5 mm wide. Flowers in a one- to three-flowered, inclined spike, white with red markings on the lower tepals, perianth tube slender, mostly 15–22 mm long, dorsal tepal largest, usually arched over the stamens, 17–27 mm long, the lower tepals arching outward; bracts ridged. Flowering September–October. Rocky sandstone slopes, SW (Cape Peninsula to Bredasdorp).

Gladiolus delpierrei Goldblatt

Plants 40–45 cm high; corm globose with woody to coarsely fibrous tunics. Leaves linear with two thickened veins, 3–4 mm wide. Flowers in a one- to three-flowered spike, bilabiate, yellowish cream with yellow and red markings on the lower tepals, perianth tube funnel-shaped, c. 8 mm long, dorsal tepal largest, suberect, c. 21 mm long, the lower tepals spreading. Flowering December–January. Marshy sandstone slopes, 1200 m, NW (Cedarberg Mountains at Sneeuberg).

Gladiolus emiliae L. Bolus

Plants 30–60 cm high; corm globose with papery to fibrous tunics. Leaves of the flowering stem sheathing, foliage leaf single, linear, lightly ribbed, sparsely hairy, 5–7 mm wide. Flowers in a 4- to 10-flowered, erect spike, yellowish to light brown, covered with brown or purplish speckles, fragrant, perianth tube slender below, curved outward and flared above, 32–45 mm long, tepals subequal, 14–20 mm long, the dorsal inclined over the stamens, the lower arching outward. Flowering March–April. Rocky loam, SW, KM, LB, SE (Riviersonderend to George and Gamkaberg).

Gladiolus engysiphon G. J. Lewis

Plants 35–50 cm high; corm globose with tunics of coarse vertical fibers. Leaves of flowering stem entirely

Gladiolus emiliae

Gladiolus engysiphon

sheathing, foliage leaf single, terete, four-grooved. Flowers in a two- to six-flowered spike, cream with red median streaks on the lower tepals, perianth tube cylindrical, usually 40–60 mm long, dorsal tepal largest, 16–20 mm long, the lower tepals narrower, directed forward. Flowering March–April. Clay and granitic loam in renosterveld and grassland, LB (Swellendam to Mossel Bay).

Gladiolus exilis G. J. Lewis

Plants 25–45 cm high; corm globose with tunics of leathery layers aging into firm vertical fibers. Leaves linear, leathery, without evident veins, the blades reduced in length, 1–1.5 mm wide. Flowers in a one- to four-flowered spike, bilabiate, white to pale blue with dark streaks on the lower tepals, fragrant, perianth tube 11–15 mm long, dorsal tepal inclined over the stamens, 22–35 mm long, the lower tepals narrow, directed forward. Flowering April–May. Clay loam in fynbos, NW, SW (Porterville to Du Toit's Kloof).

Gladiolus floribundus Jacquin

Plants 20–45 cm high; corm globose with papery tunics alternating with fibrous layers. Leaves sword-shaped, the margins and midrib thickened, 12–20 mm wide. Flowers mostly in a three- to eight-flowered, horizontal spike, white to cream or pinkish with a dark median streak on all the tepals, perianth tube cylindrical, widening above, 40–70 mm long, dorsal tepal largest, 30–45 mm long, suberect to inclined, the lower tepals shorter and narrower, arching forward. Flowering September–November. Dry clay, sandy, or limestone flats and slopes, NW, SW, AP, KM, LB, SE (Cedarberg Mountains to the Eastern Cape at Alexandria).

Gladiolus fourcadei (L. Bolus) Goldblatt & M. P. de Vos

Plants 40–60 cm high; corm globose with firm, fibrous tunics. Leaves linear, X-shaped in cross section, 2–3 mm wide. Flowers in a three- to five-flowered, erect spike, red or yellow-green, the lower tepals darkly veined, dorsal tepal largest, 15–20 mm long, more or less erect, lower tepals smaller, arching downward. Flowering September–October. Clay soils in renosterveld, KM, SE (George to Humansdorp).

Gladiolus geardii L. Bolus

Plants 80–150 cm high; corm globose with papery to fibrous tunics. Leaves sword-shaped, 14–28 mm wide. Flowers in a 6- to 10-flowered spike, pink with darker markings on the lower tepals, perianth tube slender, 30–40 mm long, dorsal tepal inclined, 40–55 mm long, the lower tepals slightly smaller, inclined toward the ground. Flowering November–January. Moist sandstone slopes, SE (Humansdorp to Uitenhage).

Gladiolus floribundus

Gladiolus gracilis

Gladiolus gracilis Jacquin
Plants 30–60 cm high; corm globose with woody tunics. Leaves linear, the margins raised into wings arching inward, the blade apparently terete but H-shaped in cross section, 1.5–2.5 mm wide. Flowers in a two- to five-flowered, inclined, strongly flexuous spike, bilabiate, blue to gray, rarely pink or yellowish, with dark streaks on the lower tepals, fragrant, perianth tube funnel-shaped, 12–18 mm long, dorsal tepal largest, inclined over the stamens, 24–33 mm long, lower tepals narrower, arching outward. Flowering June–August. Mostly clay slopes, sometimes on granite, NW, SW, AP, LB (Aurora to Albertinia).

Gladiolus grandiflorus Andrews
Plants 25–50 cm high; corm globose with papery tunics alternating with fibrous layers. Leaves sword-shaped, the margins and midrib thickened, mostly 6–15 mm wide. Flowers in a two- to nine-flowered spike, cream to greenish, sometimes with a darker median streak on the lower or all the tepals, perianth tube slender to funnel-shaped, 27–55 mm long, dorsal tepal largest, 35–44 mm long, suberect, the lower tepals slightly smaller, arching forward. Flowering September–October. Clay slopes in renosterveld, SW, KM, LB, SE (Bot River to Port Elizabeth).

Gladiolus griseus Goldblatt & J. C. Manning
Plants mostly 30–60 cm high, stem base purple, mottled with white; corm globose with tunics of fairly soft fibers. Leaves linear, the midrib prominent, the margins lightly thickened, 2–7.5 mm wide. Flowers mostly in a three- to six-flowered spike, bilabiate, gray-blue with pale yellow markings edged with dark color on the lower tepals, lightly fragrant, perianth tube 6–10 mm long, dorsal tepal arching over the stamens, 16–26 mm long, lower tepals narrow, directed forward. Flowering May–July. Calcareous coastal soils in fynbos and strandveld, SW (Saldanha to Milnerton).

Gladiolus gueinzii Kuntze
Plants 25–50 cm high; corm globose with papery tunics, producing axillary and basal cormels. Leaves linear to sword-shaped, leathery, the margins and midrib scarcely thickened, 4–6 mm wide, glaucous. Flowers mostly in a four- to eight-flowered spike, nearly actinomorphic, mauve with red-purple and white markings usually only on the lower tepals, perianth tube nearly cylindrical, 13–15 mm long, tepals subequal, 17–20 mm long. Flowering mainly October–December. Coastal sand dunes, AP, LB, SE (Agulhas and Mossel Bay to KwaZulu-Natal).

Gladiolus guthriei F. Bolus
Plants 40–70 cm high; corm globose with fibrous tunics. Leaves sword-shaped, fairly short, usually lightly hairy at least when young, 3–6 mm wide. Flowers usually in a three- to nine-flowered spike, pink to red-purple or brownish with dark speckles, fragrant, perianth tube narrowly funnel-shaped, 20–27 mm long, the dorsal tepal largest, 22–30 mm long, arching over the stamens, the lower tepals smaller, arching downward. Flowering April–June. Sandstone outcrops, 100–800 m, NW, SW, KM (Bokkeveld Mountains to Elim).

Gladiolus grandiflorus

Gladiolus guthriei

Gladiolus hirsutus

Gladiolus hirsutus Jacquin
Plants 30–50 cm high; corm globose with coarsely fibrous tunics. Leaves linear to sword-shaped, often fairly short, hairy, mostly 3–8 mm wide. Flowers in a three- to six-flowered spike, bilabiate, pink to purple or whitish, lower tepals irregularly streaked with dark color, perianth tube funnel-shaped, usually 15–25 mm long, dorsal tepal largest, mostly 19–27 mm long, arching over the stamens, the lower tepals arching outward. Flowering mainly June–October. Rocky sandstone slopes, NW, SW, LB (Citrusdal to Mossel Bay).

Gladiolus huttonii (N. E. Brown) Goldblatt & M. P. de Vos
Plants 30–60 cm high; corm ovoid with tunics of coarse fibers. Leaves linear, the midrib raised, thus X-shaped in cross section, 2–3 mm wide. Flowers in a three- to eight-flowered, erect spike, red to orange, the lower tepals sometimes yellow, the tube streaked with maroon, perianth tube cylindrical, wide and horizontal above, 50–53 mm long, dorsal tepal largest, suberect, 25–40 mm long, the lower tepals smaller, arching downward. Flowering June–September. Sandstone slopes, SE (Plettenberg Bay to Grahamstown).

Gladiolus hyalinus Jacquin
Plants 25–50 cm high; corm globose with more or less woody tunics. Leaves linear, the margins and midrib thickened, 1.7–2.5 mm wide. Flowers in a one- to six-flowered spike, green to brownish with dark speckles, rarely fragrant, perianth tube cylindrical, 25–36 mm long, the dorsal tepal largest, inclined over the stamens, 23–30 mm long, lower tepals narrower, arching downward and diverging. Flowering June–September. Shale, granite, and sandstone slopes, fynbos or renosterveld, NW, SW, SE (Namaqualand to Port Alfred).

Gladiolus inflatus Thunberg
Plants 25–60 cm high; corm globose with tunics of hard, woody fibers. Leaves terete with four longitudinal grooves, c. 1 mm diam. Flowers in a two- or three-flowered spike, bell-like, mauve to pink with yellow transverse markings edged with dark color, rarely white with red markings, perianth tube funnel-shaped, 12–25 mm

long, dorsal tepal hooded over the stamens, 22–27 mm long, the lower tepals narrower, directed forward. Flowering August–November. Rocky sandstone slopes, NW, SW, LB (Cedarberg Mountains to Swellendam).

Gladiolus inflexus Goldblatt & J. C. Manning
Plants 15–25 cm high, stem strongly flexuous; corm globose with woody to coarsely fibrous tunics. Leaves linear with lightly thickened midrib, 1–2 mm wide. Flowers in a one- to three-flowered, flexuous spike, bilabiate, pale blue to mauve with dark speckling on the lower tepals, fragrant, perianth tube funnel-shaped, 11–20 mm long, dorsal tepal largest, inclined over the stamens, 21–25 mm long, lower tepals narrow, directed downward. Flowering July–August. Rocky sandstone or limestone flats in fynbos, SW (Worcester and Bredasdorp).

Gladiolus insolens Goldblatt & J. C. Manning
Plants 30–50 cm high; corm globose with papery tunics. Leaves linear, slightly fleshy, glaucous, the midrib lightly raised, 3.5–5.5 mm wide. Flowers in a one- to three-flowered spike, tulip-shaped, scarlet, perianth tube cylindrical, c. 38 mm long, tepals subequal, 27–30 mm long, the dorsal suberect, the lower spreading. Flowering December–January. Wet sandstone cliffs and rocks, c. 1200 m, NW (Piketberg at Zebra Kop).

Gladiolus involutus D. Delaroche
Plants 30–50 cm high; corm globose with soft, papery tunics, producing cormels on long stolons. Leaves linear, thickened in the midline, 1.7–3 mm wide. Flowers in a four- to seven-flowered spike, bilabiate, white, often fading pink, with yellow-green markings on the lower tepals, perianth tube funnel-shaped, tepals attenuate, the upper three largest, 25–28 mm long, the dorsal arching over the stamens, the lower tepals narrow, channeled, arching outward. Flowering August–October. Clay slopes in renosterveld and grassland, LB, SE (Swellendam to East London).

Gladiolus jonquilliodorus Ecklon ex G. J. Lewis
Plants 30–45 cm high, flowering stem without foliage leaves; corm depressed-globose with softly papery tu-

Gladiolus hyalinus

Gladiolus insolens

nics. Leaves produced after flowering, terete and four-grooved. Flowers mostly in a 7- to 14-flowered spike, bilabiate, cream to pale yellow, fragrant, perianth tube funnel-shaped, c. 9 mm long, dorsal tepal largest, hooded over the stamens, c. 20 mm long, the lower tepals narrower, directed forward. Flowering November–December. Sandy coastal flats, SW (Darling to Cape Peninsula).

Gladiolus lapeirousioides Goldblatt

Plants 8–14 cm high; corm conical with more or less woody tunics. Leaves linear to falcate, thicker in the midline, mostly 3–5 mm wide. Flowers in a 5- to 12-flowered, nearly horizontal spike, bilabiate, creamy white, the lower tepals with a yellow spot near the base outlined in red, perianth tube elongate, cylindrical, 35–40 mm long, dorsal tepal largest, erect or recurving, 20–22 mm long, the lower tepals narrower, directed forward. Flowering late August to early October. Stony shale slopes, RV (Western Karoo near Loeriesfontein).

Gladiolus leptosiphon F. Bolus

Plants 25–45 cm high; corm globose with tunics of wiry fibers. Leaves linear and whip-like, thickened in the midline, c. 2.5 mm wide. Flowers in a six- to nine-flowered spike, cream with a purple median streak on the lower tepals, perianth tube cylindrical, 45–50 mm long, tepals narrow and attenuate, the upper three largest, 25–35 mm long, the dorsal suberect, the lower tepals narrower, channeled, arching downward. Flowering October–November. Dry, stony, sandstone slopes, KM, SE (Ladismith to Uitenhage).

Gladiolus liliaceus Houttuyn

Plants 35–70 cm high; corm globose with woody to firm, papery tunics. Leaves linear, the margins and midrib strongly thickened, 2–6 mm wide. Flowers in a one- to six-flowered spike, brown to russet or beige, turning mauve in the evening and then intensely fragrant, perianth tube cylindrical, widening above, 43–50 mm long, tepals attenuate with undulate margins, the dorsal largest, inclined over the stamens, 38–45 mm long, the lower tepals slightly smaller, arching downward. Flowering August–November. Clay slopes, mainly in renoster-

Gladiolus liliaceus

Gladiolus maculatus

veld, NW, SW, AP, KM, LB, SE (Cedarberg Mountains to Port Elizabeth).

Gladiolus longicollis Baker

Plants 35–60 cm high; corm globose with hard, wiry tunics. Leaves terete and four-grooved, c. 1.5 mm diam. Flowers mostly in a two- or three-flowered spike, brown to cream often with brownish speckling, fragrant in the evening, perianth tube cylindrical, 45–65 mm long, tepals subequal, the dorsal 30–35 mm long, inclined over the stamens, the lower tepals narrower, arching outward. Flowering September–October. Sandstone slopes, KM, SE (Swartberg Mountains to Northern Province).

Two subspecies are recognized: subspecies *longicollis* with perianth tube 45–65 mm long, flowering September–October, KM, SE (Swartberg Mountains to KwaZulu-Natal), and subspecies *platypetala* (Baker) Goldblatt & J. C. Manning with perianth tube 65–110 mm long, flowering mostly October–December, grassy clay or sandstone slopes (KwaZulu-Natal to Northern Province).

Gladiolus maculatus Sweet

Plants 30–60 cm high; corm globose with fibrous tunics. Leaves linear, the blades often short, leathery, without evident veins, 1.5–2 mm wide. Flowers in a one- to five-flowered spike, brownish to buff with dark speckling, fragrant, perianth tube 23–48 mm long, tepals unequal, the dorsal largest, 25–33 mm long, the lower tepals narrower, arching downward. Flowering March–July. Mainly clay slopes, SW, AP, KM, LB, SE (Cape Peninsula to Grahamstown).

Gladiolus marlothii L. Bolus

Plants 45–60 cm high; corm globose with fibrous tunics forming a neck. Leaves linear, the midrib strongly raised, thus X-shaped in cross section, hairy, 3–4 mm wide. Flowers in a three- to five-flowered spike, bell-like, pale blue, darkly speckled and with yellow transverse markings on the lower tepals, perianth tube funnel-shaped, 9–10 mm long, dorsal tepal largest, 24–30 mm long hooded over the stamens, the lower tepals narrow, directed downward. Flowering mainly October. Stony slopes in clay, RV (Roggeveld Escarpment).

Gladiolus martleyi L. Bolus

Plants 20–35 cm high, flowering stem without foliage leaves; corm depressed-globose with softly papery tunics. Leaves produced after flowering, one or two, terete and four-grooved, c. 1 mm diam. Flowers in a 3- to 11-flowered spike, bilabiate, pink with pale markings edged with red on the lower tepals, usually fragrant, perianth tube funnel-shaped, c. 12 mm long, the dorsal tepal largest, inclined over the stamens, 22–27 mm long, the lower tepals narrower, arching outward. Flowering February–May. Sandy and rocky flats, lower slopes, NW, SW, AP, LB (Bokkeveld Mountains to Riversdale). Page 202.

Gladiolus meliusculus (G. J. Lewis) Goldblatt & J. C. Manning

Plants 12–25 cm high; corm depressed-globose with papery tunics, often with cormels on short stolons. Leaves linear to falcate, ribbed, 2–5 mm wide. Flowers in a two- to six-flowered spike, bilabiate, pink with blackish and greenish markings on the lower tepals, fragrant, perianth tube funnel-shaped, c. 11 mm long, dorsal tepal largest, suberect, 30–38 mm long, lower tepals narrow, arching downward, filaments minutely hairy. Flowering September–October. Damp sandstone and granite slopes and flats, SW (Hopefield to Cape Peninsula). Page 202.

Gladiolus marlothii

Gladiolus martleyi

Gladiolus meliusculus

Gladiolus meridionalis

Gladiolus monticola

Gladiolus meridionalis (G. J. Lewis) Goldblatt & J. C. Manning

Plants 35–45 cm high; corm globose with papery to fibrous tunics. Leaves linear, blades usually short, leathery, without evident veins, c. 2 mm wide. Flowers in a one- to three-flowered spike, salmon pink to yellowish cream, lightly scented, perianth tube elongate, slender, 40–48 mm long, tepals subequal, 22–28 mm long, the dorsal horizontal, the lower arching outward. Flowering May–July. Sandstone slopes, SW, AP, SE (Pearly Beach to Port Elizabeth).

Gladiolus miniatus Ecklon

Plants 15–40 cm high; corm globose with firm, papery tunics alternating with fibrous layers. Leaves sword-shaped, 7–18 mm wide. Flowers in a three- to seven-flowered, horizontal spike, salmon, often red along the midline of the tepals, perianth tube cylindrical, widening above, 50–65 mm long, upper three tepals largest, 32–39 mm long, inclined to almost horizontal, lower tepals smaller, arching downward. Flowering October–November. Coastal limestone outcrops, SW, AP (Hermanus to Agulhas).

Gladiolus monticola G. J. Lewis

Plants 30–45 cm high, flowering stem bearing only sheathing leaves; corm globose with coarsely fibrous tunics. Leaf produced after flowering, solitary, linear, with thickened margins and midrib, lightly hairy, 3–6 mm wide. Flowers in a three- to nine-flowered, erect spike, pink to apricot with darker pink markings on the lower tepals, perianth tube cylindrical, 22–30 mm long, dorsal tepal largest, 20–25 mm long, arching over the stamens, the lower tepals narrower, arching outward. Flowering December–March. Rocky sandstone slopes, SW (Cape Peninsula).

Gladiolus mostertiae L. Bolus

Plants 25–30 cm high; corm globose with papery to fibrous tunics. Leaves linear, lightly hairy, the midrib thickened, 2.5–4 mm wide. Flowers in a 4- to 10-flowered spike, bilabiate, pale pink with yellow-green markings on the lower tepals, perianth tube funnel-shaped, c. 11 mm long, dorsal tepal largest, c. 20 mm long, hooded over the stamens, the lower tepals narrow, arching outward. Flowering November–December. Wet sandy soils, NW (Bokkeveld Mountains).

Gladiolus mutabilis G. J. Lewis

Plants 25–50 cm high; corm conical with fibrous to woody tunics. Leaves with short blades, linear without evident midrib, 2–3 mm wide. Flowers in a two- to five-flowered spike, bilabiate, purple to pink or brown with purple to brown streaks on the lower tepals, fragrant, perianth tube 13–17 mm long, dorsal tepal inclined over the stamens, 25–32 mm long, the lower tepals narrow, directed forward. Flowering July–August. Sandstone slopes, SW, LB, SE (Albertinia to Grahamstown).

Gladiolus nerineoides G. J. Lewis

Plants 35–60 cm high, flowering stem bearing only sheathing leaves; corm globose with fairly fine, fibrous tunics. Leaf produced after flowering, solitary, linear, lightly hairy, 3–6 mm wide. Flowers in a 3- to 10-flowered spike, crowded together, scarlet, perianth tube narrowly funnel-shaped, 25–31 mm long, tepals subequal, 19–22

Gladiolus nerineoides

Gladiolus nigromontanus

Gladiolus orchidiflorus

mm long, laxly spreading, stamens included or anthers partly exserted. Flowering January–March. Rocky sandstone slopes and cliffs, 500–1500 m, SW (Bain's Kloof to Somerset West).

Gladiolus nigromontanus Goldblatt

Plants 30–40 cm high; corm globose with woody tunics. Leaf blades short, terete, with four narrow grooves, c. 1 mm diam. Flowers in a three- to six-flowered spike, white with red median streaks on the lower tepals, perianth tube cylindrical, 17–25 mm long, dorsal tepal longest, 20–24 mm long, the lower tepals narrow, arching forward. Flowering March. Local in seeps on sandstone slopes, KM (Swartberg Mountains).

Gladiolus orchidiflorus Andrews

Plants mostly 20–50 cm high; corm globose with papery to fibrous tunics, usually with many small cormels around the base. Leaves linear to sword-shaped, glaucous, thickened in the midline, 2–10 mm wide. Flowers in a 5- to 12-flowered spike, bilabiate, windowed in profile, greenish to purple with dark purple markings on the lower tepals, fragrant, perianth tube funnel-shaped, 9–14 mm long, dorsal tepal longest, narrow, arching in a semicircle, 20–35 mm long, the lower tepals arching downward. Flowering August–October. Clay and sandstone soils, NW, SW, KM (Namibia to Cape Flats, to Free State).

Gladiolus oreocharis Schlechter

Plants 15–50 cm high; corm globose with finely fibrous tunics. Leaves linear, two-veined, 2–6 mm wide. Flowers in a two- to seven-flowered spike, bilabiate, dark pink with red and white markings on the lower tepals, perianth tube funnel-shaped, 15–24 mm long, dorsal tepal largest 18–22 mm long, inclined over the stamens, lower tepals arching outward. Flowering December–January, mostly after fire. Wet sandstone slopes, 1000–2000 m, NW, SW, LB (Cedarberg to Langeberg Mountains).

Gladiolus ornatus Klatt

Plants 40–60 cm high; corm globose with softly papery tunics, not accumulating. Leaves linear with the margins and midrib thickened, 1–2 mm wide. Flowers in a one- to three-flowered, flexuous spike, pink with white and red markings on the lower tepals, perianth tube funnel-shaped, 18–20 mm long, dorsal tepal largest, inclined over the stamens, c. 28 mm long, the lower tepals narrower, arching outward. Flowering August–November. Marshy sandstone and granite slopes, SW (Mamre to Cape Flats).

Gladiolus overbergensis Goldblatt & M. P. de Vos
Plants 35–50 cm high; corm globose with coarsely fibrous tunics. Leaves sword-shaped to linear, rough and scabrid, lightly ridged, 2.5–5 mm wide. Flowers in a two- to five-flowered, erect spike, red to orange, perianth tube cylindrical, wide and horizontal above, 46–55 mm long, dorsal tepal largest, 22–26 mm long, nearly horizontal, lower tepals smaller, arching toward the ground. Flowering July–September. Sandstone slopes, SW, AP (Hermanus to Agulhas).

Gladiolus pappei Baker
Plants 20–35 cm high; corm globose with softly papery tunics. Leaves usually linear, the margins and midrib hardly thickened, glaucous, 1.6–3 mm wide. Flowers in a two- to four-flowered spike, dark pink with red and white markings on the lower tepals, perianth tube cylindrical, 30–35 mm long, dorsal tepal largest, 26–30 mm long, suberect or inclined, lower tepals slightly smaller, arching outward. Flowering October–November, mainly after fire. Marshes on sandstone slopes, SW (Cape Peninsula and Jonkershoek Mountains).

Gladiolus patersoniae F. Bolus
Plants 30–50 cm high; corm globose with tunics of coarse fibers. Leaves terete, four-grooved, c. 2 mm diam. Flowers in a two- to five-flowered spike, bell-like, blue to pearly gray, with yellow transverse markings on the lower tepals, fragrant, perianth tube funnel-shaped, 10–15 mm long, dorsal tepal largest, hooded over the stamens, 20–30 mm long, lower tepals narrow, directed forward. Flowering August–October. Rocky sandstone slopes, NW, SW, KM, LB, SE (Worcester to Great Winterhoek Mountains).

Gladiolus pappei

Gladiolus patersoniae

Gladiolus phoenix

Gladiolus priorii

Gladiolus permeablis D. Delaroche
Plants mostly 20–40 cm high; corm globose with tunics of wiry fibers. Leaves linear and whip-like, thickened in the midline, 1–3 mm wide. Flowers in a four- to eight-flowered spike, bilabiate, windowed in profile, mauve to dull purple or cream, often with yellowish markings, usually intensely fragrant, perianth tube funnel-shaped, 9–12 mm long, tepals narrowed below, the dorsal largest, 28–35 mm long, arching over the stamens, lower tepals narrow, directed downward. Flowering August–October. Shale slopes in renosterveld, SW, LB, KM, SE (Caledon eastward through southern Africa to Zimbabwe).

Gladiolus phoenix Goldblatt & J. C. Manning
Plants 50–75 cm high; corm globose with papery tunics, bearing numerous cormels in short fascicles. Leaves sword-shaped, mostly 6–12 mm wide, the margins and midrib scarcely raised. Flowers in a 9- to 12-flowered spike, bilabiate, deep pink with red and white markings on the lower tepals, perianth tube funnel-shaped, 18–20 mm long, dorsal tepal largest, 26–28 mm long, inclined over the stamens, the lower tepals narrower, arching outward. Flowering November–December, only after fire. Wet sandstone slopes above 600 m, SW (Bain's Kloof Mountains).

Gladiolus priorii (N. E. Brown) Goldblatt & M. P. de Vos
Plants 30–40 cm high; corm globose with papery tunics aging into vertical fibers. Leaves linear with short blades, leathery, without visible veins, c. 2 mm wide. Flowers in a one- to four-flowered, flexuous spike, red with a yellow throat, perianth tube cylindrical, wide and horizontal above, 30–46 mm long, tepals unequal, the dorsal largest, 25–32 mm long, the lower slightly smaller, arching downward. Flowering April–June. Sandstone and granite slopes, SW (Saldanha to Hermanus).

Gladiolus pritzelii Diels
Plants 30–50 cm high; corm globose with woody to leathery tunics. Leaves linear, scabrid to pilose, usually with two thickened veins, 1.5–3.5 mm wide. Flowers in a one- to five-flowered spike, bell-like, yellow with red to brown transverse markings on the lower tepals, fragrant,

perianth tube funnel-shaped, c. 12 mm long, dorsal tepal largest, 16–24 mm long, hooded over the stamens, the lower tepals narrower, directed forward. Flowering August–October. Rocky sandstone slopes, 800–2000 m, NW (western Karoo, Cedarberg Mountains to Cold Bokkeveld).

Gladiolus pulcherrimus (G. J. Lewis) Goldblatt & J. C. Manning
Plants 20–60 cm high, stem compressed and angled; corm depressed globose with papery tunics, bearing cormels at the base. Leaves linear to sword-shaped, glaucous, 3–12 mm wide. Flowers in a five- to eight-flowered spike, bilabiate, orange marked yellow to greenish, fragrant, perianth tube funnel-shaped, c. 11 mm long, dorsal tepal largest, c. 40 mm long, suberect, lower tepals narrow, arching downward, filaments minutely hairy. Flowering September–October. Sandstone slopes, NW (Trawal to Piketberg).

Gladiolus quadrangularis (Burman fil.) Ker Gawler
Plants 50–90 cm high; corm globose with tunics of firm, wiry fibers. Leaves linear, the midrib strongly raised, thus X-shaped in cross section, 2.4–4 mm wide. Flowers in a 4- to 10-flowered, erect spike, red to orange, perianth tube cylindrical, wide and horizontal above, 35–55 mm long, dorsal tepal largest, 24–29 mm long, extended horizontally, the lower tepals narrower, arching downward. Flowering August–October. Rocky sandstone slopes, NW (Cold Bokkeveld to Koo).

Gladiolus quadrangulus (D. Delaroche) Barnard
Plants mostly 14–35 cm high, stem base purple, mottled with white; corm globose with fibrous tunics. Leaves linear, thickened in the midline, 1–2 mm wide. Flowers mostly in a three- to five-flowered spike, actinomorphic, lilac to pink or white, lightly fragrant, perianth tube 6–10 mm long, tepals subequal, 18–25 mm long. Flowering August–October. Wet sandy flats, SW (Darling to the Cape Flats).

Gladiolus recurvus Linnaeus
Plants 25–35 cm high; corm globose with woody tunics. Leaves linear, the margins raised into wings arching in-

Gladiolus quadrangulus

Gladiolus recurvus

ward, H-shaped in cross section, c. 3 mm wide. Flowers in a one- to four-flowered, flexuous spike, bilabiate, pale gray to cream or pinkish, with darker streaks on the lower tepals, fragrant, perianth tube cylindrical, 27–36 mm long, tepals attenuate, the dorsal largest, inclined over the stamens, 22–30 mm long, lower tepals narrower, arching downward. Flowering June–October. Clay flats and lower slopes, NW, SW (Ceres to Somerset West).

Gladiolus rhodanthus J. C. Manning & Goldblatt
Plants 30–50 cm high; corm globose with fibrous tunics. Leaves linear, lightly hairy, sometimes dry at flowering, 3–6 mm wide. Flowers in a two- to five-flowered spike, pink with red markings on the lower tepals, perianth tube slender, 25–36 mm long, dorsal tepal largest, 35–40 mm long, inclined over the stamens, lower tepals directed downward. Flowering December–January. Rocky sandstone slopes at high elevations, SW (Stettynskloof Mountains, near Villiersdorp).

Gladiolus rudis

Gladiolus rogersii Baker
Plants 30–60 cm high, stem base often purple with white speckling; corm globose with softly fibrous to more or less woody tunics. Leaves solidly terete or linear and mostly 1.5–5 mm wide, the margins and midrib lightly to heavily thickened. Flowers mostly in a three- to six-flowered spike, more or less bell-like, blue to purple with yellow or white transverse markings on the lower tepals, usually fragrant, perianth tube 12–19 mm long, dorsal tepal largest, 20–30 mm long, hooded over the stamens, the lower tepals narrow, directed forward. Flowering mainly September–October. Sandstone and limestone slopes to 1000 m, AP, KM, LB, SE (Pearly Beach to Humansdorp).

Gladiolus roseovenosus Goldblatt & J. C. Manning
Plants 20–40 cm high; corm globose with softly fibrous tunics. Leaf blades reduced, linear, the margins and midrib lightly thickened, 1.5–2 mm wide. Flowers in a two- to four-flowered spike, pink with dark streaks on the lower tepals, perianth tube funnel-shaped, 36–44 mm long, dorsal tepal largest, 34–37 mm long, inclined over the stamens, lower tepals arching downward. Flowering March–April. Sandstone slopes, SE (Outeniqua Mountains at Robinson's Pass).

Gladiolus rudis Lichtenstein ex Roemer & Schultes
Plants 20–50 cm high; corm globose with alternating papery and fibrous tunics. Leaves sword-shaped, the margins thickened, the bases strongly marked with textured white speckles, mostly 7–15 mm wide. Flowers in a two- to five-flowered spike, cream to pale pink, with spear-shaped markings on the lower tepals, perianth tube funnel-shaped, 18–21 mm long, dorsal tepal largest, 32–36 mm long, suberect, the lower tepals arching outward. Flowering September–October. Sandstone slopes in fynbos, SW (Grabouw to Elim).

Gladiolus saccatus (Klatt) Goldblatt & M. P. de Vos
Plants 25–80 cm high; corm globose with firm, papery tunics. Leaves sword-shaped, thickened in the midline, 3–15 mm wide. Flowers in an 8- to 12-flowered, strongly inclined spike, bright red, perianth tube cylindrical, slender below, abruptly expanded and spurred above, 11–20

mm long, dorsal tepal largest, 30–45 mm long, elongate, spoon-shaped, more or less horizontal, upper lateral and lower tepals reduced to short scales, all directed forward, anthers with long, free tails. Flowering June–August. Dry shale slopes, NW (Namibia to Pakhuis Mountains).

Gladiolus scullyi Baker

Plants mostly 15–40 cm high; corm globose with more or less woody to coarsely fibrous tunics. Leaves linear to falcate, thickened in the midline, 3–5 mm wide. Flowers in a five- to eight-flowered spike, bilabiate, dull yellow to light brown, the lower tepals darker yellow below, fragrant, windowed in profile, perianth tube funnel-shaped, 12–14 mm long, dorsal tepal largest, 25–40 mm long, arching over the stamens, lower tepals pinched and sharply bent below, narrow, arching downward. Flowering August–September. Silty clay and granite slopes, RV, NW (Namaqualand and western Karoo to Klawer).

Gladiolus sempervirens G. J. Lewis

Plants 40–100 cm high, more or less evergreen, spreading by thin rhizomes; corm reduced and almost rhizome-like, with soft, papery tunics. Leaves sword-shaped, the veins lightly thickened, 6–18 mm wide. Flowers in a four- to eight-flowered spike, large, carmine red with white streaks on the lower tepals, perianth tube slender, 25–42 mm long, dorsal tepal largest, 55–58 mm long, erect, lower tepals slightly smaller, spreading. Flowering March–May. Seeps on sandstone slopes, 300–1500 m, SE (George to Kareedouw).

Gladiolus speciosus Thunberg

Plants mostly 12–20 cm high, stem compressed and angled; corm depressed-globose with papery tunics, bearing cormels on long, slender stolons. Leaves linear, glaucous, 3–7 mm wide. Flowers in a two- to eight-flowered spike, bilabiate, orange marked yellow to greenish, fragrant, perianth tube funnel-shaped, 11–13 mm long, dorsal tepal 25–40 mm long, hooded over the stamens, lower tepals narrow, arching downward, filaments sparsely hairy below. Flowering September–October. Deep sandy soils in fynbos, NW, SW (Bokkeveld Escarpment to Mamre). Page 210.

Gladiolus scullyi

Gladiolus sempervirens

Gladiolus splendens (Sweet) Herbert

Plants 50–110 cm high; corm globose with papery tunics, producing cormels on long, slender stolons. Leaves sword-shaped, thickened in the midline, 4–9 mm wide. Flowers in a 6- to 14-flowered, strongly inclined spike, bright red, the lower tepals green, perianth tube slender below, abruptly expanded, 16–18 mm long, dorsal tepal largest, elongate, spoon-shaped, 28–34 mm long, horizontal, upper lateral tepals erect, lower tepals small, the lower median directed downward, anthers with long, free tails. Flowering September–October. Rocky clay, mostly near streams, RV (Roggeveld Escarpment and Calvinia district).

Gladiolus stefaniae Obermeyer

Plants 40–65 cm high; corm globose with papery tunics. Leaves produced after flowering, sword-shaped, the margins and midrib moderately thickened, c. 5 mm wide. Flowers in a two- to four-flowered spike, red with a white streak on the lower tepals, perianth tube narrowly funnel-shaped, 35–45 mm long, tepals subequal, 50–60 mm long, the dorsal lightly inclined, the lower tepals arching outward. Flowering March–April. Rocky sandstone slopes, 100–800 m, NW, SW (Montagu and Potberg).

Gladiolus stellatus G. J. Lewis

Plants 30–60 cm high; corm globose with tunics of wiry fibers. Leaves linear and whip-like, thickened in the midline, 1–3 mm wide. Flowers in a 5- to 12-flowered spike, actinomorphic, star-like, white to lilac, fragrant, perianth tube funnel-shaped, 5–7 mm long, tepals subequal, spreading, 14–20 mm long. Flowering September–November. Clay slopes in renosterveld, AP, KM, LB, SE (Swellendam to Port Elizabeth).

Gladiolus stokoei G. J. Lewis

Plants 30–45 cm high, flowering stem bearing only sheathing leaves; corm globose with fairly fine, fibrous tunics. Leaf produced after flowering, solitary, linear, lightly hairy, 2–3.5 mm wide. Flowers in a one- to three-flowered spike, tulip-shaped, scarlet, tepals subequal, 25–30 mm long, the dorsal suberect, the lower spreading. Flowering March–April. Marshy sandstone slopes, 500–1000 m, SW (Riviersonderend Mountains).

Gladiolus subcaeruleus G. J. Lewis

Plants 20–30 cm high, flowering stem bearing only sheathing leaves; corm globose with coarsely fibrous tunics. Leaf produced after flowering on a separate shoot, solitary, terete and four-grooved, thinly hairy, c. 1 mm diam. Flowers in a three- to five-flowered spike, bilabiate, pale blue to mauve with yellow markings on the lower tepals, perianth tube funnel-shaped, 15–17 mm long, dorsal tepal largest, hooded over the stamens, 20–24 mm long, the lower tepals narrower, directed forward. Flowering March–May. Sandy loam and clay slopes in renosterveld, SW (Caledon to Bredasdorp).

Gladiolus sufflavus (G. J. Lewis) Goldblatt & J. C. Manning

Plants 45–70 cm high; corm globose with leathery to fibrous tunics, often extending upward in a neck. Leaves

Gladiolus speciosus

Gladiolus splendens

Gladiolus stefaniae

Gladiolus stellatus

Gladiolus sufflavus

Gladiolus teretifolius

Gladiolus trichonemifolius

linear to terete, mostly the midrib strongly raised, thus X-shaped in cross section, hairy at least on the sheaths, 2–3 mm wide. Flowers in a four- to six-flowered spike, bell-like, greenish yellow, fragrant, perianth tube funnel-shaped, c. 15 mm long, the dorsal largest, hooded over the stamens, 18–20 mm long, the lower somewhat narrower, directed forward. Flowering August–September. Marshy sandstone soils, NW (Bokkeveld Mountains).

Gladiolus taubertianus Schlechter

Plants 18–25 cm high; corm globose with more or less woody tunics. Leaves linear, the midrib and sometimes the margins lightly thickened, 1–3 mm wide. Flowers in a one- to five-flowered spike, bilabiate, purple with dark streaks, the lower tepals with transverse yellow markings edged with dark blue, perianth tube funnel-shaped, 9–14 mm long, dorsal tepal largest, hooded over the stamens, 20–26 mm long, the lower tepals narrower, directed forward. Flowering August–September. Rocky sandstone soils, NW (Pakhuis Pass to Cold Bokkeveld).

Gladiolus teretifolius Goldblatt & M. P. de Vos

Plants 30–60 cm high; corm with hard, wiry to woody tunics. Leaves linear to terete and four-grooved, the margins and midrib heavily thickened, 1–2 mm wide. Flowers in a two- to five-flowered, erect spike, red, perianth tube cylindrical, wide and horizontal above, 35–45 mm long, dorsal tepal largest, 20–27 mm long, inclined over the stamens, lower tepals smaller, directed forward. Flowering May–August. Clay slopes in renosterveld, SW, LB (Caledon to Mossel Bay).

Gladiolus trichonemifolius Ker Gawler

Plants 10–25 cm high; corm globose with woody tunics. Leaves terete and four-grooved, 1–2 mm diam. Flowers in a one- to four-flowered spike, funnel-shaped, sometimes actinomorphic, yellow to whitish, occasionally with a dark center, usually intensely fragrant, perianth tube funnel-shaped, 16–20 mm long, tepals subequal or the dorsal largest, 24–40 mm long, suberect, the lower somewhat narrower, arching forward. Flowering July–October. Wet sandy flats, 50–1000 m, NW, SW, AP (Hopefield and Ceres to Bredasdorp).

Gladiolus tristis Linnaeus

Plants 40–150 cm high; corm globose with woody to coarsely fibrous tunics. Leaves linear, the midrib strongly raised, thus X-shaped in cross section, 2–4 mm wide. Flowers in a two- to five-flowered, erect spike, cream with brown shading, fragrant in the evening, perianth tube cylindrical, 40–63 mm long, flaring above, dorsal tepal largest, suberect, 22–28 mm long, the lower tepals slightly smaller. Flowering August–December. Usually marshy sites on sandstone, clay, or limestone soils, NW, SW, AP, KM, LB, SE (Bokkeveld Mountains to Port Elizabeth).

Gladiolus uitenhagensis Goldblatt & Vlok

Plants 35–60 cm high; corm ovoid with tunics of wiry fibers. Leaves linear, whip-like, thickened in the midline, c. 2 mm wide. Flowers in a five- to eight-flowered spike, bilabiate, windowed in profile, gray-blue with yellow markings, perianth tube 28–35 mm long, tepals narrowed below, the dorsal largest, 28–30 mm long, inclined over the stamens, lower tepals narrower, directed downward. Flowering September–October, only after fire. Rocky sandstone slopes, SE (Uitenhage).

Gladiolus undulatus Linnaeus

Plants mostly 40–80 cm high; corm globose with papery tunics. Leaves sword-shaped, glaucous, the margins and midrib usually lightly thickened, 5–12 mm wide. Flowers in a 3- to 12-flowered spike, whitish to cream, rarely pale mauve, often with faint pink markings on the lower tepals, perianth tube cylindrical, 52–75 mm long, tepals attenuate with undulate margins, dorsal tepal largest, 40–50 mm long, arching over the stamens, the lower tepals slightly smaller, directed forward. Flowering November–December. Marshy sandstone slopes, NW, SW (Kamiesberg, Bokkeveld Mountains to Stellenbosch).

Gladiolus uysiae L. Bolus ex G. J. Lewis

Plants 7–15 cm high; corm depressed-globose with papery tunics, producing cormels on long, slender stolons. Leaves linear-falcate, plane, 3–8 mm wide. Flowers in a one- to three-flowered spike, bilabiate, brownish purple with conspicuous dark veining, fragrant, perianth tube

Gladiolus tristis

Gladiolus undulatus

funnel-shaped, 10–12 mm long, dorsal tepal erect, the margins curved back, 28–35 mm long, the lower tepals narrow, arching downward. Flowering August–September. Clay slopes in renosterveld, 600–1000 m, RV, NW (Bokkeveld Escarpment and western Karoo to Ceres).

Gladiolus uysiae

Gladiolus variegatus

Gladiolus vaginatus F. Bolus

Plants mostly 30–50 cm high; corm globose with fibrous tunics. Leaves only two, both entirely sheathing or the lower with a short free tip, leathery and without visible veins, 1–1.5 mm wide. Flowers mostly in a two- to six-flowered spike, bilabiate, blue to gray with dark streaks on the lower tepals, fragrant, perianth tube 6.5–20 mm long, dorsal tepal inclined over the stamens, 18–27 mm long, the lower tepals narrow, directed forward. Flowering February–April. Limestone and clay-loam slopes, fynbos and renosterveld, SW, LB, SE (Cape Peninsula, Caledon to Knysna).

Gladiolus vandermerwei (L. Bolus) Goldblatt & M. P. de Vos

Plants 30–60 cm high; corm globose with soft, papery tunics, producing cormels on long stolons. Leaves sword-shaped to linear, thickened in the midline, 2–5 mm wide. Flowers in a three- to eight-flowered spike, bright red, the lower tepals yellowish in the lower half, perianth tube cylindrical, wide and horizontal above, 35–45 mm long, dorsal tepal largest, 23–28 mm long, inclined to horizontal, the lower tepals short and narrow, arching outward. Flowering August–September. Shale slopes in renosterveld, SW, LB (Bot River to Heidelberg).

Gladiolus variegatus (G. J. Lewis) Goldblatt & J. C. Manning

Plants 20–40 cm high; corm globose with woody to coarsely fibrous tunics. Leaves linear, the midrib but not the margins thickened, 1.5–2.5 mm wide. Flowers in a one- to four-flowered spike, white to pale pink, the lower tepals irregularly spotted with dark red, perianth tube cylindrical, 14–20 mm long, dorsal tepal largest, 25–30 mm long, arching over the stamens, the lower tepals directed forward. Flowering September–October. Limestone outcrops, AP (Gansbaai to Cape Agulhas).

Gladiolus venustus G. J. Lewis

Plants mostly 12–35 cm high; corm conical with more or less woody tunics. Leaves linear to falcate, thicker in the midline, mostly 2–5 mm wide. Flowers in a five- to eight-flowered, flexuous spike, bilabiate, purple to pink with yellow markings on the lower tepals, fragrant, perianth tube funnel-shaped, 12–17 mm long, dorsal tepal largest,

30–37 mm long, inclined over the stamens, upper lateral tepals curving back, lower tepals pinched and sharply bent below, narrow, directed downward. Flowering August–October. Clay and sandstone slopes, NW, SW, KM, LB (Bokkeveld Escarpment to Swellendam).

Gladiolus vigilans Barnard

Plants 30–40 cm high; corm globose with woody, ridged tunics. Leaves linear, margins and midribs strongly thickened, c. 1.5 mm wide. Flowers in a one- to three-flowered, inclined spike, pink with darker, spear-shaped markings on the lower tepals, perianth tube slender, 35–40 mm long, dorsal tepal largest, c. 28 mm long, inclined over the stamens, the lower tepals directed forward. Flowering October–November. Sandstone slopes, SW (Cape Peninsula, Kogelberg?).

Gladiolus violaceolineatus G. J. Lewis

Plants 35–60 cm high; corm conical with tunics of coarse fibers. Leaves linear, midrib winged on one side, 1.5–4 mm wide. Flowers in a one- to four-flowered spike, bilabiate, pale blue with violet veins, fragrant, perianth tube funnel-shaped, 12–15 mm long, tepals attenuate, the dorsal largest, 26–39 mm long, inclined over the stamens, the lower tepals arching downward. Flowering July–August. Rocky sandstone slopes, 500–1000 m, NW (Gifberg to Cedarberg Mountains).

Gladiolus virescens Thunberg

Plants 10–25 cm high; corm depressed-globose with soft, papery to fibrous tunics. Leaves linear, ribbed to terete with narrow longitudinal grooves, 2–4 mm wide. Flowers in a three- to seven-flowered spike, bilabiate, yellow to pink with dark veins, fragrant, perianth tube funnel-shaped, 9–15 mm long, dorsal tepal largest, 20–48 mm long, erect, the margins recurved, the lower tepals narrow, arching downward. Flowering August–September. Sandstone or clay slopes, NW, SW, KM, LB, SE (Ceres to Humansdorp).

Gladiolus virgatus Goldblatt & J. C. Manning

Plants 30–60 cm high; corm globose with woody to coarsely fibrous tunics. Leaves linear, the margins and

Gladiolus venustus

Gladiolus virescens

216 *Gladiolus virgatus*

midrib lightly thickened, 1.5–2.5 mm wide. Flowers in a two- to four-flowered, inclined spike, bilabiate, pale to deep pink with red markings on the lower tepals, perianth tube slender, 22–27 mm long, dorsal tepal largest, 30–37 mm long, inclined over the stamens, the lower tepals slightly smaller than the dorsal, arching forward; bracts ridged. Flowering September–November. Rocky sandstone slopes, SW (Du Toit's Kloof to Somerset West).

Gladiolus viridiflorus G. J. Lewis

Plants 10–20 cm high, stem base purple, speckled with white; corm ovoid with tough, fibrous to woody tunics. Leaves sword-shaped to linear, loosely twisted above, 2.7–6 mm wide. Flowers in a three- to eight-flowered, flexuous, inclined spike, bilabiate, greenish with transverse purple markings on the lower tepals, fragrant, perianth tube funnel-shaped, 12–17 mm long, dorsal tepal largest, 23–31 mm long, arching over the stamens, the lower tepals narrow, arching downward. Flowering May–July. Rocky sandstone slopes, NW (Orange River to Clanwilliam).

Gladiolus virgatus

Gladiolus watermeyeri

Gladiolus watsonius

Gladiolus watermeyeri L. Bolus

Plants 10–30 cm high; corm depressed-globose with soft, papery tunics. Leaves linear, ribbed, 3–11 mm wide. Flowers in a one- to six-flowered spike, bilabiate, pearly gray with dark veins, the lower tepals green, intensely fragrant, perianth tube funnel-shaped, 14–16 mm long, dorsal tepal largest, 27–35 mm long, hooded over the stamens, the lower tepals narrow, arching downward. Flowering July–September. Rocky sandstone slopes, NW (Bokkeveld Mountains to Wuppertal).

Gladiolus watsonius Thunberg

Plants 30–70 cm high; corm globose with hard, woody tunics. Leaves linear, the margins and midrib strongly thickened, 3–6 mm wide. Flowers in a two- to six-flowered, erect spike, red to orange, perianth tube cylindrical, wide and horizontal above, 43–55 mm long, dorsal tepal largest, 26–33 mm long, more or less horizontal, lower tepals slightly smaller, arching downward. Flowering July–September. Clay and granite slopes in renosterveld, NW, SW (Piketberg to Stellenbosch).

Gladiolus wilsonii (Baker) Goldblatt & J. C. Manning

Plants mostly 20–40 cm high; corm globose with tunics of fine to coarse fibers. Leaves linear and whip-like, thickened in the midline, 1–3 mm wide. Flowers in a 4- to 12-flowered spike, bilabiate, cream, often flushed pink on the outside, usually fragrant, perianth tube funnel-shaped, 6–13 mm long, tepals narrowed below, the dorsal largest, 20–30 mm long, hooded over the stamens, lower tepals narrow, directed forward. Flowering October–November. Grassy flats, SE (Humansdorp to Transkei).

Haemanthus

COMMON NAMES paintbrush lily, powderpuff lily, FAMILY Amaryllidaceae. Deciduous or evergreen perennials. ROOTSTOCK a bulb with thick fleshy tunics or two-ranked scales. LEAVES two, sometimes single or as many as six, dry or green at flowering, erect to prostrate, strap-shaped to elliptical, often barred with dark green or red, fleshy, sometimes hairy. INFLORESCENCE a compact to spreading umbel on a stout, somewhat compressed fleshy scape; spathe bracts four or more, often fleshy, erect or spreading, white, pink, or red. FLOWERS actinomorphic, narrowly or broadly funnel-shaped, erect or spreading, the perianth tube short, cylindrical or bell-shaped, the tepals narrowly oblong to lanceolate. STAMENS inserted in the throat, usually longer than the tepals, the anthers dorsifixed. OVARY with one or two ovules per locule; STYLE straight, as long as the stamens, the stigma minutely tricuspidate. FRUIT usually fleshy, ovoid to globose, white, orange, or pink, often aromatic when ripe. SEEDS ovoid, fleshy, red, green, or ivory, the embryo green. Basic chromosome number $x = 8$. Endemic to southern Africa, where most species are located in the winter-rainfall region; 22 spp., 11 in the Cape.

The specialized berry-like fruits of *Haemanthus* are shared with *Apodolirion*, *Clivia*, *Cryptostephanus*, *Gethyllis*, and *Scadoxus* and this feature points to the close alliance between these genera. The fruit of *H. tristis* differs from those of other *Haemanthus* species in having a dull, leathery, brown to maroon wall—a novel camouflage that renders the fruits indistinguishable from the droppings of small antelope. All other species of *Haemanthus*, in contrast, have attractive, fleshy, orange to pink or opalescent fruit walls. This variation in fruit texture is also known in *Apodolirion*, *Crinum*, and *Gethyllis*.

Widely cultivated, *Haemanthus* was among the first Cape bulbs to be transported to Europe by Dutch seafarers. First grown in the Netherlands, *H. coccineus* and *H. sanguineus* found such favor that they were illustrated as early as 1605 under the name *Narcissus africanus bifolius*. Residents of the Cape popularly refer to *Haemanthus* as the paintbrush, a name that emphasizes the plant's distinctive floral form and the bright splashes of red that they bring to the dry autumn landscape. The red-flowered species are visited by sunbirds and the large satyrid butterfly known as the pride of Table Mountain, *Aeropetes tulbaghia*. Pink-flowered species are probably pollinated by bees. *Haemanthus* has several representatives with extremely elegant leaves, many of which deserve to be grown for their foliage alone. The most widely cultivated species is *H. albiflos*, an evergreen plant suited to shady conditions.

Haemanthus albiflos (Colin Paterson-Jones)

Haemanthus amarylloides subsp. *toximontana*

FURTHER READING. *Haemanthus* was revised by Snijman (1984) in a beautifully illustrated monograph. Since then, Snijman and van Wyk (1993) described a further summer-rainfall species. The cytology of *Haemanthus* was investigated by Vosa and Snijman (1984). O'Neill (1991) dealt briefly with the cultivation of *Haemanthus*, and Rabe and van Staden (1999) reported on micropropagation techniques.

Haemanthus albiflos Jacquin

Plants to 35 cm high; bulbs often with green tunics. Leaves two, four, or six, green at flowering, erect to prostrate, oblong to elliptical, 25–115 mm wide, smooth, hairy or fringed, unmarked. Umbel somewhat compact on a green scape, spathe bracts four to eight, slightly spreading, blunt, shorter or slightly longer than the flowers, white with green veins, flowers 16–23 mm long, white, with a tube 4–7 mm long, stamens and style slightly exserted. Flowering April–August. Coastal and riverine scrub, AP, KM, SE (Still Bay and Oudtshoorn to KwaZulu-Natal).

Haemanthus amarylloides Jacquin

Plants to 25 cm high; bulb with unequal, cream tunics. Leaves two, sometimes three, dry at flowering, erect to prostrate, strap-shaped to elliptical, 8–120 mm wide, smooth, unmarked, the margin sometimes red. Umbel somewhat lax on a wine red scape, spathe bracts four to nine, widely spreading, acute, shorter or as long as the flowers, pale to deep pink and thin textured, flowers 7–19 mm long, pale to dark pink with a tube 0.5–3 mm long, stamens and style exserted. Flowering February–April. Seasonally moist sites, NW (Namaqualand to Clanwilliam).

Three subspecies are recognized: subspecies *amarylloides* with erect or recurved, firm-textured leaves 8–40 mm wide, four to six spathe bracts, flowers 12–19 mm long, tepals lanceolate, erect or slightly spreading, granite or sandstone soils (Namaqualand and Bokkeveld Mountains), subspecies *polyanthus* Snijman with erect, soft-textured leaves 25–50 mm wide, six to nine spathe bracts, flowers 7–10 mm long, tepals linear, spreading, granite soils (Namaqualand), and subspecies *toximontanus*

Snijman with prostrate succulent leaves 55–120 mm wide, four to six spathe bracts, flowers 12–19 mm long, tepals lanceolate, erect or slightly spreading, sandstone pavement and rock flushes (Gifberg).

Haemanthus barkerae Snijman

Plants to 20 cm high; bulbs extended into a neck. Leaves two, dry at flowering, suberect to recurved, strap- to tongue-shaped, 7–80 mm wide, smooth or shortly hairy, whitish and barred with dark green and maroon near the base beneath. Umbel more or less spreading on a deep to pale pink scape, spathe bracts four to six, spreading, shorter to longer than the flowers, acute, pink, flowers 11–21 mm long, pale to deep pink, with a tube 1.5–3 mm long, stamens and style exserted. Flowering March–April. Among rocks in heavy soils, RV, NW (Bokkeveld Mountains and western Karoo).

Haemanthus canaliculatus Levyns

Plants to 20 cm high; bulbs compressed with thick, cream tunics. Leaves usually two, dry at flowering, suberect to recurved, strap-shaped, 5–27 mm wide, channeled, smooth, barred with red or dark green near the base beneath. Umbel more or less compact on a deep red scape, spathe bracts five to seven, slightly spreading, acute, slightly shorter or longer than the flowers, bright red or rarely pink, flowers 20–30 mm long, bright red or rarely pink, with a tube 3–6 mm long, stamens and style exserted. Flowering December–March, after fire. Swampy coastal flats, SW (Rooi Els to Betty's Bay).

Haemanthus coccineus Linnaeus

Plants variable in size, to 40 cm high; bulbs with thick, cream tunics. Leaves usually two, dry at flowering, suberect to prostrate, strap- to tongue-shaped, (25–)85–150(–210) mm wide, fleshy, smooth or hairy, barred with maroon or dark green beneath, sometimes on a whitish background, the margin often rolled back. Umbel more or less compact on a stout, spotted or rarely plain red scape, spathe bracts (4–)6–9(–13), erect, overlapping, shorter to longer than the flowers, bright red, stiff and fleshy, flowers 14–30 mm long, scarlet, with a tube 2–5 mm long, stamens and style exserted. Flowering Febru-

Haemanthus canaliculatus (Colin Paterson-Jones); see also page 18

Haemanthus coccineus (Colin Paterson-Jones)

Haemanthus coccineus fruit and foliage

Haemanthus crispus (Colin Paterson-Jones)

ary–April. Coastal scrub and rocky slopes, NW, SW, AP, KM, LB, SE (southern Namibia to Port Elizabeth).

Haemanthus crispus Snijman
Small plants, at most 15 cm high; bulbs more or less globose with a long, slender neck. Leaves usually two, dry at flowering, suberect to recurved, strap-shaped, 7–33 mm wide, channeled, with undulate edges, smooth or covered with short stiff hairs, blotched with maroon or dark green beneath. Umbel compact on a dark red or pink scape, spathe bracts four or five, sometimes six, erect, as long as or longer than the flowers, overlapping, broadest above the middle, waxy, red or rarely pink, flowers 15–26 mm long, red or sometimes pink, on short pedicels mostly less than 4 mm long, the tube 1.5–9 mm long, stamens and style exserted. Flowering March–April. Stony lower slopes, usually in heavy soils, NW (Namaqualand to Olifants River Valley).

Haemanthus nortieri Isaac
Plants to 30 cm high; bulbs with dark outer tunics. Leaf single, dry at flowering, erect, broadly elliptical, 40–150 mm wide, often narrowly strap-shaped near the base, dark green, somewhat rough and sticky, often covered with sand. Umbel compact on a dark red scabrid scape, spathe bracts five to eight, as long as or longer than the flowers, acute, leathery, deep red to dusky pink, flowers 14–18 mm long, pale red, stamens and style exserted. Flowering February–March. Seasonal washes, often near exposed rocks with succulent shrubs, NW (Nardouw Mountains).

Haemanthus pubescens Linnaeus fil.
Plants to 30 cm high; bulb with thick, cream tunics, forming bulblets. Leaves usually two, dry at flowering, recurved to prostrate, strap-shaped, (10–)15–45(–85) mm wide, smooth or hairy; sometimes finely speckled with red toward the base beneath, fringed. Umbel compact on a red, sometimes hairy scape, spathe bracts four or five, rarely more, erect, as long as or longer than the flowers, broadest in the upper half with a distinct point at the apex, red or rarely pink, fleshy, flowers 10–30 mm long, red or sometimes pink with a tube 2–5 mm long, sta-

mens and style longer than the perianth. Flowering February–April. Sandy flats, NW, SW (southern Namibia to Cape Peninsula).

Three subspecies are recognized: subspecies *arenicola* Snijman has channeled, recurved leaves, often softly hairy beneath (southern Namibia to northern Namaqualand), subspecies *leipoldtii* Snijman has flat, prostrate, hairless leaves, NW (southern Namaqualand), and subspecies *pubescens* has scale-like bulb tunics and leaves that are densely hairy above, SW (Vredenburg to Cape Peninsula).

Haemanthus pumilio Jacquin

Slender plants to 20 cm high; bulbs compressed with cream tunics. Leaves two, suberect, dry at flowering, strap-shaped, 2.5–15 mm wide, twisted, slightly channeled, smooth, with red bars near the base beneath. Umbel loose on a slender, deep pink scape, spathe bracts four to six, slightly spreading, acute, pale to deep pink, flowers 8–12 mm long, delicate to dark pink or white with a tube 1–1.5 mm long, stamens and style exserted. Flowering March–April, after fire. Seasonally waterlogged clay flats, SW (Hermon, Paarl, Stellenbosch).

Haemanthus sanguineus Jacquin

Plants variable in size, to 30 cm high; bulbs with cream tunics. Leaves two, dry at flowering, pressed to the ground, 35–280 mm across, often broader than long, leathery, the upper surface dark green and often rough, with a short, red or opaque, cartilaginous fringe. Umbel somewhat compressed, compact to slightly spreading, on a compressed and furrowed, red to pink scape, spathe bracts 5–11, erect to slightly spreading, shorter than the flowers, laterally keeled, red to pink and leathery, flowers 15–32 mm long, bright red to pale pink, with a tube 2–9 mm long, stamens and style exserted. Flowering January–April, after fire. Seasonally moist habitats on mountains and coastal flats, NW, SW, AP, KM, LB, SE (Nardouw Mountains to Port Elizabeth). Page 222.

Haemanthus tristis Snijman

Plants to 10 cm high; bulbs ellipsoidal with a long, slender neck. Leaves two, dry at flowering, recurved, strap-

Haemanthus nortieri foliage (Colin Paterson-Jones)

Haemanthus pubescens subsp. *pubescens* (Colin Paterson-Jones)

Haemanthus pumilio (Colin Paterson-Jones)

Haemanthus sanguineus

shaped, 7–16 mm wide, channeled, fleshy, grayish green with red margins, smooth. Umbel loose on a slender, pale green to pink scape, spathe bracts four or five, spreading, acute, shorter or as long as the flowers, pale, flowers 8–11 mm long, white, cream, or pink, with a tube 1.5–3 mm long, stamens and style exserted. Flowering March. Seasonal washes in open succulent veld, RV (Tanqua Karoo).

Hesperantha

COMMON NAME hesperantha, FAMILY Iridaceae. Deciduous perennials. ROOTSTOCK a corm, rarely the corm reduced and rhizome-like, globose to ovoid or bell-shaped with a flat base, sometimes with a basal ridge from which the roots emerge, basal in origin, the tunics woody or rarely firm-papery, concentric or overlapping and then notched below. LEAVES few to several, the lower two or three forming membranous cataphylls, foliage leaves two to several, unifacial with a definite midrib, the blades plane to terete, sometimes the margins and or midrib thickened, sometimes hairy; stem aerial or subterranean, simple or branched, terete. INFLORESCENCE a spike, sometimes with only one or two flowers; bracts green and soft textured, sometimes becoming dry from the tips, the inner bract smaller than the outer and notched apically. FLOWERS rotate to salverform or nodding, mostly white or pink, also yellow or blue to violet, purple, or red, usually actinomorphic, often fragrant and then usually in the evening; perianth tube cylindrical, short or long, sometimes curved near the apex; tepals subequal, spreading, rarely recurved. STAMENS symmetrically disposed or rarely unilateral and arching downward; filaments sometimes very short, erect or drooping; anthers erect and facing inward or articulated on the filament apices and horizontal, drooping when the perianth tube is curved, rarely included in the tube. STYLE filiform, dividing at or below the mouth of the tube, the branches filiform, long and slender, ascending or spreading, stigmatic adaxially along their entire length. FRUIT a globose to oblong or cylindrical capsule, sometimes splitting only in the upper third. SEEDS globose to angular, flattened at the chalazal end, sometimes lightly winged on the angles, matte. Basic chromosome number $x = 13$. Southwestern Cape and Namaqualand to Ethiopia with major centers in the southwestern Cape, the western Karoo, and the Drakensberg Mountains; c. 77 spp., 34 in the Cape.

Hesperantha is most closely related to *Geissorhiza* and the two genera share a similar, specialized corm morphology. The two genera are often confused with each other, but *Hesperantha* is distinguished by its specialized style, which divides at the mouth of the perianth tube into long, filiform style branches. In the winter-rainfall species, white to cream flowers that open in the late afternoon and evening are most common but there are also several day-blooming species with pink, blue, or yellow flowers. In contrast, most of the species in the summer-rainfall area are day blooming, usually with pink flowers but sometimes with white to cream flowers.

Although *Hesperantha* has been thought in the past to be primarily pollinated by small moths, little is actually known. Some species with white flowers that open in the late afternoon are pollinated by long-tongued bees as well as noctuid moths, and only the few species that flower at or after sunset are exclusively pollinated by moths. The long-tubed pink- or purple-flowered species in Namaqualand and the Drakensberg Mountains are pollinated by long-proboscid flies of the genus *Prosoeca* (Nemestrinidae).

Hesperanthas are easily cultivated, but the smaller species are better treated as pot plants. The eastern southern African *Hesperantha coccinea*, previously known as *Schizostylis coccinea*, is widely cultivated and makes a valuable addition to the garden, especially when grown at the edges of ponds. Both the pink- and red-flowered forms are available in the nursery trade, and we have seen plants successfully grown in herbaceous borders or along streams in western Canada and the northwestern United States as well as in Britain and South Africa. The Cape hesperanthas have not been accorded much horticultural attention. We have grown several Cape species in pots and have been delighted at the successful flowering of several species.

All the species are worth trying in cultivation, bearing in mind that most are miniatures and have idiosyncratic flowering schedules. As a rule, the species with colorful flowers open during the day, and those with white flowers in the evening. The evening-flowering *Hesperantha bachmannii* and *H. radiata* flower well and can be brought indoors in the evening where their delicate form and fragrance may be enjoyed. Their delightful scent is best appreciated at close quarters. Note that it is important to place the pots where they can enjoy full daylight or their evening-blooming habit may become disrupted. *Hesperantha cucullata* is especially desirable, for the flowers open at about 4 o'clock and make a fine show as the sun sets. It is recommended as an unusual subject for a rock garden or in front of plantings of small shrubs, where the snowy flowers will make an arresting sight against a dark background. Most of the day-flowering species are ideal subjects for the rock garden. In the wild, the large pink-flowered *H. pauciflora* makes showy displays at the edges of plowed fields and in heavily grazed bush and will do as well in the garden. *Hesperantha vaginata* is another lovely, day-blooming species with tulip-like flowers deep yellow in color, usually with chocolate brown markings in a harlequin pattern. Unfortunately, the flowers open only on warm afternoons between 2 and 5 o'clock.

FURTHER READING. The significance of corm structure in the classification of *Hesperantha* was first discussed by Goldblatt (1982b) in preparation for the monograph that followed (Goldblatt 1984a). Since then, the genus *Schizostylis* has been incorporated into *Hesperantha* and new species described (Goldblatt 1987a, Goldblatt and Manning 1996a). These changes have culminated in a synoptic treatment of the genus that includes changes to the taxonomy and the description of additional species (Goldblatt 2002).

Hesperantha acuta (Lichtenstein ex Roemer & Schultes) Ker Gawler

Plants 10–30 cm high; corm rounded with concentric tunics. Leaves linear to sword-shaped, the uppermost leaf sheathing the stem. Flowers mostly three to six per spike, yellow or white, sweetly fragrant at night, perianth tube mostly 8–11 mm long, tepals spreading, mostly 10–17 mm long; bracts distant, green. Flowering July–September. Clay slopes in renosterveld and succulent karoo, NW, KM, SE (Worcester to George, southern Karoo).

Hesperantha bachmannii Baker

Plants 15–30 cm high; corm rounded, tunics overlapping, notched into segments below. Leaves three or four, linear to sword-shaped, fairy soft in texture. Flowers mostly three to six per spike, white, nodding on a recurved tube, sweetly scented when open, afternoon and evening, perianth tube c. 10 mm long, tepals reflexed, 14–20 mm long; bracts green or becoming membranous. Flowering July–September. Mostly clay slopes in renosterveld, or along streams, RV, NW, SW, KM, LB, SE (widespread, Namaqualand to East London). Page 224.

Hesperantha brevifolia Goldblatt

Plants 15–40 cm high; corm bell-shaped with oblique, flat base, the tunics prominently ridged. Leaves short, linear to narrowly sword-shaped. Flowers two to five per spike, white, often red on the outside of the outer tepals,

Hesperantha bachmannii

Hesperantha cucullata

facing to the side or half-nodding, lightly scented in the evening when open, perianth tube curved near the apex, 6–8 mm long, tepals 8–13 mm long; bracts green, prominently veined, the margins united toward the base around the spike axis. Flowering September–November. Shale and sandstone slopes, NW, SW (Nardouw Mountains to Bain's Kloof).

Hesperantha cedarmontana Goldblatt
Plants 12–25 cm high; corm bell-shaped with a flat base, the margins fringed. Leaves sword-shaped, obtuse. Flowers mostly two to four per spike, white, stamens included in the tube, sweetly clove scented when open in the later afternoon and evening, perianth tube 10–13 mm long, tepals spreading, 10–12 mm long; bracts green. Flowering September–October. Sandstone rocks, NW (Pakhuis Mountains to Cold Bokkeveld and Piketberg).

Hesperantha ciliolata Goldblatt
Plants 15–30 cm high, stem with a membranous, scale-like bract below the spike; corm rounded, the tunics concentric. Leaves three, linear to sword-shaped, hollow, blades finely grooved and ridged, shortly hairy along the ridges, the uppermost leaf sheathing the lower half of the stem. Flowers mostly two or three per spike, pink to light blue or violet, open during the day and musk scented, perianth tube 4–6 mm long, tepals 12–15 mm long, lightly reflexed; bracts green to membranous. Flowering September–October. Rocky slopes in clay soil, RV (Roggeveld Escarpment).

Hesperantha cucullata Klatt
Plants 15–30 cm high; corm rounded with an oblique flat side, tunics overlapping, notched into segments below. Leaves three or four, sword-shaped to falcate. Flowers mostly three to eight per spike, white, red to brown on the outside, fragrant when open in the late afternoon and evening, perianth tube 6–9 mm long, tepals spreading, 15–20 mm long; bracts green. Flowering mainly August–September. Sandy and shale slopes, mostly renosterveld, RV, NW (western Karoo and Bokkeveld Mountains to Biedouw valley).

Hesperantha elsiae Goldblatt

Plants 25–30 cm high; corm bell-shaped with an oblique flat base, tunics overlapping, notched below. Leaves linear. Flowers one to four per spike, bright pink, facing to the side, stamens and style branches included in the tube, unscented and open during the day, perianth tube 13–21 mm long, tepals spreading, 13–15 mm long; bracts green or becoming dry, the lower margins united around the spike axis. Flowering December. Rocky sandstone slopes, NW (Cedarberg Mountains).

Hesperantha erecta (Baker) Bentham ex Baker

Plants 10–22 cm high; corm rounded, the tunics concentric. Leaves narrowly sword-shaped. Flowers mostly three to six per spike, cream, sometimes white, lightly musk scented when open in the afternoon, perianth tube 8–10 mm long, tepals spreading, 10–15 mm long; bracts distant, green or submembranous. Flowering August–September. Granite outcrops and granitic sands, sandveld and renosterveld, NW, SW (Klawer to Mamre).

Hesperantha falcata (Linnaeus fil.) Ker Gawler

Plants mostly 25–30 cm high; corm bell-shaped with a flat base, tunics usually smooth. Leaves three to five, sword-shaped to falcate. Flowers three to eight per spike, white or yellow, outer tepals red to brown on the outside, white-flowered plants sweetly fragrant in the late afternoon and evening when open, yellow-flowered open during the middle of the day and unscented, perianth tube straight, 4–9 mm long, tepals spreading, mostly 12–15 mm long; bracts green. Flowering July–October. Sandstone and shale slopes and coastal flats, widespread, NW, SW, LB, SE (Gifberg to Port Elizabeth).

Hesperantha falcata

Hesperantha fibrosa Baker

Plants 8–30 cm high; corm rounded, the tunics concentric, drawn into fine fibers above and sheathing the stem base. Leaves three, linear to sword-shaped, fleshy and with thickened margins, the uppermost sheathing the lower half of the stem. Flowers two to six per spike, light mauve to purple, sometimes white, usually scentless and open during the middle of the day, perianth tube 7–10 mm long, tepals spreading, c. 10 mm long; bracts green.

Hesperantha fibrosa

Flowering August–September. Clay slopes in renosterveld, SW, LB (Caledon to Bredasdorp and Heidelberg).

Hesperantha flava G. J. Lewis

Plants 4–6 cm high, stemless; corm rounded with an oblique flat side, the tunics overlapping, notched below. Leaves mostly two, falcate. Flowers one or two per spike, yellow, flushed brown on the outside, opening at sunset and then sweetly scented, perianth tube 18–28 mm long, tepals widely cupped to spreading, 13–15 mm long; bracts overlapping, green and firm. Flowering May–August. Clay flats, RV (northern Namaqualand to Matjiesfontein).

Hesperantha hantamensis Schlechter

Plants 4–6 cm high, stemless or nearly so; corm rounded with an oblique flat side, tunics overlapping, notched below. Leaves mostly three, falcate. Flowers one to three per spike, the axis hidden in the leaf sheaths, white, opening in the early afternoon and then sweetly scented, perianth tube 14–20 mm long, tepals spreading, 8–12 mm long; bracts overlapping, keeled, green, firm. Flowering July–August. Shale flats, mainly in renosterveld, RV (western Karoo in the Calvinia district).

Hesperantha humilis Baker

Plants 3–8 cm high, stemless or nearly so; corm rounded with an oblique flat side, tunics overlapping, notched below. Leaves two or three, falcate, glaucous. Flowers one to three per spike, axis hidden in the leaf sheaths, deep pink to reddish, unscented and open during the day, perianth tube 17–24 mm long, tepals spreading, 17–25 mm long; bracts overlapping, green and firm, often keeled. Flowering July–September. Sandstone and shale slopes, mainly in renosterveld, RV, NW, KM (western Karoo and Hex River Mountains to the Witteberg).

Hesperantha juncifolia Goldblatt

Plants 18–20 cm high; corm bell-shaped with a flat base, tunics concentric. Leaves terete. Flowers four to eight per spike, white, pink on the outside, lightly scented when open in the evening, perianth tube c. 6 mm long, tepals spreading, 13–15 mm long; bracts distant, submembranous, the lower margins sheathing the spike axis. Flowering September–October. Limestone flats, AP (Agulhas coast).

Hesperantha karooica Goldblatt

Plants 6–8 cm high; corm rounded with an oblique flat side, tunics overlapping. Leaves usually four, sword-shaped to falcate, gray-green. Flowers mostly one or two per spike, yellow, probably unscented and open in the mid- to late afternoon, perianth tube c. 5 mm long, tepals c. 20 mm long; bracts green with dry tips. Flowering August–September. Shale flats, RV (western Karoo at Calvinia).

Hesperantha luticola Goldblatt

Plants to 10 cm high, stemless; corm bell-shaped with a flat base, the tunic margins with projecting teeth. Leaves sword-shaped to falcate. Flowers one or two per spike, white with dark purple blotches at the tepal bases, unscented, open during the day, perianth tube straight, mostly 30–45 mm long, tepals spreading, 13–15 mm long; bracts membranous, overlapping, concealed by the leaves. Flowering mostly July or early August. Stony flats in seasonal pools or watercourses, RV (Hantamsberg to Roggeveld Escarpment at Sneeukrans).

Hesperantha marlothii R. C. Foster

Plants 4–15 cm high; corm bell-shaped with a flat base, tunics lightly ridged, the margins with projecting teeth.

Hesperantha humilis

Leaves linear, fleshy. Flowers mostly three to six per spike, nodding on a recurved tube, cream, brown or red on the outside, perianth tube 10–12 mm long, tepals 10–15 mm long; bract margins often united near the base around the spike axis, membranous, distant. Flowering July–September. Mostly rocky pavement, RV, NW (Bokkeveld Mountains to Cold Bokkeveld and western Karoo).

Hesperantha montigena Goldblatt
Plants 5–15 cm high; corm conical, tunics concentric. Leaves oblong, lower two often prostrate, with thickened margins, the uppermost leaf entirely sheathing. Flowers mostly one to three per spike, white, outer tepals red on the outside, opening at sunset, perianth tube 10–12 mm long, tepals spreading, c. 15 mm long; bracts green. Flowering October–November. Sandstone outcrops, 1000–1600 m, NW, SW (Hex River Mountains to Jonkershoek and Riviersonderend Mountains).

Hesperantha muirii (L. Bolus) G. J. Lewis
Plants 10–20 cm high; corm with a flat base, tunics overlapping. Leaves linear, relatively short. Flowers one to three per spike, large, nodding on a curved tube, cream with pink veins, open during the day and scentless, perianth tube curved near the apex, 15–25 mm long, tepals spreading, 15–25 mm long; bracts submembranous, overlapping, the margins united below around the spike axis. Flowering October–November. Clay slopes in renosterveld, SW, LB (Bredasdorp to Albertinia).

Hesperantha oligantha (Diels) Goldblatt
Plants 6–10 cm high; corm rounded with an oblique flat side, tunics overlapping, notched below. Leaves linear to falcate. Flowers one to three per spike, dark purple with a pale throat, open during the day and unscented, perianth tube 25–35 mm long, tepals spreading, 15–18 mm long, narrow; bracts green. Flowering September–October. Stream banks and marshy ground, RV (Hantamsberg).

Hesperantha pallescens Goldblatt
Plants 10–20 cm high; corm rounded, tunics overlapping, notched into segments below. Leaves four or five,

Hesperantha luticola

Hesperantha oligantha

Hesperantha paucifora; see also page 22

Hesperantha pilosa

linear, fairly soft. Flowers one to four per spike, pale yellow, opening in the early morning and closing before sunset, unscented, perianth tube straight, mostly 15–20 mm long, tepals widely cupped, c. 16 mm long; bracts green. Flowering August–September. Clay slopes in renosterveld, NW (Olifants River Mountains).

Hesperantha pauciflora (Baker) G. J. Lewis
Plants 8–24 cm high; corm bell-shaped with a flat base, the tunic margins with thick spines. Leaves sword-shaped. Flowers mostly two to four per spike, pink to purple, rarely pale yellow, opening in the afternoon and unscented, perianth tube straight, 6–11 mm long, tepals spreading, 18–26 mm long; bracts submembranous, distant. Flowering August–September. Mainly in sandy soils, NW (Namaqualand to Bokkeveld Plateau).

Hesperantha pilosa (Linnaeus fil.) Ker Gawler
Plants 10–30 cm high, stem bearing a scale-like leaf as much as 5 mm long below the spike; corm rounded, tunics concentric. Leaves linear to sword-shaped, pilose on the margins, midrib, and secondary veins. Flowers mostly three to eight per spike, white, opening in the evening and sweetly scented, or blue to purple, opening in the day and unscented, perianth tube 6–10 mm long, tepals spreading, 10–15 mm long; bracts green. Flowering August–October. Sandstone soils, RV, NW, SW (Bokkeveld Mountains to Bredasdorp, and western Karoo).

Hesperantha pseudopilosa Goldblatt
Plants 12–25 cm high, stem bearing a scale-like leaf 5–10 mm long below the spike; corm rounded, tunics concentric. Leaves sword-shaped to oblong, pilose on the margins and midrib. Flowers mostly three to six per spike, white, greenish to brown on the reverse, opening in the evening and sweetly scented, perianth tube 6–10 mm long, tepals spreading, 10–15 mm long; bracts green. Flowering August–September. Clay soils in renosterveld, RV, NW, KM (Bokkeveld Escarpment and western Karoo to the Kleinswartberg).

Hesperantha purpurea Goldblatt
Plants 8–25 cm high; corm rounded with an oblique flat

side, tunics overlapping, notched below. Leaves four or five, lanceolate to falcate. Flowers one to three per spike, dark red-purple with darker markings at the mouth of the tube, unscented and open during the day, perianth tube c. 20 mm long, tepals spreading, 16–20 mm long; bracts green. Flowering August–September. Stony slopes in clay soil, RV (western Karoo NW of Calvinia).

Hesperantha quadrangula Goldblatt
Plants 10–30 cm high; corm rounded, the tunics concentric. Leaves three, the lower two oblong, obtuse, the uppermost sheathing the stem, inflated and four-angled. Flowers two to seven per spike, small, white, scented when open in the late afternoon and early evening, perianth tube straight, 2–3 mm long, tepals spreading, 9–12 mm long; bracts green, membranous. Flowering July–August. Stony clay slopes, RV (Hantamsberg and Roggeveld Escarpment).

Hesperantha radiata (Jacquin) Ker Gawler
Plants 20–40 cm high; corm obliquely flattened below, tunics overlapping, the margins fringed, serrated, or toothed. Leaves short, linear, fleshy. Flowers mostly many per spike, nodding on a recurved tube and tepals reflexed, white to cream, outer tepals red to brown on the outside, mostly opening after sunset and sweetly scented, perianth tube curved in the upper third, 10–18 mm long, tepals lightly reflexed, 7–15 mm long; bracts green or submembranous, often almost overlapping, the margins united in the lower half around the spike axis. Sandstone, granite, and clay soils, fynbos and renosterveld, RV, NW, SW, KM, LB, SE (widespread, Namaqualand to Swaziland).

Hesperantha radiata

Hesperantha rivulicola Goldblatt
Plants 15–30 cm high; corm rounded, tunics concentric. Leaves three or four, slightly fleshy, elliptical in cross section and hollow. Flowers two to five per spike, white, outer tepals brown on the reverse, opening in the late afternoon and then lightly sweetly scented, perianth tube 7–10 mm long, tepals spreading, c. 15 mm long; bracts green. Flowering September. Along streams, RV, NW (Bokkeveld Mountains to Calvinia).

Hesperantha rivulicola; see also page 2

Hesperantha saldanhae Goldblatt

Plants 12–35 cm high; corm bell-shaped with a flat base, tunics concentric. Leaves sword-shaped. Flowers five to eight per spike, small, white, with the stamens and style branches included in the tube, probably open in the evening and scented, perianth tube 9–12 mm long, tepals spreading, 9–10 mm long; bracts green. Flowering August. Granite rocks, SW (Vredenburg).

Hesperantha spicata (Burman fil.) N. E. Brown

Plants 12–35 cm high; corm bell-shaped with an oblique flat base, tunics concentric. Leaves lanceolate to falcate and margins sometimes crisped, or terete and hollow. Flowers mostly many in a secund spike, small, white, dark on the outside, sweetly cinnamon or clove scented when open in the evening, perianth tube slightly curved, 4–6 mm long, tepals spreading, 4–7(–9) mm long; bracts green, distant. Flowering August–September. Clay and sandy soils, NW, SW (Piketberg to Cape Peninsula).

Hesperantha vaginata; see also page 25

Three subspecies are recognized: subspecies *fistulosa* (Baker) Goldblatt with leaves round in section and hollow, wet sand and loam, NW, SW (Porterville and near Paarl), subspecies *graminifolia* (Sweet) Goldblatt with leaves narrow, soft textured, with smooth margins, mostly sandstone soils, SW (Darling to Cape Peninsula and Franschhoek), and subspecies *spicata* with leaves firm, erect or falcate, margins crisped or undulate, sandstone and clay slopes, NW, SW (Piketberg to Gordon's Bay).

Hesperantha sufflava Goldblatt

Plants mostly 8–12 cm high; corm bell-shaped with a flat base, tunics usually smooth, the edges lightly toothed. Leaves three, sword-shaped to falcate. Flowers mostly three to six per spike, pale yellow, the outer tepals brownish on the outside, musk scented when open in the late afternoon and evening, perianth tube straight, 12–16 mm long, tepals spreading, 7–10 mm long; bracts green. Flowering July–August. Granitic gravel slopes in renosterveld, SW (Malmesbury hills).

Hesperantha teretifolia Goldblatt

Plants mostly 30–40 cm high, stem bearing a short, membranous, scale-like leaf just below the spike; corm rounded with overlapping tunics irregularly notched below. Leaves three, blades terete and hollow, with fine, narrow, vertical grooves and ridges and minutely scabrid on the ridges. Flowers mostly 5–10 per spike, white to cream, opening in the late afternoon and sweetly scented, perianth tube c. 9 mm long, tepals spreading, c. 13 mm long; bracts green to membranous. Stony slopes, often growing in rock crevices, RV (Roggeveld Escarpment).

Hesperantha truncatula Goldblatt

Plants 8–12 cm high, stem bearing a short, membranous, scale-like leaf just below the spike; corm rounded, tunics overlapping, irregularly notched below. Leaves three, the lower two short, oblong, and obtuse, the third inflated and sheathing the lower half of the stem, and without a free tip. Flowers mostly two to five per spike, pale blue-mauve, unscented and open during the day, perianth tube straight, c. 7 mm long, tepals spreading, c. 12 mm long; bracts green. Flowering August–September. Dry, north-facing, shale slopes in renosterveld, KM (Kleinswartberg foothills).

Hesperantha vaginata (Sweet) Goldblatt
Plants 12–18 cm high; corm rounded with an oblique flat side, tunics overlapping. Leaves four or five, sword-shaped, gray-green. Flowers mostly two to four per spike, large, cup-shaped, yellow, often marked with dark brown in the center and toward the tips of the outer tepals, unscented when open in the mid- to late afternoon, perianth tube 5–8 mm long, tepals 25–35 mm long; bracts green, dry at the tips. Flowering August–September. Heavy clay soil, RV, NW (Bokkeveld Escarpment and western Karoo).

Hessea
COMMON NAME umbrella lily, FAMILY Amaryllidaceae. Small deciduous perennials. ROOTSTOCK a bulb with parchment to felt-like outer tunics producing extensible threads when torn. LEAVES two, sometimes three, dry or emerging at flowering, spreading, linear to narrowly strap-shaped, smooth or rarely shortly pilose, surrounded by a sometimes prominent basal sheath. INFLORESCENCE a widely spreading, conical to hemispherical umbel, 3- to 120-flowered, on a firm, slender scape; spathe bracts two, rapidly withering. FLOWERS actinomorphic, star- to funnel-shaped, pink, white, or occasionally pale lemon, sometimes with dark central markings, the pedicels radiating, much longer than the flowers, the tepals free or united into a tube as much as 12 mm long, spreading, sometimes crisped. STAMENS united into a tube at the base, then spreading, the filaments sometimes hooked on the inner surface, the anthers subcentrifixed to centrifixed. OVARY with as many as four ovules per locule, sometimes as many as seven; STYLE slender and straight, the stigma distinctly to minutely trifid. FRUIT a small, thin-walled capsule. SEEDS fleshy, ovoid, reddish green, 3–4 mm diam., the embryo green. Basic chromosome number $x = 11$. Southern Africa, mostly in the winter-rainfall region; 13 spp., 8 in the Cape.

Although *Hessea* species have small flower heads they are communal, sometimes forming large colonies. The bulbs flower synchronously in autumn and in good seasons transform the dry landscape into patches of pink and white. Most species flower freely in cultivation, but exceptions are *H. cinnamomea* and *H. monticola,* which are restricted to fire-prone habitats. These two species favor marshy situations on the Cape Peninsula and Western Cape mountains, where they flower in their thousands after wildfires. Several species are now rare in nature, the result of urban sprawl and mining. *Hessea mathewsii,* a limestone endemic on the western coast, is seriously threatened and if the current trends in habitat loss continue, it may become extinct in the wild.

Several of the species, particularly those with appendaged stamens, are pollinated by flies, but the remainder are probably pollinated by bees and other insects. Propagation is easy from seed, and flowers can be expected from the third season onward. Most species flower well in pots.

FURTHER READING. *Hessea* was revised by D. and U. Müller-Doblies (1985), followed by a more complete, well-illustrated treatment by Snijman (1994). An additional species and further notes on the genus were published by Snijman (1999b).

Hessea breviflora Herbert
Plants to 20 cm high; bulb extended into a stout neck. Leaves two, sometimes three, often emerging at flowering, spreading, strap-shaped, 4–16 mm wide, shiny green, flushed with red basally, enclosed in an exserted brownish red sheath. Flowers 10–55, spreading, star-shaped to widely funnel-shaped, 7–15 mm long, pale to deep pink, sometimes scented, stamens slightly shorter to longer than the tepals, spreading, with a filament tube 1–4.5 mm long. Flowering April–May. Sandy pockets between rocks on lower slopes, NW, SW (Namaqualand, Olifants River Valley to Hopefield). Page 232.

Hessea cinnamomea (L'Héritier) Durand & Schinz
Plants to 15 cm high; bulb extended into a slender neck. Leaves two, sometimes single, dry or emerging at flowering, suberect, linear, 1–2.5 mm wide, dark shiny green. Flowers 5–27, spreading to one side, widely funnel-

Hessea breviflora

Hessea mathewsii

Hessea cinnamomea (Colin Paterson-Jones)

Hessea monticola (Colin Paterson-Jones)

shaped, 10–14 mm long, glistening white to pink with a wine red center, scented of spice, tepals crisped, the outer whorl with a short point on the apex, stamens shorter than the perianth, filament tube to 0.5 mm long. Flowering May–June, after fire. Peaty lowlands, SW (Cape Peninsula).

Hessea mathewsii W. F. Barker
Plants to c. 19 cm high; bulb with a slender neck. Leaves two, sometimes three, dry or emerging at flowering, narrowly strap-shaped, 2–5 mm wide. Flowers 5–18, spreading, star-shaped, white to delicate pink with a deep pink to crimson center and midrib, unpleasantly scented, tepals 6–8.5 mm long, exceeding the outspread stamens, the filaments united at the extreme base, with the basal third densely papillate on the inner surface and bearing a fleshy, inward-curved hook. Flowering May. Limestone flats, SW (Saldanha Bay).

Hessea monticola Snijman
Plants to 25 cm high; bulb with a long neck. Leaves usually two, dry at flowering, spreading, narrowly strap-shaped, 1.5–3 mm wide. Flowers usually 10–30, spreading, star-shaped, white to pink with deep pink stripes leading down the throat, unpleasantly scented, tepals 10–25 mm long with crisped edges, stamens spreading, shorter than the tepals, the filaments basally united into a tube 1 mm long. Flowering March–May, usually after fire. Rocky slopes or seasonally wet valleys, NW, SW (Piketberg and Cedarberg to Riviersonderend Mountains).

Hessea pulcherrima (D. & U. Müller-Doblies) Snijman
Plants to c. 10 cm high; bulb with a slender neck. Leaves two, dry at flowering, spreading, linear, 1–2 mm wide, spirally twisted apically. Flowers 4–20, spreading on wiry pedicels, star-shaped, white, often with crimson in the center and on the tips of the outer tepals, rarely pure white, faintly scented, tepals 4.5–6 mm long, twisted, about as long as the stamens, the filaments free or united at the extreme base, the basal third densely papillate on the inner surface and bearing a fleshy, inward-curved hook. Flowering May. Clay flats, RV, NW (Bokkeveld Escarpment and western Karoo).

Hessea pusilla Snijman
Plants to c. 12 cm high; bulb with a slender neck. Leaves two, dry at flowering, spreading, linear, 0.5–1 mm wide. Flowers 4–11, spreading, widely funnel-shaped, 6–8 mm long, glistening pale pink with a deep pink star-like center, scentless, tepals usually with slightly undulate edges, stamens about as long as the tepals, the filaments united into a basal tube 2 mm long. Flowering April–May. Sandy sandstone plateaus, NW (Bokkeveld Escarpment).

Hessea stellaris (Jacquin) Herbert
Plants to c. 20 cm high; bulb with a slender neck. Leaves two, dry or emerging at flowering, recurved, narrowly strap-shaped, 1–7 mm wide. Flowers 6–30, spreading, star-shaped, pale to deep pink with a darker pink star-shaped center, sometimes scented, tepals 7–12 mm long,

Hessea stellaris

Hessea undosa (Colin Paterson-Jones)

sometimes slightly undulate near base, stamens spreading, slightly shorter to longer than the tepals, the filaments united into a basal tube 1 mm long. Flowering April–June. Sandy or clay flats, RV, NW, KM (western Karoo, Karoopoort to Oudtshoorn).

Hessea undosa Snijman

Plants to 23 cm high; bulb with a slender neck. Leaves two, dry at flowering, spreading, linear, 1–2 mm wide. Flowers 7–20, spreading, stellate, glistening pale to deep pink, with a reddish center, scentless, tepals 6.5–8 mm long with crisped edges, about as long as the spreading stamens, the filaments united into a basal tube to 1 mm long. Flowering June–July. Seasonally waterlogged sandstone rock pockets, NW (Gifberg).

Hypoxis

COMMON NAME star grass, FAMILY Hypoxidaceae. Deciduous or rarely evergreen perennials usually with hairs on leaves, pedicels, and ovary or at least on the backs of outer tepals, the hairs branched, whitish to reddish brown, with the arms often radiating. ROOTSTOCK a slow-growing vertical rhizome, often large, subglobose to elongated, often with yellow flesh; roots stout, contractile, present mostly in upper half of the rhizome. LEAVES few to many in a basal cluster, green at flowering, strongly veined, linear to ovate, clasping basally, often surrounded by dry fibers. INFLORESCENCE a raceme, corymb, or rarely single-flowered on a long scape; bracts narrow, one, sometimes two, subtending each flower. FLOWERS star-shaped, opposite, alternate or in a whorl, yellow or occasionally white, green and hairy on the outside, on long or short pedicels, the tepals six, rarely four, free, subequal, narrowly ovate, spreading. STAMENS six, rarely four, inserted at the tepal bases, spreading to erect, the filaments short, filiform to subulate, attached to anther base, the anthers latrorse, more or less versatile when older. OVARY three-locular with many axile ovules; STYLE short, cylindrical, the stigma obconical, three-grooved. CAPSULE top-shaped to obovoid, thin-walled, opening apically by means of a lid and then often splitting longitudinally. SEEDS subglobose, black to dark brown, shiny or dull with a warty surface, raphe and hilum distinct. Basic chromosome numbers $x = 7, 8, 9, 11, 19$ (with much polyploidy and aneuploidy). Southern Africa (c. 45 spp., 7 in the Cape) with as many species elsewhere in sub-Saharan Africa, the Americas, Southeast Asia, and Australia.

Despite the widespread medicinal use of some African species of *Hypoxis*, the genus is poorly known taxonomically and horticulturally. The prevalence of apomixis in the genus makes species delimitation problematic because minor variants may multiply through seeds. Furthermore, the flowers of *Hypoxis* are self-compatible, and both outcrossing and selfing are possible.

Many popular reports suggest that extracts of *Hypoxis hemerocallidea* Fischer & C. A. Meyer may inhibit cancer, but clinical studies indicate that these extracts can be harmful to humans. To meet the need for reliable information on *Hypoxis* in Africa, systematic studies are underway.

Many representatives of *Hypoxis* tolerate dry conditions, making them ideal horticultural subjects for temperate and subtropical climates. In cultivation, the seeds are slow to germinate, and once released they remain dormant for a year. In nature, however, the seeds of some species germinate readily in response to fire. The brilliant yellow flowers open for only a day, if sufficiently sunny, but their sequential flowering pattern usually keeps the plants colorful for several weeks. Many species of *Hypoxis*, such as *H. villosa* and several others from outside the Cape, have densely hairy, silver or rufous foliage, which gives them extra horticultural merit.

FURTHER READING. *Hypoxis* in southern African was last revised by Baker (1896), who had a broader concept of the genus than we do today; the species currently placed in *Hypoxis* formed his subgenus *Eurypoxis*. More recently, notes on pollination and medicinal uses were published by Singh (1999), and the difficulties in germination were studied by Hammerton and van Staden (1988). Judd (2000) summarized studies of several North American *Hypoxis* species.

Hypoxis angustifolia Lamarck

Plants 15–25 cm high; rhizome often with a brown papery neck. Leaves 6–12, recurved, linear-lanceolate, 2–6 mm wide, margin and midrib usually softly hairy. Flowers two or three per scape, tepals 5–10 mm long, yellow. Flowering September–February. In grassy damp depressions or rock crevices, LB, SE (Mossel Bay to tropical Africa, Mauritius, and Madagascar).

Hypoxis argentea Harvey ex Baker

Plants 15–25 cm high; rhizome usually with a bristly neck. Leaves 6–12, mostly suberect, linear-lanceolate, 2–5 mm wide, strongly veined, gray-green with at least the undersurface persistently silky. Flowers two per scape or sometimes as many as four, tepals 5–10 mm long, yellow. Flowering October–March. Grassland and low scrub in poorly drained sites, LB, SE (Swellendam to Port Elizabeth, Eastern Cape to Gauteng).

Hypoxis floccosa Baker

Plants 5–20 cm high; rhizome neck dark and papery. Leaves 3–10, recurved, linear, 1–3 mm wide, both surfaces softly shaggy. Flowers one or two per scape, tepals 5–10 mm long, yellow. Flowering September–April. Coastal flats in seasonally moist depressions, SW, AP, SE (Gordon's Bay to the Eastern Cape).

Hypoxis longifolia Baker

Plants 25–40 cm high; rhizome neck densely surrounded by fibrous bristles. Leaves three to nine, sub-

Hypoxis argentea

Hypoxis floccosa

Hypoxis longifolia

erect, 1–3 mm wide, strongly veined, reaching well above the flowers, smooth when mature. Flowers two to four per scape, tepals 10–15 mm long, yellow. Flowering November–February. Seasonally damp grassy flats and slopes, SE (Knysna to the Eastern Cape).

Hypoxis setosa Baker

Plants 15–25 cm high; rhizome with a broad fibrous neck. Leaves six to eight, lanceolate, 5–25 mm wide, recurved, leathery, many-veined, both surfaces smooth, margins hairy. Flowers two to six per scape, tepals 10–15 mm long, yellow. Flowering January–April. Sandy flats and slopes, LB, SE (Swellendam to the Eastern Cape).

Hypoxis stellipilis Ker Gawler

Plant 20–30 cm high; rhizome large with a bristly neck. Leaves 12 or more, spreading, lanceolate, 8–18 mm wide, overtopping the flowers, green above, persistently pilose with a dense mat of silver-white hairs beneath. Flowers two to four per scape, tepals 10–20 mm long, yellow. Flowering October–April. Grassy fynbos, SE (Humansdorp to Port Elizabeth).

Hypoxis villosa Linnaeus fil.

Plants 15–20 cm high; rhizome with a bristly neck. Leaves 12 or more, spreading to recurved, lanceolate, 10–20 mm wide, both surfaces covered with tufted, often rust-colored hairs. Flowers two to seven per scape, tepals 10–20 mm long, yellow. Flowering March–April. Southern slopes, LB, SE (Swellendam to KwaZulu-Natal).

Ixia

COMMON NAME ixia, FAMILY Iridaceae. Deciduous perennials. ROOTSTOCK a globose corm, rooting from below, basal in origin, with tunics of fine to moderately coarse fibers. LEAVES several, lower two or three forming cataphylls, foliage leaves unifacial with a definite midrib, blades usually plane, rarely H-shaped in cross section with winged margins, sword-shaped, falcate or linear, sometimes the margins thickened, occasionally crisped; stem aerial, rarely subterranean, usually slender and wiry, terete, usually branched, branching often divaricate. IN-

FLORESCENCE a spike, often flexuous; flowers spirally arranged, occasionally two-ranked, bracts membranous, occasionally scarious, short, outer usually three-cuspidate, inner smaller than outer and bicuspidate. FLOWERS usually actinomorphic, rarely weakly zygomorphic, variously colored, often pink, mauve, or yellow, sometimes darker in the center, sometimes fragrant, sometimes with nectar from septal nectaries; perianth tube funnel-shaped or cylindrical or filiform, short or elongate; tepals subequal, usually spreading. STAMENS symmetrically disposed, arising in throat or at top of tube; filaments included or exserted, sometimes partly or entirely united; anthers diverging or contiguous, sometimes incompletely dehiscent, occasionally with a bend near base. STYLE included or exserted, dividing at or well above mouth of tube, branches slender, channeled and slightly broadened above or involute and stigmatic apically. FRUIT a globose cartilaginous capsule. SEEDS globose or lightly angled, mostly smooth, hard and shiny, raphal vascular trace excluded. Basic chromosome number $x = 10$. Mainly the winter-rainfall region, extending from Namaqualand and the western Karoo through the southwestern Cape into Eastern Cape Province, most diverse in the southwestern Cape; 50 spp.

Ixia is concentrated in the southwestern Cape with a few species extending to the extremes of its limits in the north or east. Less specialized species of the genus have an open perianth tube containing nectar. The short-tubed flowers of this kind are pollinated by bees in search of pollen and nectar, but the long-tubed species are pollinated by long-proboscid flies. *Ixia paniculata*, which has by far the longest perianth tube of all the species, is pollinated by the long-proboscid flies *Moegistorhynchus longirostris* (Nemestrinidae) and *Philoliche rostrata* (Tabanidae) whereas other long-tubed species, including *I. bellendenii* and *I. pauciflora*, are pollinated by *P. gulosa*. The remaining species (subgenus *Ixia*) have specialized flowers in which the perianth tube is extremely narrow and does not contain nectar. Among these species, those with dark central markings are pollinated by monkey beetles (Scarabaeidae: Hopliini) whereas buzz pollination appears to be characteristic of section *Dichone* of subgenus *Ixia*. Buzz pollination is a specialized system in which pollen can only be released from the anthers if they are vibrated at a high frequency by visiting bees (see also *Cyanella*).

Many ixias make charming and sometimes striking garden subjects. In most species the flowers are crowded at the tops of slender stalks and make a dazzling display in sunny weather but do close in cold or overcast weather. A series of hybrids in a wide range of colors is available in the bulb trade, mostly with *Ixia lutea* as the dominant parental species. These hybrids are becoming more common as cut flowers for sale in markets. Of the wild species, among the most desirable is undoubtedly *I. viridiflora*, the green ixia. This positively ethereal species produces long, slender spikes bearing flowers of a remarkable turquoise green with black centers. There are reports that it is one of the more difficult species to grow and is best grown outdoors in a rock garden. Several other species with brightly colored flowers and contrasting dark eye make attractive garden or pot subjects. The orange-flowered *I. maculata* and the bluish *I. monadelpha* were favorite cultivated plants in Europe in the 18th and 19th centuries and continue to deserve attention today. Another attractive species is *I. leipoldtii*, which has large white flowers with a brilliant royal purple center on rather short stems. The species has only relatively recently been rediscovered in the wild and has been brought into cultivation at Kirstenbosch botanical garden. *Ixia rapunculoides* has large, half-nodding to drooping, mauve or blue flowers and has a wide range of forms, nearly all from dry parts of the Cape Floral Region. It is thus drought and cold tolerant to a greater degree than most species of the genus. Wild plants of this charming species appear in drifts across stony plains and road verges in the western Karoo. These lovely displays should easily be duplicated in a rock garden. Another species that warrants attention is *I. scillaris*, which bears numerous pink flowers in slender spikes. It, too, is occasionally common, especially in cleared or burned slopes. Ixias mostly have small corms that should reach flowering size in the second year after seeds germinate. All require a well-drained soil. A mix of equal parts of sand, peat moss or leaf mold, and loam has produced excellent results for us.

FURTHER READING. *Ixia* was revised by Lewis (1962) and more recently by De Vos (1999a). Changes to the taxonomy were made by Goldblatt and Manning (1999) and an additional species was described by Manning and Goldblatt (2001a). The diverse methods of pollination in the genus were studied by Goldblatt et al. (2001).

Ixia atrandra Goldblatt & J. C. Manning
Plants 20–50 cm high, sometimes with one or two short lateral branchlets. Leaves narrowly lanceolate. Flowers 4–10 per spike, crowded, pink or white with a large dark center, perianth tube filiform, 6–9 mm long, tepals spreading, 11–14 mm long, stamens fully exserted, black, with broadened, arrow-shaped anthers. Flowering September–October. Clay slopes, SW (Villiersdorp).

Ixia aurea J. C. Manning & Goldblatt
Plants 15–40 cm high, occasionally with one short branchlet. Leaves sword-shaped, loosely coiled above. Flowers mostly 10–16 per spike, crowded, yellowish orange, perianth tube narrowly funnel-shaped (nearly cylindrical), 8–11 mm long, tepals spreading, 16–23 mm long, filaments largely exserted; bracts translucent. Flowering September–October. Granite slopes, SW (Darling).

Ixia brevituba Baker
Plants 25–50 cm high, usually with one or two short, spreading branchlets. Leaves linear to sword-shaped, prominently veined. Flowers 5–10 per spike, axis lax, flexuous, pale pink or mauve, perianth tube filiform, c. 1.5 mm long, tepals spreading, 10–12 mm long, stamens fully exserted, anthers ovoid. Flowering July–September. Rocky flats and slopes, RV (Roggeveld Escarpment).

Ixia brunneobractea G. J. Lewis
Plants 25–45 cm high, sometimes with one or two short branchlets. Leaves linear or narrowly sword-shaped. Flowers two to five per spike, usually half-nodding, cream, the tepals tinged with pink on the outside, perianth tube funnel-shaped, 5–7 mm long, tepals laxly spreading, 12–15 mm long; bracts glossy dark brown. Flowering September–October. Sandstone soils, mostly in marshes or seeps, NW (Bokkeveld Mountains).

Ixia campanulata Houttuyn
Plants 10–35 cm high, stem usually unbranched. Leaves linear. Flowers mostly three to eight per spike, congested, mostly deep red, sometimes white, perianth tube filiform, 2–3 mm long, tepals spreading, 12–25 mm long, stamens fully exserted; bracts whitish or flushed pink. Flowering October–November. Damp sandstone slopes, NW, SW (Tulbagh to Villiersdorp).

Ixia capillaris Linnaeus fil.
Plants 20–45 cm high, often with a few short branchlets. Leaves linear, to 2 mm wide. Flowers mostly two to four per spike, white to blue-mauve, perianth tube funnel-shaped, 5–7 mm long, tepals spreading, 10–15 mm long, filaments usually included or half-exserted. Flowering July–September. Sandy or clay slopes, NW, SW, KM, LB (Citrusdal to Ladismith).

Ixia aurea

Ixia cochlearis G. J. Lewis

Plants 20–40 cm high, stem unbranched. Leaves linear, 1–3 mm wide. Flowers 4–12 per spike, rose to salmon pink with dark veins, perianth tube narrowly funnel-shaped, 10–18 mm long, tepals slightly cupped, 12–17 mm long, filaments well exserted. Flowering mainly November. Lower mountain slopes, SW (Stellenbosch Mountains).

Ixia collina Goldblatt & Snijman

Plants 50–90 cm high, stem usually with two or three short, sharply diverging branchlets. Leaves linear to sword-shaped. Flowers 6–10 per spike, axis flexuous, pale pink, perianth tube filiform, c. 5 mm long, tepals subequal, spreading, 9–12 mm long, stamens unilateral, filaments fully exserted, bent at right angles in the upper third, anthers broadly oblong with a right-angled bend near base, splitting incompletely. Flowering August–September. Shale hills in renosterveld, SW (Breede River Valley near Worcester).

Ixia curta Andrews

Plants 15–40 cm high, stem rarely with one short branchlet. Leaves sword-shaped. Flowers four to eight per spike, crowded, orange with a brownish center, perianth tube filiform, 10–15 mm long, tepals spreading, 20–25 mm long, stamens fully exserted, filaments united; bracts pallid. Flowering September–October. Sandy flats and slopes, SW (Hopefield to Darling).

Ixia curvata Baker

Plants 25–50 cm high, sometimes with one or two short branchlets. Leaves linear, rigid, to 4 mm wide. Flowers 6–10 per spike, axis lax, deep pink, perianth tube filiform, 3–5 mm long, tepals spreading, 9–14 mm long, stamens fully exserted, anthers oblong. Flowering July–September. Rocky slopes, RV (western Karoo in the Calvinia district).

Ixia dubia Ventenat

Plants 25–60 cm high, stem sometimes with one or two short branchlets. Leaves sword-shaped to nearly linear. Flowers mostly 4–10 per spike, crowded, orange to yel-

Ixia curta with *Drosera cistiflora* (sticky leaves) and, below, *Geissorhiza eurystigma* (red centers) and *G. monanthos*

Ixia curvata

low, often dark in the center, perianth tube usually filiform, 6–14 mm long, tepals spreading, 10–15 mm long, stamens fully exserted, the filaments sometimes united at the base; bracts translucent pink. Flowering October–December. Sandstone and granite flats and slopes, NW, SW, AP (Piketberg to Caledon).

Ixia erubescens Goldblatt

Plants 12–30 cm high, stem unbranched. Leaves sword-shaped with undulate to crisped margins. Flowers mostly 4–10 per spike, axis fairly lax, flexuous, pink, perianth tube filiform, c. 2.5 mm long, tepals more or less vertical, spreading, 8–11 mm long, stamens fully exserted, anthers spherical. Flowering August–September. Clay flats and slopes in renosterveld, NW, SW (Piketberg to Caledon).

Ixia esterhuyseniae M. P. de Vos

Plants 10–15 cm high, sometimes with a short branchlet. Leaves sword-shaped. Flowers two to four per spike, fairly crowded, yellow, reddish on the outside, lily scented, perianth tube funnel-shaped, 4–5 mm long, tepals spreading, 10–11 mm long, filaments largely exserted. Flowering December–January. Seasonally wet sandstone pavement, SW (Jonkershoek and Hottentots Holland Mountains).

Ixia flexuosa Linnaeus

Plants 35–65 cm high, stems wiry, often unbranched. Leaves linear to sword-shaped. Flowers mostly 4–12 per spike, congested, pink, mauve, or white with darker streaks, with a light musky odor, perianth tube filiform, 4–6 mm long, tepals spreading, 10–16 mm long, stamens fully exserted. Flowering mainly August–September. Mostly clay flats and slopes, SW, AP, LB (Cape Peninsula to Riversdale).

Ixia fucata Ker Gawler

Plants mostly 20–50 cm high, occasionally with one short branchlet. Leaves linear to needle-like, 0.5–3 mm wide. Flowers mostly two to four per spike, crowded, white to pale pink, with darker veins, perianth tube cylindrical, 12–15 mm long, tepals spreading, filaments exserted. Flowering September–November. Sandstone mountain slopes, NW, SW, KM (Ceres to Caledon and Montagu).

Ixia gloriosa G. J. Lewis

Plants 35–65 cm high, stems wiry, sometimes with one to three short, wiry branches. Leaves linear, to 3 mm wide. Flowers mostly 5–10 per spike, axis lax, flexuous, deep pink with a shining purple-black center, perianth tube filiform, 3–6 mm long, tepals spreading, 15–20 mm long, stamens fully exserted; bracts pellucid. Flowering August–September. Clay slopes in renosterveld, KM (Barrydale district).

Ixia latifolia D. Delaroche

Plants 20–50 cm high, stem with few to many short branchlets. Leaves sword-shaped to falcate, often fairly broad, to 20 mm wide. Flowers four to seven per main spike, usually erect, deep pink to purple or mauve, perianth tube narrowly funnel-shaped, 10–20 mm long, tepals spreading, 12–20 mm long, filaments well exserted. Flowering September–November. Mostly clay soils in renosterveld, RV, NW, SW, KM (Namaqualand to Paarl, Montagu and western Karoo).

Ixia leipoldtii G. J. Lewis

Plants 11–25 cm high, sometimes with one or two short branchlets. Leaves lanceolate, the margins fairly prominent. Flowers mostly three or four per spike, erect, white with a dark red-purple center, perianth tube funnel-shaped, 10–12 mm long, tepals spreading, 15–17 mm long, filaments included, anthers half-exserted. Flowering August–September. Stony clay soils in renosterveld, KM (Barrydale to Prince Albert).

Ixia longituba N. E. Brown

Plants 35–70 cm high, usually with one to three short branchlets. Leaves sword-shaped, the margins usually prominent. Flowers 5–12 per spike, fairly crowded, white flushed pink to deep pink, perianth tube cylindrical, often elongate, 18–35 mm long, tepals spreading, 12–20 mm long, filaments exserted; bracts pellucid, dry, fairly short. Flowering September–October. Shale slopes, SW, AP, LB (Caledon to Swellendam).

Ixia lutea Ecklon

Plants 15–35 cm high, stem unbranched. Leaves sword-shaped to lanceolate. Flowers mostly five to eight per spike, axis crowded, red to purple or cream to yellow, with a dark center, perianth tube filiform, 6–9 mm long, tepals spreading, 14–25 mm long, stamens fully exserted. Flowering August–October. Clay flats and slopes in renosterveld, NW, SW (Citrusdal to Paarl). Page 242.

Ixia maculata Linnaeus

Plants 20–50 cm high, stem unbranched; corms with stolons bearing a single cormel. Leaves sword-shaped, lightly twisted above. Flowers four to many per spike, crowded, orange to yellow with a dark, star-like center, perianth tube filiform, 5–8 mm long, tepals spreading, 15–30 mm long, stamens fully exserted, filaments usually united below, sometimes to the middle; bracts large, truncate, rust brown. Flowering September–October. Granite and sandstone flats and slopes, mostly fynbos, NW, SW (Clanwilliam to Melkbos, extinct on the Cape Peninsula). Page 242.

Ixia longituba

Ixia lutea

Ixia maculata; see also page 21

Ixia metelerkampiae

Ixia micrandra

Ixia marginifolia (Salisbury) G. J. Lewis
Plants to 75 cm high, stem with several short, spreading branchlets. Leaves sword-shaped to falcate, the margins and midrib conspicuously thickened. Flowers mostly two or three per spike, pale blue to mauve or gray, perianth tube widely funnel-shaped, 4–7 mm long, tepals 10–14 mm long, filaments well exserted. Flowering September–October. Mostly in renosterveld on stony slopes, RV (Calvinia to Tweedside).

Ixia metelerkampiae L. Bolus
Plants 35–70 cm high, stem usually subdivaricately one- to three-branched. Leaves linear to sword-shaped. Flowers 5–15 per spike, axis congested, pale pink to lilac, with a small dark pink or purple center sometimes outlined with white, perianth tube filiform, 3–4 mm long, tepals spreading, 14–22 mm long, stamens fully exserted; bracts pellucid. Flowering November–December. Sandstone slopes, SW (Bain's Kloof to Paarl).

Ixia micrandra Baker
Plants 25–50 cm high, stem slender, unbranched. Leaves linear, mostly less than 1.5 mm wide. Flowers two to six per spike, pink, perianth tube filiform, 3–5 mm long, tepals spreading, mostly 10–16 mm long, stamens fully exserted, anthers oblong. Flowering July–September. Rocky sandstone slopes and flats, SW, AP, KM, LB (Paarl to Oudtshoorn).

Ixia monadelpha D. Delaroche
Plants 15–40 cm high, stem mostly with one or two spreading branchlets. Leaves sword-shaped. Flowers mostly 6–12 per spike, crowded, turquoise to purple, rarely whitish, with a blackish center, perianth tube filiform, 10–18 mm long, tepals spreading, 13–20 mm long, stamens fully exserted, filaments more or less united, black. Flowering September–October. Wet sandy flats and lower slopes, SW (Darling to Cape Peninsula).

Ixia mostertii M. P. de Vos
Plants to 45 cm high, stem with a fibrous neck, unbranched. Leaves sword-shaped to linear, the margins and midvein prominently thickened. Flowers 5–12 per spike, usually compact, pink, mauve, or white, with a dark center, perianth tube filiform, 4–7 mm long, tepals widely cupped, 15–22 mm long, stamens fully exserted. Flowering September–October. Clay slopes in renosterveld, NW (Roman's River to Worcester).

Ixia odorata Ker Gawler
Plants 30–60 cm high, sometimes with one or two short lateral branchlets. Leaves linear to lanceolate, often loosely coiled above. Flowers 5–12 per spike, crowded, small, pale yellow or cream, sweetly fragrant, perianth tube narrowly funnel-shaped, 5–11 mm long, tepals spreading, mostly 12–15 mm long, filaments shortly exserted. Flowering September–November. Sandstone and granite slopes, NW, SW (Citrusdal to Hermanus). Page 244.

Ixia orientalis L. Bolus
Plants 25–70 cm high, stem sometimes with one to three filiform branchlets. Leaves linear, mostly 1.5–5 mm long.

Ixia monadelpha

Ixia odorata

Ixia paniculata

Flowers mostly 5–10 per spike, fairly crowded, cream to mauve-pink, perianth tube narrowly funnel-shaped, mostly 7–10 mm long, tepals spreading, 10–18 mm long, filaments exserted. Flowering September–October. Flats and slopes, SW, AP, KM, LB, SE (Villiersdorp to Port Alfred).

Ixia paniculata D. Delaroche

Plants 40–100 cm high, usually with as many as three spreading branchlets. Leaves sword-shaped. Flowers mostly 6–12 per spike, axis fairly lax, cream to biscuit colored, perianth tube elongate-cylindrical, 40–70 mm long, tepals spreading, 15–25 mm long, stamens included or the anthers partly exserted. Flowering October–December. Moist sandy slopes and flats, NW, SW (Bokkeveld Mountains to False Bay).

Ixia patens Aiton

Plants 20–50 cm high, sometimes with one or two short erect branchlets. Leaves sword-shaped to linear, the margins often prominent. Flowers 5–15 per spike, the axis lax and flexuous, sometimes compact, usually red or pink, sometimes with a whitish center, perianth tube filiform, 4–6 mm long, tepals spreading, 16–24 mm long, stamens fully exserted. Flowering September–October. Clay slopes in renosterveld, NW, SW (Clanwilliam to Riviersonderend).

Ixia pauciflora G. J. Lewis

Plants 20–40 cm high, sometimes with one or two short branchlets. Leaves linear, half as long as the stem, to 1 mm wide. Flowers one to three per spike, cream or pink to violet, usually fragrant, perianth tube cylindrical below, flared above, c. 15 mm long, tepals spreading, 15–18 mm long, stamens slightly to well exserted, declinate. Flowering August–September. Sandstone soils in fynbos, NW (Cedarberg Mountains to Cold Bokkeveld).

Ixia paucifolia G. J. Lewis

Plants 12–55 cm high, stem mostly with one to three short branchlets. Leaves linear to lanceolate, or falcate. Flowers mostly four to eight per spike, white to pink, tube elongate-cylindrical, 16–33 mm long, tepals spreading,

7–12 mm long, filaments shortly exserted. Flowering September–November. Stony, middle to upper mountain slopes, NW, KM (Cedarberg Mountains to Ladismith).

Ixia polystachya Linnaeus
Plants 40–80 cm high, sometimes with one to three short, suberect branchlets; corms with stolons. Leaves sword-shaped to lanceolate. Flowers few to many in dense or lax spikes, white to pink or mauve, often with a darker center, sometimes yellow, rarely lightly fragrant, perianth tube cylindrical-filiform, 5–14 mm long, tepals spreading, 10–12 mm long, stamens fully exserted. Flowering October–December. Granitic and sandstone slopes and flats, NW, SW (Cedarberg to Betty's Bay and Riviersonderend Mountains).

Ixia pumilio Goldblatt & Snijman
Plants 12–20 cm high, simple or with as many as three short branches. Leaves linear to sword-shaped, 2–5 mm wide, often twisted toward the tips. Flowers in short spikes, brick red, tube funnel-shaped, 8–10 mm long, wide and cup-like in the upper half, tepals subequal, mostly 12–15 mm long, spreading, style dividing opposite the middle of the anthers; bracts membranous, becoming dry as the flowers fade. Flowering August–September. Sandy alluvial flats, SW (Breede River Valley near Worcester).

Ixia purpureorosea G. J. Lewis
Plants 20–60 cm high, stem unbranched. Leaves sword-shaped, fairly soft textured. Flowers 3–12 per spike, axis congested, mauve-pink with a blackish center, perianth tube filiform, barely expanded at the throat, tepals spreading, 15–20 mm long, stamens fully exserted; bracts pale. Flowering September–October. Limestone and calcareous sands in strandveld, SW (Saldanha Bay).

Ixia rapunculoides Delile
Plants 15–70 cm high, stem usually with several short, few-flowered branches. Leaves sword-shaped to falcate. Flowers mostly one to four per spike, blue, mauve, cream, or pink, suberect to nodding, perianth tube funnel-shaped, 5–9 mm long, including the filaments, tepals

Ixia paucifolia

Ixia polystachya

spreading, 12–18 mm long, anthers usually partly included. Flowering August–September. Mostly clay soils in renosterveld or karroid scrub, RV, NW, KM (Namaqualand to Oudtshoorn and western Karoo).

Ixia rouxii G. J. Lewis
Plants 35–50 cm high, stem with one to three short, spreading branchlets. Leaves linear to sword-shaped. Flowers three to nine per spike, axis congested, white, pink, or bluish, with dark center, perianth tube filiform, 5–7 mm long, tepals spreading, 15–20 mm long, stamens fully exserted, with dark anthers. Flowering October–November. Clay flats, NW (Porterville to Wolseley).

Ixia scillaris Linnaeus
Plants 25–50 cm high, often with one to three short branchlets. Leaves sword-shaped, the margins sometimes undulate. Flowers 7–20 per spike, axis lax, pale or deep pink, perianth tube filiform, 3–4 mm long, tepals more or less vertical, spreading, 8–16 mm long, stamens fully exserted, unilateral, anthers oblong, nodding, splitting incompletely from the base. Flowering September–November. Stony granite, sandstone, and clay flats and slopes, NW, SW (Namaqualand to Caledon).

Ixia splendida G. J. Lewis
Plants 30–60 cm high, stem unbranched. Leaves linear. Flowers five to seven per spike, congested, pale pink, perianth tube elongate-cylindrical, 22–28 mm long, tepals spreading, 15–18 mm long, stamens included in tube. Flowering October–November. Mountain slopes, SW (Piketberg at Zebra Kop).

Ixia stohriae L. Bolus
Plants 15–30 cm high, sometimes with one or two short, spreading branchlets. Leaves linear to narrowly sword-shaped, soft textured. Flowers mostly three to eight per spike, fairly crowded, pink or white flushed pink outside, perianth tube narrowly funnel-shaped to almost cylindrical, 10–16 mm long, tepals spreading, 9–14 mm long, stamens fully included or the anthers exserted. Flowering September–October. Sandstone slopes, 300–800 m, mainly after wildfires, LB (Langeberg Mountains from Tradouw Pass to Heidelberg).

Ixia stolonifera G. J. Lewis
Plants 20–50 cm high, sometimes with a short branchlet; corms with stolons bearing clusters of cormels. Leaves sword-shaped, fairly soft textured. Flowers 6–12 per spike, congested, mauve with a small purple center, perianth tube filiform-cylindrical, 2–4 mm long, tepals spreading, 9–12 mm long, stamens fully exserted; bracts bearing long, setaceous cusps. Flowering September. Sandstone slopes, c. 1000 m, KM (Kiesiesberg, Montagu district).

Ixia stricta (Ecklon ex Klatt) G. J. Lewis
Plants 35–55 cm high, often with one to three short, spreading branchlets. Leaves sword-shaped with rigid, thickened margins, often becoming dry at flowering. Flowers 6–15 per spike, axis fairly lax, flexuous, pale to

Ixia rapunculoides; see also page 25

deep pink, perianth tube filiform, c. 5 mm long, stamens fully exserted, anthers ovoid. Flowering November–December. Lower sandy loam slopes in renosterveld, SW (Caledon to Bredasdorp).

Ixia tenuifolia Ventenat
Plants 15–40 cm high, unbranched. Leaves linear, wiry, 1–2 mm wide. Flowers mostly three to eight per spike, crowded, erect, orange to brick red, with a dark center, perianth tube narrowly funnel-shaped, almost cylindrical, only slightly wider above, 15–20 mm long, tepals spreading, 15–24 mm long, filaments included or shortly exserted. Flowering September–October. Sandy flats, SW (Darling and Kalbaskraal).

Ixia thomasiae Goldblatt
Plants 50–80 cm high, stem with short, nodding branches. Leaves linear with thickened margins and midrib, the margins winged, 3–5 mm wide. Flowers mostly 6–10 per spike, nodding, pink, perianth tube funnel-shaped, 7 mm long, tepals spreading, 20–25 mm long, filaments partly exserted. Flowering September–October. Stony clay flats and slopes, RV (Roggeveld Escarpment).

Ixia trifolia G. J. Lewis
Plants 25–30 cm high, often with one to three short, spreading branchlets. Leaves linear to falcate, the margins prominently thickened. Flowers five to nine per spike, axis lax, deep pink, perianth tube filiform, 3–4 mm long, tepals spreading, 14–20 mm long, stamens fully exserted, anthers oblong. Flowering July–September. Sandstone slopes, RV (Roggeveld Escarpment to Tweedside).

Ixia trinervata (Baker) G. J. Lewis
Plants 20–40 cm high, unbranched. Leaves only two, the upper mostly sheathing, the lower lanceolate, stiff and leathery, with three prominent hyaline veins, often becoming dry at flowering. Flowers 3–12 per spike, often fairly lax, pink to purplish, perianth tube filiform, c. 5 mm long, tepals spreading, 12–15 mm long, stamens fully exserted, anthers oblong, dehiscing from the base. Flowering September–October. Stony clay slopes, SW (Elgin to Riviersonderend).

Ixia scillaris

Ixia tenuifolia, different color forms

Ixia versicolor, different color forms

Ixia viridiflora

Ixia vanzijliae L. Bolus
Plants 18–40 cm high, occasionally with a short erect branch. Leaves sword-shaped, loosely twisted above, the margins undulate. Flowers mostly three to seven per spike, crowded, pinkish with a darker center, perianth tube filiform, 8–10 mm long, tepals spreading, 8–11 mm long, stamens fully exserted. Flowering August–September. Clay flats, LB (Bonnievale).

Ixia versicolor G. J. Lewis
Plants 15–35 cm high, stem unbranched. Leaves linear to sword-shaped, loosely twisted above. Flowers mostly four to seven per spike, axis congested, white or purple with a dark center, perianth tube filiform, 8–12 mm long, tepals spreading, 12–17 mm long, stamens fully exserted, black. Late September–October. Sandy flats, SW (Simondium to Gordon's Bay).

Ixia vinacea G. J. Lewis
Plants 40–45 cm high, stem with a fibrous neck, unbranched. Leaves linear, 2–3 mm wide, longer than the stem. Flowers three to nine per spike, compact, red with a dark center, perianth tube filiform, 4–7 mm long, tepals spreading, 17–20 mm long, stamens fully exserted. Flowering August–September. Stony clay flats, NW (Tulbagh).

Ixia viridiflora Lamarck
Plants 50–100 cm high, sometimes with one or two short erect branchlets. Leaves linear, to 4 mm wide. Flowers 12 to many per spike, fairly lax on an elongate axis, green or turquoise, with a dark purple to blackish center, perianth tube filiform, 6–9 mm long, tepals spreading, 16–25 mm long, stamens fully exserted. Flowering September–October. Rocky clay and granite slopes, NW, SW (Malmesbury Paardeberg and Tulbagh valley).

Kniphofia
COMMON NAME red-hot poker, FAMILY Asphodelaceae. Tufted evergreen or deciduous perennials, solitary or clump-forming, rarely with a well-developed stem. ROOTSTOCK a thick rhizome. LEAVES several, usually spirally arranged, strap-like and usually keeled, the mar-

gin smooth or minutely toothed. INFLORESCENCE a lax or dense raceme, sometimes subspicate; bracts papery. FLOWERS tubular or rarely funnel-shaped, spreading or more usually nodding, the tepals united most of their length, with short free lobes, white, yellow, brownish, or various shades of red, the red pigment often more conspicuous in the buds, giving the raceme a bicolored appearance, unscented. STAMENS inserted below the ovary, the inner longer, sometimes well exserted at first but later withdrawn. OVARY ovoid with numerous ovules per locule; STYLE slender. FRUIT a globose or ovoid capsule. SEEDS several per locule, somewhat flattened and three-angled or winged, black. Basic chromosome number $x = 6$. Sub-Saharan Africa and southern Arabia; c. 70 spp., 5 in the Cape.

In contrast to most genera of the family Asphodelaceae, which have a basic chromosome number $x = 7$, *Kniphofia* has $x = 6$, which is otherwise recorded in some species of *Bulbinella*. *Kniphofia* is distinguished by its channeled, fibrotic leaves, V-shaped in cross section, and it seems to be somewhat isolated in the family. Relationships between the genera of Asphodelaceae are not yet resolved, although the succulent genera centered around *Aloe* are all clearly very closely related.

Most species of *Kniphofia* are adapted for sunbird pollination, although those with rather short-tubed flowers and conspicuously protruding stamens are more likely to be visited by short-beaked nectar-feeding birds or even bees. Some of the orange- or red-flowered species are also visited by the large satyrid butterfly known as the pride of Table Mountain, *Aeropetes tulbaghia*, which is a specialist pollinator of various red-flowered plants in southern Africa.

Species of *Kniphofia* grow mainly at moderate or higher elevations and in moist places. Many are very striking in appearance, ranging from small, slender, mostly solitary plants to robust, almost tussock-forming ones. The drooping, tubular flowers, often colored red, orange, or yellow, resemble those of the *Aloe* and represent similar adaptations to bird pollination. Forms or hybrids of *K. praecox*, *K. linearifolia* Baker, and *K. uvaria* are commonly found in South African gardens, even in drier areas, providing brilliant color through summer and winter.

All species of *Kniphofia* are recommended for cultivation, preferably in the garden where they can establish themselves without disturbance. They require good light and will tolerate waterlogging of the soil. Flowering in the two Cape species that favor sandstone soils, *K. tabularis* and *K. uvaria*, is greatly stimulated in the wild by burning. In the season following a fire, they will send up their inflorescences in a mass, painting the blackened landscape with swaths of color. The long-lived inflorescences of all species are ideal for the vase.

FURTHER READING. The South African species of *Kniphofia* were revised by Codd (1968) in a well-illustrated monograph.

Kniphofia citrina Baker

Plants 40–65 cm high, forming clumps. Leaves strap-shaped, coarsely fibrous, keeled, margins finely serrate or

Kniphofia citrina

Kniphofia praecox

Kniphofia sarmentosa; see also page 12

Kniphofia tabularis

Kniphofia uvaria

smooth. Flowers in globose racemes 4–5 × 5–5.5 cm on pedicels 1.5–2.5 mm long, yellow, 22–27 mm long, anthers exserted 4–6 mm; bracts ovate-oblong, 4.5–5 mm long. Flowering March–May. Grassland, SE (Humansdorp to Grahamstown).

Kniphofia praecox Baker

Plants 1.5–2 m high, forming clumps. Leaves strap-shaped, keeled, margins finely serrate. Flowers in cylindrical racemes 12–30 × 6–7 cm on pedicels 4–5(–8) mm long, reddish in bud, opening yellow to yellow-green, 25–35 mm long, anthers exserted 4–15 mm; bracts linear-lanceolate, 8–12 mm long. Flowering November–January. Streambanks and wet hollows, SE (George to Komga).

Kniphofia sarmentosa (Andrews) Kunth

Plants to 1 m high. Leaves grayish, strap-shaped, keeled, margins smooth. Flowers in ovoid to cylindrical racemes 8–30 × 5–6.5 cm on pedicels 1–3 mm long, reddish in bud, opening buff, anthers exserted 2–5 mm at flowering but later withdrawn; bracts lanceolate, 11–15 mm long. Flowering June–October. Mountain streams and moist hollows, RV, NW, KM (western Karoo to Hex River Mountains).

Kniphofia tabularis Marloth

Plants 60–120 cm high, often drooping from cliffs. Leaves strap-shaped, bright green, somewhat succulent, keeled, margins smooth. Flowers in laxly cylindrical racemes 10–5 × 5.5–7 cm on pedicels 5–7 mm long, dull orange, buds with blackish tips, anthers not or slightly exserted; bracts linear-lanceolate, 7–11 mm long. Flowering December–January. Wet, mossy, sandstone cliffs, NW, SW (Tulbagh to Kogelberg and Cape Peninsula).

Kniphofia uvaria (Linnaeus) Oken

Plants 50–120 cm, in small clumps. Leaves strap-shaped, fibrous, keeled, margins smooth or sparsely serrate. Flowers in oblong to globose racemes 4.5–11 × 6 cm on pedicels (1.5–)3–5 mm long, orange to greenish yellow, anthers not or slightly exserted at flowering but later withdrawn; bracts ovate, 3–9 mm long. Flowering mostly October–December. Seeps, marshes, and streams on sandstone slopes, NW, SW, KM, LB, SE (Namaqualand to Barkly East).

Lachenalia

COMMON NAME Cape cowslip, FAMILY Hyacinthaceae. Deciduous perennials. ROOTSTOCK a pear-shaped, globose, or flattened bulb, often forming bulblets at the base, usually with pale membranous outer tunics, sometimes the outer tunics papery and dark brown or black and then often forming a fibrous neck around the base of the stem. LEAVES one to several, usually two, surrounded by a membranous cataphyll extending above the bulb, terete or linear to lanceolate or heart-shaped, suberect or prostrate, smooth or pustulate, rarely with simple or star-shaped hairs, sometimes spotted or banded, especially on the sheath. INFLORESCENCE a few- to many-flowered raceme or spike, sometimes condensed, the upper flowers often vestigial, the peduncle sometimes swollen and club-shaped, sometimes spotted or marked; bracts small, membranous. FLOWERS more or less weakly zygomorphic with the lower inner tepal larger, suberect or more or less nodding, bell-shaped to tubular cylindrical or urn-shaped, variously colored, often scented, the tepals spreading or suberect, shortly united below into an oblique cup or tube, the inner usually longer than the outer, which are often swollen at the tips. STAMENS usually more or less declinate, filaments filiform or somewhat swollen above, joined to the base of the tepals, inserted obliquely or more or less in two series at different levels, included or exserted, sometimes unequal. OVARY subglobose with several ovules per locule; STYLE slender, longer than the ovary. FRUIT an ovoid, three-angled or three-winged capsule, membranous or papery. SEEDS several per locule, subglobose to pear-shaped, glossy black. Basic chromosome numbers x = 5–15. Namibia and South Africa; c. 110 spp., 80 in the Cape.

Essentially plants of the winter-rainfall region of southern Africa, the vast majority of species of *Lachenalia* occur in southern Namaqualand and the Western Cape. The genus is closely related to the other winter-rainfall genera that produce glossy, subglobose or pear-shaped seeds, particularly *Polyxena*. Most species favor open habitats, sometimes on rock sheets, and can occur in dense stands numbering hundreds or thousands of plants. The variability of many of the species can make accurate identification difficult. The species are extremely variable in flower form and foliage, the latter often attractively mottled or banded. Almost all the species are pollinated by bees of the family Apidae (Anthophorinae). The exceptions are the species with large, tubular flowers, which are pollinated by sunbirds; these include *L. aloides, L. bulbifera, L. reflexa, L. rubida,* and *L. viridiflora*.

Easy to grow and often very attractive, the majority of species of *Lachenalia* are well worth cultivating, particularly those with large, brightly colored or heavily scented flowers. Their small stature, combined with their variously colored flowers, make them ideal pot subjects, although massed plantings of some of the species will ensure a brilliant display in rock gardens or containers. The large, nodding-flowered species *L. aloides* and *L. bulbifera* are particularly effective. The range of flower shapes and colors in the genus, combined with often interesting foliage, make *Lachenalia* a treasure trove for bulb enthusiasts. A particular gem is the early-flowering *L. viridiflora* with large, startlingly colored sea green or turquoise flowers. Now restricted in the wild to a single population, it is fortunately easily grown. Another very attractive species almost extinct in the wild is *L. mathewsii,* which produces clusters of bright yellow flowers tipped with green. It multiplies rapidly by division and is delightful for containers. A particularly effective mixed planting at Kirstenbosch botanical garden featured this species combined with pink-flowered *Gladiolus carneus* or *Onixotis triquetra*. Perhaps the most striking of the species with patterned foliage, *L. zebrina* produces an elegant, arched leaf, boldly banded with gray and maroon. Unfortunately, this species, like *L. nervosa,* is reluctant to sprout every season. Fragrance is an attractive feature of many Cape bulbs, including *Lachenalia*. Both *L. peersii* and *L. nervosa* produce a strong, spicy, carnation-like scent redolent of cloves, whereas *L. congesta, L. fistulosa,* and *L. orchioides* are sweetly scented, *L. fistulosa* almost unbearably so.

Propagation is best from seed, and species will flower in their second or third season. Several of the species produce bulblets at the base of the bulb or even on the leaves whereas some of the broad-leaved species can be propagated from leaf cuttings. Species of *Lachenalia* should be grown in a well-drained medium, reducing the loam content substantially or even entirely if necessary. Water sparingly and only when the soil is dry. The bulbs are particularly susceptible to infestations by mealybugs and *Fusarium*. Like most Cape bulbs, *Lachenalia* must be grown at moderate temperatures of 12–17°C (54–62°F). Plants grown at higher temperatures produce large, weak leaves, do not flower, and enter dormancy earlier. The early-flowering species should be potted somewhat earlier than usual for Cape bulbs, in August or September rather than October in the Northern Hemisphere.

FURTHER READING. No complete revision of *Lachenalia* exists although the well-illustrated handbook by Duncan (1988) covers the majority of species and provides extensive cultivation notes. Since then, several further species have been described (Barker 1989, Duncan 1993, 1996, 1998b). Various species have also been illustrated separately with accompanying cultivation notes (Duncan 2001, Duncan and Anderson 1997, 1999, Duncan and Linder Smith 1999a, b).

Lachenalia alba W. F. Barker ex G. D. Duncan
Plants 10–33 cm high. Leaves two, lanceolate. Flowers on short to long pedicels, narrowly bell-shaped, white, perianth 9–11 mm long, anthers shortly exserted. Flowering August–October. Clay flats in renosterveld, RV (Nieuwoudtville to Calvinia).

Lachenalia algoensis Schönland
Plants 6–30 cm high. Leaves one or two, linear, lanceolate, or strap-shaped. Flowers shortly pedicellate, erect, yellow to greenish yellow, fading to dull red, perianth 20–28 mm long, anthers included. Flowering July–August. Coastal grassland, SE (Knysna to Eastern Cape).

Lachenalia aloides (Linnaeus fil.) Engler
Plants 5–31 cm high. Leaves one or two, lanceolate or strap-shaped, plain or densely spotted with green or purple. Flowers on long pedicels, nodding, cylindrical, in combinations of orange, red, yellow, or greenish blue, with

greenish markings, perianth 20–35 mm long, anthers included. Flowering May–October. Granite and sandstone outcrops, NW, SW (Lambert's Bay to Bredasdorp).

Lachenalia ameliae W. F. Barker

Plants 4–11 cm high. Leaves one or two, broadly lanceolate, smooth or hairy. Flowers sessile, urn-shaped to bell-shaped, greenish yellow with or without purple tips, perianth 9 mm long, anthers included. Flowering August–September. Clay flats, RV, NW, KM (Ceres to Montagu and Touws River).

Lachenalia anguinea Sweet

Plants 10–35 cm high. Leaf single, narrowly lanceolate, banded green and maroon. Flowers on long pedicels, bell-shaped, cream with green markings, perianth 6–8 mm long, anthers well exserted. Flowering July–September. Deep coastal sands, NW (Richtersveld to Klawer).

Lachenalia arbuthnotiae W. F. Barker

Plants 18–40 cm high. Leaves one or two, lanceolate, plain or densely spotted. Flowers sessile, shortly cylindrical, yellow with pale green markings, perianth 9–13 mm long, anthers included. Flowering August–October. Marshy flats, SW (Cape Flats).

Lachenalia attenuata W. F. Barker ex G. D. Duncan

Plants 7–22 cm high. Leaf single, linear, suberect, lower surface banded with dark green and magenta. Flowers on long white pedicels, spreading or slightly nodding, tubular, pale blue and greenish yellow, perianth 6–7 mm long, anthers included. Flowering August–September. Loamy clay slopes, RV, KM, LB (Roggeveld and Little Karoo to Riversdale).

Lachenalia aurioliae G. D. Duncan

Plants 6–38 cm high. Leaves one or two, suberect, lanceolate to ovate-lanceolate, upper surface usually unmarked. Flowers sessile or subsessile, urn-shaped, cream or yellowish green to brownish blue, perianth 8–10 mm long, anthers included or scarcely exserted. Flowering July–August. Stony and sandy slopes, KM, SE (southern Karoo and Montagu to Kammanassie Mountains).

Lachenalia bachmannii Baker

Plants 15–30 cm high. Leaves two, linear. Flowers shortly pedicellate, bell-shaped, white with brownish markings, perianth 7–9 mm long, anthers included. Flowering August–September. Edges of seasonal pools, SW (Piketberg to Stellenbosch). Page 254.

Lachenalia barkeriana U. Müller-Doblies, B. Nordenstam & D. Müller-Doblies

Plants stemless, 1.5–2 cm high. Leaves 3–10(–30), suberect, linear-canaliculate, dark green. Flowers congested at ground level, subsessile, cylindrical, white, heavily scented, perianth c. 9 mm long, anthers exserted. Flowering May–July. Sandy flats and slopes, RV (Knersvlakte to Loeriesfontein).

Lachenalia aloides

Lachenalia bachmannii

Lachenalia bulbifera

Lachenalia bolusii W. F. Barker
Plants 10–35 cm high. Leaf single, ovate-lanceolate or strap-shaped, banded maroon below. Flowers on long pedicels, bell-shaped, nodding, pale blue and white with brownish markings, perianth 7–9 mm long, anthers included. Flowering August–September. Rocky outcrops, NW (Richtersveld to Clanwilliam).

Lachenalia bowkeri Baker
Plants 10–26 cm high. Leaves one or two, lanceolate. Flowers shortly pedicellate, narrowly bell-shaped, pale blue and white with purple markings, perianth 9–11 mm long, anthers included. Flowering August. Sandy soil, LB, SE (Riversdale to Riebeek East).

Lachenalia bulbifera (Cirillo) Engler
Plants 8–30 cm high. Leaves one or two, lanceolate, strap-shaped, or ovate, plain or blotched. Flowers on fairly long pedicels, cylindrical, nodding, orange to red with darker red or brown markings and green tips, perianth 20–35 mm long, anthers included. Flowering April–September. Sandy slopes and flats, mainly coastal, NW, SW, AP (Klawer to Mossel Bay).

Lachenalia capensis W. F. Barker
Plants 15–25 cm high. Leaves one or two, lanceolate or strap-shaped, with or without brown blotches. Flowers sessile or shortly pedicellate, shortly cylindrical, white or cream, perianth 15–17 mm long, anthers included. Flowering September–October. Sandstone slopes, SW (Cape Peninsula).

Lachenalia comptonii W. F. Barker
Plants 5–20 cm high. Leaf single, spreading, lanceolate, flushed maroon beneath, upper surface and margins pilose with long and short hairs. Flowers shortly pedicellate, widely bell-shaped, white with green marks at the tips, strongly scented, perianth 5–6 mm long, anthers exserted on dark mauve filaments. Flowering September–October. Sandy flats, RV, KM (Roggeveld Escarpment and Little Karoo).

Lachenalia congesta W. F. Barker
Plants 6–14 cm high. Leaves two, ovate, leathery, with thickened margins, maroon beneath. Flowers sessile, crowded, narrowly bell-shaped with tips recurved, pale yellow, strongly sweetly scented, perianth 10–12 mm long, anthers included. Flowering June–August. Stony flats, RV (Calvinia to Komsberg Pass).

Lachenalia contaminata Aiton
Plants 6–25 cm high. Leaves several, subterete, erect. Flowers shortly pedicellate, bell-shaped, white with brown or reddish markings, perianth 5–9 mm long, anthers included or exserted. Flowering August–October. Wet places, often common, NW, SW, AP (Citrusdal to Bredasdorp).

Lachenalia dehoopensis W. F. Barker
Plants 8–16 cm high. Leaves two, linear, banded with green and maroon. Flowers shortly pedicellate, narrowly bell-shaped, pale blue and cream with reddish markings, perianth 8–9 mm long, anthers included. Flowering August–September. Sandy flats, AP (De Hoop, Bredasdorp).

Lachenalia doleritica G. D. Duncan
Plants 12–18 cm high. Leaves two, ovate, spreading with the tips recurved and touching the ground. Flowers shortly pedicellate, narrowly bell-shaped, yellowish green with darker marks at the tips, perianth 9–11 mm long, anthers included. Flowering September–October. Dolerite flats, RV (Calvinia).

Lachenalia elegans W. F. Barker
Plants 10–30 cm high. Leaves one or two, lanceolate to ovate-lanceolate, with or without green or maroon spots. Flowers sessile, urn-shaped, in shades of yellow, blue, mauve, or purple, with white tips, perianth 6–10 mm long, anthers included. Flowering July–October. Sandy, mostly moist slopes, often in large colonies, RV, NW (Bokkeveld Mountains and western Karoo to Clanwilliam).

Lachenalia fistulosa Baker
Plants 8–30 cm high. Leaves two, strap-shaped, plain or spotted with brown. Flowers sessile, narrowly bell-shaped, cream, yellow, blue, lilac, or violet, with pale brown markings, heavily scented, perianth 8–10 mm long, anthers included. Flowering September–October. Rocky mountain slopes, NW, SW (Piketberg to Caledon).

Lachenalia gillettii W. F. Barker
Plants 12–22 cm high. Leaves two, strap-shaped. Flowers shortly pedicellate, narrowly bell-shaped, white and lilac with green markings, perianth 6–8 mm long, anthers exserted. Flowering August–September. Clay soils, often in large colonies, NW (Piketberg to Citrusdal).

Lachenalia haarlemensis Fourcade
Plants 12–22 cm high. Leaves one or two, linear-lanceolate, erect, banded with maroon at base. Flowers shortly pedicellate, bell-shaped, greenish gray, perianth 5–7 mm long, anthers exserted and mauve. Flowering September–October. Mainly stony clay slopes, SE (Kammanassie Mountains to Long Kloof).

Lachenalia hirta (Thunberg) Thunberg
Plants 10–30 cm high. Leaf single, linear, with stiff hairs on margins and beneath, banded with maroon. Flowers on long pedicels, narrowly bell-shaped, blue to blue-gray with brown markings and pale yellow tips, perianth 8–9 mm long, anthers usually included, sometimes exserted. Flowering August–September. Often in sandy soil in large colonies, NW, SW (Namaqualand to Malmesbury).

Lachenalia isopetala Jacquin
Plants 10–30 cm high, the leaf bases persisting as a straw-like neck. Leaves two, lanceolate, withering at flowering. Flowers numerous, shortly pedicellate, suberect, narrowly cylindrical, brownish to maroon, perianth 10–12 mm long, anthers scarcely exserted. Flowering October–November. Dolerite flats, NW, RV (Nieuwoudtville and Calvinia to Roggeveld Escarpment). Page 256.

Lachenalia juncifolia Baker
Plants 7–40 cm high. Leaves two, linear, filiform, terete or subterete, with maroon bands. Flowers on long pedicels, narrowly bell-shaped, white or pink, tinged darker pink or blue, with purple or green markings, perianth

5–7 mm long, anthers exserted. Flowering August–November. Often in sand in large colonies, NW, SW, AP (Cedarberg Mountains to Stilbaai).

Lachenalia karooica W. F. Barker ex G. D. Duncan
Plants 4–22 cm high. Leaves one or two, lanceolate, with blotches on upper surface. Flowers sessile or shortly pedicellate, narrowly bell-shaped, greenish white and pale blue with maroon or brown markings, perianth 7–10 mm long, anthers exserted. Flowering June–September. Rocky outcrops, NW (Worcester district and Great Karoo to western Free State).

Lachenalia lactosa G. D. Duncan
Plants 10–25 cm high. Leaves one or two, oblong, maroon beneath. Flowers pedicellate, urn-shaped, bluish or greenish white, perianth 6–8 mm long, anthers shortly exserted, peduncle heavily blotched. Flowering September–October. Sandy coastal flats, SW (Bot River to Elim).

Lachenalia latimerae W. F. Barker
Plants 15–28 cm high. Leaves one or two, linear-lanceolate. Flowers on long pedicels, bell-shaped, pale pink with greenish brown markings, perianth 5–7 mm long, anthers exserted. Flowering July–August. Sand, in large colonies, KM, SE (Swartberg and Kouga Mountains).

Lachenalia leipoldtii G. D. Duncan
Plants 10–28 cm high; peduncle sometimes inflated. Leaf single, lanceolate, spotted. Flowers subsessile, bell-shaped, cream to greenish yellow, perianth 7–9 mm long, anthers well exserted. Flowering August–September. Sandstone slopes, NW, KM (Biedouw to Waboomsberg).

Lachenalia leomontana W. F. Barker
Plants 10–30 cm high. Leaf single, lanceolate or strap-shaped, plain or with purple spots on upper surface. Flowers on long pedicels, tubular to bell-shaped, white with pale green markings, perianth 7–8 mm long, anthers included. Flowering October–November. Sandstone slopes, LB (Langeberg Mountains in the Swellendam district).

Lachenalia liliiflora Jacquin
Plants 10–20 cm high. Leaves two, lanceolate, usually densely pustulate on upper surface. Flowers shortly pedicellate, narrowly bell-shaped, white with brownish markings and dark magenta tips, perianth 15–20 mm long, anthers included. Flowering September–October. Hilly slopes in renosterveld, SW (Tygerberg to Paarl).

Lachenalia longibracteata E. Phillips
Plants 7–35 cm high. Leaves one or two, lanceolate, leathery, plain or spotted. Flowers sessile or shortly pedicellate, narrowly bell-shaped, each flower with a long bract at the base, pale blue or yellow with a blue base, with brown or green markings, perianth 10–14 mm long, anthers included. Flowering July–September. Clay flats and slopes, NW, SW (Piketberg to Malmesbury).

Lachenalia isopetala

Lachenalia macgregoriorum W. F. Barker
Plants 16–36 cm high. Leaves two, narrowly lanceolate, suberect, lower surface mottled dark maroon toward the base, withering at flowering. Flowers pedicellate, widely bell-shaped, maroon, perianth 6–8 mm long, anthers exserted. Flowering October–November. Heavy clay flats, RV (Bokkeveld Plateau).

Lachenalia margaretae W. F. Barker
Plants 3–12 cm high. Leaves one or two, strap-shaped, sometimes spotted. Flowers shortly pedicellate, bell-shaped, white with large brown or green markings, perianth c. 5 mm long, anthers very shortly exserted. Flowering October–December. Rock ledges in partial shade, NW (Cedarberg Mountains).

Lachenalia marginata W. F. Barker
Plants 11–30 cm high. Leaf single, ovate to lanceolate, glaucous, marked brown or green, margins thickened. Flowers sessile, shortly cylindrical, greenish yellow with large, dark brown markings, perianth 15–20 mm long, anthers included. Flowering July–August. Sandy flats or slopes, NW (Bokkeveld Mountains to Clanwilliam).

Lachenalia marginata

Lachenalia marlothii W. F. Barker ex G. D. Duncan
Plants 9–16 cm high. Leaf single, suberect or spreading, ovate to broadly lanceolate, leathery, banded with green and magenta beneath. Flowers sessile or subsessile, narrowly urn-shaped with purple markings, heavily scented, perianth 8–12 mm long, anthers included. Flowering July–September. Clay slopes, RV (Roggeveld Escarpment).

Lachenalia martinae W. F. Barker
Plants 10–25 cm high. Leaf single, ovate-lanceolate with maroon bands on clasping base, margins undulate. Flowers shortly pedicellate, narrowly bell-shaped, dull white and gray with greenish brown markings, perianth 10–12 mm long, anthers included. Flowering July–August. Sandstone outcrops, NW (Olifants River Valley and Mountains).

Lachenalia martinae

Lachenalia mathewsii W. F. Barker
Plants 10–20 cm high. Leaves two, narrowly lanceolate tapering to a long, terete apex. Flowers shortly pedicellate, yellow with green markings, perianth 9–10 mm long, anthers exserted. Flowering September. Moist lower slopes, SW (Vredenburg).

Lachenalia maximiliani Schlechter ex W. F. Barker
Plants 10–20 cm high. Leaf single, lanceolate. Flowers shortly pedicellate, narrowly bell-shaped, pale blue and white with magenta tips, perianth c. 8 mm long, anthers included. Flowering July–August. Sandy slopes, often in large colonies, NW (Cedarberg Mountains).

Lachenalia mediana Jacquin
Plants 20–40 cm high. Leaves one or two, lanceolate. Flowers shortly pedicellate, narrowly bell-shaped, pale blue and white, or in shades of pinkish blue, with green or purplish markings, perianth 9–10 mm long, anthers included. Flowering August–September. Clay soil, often in large colonies, NW, SW (Porterville to Cape Peninsula and Caledon).

Lachenalia moniliformis W. F. Barker
Plants 12–17 cm high, producing bulblets on long stolons. Leaves several, terete with circular, raised, fleshy bands along upper two-thirds. Flowers on long pedicels, pale blue and pink with reddish brown markings, perianth 5–7 m long, anthers well exserted. Flowering September. Sandy flats, NW (Worcester district).

Lachenalia montana Schlechter ex W. F. Barker
Plants 10–33 cm high. Leaves two, linear, the margins folded together. Flowers on long magenta pedicels, bell-shaped, nodding, cream or pink with large, brownish green markings, perianth 8–9 mm long, anthers exserted. Flowering October–December, only after fire. Sandy mountain slopes, SW (Franschhoek to Hermanus).

Lachenalia muirii W. F. Barker
Plants 10–25 cm high. Leaves one or two, linear, withered at flowering time. Flowers sessile, urn-shaped to shortly cylindrical, pale blue and white with brown or maroon markings, perianth 10–12 mm long, anthers included. Flowering October–December. Limestone hills and flats, AP (Bredasdorp to Stilbaai).

Lachenalia multifolia W. F. Barker
Plants 7–20 cm high. Leaves 8–10, erect or suberect, terete, glaucous. Flowers congested, pedicellate, suberect, widely bell-shaped, white, heavily scented, perianth 5–6 mm long, anthers exserted. Flowering September–October. Rocky slopes in crevices, RV (Tanqua Karoo and Roggeveld).

Lachenalia mutabilis Sweet
Plants 10–45 cm high. Leaf single, lanceolate, erect, with crisped margins. Flowers narrowly urn-shaped, pale blue and white with yellow tips, or yellowish green, with brown markings, perianth 8–10 mm long, anthers included. Flowering July–September. Sandy and stony slopes, NW, SW (Namaqualand to Langebaan, Worcester, and Riviersonderend).

Lachenalia neilii W. F. Barker ex G. D. Duncan
Plants 12–32 cm high, producing numerous bulblets at the base. Leaves two, lanceolate. Flowers pedicellate, narrowly bell-shaped, greenish white, perianth 8–10 mm long, anthers shortly exserted. Flowering August–October. Dolerite flats, RV (Nieuwoudtville to Calvinia).

Lachenalia nervosa Ker Gawler
Plants 15–30 cm high. Leaves two, ovate, prostrate, sometimes with pustules on upper surface. Flowers shortly pedicellate, bell-shaped, white with reddish pink markings, perianth 6–8 mm long, anthers exserted. Flowering September–November. Coastal grassland, AP, LB, SE (Swellendam to George).

Lachenalia obscura Schlechter ex G. D. Duncan
Plants 6–38 cm high. Leaves one or two, suberect, lanceolate to ovate, upper surface usually unmarked, heavily banded with green beneath, becoming magenta toward the base. Flowers sessile or subsessile, narrowly bell-shaped, cream or yellowish green to brownish blue, sometimes with magenta tips, perianth 8–12 mm long,

anthers included or scarcely exserted. Flowering June–October. Stony karroid flats, RV, NW, KM (Namaqualand and western Karoo to Little Karoo).

Lachenalia orchioides (Linnaeus) Aiton
Plants 10–40 cm high. Leaves one or two, lanceolate or strap-shaped, plain or densely spotted. Flowers suberect, sessile, shortly cylindrical, greenish yellow or pale to dark blue, perianth 15–20 mm long, anthers included. Flowering August–October. In heavy soil, often in partial shade, in large colonies, NW, SW, AP, KM (Gifberg to Albertinia and Little Karoo).

Lachenalia orthopetala Jacquin
Plants 9–27 cm high. Leaves several, grass-like, sometimes with brown spots. Flowers shortly pedicellate, narrowly bell-shaped, facing upward, white with maroon markings, perianth 12–15 mm long, anthers included. Flowering September–October. Clay soils in large colonies, NW, SW (Piketberg to Durbanville).

Lachenalia pallida Aiton
Plants 12–30 cm high. Leaves one or two, lanceolate, sometimes with pustules above. Flowers shortly pedicellate, narrowly bell-shaped, cream to dark yellow with brown or green markings, perianth 8–10 mm long, anthers included. Flowering August–October. Clay flats in large colonies, NW, SW (Piketberg to Stellenbosch).

Lachenalia peersii Marloth ex W. F. Barker
Plants 15–30 cm high. Leaves one or two, strap-shaped, green or purplish. Flowers on fairly long pedicels, urn-shaped, cream or white with greenish brown markings, strongly carnation scented, perianth c. 8 mm long, anthers included. Flowering October–November. Often in partial shade, sandy soil, SW (Cape Hangklip to Hermanus).

Lachenalia perryae G. D. Duncan
Plants 12–32 cm high. Leaf single, narrowly lanceolate, banded beneath with green, shading to maroon on the sheath. Flowers shortly pedicellate, pale blue and white with green or brown markings, perianth 7–9 mm long,

Lachenalia mutabilis

Lachenalia pallida

anthers included. Flowering July–September. Clay or sandy soil among succulents, NW, SW, LB (Worcester to Albertinia, Eastern Cape?).

Lachenalia physocaulos W. F. Barker

Plants 13–30 cm high; peduncle heavily spotted, swollen. Leaf single, linear, widening abruptly into a white, clasping base. Flowers shortly pedicellate, bell-shaped, pale magenta with brownish green markings, perianth 6–8 mm long, anthers exserted. Flowering August–September. Sandy flats and slopes, NW, LB (Robertson to Swellendam).

Lachenalia polyphylla Baker

Plants 6–18 cm high. Leaves five to nine, erect, terete. Flowers on long pedicels, narrowly bell-shaped, pale blue and pink with brownish markings, perianth 5–6 mm long, anthers exserted. Flowering September–October. Gravel flats, NW (Piketberg to Tulbagh).

Lachenalia pusilla

Lachenalia purpureocaerulea Jacquin

Plants 10–28 cm high. Leaves two, lanceolate or strap-shaped, densely pustulate. Flowers bell-shaped, white and purplish blue with greenish brown markings, perianth 6–8 mm long, anthers exserted. Flowering October–November. Gravel flats, SW (Darling and Mamre).

Lachenalia pusilla Jacquin

Plants stemless, 1–4 cm high. Leaves in a rosette, prostrate, linear to lanceolate, plain or spotted. Flowers subsessile, cylindrical, erect, borne at ground level in a congested raceme, white, heavily scented, perianth 8–10 mm long, anthers exserted. Flowering April–June. Common on sandy flats and slopes, NW, SW, AP, LB (Bokkeveld Mountains to Swellendam).

Lachenalia pustulata Jacquin

Plants 15–35 cm high. Leaves one or two, lanceolate or strap-shaped, smooth or densely pustulate. Flowers on long pedicels, narrowly bell-shaped, shades of cream, blue, or pink with green or brownish markings, perianth 7–9 mm long, anthers shortly or well exserted. Flowering August–October. Often in large colonies in heavy soil, SW (St. Helena Bay to Cape Peninsula).

Lachenalia reflexa Thunberg

Plants 3–19 cm high. Leaves one or two, lanceolate or strap-shaped, plain or densely spotted on upper surface. Flowers shortly pedicellate, erect, cylindrical to narrowly urn-shaped, bright yellow, perianth 20–25 mm long, anthers included. Flowering June–August. Wet sandy flats in large colonies, SW (Malmesbury to Cape Peninsula and Franschhoek).

Lachenalia rosea Andrews

Plants 8–30 cm high. Leaves one or two, lanceolate, plain or blotched with maroon or brown. Flowers shortly pedicellate, narrowly bell-shaped, pink or combinations of pink and blue, with darker pink markings, perianth 9–11 mm long, anthers included. Flowering August–December. Mainly coastal, on moist flats, SW, AP, KM, LB, SE (Cape Peninsula to Knysna, Montagu, and Ladismith).

Lachenalia rubida Jacquin

Plants 6–25 cm high. Leaves one or two, lanceolate or strap-shaped, plain green or spotted with darker green or purple. Flowers shortly pedicellate, nodding, cylindrical, plain or densely spotted with pink or red, perianth 20–32 mm long, anthers included. Flowering March–July. Sandy flats and slopes, NW, SW, AP, SE (Hondeklip Bay to Cape Peninsula to George).

Lachenalia salteri W. F. Barker

Plants 15–35 cm high. Leaves two, lanceolate, leathery, plain or with large brown blotches. Flowers shortly pedicellate, narrowly bell-shaped, cream, reddish purple, or a combination of pale blue and pink, perianth 9–11 mm long, anthers exserted. Flowering October–December. Marshy areas around seasonal pools, SW, AP (Cape Peninsula to Bredasdorp).

Lachenalia sargeantii W. F. Barker

Plants 20–30 cm high. Leaves two, linear-lanceolate. Flowers on long pedicels, nodding, cream or pale green with green or brown markings, perianth 20–25 mm long, anthers included. Flowering November, only after fire. Sandstone slopes, SW (Bredasdorp Mountains).

Lachenalia schelpei W. F. Barker

Plants 10–25 cm high. Leaves two, lanceolate, upper and lower surfaces with dark green blotches, sheath banded with maroon. Flowers subsessile, narrowly urn-shaped, white with greenish brown marks at the tips, scented, perianth 9–11 mm long, anthers spreading, shortly exserted; bracts conspicuous. Flowering June–July. Dolerite flats, RV (Hantamsberg near Calvinia).

Lachenalia splendida Diels

Plants 6–25 cm high; peduncle swollen just below base of inflorescence. Leaves two, lanceolate. Flowers sessile, narrowly bell-shaped, pale blue and bright lilac with greenish brown markings, perianth 9–11 mm long, anthers exserted. Flowering July–August. Usually on quartzite flats, NW (Garies to Klawer).

Lachenalia pustulata

Lachenalia reflexa

Lachenalia stayneri W. F. Barker
Plants 12–30 cm high. Leaves two, lanceolate or strap-shaped, prostrate, with large pustules on upper surface. Flowers on long pedicels, bell-shaped, pale blue and cream with reddish markings, perianth 5–7 mm long, anthers exserted. Flowering August–September. Karroid flats, NW (Worcester to Robertson).

Lachenalia thomasiae W. F. Barker ex G. D. Duncan
Plants 12–38 cm high. Leaves two, lanceolate or strap-shaped, yellowish green. Flowers on long pedicels, narrowly bell-shaped, white with green or brown markings, perianth 5–7 mm long, anthers well exserted. Flowering September–October. Rocky sandstone slopes, NW (Clanwilliam district).

Lachenalia trichophylla Baker
Plants 8–20 cm high. Leaf single, heart-shaped, prostrate with stellate hairs on upper surface and margin. Flowers sessile or with short to long pedicels, shortly cylindrical, shades of yellow, or yellow flushed with pink, with green markings, perianth 15–20 mm long, anthers included. Flowering August–September. Sandy slopes, NW (Namaqualand to Citrusdal).

Lachenalia trichophylla

Lachenalia undulata Masson ex Baker
Plants 10–30 cm high. Leaves one or two, lanceolate to ovate-lanceolate, spreading or suberect, plain or spotted with brownish purple, the margin sometimes undulate or crisped. Flowers sessile, narrowly urn-shaped, greenish white, perianth 10–11 mm long, anthers included. Flowering May–June. Clay flats and lower slopes, NW (Namaqualand to Klawer).

Lachenalia unicolor Jacquin
Plants 8–30 cm high. Leaves two, lanceolate or strap-shaped, densely pustulate on upper surface. Flowers on long pedicels, cream, lilac, pink, magenta, blue, or purple, with green or purplish markings, perianth 7–10 mm long, anthers exserted. Flowering September–October. Heavy soil in large colonies, NW, SW (Bokkeveld Mountains to Somerset West).

Lachenalia unifolia Jacquin
Plants 10–35 cm high. Leaf single, linear, banded with green and maroon. Flowers variable, on short or long pedicels, narrowly bell-shaped, blue, pink, or pale yellow, with white tips, perianth 8–15 mm long, anthers included. Flowering August–October. Sandy granitic or sandstone soils, NW, SW, AP (Namaqualand to Bredasdorp).

Lachenalia variegata W. F. Barker
Plants 10–40 cm high. Leaf single, lanceolate or strap-shaped, margins thickened, undulate. Flowers shortly pedicellate, narrowly bell-shaped, greenish gray with darker green, blue, purple, or brown markings and white tips, perianth 8–10 mm long, anthers included. Flowering August–October. Mainly coastal, in deep sand, NW, SW (Clanwilliam to Cape Peninsula).

Lachenalia ventricosa Schlechter ex W. F. Barker
Plants 20–48 cm high. Leaf single, lanceolate to strap-shaped, margins undulate. Flowers sessile, narrowly urn-shaped, pale yellow with white tips, perianth 8–13 mm long, anthers exserted. Flowering August–September. Usually in sand in large colonies, NW (Nardouw and Pakhuis Mountains).

Lachenalia violacea Jacquin
Plants 10–35 cm high. Leaves one or two, lanceolate, plain or heavily spotted. Flowers on long pedicels, bell-shaped, bluish green at base with magenta or purple tips, perianth 5–6 mm long, anthers mauve, magenta, or white, exserted. Flowering July–September. Habitat variable, usually in rocky places, NW (Namaqualand to Clanwilliam).

Lachenalia viridiflora W. F. Barker
Plants 8–20 cm high. Leaves two, lanceolate, plain or spotted. Flowers shortly pedicellate, elongate, urn-shaped, turquoise, perianth 17–25 mm long, anthers included. Flowering May–July. Granite outcrops, SW (St. Helena Bay).

Lachenalia whitehillensis W. F. Barker
Plants 15–36 cm high. Leaf single, narrowly lanceolate, heavily banded with maroon beneath. Flowers pedicellate, nodding, bell-shaped, pale blue and white with

Lachenalia violacea

Lachenalia unifolia

Lachenalia viridiflora

brown marks at the tips, scented, perianth 5–6 mm long, anthers exserted. Flowering September. Sandy flats, RV (Sutherland and Matjiesfontein).

Lachenalia youngii Baker
Plants 7–30 cm high. Leaves two, narrowly lanceolate. Flowers on fairly long pedicels, bell-shaped, pale blue and pink with darker purplish pink markings, perianth 6–7 mm long, anthers included. Flowering July–November. Coastal areas, SE (Mossel Bay to Humansdorp).

Lachenalia zebrina W. F. Barker
Plants 10–30 cm high. Leaf single, lanceolate, arching, channeled or margins folded together, glaucous, banded with maroon beneath. Flowers on long pedicels, nodding, narrowly urn-shaped, cream, tinged green or brown, perianth 5–7 mm long, anthers well exserted. Flowering August–October. Stony clay flats, RV (western Karoo).

Lachenalia zeyheri Baker
Plants 6–20 cm high. Leaves one or two, subterete. Flowers shortly pedicellate, bell-shaped, white with reddish brown or green markings, perianth c. 5 mm long, anthers included. Flowering September–October. Marshes and seeps, NW (Elandskloof to Ceres).

Lanaria

COMMON NAME kapok lily, FAMILY Lanariaceae. Evergreen perennial. ROOTSTOCK a short rhizome covered with hard fibers; roots rough, hard. LEAVES several, channeled and keeled, linear, stiff and fibrotic, finely serrated, clasping, the inner leaves thickly hairy basally. INFLORESCENCE a rounded paniculate thyrse, the axis thickly white plumose-woolly above; bracts small and narrow, more or less dry and membranous, plumose-woolly beneath. FLOWERS star-shaped, the tepals united below into a narrow tube, plumose-woolly outside, pinkish mauve, lightly scented. STAMENS inserted on the tepals just above the mouth of the tube, filaments slender, unequal, the three inner slightly shorter. OVARY inferior, subglobose with two ovules per locule, plumose-woolly; STYLE slender. FRUIT indehiscent, thin-walled and fragmenting with age, closely covered by the plumose-woolly perianth, typically only one ovule maturing and the remaining locules aborting. SEED one per capsule, obovoid to globose, glossy black. Basic chromosome number x = 18. Western and Eastern Cape Provinces; 1 sp.

Although *Lanaria* was formerly and always somewhat incongruously included in either of the families Haemodoraceae or Tecophilaeaceae, more recent data indicate that it is actually most closely related to the Hypoxidaceae. Flowering is strongly stimulated by fire, and the white woolly flowering stems are particularly conspicuous against the charred slopes in summer when they may cover the ground in their thousands. The fruits are highly unusual, remaining concealed within the persistent, woolly perianth and containing a single large, glossy

Lachenalia zebrina

Lanaria lanata, flowering after a burn on Bain's Kloof Pass near Wellington

Lanaria lanata

black seed. Fruits are indehiscent but the papery fruit wall and dry perianth covering are easily broken to expose the plump seed.

The small flowers are inconspicuous among the characteristic plumose hairs that cover the inflorescence, but honeybees are attracted by the light honey-like scent and nectar, and various monkey beetles (Scarabaeidae: Hopliini) are also common visitors to the congested inflorescences.

Lanaria lanata (Linnaeus) Durand & Schinz

Plants 30–80 cm high. Leaves tufted, narrow, channeled, fibrotic, margins minutely serrate, 5–8 mm wide. Flowers in white woolly, congested thyrses, mauve, tube 4–5 mm long, tepals 5–7 × 1–1.5 mm, stamens 3–4 mm long. Flowering November–January. Clay and sandstone slopes, SW, AP, LB, SE (Bain's Kloof to Grahamstown).

Lapeirousia

COMMON NAMES cabong, lapeirousia, painted petals (for some species), FAMILY Iridaceae. Deciduous perennials. ROOTSTOCK a bell-shaped corm with a flat base, rooting from the edges, axillary in origin, the tunics of densely compacted fibers or woody. LEAVES several, lower two or three forming cataphylls, foliage leaves unifacial, sometimes with a definite midrib, few, sometimes solitary, lowermost longest and arising on stem near ground level, upper leaves cauline and progressively smaller, blade either plane, or shallowly pleated to corrugated, or terete; stem aerial or subterranean, compressed and angled to winged, usually branched, sometimes repeatedly. INFLORESCENCE either a simple to branched spike or panicle-like, then usually ultimate branches with sessile flowers, or flowers clustered at ground level in a basal tuft; bracts green and firm to soft textured, outer sometimes ridged, keeled, crisped or toothed, inner shorter than outer and notched or forked apically. FLOWERS zygomorphic or actinomorphic, bell-shaped to salverform, blue, purple, red, pink, or white, lower or all tepals usually with contrasting darker or lighter markings, sometimes sweetly scented, with nectar from septal nectaries; perianth tube cylindrical or funnel-shaped, short to extremely long; tepals subequal or unequal and then often bilabiate. STAMENS symmetrically disposed around style or unilateral and arcuate; filaments arising shortly below mouth of tube; anthers exserted. STYLE filiform, exserted, branches usually forked as much as half their length, occasionally entire or barely forked. FRUIT a membranous to cartilaginous capsule, more or less globose. SEEDS more or less globose, flattened at chalazal end, smooth, matte. Basic chromosome number $x = 10$, other base numbers 9, 8, 7, 6, 5, 4, 3. Widespread across sub-Saharan Africa from Nigeria and Ethiopia to the southwestern Cape, most diverse in Namaqualand and the northwestern Cape in semiarid habitats; 40 spp., 35 in southern Africa, 15 in the Cape.

Lapeirousia is best represented in more arid habitats and favors gritty or clay soils. A few species are restricted to acidic, nutrient-poor, sandy soils, and these species invariably flower best in the wild after a fire has cleared and fertilized the soil. The flowers of *Lapeirousia* are highly variable, reflecting adaptations to a range of pollinators. Short-tubed flowers are visited by bees, bombyliid flies, noctuid moths, and butterflies whereas long-tubed species are adapted to pollination by long-proboscid flies of the genera *Philoliche* (Tabanidae) and *Prosoeca* and *Moegistorhynchus* (both Nemestrinidae).

Most of the Cape species of this widespread African genus are small plants and perhaps best reserved for pot culture. A few of the larger species, *Lapeirousia anceps* and *L. fabricii*, for example, can grow to a fair size and produce dozens of large creamy pink flowers each season. These species would make a fine addition to a rock garden. Two low-growing but floriferous species, *L. azurea*, which has delphinium blue flowers marked with black, and *L. fastigiata*, which has yellow flowers, are especially recommended. Both have large flowers and three or four corms would be sufficient to give a fine display in a pot or planter. The more common *L. corymbosa* has smaller, light blue flowers with a central white star. A particularly striking species is *L. oreogena* from the Bokkeveld Plateau east of Nieuwoudtville. The tufted plants become covered with midnight blue flowers, each with a white central star bearing black chevrons. Well-grown specimens form brilliant cushions of color. The white- and pale blue-flowered forms of *L. pyramidalis* are recommended for their heady clove-like scent. All lapeirousias are drought tolerant and thrive on low rainfall. Water should be withheld at the beginning of the dormant period to force the corms to go dormant. Corms should not be lifted when dormant. Seeds germinate readily when ripe, and plants may be persuaded to flower in their second growing season although three seasons is more usual.

FURTHER READING. Since the Cape species of *Lapeirousia* were revised by Goldblatt (1972b), several changes to the taxonomy have been made, including the description of additional species (Goldblatt and Manning 1992, 1994). The diverse methods of pollination and their effects on speciation in subgenus *Lapeirousia* were studied by Goldblatt et al. (1995) and Goldblatt and Manning (1996b).

Lapeirousia anceps (Linnaeus fil.) Ker Gawler

Plants 10–30 cm high; corm tunics brown, with thickened, crenate margins. Leaves linear, mostly 4–10 mm wide, ribbed. Flowers in short spikes on a branched stem, cream to pink with red markings on lower tepals, perianth tube cylindrical and slender, (25–)40–80 mm long, tepals 10–12 mm long; bracts fairly short. Flowering September–November. Deep sand or stony slopes in fynbos, NW, SW, AP, LB (southern Namaqualand to Mossel Bay).

Lapeirousia azurea (Ecklon ex Baker) Goldblatt

Plants 6–12 cm high; corm with blackish, rough tunics. Leaves plane, falcate, to 15 mm wide, margins undulate and crisped. Flowers in a dense, flat-topped panicle, zygomorphic, deep blue with blackish markings, perianth tube funnel-shaped, 8–12 mm long, tepals subequal, mostly 14–20 mm long, stamens unilateral, pollen dark blue to brown. Flowering September–October. Granitic soils in renosterveld, SW (Gouda to Paarl). Page 268.

Lapeirousia corymbosa (Linnaeus) Ker Gawler

Plants 5–15 cm high; corm with blackish, rough tunics. Leaves plane, mostly 4–8 mm wide, falcate, often undulate or crisped. Flowers in a dense, flat-topped panicle, actinomorphic, pale to deep blue with white central star, perianth tube funnel-shaped, 4–7 mm long, tepals subequal, 7–10 mm long, stamens symmetrically arranged. Flowering mainly September–November. Sandy and granitic slopes, NW, SW, AP (Piketberg to Agulhas).

Lapeirousia anceps

Lapeirousia azurea

Lapeirousia corymbosa

Lapeirousia divaricata

Lapeirousia fabricii

Lapeirousia divaricata Baker

Plants 7–25 cm high; corm tunics blackish, the margins with small teeth. Leaves lanceolate, 2–5 mm wide, ribbed. Flowers in a short spike, bilabiate, white to pale pink, fragrant, perianth tube short, c. 12 mm long, tepals unequal, the dorsal c. 16 mm long; bracts short, translucent toward the base. Flowering August–October. Damp sandy places, NW (Bokkeveld Mountains to Citrusdal).

Lapeirousia fabricii (D. Delaroche) Ker Gawler

Plants 15–25 cm high; corm tunics brown, with toothed to spiny margins. Leaves linear, 5–12 mm wide, ribbed. Flowers in short spikes on a branched stem, cream to pink with red markings on the lower tepals, perianth tube slender below, widening above, 30–50 mm long, tepals unequal, the dorsal 15–20 mm long, lower tepals often with claw-like appendages; bract keels serrated or crisped. Flowering September–October. Stony sandstone and granitic slopes, NW, SW (southern Namaqualand to Worcester).

Lapeirousia falcata (Linnaeus fil.) Ker Gawler

Plants 5–8 cm high; corm with blackish, rough tunics. Leaf blades plane, to 8 mm wide, falcate, margins undulate. Flowers in a short spike, pink to mauve with red markings on the lower three tepals, actinomorphic, perianth tube cylindrical, 12–20 mm long, tepals c. 8 mm long, stamens unilateral. Flowering September–October, mainly after fire. Rocky sandstone slopes in shallow sand, NW (Cold Bokkeveld to Worcester).

Lapeirousia fastigiata (Lamarck) Ker Gawler

Plants 5–9 cm high; corm with blackish, rough tunics. Leaves plane, falcate, mostly 10–12 mm wide, margins straight or undulate, sometimes loosely crisped. Flowers in a dense, flat-topped panicle, actinomorphic, pale yellow with brown markings, perianth tube funnel-shaped, 6.5–8 mm long, tepals subequal, 12–15 mm long, stamens symmetrically arranged. Flowering September–October. Clay slopes and flats in renosterveld, to 300 m, NW, SW (Piketberg to Malmesbury).

Lapeirousia jacquinii N. E. Brown

Plants 8–12 cm high, branching from the base; corm tunics brown, the margins with short, down-pointed teeth. Leaves linear, 3–8(–15) mm wide, ribbed. Flowers in short spikes on a branched stem, dark purple with whitish and red to purple streaks on the lower tepals, perianth tube cylindrical, 30–40 mm long, tepals unequal, the dorsal 9–12 mm long; bracts two-keeled below, broadly obtuse. Flowering August–September. Sandstone soils, NW, SW (southern Namaqualand to Worcester). Page 270.

Lapeirousia micrantha (E. Meyer ex Klatt) Baker

Plants 15–35 cm high; corm with rough, blackish tunics. Leaves plane, falcate, 8–16 mm wide, margins crisped. Flowers in a flat-topped panicle, actinomorphic, small, cream to maroon, perianth tube cylindrical, 8–10 mm long, tepals subequal, 3–5 mm long, strongly fragrant,

Lapeirousia falcata

Lapeirousia jacquinii

Lapeirousia micrantha

Lapeirousia montana

Lapeirousia neglecta

stamens mostly unilateral. Flowering October–November, only after fire. Rocky sandstone soils in fynbos, NW, SW, LB (Gifberg to Riversdale).

Lapeirousia montana Klatt
Plants 5–10 cm high, stemless; corm tunics brown, with thickened margins. Leaves linear-falcate, 2–3 mm wide, ribbed. Flowers in a basal rosette, actinomorphic, pale blue to whitish, often with darker blue markings, narcissus scented, perianth tube cylindrical, c. 40 mm long, tepals subequal, c. 12 mm long. Flowering August–September. Clay soils, RV (Roggeveld Escarpment and western Karoo).

Lapeirousia neglecta Goldblatt & J. C. Manning
Plants 30–80 cm high; corm with brown tunics and surrounded by numerous cormels. Leaves plane, sword-shaped to falcate, 7–15 mm wide. Flowers in an open, rounded panicle, white or blue, the lower tepals with darker markings, perianth tube cylindrical, 10–14 mm long, tepals subequal, 9–13 mm long, stamens unilateral. Flowering November–December, only after fire. Rocky sandstone slopes above 800 m, SW (Bain's Kloof to Hottentots Holland Mountains).

Lapeirousia oreogena Schlechter ex Goldblatt
Plants 5–10 cm high, stemless; corm tunics brown, with thickened, crenate margins. Leaves linear to sword-shaped, 2–3 mm wide, ribbed. Flowers in a basal rosette, actinomorphic, violet with cream and blackish markings, perianth tube cylindrical, 45–60 mm long, tepals subequal, c. 13 mm long; bracts leafy, margins crisped. Flowering August–September. Clay soils, NW (Bokkeveld Plateau and western Karoo).

Lapeirousia plicata (Jacquin) Diels
Plants 3–5 cm high, stemless; corm tunics brown, with thickened, crenate margins. Leaves linear to sword-shaped, 2–6 mm wide, ribbed. Flowers in a basal tuft, actinomorphic, pale blue to whitish, tepals spreading, perianth tube cylindrical, 12–25(–35) mm long, tepals subequal, lanceolate, 6–10 mm long; bracts large and leafy, usually undulate or crisped. Flowering July–Sep-

Lapeirousia oreogena

Lapeirousia plicata

Lapeirousia pyramidalis subsp. *pyramidalis*

Lapeirousia pyramidalis subsp. *regalis*

tember. Dry shale flats, succulent karoo or renosterveld, RV, NW, KM (Namibia and Bushmanland to the Karoo, Worcester and Little Karoo).

Lapeirousia pyramidalis (Lamarck) Goldblatt
Plants 5–10 cm high; corm tunics with crenate margins. Leaves linear, mostly 2–6 mm wide, ribbed. Flowers in a short, often dense spike, cream to bluish and fragrant, or dark purplish to magenta and scentless, perianth tube cylindrical, 20–40 mm long, tepals subequal, 7–9 mm long; bracts spreading, broad and retuse above. Flowering July–September. Shale and sandstone soils, fynbos and renosterveld, RV, NW, SW, AP, KM, LB (southern Namaqualand to Oudtshoorn).

Two subspecies are recognized: subspecies *pyramidalis* with cream to bluish, intensely fragrant flowers, RV, NW, SW, AP, KM, LB (southern Namaqualand to Little Karoo), and subspecies *regalis* Goldblatt & J. C. Manning with dark purplish to magenta, scentless flowers, stony sandstone slopes, NW (Olifants River Valley and nearby).

Lapeirousia violacea Goldblatt
Plants 8–10 cm high, often branching from the base; corm blackish, with spiny margins. Leaves sword-shaped, 3–6 mm wide, ribbed. Flowers in a short spike, violet with dark red markings on lower tepals, perianth tube cylindrical, 30–40 mm long, tepals unequal, c. 12 mm long; bracts large and inflated. Flowering August–September. Sandstone soils in renosterveld and arid fynbos, NW (Bokkeveld Escarpment to Biedouw valley).

Ledebouria

COMMON NAME African squill, FAMILY Hyacinthaceae. Deciduous or weakly evergreen perennials. ROOTSTOCK a bulb, the scales sometimes loosely overlapping, occasionally producing fibrous threads when torn. LEAVES one to several, green or emergent at flowering, rarely dry, linear to ovate, rarely pseudopetiolate, fleshy or leathery, hairless, suberect or spreading, rarely twisted, often spotted with darker green or purple. INFLORESCENCES one to several racemes with few to many flowers, sometimes congested and subcorymbose, the pedicels mostly long;

bracts usually small, membranous, with or without lateral inner bracts, rarely vestigial. FLOWERS usually nodding, cup- or bell-shaped, the tepals more or less erect below and usually recurved above, united at the base, green to purple, usually unscented, the filaments more brightly colored. STAMENS with filaments joined to the base of the tepals, filiform or swollen below. OVARY stalked, subglobose to top-shaped, three- or six-lobed, the lobes often with swollen nectar-producing lobules below, with one or two ovules per locule; STYLE slender, usually shorter than the perianth. FRUIT a globose to obovoid or club-shaped capsule. SEEDS one or two per locule, subglobose, black. Basic chromosome number $x = 10$. India, Madagascar, and sub-Saharan Africa, mainly southern Africa; c. 30 spp., 5 in the Cape.

Largely restricted to areas of summer rainfall, the genus *Ledebouria* is best developed in the subtropical savannas and grasslands in the eastern and northeastern parts of southern Africa. Most species favor stony slopes on a variety of more or less fine-grained substrates. The taxonomic status of *Ledebouria* as a genus apart from African members of *Scilla* was established relatively recently, and subsaharan scillas are distributed among three other genera. True scillas are Northern Hemisphere. *Ledebouria* is mostly separable from *Scilla* by its spotted leaves, several flaccid inflorescences, and stalked ovary with one or two ovules per locule. Although the bulbs of at least one Kalahari species form part of the traditional tribal diet, several species are known to contain alkaloids, including cardiac toxins. The small, dull flowers of most species are livened by their pink or magenta filaments and are pollinated mainly by bees.

These small bulbs are best treated as pot subjects. They are drought resistant and easily grown as long as they are not overwatered. Although *Ledebouria undulata* requires a dry dormancy during the summer, the other species will remain more or less evergreen if watered lightly throughout the year. The bulbs of most species should be planted near or at the surface. The leaves, which are variously spotted, are the most interesting feature. The plants should be grown in high light intensity for the best development of the leaf markings and other foliage features such as twisting or crisping.

FURTHER READING. The last published revision of *Ledebouria* (Jessop 1970) is very inadequate. Since then, the genus has been revised in an unpublished thesis by Venter (1993) but that work is not generally available and is itself not entirely free of problems.

Ledebouria ovalifolia (Schrader) Jessop

Plants 7–12 cm high; bulb subglobose, $1–2 \times 1–1.5$ cm. Leaves emergent at flowering, ascending, soft, lanceolate to ovate, narrowed below, reddish or purple beneath, $3–5 \times 2–3$ cm. Flowers in broad racemes, nodding on pedicels 4–7 mm long, purple or pink and white, unscented, tepals recurved, 3.5–4 mm long, ovary subglobose, broadly three-lobed but the lobes longitudinally channeled. Flowering December–April. Rocky places, often coastal limestone, NW, SW, AP, SE (Hex River Valley to Humansdorp).

Ledebouria ovalifolia

Ledebouria ovatifolia (Baker) Jessop
Plants 4–15 cm high; bulb subglobose, 4–7 × 3–5 cm, scales loosely arranged, fleshy, producing copious threads when torn. Leaves usually prostrate, firm, ovate, often faintly speckled, margins hyaline, 5–12 × 3.5–6 cm. Flowers in broad racemes, nodding on pedicels 7–12 mm long, mauve to greenish, tepals recurved, 5 mm long, ovary depressed and top-shaped, six-lobed, lobes rounded above. Flowering September–October. Stony slopes, SE (Port Elizabeth to tropical Africa to Sri Lanka).

Ledebouria revoluta (Linnaeus fil.) Jessop
Plants to 15 cm high; bulb subglobose, 6–8 × 4–6 cm, scales producing sparse threads when torn. Leaves spreading, lanceolate, firm, spotted with red, margins hyaline, often slightly crisped and minutely hairy, 8–13 × 3–9 cm. Flowers in broad racemes, nodding on pedicels 10–13 mm long, purple and greenish, unscented, tepals recurved, 5 mm long, ovary depressed and top-shaped, six-lobed, the lobes rounded above. Flowering mainly October–December. Stony slopes, LB (Swellendam to Riversdale, eastern southern Africa to India).

Ledebouria undulata (Jacquin) Jessop
Plants 10–15 cm high; bulb subglobose, 5–6 × 3–5 cm, scales loosely arranged, fleshy. Leaves dry at flowering, ascending, narrowly lanceolate, mottled with dark green, margins undulate, 7–11 × 0.5–1 cm. Flowers in dense racemes, spreading on pedicels 3–7 mm long, whitish and green or purple-pink, channeled, lightly acridly scented, tepals recurved, 5–6 mm long, ovary subglobose, broadly three-lobed but the lobes longitudinally channeled. Flowering November–January. Rocky places, including limestone, RV, NW, SW (Namaqualand and western Karoo to Darling).

Ledebouria sp. 1
Synonym, *Scilla ensifolia* (Ecklon) Britten. Plants to 15 cm high; bulb cylindrical, scales papery and forming a neck. Leaves ovate to lanceolate, firm, often spotted with red, margins hyaline, 8–15 × 1.5–4 cm. Flowers in narrow racemes, nodding on pedicels 3–4 mm long, purple and greenish, tepals recurved, 3 mm long, ovary top-shaped, six-lobed, the lobes tapering above. Flowering August–December. Stony slopes, SE (Humansdorp to Eastern Cape).

Massonia

COMMON NAME hedgehog lily, FAMILY Hyacinthaceae. Deciduous perennials. ROOTSTOCK a globose bulb with pale, papery or thinly leathery outer tunics lightly barred above and sometimes extended as a short neck, with a tubular membranous cataphyll. LEAVES two, prostrate, oblong to broadly elliptical, subsucculent or leathery, hairless or variously pustulate-hairy or bristly. INFLORESCENCE a condensed, corymbose or subcapitate raceme, the pedicels elongating in fruit; bracts large or the upper smaller, green or membranous. FLOWERS tubular or rarely cup-shaped, the tepals united at the base into a short or long and often delicate tube, spreading or sharply recurved at the base then sharply inflexed in a transverse, sigmoid fold, white to pink, usually scented. STAMENS with firm filaments, sometimes the inner shorter, more or less united into a shallow cup inserted at the mouth of the perianth tube. OVARY ovoid or obtriangular, with several ovules per locule; STYLE as long as the ovary or much longer, slender, the stigma minute. FRUIT a papery capsule, inflated, obtriangular and three-angled or three-winged, loculicidal. SEEDS several per locule, subglobose, black, smooth or finely wrinkled. Basic chromosome numbers $x = 13, 11, 10, 9$. Widespread in dry areas, southern Namibia and Western Cape to Lesotho; c. 6 spp., 4 in the Cape.

One of a small group of genera typical of the winter-rainfall region of southern Africa that share papery, three-angled capsules containing globose, often smooth and glossy seeds, *Massonia* is recognized by its two prostrate or spreading leaves, the head-like inflorescence borne at ground level in which the bracts are large and leafy, and the more or less tubular flowers with the filaments shortly joined together at the base. DNA sequence studies indicate that the yellow-flowered plant called M. *angustifolia* Linnaeus fil. in the past by some (now known to be a synonym of M. *echinata*) is actually more closely related to *Daubenya* than to other species of *Massonia* and it is placed there. It was anomalous in *Massonia* in its small bracts, yellowish flowers, and longitudinally striate leaves. Although *Massonia* is most often found on stony clay or dolerite flats, some species grow equally or solely on more sandy soils. In an effective mode of seed dispersal, the peduncles and pedicels elongate to lift the more or less three-winged, papery capsules and their dry, sail-like bracts above the drying leaves, where they form a light, balloon-like ball, which is easily detached and blown away by the wind, dispersing seeds along its path.

Most of the species of *Massonia* are not highly specialized for pollination, and the pleasantly fragrant flowers of the long-tubed species are visited by honeybees, also butterflies, in search of the nectar held in the bottom of the elongate floral tubes. *Massonia depressa*, with its broad perianth tube, copious nectar, and a faint yeasty scent, has a much more unusual pollination biology. It is specialized for pollination by rodents, a strategy developed among various Proteaceae but otherwise unknown among geophytes.

All species of *Massonia* are amenable to pot culture. Their main horticultural interest lies in their unusual growth form and often patterned or pustulate leaves. Most of the species flower in the winter and should be potted somewhat earlier than usual for Cape bulbs, in August or September in the Northern Hemisphere. They require a sandy, well-drained soil, and water should be withheld at the beginning of the dormant period to force the plants to go dormant. *Massonia echinata* makes a particularly attractive pot plant when in flower in the winter in the Alpine House at the Royal Botanic Gardens, Kew.

FURTHER READING. The revision of *Massonia* by Jessop (1976), although somewhat lacking, is marginally preferable to the later work by U. and D. Müller-Doblies (1997), which is marred by an overzealous fragmentation of species.

Massonia depressa Houttuyn

Plants to 5 cm high. Leaves smooth or rarely pustulate-hairy, sometimes spotted, 5–25 × 4–15 cm. Flowers green, cream, white, or pink, yeast scent, tube 3–17 × 3–8 mm, tepals sigmoid, oblong, 6–12 mm long, filaments 8–18 mm long, united below as much as 2 mm, style 5–14 mm long; bracts green, obovate, the lower 15–50 mm long. Capsule obovoid, three-winged. Flowering May–July. Widespread in dry areas, RV, NW, SW, AP, KM, SE (Namaqualand to Long Kloof, Eastern Cape, Karoo).

Massonia echinata Linnaeus fil.

Plants to 5 cm high. Leaves smooth, hairy or pustulate-hairy, sometimes spotted, margins smooth or hairy, 2–15 × 1–13 cm. Flowers cream to white fading pink, honey scented, tube 5–15 × 1–2 mm, tepals recurved below or almost sigmoid, oblong, 4–9 mm long, filaments 4–10 mm long, free or united below as much as 1 mm, style 5–10 mm long; bracts green, obovate, smooth or hairy, sometimes only on the margins, 10–30 mm long. Capsule obovoid, three-winged. Flowering May–July. Widespread in dry areas, RV, NW, SW, AP, KM, LB, SE (Bokkeveld Mountains to Eastern Cape, Karoo).

Massonia depressa

Massonia echinata

Massonia pustulata Jacquin
Plants to 5 cm high. Leaves smooth or pustulate-hairy, sometimes spotted, margins mostly minutely hairy, 3–15 × 2–13 cm. Flowers cream to pink, rose scented, tube 6–15 × 1.5–2.5 mm, tepals recurved below or almost sigmoid, oblong, 5–15 mm long, filaments (10–)15–24 mm long, free or united below as much as 1 mm, style 15–30 mm long; bracts green, obovate, 12–45 mm. Capsule obovoid, three-winged. Flowering June–September. Often coastal sands, NW, SW, AP, KM, SE (Namaqualand to Port Elizabeth and Karoo).

Massonia pygmaea Kunth
Plants to 5 cm high. Leaves smooth or pustulate, sometimes spotted, 1.5–4 × 1–2 cm. Flowers white to pink, scented, tube 6–17 × 0.5–1.5 mm, tepals recurved below or almost sigmoid, linear-oblong, 4–7 mm long, filaments 3–8 mm long, the inner shorter, free or united below as much as 1 mm, style 11–12 mm long; bracts oblanceolate, membranous, the lower 12–20 mm long. Capsule obovoid. Flowering April–May. Mountains, NW, SW (Kamiesberg and Cedarberg Mountains to Villiersdorp).

Melasphaerula

COMMON NAME fairy bells, FAMILY Iridaceae. Deciduous perennial. ROOTSTOCK a bell-shaped corm with a flat base, rooting from the base, the tunics woody to firm-papery and concentric. LEAVES several, the lower two or three forming sheathing, membranous cataphylls, foliage leaves unifacial with a midrib, in a two-ranked fan, the blades lanceolate, plane, soft textured; stem aerial, terete and wiry, many-branched, the branching divaricate. INFLORESCENCE a lax compound spike; bracts green, soft textured, short, the inner shorter to about as long as the outer, notched apically. FLOWERS zygomorphic and bilabiate; perianth tube very short; TEPALS unequal, lanceolate-attenuate, the dorsal tepal largest and arcuate. STAMENS unilateral and arcuate; anthers parallel, lying under the dorsal tepal. OVARY prominently three-angled; STYLE exserted, the branches expanded above and recurved. FRUIT a leathery capsule with three

Massonia echinata

Massonia pustulata

prominent wing-like lobes, wider than high. SEEDS globose, two per locule, smooth, matte. Basic chromosome number $x = 10$. Widespread in the winter-rainfall region of southern Africa, extending from southern Namibia to the Agulhas Peninsula, in sheltered shady places; 1 sp.

The distinctive *Melasphaerula*, with but a single species, has an unusual combination of characteristics: woody corm tunics, a short-tubed bilabiate flower with short filiform style branches, and winged capsules. Its closest relatives are not clear, but on the basis of its woody corm tunics and soft-textured bracts, *Melasphaerula* is regarded as most closely related to *Geissorhiza* and *Hesperantha*. It is widespread in sheltered, damp situations among rocks or on the edge of scrub. The flowers are probably pollinated by small flies attracted by the sour, musk-like odor.

A much undervalued species, *Melasphaerula ramosa* is barely known in horticulture. Each plant produces numerous flowers in a loose, graceful arrangement on delicate, much branched stems. Well-grown specimens are extremely elegant and have the aspect of *Gypsophila* (baby's breath). The species is easy to grow in pots and in the garden. It should do well among small shrubs in the open ground. It grows in stony ground on cooler slopes, often among light brush in the wild. It seems to favor richer soils of clay and loam but will even grow on limestone.

Melasphaerula ramosa (Burman fil.) N. E. Brown

Plants mostly 30–50 cm high, rarely as high as c. 1 m; corm bell-shaped, often with small cormels around the base. Flowers many in a lax, compound spike, small, zygomorphic, the lower tepals forming a lip, cream to pale yellow, with dark median streaks, with a strong, sour, musk-like scent, perianth tube c. 1 mm long, tepals unequal, the dorsal tepal largest, 10–15 mm long; bracts submembranous, distant. Flowering August–September. Stony slopes, mostly on cooler south- or east-facing hillsides, NW, SW (southern Namibia to Bredasdorp).

Micranthus

COMMON NAME combflower, FAMILY Iridaceae. Deciduous perennials. ROOTSTOCK a globose corm, rooting from below, axillary in origin, tunics densely fibrous. LEAVES few, lower two or three forming cataphylls, foliage leaves either unifacial and with a definite midrib, blades falcate or linear, or terete, then sometimes hollow, margins occasionally thickened, lowermost longest, arising on stem above corm, the remaining leaves arising above ground and smaller than the basal; stem aerial, usually simple, or few-branched, terete. INFLORESCENCE a spike, flowers in two ranks and crowded; bracts firm textured, short, overlapping, dry and brown with broad membranous margins. FLOWERS blue, white, or purple, scented or not, zygomorphic, stamens arcuate, with nectar from septal nectaries; perianth tube short, curving outward and more or less cylindrical; tepals subequal, dorsal, arching over stamens. STAMENS unilateral and arcuate. STYLE filiform, branches deeply divided and recurved. FRUIT a small, woody, oblong capsule. SEEDS slender, lightly striate and matte. Basic chromosome number $x = 10$. Southwestern Cape, mostly in sandstone

Melasphaerula ramosa

Micranthus alopecuroides

Micranthus junceus

soils and often in damp sites, unusual in blooming in the early summer; 3 spp.

The three species of *Micranthus* all have blue or rarely white flowers densely crowded in long, slender spikes. The flowers are the smallest of any of the Cape Iridaceae and are individually inconspicuous. The plants favor damper, sandy or gritty soils and are conspicuously communal. The flowers of all the species are alike and are visited by a variety of insects, including bees, wasps, butterflies, noctuid moths, and bombyliid flies.

Combflowers have attracted little attention from gardeners but should thrive in a rock garden. They deserve serious consideration as an interplanting among spring-flowering bulbs because of their late flowering period. The flowers are very attractive to butterflies, which is another reason to grow them. Plants are most easily grown from the cormels produced in the leaf axils as the capsules mature, and corms reproduce vegetatively as well, one main corm fragmenting into several each year, a strategy that explains the communal habit of the plants. In the wild, *Micranthus junceus* favors seasonal marshes or seeps whereas the other species grow on heavy clay, which bakes as hard as concrete in the summer.

Micranthus alopecuroides (Linnaeus) Rothmaler

Plants 25–40 cm high; corm globose with tough fibrous tunics. Leaves sword-shaped, plane with distinct midvein, 5–12 mm wide. Flowers in dense, two-ranked spikes, c. 8 mm long, pale to deep blue; bracts dry, rigid, brown with broad membranous margins. Flowering October–December. Sandstone soils, SW (Bain's Kloof to Elgin and Cape Peninsula).

Micranthus junceus (Baker) N. E. Brown

Plants 25–45 cm high; corm globose with tough fibrous tunics. Leaves terete, slender, and hollow, mostly 3–6 mm diam. Flowers in dense, two-ranked spikes, c. 8 mm long, usually dark blue, occasionally white; bracts dry, rigid, brown with broad membranous margins. Flowering November–January. Wet sites on granite or sandstone soils, NW, SW, AP, LB (Bokkeveld Mountains to Riversdale).

Micranthus tubulosus (Burman) N. E. Brown

Plants 25–45 cm high; corm globose with tough fibrous tunics. Leaves tubular, hollow, mostly 8–14 mm diam., truncate and apiculate at the tip. Flowers in dense, two-ranked spikes, c. 8 mm long, blue to mauve, fragrant; bracts dry, rigid, brown with broad membranous margins. Flowering November–December. Mainly clay and granitic soils in renosterveld, NW, SW (Gifberg to Cape Peninsula).

Moraea

COMMON NAMES moraea, peacock iris (some species) FAMILY Iridaceae. Deciduous perennials, sometimes stemless and tufted. ROOTSTOCK a corm, usually replaced annually, rooting from an apical bud, tunics persistent, mostly of coarse, netted fibers. LEAVES several to few or one, usually bifacial and channeled, without a midrib, sometimes terete, the margins sometimes rolled inward or undulate to crisped, when terete sometimes twisted or coiled; sometimes only the lowermost leaf with a blade, the remainder entirely sheathing and bract-like; stems sometimes subterranean, simple or branched. INFLORESCENCES of several flowers in an umbellate cluster (a rhipidium) enclosed by large opposed bracts (spathes), clusters mostly single and terminal on branches, rarely apically crowded in a fascicle on short branches; spathes usually firm to leathery, the inner exceeding the outer, acute or attenuate, rarely truncate. FLOWERS usually pedicellate, rarely sessile, exserted or included in the spathes, fugacious or lasting as long as 3 days, often blue or yellow, also other colors, mostly more or less *Iris*-like with clawed tepals, usually only outer with nectar guides, sometimes sweetly or unpleasantly scented, often with nectar from perigonal nectaries at the tepal bases; tepals free, rarely united in a short tube, claws ascending to erect, often long, or short, limbs spreading to reflexed, or the inner tepal limbs erect, inner tepals sometimes tricuspidate, filiform, hair-like, or lacking. STAMENS with filaments usually united below, or entirely; anthers usually appressed to style branches, often concealed by the outer tepal claws but prominent when the style branches narrow or reduced. OVARY mostly ovoid and exserted, sometimes included, then often with a beak or tubular and sterile in the upper half; STYLE filiform, usually enclosed by the filaments and dividing shortly beyond the filament column, style branches usually flattened and petaloid with paired terminal petaloid crests, stigma a transverse lobe on abaxial surface at base of crests, terminal when style branches narrow or filiform, rarely style branches filiform or divided to base into paired filiform arms. FRUIT mostly a club-shaped capsule, truncate or shortly beaked, the beak sometimes tubular. SEEDS angular to fusiform or compressed and discoid. Basic chromosome number $x = 10$, other numbers 9, 8, 6, 5, 4. Throughout sub-Saharan Africa (2 spp. in Eurasia), concentrated in the southwestern Cape, occurring in a variety of open habitats, never in forest; c. 195 spp., 123 in the Cape.

Resembling *Iris* in many ways, *Moraea* is not immediately related to that Northern Hemisphere genus but is more closely allied to *Dietes* and *Ferraria*. All these genera have specialized style branches, which are flattened and petaloid with paired terminal crests and bearing an abaxial transverse stigma lobe. Among this alliance, *Moraea* and *Ferraria* differ from *Iris* and *Dietes* in having a corm, and *Moraea* alone has a bifacial leaf. The genus is diverse; five subgenera are recognized. Until 1998, several other southern African genera of Iridaceae tribe Irideae with corms and bifacial leaves were recognized, but these are now included within *Moraea*. These segregate genera were recognized on the basis of floral characteristics that are now seen to be recurrently evolving specializations for different pollination strategies. A frequent floral specialization in *Moraea* is for the tepals of both the inner and outer perianth whorls to become nearly equal and bear nectar guides. In these species, the filaments are often united entirely and style branches and crests reduced in size, sometimes to filiform structures. Such flowers defined the formerly segregated genera *Galaxia*, *Hexaglottis*, and *Homeria*. *Barnardiella* and *Gynandriris*, on the other hand, were defined by an ovary with a sterile tubular extension and subsessile flower.

Pollination in *Moraea* is diverse. The ancestral condition appears to be pollination by long-tongued bees foraging for nectar. Several southwestern Cape species are pollinated by monkey beetles (Scarabaeidae: Hopliini) whereas *M. lurida* has fetid-smelling flowers probably pollinated by carrion flies (Calliphoridae). Species that have prominently displayed anthers are pollinated by bees foraging for pollen.

Many species of *Moraea* are worth growing; we can mention only the most attractive ones here. Among the most striking are the so-called peacock moraeas, which have large, spreading outer tepals with bold, often iridescent central markings and inconspicuous, three-lobed inner tepals. Best known is *M. villosa*, the most common form of which has purple tepals with dark blue-black central marks. Less well known but deserving of attention are the larger-flowered forms of *M. tulbaghensis* (previously regarded as a separate species, *M. neopavonia*), which bear large, orange, *Tigridia*-like flowers with navy blue central markings. These two species are native to heavier soils of sandy loam or clay and respond well to garden conditions. For many years, white-flowered *M. aristata* (better known as *M. glaucopis*) was offered in bulb catalogs, and the flowers, with their deep turquoise or navy blue central eye, are certainly attractive; the plant is virtually extinct in the wild. Another peacock moraea, *M. loubseri*, may also be extinct in its native habitat in the Western Cape but its curious, dark blue-purple flowers, with the tepals densely covered with blackish hairs, have so far ensured its survival in gardens. Like other peacock moraeas, it grows easily in pots and in the open garden.

Other attractive moraeas are the stemless species such as *Moraea ciliata*, which has blue, yellow, or sometimes white flowers scented of vanilla, the yellow- or pink-flowered *M. tricolor*, and the white-flowered *M. falcifolia*. All produce numerous flowers, each lasting a day. Just a few plants will fill a small pot or corner of the rock garden with bright color. The plants have the curious habit of producing flowers simultaneously on certain days, none on others. The reason for this carefully orchestrated flowering is not yet understood but may be related to the cycles of passing cold fronts and low atmospheric pressure. Species of the *Galaxia* group show this same pattern of growth and flowering and are also best displayed in small pots. Many species of the *Galaxia* group have bright yellow flowers but *M. barnardiella* and *M. melanops* have large, deep pink flowers with a dark purple center that make an arresting show on the days that they open.

Among the large-flowered species in *Moraea* subgenus *Grandiflora*, only *M. spathulata* occurs in the Cape Floral Region, but it has handsome yellow flowers very like those of *Iris orientalis*. In addition, the plants form large clumps within a few seasons. Each stalk produces several flowers and each flower lasts 3 days, extending the flowering period over several weeks. This species may be either weakly or very strongly cold tolerant, depending on the origin of the material. It thrives in the Royal Botanic Garden, Edinburgh, for instance, which has a climate far more severe than anywhere at the Cape. We recommend it highly for garden cultivation. This species produces corms that are rather small and that dry out rapidly, so it is better to start plants from seeds or established seedlings.

Species of the *Homeria* group are overlooked as potential horticultural subjects at the Cape because there they are regarded as weeds. Their leaves can be poisonous and are avoided by sheep and cattle, leaving the plants to multiply freely in overgrazed pastures. One or two species are available in the nursery trade, including *Moraea ochroleuca*, one of the most attractive species in the genus. This species grows well in both the open garden and in the greenhouse. The yellow, orange, or bicolored flowers resemble small-flowered tulips but the habit of the plants is looser, with a slender, graceful stem and branches. Almost any species of the *Homeria* group merits garden attention, although the small-flowered *M. brachygyne* and *M. demissa* are more of a curiosity. Two particularly handsome species that deserve horticultural attention because of their large, scented flowers are *M. elegans* with striking green- and orange-spotted flowers, and *M. comptonii* with large, yellow or pink, coconut-scented flowers.

Among the small group of species previously placed in the genus *Gynandriris*, *Moraea pritzeliana* deserves special mention. This plant has large purple flowers with white markings and fascinatingly coiled leaves that have a central white band running their entire length. The species has the habit of forming clumps as the corms multiply vegetatively. It is both cold and drought tolerant. The leaves tend to be less coiled if plants are shaded or watered too generously. Another attractive species with coiled leaves is *M. tortilis*.

Moraeas should be grown in well-drained heavy soils and benefit from feeding during their growing season. The smaller species may flower in their second season but it is more realistic to expect good flowering in the third year from seed. Corms of a few species are available in the nursery trade.

FURTHER READING. The circumscription of *Moraea* has been significantly widened to include several previously separate genera (Goldblatt 1998). Comprehensive and in some cases lavishly illustrated revisions exist for all the component genera now included in *Moraea* (Goldblatt 1979, 1980, 1981c, 1986, 1987b). More recently discovered species were described by Goldblatt (1984b) and Goldblatt and Manning (1995b, 2000b).

Moraea albiflora (G. J. Lewis) Goldblatt
Plants 2–3 cm high, stemless. Leaves several, oblong, channeled, usually prostrate. Flowers in a basal tuft, white with yellow center, tepals cupped, 9–12 mm long, filaments united in a column, style shorter than the stamens, stigmas fringed. Flowering May–August. Coastal, on sand or granite or limestone outcrops, SW, AP (St. Helena Bay to Agulhas).

Moraea algoensis Goldblatt
Plants 20–40 cm high; corm tunics of gray, netted fibers. Leaf single, linear, channeled, trailing above. Flowers enclosed in firm, attenuate spathes, purple with cream to yellow nectar guides on the outer tepals, tepals unequal, the outer to 30 mm long, limbs lightly reflexed, the inner erect, lanceolate to rhombic, sometimes obscurely three-lobed, filaments united in the lower two-thirds, anthers appressed to narrow style branches, crests linear, to 8 mm long. Flowering July–September. Clay slopes in renosterveld, NW, KM, LB, SE (Worcester to Port Elizabeth).

Moraea amissa Goldblatt
Plants 20–30 cm high; corm tunics of brown, netted fibers. Leaf single, linear, channeled, trailing above. Flowers enclosed in brown-tipped, attenuate spathes, mauve to purple with pale nectar guides edged with darker color on both inner and outer tepals, tepals slightly unequal, the outer larger, 17–20 mm long, the limbs spreading, inner tepals with similarly spreading limbs, filaments almost fully united, anthers appressed to narrow style branches, crests erect, to 4 mm long. Flowering October. Stony granitic slopes, SW (Malmesbury hills).

Moraea angulata Goldblatt
Plants 2–4 cm high, stemless; corm tunics corky and vertically winged. Leaves terete, falcate. Flowers in a basal tuft, yellow or white, tepals cupped, 13–19 mm long, filaments united in a column, style exceeding the anthers, stigmas fringed. Flowering June–August. Wet sandy flats, SW (Malmesbury to Gordon's Bay).

Moraea angusta (Thunberg) Ker Gawler
Plants 20–40 cm high, stem unbranched, the nodes sticky; corm tunics of soft, brown, more or less fibrous layers. Leaf single, terete, rigid. Flowers enclosed in leathery, truncate spathes, yellow to brownish, sometimes flushed with mauve, tepals unequal, the outer 30–50 mm long, limbs laxly spreading, inner tepals often erect, filaments united basally, anthers appressed to broad style branches, crests to 20 mm long; ovary three-angled. Flowering August–November. Rocky sandstone flats and slopes, NW, SW, LB, SE (Cedarberg Mountains to Knysna).

Moraea albiflora

Moraea angusta

Moraea aristata (D. Delaroche) Ascherson & Graebner
Plants 25–35 cm high; corm tunics of pale, coarse fibers. Leaf single, linear, channeled, trailing above. Flowers enclosed in green, attenuate spathes, white, the outer tepals with dark blue to emerald nectar guides, tepals unequal, the outer larger, 30–35 mm long, the limbs broad, spreading, inner tepals tricuspidate with a long, straight central cusp, filaments united, the tips free, anthers appressed to broad style branches, crests erect, to 7 mm long. Flowering September. Clay soils, SW (Cape Peninsula at the Royal Observatory).

Moraea aspera Goldblatt
Plants 10–30 cm high, stem minutely hairy; corm tunics of wiry, black fibers. Leaves three, linear, more or less plane, loosely coiled. Flowers enclosed in green, attenuate spathes, salmon, tepals subequal, 16–23 mm long with short ascending claws, limbs spreading, filaments united in a slightly bulbous column, anthers coherent, concealing the style branches. Flowering August–September. Clay slopes in renosterveld, NW (Bokkeveld Escarpment).

Moraea atropunctata Goldblatt
Plants 15–20 cm high. Leaf single, linear, channeled, usually erect, hairy on the margins. Flowers enclosed in green, long-attenuate spathes, gray-white with dark speckles in the center, brownish on the reverse, tepals unequal, the outer larger, 20–24 mm long, the limbs spreading, inner tepals tricuspidate with a long, spreading central cusp, filaments united, free only near the tips, anthers appressed to narrow style branches, crests narrow, c. 4 mm long. Flowering August–September. Clay slopes, SW (Caledon in the Eseljacht Mountains).

Moraea australis (Goldblatt) Goldblatt
Plants mostly 12–25 cm high; corm with pale, soft tunic fibers. Leaf single, linear, channeled, trailing above. Flowers enclosed by translucent spathes, large, pale blue or deep blue with cream nectar guides, outer tepals 23–28 mm long, limbs reflexed, inner tepals smaller, suberect, style crests 8–12 mm long; ovary with a tubular beak.

Moraea aristata (Colin Paterson-Jones)

Moraea anomala G. J. Lewis
Plants 20–40 cm high, stem unbranched, the nodes sticky; corm tunics of soft, brown layers. Leaf single, terete, rigid. Flowers enclosed in leathery, truncate spathes, yellow with darker yellow nectar guides on the outer tepals, tepals unequal, the outer larger, 30–45 mm long, limbs weakly reflexed, inner tepals suberect or limbs also reflexed, filaments united in the lower third, anthers appressed to broad style branches, crests 10–15 mm long; ovary three-angled. Flowering September–November. Mountains and flats, often on clay, NW, SW (Pakhuis Pass to Cape Peninsula, Caledon).

Flowering September–November. Coastal sand dunes and rocky flats, SE (George to Humansdorp).

Moraea autumnalis (Goldblatt) Goldblatt
Plants 20–30 cm high; corm tunics of wiry, black fibers. Leaf single, linear, trailing above. Flowers enclosed in green, attenuate spathes, yellow, tepals subequal, 30–40 mm long, claws ascending, forming a narrow cup, filaments united in a slender column, anthers partly exserted, appressed to narrow, barely diverging style branches and slightly exceeding them, crests erect, c. 2 mm long. Flowering April–July. Sandstone slopes, NW (Elandskloof, Cold Bokkeveld).

Moraea barkerae Goldblatt
Plants 15–40 cm high; corm tunics of brown, netted fibers. Leaf single, linear, channeled, trailing above. Flowers enclosed in green, attenuate spathes, pale salmon pink, the outer tepals with purple and white nectar guides, tepals unequal, the outer larger, c. 30 mm long, limbs only slightly longer than the claws, spreading, inner tepals erect, attenuate, filaments united in the lower two-thirds, anthers appressed to narrow style branches, crests erect, to 10 mm long. Flowering October–November. Rocky sandstone slopes, common after fire, NW (Cedarberg and Cold Bokkeveld Mountains).

Moraea barnardiella Goldblatt
Plants 3–5 cm high, stemless. Leaves broadly lanceolate, margins undulate, often prostrate. Flowers in a basal tuft, pink to purple, with a blackish center, tepals spreading horizontally, 18–25 mm long, filaments united in a column, style reaching the middle of the anthers, stigmas lobed. Flowering August–September. Clay flats and hills, renosterveld, SW (Villiersdorp to Caledon).

Moraea barnardii L. Bolus
Plants 15–30 cm high, stem usually unbranched; corm tunics of pale, netted fibers. Leaf single, linear, narrowly channeled, trailing above. Flowers enclosed in green, attenuate spathes, white streaked with blue, the outer tepals with cream nectar guides outlined in dark blue, outer tepals c. 20 mm long, margins undulate, the limbs spreading, inner tepals absent, filaments united in the lower third, anthers red, appressed to narrow style branches, crests curving inward, c. 6 mm long. Flowering September–October. Rocky sandstone slopes, SW (Caledon at Shaw's Pass).

Moraea aspera

Moraea barnardiella

Moraea bellendenii

Moraea bifida

Moraea bellendenii (Sweet) N. E. Brown
Plants 50–100 cm high, stem slender and willowy; corm tunics of pale, netted fibers. Leaf single, linear, channeled, trailing above. Flowers enclosed in green, attenuate spathes, yellow, the outer tepals darkly speckled in the middle, tepals unequal, the outer larger, 22–33 mm long, the limbs spreading, the inner tricuspidate with a short, obliquely twisted central cusp, filaments united in the lower two-thirds, anthers appressed to narrow style branches, style crests short, mostly 3–5 mm. Flowering October–November. Mainly granitic or clay slopes, SW, AP, LB, SE (Darling to Plettenberg Bay).

Moraea bifida (L. Bolus) Goldblatt
Plants to 50 cm high; corm tunics of wiry, black fibers. Leaf single, fairly broad below and clasping the lower half of the stem, linear, channeled, trailing above. Flowers enclosed in green, attenuate spathes, yellow or pink, minutely speckled in the center, tepals subequal, 16–20 mm long with short clasping claws, limbs spreading, filament column bulbous below, anthers cohering, concealing the style branches, crests lacking. Flowering August–September. Clay soils in renosterveld, RV, NW (eastern Namaqualand and western Karoo to Pakhuis Pass).

Moraea bipartita L. Bolus
Plants 15–45 cm high, stem much branched; corm tunics of wiry, black fibers. Leaves two to four, linear, channeled, often trailing above. Flowers enclosed in green, attenuate spathes, blue with yellow nectar guides on the outer tepals, tepals unequal, the outer larger, 16–23 mm long, both inner and outer tepals with claws spreading to reflexed, filaments united in the lower half, anthers appressed to narrow style branches, crests 5–8 mm long. Flowering June–November. Clay flats, KM, LB, SE (Ladismith to Eastern Cape and southern Karoo).

Moraea bituminosa (Linnaeus fil.) Ker Gawler
Plants 25–50 cm high, stem branched, sticky; corm tunics of gnarled, woody to coarsely fibrous, brown layers. Leaves two or three, linear, channeled, trailing above. Flowers enclosed in fibrotic, acute spathes, fairly large, yellow, rarely mauve, tepals unequal, the outer larger,

20–30 mm long, both inner and outer tepal limbs spreading, filaments free but contiguous, anthers appressed to broad style branches, crests lanceolate, to 10 mm long. Flowering October–December. Granitic and sandstone slopes and flats, NW, SW (Grootwinterhoek Mountains to Agulhas).

Moraea brachygyne (Schlechter) Goldblatt
Plants 8–25 cm high, stem flexed outward above the leaf sheath; corm tunics of wiry, black fibers. Leaf single, linear, channeled, trailing above. Flowers enclosed in green, attenuate spathes, small, stellate, pink with yellow, speckled center, tepals subequal, 18–22 mm long, with short erect claws, limbs spreading, filaments united in a slender, cylindrical column, shortly hairy below, anthers erect, concealing the style branches, crests lacking. Flowering July–September. Rocky sandstone slopes, NW (Bokkeveld Mountains to Clanwilliam).

Moraea britteniae (L. Bolus) Goldblatt
Plants 20–45 cm high; corm tunics of wiry, black fibers. Leaf single, clasping the lower half of the stem, channeled, trailing above. Flowers enclosed by green, attenuate spathes, pale yellow to cream, tepals subequal, 21–35 mm long, the claws ascending, forming a narrow cup, limbs spreading, filaments united in a slender column, anthers included, appressed to narrow, barely diverging style branches and slightly exceeding them, crests 1–2 mm long. Flowering September–October. Sandy slopes, SE (Knysna to Grahamstown).

Moraea bubalina Goldblatt
Plants 30–45 cm high, stem branched, sticky; corm tunics of gnarled, woody to coarsely fibrous, brown layers. Leaves two to five, linear, channeled, trailing above. Flowers enclosed in fibrotic, acute spathes, brownish with yellow to cream nectar guides on the inner and outer tepals, the outer larger, 22–33 mm long, both inner and outer tepals with widely cupped claws and spreading limbs, filaments free but contiguous, anthers appressed to narrow style branches, crests c. 3 mm long. Flowering October–November. Rocky sandstone or shale slopes, RV, NW (Gifberg to Botterkloof and western Karoo).

Moraea bulbillifera (G. J. Lewis) Goldblatt
Plants 30–50 cm high, stems often with clusters of cormels at the nodes; corm tunics of wiry, black fibers. Leaf single, linear, trailing. Flowers enclosed in green, attenuate spathes, yellow to salmon, tepals subequal, 23–38 mm long, with short ascending claws forming a shallow cup, filaments united in a slender column, anthers appressed to narrow, diverging style branches, crests 1–2 mm long. Flowering August–September. Sandstone and limestone soils, mainly coastal, SW, AP, LB, SE (Cape Peninsula to Alexandria).

Moraea caeca Barnard ex Goldblatt
Plants 20–40 cm high, stem usually smooth, rarely velvety hairy; corm tunics of light brown, fairly coarse fibers. Leaf single, linear, channeled, trailing above. Flowers enclosed in brown-tipped, attenuate spathes, mauve, the outer tepals with a small, dark or sometimes yellow nectar guide, tepals unequal, the outer larger, 23–28 mm long, the limbs spreading, inner tepals tricuspidate with a long, spreading central cusp, filaments almost completely united, anthers appressed to broad style branches, crests erect, c. 6 mm long. Flowering September–October. Rocky sandstone slopes in fynbos, NW (Piketberg to Porterville Mountains).

Moraea calcicola Goldblatt
Plants 30–40 cm high, stem velvety; corm tunics of brown, netted fibers. Leaf single, linear, channeled, trailing above, hairy on the outer surface. Flowers enclosed in brown-tipped, attenuate spathes, mauve to purple, the outer tepals with dark blue nectar guides, tepals unequal, the outer larger, 20–35 mm long, the limbs spreading, inner tepals tricuspidate with a long, straight central cusp, filaments united, the tips free, anthers red, appressed to broad style branches, crests broad, to 4 mm long. Flowering August–September. Limestone hills, SW (St. Helena Bay to Saldanha). Page 286.

Moraea cantharophila Goldblatt & J. C. Manning
Plants 20–40 cm high; corm tunics of pale brown, netted fibers. Leaf single, linear, channeled, trailing above. Flowers enclosed by green, attenuate spathes, white or cream,

inner tepal claws with a dark central streak, style crests yellow to salmon, tepals unequal, the outer larger, 28–30 mm long, the claws shorter than the limbs, limbs spreading, inner tepal limbs fairly short, filaments united, anthers appressed to broad style branches, style crests short, to 3 mm long. Flowering August–October, mainly after fire. Rocky granitic and shale slopes in fynbos, SW (Sir Lowry's Pass to Sandy's Glen).

Moraea calcicola

Moraea cedarmontana (Goldblatt) Goldblatt
Plants 10–30 cm high; corm with gray, mealy tunic fibers. Leaves two, linear, channeled, trailing above. Flowers enclosed by translucent spathes, white with yellow nectar guides, opening in the late afternoon, sweetly scented, outer tepals 24–27 mm long, limbs laxly spreading, inner tepals smaller, suberect, crests 7–11 mm long; ovary with a tubular beak. September–October. Streambanks in sandy soils, NW (Pakhuis Mountains to Citrusdal).

Moraea cedarmonticola Goldblatt
Plants 70–100 cm high; corm tunics of wiry, black fibers. Leaves two or three, linear-lanceolate, channeled, trailing above, glaucous. Flowers enclosed in green, attenuate spathes, yellow, tepals subequal, c. 40 mm long, with long claws forming a narrow cup including the stamens, filaments united in a slender column, anthers appressed to weakly diverging style branches, crests incurving, c. 2.5 mm long. Flowering August–October, only after fire. Rocky sandstone slopes, 1000–1500 m, NW (Cedarberg Mountains).

Moraea ciliata (Linnaeus fil.) Ker Gawler
Plants 5–10(–20) cm high, stemless; corm tunics of pale, coarse, netted fibers. Leaves three to five, overlapping, channeled above, sparsely to densely hairy, usually gray. Flowers enclosed in large, lightly hairy spathes similar to the leaves, blue or yellow, rarely white, spicy fragrant, tepals unequal, the outer larger, 25–35 mm long, the limbs spreading to lightly reflexed, inner tepals erect or laxly spreading, filaments united in the lower third, anthers appressed to broad style branches, crests linear, to 15 mm long. Flowering July–September. Sandy and clay slopes, RV, NW, SW, AP, KM, LB (Namaqualand and Karoo to Riversdale).

Moraea citrina (G. J. Lewis) Goldblatt
Plants 3–6 cm high, stemless. Leaves few, oblong, chan-

Moraea ciliata

neled. Flowers in a basal tuft, yellow, tepals cupped, 18–30 mm long, filaments united in a column, style exceeding the anthers, stigmas lobed. Flowering July–October. Shallow, sandy or stony soils, 500–1000 m, NW (Bokkeveld Mountains to Gydo Pass).

Moraea collina Thunberg

Plants 20–50 cm high, stem flexed outward above the leaf sheath; corm tunics of wiry, black fibers. Leaf single, inserted above the ground, linear, channeled, glaucous, trailing above. Flowers enclosed in gray, attenuate spathes, yellow or salmon, lightly scented, tepals subequal, 25–35 mm long, the claws forming a deep cup including the stamens, filaments united in a slender column, anthers appressed to weakly diverging style branches, crests suberect, c. 1 mm long. Flowering July–September, common after fire. Lower mountain slopes and flats on sand or clay, SW (Bain's Kloof to Caledon).

Moraea comptonii (L. Bolus) Goldblatt

Plants 18–40 cm high; corm tunics of wiry, black fibers. Leaf single, glaucous, clasping the stem below, linear, channeled and trailing above. Flowers enclosed in green, attenuate spathes, yellow or salmon with a yellow center, tepals often with a large, central green mark, intensely fragrant of coconut, tepals subequal, 30–50 mm long, claws forming a wide, shallow cup, limbs spreading, filaments united in a stout column, anthers appressed to narrow, diverging style branches, crests incurved, c. 1 mm long. Flowering August–September. Clay slopes in renosterveld, SW (Villiersdorp to Stanford).

Moraea contorta Goldblatt

Plants 20–30 cm high; corm with blackish, wiry tunics. Leaf single, linear, channeled, trailing above. Flowers enclosed by translucent spathes, deep blue-violet with white nectar guides, outer tepals 21–26 mm long, limbs weakly reflexed, inner tepals slightly smaller, limbs similarly reflexed, style crests c. 10 mm long; ovary with a long tubular beak. Flowering September–October. Stony, clay flats and slopes, RV (Hantamsberg to Roggeveld Escarpment at Ganagga Pass).

Moraea comptonii

Moraea contorta

Moraea cookii (L. Bolus) Goldblatt
Plants 30–60 cm high; corm tunics of wiry, black fibers. Leaf single, clasping the lower half of the stem, channeled and trailing above, fairly broad, margins undulate. Flowers enclosed in glaucous, attenuate spathes, yellow with a darker yellow, speckled center, tepals subequal, 30–40 mm long, with short clasping claws, limbs spreading, filaments united in a thick column, anthers appressed to diverging style branches, crests incurved, 2–4 mm long. Flowering August–September. Rocky sandstone slopes, RV, NW, KM, SE (Cedarberg Mountains to Karoo and Lesotho).

Moraea cooperi Baker
Plants 20–35 cm high, stem much branched; corm tunics of dark brown, woody to fibrous layers. Leaves two or three, linear, channeled, trailing above. Flowers enclosed in green, attenuate spathes, yellow, tepals united in a tube, the outer 33–40 mm long, the limbs lightly reflexed, inner tepals absent, filaments united in the lower third, anthers appressed to the narrow style branches, crests lanceolate, to 10 mm long; ovary subsessile and capsules fusiform, concealed in the spathes. Flowering September–October. Rocky sandstone slopes and flats, often near water, NW, SW (Tulbagh to Stanford).

Moraea crispa Thunberg
Plants 8–20 cm high; corm tunics of wiry, blackish fibers. Leaf usually single, linear, channeled, often lightly twisted, margins rarely crisped or tightly rolled inward. Flowers enclosed in more or less dry, attenuate spathes, tiny, blue-mauve with yellow to orange nectar guides on the inner and outer tepals, opening in the late afternoon, tepals subequal, 11–21 mm long, claws suberect, filaments united in the lower half or almost free to the base, anthers coherent or diverging, mostly concealing the reduced style branches, crests vestigial. Flowering mostly October–November. Mainly clay slopes in renosterveld, RV, NW, KM, SE (western Karoo to Baviaanskloof and southern Karoo).

Moraea debilis Goldblatt
Plants 15–40 cm high; corm tunics of pale, netted fibers. Leaf single, linear, channeled, hairy on the outside. Flowers enclosed in partly dry, attenuate spathes, blue-mauve, becoming darkly mottled with age, tepals unequal, the outer larger, c. 20 mm long, the limbs laxly spreading, the inner tricuspidate with a straight, filiform central cusp, filaments united in the lower half, anthers appressed to narrow style branches, style crests narrow, to 7 mm long. Flowering September–October. Clay slopes in renosterveld, SW, LB (Bot River to Swellendam).

Moraea deltoidea Goldblatt & J. C. Manning
Plants, 30–40 cm high; corm tunics of pale, fine, netted fibers. Leaf single, narrow, channeled, trailing above. Flowers enclosed in green, attenuate spathes, creamy yellow, tepals unequal, the outer larger, 19–21 mm long, limbs laxly spreading, the inner erect, oblanceolate-rhomboid, filaments united in the lower two-thirds, anthers appressed to narrow style branches, crests short, c.

Moraea cooperi

1 mm long. Flowering October–November. Marshy sandstone slopes, SW (Kogelberg to Hermanus).

Moraea demissa Goldblatt
Plants 7–20 cm high, stem flexed sharply outward above the leaf sheath; corm tunics of wiry, black fibers. Leaf single, linear, channeled. Flowers enclosed by green, attenuate spathes, small, pale yellow, rarely salmon, tepals subequal, 10–12 mm long, claws ascending, forming a shallow cup, filaments united in a stout column, anthers appressed to narrow, weakly diverging style branches, crests obscure. Flowering August–September. Rocky sandstone slopes, 400–1400 m, NW (Gifberg to Citrusdal).

Moraea elegans Jacquin
Plants 18–40 cm high; corm tunics of wiry, black fibers. Leaf single, glaucous, clasping the lower half of the stem, linear, channeled, trailing above. Flowers enclosed in green, attenuate spathes, yellow with outer tepals usually orange and with prominent green blotches, intensely fragrant, tepals unequal, the outer obovate to oblong, often smaller than the narrow inner tepals, 28–35 mm long, claws forming a wide, poorly defined, shallow cup, limbs spreading, filaments united in a stout column, anthers appressed to narrow, weakly diverging style branches and exceeding them, crests incurved, c. 2 mm long. Flowering August–September. Clay slopes in renosterveld, SW (Teslaarsdal to Bredasdorp).

Moraea elliotii Baker
Plants 15–50 cm high; corm tunics of dark brown, wiry fibers. Leaf single, linear, channeled, trailing above. Flowers enclosed in green, attenuate spathes, blue-violet, the outer tepals with yellow nectar guides, tepals unequal, the outer larger, 20–30 mm long, both inner and outer tepal limbs spreading, filaments united in the lower half, anthers appressed to broad style branches, crests erect, to 10 mm long. Flowering mostly October–November. Grassy sandstone slopes, LB, SE (Mossel Bay to Malawi).

Moraea elsiae Goldblatt
Plants 20–40 cm high, stem branched, sticky; corm tunics of gnarled, woody to coarsely fibrous, brown layers. Leaves two or three, linear, channeled, trailing above. Flowers enclosed in fibrotic, obtuse spathes, yellow with dark speckles in the center, tepals subequal, 14–22 mm long, limbs spreading, filaments free but contiguous, anthers diverging, as wide as the style branches, crests vestigial. Flowering November–December. Deep sandy soils, SW (Cape Peninsula to Bredasdorp).

Moraea demissa

Moraea elegans

Moraea exiliflora Goldblatt

Plants 15–25 cm high; corm tunics of dark brown, wiry fibers. Leaf single, linear, channeled, trailing above. Flowers enclosed in green, attenuate spathes, blue-mauve, the outer tepals with yellow nectar guides, tepals unequal, the outer larger, c. 15 mm long, both inner and outer tepal limbs spreading, filaments united in the lower half, anthers appressed to broad style branches, crests erect, to 5 mm long. Flowering September. Sandstone outcrops in fynbos, KM (Swartberg Mountains).

Moraea falcifolia Klatt

Plants to 5 cm high, stemless; corm tunics of tough, wiry, blackish fibers. Leaves several in a basal rosette, spreading, channeled and somewhat twisted, the margins undulate. Flowers in a basal tuft, white with yellow nectar guides on the outer tepals and purple or yellow blotches on the inner tepals, tepals unequal, the outer 15–22 mm long, both inner and outer tepal limbs spreading, filaments united in the lower half, anthers appressed to broad style branches, crests lanceolate, 5–8 mm long. Flowering May–August. Sandy or clay slopes and flats, RV, NW, SW (southern Namibia to Bredasdorp and Karoo to Alexandria).

Moraea falcifolia

Moraea fenestrata (Goldblatt) Goldblatt

Plants 10–30 cm, high, stem flexed above the leaf sheaths; corm tunics of wiry, black fibers. Leaves three, linear, channeled. Flowers enclosed in green, attenuate spathes, salmon with yellow nectar guides, rarely uniformly yellow, tepals subequal, 15–21 mm long, with short diverging claws, limbs spreading, filaments united in a slightly bulbous column, anthers coherent, concealing the style branches, crests vestigial. Flowering August–September. Clay slopes in renosterveld, RV (western Karoo in the Tanqua and Doorn River Basins).

Moraea fergusoniae L. Bolus

Plants 12–20 cm high, branching only near the base; corm tunics of netted fibers. Leaves several, linear-lanceolate, channeled, suberect, margins undulate, sometimes crisped. Flowers enclosed in green, attenuate spathes, white, sometimes blue, the outer tepals with yellow nectar guides, outer tepals larger, c. 20 mm long, the limbs spreading, inner tepals erect, lanceolate or tricuspidate, filaments united in the lower half, anthers appressed to narrow style branches, crests lanceolate, to 7 mm long. Flowering July–August. Clay slopes in renosterveld, SW, LB (Bot River to Mossel Bay).

Moraea fistulosa (Goldblatt) Goldblatt

Plants 15–25 cm high, stem bearing sheathing, bract-like leaves with one or two branches; corm with wiry tunics. Leaf single, terete, hollow, erect. Flowers enclosed in green attenuate spathes, blue with small orange nectar guides, tepals subequal, 16–18 mm long with short claws forming a narrow cup, limbs spreading, stamens free, diverging, style dividing into three filiform branches extending between the anthers. Flowering October–November. Dry stony flats, RV (Roggeveld Escarpment).

Moraea flaccida Sweet

Plants 35–60 cm high, stem flexed outward above the leaf sheath; corm tunics of wiry, black fibers. Leaf single, linear, channeled, trailing above. Flowers enclosed in green, attenuate spathes, salmon with a yellow center or entirely yellow, tepals subequal, 35–40 mm long, claws forming a wide, shallow cup, filaments united in a slender column, anthers appressed to narrow, weakly diverging style branches, crests erect, c. 1 mm long. Flowering August–October. Wet sandstone and granitic slopes and flats, often in seeps or near streams, NW, SW (Bokkeveld Mountains to Caledon).

Moraea flavescens (Goldblatt) Goldblatt
Plants 12–30 cm high, stem flexed sharply outward above the leaf sheath; corm tunics of wiry, black fibers. Leaf single, linear, channeled, trailing above. Flowers enclosed in green, attenuate spathes, yellow with a greenish speckled center, tepals subequal, 16–24 mm long, claws forming a shallow cup, filaments united in a slender column, anthers appressed to narrow, weakly diverging style branches, crests obscure. Flowering August–September. Rocky sandstone slopes, NW (Bokkeveld to Cedarberg Mountains).

Moraea fragrans Goldblatt
Plants 30–50 cm high; corm tunics of wiry, black fibers. Leaf single, fairly broad below and clasping the lower half of the stem, linear, channeled, trailing above. Flowers enclosed in green, attenuate spathes, pale yellow, sweetly fragrant, tepals subequal, 23–25 mm long, the claws forming a deep cup enclosing the stamens, limbs spreading, filaments united in a column bulbous below, anthers cohering, concealing the style branches, crests lacking. Flowering August–September. Mainly clay soils in renosterveld, NW (Bokkeveld Plateau and western Karoo).

Moraea fugacissima (Linnaeus fil.) Goldblatt
Plants to 3–6 cm high, stemless. Leaves several, linear to terete, more or less erect, channeled below. Flowers in a basal tuft, yellow, fragrant, tepals subequal, widely cupped, 11–19 mm long, filaments united in a column, style exceeding the anthers, style lobes fringed. Flowering July–September. Wet sand and clay flats, NW, SW, AP, LB, SE (Namaqualand to Humansdorp). Page 292.

Moraea flaccida

Moraea fragrans; see also page 25

Moraea fugax (D. Delaroche) Jacquin

Plants 12–80 cm high, branches often crowded above the leaves. Leaves one or two, inserted well above the ground, linear to filiform, channeled, trailing above. Flowers enclosed in partly dry, attenuate spathes, blue, white, or yellow, spicy fragrant, tepals unequal, the outer larger, 20–30 mm long, both inner and outer tepal limbs spreading to lightly reflexed, filaments united in the lower half, anthers appressed to broad style branches, crests lanceolate, to 15 mm long; ovary and capsules beaked. Flowering August–November. Deep sands and rocky sandstone and granitic soils, NW, SW, AP, LB (Namaqualand to Mossel Bay).

Moraea fuscomontana (Goldblatt) Goldblatt

Plants 10–25 cm high, stem flexed sharply outward above the leaf sheath; corm tunics of wiry, black fibers. Leaf single, linear, channeled, trailing above. Flowers enclosed in green, attenuate spathes, pale yellow with a greenish, speckled center, tepals subequal, 20–22 mm long, with short clasping claws, limbs spreading, filaments united in a slender column, anthers coherent, concealing the style branches. Flowering September. Rocky sandstone slopes in dry fynbos, NW (Swartruggens).

Moraea galaxia (Linnaeus fil.) Goldblatt & J. C. Manning

Plants 2–4 cm high, stemless. Leaves few, ovate, prostrate, margins thickened and shortly hairy or smooth. Flowers in a basal tuft, yellow, tepals subequal, widely cupped, 16–20 mm long, filaments united in a column, style exceeding the anthers, stigmas fringed. Flowering July–September. Flats and plateaus, mainly on sandstone soils, NW, SW, AP (Cedarberg Mountains to Bredasdorp).

Moraea gawleri Sprengel

Plants 15–45 cm high; corm tunics of firm, vertical fibers. Leaves mostly two, linear, channeled, often trailing from the base, the margins often crisped. Flowers enclosed in green, acute spathes, yellow, cream, or brick red, sometimes bicolored, tepals unequal, the outer larger, mostly 18–25 mm long, both inner and outer tepal limbs reflexed, filaments united in the lower half, anthers appressed to broad style branches, crests lanceolate, to 12 mm long. Flowering July–October. Sandy or clay slopes, usually in renosterveld, NW, SW, AP, KM, LB (northern Namaqualand to Humansdorp).

Moraea gigandra L. Bolus

Plants 20–40 cm high, stem minutely velvety; corm tunics of brown, netted fibers. Leaf single, linear, channeled,

Moraea fugacissima

Moraea fugax

trailing above, smooth or sparsely hairy on the outside. Flowers enclosed in green, attenuate spathes, blue, rarely white or orange, the outer tepals with dark blue to brown nectar guides, tepals unequal, the outer larger, 30–45 mm long, the limbs round, spreading, inner tepals tricuspidate with a long, spreading central cusp, filaments united, the tips free, anthers appressed to narrow style branches and exceeding them, style crests short, c. 2 mm long. Flowering September–October. Clay soils, NW (Piketberg to Porterville).

Moraea gracilenta Goldblatt
Plants 12–80 cm high, repeatedly branched; corm tunics of pale, netted fibers. Leaves one or two, inserted well above the ground, linear, channeled, trailing above. Flowers enclosed in partly dry, attenuate spathes, blue or white, fragrant, opening in the late afternoon, tepals unequal, the outer larger, 18–28 mm long, both inner and outer tepal limbs spreading, filaments united in the lower half, anthers appressed to broad style branches, crests linear, to 12 mm long; ovary and capsules beaked. Flowering September–October. Sandy soils, NW (Clanwilliam to Tulbagh).

Moraea hesperantha (Goldblatt) Goldblatt
Plants 40–60 cm high; corm with grayish, mealy tunics. Leaves two, linear, channeled, with margins rolled inward, trailing above. Flowers enclosed in translucent spathes, dark blue-purple, opening in the late afternoon, outer tepals 26–29 mm long, the limbs weakly reflexed, inner tepals slightly smaller, limbs similarly reflexed, crests 7–10 mm long; ovary with a long tubular beak. Flowering October–November. Heavy clay slopes in renosterveld, RV, NW (Bokkeveld Plateau and western Karoo).

Moraea inconspicua Goldblatt
Plants 20–45 cm high, stem branched, sticky; corm tunics of gnarled, woody to coarsely fibrous, brown layers. Leaves two or three, linear, channeled, trailing or flat and loosely coiled. Flowers enclosed in fibrotic, acute spathes, tiny, yellow to brown or cream, tepals unequal, the outer larger, 13–18 mm long, both inner and outer tepal limbs laxly to strongly reflexed, filaments free but contiguous, anthers appressed to narrow style branches, crests linear, 3–6 mm long. Flowering September–November. Sandy and clay slopes, NW, SW, AP, KM, LB, SE (Namaqualand to Port Elizabeth). Page 294.

Moraea gawleri

Moraea gigandra (Colin Paterson-Jones)

Moraea inconspicua

Moraea incurva

Moraea insolens

Moraea lewisiae subsp. *secunda*

Moraea incurva G. J. Lewis

Plants 35–40 cm high; corm tunics of brown, netted fibers extending upward in a neck. Leaf single, linear, channeled, trailing above. Flowers enclosed in partly dry, attenuate spathes, blue, the outer tepals with cream to yellow nectar guides, tepals unequal, the outer larger, c. 20 mm long, the limbs lightly reflexed, inner tepals erect, filaments united almost to the tips, anthers red, appressed to broad style branches, crests to 4 mm long. Flowering October–November. Stony, clay flats in renosterveld, NW (Tulbagh valley).

Moraea insolens Goldblatt

Plants 20–35 cm high; corm tunics of coarse, light brown, netted fibers. Leaf single, linear, channeled, often trailing above. Flowers enclosed in brown-tipped, attenuate spathes, deep orange or cream with brown center, tepals subequal, spreading from the base, 25–30 mm long, filaments united, anthers appressed to narrow style branches and slightly exceeding them, crests c. 1.5 mm long. Flowering September. Clay slopes in renosterveld, SW (Caledon Swartberg).

Moraea karooica Goldblatt

Plants 15–30 cm high; corm tunics of wiry, black fibers. Leaf usually single, clasping the stem below, linear, channeled, often trailing above. Flowers enclosed in brown-tipped, attenuate spathes, salmon to deep pink with a yellow center edged in red or purple, tepals subequal, 18–24 mm long, the claws forming a shallow cup, limbs spreading, filaments united in a slender column, anthers parallel and coherent, concealing the style branches, crests lacking. Flowering September–October. Clay soils in renosterveld and karroid bush, RV, NW, KM (Ceres to Barrydale and western Karoo).

Moraea lewisiae (Goldblatt) Goldblatt

Plants 20–90 cm high, stem with sessile lateral flower clusters; corm with wiry tunics. Leaves two or three, sometimes single, linear, channeled and trailing above, or flat and somewhat twisted. Flowers enclosed by green, attenuate spathes, yellow, speckled with black in the center, fragrant, tepals 19–24 mm long, style with six filiform arms extending between the filaments. Flowering October–December. Various soils and habitats, mostly dry sites, RV, NW, SW, KM, LB, SE (Namaqualand to Humansdorp).

Two subspecies are recognized: subspecies *secunda* Goldblatt with capsules oblong to ellipsoid, outer tepals 24–30 mm long, stony slopes and flats, RV, NW (Namaqualand to Bokkeveld Mountains), and subspecies *lewisiae* with capsules cylindrical or nearly so, outer tepals 19–24 mm long, dry sandstone and clay slopes, NW, SW, KM, LB, SE (Clanwilliam to Humansdorp).

Moraea lilacina Goldblatt & J. C. Manning

Plants 20–35 cm high; corm tunics of brown, netted fibers. Leaf single, linear, channeled, trailing above. Flowers enclosed in green, attenuate spathes, pale pink, the outer tepals with bright yellow nectar guides, tepals unequal, the outer larger, 26–28 mm long, inner tepals tricuspidate with a long, suberect central cusp, filaments c. 7 mm long, anthers appressed to narrow style branches, crests slender, 4–8 mm long. Flowering August–September. Clay slopes, LB (Langeberg Mountains near Robinson's Pass).

Moraea linderi Goldblatt

Plants 35–45 cm high, stem with an elongate basal internode, branches short and crowded; corm tunics brown, woody, becoming fragmented with age. Leaves two or three, linear, channeled. Flowers enclosed in leathery, truncate to acute spathes, the outer spathe often not sheathing above, yellow, the outer tepals with darker yellow nectar guides, tepals unequal, the outer larger, c. 35 mm long, the limbs spreading to weakly reflexed, limbs of the inner tepals also weakly spreading, filaments united in the lower third, anthers appressed to broad style branches, crests erect, c. 10 mm long. Flowering October–December. Seasonally moist, poorly drained, sandy flats, NW (Piketberg and Cold Bokkeveld).

Moraea longiaristata Goldblatt

Plants 15–30 cm high, stem usually unbranched; corm tunics of dark brown, netted fibers. Leaf single, linear, narrowly channeled, trailing above. Flowers enclosed in green, attenuate spathes, white, the outer tepals with yellow nectar guides outlined in dark blue, and darkly veined, tepals unequal, the outer larger, 23–30 mm long, the limbs spreading, inner tepals elongate-filiform, filaments united in the lower half, anthers red, appressed to narrow style branches, crests erect, c. 5 mm long. Flowering September–October. Rocky sandstone lower slopes, SW (Caledon Swartberg).

Moraea longifolia (Jacquin) Persoon
Plants 60–150 cm high, stem with sessile lateral flower clusters; corm with wiry tunics. Leaves three to five, linear, channeled, trailing above. Flowers enclosed by green, attenuate spathes, pale yellow, unscented, tepals subequal, 20–28 mm long, spreading, style with six filiform arms extending between the filaments. Flowering October–November. Shady, moist sites on sandstone, SW (Cape Peninsula to Du Toit's Kloof).

Moraea longistyla (Goldblatt) Goldblatt
Plants 15–30 cm high, stem flexed outward above the leaf sheath; corm tunics of black, wiry fibers. Leaf single, linear, channeled, trailing above. Flowers enclosed in green, attenuate spathes, yellow or salmon, tepals subequal, 25–35 mm long, the claws forming a deep cup including the stamens, anthers appressed to suberect style branches usually united in the lower half, crests short or vestigial. Flowering August–October. Mainly clay soils, renosterveld or arid fynbos, NW, SW, KM (Ceres to Montagu and Caledon).

Moraea loubseri Goldblatt
Plants 15–20 cm high, stem velvety hairy; corm tunics of brown, netted fibers. Leaf single, linear, channeled, trailing above, hairy on the outside. Flowers enclosed in brown-tipped, attenuate spathes, deep blue to purple, with blackish purple hairs on the outer tepals, tepals unequal, the outer larger, 20–24 mm long, the limbs laxly spreading, the inner tepals tricuspidate with a long, laxly spreading central cusp, filaments united in the lower two-thirds, anthers appressed to narrow style branches, style crests arching outward, c. 2 mm long: Flowering August–September. Limestone and calcareous sand on granite hills, SW (Saldanha Bay).

Moraea louisabolusiae Goldblatt
Plants 15–40 cm high, stem sharply flexed above the leaf sheaths; corm tunics of wiry, black fibers. Leaf single, sometimes as many as three leaves, linear, channeled, trailing above. Flowers enclosed in green, attenuate spathes, yellow, rarely salmon, speckled in the center, tepals subequal, c. 28 mm long, with short, cupped claws, limbs spreading, filaments united in a slender column, partly included in the tepal cup, anthers appressed to weakly diverging style branches and exceeding them, crests c. 1 mm long. Flowering August–September. Rock outcrops, NW (Namaqualand to Nardouw Mountains).

Moraea lugubris (Salisbury) Goldblatt
Plants 6–16 cm high; corm tunics forming a basket-like network. Leaves two, linear, channeled, glossy green. Flowers enclosed in glossy, acute spathes, deep blue, the outer tepals with yellow nectar guides, tepals unequal, the outer larger, to 18 mm long, both inner and outer tepal

Moraea lugubris

limbs spreading, filaments united in the lower two-thirds, anthers appressed to narrow style branches, style crests feathery. Flowering August–November, mainly after fire. Mostly damp sandstone soils, NW, SW, AP (Bokkeveld Mountains to Bredasdorp).

Moraea lurida Ker Gawler

Plants 20–30 cm high; corm tunics of gray to brown, netted fibers. Leaf single, linear, channeled, trailing above. Flowers enclosed by green, attenuate spathes, dull maroon or violet, sometimes the tepal edges with yellow to orange, usually fetid smelling, tepals unequal, the outer larger, 22–30 mm long, with claws exceeding the limbs, limbs spreading, inner tepal limbs fairly short, sometimes more or less trilobed, the central cusp longer, filaments united, anthers appressed to broad style branches, style crests short, to 3 mm. Flowering August–October, mainly after fire. Rocky sandstone and granitic slopes in fynbos, SW (Kogelberg to Bredasdorp).

Moraea luteoalba (Goldblatt) Goldblatt

Plants 2–5 cm high, stemless. Leaves few, ovate and prostrate, margins conspicuously hairy. Flowers in a basal tuft, yellow fading to white at edges, tepals shallowly cupped, 15–21 mm long, stamens free, style exceeding the anthers, stigmas fringed. Flowering July–September. Sandstone outcrops, 400–1000 m, NW (Matsikamma to Cedarberg Mountains).

Moraea macgregorii Goldblatt

Plants 20–50 cm high; corm tunics of soft, brown fibers, extending upward in a neck. Leaf single, channeled, the margins rolled inward. Flowers enclosed in leathery, attenuate spathes, mauve, the outer tepals with orange and white nectar guides, opening in the late afternoon, tepals unequal, the outer larger, c. 30 mm long, claws unusually long, both inner and outer tepal limbs spreading, filaments united in the lower two-thirds, anthers appressed to narrow style branches, crests linear, to 10 mm long; ovary and capsules beaked. Flowering September–October. Stony, clay slopes, NW (lower slopes of the Bokkeveld Mountains).

Moraea lurida

Moraea luteoalba

Moraea macrocarpa

Moraea macronyx

Moraea macrocarpa Goldblatt

Plants 8–12 cm high, stemless; corm tunics of pale, coarse, netted fibers. Leaf single, linear, channeled, trailing above. Flowers enclosed in green, attenuate spathes, violet, the outer tepals with yellow nectar guides, tepals unequal, the outer 20–30 mm long, limbs laxly spreading, inner tepals also laxly spreading, filaments united in the lower half, style crests 12–18 mm long; ovary and capsules elongate, beaked, partly concealed. Flowering September. Deep sand in arid fynbos, NW (Lambert's Bay to Worcester).

Moraea macronyx G. J. Lewis

Plants 9–15 cm high, stemless; corm tunics of pale, spongy layers or netted fibers. Leaves three, overlapping, channeled above, lightly hairy, usually gray. Flowers enclosed in large, lightly hairy spathes similar to the leaves, deep yellow, the outer tepals with white nectar guides speckled with dark spots, spicy fragrant, tepals unequal, the outer larger, 40–60 mm long, claw longer than the limb, limbs spreading, inner tepals erect, filaments united in the lower half, anthers appressed to broad style branches, crests lanceolate, to 25 mm long. Flowering September–October. Rocky sandstone slopes, NW, LB, SE (Cold Bokkeveld to Avontuur).

Moraea marlothii (L. Bolus) Goldblatt

Plants 50–75 cm high; corm tunics of wiry, black fibers. Leaf single, clasping the lower half of the stem, broad, glaucous, channeled and trailing above. Flowers enclosed in attenuate spathes, yellow or salmon pink, tepals subequal, 26–34 mm long, with short clasping claws, limbs spreading, filaments united in a stout column, anthers appressed to narrow, weakly diverging style branches and exceeding them, crests incurved, c. 3 mm long. Flowering August–October. Sandstone rocks or heavy clay soils, RV, NW (western Karoo and Bokkeveld Mountains).

Moraea maximiliani (Schlechter) Goldblatt & J. C. Manning

Plants 15 cm high, stem usually branched above the leaves and branches short, crowded in a fascicle. Leaves two to several, clustered well above the ground, linear, channeled, often trailing above. Flowers enclosed in leathery, truncate spathes, buff-yellow, tepals subequal, 16–24 mm long, limbs spreading, filaments united in a slender column, anthers erect, exceeding and concealing the short style branches, crests vestigial. Flowering August–September. Sandstone slopes and flats, NW (Pakhuis Mountains).

Moraea melanops Goldblatt & J. C. Manning

Plants 2–4 cm high, stemless. Leaves few, broadly lanceolate, prostrate. Flowers in a basal tuft, purple with a blackish center, tepals shallowly cupped to laxly spreading, c. 16 mm long, filaments united in the lower half or free almost to the base, style exceeding the anthers, stigmas lobed. Flowering August–September. Clay slopes in renosterveld, SW (Shaw's Pass to Potberg).

Moraea miniata Andrews

Plants 15–60 cm high; corm tunics of wiry, black fibers. Leaves two or three, linear, channeled, trailing above. Flowers enclosed in glaucous, attenuate spathes, usually salmon, sometimes yellow, rarely white, minutely speckled in the center, tepals subequal, mostly 15–24 mm long, with short clasping claws, limbs spreading, filaments united in a bulbous column, anthers erect, concealing the style branches, crests lacking. Flowering August–September. Mainly clay slopes, renosterveld and karroid scrub, RV, NW, SW, LB (Namaqualand to Riversdale, and Karoo).

Moraea minima Goldblatt

Plants 2–3 cm high, stemless. Leaves few, lanceolate, spreading, margins undulate. Flowers in a basal tuft, tiny, white marked with green, tepals cupped, to 12 mm long, filaments united in a column, style reaching the middle of anthers, stigmas lobed. Flowering July–August. Clay flats in renosterveld, SW (Bredasdorp).

Moraea minor Ecklon

Plants 15–30 cm high, stem flexed outward above the leaf sheath; corm tunics of wiry, black fibers. Leaf single, linear, channeled, trailing above, glaucous. Flowers enclosed in gray, attenuate spathes, yellow or salmon, tepals subequal, 21–37 mm long, claws forming a deep cup including the stamens, limbs spreading, filaments united in a slender column, anthers appressed to narrow, weakly diverging style branches, crests c. 1 mm long; ovary and capsules elongate and cylindrical. Flowering August–September. Sandstone and granitic slopes and flats, NW, SW (Gifberg to Cape Peninsula).

Moraea melanops

Moraea miniata

Moraea nana

Moraea neglecta

Moraea monticola Goldblatt
Plants 10–15 cm high with one or two branches, the stem bearing sheathing, bract-like leaves; corm with blackish, wiry tunics. Leaf single, terete, often trailing above. Flowers enclosed in green attenuate spathes, blue or white, with yellow nectar guides, tepals subequal, 13–15 mm long, with short claws forming a narrow cup, limbs spreading, stamens free, diverging, style with three filiform branches extending between the anthers. Flowering November–December. Rocky lower slopes, KM (Kamiesberg and southern Karoo to Swartberg Mountains).

Moraea nana (L. Bolus) Goldblatt & J. C. Manning
Plants 10–30 cm high, stem with an elongate basal internode, and branches crowded in a fascicle above the leaves; corm with brown, woody tunics. Leaves two to several, clustered well above the ground, linear, channeled, often trailing above. Flowers enclosed by blunt, leathery spathes, pale yellow or salmon, tepals 19–23 mm long with short clasping claws, limbs spreading, style with six filiform arms extending between the stamens. Flowering September–November. Rocky granite and sandstone slopes, NW, KM (Namaqualand to Citrusdal).

Moraea neglecta G. J. Lewis
Plants 20–50 cm high, stem unbranched, the nodes sticky; corm tunics of soft, brown, more or less fibrous layers. Leaf single, terete, often rigid. Flowers enclosed in leathery, truncate spathes, yellow with darkly stippled markings on the outer tepals, fragrant, tepals unequal, the outer 38–50 mm long, limbs spreading, inner tepals erect, filaments united basally, anthers appressed to broad style branches, crests 12–22 mm long; ovary three-angled. Flowering September–November. Usually deep sandy soils, NW, SW, AP (Bokkeveld Mountains to Agulhas coast).

Moraea nubigena Goldblatt
Plants 3–5 cm high, nearly stemless; corm tunics of fine, dark, netted fibers. Leaf single, linear-lanceolate, channeled, spreading, shiny. Flowers enclosed in shiny, acute spathes, small, blue-mauve with orange nectar guides on the outer tepals, tepals unequal, the outer larger, 10–14

mm long, both inner and outer tepals with limbs spreading, filaments united in the lower half, anthers appressed to broad style branches, crests short, c. 2 mm long. Flowering September–October. Rock seeps at 1200 m, NW (Worcester at Fonteintjiesberg).

Moraea ochroleuca (Salisbury) Drapiez

Plants 35–75 cm high; corm tunics of wiry, black fibers. Leaf single, rarely two leaves, linear, channeled, trailing above. Flowers enclosed in green, attenuate spathes, yellow to orange or bicolored, fetid smelling, tepals subequal, 30–40 mm long, the claws forming a wide cup, limbs laxly spreading, filaments united in a slender column, anthers appressed to narrow, diverging style branches, crests rounded, short. Flowering mainly August–November, mostly after fire. Rocky sandstone slopes, NW, SW (Citrusdal to Caledon).

Moraea papilionacea (Linnaeus fil.) Ker Gawler

Plants 10–20 cm high, branching mainly from the base; corm tunics of soft, brown fibers. Leaves three or four, usually hairy, channeled, trailing above. Flowers enclosed in green, attenuate spathes, yellow or salmon, the outer tepals with yellow nectar guides, outer tepals larger, c. 25 mm long, both inner and outer tepal limbs spreading, filaments united near the base, anthers appressed to broad style branches, style crests lanceolate, to 15 mm long. Flowering August–October. Mostly sandstone soils, sometimes granite or clay, in renosterveld and transitional fynbos, to 500 m, NW, SW (Cedarberg Mountains to Bredasdorp).

Moraea patens (Goldblatt) Goldblatt

Plants 25–45 cm high, stem flexed sharply outward above the leaf sheath; corm tunics of wiry, black fibers. Leaf single, channeled, trailing above. Flowers enclosed in green, attenuate spathes, yellow or salmon pink, tepals subequal, 24–27 mm long, claws ascending, forming a short cup, filaments united in a slender column, anthers appressed to narrow, weakly diverging style branches, crests c. 0.5 mm long. Flowering August–September. Sandstone soils, NW (Nardouw and Pakhuis Mountains).

Moraea ochroleuca

Moraea papilionacea

Moraea polystachya

Moraea pritzeliana

Moraea pilifolia Goldblatt
Plants to 4 cm high, stemless. Leaves several, ovate-oblong, spreading to prostrate, the margins with thickened, densely hairy margins with hairs longer than the width of the thickened margins. Flowers in a basal tuft, yellow, tepals cupped, 14–16 mm long, filaments united in a column, style exceeding the anthers, style lobes fringed. Flowering June–July. Stony slopes, NW (Namaqualand to Gifberg).

Moraea polyanthos Linnaeus fil.
Plants 15–60 cm high, stem often much branched; corm tunics of dark brown, wiry fibers. Leaves several, linear, channeled. Flowers blue or white, with yellow nectar guides on the inner and outer tepals, tepals subequal, 23–40 mm long, the claws forming a narrow cup, the limbs spreading, filaments united in a slender column, anthers diverging, about as wide as the style branches, style crests vestigial. Flowering August–September. Flats and lower slopes, mainly clay, NW, KM, LB, SE (Worcester to Eastern Cape).

Moraea polystachya (Thunberg) Ker Gawler
Plants 50–80 cm high, much branched; corm tunics of dark brown, wiry fibers. Leaves several, linear, channeled, often trailing above. Flowers enclosed in green, attenuate spathes, blue, the outer tepals with yellow nectar guides, tepals unequal, the outer larger, 36–55 mm long, the limbs spreading, the inner erect, or the claws also spreading, filaments united in the lower two-thirds, anthers appressed to broad style branches, crests prominent, to 20 mm long. Flowering mainly March–June. Dry karroid slopes, KM (Ladismith to Oudtshoorn, Karoo to southern Namibia).

Moraea pritzeliana Diels
Plants 10–35 cm high; corm with wiry, often mealy tunics. Leaves two, flat and translucent along the midline, entire blade helically coiled, often tightly. Flowers enclosed in translucent spathes, dark blue with cream nectar guides, outer tepals 21–30 mm long, limbs weakly reflexed, inner tepals smaller, limbs similarly reflexed,

crests 7–11 mm long; ovary with a long tubular beak. Flowering September–October. Sandstone and clay soils, mainly in renosterveld, RV, NW (Bokkeveld Plateau and western Karoo).

Moraea pseudospicata Goldblatt

Plants 25–50 cm high, lateral inflorescences sessile; corm tunics of tough, wiry, dark fibers forming a thick mass. Leaf single, terete, long and trailing, often dry at flowering. Flowers enclosed in more or less dry, acute spathes, tiny, violet with orange nectar guides on the inner and outer tepals, tepals subequal, 12–17 mm long, with short suberect claws, filaments united in a slender column, anthers parallel, concealing the narrow style branches, crests vestigial. Flowering mainly December–March. Stony clay slopes in karroid scrub, RV (Bokkeveld Plateau).

Moraea pyrophila Goldblatt

Plants 15–30 cm high, stem flexed outward above the leaf sheath; corm tunics of wiry, black fibers. Leaf single, inserted above the ground, linear, channeled, fairly short, the apex often flattened. Flowers enclosed in green, attenuate spathes, pale yellow, tepals subequal, 28–33 mm long, claws forming a narrow cup including the stamens, filaments united in a slender, sparsely hairy column, anthers appressed to narrow, suberect style branches, crests incurved, c. 1 mm long. Flowering mainly March–June, only after fire. Rocky sandstone slopes, NW, SW (Piketberg to Bredasdorp).

Moraea radians (Goldblatt) Goldblatt

Plants 12–25 cm high, stem flexed sharply outward above the leaf sheath; corm tunics of wiry, black fibers. Leaf single, linear, channeled, glaucous, trailing above. Flowers enclosed in glaucous, attenuate spathes, cream with a yellow center, tepals subequal, 30–34 mm long, with short suberect claws, limbs spreading, filaments free, style branches subsessile, bilobed, shorter than the stamens, crests lacking. Flowering August–September. Clay soils in renosterveld, SW (northern foothills of the Riviersonderend Mountains).

Moraea ramosissima (Linnaeus fil.) Druce

Plants 50–120 cm high, much branched, roots spiny; corm with brown, cartilaginous tunics. Leaves several in a two-ranked fan, linear, channeled, shiny green. Flowers enclosed in pale green, acute spathes, yellow with darker yellow nectar guides on the outer tepals, tepals unequal, the outer larger, c. 30 cm long, limbs of both inner and outer tepals reflexed, filaments free or basally united, anthers appressed to broad style branches, crests lanceolate, to 15 mm long. Flowering October–December, mainly after fire. Damp sandy or stony flats and slopes, NW, SW, LB, SE (Gifberg to Eastern Cape). Page 304.

Moraea reflexa Goldblatt

Plants 17–110 cm high; corm tunics of wiry, black fibers. Leaf single, linear, channeled, glaucous, broad and clasping the stem below. Flowers enclosed in pale green, attenuate spathes, nodding on recurved pedicels, pale yel-

Moraea pseudospicata

low with dark spots near the base of the tepals, tepals subequal, 27–34 mm long, with short, suberect, clasping claws, the limbs reflexed, filaments united in a bulbous column, anthers appressed to and slightly exceeding the narrow, diverging style branches, crests linear, prominent. Flowering October–November. Rocky doleritic soils, RV (western Karoo on the Hantamsberg).

Moraea regalis Goldblatt & J. C. Manning

Plants 18–25 cm high; corm tunics of brown, netted fibers. Leaf single, linear, channeled, trailing above. Flowers enclosed in brown-tipped, attenuate spathes, deep violet, the outer tepals each with a small white nectar guide outlined in dark purple, tepals unequal, the outer larger, 26–40 mm long, the limbs reflexed, the inner almost linear to tricuspidate, then with a slender, incurving central cusp, filaments united in the lower two-thirds, anthers appressed to narrow, spreading style branches, style crests erect, 5–8 mm long. Flowering August–September. Rocky slopes, KM (De Rust).

Moraea riparia (Goldblatt) Goldblatt

Plants 45–90 cm high, stem with sessile lateral flower clusters; corm with wiry tunics. Leaves two or three, linear, channeled, trailing above. Flowers enclosed in green, attenuate spathes, yellow, strongly fragrant, tepals subequal, 16–21 mm long, spreading, style with six filiform arms extending between the filaments. Flowering October–November. Along streams and rivers in rocky sandstone, NW (Clanwilliam to Tulbagh).

Moraea serpentina Baker

Plants 4–15 cm high, branching mainly from the base; corm tunics of wiry, blackish fibers. Leaves mostly two to four, linear, twisted or coiled, the margins often rolled inward. Flowers enclosed in green to dry, attenuate spathes, white and yellow, often flushed violet, tepals unequal, the outer larger, 24–30 mm long, the limbs laxly reflexed, inner tepals erect, spathulate, filaments united in the lower half, anthers appressed to narrow style branches, crests lanceolate, 4–8 mm long. Flowering September–October. Dry stony flats, NW (Namaqualand and Karoo to the Olifants River Valley).

Moraea ramosissima

Moraea serpentina

Moraea setifolia (Linnaeus fil.) Druce
Plants mostly 5–16 cm high; corm with pale, soft tunic fibers. Leaves one or two, linear, channeled, trailing above. Flowers enclosed by translucent spathes, small, pale mauve with orange and white nectar guides, outer tepals 12–18 mm long, limbs weakly reflexed, inner tepals slightly smaller, limbs similarly reflexed, crests 4–7 mm long; ovary with a long tubular beak. Flowering September–November. Sandy and gravelly flats and slopes, NW, SW, AP, KM, LB (Namaqualand to Grahamstown).

Moraea spathulata (Linnaeus fil.) Klatt
Plants 80–100 cm high, stem unbranched and sheathed with large, overlapping bracts; corm tunics of coarse, brown fibers, extending upward in a neck. Leaf single, linear, flat or channeled, often fairly broad, trailing above. Flowers enclosed in green, acute spathes, large, yellow, the outer tepals with dark yellow nectar guides, tepals unequal, the outer longer, 35–50 mm, the limbs laxly spreading, inner tepals erect, filaments united in the lower half, anthers appressed to broad style branches, crests erect, to 12 mm long. Flowering June–September in the Cape, other months elsewhere in southern Africa. Sandstone and peaty slopes and flats, KM, SE (Kammanassie Mountains and George to Zimbabwe and Mozambique).

Moraea speciosa (L. Bolus) Goldblatt
Plants 40–70 cm high, stem often much branched; corm tunics of wiry, blackish fibers. Leaves several, strap-like, channeled, often twisted above. Flowers enclosed in green, attenuate spathes, blue with a pale cup, both inner and outer tepals with yellow nectar guides, tepals subequal, 35–45 mm long, the claws forming a wide cup, limbs spreading, filaments united in a slender column, anthers cohering or weakly diverging, partly concealing the narrow style branches, style crests vestigial. Flowering mostly July–August. Flats and lower slopes, mainly clay, RV (Tanqua Basin and southern Karoo).

Moraea stagnalis (Goldblatt) Goldblatt
Plants to 2–4 cm high, stemless. Leaves several, linear to lanceolate. Flowers in a basal tuft, yellow, tepals widely cupped, 10–15 mm long, filaments united in a column, style reaching the anther apices, style lobes fringed and arching over the anthers. Flowering June–August. Wet sites on sandstone soils, 400–800 m, NW (Namaqualand to Pakhuis Pass).

Moraea thomasiae Goldblatt
Plants 15–30 cm high; corm tunics of brown to gray, netted fibers. Leaf single, linear, channeled, to flat, trailing above. Flowers enclosed in narrow, partly dry, attenuate spathes, pale yellow with dark veins, the outer tepals with darker yellow nectar guides, tepals unequal, the outer larger, 26–37 mm long, the limbs lightly reflexed, the inner initially erect, spreading later, filaments barely united at the base, anthers appressed to narrow style branches, crests prominent, to 10 mm long. Flowering August–September. South-facing shale slopes in renosterveld, NW, KM (Worcester to Barrydale).

Moraea tricolor Andrews
Plants 5–15 cm high, stemless; corm tunics of pale, netted fibers. Leaves three to five, overlapping, channeled

Moraea speciosa

above, almost hairless to densely hairy, dark green to gray. Flowers enclosed in large, almost hairless to hairy spathes similar to the leaves, pink, red, purple, or yellow, with yellow nectar guides on the outer tepals, fragrant, tepals unequal, the outer larger, 20–25 mm long, the limbs spreading, both inner and outer tepal limbs spreading, filaments united in the lower third, anthers appressed to broad style branches, crests broadly triangular, serrated, c. 10 mm long. Flowering July–September. Wet sandy flats, SW (Hopefield to Napier).

Moraea tricuspidata (Linnaeus fil.) G. J. Lewis

Plants 25–60 cm high; corm tunics of pale, netted, often soft fibers. Leaf single, linear, channeled, trailing above. Flowers enclosed in green, attenuate spathes, white to cream, the outer tepals with darkly speckled claws, smelling sour, tepals unequal, the outer larger, 26–30 mm long, the limbs spreading, inner tepals tricuspidate with a short, obliquely twisted central cusp, filaments united in the lower half, anthers appressed to narrow style branches, crests c. 6 mm long. Flowering mainly September–October, especially after fire. Sandstone, granite, or sometimes clay slopes, NW, SW, LB, SE (Cedarberg to Grahamstown).

Moraea tripetala (Linnaeus fil.) Ker Gawler

Plants 20–45 cm high; corm tunics of pale or dark brown, netted tunics. Leaf single, linear, channeled, trailing above, occasionally hairy on the outside. Flowers enclosed in green or partly dry, attenuate spathes, blue to violet, rarely white or yellowish, the outer tepals with cream nectar guides, tepals unequal, the outer larger, 20–35 mm long, the limbs spreading to laxly reflexed, inner tepals reduced to a short tooth, rarely filiform, absent, or trifid with filiform lobes, filaments barely united at the base, anthers often red, appressed to narrow style branches, crests erect, to 10 mm long. Flowering August–September. Rocky sandstone and clay soils, to 1200 m, RV, NW, SW, AP, KM, LB (Bokkeveld Mountains and western Karoo to Riversdale and Swartberg Mountains).

Moraea tulbaghensis L. Bolus

Plants 25–50 cm high, stem minutely velvety hairy; corm tunics of brown, netted fibers. Leaf single, linear, channeled, trailing above, hairy on the outer surface. Flowers enclosed in brown-tipped, attenuate spathes, orange to reddish, the outer tepals with iridescent blue or green or darkly speckled markings, tepals unequal, the outer larger, 20–40 mm long, the limbs spreading or arching upward, inner tepals lanceolate to tricuspidate with a long, straight central cusp, filaments united, the tips free, anthers appressed to narrow style branches and exceeding them, crests erect, c. 2 mm long. Flowering September. Clay flats in renosterveld, NW, SW (Piketberg to Paarl).

Moraea umbellata Thunberg

Plants 15–45 cm high, stem usually branched above the leaves and branches short, crowded in a fascicle. Leaves two to several, clustered above ground, linear, channeled, trailing above. Flowers enclosed in leathery, truncate spathes, pale yellow, tepals subequal, 19–27 mm long, limbs spreading, filaments united in a slender column, anthers appressed to and exceeding the narrow style branches, crests vestigial. Flowering September–No-

Moraea tricuspidata

vember. Seasonally wet sandstone flats and plateaus, NW, SW (Piketberg to Caledon).

Moraea unguiculata Ker Gawler

Plants 20–50 cm high; corm tunics of brown, netted fibers. Leaf single, narrow, channeled, trailing above. Flowers enclosed in partly dry, attenuate spathes, white to cream, brownish, rarely violet, the outer tepals usually with pale nectar guides, tepals unequal, the outer larger, mostly 15–20 mm long, the limbs spreading to fully reflexed, inner tepals erect, tricuspidate with a long, central cusp rolled inward, filaments free only near the tips, anthers appressed to narrow style branches, crests erect, to 4 mm long. Flowering September–November. Mostly shale slopes in renosterveld, RV, NW, SW, AP, LB, SE (Namaqualand to Port Elizabeth and isolated Karoo mountains).

Moraea vallisavium Goldblatt

Plants 10–35 cm high, stem unbranched; corm with brown, netted fibers. Leaf single, linear. Flowers enclosed in green, obtuse to truncate spathes, yellow with brown spotted nectar guides on the outer tepals, tepals unequal, the outer larger, 20–24 mm long, the limb spreading, inner tepals narrower, the limbs also spreading, filaments united in the lower third, appressed to broad style branches, crests erect, 6–10 mm long; ovary three-angled. Flowering December–January. Sandstone rocks, 500–1000 m, SW, LB (Klein River Mountains and Langeberg Mountains).

Moraea vallisbelli (Goldblatt) Goldblatt

Plants 15–30 cm high, stem flexed outward above leaf sheath; corm tunics of wiry, black fibers. Leaf single, linear, channeled, glaucous. Flowers enclosed in gray, attenuate spathes, yellow or pink with darkly outlined yellow nectar guides, tepals subequal, c. 25 mm long, claws forming a narrow cup, filaments united in a slender column, anthers partly exserted, appressed to narrow, weakly diverging style branches, crests obscure. Flowering July–September. Rocky sandstone soils, NW (Bokkeveld Mountains to Botterkloof).

Moraea tripetala; see also page 19

Moraea tulbaghensis; see also page 20

Moraea variabilis (G. J. Lewis) Goldblatt
Plants 2–5 cm high, stemless. Leaves several, ovate to oblong, channeled, mostly prostrate. Flowers in a basal tuft, purple to mauve, with yellow center, tepals cupped, 20–30 mm long, filaments united in a column, anthers sessile, style exceeding the anthers, stigmas lobed. Flowering September–October. Mainly clay soils, 400–1000 m, NW (Cold Bokkeveld to Ceres).

Moraea vegeta Linnaeus
Plants 15–30 cm high, stem minutely hairy; corm tunics of soft, pale fibers. Leaves three or four, linear-lanceolate, channeled, glaucous. Flowers enclosed in glaucous, acute spathes, buff to dull purple-brown, the outer tepals with yellow nectar guides, outer tepals larger, 20–25 mm long, both inner and outer tepal claws lightly reflexed, filaments united in the lower half, anthers appressed to broad style branches, crests lanceolate, to 10 mm long. Capsules nodding. Flowering September–October. Damp clay or granite slopes and flats, SW (Darling to Caledon).

Moraea verecunda Goldblatt
Plants 15–25 cm high; corm tunics of wiry, blackish fibers. Leaf single, linear, channeled, the margins rolled inward, long and trailing above. Flowers enclosed in more or less dry, attenuate spathes, tiny, violet with yellow nectar guides on the inner and outer tepals, tepals subequal, 9–13 mm long, with short suberect claws, filaments united in a slender column, free in the upper third, anthers coherent, concealing the narrow style branches, crests vestigial. Flowering October–November. Rocky sandstone flats in arid fynbos, NW (Bokkeveld Mountains).

Moraea versicolor (Salisbury ex Klatt) Goldblatt
Plants 2–5 cm high, stemless. Leaves several, ovate to lanceolate, prostrate or spreading, margins undulate. Flowers in a basal tuft, pink to purple, often with a yellow center, tepals cupped, 14–22 mm long, filaments united in a column, style exceeding the anthers, stigmas lobed. Flowering August–September. Clay and granite flats and slopes, to 300 m, SW (Tulbagh to Cape Peninsula and Houwhoek).

Moraea vespertina Goldblatt & J. C. Manning
Plants 45–60 cm high, stems branched, sticky; corm tunics of gnarled, woody to coarsely fibrous, brown layers. Leaves four to six, linear, channeled, trailing above. Flowers enclosed in fibrotic, acute spathes, white, fragrant, opening in the late afternoon, tepals unequal, the outer larger, 40–43 mm long, both inner and outer tepal limbs laxly spreading, filaments free but contiguous, anthers appressed to narrow style branches, crests c. 15 mm long. Flowering September–December. Seasonally wet clay around large dolerite boulders, RV (Bokkeveld Plateau).

Moraea villosa (Ker Gawler) Ker Gawler
Plants 30–40 cm high, stem velvety hairy; corm tunics of pale, netted fibers. Leaf single, hairy on the outer surface, linear, channeled, trailing above. Flowers enclosed in brown-tipped, attenuate spathes, purple, blue, pinkish, or orange, the outer tepals with prominent, dark markings and a yellow claw, tepals unequal, the outer larger, 30–40 mm long, with spreading, round limbs, inner tepals tricuspidate with a long, spreading central cusp, filaments united, the tips free, anthers often red, appressed to broad style branches, crests erect, 3–7 mm long. Flowering August–September. Stony granite and clay slopes and flats, NW, SW (Piketberg to Gordon's Bay and Ceres).

Moraea versicolor

Moraea virgata Jacquin

Plants 30–85 cm high, stem with sessile lateral flower clusters; corm with wiry tunics. Leaves mostly two to four, linear, channeled, trailing above. Flowers enclosed by dry, attenuate spathes, yellow, unscented, with a filiform perianth tube 4–9 mm long, tepals spreading, 14–32 mm long; ovary sessile, style with six filiform arms extending between the filaments. Capsules narrowly ellipsoidal, enclosed in the spathes. Flowering mainly September–November. Shale and granite soils, rarely sandstone, RV, NW, SW, AP, LB, SE (southern Namaqualand and western Karoo to Port Elizabeth).

Two subspecies are recognized: subspecies *karooica* Goldblatt with tepals 23–32 mm long, stony dolerite slopes and flats, RV (Roggeveld Escarpment), and subspecies *virgata* with tepals 14–22 mm long, mostly granitic and clay soils, NW, SW, AP, LB, SE (southern Namaqualand to Port Elizabeth).

Moraea viscaria (Linnaeus fil.) Ker Gawler

Plants 20–45 cm high, stems sticky; corm tunics of gnarled, woody to coarsely fibrous, brown layers. Leaves two or three, linear, channeled, trailing above. Flowers enclosed in fibrotic, acute spathes, white, brownish beneath, opening in the later afternoon, fragrant, tepals unequal, the outer larger, 15–23 mm long, both inner and outer tepal limbs spreading, filaments free but contiguous, anthers appressed to narrow style branches, crests c. 6 mm long. Flowering September–December. Sandy flats, SW, AP (Saldanha to Cape Agulhas).

Moraea vlokii Goldblatt

Plants 15–20 cm high; corm tunics of rigid, pale fibers. Leaves one or two, linear, channeled. Flowers enclosed in green, obtuse to acute spathes, tiny, yellow, opening in the early morning and fading soon after midday, tepals subequal, 10–14 mm long, the claws short, forming a narrow cup, limbs spreading, filaments united in a slender column, free in the upper 1 mm, anthers appressed to short, narrow style branches and exceeding them, crests vestigial. Flowering October. Rocky sandstone slopes in arid fynbos, KM (Montagu to Swartberg Mountains).

Moraea worcesterensis Goldblatt

Plants mostly 15–20 cm high; corm tunics of brown, netted fibers. Leaf single, linear, channeled, often trailing above. Flowers enclosed by partly dry, attenuate spathes, purple with pale, diamond-shaped markings on the inner and outer tepals, tepals unequal, the outer larger, c. 16 mm long, spreading from the base, inner tepals similarly

Moraea villosa

Moraea worcesterensis

spreading, filaments united almost to the tips, anthers appressed to narrow style branches, crests vestigial, overtopped by the anthers. Flowering September–October. Rocky slopes and flats in fynbos or karroid bush, NW (low hills near Worcester).

Neodregea

COMMON NAME mosquito lily, FAMILY Colchicaceae. Deciduous perennial. ROOTSTOCK an asymmetric ovoid corm covered with dark, leathery or cartilaginous tunics. LEAVES three, scattered along the stem, lanceolate, only the lowermost clasping and the uppermost reduced and bract-like. INFLORESCENCE a bractless spike-like cyme with the lowermost flower subtended by the uppermost leaf. FLOWERS one to three, erect, sessile, star-like, the tepals free, slender and attenuate, narrowed and clawed below with a nectary on each of two conspicuous lobes curved upward above the claw, persistent and reflexed in fruit, yellowish. STAMENS arising midway along the claws. OVARY deeply lobed with several ovules per locule; STYLES three, short and hook-like, subterminal on each lobe. FRUIT an oblong septicidal capsule. SEEDS several per locule, globose or subglobose, brown. Basic chromosome number $x = 11$ or 10. South Africa; 1 sp.

Neodregea glassii

The curious little *Neodregea* is rarely collected, largely because of its inconspicuous appearance and early flowering, but it has been found scattered all along the southern Cape coast from the slopes of the Helderberg at Somerset West to Grahamstown. It is closely related to *Wurmbea* but differs most obviously from it in the completely free tepals. The curiously shaped flowers suggest pollination by gnats or other small flies.

FURTHER READING. *Neodregea* was reviewed by Garside (1935).

Neodregea glassii C. H. Wright

Plants to 4 cm high. Leaves three, lanceolate. Flowers one to three, yellow, tepals spreading, blades slender and thread-like but conspicuously eared at the top of the claw, 5–6 mm long, claw c. 1 mm long, filaments c. 0.8 mm long, anthers 0.2 mm long, styles c. 0.5 mm long. Flowering May–June. Mainly clay slopes in renosterveld under bushes, SW, LB, SE (Somerset West to Eastern Cape at Grahamstown).

Neopatersonia

COMMON NAME fly lily, FAMILY Hyacinthaceae. Deciduous perennials. ROOTSTOCK an ovoid bulb with pale, papery or thinly leathery outer tunics lightly barred above and extending as a short or long neck. LEAVES one to three, suberect or falcate to spreading, straight or curled, linear to lanceolate, more or less channeled, the margins rarely crisped or fringed below. INFLORESCENCE a few- to many-flowered raceme, usually subcorymbose; bracts pale and membranous or green and slightly fleshy, ovate to attenuate, sometimes more or less auriculate and fimbriate below. FLOWERS suberect, star-shaped, the tepals shortly united at the base, pale whitish green, sometimes marked with brown or purple, unpleasantly scented, the pedicels rather stout. STAMENS with filaments conspicuously broadened and sometimes fleshy below, sometimes distinctly toothed or shouldered, and united below and joined to the base of the tepals, slender and slightly incurved above. OVARY ovoid with few ovules per locule; STYLE slightly longer than the ovary, the stigma three-branched, the branches short or long, spreading and slightly decurved. FRUIT an ovoid to conical capsule, sometimes rather pointed. SEEDS few to several per locule, pear-shaped, black. Basic chromosome number *x* unknown. Southern Namibia to Eastern Cape; 3 spp., 1 in the Cape.

The curious genus *Neopatersonia* is endemic to the winter-rainfall region of southern Africa. It was first allied with *Whiteheadia* on the basis of the basally united stamens and pear-shaped seeds but this supposed relationship is a spurious one. Results from DNA sequence studies indicate that it is part of the alliance that includes *Albuca*, *Galtonia*, and *Ornithogalum*. *Neopatersonia* has an unusual distribution with a single species extending from the Little Karoo to Port Elizabeth and the other two recorded only from southern Namibia and northern Namaqualand. It is typically found in arid habitats, and although *N. uitenhagensis* occurs in a region of rather higher rainfall than the other species, it favors drier limestone outcrops or well-drained calcareous sands. For some time thought to be a rare species from around Port Elizabeth, *N. uitenhagensis* is now known from as far west as Robertson and De Hoop in the Western Cape. The greenish flowers with their unpleasant smell are visited by various muscid flies for the nectar that accumulates in the open cup formed by the united tepals and filaments.

FURTHER READING. *Neopatersonia* was described and illustrated by Schönland (1912) and further species were added by Lewis (1952). A color illustration of *N. uitenhagensis* accompanies an account of the species by Archibald (1956).

Neopatersonia uitenhagensis Schönland

Plants 15–20 cm high. Leaves two or three, ascending or falcate, lanceolate and channeled, somewhat glaucous. Flowers 12–15 mm diam., greenish with white stamens, smelling of fish, filaments fleshy and lobed below; stigma shortly three-branched. Flowering September–October. Stony, mostly limestone slopes, NW, AP, LB, SE (Robertson to Addo).

Nerine

COMMON NAME nerine, FAMILY Amaryllidaceae. Evergreen or deciduous perennials. ROOTSTOCK a bulb covered with soft, felt-like tunics, producing extensible threads when torn. LEAVES four to six, sometimes as few as two or as many as eight, green or rarely dry at flowering, suberect to spreading, linear to strap-shaped, smooth. INFLORESCENCE a conical to hemispherical umbel with 1–75 flowers, on a slender to stout, more or less compressed scape, the scape smooth or sometimes minutely hairy; spathe bracts two, rapidly withering. FLOWERS zygomorphic, trumpet-shaped to widely flared, pink, red or white, the pedicels spreading, as long as or rarely somewhat longer than the flowers, the tepals united into a short tube, recurved, margins usually undulate or crisped. STAMENS shortly united basally, inserted near tepal base, tightly clustered, upturned toward the tips, often with short lateral appendages at the base; anthers dorsifixed. OVARY with as many as four ovules per locule; STYLE filiform, declinate or sometimes central the stigma minutely trifid or three-lobed. FRUIT a small, subglobose capsule with membranous walls, readily disintegrating. SEEDS fleshy, ovoid, 3–7 mm diam., reddish green, the embryo green. Basic chromosome

Neopatersonia uitenhagensis

Nerine humilis (Colin Paterson-Jones)

Nerine pudica (Colin Paterson-Jones)

Nerine sarniensis (Colin Paterson-Jones)

number $x = 11$. Southern Africa, mostly in the eastern summer-rainfall region; c. 23 spp., 4 in the Cape.

The genus *Nerine* is richly represented in the damp grasslands of eastern southern Africa and the mountains of the southwestern Cape, but a few species tolerate the extremely arid conditions of the Kalahari and Great Karoo. The genus is curiously absent from the semiarid winter-rainfall area of Namaqualand. Scarlet is the dominant flower color for *N. sarniensis* in nature but several populations on the Cape Peninsula have carmine to dusky pink flowers. The most notable feature of these strikingly beautiful flowers is the glitter of reflected sunlight on the tepal surface. As in *Brunsvigia*, the red- and pink-flowered species attract different pollinators. *Nerine sarniensis* belongs to a guild of red-flowered, summer-flowering plants pollinated by the large satyrid butterfly known as the pride of Table Mountain, *Aeropetes tulbaghia*.

Nerine has held the attention of plant breeders more than any other southern African genus of Amaryllidaceae. *Nerine sarniensis*, which has given rise to most cultivated *Nerine* hybrids, has been grown in Britain since the early 17th century. More recent breeding efforts, however, have focused on improving the flowering performance of the hardy cultivars and generally on raising deeper color forms and more good whites. Several hundred cultivars have been named, many of which produce excellent cut flowers.

FURTHER READING. *Nerine* was last reviewed by Traub (1967), who carefully researched the early literature, and by Norris (1974), who examined many species in the wild. More recently, a rare drought-tolerant species was described by Snijman (1995). Duncan (2002) has published a well-illustrated guide to the species and their cultivation and propagation in southern Africa. The growing and breeding of nerines in Britain was described by Smee (1984) and Toogood and Hide (1996). A detailed account of the reproductive biology of *Nerine* was given by Brown et al. (1999a, b).

Nerine humilis (Jacquin) Herbert

Plants of varying size, 10–40 cm high. Leaves four to six, dry or green at flowering, spreading to prostrate, strap-shaped, 4–10(–15) mm wide, dull green. Flowers 1–8(–12) in a loose umbel, tepals lanceolate, flared upward, 3–5 mm wide, pale to deep pink, margins undulate, stamens in a horizontal cluster, slightly shorter than the tepals, style exceeding the stamens. Flowering April–June. Loamy and sandstone soils among rocks on flats and lower slopes, NW, SW, AP, KM, LB, SE (Clanwilliam to Worcester, Bredasdorp, Montagu, and Baviaanskloof Mountains).

Nerine pudica Hooker fil.

Plants 30 cm high. Leaves usually two, emerging at flowering, narrowly strap-shaped, c. 3 mm wide. Flowers one to six, spreading horizontally, tepals lanceolate, spreading more or less regularly or four slightly curved upward, c. 6 mm wide, margins plane, pale pink with dark keels, stamens in a horizontal cluster, shorter than the tepals, style slightly longer than the tepals. Flowering March–May, usually after fire. Rocky slopes at high elevations, SW (Du Toit's Kloof Mountains to Caledon).

Nerine ridleyi E. Phillips

Robust plants to 75 cm high. Leaves usually three, green at flowering, recurved, broadly strap-shaped, 15–25 mm wide. Flowers 4–11, deep pink, on spreading pedicels 80 mm long, tepals lanceolate, flared upward, mostly 5–7 mm wide with undulate margins, stamens in a horizontal cluster, slightly shorter than the tepals, style exceeding the stamens. Flowering February–April. Steep south-facing sandstone ledges at high elevations, NW (Cold Bokkeveld to Hex River Mountains).

Nerine sarniensis (Linnaeus) Herbert

Striking plants 15–45 cm high. Leaves four to seven, dry or green at flowering, recurved, broadly strap-shaped, 5–25 mm wide. Flowers 5–15, bright red with a golden luster, rarely pale to dark pink or white, tepals lanceolate, regularly arranged, 4–10 mm wide, recurved, with the margins undulate toward the apex, stamens suberect, prominent, slightly curved toward the apex, style exceeding the stamens. Flowering March–May. Shaded rocky slopes in loamy soil, NW, SW (Citrusdal to Caledon).

Onixotis

COMMON NAME water phlox, FAMILY Colchicaceae. Deciduous perennials. ROOTSTOCK an asymmetric ovoid corm covered with dark, leathery or cartilaginous tunics. LEAVES three, scattered along the stem, lanceolate, the uppermost smaller and bract-like. INFLORESCENCE a bractless spike-like scorpioid cyme. FLOWERS few to many, suberect, sessile, star-like, the tepals free, narrowed and somewhat clawed below, with a more or less narrowly pouch-like nectary above each of two conspicuous lobes curved upward above the claw, deciduous, white to pink, often with dark nectaries, unscented or faintly fragrant. STAMENS arising on the tepal claws. OVARY cylindrical with several ovules per locule; STYLES three, sometimes shortly united below, slender. FRUIT an oblong septicidal capsule. SEEDS several per locule, globose or subglobose, brown. Basic chromosome number $x = 10$. Winter-rainfall South Africa; 2 spp.

Onixotis punctata

Onixotis stricta; see also page 11

Both species of *Onixotis* are restricted to the winter-rainfall region of South Africa. The paired, auriculate nectaries recall those of *Neodregea*, but in that genus the styles are short, hook-like, and always borne separately on the lobed ovary, and the tepals are persistent in fruit. The flowers of *O. stricta* are visited by various bees, including honeybees in search of nectar, and it is likely that *O. punctata* is also bee pollinated.

Onixotis stricta (known for more than 250 years by the epithet *triquetra* and until relatively recently as *Dipidax triquetra*) is the larger and more attractive of the species. It can blanket the small pools in which it grows with spikes of cherry-like flowers. It is a valuable addition to water gardens, where it can be grown in pots immersed during the growing season but lifted out for dry storage in the summer.

Onixotis punctata (Linnaeus) Mabberley

Plants 10–20 cm high; corm tunics black, leathery or cartilaginous. Leaves three, lanceolate to narrowly lanceolate, the margins minutely hairy, the uppermost set about halfway up the stem. Flowers sessile in short spikes, white to maroon, tepals 7–12 mm long, claws 1.5–2 mm long, filaments 2–3 mm long, anthers c. 1 mm long, styles free, 2–2.5 mm long. Flowering July–September. Damp sandstone and clay slopes, NW, SW, AP, KM, LB (Bokkeveld Mountains to Swellendam).

Onixotis stricta (Burman fil.) Wijnands

Plants 20–50 cm high; corm tunics brown, papery. Leaves three, the lowermost basal and the upper two set just below the spike, the lower two with slender subterete blades triangular in cross section, the uppermost without a blade and clasping. Flowers sessile in short or long spikes, pink with cherry red nectar guides, tepals 8–12 mm long, claws c. 2 mm long, filaments 4–5 mm long, anthers c. 1.5 mm long, styles shortly united below, 1.5–2 mm long. Flowering August–October. Marshes and pools, NW, SW (Namaqualand to Cape Peninsula and Worcester).

Ornithogalum

COMMON NAME chincherinchee (or chincherichee), Eurasian species often called star-of-Bethlehem, FAMILY Hyacinthaceae. Deciduous or rarely evergreen perennials. ROOTSTOCK a globose bulb, rarely poorly developed and the rootstock rhizomatous, subterranean or partially exposed, the tunics sometimes scale-like. LEAVES one to several, green or dry at flowering, erect or spreading, linear to oblong or filiform, sometimes very succulent, hairless or hairy, the margins smooth, hairy, fringed, or hyaline, the sheaths sometimes persistent and forming a papery or weakly or strongly fibrous, sometimes horizontally barred sheath around the base of the stem. INFLORESCENCE a several- to many-flowered raceme, sometimes subcorymbose with shortened axis; bracts membranous or leafy, small or large. FLOWERS suberect or spreading, star- or cup-shaped, tepals more or less shortly united at the base, rarely into a distinct tube, white, yellow, orange, or yellowish green, with or without darker keels, scented or unscented, closing at night or rarely nocturnal. STAMENS with filaments joined to the base of the tepals, free or rarely united below, filiform to lanceolate, similar or the inner usually broader, both whorls or more usually the inner variously expanded or toothed below. OVARY ovoid to globose, sometimes shortly stalked, with few to many ovules per locule; STYLE vestigial to long, cylindrical, sometimes slightly deflexed, stigma small and three-lobed to large and head-like. FRUIT a fusiform, ovoid to globose capsule, more or less three-angled or three-lobed, membranous or leathery, enclosed in the dry perianth or exposed. SEEDS few to many per chamber, angled to discoid, black. Basic chromosome number $x = 9$, other base numbers 8, 7, 6. Africa and Eurasia, mainly southern Africa; c. 120 spp., 43 in the Cape.

The large genus *Ornithogalum* has been divided into numerous subgenera, several of which have also been recognized as genera in their own right. Species of *Ornithogalum* are found in a wide range of habitats, including dry stony slopes, deep coastal sands or limestone, rock pavement, seeps, and forest margins. Although widespread across Africa, the genus is best developed in the drier parts of the winter-rainfall region of southern Africa, and the majority of the larger-flowered species occur there.

The flowers are usually unscented or weakly scented but species of *Ornithogalum* subgenus *Osmyne* are often very fragrant. These are probably visited by long-tongued bees (Apidae: Anthophorinae) but the smaller flowers of the majority of species are likely to be visited by a range of insects. The larger-flowered species with dark eyes, including *O. dubium* and *O. thyrsoides*, are adapted for pollination by monkey beetles (Scarabaeidae: Hopliini).

Although the flowers of all species close at night, they soon lose this ability if kept indoors and are long-lasting and rewarding in the vase. Relatively few species have flowers distinctive enough to warrant cultivation, but there are startling exceptions, and the florists' chincherinchee, *Ornithogalum thyrsoides*, is justifiably widely grown. Their long-lasting beauty and carrying qualities fitted them ideally for travel, and sheaves of their handsome inflorescences, sent from the Cape, graced Victorian homes through the northern winters. This species and its hybrids are now cultivated throughout the world. Other handsome species are *O. dubium*, which has yellow or orange as well as white flowers, and *O. maculatum*, the best form of which has brilliant orange-red flowers boldly spotted with black at the tips. A few other species are worth growing for their flowers but *O. longibracteatum*, the pregnant onion, is cultivated as a curiosity for its large, smooth bulb, which is exposed above the soil. Many species of *Ornithogalum* are poisonous, and all parts of *O. thyrsoides* are toxic to stock. That species in particular thrives on overgrazed lands where it is avoided by the animals. It is a common sight on the outskirts of Cape Town, where it flowers in dense stands in early summer.

FURTHER READING. The revision of the South African species of *Ornithogalum* by Obermeyer (1978) is somewhat outdated but a more recent treatment by U. and D. Müller-Doblies (1996) is marred by an overzealous fragmentation of species.

Ornithogalum bicornutum F. M. Leighton

Plants 10–16 cm high; outer bulb tunics leathery, brown. Leaves two to four, narrowly ovate to linear with tubular sheathing bases, the margins often thickened and shiny with backward-pointing bristles above and below, c. 10 mm long, dry at flowering. Flowers in a narrow raceme, nocturnal, white, tepals 5–7 mm long, filaments expanded below into two spreading horns, pedicels 4–6 mm long. Capsules ovoid, pointed, 4 mm long. Flowering October–December. Dry stony places, RV, NW (Botterkloof and western Karoo).

Ornithogalum ciliiferum U. & D. Müller-Doblies

Plants 10–20 cm high, peduncles and pedicels minutely punctate; outer bulb tunics leathery, dark brown. Leaves two to five, ovate to linear with tubular sheathing bases, the margins thickened and papillate or with two rows of minute slender hairs, 1–5 cm long, dry at flowering. Flowers in a narrow raceme with conspicuously fringed bracts, white, tepals 7–14 mm long, filaments filiform, the inner broader below, pedicels 6–25 mm long. Capsules ovoid, 3–4 mm long. Flowering November–December. Stony slopes, RV, NW (Namaqualand to Clanwilliam).

Ornithogalum comptonii F. M. Leighton

Plants 5–10 cm high; outer bulb tunics pale or gray. Leaves three to eight, curved, narrowly oblong, channeled and keeled, fibrotic, 2–6 cm long, the margins with stiff backward-pointing hairs. Flowers in a dense subcorymbose raceme, white with brown keels, tepals c. 6 mm long, filaments lanceolate, the inner broader, pedicels 6–12 mm long. Capsules ovoid. Flowering October–July. Shale flats, RV, KM (western and Little Karoo).

Ornithogalum concordianum (Baker) U. & D. Müller-Doblies

Plants 10–20 cm high. Leaves 8–10, strap-shaped, corkscrew-coiled throughout, flat or channeled, 3–20 cm long. Flowers spreading, firm, yellow with broad green keels, tepals c. 10 mm long, filaments awl-shaped, pedicels c. 10 mm long. Capsules oblong-globose, c. 20 mm long. Flowering August–September. Stony flats, RV, NW, KM, SE (southern Namibia and western Karoo to Clanwilliam through Little Karoo to Uniondale).

Ornithogalum conicum Jacquin

Plants 40–100 cm high; outer bulb tunics pale. Leaves 6–12, lanceolate, green or drying at flowering. Flowers in a conical or cylindrical raceme, white, tepals 10–20 mm long, filaments filiform to awl-shaped, the inner sometimes with an ovate or square basal expansion, pedicels 10–60 mm long. Capsules fusiform to ovoid or oblong, pointed. Flowering November–December. Clay or loam flats, often moist, RV, NW, SW, KM, SE (Bokkeveld Plateau and western Karoo to Cape Peninsula, and Eastern Cape).

Two subspecies are recognized: subspecies *conicum* with a conical inflorescence 60–120 cm tall, pedicels 10–60 mm long, moist hollows or sandy flats, SW, SE (Cape Peninsula, Eastern Cape), and subspecies *strictum* (L. Bolus) Obermeyer with a narrowly cylindrical inflorescence to 30 cm tall, pedicels 5–15 mm long, clay or loam flats, RV, NW, KM (Bokkeveld Plateau and western Karoo to Montagu).

Ornithogalum concordianum

Ornithogalum constrictum F. M. Leighton
Plants 20–40 cm high; outer bulb tunics pale yellow. Leaves one to three, dry at flowering, prostrate, oblong, the margins minutely fimbriate. Flowers suberect in a spike-like raceme, white with greenish keels below, tepals 10–15 mm long, stamens unequal, dimorphic, the outer shorter with filaments oblong or tapering, the inner expanded above, pedicels 8–22 mm long. Capsules fusiform, beaked, 8–10 mm long. Flowering November–February. Clay soils in renosterveld, AP, KM, SE (Worcester, Little Karoo, Bredasdorp to Lesotho).

Ornithogalum diluculum Obermeyer
Plants to 25 cm high. Leaf single, oblong, leathery, margin cartilaginous, to 80 × 15 mm. Flowers slightly nodding, firm, yellow with green keels, tepals 15 mm long, filaments awl-shaped, pedicels c. 20 mm long. Capsules oblong-globose, 7–10 mm long. Flowering September–October. Dry slopes and flats, RV, KM (western Karoo to Montagu).

Ornithogalum dregeanum Kunth
Plants to 50 cm high; bulb deep-seated, small. Leaves three to seven, wiry, subterete or lightly grooved, often loosely twisted, 20–60 cm long, forming a long narrow neck often faintly orange-spotted and decaying into thin netted strips. Flowers in a subspicate raceme, suberect, white, tepals c. 9 mm long, filaments awl-shaped, pedicels c. 5 mm long. Capsules ovoid, trigonous, c. 10 mm long. Flowering December–January. Sandy, often wetter sites, NW, SW (Tulbagh to Klein River Mountains).

Ornithogalum dubium Houttuyn
Plants 10–50 cm high; outer bulb tunics brown. Leaves three to eight, linear to ovate, the margins minutely hairy, 5–20 cm long. Flowers in a subcorymbose or conical raceme, yellow to orange or rarely white, often with a green or brown center, tepals 10–20 mm long, filaments fleshy, the inner with eared expansions folded around the ovary, style very short. Capsules oblong, c. 15 mm long. Flowering August–December. Mountains and flats, NW, SW, AP, KM, LB, SE (Clanwilliam to Paarl, Caledon to Port Elizabeth, western Karoo, Eastern Cape).

Ornithogalum conicum subsp. *strictum*

Ornithogalum dubium

Ornithogalum esterhuyseniae Obermeyer

Plants 50–70 cm high; bulb often poorly developed and rhizomatous below. Leaves erect, three to five, linear-oblong, to 40 cm long. Flowers subcorymbose, suberect, white, tepals c. 12 mm long, filaments awl-shaped, the inner broader, ovary stalked, pedicels 10–50 mm long. Capsules obovoid to triangular, stalked, c. 10 mm long. Flowering December–February, usually after fire. Wet places at high elevations, NW, SW (Hex River Mountains to Hottentots Holland Mountains).

Ornithogalum fimbrimarginatum F. M. Leighton

Plants 20–45 cm high; outer bulb tunics hard and dark. Leaves about five, usually dry at flowering, oblong or narrowly ovate, 5–10 cm long, the margins usually minutely fringed or hairy. Flowers in a subcorymbose to conical raceme, white with or without a dark center, lightly scented, tepals 10–20 mm long, filaments awl-shaped or ovate-acuminate, the inner broader, pedicels to 30 mm long. Capsules ovoid, c. 10 mm long. Flowering September–January. Widespread, NW, SW, KM, SE (Gifberg to Eastern Cape).

Ornithogalum flexuosum (Thunberg) U. & D. Müller-Doblies

Plants 20–45 cm high, gregarious; bulb relatively small. Leaves two to nine, semiterete to channeled, succulent, to 45 cm long, forming a long neck. Flowers subcorymbose at first, the raceme becoming lax and cylindrical, spreading, tepals 6–7 mm long, filaments awl-shaped, ovary narrowed below, pedicels 20–60 mm long. Capsules obovoid to globose, trigonous, 6–9 mm long. Flowering November–March. Marshes and riverbanks, LB, SE (Riversdale to Port Elizabeth to Malawi).

Ornithogalum graminifolium Thunberg

Plants 10–40 cm high; outer bulb tunics brown. Leaves three, sometimes two or as many as five, linear to lanceolate, channeled, 8–25 cm long, dry or green at flowering, hairless or with long hairs, often along the margins near the base, surrounded by a brittle, often purplish sheath or cataphyll. Flowers in a subspicate raceme on a long peduncle, white or pinkish with dark keels, tepals 5–10 mm long, filaments linear, the inner ovate-acuminate, pedicels 1–6 mm long. Capsules ovoid, c. 9 mm long. Flowering December–March. Stony clay flats and slopes, often moist sites, RV, NW, SW, AP, KM, LB, SE (western Karoo and Bokkeveld Mountains to KwaZulu-Natal).

Ornithogalum hispidum Hornemann

Plants 10–40 cm high; outer bulb tunics gray. Leaves three to six, ovate to linear with tubular, often with spotted sheathing bases, sparsely to densely hairy, to 10 cm long, green or dry at flowering, the margins thickened and minutely bristly. Flowers in a narrow raceme, white, tepals spreading or reflexed, 8–18 mm long, filaments filiform or awl-shaped, the inner sometimes expanded below, pedicels 10–20 mm long. Capsules ovoid, beaked. Flowering August–January. Clay flats or rock outcrops, NW, SW, KM (Namaqualand to Cape Peninsula to Little Karoo).

Two subspecies are recognized: subspecies *bergii* (Schlechtendal) Obermeyer with flowers with the inner

Ornithogalum hispidum subsp. *hispidum*

filaments winged below, seeds densely prickly, flowering December–January, mainly montane on sandstone outcrops, SW (Darling to Hermanus), and subspecies *hispidum* with flowers with the inner filaments filiform or widened below, seeds smooth, warty, or sparsely prickly, flowering August–October, clay flats and stony clay slopes, NW, KM (Namaqualand to Worcester).

Ornithogalum inclusum F. M. Leighton

Plants to 30 cm high; outer bulb tunics white. Leaves 4–14, drying at flowering, suberect, lanceolate-attenuate, margins minutely fimbriate, usually crisped. Flowers suberect in a subspicate raceme, white with greenish keels below, tepals 10–12 mm long, stamens unequal, dimorphic, the outer shorter with filaments oblong or tapering, the inner expanded above, pedicels 2–8 mm long. Capsules oblong-globose, 10 mm long. Flowering August–September. Karroid flats, NW (Botterkloof Valley at Doornbosch).

Ornithogalum juncifolium Jacquin

Plants 10–40 cm high; outer bulb tunics pale to gray. Leaves several, linear to filiform, usually fibrotic and ribbed, sometimes twisted, 10–20 cm long, usually with rows of small hairs, the bases usually persisting as a finely fibrous neck. Flowers in a dense spike-like raceme, white with darker keels, faintly honey scented, tepals 7–10 mm long, filaments linear to ovate-acuminate, pedicels 2–7 mm long. Capsules ovoid, c. 5 mm long. Flowering November–March. Dry flats or exposed rocky slopes, SW, AP, KM, LB, SE (Little Karoo and Caledon to eastern southern Africa).

Ornithogalum longibracteatum Jacquin

Plants to 1.5 m high, gregarious; bulbs often exposed and green, forming bulblets. Leaves 8–12, spreading, lanceolate, often flaccid, 40–100 cm long. Flowers in a dense raceme with long-attenuate bracts, whitish with broad green keels, smelling musty, tepals c. 9 mm long, filaments ovate-acuminate or with short basal extensions, pedicels 5–15 mm long. Capsules globose-trigonous, c. 10 mm long. Flowering August–May. Shaded slopes and forest margins, SE (Mossel Bay to tropical East Africa).

Ornithogalum maculatum Jacquin

Plants 8–50 cm high; outer bulb tunics pale or brown. Leaves two to five, grayish and leathery, to 15 cm long. Flowers in a subcorymbose raceme, orange to orange-red or yellow, rarely buff, outer tepal tips often with a dark or transparent blotch, tepals 10–25 mm long, filaments awl-shaped, the inner often broader, style very short, pedicels 10–30 mm long. Capsules ellipsoidal. Flowering September–October. Usually sandy soils, often on rocks, RV, NW, SW (Namaqualand to Paarl, western Karoo). Page 320.

Ornithogalum multifolium Baker

Plants 3–25 cm high; outer bulb tunics thin, brown. Leaves 2–10, terete, succulent, often twisted, to 10 cm long. Flowers in a subcorymbose raceme, yellow to orange, tepals 6–15 mm long, filaments narrowly ovate, the inner slightly wider, style very short, pedicels to 20 mm long. Capsules oblong to ovoid, 10 mm long. Flow-

Ornithogalum longibracteatum

Ornithogalum maculatum

Ornithogalum multifolium

ering September–October. Shallow soil on rocks, RV, NW, SW (Namaqualand, Bokkeveld Mountains to Mamre, western Karoo).

Ornithogalum nannodes F. M. Leighton

Plants to 15 cm high; outer bulb tunics pale dull gray, forming a wrinkled neck sheathing the fibrous leaf bases. Leaves 2–30, semiterete to subfiliform, minutely toothed in rows, 10–60 mm long, usually dry at flowering. Flowers in a lax, usually subcorymbose wiry raceme, whitish with brown midribs, tepals c. 5 mm long, filaments lanceolate, pedicels 8–20 mm long. Capsules oblong to ovoid, 5–7 mm long. Flowering October–December. Hard, stony soil, RV, NW, SW (Namaqualand and western Karoo to Stellenbosch).

Ornithogalum paludosum Baker

Plants 20–50 cm high, stiffly erect; bulb elongate and poorly developed, somewhat rhizomatous below. Leaves two to six, sometimes as many as nine, erect, linear, 8–20 cm long, the margins often rolled inward, fibrotic. Flowers in a subspicate raceme, suberect, white, tepals 6–12 mm long, filaments awl-shaped, the inner broader, ovary stalked, pedicels 2–4 mm long. Capsules ovoid, trigonous, c. 10 mm long. Flowering October–January. Wet grassy slopes, SW, KM, SE (Caledon to Mpumalanga).

Ornithogalum pentheri A. Zahlbruckner

Plants 10–50 cm high; leaves, scape, bracts, and pedicels sparsely glandular hairy. Leaves two to five, sometimes as many as seven, linear, channeled, finely ribbed or striate, clasping below, glandular hairy, 10–40 cm long. Flowers spreading, firm, yellow with broad green keels, tepals c. 12 mm long, filaments expanded below. Capsules ovoid, trigonous, 10–20 mm long. Flowering August–October. Stony and sandy slopes, RV, NW (Calvinia to Citrusdal).

Ornithogalum pilosum Linnaeus fil.

Plants 15–30 cm high, often with more than one raceme, peduncles and pedicels minutely punctate; outer bulb tunics hard, shiny black, sometimes forming a neck. Leaves usually four, lanceolate, sheathing below, to 15 cm long, green or dry at flowering, the margin with even stiff hairs

0.5–3 mm long. Flowers in a narrow raceme, white with pinkish reverse, tepals spreading or reflexed, c. 10 mm long, filaments linear, the inner ovate-acuminate. Capsules ovoid, 7 mm long. Flowering October–December. Clay flats and lower slopes, NW, SW, KM, LB (Pakhuis Mountains to Riversdale).

Ornithogalum polyphyllum Jacquin
Plants 25–60 cm high. Leaves 8–20, terete to linear, loosely coiled above on drying, 10–40 cm long. Flowers spreading, firm, yellow or white with green keels, violet scented, tepals c. 12 mm long, filaments slightly widened below, pedicels to 20 mm long. Capsules oblong-globose, c. 20 mm long. Flowering August–September. Stony slopes, RV, NW (Namaqualand to Cold Bokkeveld).

Ornithogalum pruinosum F. M. Leighton
Plants 10–30(–60) cm high; outer bulb tunics hard and brown. Leaves three to six, erect, oblong to obovate, gray and firm, 6–14 cm long. Flowers in a subcorymbose to cylindrical raceme, white, rarely with a dark center, tepals c. 15 mm long, filaments dimorphic, the outer filiform, the inner awl-shaped or winged below, pedicels 10–20 mm long. Capsules ovoid. Flowering September–October. Rocky slopes and flats, RV (Namaqualand to western Karoo).

Ornithogalum pullulatum F. M. Leighton
Plants 15–30 cm high, peduncles and pedicels minutely punctate; outer bulb tunics hard, shiny black, sometimes forming a neck. Leaves usually four, lanceolate, sheathing below, to 15 cm long, green or dry at flowering, the margin with two rows of uneven soft hairs 3–5 mm long. Flowers in a narrow raceme, white with pinkish reverse, tepals spreading or reflexed, c. 10 mm long, filaments linear, the inner ovate-acuminate, style sharply deflexed at the base, then erect in younger flowers. Capsules ovoid, 7 mm long. Flowering October–December. Clay flats and lower slopes, RV (Namaqualand to western Karoo).

Ornithogalum rotatum U. & D. Müller-Doblies
Plants 5–15 cm high; outer bulb tunics grayish and leathery. Leaf single, elliptical to ovate, 50–70 mm long. Flow-

Ornithogalum pentheri

Ornithogalum polyphyllum

ers in a subumbellate raceme on pedicels 10–30 mm long, suberect, cream, flushed gray, tepals 9–10 mm long, united into a tube 4–5 mm long, filaments inserted at the mouth of the tube, ovate, shortly joined at the base. Capsules ovoid, 10 mm long. Flowering September–October. Gravelly flats, RV (Namaqualand to Calvinia, western Karoo).

Ornithogalum rupestre Linnaeus fil.
Plants 2–10 cm high; outer bulb tunics white. Leaves one to three, linear-filiform, flat or margins rolled inward, succulent, 10–40 mm long. Flowers in a subumbellate raceme, white, often flushed pink, tepals 5–7 mm long, filaments narrowly ovate, the inner broader, style very short. Capsules ovoid. Flowering September–December. Sandy pockets on granite boulders, NW, SW (Bokkeveld Mountains to Saldanha).

Ornithogalum sabulosum U. & D. Müller-Doblies
Plants 10–50 cm high. Leaves two, suberect, tapering, channeled, ribbed, glandular-papillate with adhering sand. Flowers spreading, firm, yellow with broad green keels, tepals c. 12 mm long, filaments awl-shaped or expanded below, pedicels to 30 mm long in fruit. Capsules ovoid, trigonous, 10–20 mm long. Flowering September–October. Deep sands, NW, SW (Namaqualand to Yzerfontein).

Ornithogalum sardienii Van Jaarsveld
Plants to 4 cm high, evergreen; bulb borne above ground, outer tunics gray or green. Leaves 20–50, *Haworthia*-like, 15–25 mm long, triangular in cross section with as many as six rows of short, stiff white bristles. Flowers in a delicate raceme, white, tepals 5–6 mm long, filaments linear, the inner broader, pedicels 10–20 mm long. Capsules ovoid, 3.5 mm long. Flowering January–March. Enon conglomerate hills, KM (Oudtshoorn).

Ornithogalum schlechterianum Schinz
Plants (5–)10–30 cm high, peduncle straggling or flexuous; outer bulb tunics pale. Leaves 3–10, linear to narrowly lanceolate, hairless or the margins minutely hairy, soft and spreading, to 30 cm long. Flowers in a subcorymbose raceme on a flaccid peduncle, white, tepals 5–7 mm long, filaments lanceolate, pedicels 10–30 mm long. Capsules ovoid to globose, 6 mm long. Flowering December–February. Rock ledges at middle to upper elevations, often damp, SW, KM, LB, SE (Cape Peninsula to Outeniqua and Swartberg Mountains).

Ornithogalum secundum Jacquin
Plants to 50 cm high, often reddish. Leaves dry at flowering, c. 10, oblong, 5–15 cm long, the margins often hyaline and fimbriate or entire. Flowers spreading or slightly nodding, firm, yellow with green keels, 12–15 mm long, filaments awl-shaped, pedicels to 50 mm long in fruit. Capsules ovoid, c. 12 mm long. Flowering August–November. Stony slopes and flats, RV, NW, SW (Namaqualand and western Karoo to Saldanha).

Ornithogalum suaveolens Jacquin
Plants 10–50 cm high. Leaves two to seven, linear channeled, clasping below, 10–40 cm long. Flowers spreading or nodding, firm, yellow with green keels, tepals 12–15

Ornithogalum schlechterianum

mm long, filaments awl-shaped or the inner expanded below, pedicels to 30 mm long in fruit. Capsules ovoid, trigonous, 10–20 mm long. Flowering September–November. Dry slopes and flats, NW, SW, AP, KM, LB, SE (Namibia, Namaqualand, and western Karoo to Humansdorp).

Ornithogalum subcoriaceum L. Bolus
Plants to 20 cm high; outer bulb tunics hard and dark. Leaves two to five, oblong to narrowly ovate, somewhat leathery, 3–8 cm long, the margins smooth or fimbriate. Flowers in a short raceme, white, tepals 8–14 mm long, filaments awl-shaped or ovate-acuminate, pedicels to 20 mm long. Capsules spindle-shaped. Flowering September–October. Sandy middle to upper slopes and plateaus, NW (Bokkeveld Plateau to Gydo Pass).

Ornithogalum synadelphicum U. & D. Müller-Doblies
Plants 10–20 cm high; outer bulb tunics pale to gray. Leaves two to six, semiterete, 50–70 mm long, with several rows of minute, recurved hairs. Flowers in a narrow raceme, white, tepals 4–5 mm long, filaments abruptly expanded at the base and united into a cup c. 2 mm deep, pedicels 2–4 mm long. Capsules ovoid. Flowering September–December. Shale flats, KM (Ladismith to Oudtshoorn).

Ornithogalum tenuifolium F. Delaroche
Plants 10–60 cm high. Leaves suberect, few to many, linear to filiform, sometimes forming a neck. Flowers suberect, whitish with green keels, tepals 6–10 mm long, filaments ovate-acuminate, the inner sometimes with basal lobes, pedicels 2–5 mm long. Capsules ovoid, trigonous. Flowering November–March. Grassland, SE (Humansdorp to tropical Africa).

Two subspecies are recognized: subspecies *aridum* Obermeyer with many filiform leaves 2–4 mm wide near the middle, the old bases forming a neck, stony soil in dry grassland (southern Namibia and Northern Cape), and subspecies *tenuifolium* with about five linear leaves, the old bases not forming a neck, grassland (Humansdorp through eastern South Africa).

Ornithogalum thermophilum F. M. Leighton
Plants 10–30 cm high; outer bulb tunics gray. Leaves three or four, ovate to linear with tubular, often spotted sheathing bases, to 10 cm long, dry at flowering, sparsely hairy, the margins bristly. Flowers in a narrow raceme, white with orange midribs, tepals spreading or reflexed, c. 6 mm long, filaments awl-shaped, the inner ovate-acuminate, pedicels 5–10 mm long. Capsules ovoid. Flowering December. Rocky slopes, NW (Namaqualand to Clanwilliam).

Ornithogalum thyrsoides Jacquin
Plants 20–80 cm high; outer bulb tunics soft, whitish. Leaves about seven, linear to lanceolate, sometimes dry at flowering, 15–30 cm long. Flowers in a subcorymbose or cylindrical raceme, white, usually with a dark center,

Ornithogalum suaveolens

Ornithogalum thyrsoides

tepals 15–30 mm long, filaments dimorphic, the outer awl-shaped, the inner with an eared basal expansion curled inward over the ovary, pedicels (10–)20–40 mm long. Capsules oblong to ovoid, pointed, c. 15 mm long. Flowering October–December. Sandy flats and lower slopes, often in marshes, NW, SW, AP (Namaqualand to Pearly Beach).

Ornithogalum tortuosum Baker

Plants 10–20 cm high; outer bulb tunics pale. Leaves 4–20, semiterete, minutely hairy in rows on the underside, 30–60 mm long. Flowers in a lax, wiry raceme, white with green keels, tepals c. 5 mm long, filaments lanceolate, pedicels 5–7 mm long. Capsules ovoid. Flowering August–February. Clay flats, NW, KM, LB, SE (western Karoo and Worcester to Steytlerville).

Ornithogalum unifolium Retzius

Plants 6–30 cm high. Leaf usually dry at flowering, one or two, sometimes three, spreading, oblong to ovate, firm, smooth or striate, 5–12 cm long. Flowers pale yellow to cream or buff with broad dark keels, tepals c. 10 mm long, filaments ovate, pedicels 5–15 mm long. Capsules globose-trigonous, c. 8 mm long. Flowering September–November. Dry karroid places, RV, NW (Namibia, Namaqualand and western Karoo to Robertson).

Ornithogalum xanthochlorum Baker
Robust plants to 60 cm high. Leaves 9–14, oblong, 20–50 cm long. Flowers in a dense cylindrical raceme, spreading, green, sweetly scented, tepals c. 15 mm long, filaments ovate-acuminate, pedicels to 30 mm long in fruit. Capsules globose, three-ribbed, 15 × 10 mm. Flowering August–September. Sandy flats, RV (Namaqualand to Tanqua Karoo).

Ornithogalum zebrinellum U. & D. Müller-Doblies
Plants 4–6 cm high; outer bulb tunics brown. Leaves two to four, filiform, 10–15 cm long, dry at flowering, surrounded by a pale, papery, horizontally barred sheath. Flowers in a lax raceme, white, tepals 4–5 mm long, filaments linear, the inner ovate-acuminate, pedicels 3–5 mm long. Capsules ovoid, 5 mm long. Flowering February–March. Stony slopes, RV, NW (Namaqualand and western Karoo to Hex River Mountains).

Ornithogalum sp. 1
Plants 8–15 cm high; outer bulb tunics pale gray. Leaves two to four, filiform, 15–20 cm long, dry at flowering, surrounded by a pale, conspicuously papillate-hairy sheath, the hairs more or less tufted. Flowers in a lax raceme, white, tepals c. 8 mm long, filaments linear, inner broader below, pedicels 2–5 mm long. Capsules ovoid, c. 7 mm long. Flowering April. Tillite flats, RV (Nieuwoudtville).

Ornithoglossum
COMMON NAME snake lily, FAMILY Colchicaceae. Deciduous, often glaucous perennials, rarely stemless. ROOTSTOCK a subglobose or ovoid corm, simple or lobed, covered with papery tunics. LEAVES few to several, usually scattered along the stem, linear to lanceolate, clasping below. INFLORESCENCE a bracteate raceme, the bracts leaf-like and successively smaller, the flowers actually axillary but apparently bract-opposed through coalescence of the lower part of the pedicel to the stem. FLOWERS usually nodding on slender, sharply spreading pedicels; usually actinomorphic and star- or cup-shaped but rarely slightly zygomorphic, the tepals free, somewhat narrowed and clawed below with a channel-, pouch-, or pocket-like nectary on the claw, yellow or cream, green, brown, or purple, often bicolored, rarely scented. STAMENS inserted below the ovary, sometimes slightly swollen near the middle. OVARY globose, ovoid or oblong with few to many ovules per locule; STYLES three, slender and usually sharply spreading. FRUIT a globose to oblong loculicidal capsule. SEEDS several per chamber, globose or subglobose, brown. Basic chromosome number $x = 12$. Southern and tropical Africa; 8 spp., 5 in the Cape.

Largely found in the arid regions of southern Africa, the small genus *Ornithoglossum* is best developed in the winter-rainfall parts of South Africa and Namibia. The single species widespread in tropical Africa, *O. vulgare*, is also the most primitive species of the genus, suggesting that the genus probably originated in tropical Africa and moved southward into more arid areas. The nodding flowers on slender pedicels are typical of the other genera of Colchicaceae tribe Iphigenieae (which includes *Gloriosa*, *Littonia*, and *Sandersonia*), and the genus is most closely related to the Namibian and northern Namaqualand genus *Hexacyrtis*, which has a single species. The shape of the small, often curiously formed nectary located at the base of each tepal blade can be quite specific to each species. Like most genera of the Colchicaceae, species of *Ornithoglossum* contain colchicine-type alkaloids and the common name, snake lily, derives from their toxic properties. The widespread *O. vulgare* in particular has been implicated in severe stock losses.

At least one of the species with small, dull flowers, *Ornithoglossum parviflorum*, is visited by muscid flies, but *O. undulatum*, with more showy flowers, is most likely to be visited by long-tongued solitary bees (Apidae: Anthophorinae). Although the flowers are typically dull and inconspicuous, they are appreciably bigger and brighter in *O. undulatum* and also sweetly scented. The tepals of *O. undulatum* are also attractively arranged fan-wise above the flower, making it the most desirable species for cultivation. It also has the advantage of flowering early.

FURTHER READING. *Ornithoglossum* was monographed by Nordenstam (1982).

Ornithoglossum undulatum

Ornithoglossum viride

Ornithoglossum gracile B. Nordenstam
Plants 2–10 cm high. Leaves three or four, lanceolate, conspicuously undulate or crisped. Flowers few to several, nodding, actinomorphic, the tepals spreading, 14–18 × 1.5–2.5 mm, pale green, freesia scented, the nectary narrowly pouch-like with the upper margin tongue-like, filaments 10–12 mm long, often with a hump-like swelling near the middle, whitish near the base but sometimes darker above, anthers 2.5–4 mm long. Flowering April–May. Rocky sandstone or quartzite slopes, NW (Vanrhyn's Pass to Botterkloof).

Ornithoglossum parviflorum B. Nordenstam
Plants to 20 cm high. Leaves two to four, linear-lanceolate, often undulate. Flowers few to many, nodding, actinomorphic, the tepals spreading or reflexed, 6–15 × 1–2.5 mm, green and purple, unscented, the nectary pouch-like, filaments 2–5 mm long, swollen, whitish near the base but darker above, anthers 1–2 mm long. Flowering June–October. Stony slopes, RV, NW, KM (Namaqualand and western Karoo to Worcester).

Ornithoglossum vulgare

Ornithoglossum undulatum Sweet
Plants 5–20 cm high. Leaves two to four, lanceolate, often crisped or undulate. Flowers few to several, nodding, zygomorphic, the lower one or two tepals spreading and the remaining erect-recurved fan-wise above the flower, 16–30 × 2–5 mm, white to pink, with purple or maroon tips, freesia scented, the nectary narrowly pouch-like with the upper margin sometimes tongue-like, filaments 15–25 mm long, filiform or slightly swollen, whitish or pink, rarely darker near the tips, anthers 3–5.5 mm long. Flowering April–July. Rocky sandstone and granite slopes, RV, NW, KM, LB, SE (southern Namibia to Somerset East).

Ornithoglossum viride (Linnaeus fil.) Aiton
Plants 5–30 cm high. Leaves two or three, linear-lanceolate. Flowers few to many, nodding, actinomorphic, the tepals spreading-reflexed, 5.5–15 × 1.5–3.5 mm, green or purplish, with maroon margins, unscented, the nectary a small round pocket or mouth-like flap much narrower than the tepal claw, filaments 2.5–4.5 mm long, swollen, greenish yellow near the base but often darker above, anthers c. 1 mm long. Flowering July–October. Mostly deep sandy soils, NW, SW, AP, LB (Clanwilliam to Riversdale).

Ornithoglossum vulgare B. Nordenstam
Plants 7–70 cm high. Leaves 2–12, lanceolate, rarely somewhat undulate. Flowers few to many, nodding, actinomorphic, the tepals spreading or slightly reflexed, 8–25 × 1.5–3.5 mm, dull olive green but often reddish or purple above, unscented, the nectary pouch-like, filaments 5–16 mm long, slender or slightly swollen, whitish near the base but usually purplish above, anthers 2–6 mm long. Flowering August–October. Stony slopes, RV, KM (western and Little Karoo to tropical Africa).

Pauridia

COMMON NAME little star, FAMILY Hypoxidaceae. Diminutive deciduous plants. ROOTSTOCK a corm. LEAVES four to eight, green at flowering, in a basal tuft, linear to narrowly lanceolate, smooth. INFLORESCENCE single-flowered, sometimes two-flowered, several per corm, the scape shortly exserted from the leaves, terminated by two linear bracts. FLOWERS bell- to funnel-shaped, white to pale pink, on short to long pedicels, the tepals united into a short to long tube, narrowly ovate. STAMENS inserted in the perianth throat below the inner tepals, slightly exserted from the throat, the filaments attached to the base of the anthers, the anthers lobed above and below; staminodes three, joined to the lower part of the style. OVARY three-locular with many axile ovules; STYLE slender, the stigma three-lobed. FRUIT indehiscent, thin-walled, bearing the persistent perianth tube, disintegrating irregularly. SEEDS shiny black with a nodular surface. Basic chromosome number x unknown. Western Cape; 2 spp.

Pauridia may lack the horticultural potential of other genera of the family Hypoxidaceae but has its own charm in its diminutive form. When first writing of the genus in 1838, William Harvey captured the essence of the plants when he described the flowers as "snow-white and covering the ground like a shower of brilliant little stars." In some places, the plants of *P. minuta* grow so densely together that Erika I. Markötter of Stellenbosch once counted 450 flowers in an area of 643 cm^2. At the height of their season, the plants have as many as four flowers open at a time, each flower lasting as long as 5 days. The flowers close at night and only open on warm, sunny days, when they attract a variety of insects, including bees and flies. These are among the smallest geophytic plants in southern Africa.

FURTHER READING. *Pauridia* was revised by Thompson (1979) whereas Rand (1980) described the natural history of the genus.

Pauridia longituba M. F. Thompson
Plants 2–8 cm high. Leaves 3–8(–11), suberect, tufted, filiform, overtopping the flowers, c. 1 mm wide. Flowers white, funnel-shaped, tepals 7–9 mm long, spreading, narrowly ovate, a third to half as long as the narrowly cylindrical tube, stamens inserted in the throat, style slightly shorter than the tube. Flowering May–June. Seasonally wet sites below and on top of granite boulders, SW (St. Helena Bay to Saldanha).

Pauridia longituba

Pauridia minuta

Pauridia minuta (Linnaeus fil.) Durand & Schinz
Plants 2–8 cm high. Leaves three to five, linear, 1–5 mm wide, as long as or longer than the flowers. Flowers white to pale pink, bell-shaped, unscented, tepals 5–9 mm long, ovate, stamens inserted in the short tube, style slightly shorter than the tube. Flowering April–June. Damp flats and lower slopes, SW, AP, LB (Langebaan to Riversdale).

Pillansia

COMMON NAME pillansia, FAMILY Iridaceae. Evergreen perennial. ROOTSTOCK a depressed globose corm rooting from below, axillary in origin, those of past seasons not resorbed, the tunics fibrous. LEAVES few, lower two or three forming cataphylls, foliage leaves unifacial without a definite midrib, linear, usually one basal per plant and one or two cauline and smaller, leathery and fibrotic; stem erect, aerial, branched above, terete. INFLORESCENCE a panicle, each flower stalked; bracts leathery and green with reddish brown margins, mucilaginous on inside, inner more or less as long as outer, notched apically. FLOWERS actinomorphic, orange, bell-shaped, scentless, with nectar from septal nectaries; perianth tube short, funnel-shaped, the tepals subequal, spreading. STAMENS symmetrically disposed around style; filaments arising in throat; anthers exserted. STYLE filiform, exserted, branches notched apically a quarter to a third of their length. FRUIT an obovoid and truncate woody capsule. SEEDS large and angular with a chalazal crest, smooth and shiny, one to three per locule. Basic chromosome number $x = 20$. Restricted to the Caledon district in the southwestern Cape, coastal to c. 700 m, in seeps or areas of poor drainage; 1 sp.

Pillansia is exceptional in Iridaceae subfamily Crocoideae in its leaves, which lack a definite midrib, and in its inflorescence, which is a panicle rather than a spike. Chloroplast DNA sequence analysis shows the genus to be allied to *Micranthus* and *Thereianthus*. *Pillansia* is typical of many Cape geophytes that are restricted to nutrient-poor, sandstone soils in that it flowers poorly or not at all unless the surrounding vegetation has been burned. In the season following a burn, however, thousands of plants will flower. *Pillansia* appears to be pollinated by bees (Apidae and Halictidae) and monkey beetles (Scarabaeidae: Hopliini).

Like several Cape mountain species of sandstone soils, *Pillansia* does not respond well to cultivation. This is unfortunate as a well-grown *Pillansia* plant produces a flowering stem about 0.6 m high, bearing dozens of large, bright orange, starry flowers that each last several days, a dramatic sight in the field.

FURTHER READING. *Pillansia* was discussed and well illustrated by Obermeyer (1962).

Pillansia templemannii (Baker) L. Bolus

Plants 60–90 cm high, evergreen; corms depressed-globose. Leaves linear, strap-like, loosely twisted, fibrotic, without a midrib. Flowers in flat-topped panicles, tube funnel-shaped, 6–8 mm long, tepals subequal, 16–20 mm long, bright orange; bracts leathery and fibrotic. Flowering October–November, after fire. Sandstone slopes, SW (Kogelberg to Klein River Mountains).

Pillansia templemannii

Polyxena

COMMON NAME Cape hyacinth, FAMILY Hyacinthaceae. Deciduous perennials. ROOTSTOCK a globose bulb with pale, papery or thinly leathery outer tunics lightly barred above and sometimes extended as a short neck. LEAVES two to six, erect to spreading or almost prostrate, surrounded by a conspicuous tubular, membranous cataphyll extending above the bulb, linear and channeled to broadly lanceolate, subsucculent or leathery, the veins sometimes depressed. INFLORESCENCE a condensed, corymbose, or subcapitate raceme, the flowers more or less clustered between the leaves but the peduncle elongating in fruit; bracts inconspicuous, deltoid to ovate, membranous. FLOWERS funnel-shaped, tepals united below into a short or long tube, usually suberect but sometimes recurved, white to mauve or purple, honey scented. STAMENS inserted in two series, the outer lower than the inner and usually slightly shorter, inserted within the tube or on the base of the tepals above the mouth of the tube, the filaments slender, free, usually exserted. OVARY ovoid with several ovules per locule; STYLE usually much longer than the ovary, rarely shorter, slender, the stigma minute or capitate. FRUIT a papery capsule, ovoid or oblong, loculicidal. SEEDS several per locule, subglobose, smooth, black. Basic chromosome number x unknown. Winter-rainfall South Africa; 5 spp.

The small genus *Polyxena* is part of the alliance that includes *Lachenalia* and *Massonia* and is distinguished from *Lachenalia* primarily by its tubular flowers. Although the stamens in both genera are in two series inserted at different levels on the perianth, the outer lower than the inner, this is more obvious in the species placed in *Polyxena* by virtue of their longer perianth tube. DNA sequence research indicates that the genus is more properly included in *Lachenalia* and it is only a matter of time before the two are formally united. Species of *Polyxena* are all communal and form more or less dense stands in suitable habitats, usually seasonally moist clay or loamy flats. They are all early blooming, flowering at the start of the rainy season in autumn or early winter. Although the flowering axis is much condensed in flower, the peduncle elongates rapidly just before the seeds are shed, carrying the capsules well above the ground as an aid to dispersal. This strategy is best developed in *P. ensifolia* and *P. maughanii*. In those species, the broad leaves are so tightly clasping at the base that they are torn free from the bulb by the elongating peduncle and hoisted above the surface, acting as sails in an unusual form of wind dispersal of the entire infructescence. The honey-scented flowers of all the species are pollinated primarily by honeybees but are also visited by the widespread painted lady butterfly, *Vanessa cardui*.

All species of *Polyxena* are easily cultivated and ideal for pots or rock gardens. The brilliant purple flowers of *P. paucifolia* and some populations of *P. ensifolia* are very striking. The three species with narrow leaves, *P. corymbosa*, *P. longituba*, and *P. paucifolia*, are particularly recommended because they will rapidly fill a pot if left to multiply through seed. The resulting massed display of flowers is quite outstanding. Most species favor gritty or sandy substrates derived from granite or sandstone, but *P. longituba* and *P. maughanii* grow in fine-grained clays derived from shale or dolerite. Because the species flower in the autumn and winter, they should be potted somewhat earlier than usual for Cape bulbs, in August or September in the Northern Hemisphere.

FURTHER READING. No adequate account of the species of *Polyxena* exists. The revision of the genus by Jessop (1976) adopted far too broad a view whereas the later account by U. and D. Müller-Doblies (1997) is marred by an unwarranted fragmentation of the species and their placement in different genera. A more recently discovered species was described by van der Merwe and Marais (2001).

Polyxena corymbosa (Linnaeus) Jessop

Plants to 15 cm high. Leaves two or three, sometimes as many as six, suberect, linear, channeled, 1–5 mm wide. Flowers in a short raceme, pale lilac with dark keels, perianth tube shorter than the tepals, 3.5–6 mm, tepals 6–9 mm long, filaments 4–5 mm long, the outer inserted in the middle of the tube and shortly exserted, the inner inserted in the upper third and exserted, style much longer than the subglobose ovary, 7–8 mm. Flowering April–June. Seasonally moist sandy or loam flats, NW, SW (Citrusdal to Gordon's Bay).

Polyxena ensifolia (Thunberg) Schönland

Plants to 5 cm high. Leaves two, sometimes three, spreading to prostrate, lanceolate to ovate, 10–30 mm wide. Flowers in a corymbose raceme, clustered between the leaves, white to mauve or pale blue, perianth tube slender, longer than the tepals, 12–25 mm, tepals 6–9 mm long, filaments 4–6.5 mm long, both series inserted on the tepals just above the mouth of the tube, well exserted, style much longer than the ellipsoidal ovary, 15–27 mm. Flowering April–June. Clay or granite flats, RV, NW, SW, AP, KM, LB, SE (Namaqualand and western Karoo to Port Elizabeth).

Polyxena longituba A. M. van der Merwe

Plants to 7 cm high. Leaves two, suberect or falcate, narrowly lanceolate, 2–10 mm wide. Flowers in a corymbose raceme, clustered between the leaves, white to mauve, perianth tube slender, longer than the tepals, 15–25 mm, tepals 9–11 mm long, filaments 4–5 mm long, the outer inserted just within the mouth of the tube, shortly exserted, the inner inserted on the tepals just above the mouth of the tube, exserted, style much longer than the ellipsoidal ovary, 18–22 mm. Flowering May–June. Seasonally waterlogged loamy flats along streams, RV (Sutherland to Komsberg).

Polyxena maughanii W. F. Barker

Plants to 5 cm high. Leaves two, spreading to prostrate, lanceolate to ovate, 15–40 mm wide. Flowers in a corymbose raceme, clustered between the leaves, white, perianth tube slender, longer than the tepals, 17–25 mm, tepals c. 6 mm long, filaments 1.5–2 mm long, the outer inserted in the upper third of the tube and included, the inner inserted just below the mouth and included or shortly exserted, style longer than the ellipsoidal ovary, 10–15 mm long. Flowering May–June. Dolerite or rarely sandstone flats, RV, NW (western Karoo and Bokkeveld Mountains).

Polyxena paucifolia (W. F. Barker) A. M. van der Merwe & J. C. Manning

Plants to 7 cm high. Leaves two or three, suberect, linear-lanceolate, channeled, 3–10 mm wide. Flowers in a sub-

Polyxena corymbosa

Polyxena ensifolia

Polyxena longituba

Polyxena maughanii

Polyxena paucifolia

corymbose raceme, clustered between the leaves, pale to deep lilac, perianth tube about as long as the tepals, 6–7 mm long, tepals 6–8 mm long, filaments 1–2 mm long, the outer inserted in the middle to upper third of the tube and included, the inner inserted in the upper third to just below the mouth and shortly exserted, style shorter than the subglobose ovary, 1–2.5 mm. Flowering April–June. Coastal granite and limestone outcrops, SW (Paternoster to Langebaan).

Romulea

COMMON NAME romulea, FAMILY Iridaceae. Deciduous perennials, the stem short and subterranean or aerial, rarely hairy. ROOTSTOCK a globose, bell-shaped to top-shaped, compressed, or asymmetric corm with a circular to crescent-shaped basal ridge, the tunics cartilaginous or woody, rarely fibrous. LEAVES one to several, usually unifacial with the margins and midrib thickened or winged, the blade thus oval or round in cross section and four-grooved or four-winged, occasionally three-grooved or as much as eight-grooved, rarely bifacial and channeled, usually hairless but occasionally hairy on the margins. INFLORESCENCE condensed, of solitary flowers; bracts green, the margins of the inner and sometimes the outer membranous to dry, occasionally the inner bract entirely membranous. FLOWERS actinomorphic, cup- or star-shaped, the tepals united below into a short cup or rarely a long slender tube, yellow, white, pink to red, or blue, often yellow in the cup and with darker markings, usually unscented. STAMENS inserted near the top of the tube, filaments usually somewhat swollen and hairy below. OVARY inferior with several ovules per locule; STYLE slender, three-branched, the branches usually divided half their length, rarely fringed at the tips. FRUIT an oblong or subglobose loculicidal capsule. SEEDS several per locule, subglobose or weakly angled. Basic chromosome numbers $x = 9$–14. South Africa to the Middle East, mainly Western Cape; c. 95 spp., 64 in the Cape.

Centered in the southern African winter-rainfall region, *Romulea* is best represented in the drier, semiarid parts of the Western Cape and Northern Cape. The flowers vary greatly in color and markings, even within species, and characters of the corm and bracts are essential for identifying the species. The four-grooved leaves, round to oblong in cross section, are characteristic of the genus, and few species differ in their leaf shape although there may be marked differences in details of their anatomy. Many of the species favor seasonally slightly damper places and are highly communal, forming brilliant carpets of color when in flower (pages 22, 24). The flowers open only on warm, sunny days, usually around midday but later in some species. The peduncles of most species are highly mobile and bend down after pollination, straightening again when the seeds are mature and ready to be shed. In some species the peduncles roll up tightly when dry but unroll when dampened. These movements are an aid to seed dispersal. Although many of the species are quite widespread, several are very local endemics restricted to specialized habitats. These include the two aquatic species, *R. aquatica* and *R. multisulcata*, the limestone endemic *R. barkerae*, and *R. elliptica* and *R. saldanhensis* of the Saldanha district of the Western Cape's western coast.

The majority of species are pollinated by honeybees in search of pollen. The bases of the filaments in most species are swollen and covered with yellow hairs, which are thought to mimic pollen, and little or no nectar is produced. At least some populations of the early yellow- or white-flowered species are lightly scented, and in the field it is striking how often similarly colored species of *Romulea* and *Oxalis* co-occur. Several of the darker-flowered species, in particular those with large red flowers, have shifted to pollination by scarab beetles whereas *R. hantamensis* has become specialized for pollination by nectar-feeding long-proboscid flies of the family Nemestrinidae and is one of a few species that produce appreciable quantities of nectar.

Vastly more variable in their flowers than the related genus *Crocus*, *Romulea* is much undervalued horticulturally. The species do well in pots, and the potential exists for growing them in the open ground, either in beds or lawns. Flower colors range from white through lilac and pink to yellow, orange, and scarlet, and the flowers are often attractively marked in the cup. The large, scarlet-flowered species from the Bokkeveld and Roggeveld Escarpments, especially *R. amoena*, *R. monadelpha*, *R. sabulosa*, and *R. unifolia*, are among the most spectacular of all Cape bulbs.

FURTHER READING. The South African species of *Romulea* were thoroughly revised by De Vos (1972, 1983b). A more recent synopsis includes a revised classification and several new species (Manning and Goldblatt 2001c).

Romulea albiflora Goldblatt & J. C. Manning

Plants often in clumps, 12–20 cm high; corm rounded at base, with curved acuminate teeth. Leaves about five, basal, filiform, softly hairy, narrowly four-grooved, 1.5–2 mm diam. Flowers salverform, white, tube 20–33 mm long, tepals 12–20 mm long, elliptical, filaments c. 4 mm long, anthers 6–7 mm long; bracts with narrow white membranous margins, inner bracts with white, broader, membranous margins. Flowering September–October. Damp clay flats, RV (Middelpos).

Romulea albomarginata M. P. de Vos

Plants 12–25 cm high, sometimes the stem to 5 cm high; corm with an oblique basal ridge of fibril clusters. Leaves three or four, basal and cauline, narrowly four-grooved, 1 mm diam. Flowers white or pink to magenta with dark veins around the orange-yellow cup, tepals 15–25 mm long, elliptical, filaments 4–5 mm long, anthers 4–7 mm long; bracts with narrow membranous margins, inner bracts with wide membranous margins. Fruiting peduncles spreading at first, later suberect. Flowering August–October. Sandstone flats, NW (Cold Bokkeveld and Hex River Mountains).

Romulea amoena Schlechter ex Béguinot

Plants 8–15 cm high, sometimes branching above ground; corms symmetrical, bell-shaped, with a circular fringe of fibril clusters. Leaves three or four, usually all basal, narrowly four-grooved, c. 1 mm diam. Flowers deep rose pink to red with black blotches and stripes in a cream or yellow cup, tepals elliptical, 18–35 mm long, fil-

Romulea albiflora

aments 3–5 mm long, anthers 8–10 mm long; bracts with narrow or scarcely visible membranous margins, inner bracts with wide membranous margins. Flowering August–September. Damp sandstone soils, NW (Bokkeveld Mountains).

Romulea aquatica G. J. Lewis

Plants 20–60 cm high, stem 12–35 cm high; corm with an oblique basal ridge. Leaves two or three, lower one basal, narrowly five- to eight-grooved, 0.8–1.5 mm diam. Flowers white with yellow cup and lower parts of the tepals, honey scented, tepals obovate, 16–20 mm long, filaments 2–3 mm long, anthers 3–5 mm long; bracts with narrow membranous margins, inner bracts with wide membranous margins. Fruiting peduncles short, erect. Flowering August–September. Seasonal pools, NW, SW (Pools to Hopefield).

Romulea atrandra G. J. Lewis

Plants mostly 6–12 cm high; corm rounded at base, with curved acuminate teeth. Leaves (2–)4–10, basal, narrow or somewhat swollen, narrowly or widely four-grooved, rarely minutely hairy, 1–4 mm diam. Flowers magenta to pale pink or white, with dark veins and dark blotches around the yellow, often longitudinally veined cup, tepals 18–30 mm long, obovate, filaments 4–8 mm long, anthers 5–10 mm long; bracts with brownish membranous margins and prominent membranous tip, inner bracts with wide, brownish, membranous margins. Fruiting peduncles recurved and later coiled. Flowering July–October. Clay soils, RV, NW, SW, KM, LB, SE (western Karoo and Gifberg to Eastern Cape).

Romulea austinii E. Phillips

Plants 6–10 cm high; corm with a wide, oblique basal ridge. Leaves three to six, basal, narrowly four-grooved, channeled above, 0.5–1 mm diam. Flowers yellow, usually with brown blotches in the throat, honey scented, tepals 14–25 mm long, elliptical, filaments 5–7 mm long, anthers 3–6 mm long; bracts with narrow membranous margins, sometimes submembranous below, inner bracts with wide brown-flecked membranous margins. Fruiting peduncles curved, slightly flexuous. Flowering May–July. Damp stony flats, RV, KM (western and southern Karoo to Uniondale).

Romulea barkerae M. P. de Vos

Plants 8–12 cm high, stem to 3 cm high; corm with an oblique basal ridge. Leaves two or three, lower one basal, broadly two-grooved, T-shaped in cross section, 1.5–2.5 mm diam. Flowers white with large black blotches edged in yellow in the throat, tepals 18–28 mm long, oblanceolate, filaments 5–6 mm long, anthers 5–6 mm long; bracts with hardly visible membranous margins, inner bracts membranous, sometimes with reddish veins. Fruiting peduncles recurved, later erect. Flowering July–August. Limestone rocks, SW (Paternoster to Saldanha).

Romulea biflora (Béguinot) M. P. de Vos

Plants mostly 5–10 cm high, stem 2–5(–15) cm high; corm with an oblique basal ridge. Leaves three to six, lower two basal, filiform, narrowly four-grooved, 0.5–1.5 mm diam. Flowers pink to rose with purple blotches around the yellow cup, tepals 18–35 mm long, elliptical, filaments 5–7 mm long, anthers 5–8 mm long; bracts with hardly visible membranous margins, inner bracts

Romulea amoena

Romulea aquatica

Romulea atrandra

Romulea barkerae

Romulea biflora

Romulea cruciata

Romulea discifera

with wide membranous margins. Fruiting peduncles bent or suberect. Flowering July–September. Clay foothills, NW (Gifberg and Biedouw valley).

Romulea cedarbergensis M. P. de Vos

Plants 3–15 cm high; corm rounded at base, with curved acuminate teeth. Leaves one or two, sometimes three, basal, filiform, narrowly four-grooved, 0.5–1 mm diam. Flowers solitary, sometimes two, white to pale pink, with a yellow cup, tepals 7–16 mm long, elliptical, filaments 4–6 mm long, anthers 2–3.5 mm long; bracts submembranous, often purplish with narrow, colorless, membranous margins, inner bracts with wide brown-speckled membranous margins. Fruiting peduncles suberect. Flowering July–September. Damp sandstone rock sheets, NW (Cedarberg Mountains).

Romulea cruciata (Jacquin) Baker

Plants mostly 5–10 cm high, rarely as high as 40 cm; corm pointed at base, with straight acuminate teeth. Leaves two to eight, basal, narrowly or widely four-grooved, 1–4 mm diam. Flowers magenta to lilac with dark blotches around the dark yellow cup, tepals 20–35 mm long, oblanceolate, filaments 3–6 mm long, anthers 4–8 mm long; bracts with narrow, hardly visible membranous margins, inner bracts submembranous with wide membranous margins. Fruiting peduncles remaining erect or slightly spreading. Flowering July–September. Sandstone and granite slopes and rocks, NW, SW, AP, LB (Bokkeveld Mountains to Gourits River).

Romulea dichotoma (Thunberg) Baker

Plants to 35 cm high; corm with an oblique basal ridge of fibril clusters. Leaves two or three, lowest one, rarely two, basal, but then lowermost shorter, narrowly or widely four-grooved, sometimes minutely hairy, 1–2 mm diam. Flowers pink with yellowish cup, tepals 16–32 mm long, elliptical, filaments 4–8 mm long, anthers 4–7 mm long; bracts with narrow membranous margins, inner bracts with wide brown-speckled membranous margins. Fruiting peduncles spreading. Flowering September–October. Sandy flats and slopes, SW, AP, LB, SE (Stanford to Humansdorp).

Romulea discifera J.C. Manning & Goldblatt

Plants 10–15 cm high; corms symmetrical, depressed-discoid, with a wide circular rim of fibers. Leaves three to five, basal and cauline, narrowly four-grooved, 0.5–1 mm diam. Flowers yellow, mostly with dark markings around the dark yellow cup, tepals 25–35 mm long, oblanceolate, filaments c. 5 mm, anthers c. 6 mm; bracts with narrow membranous margins, inner bracts with narrow membranous margins. Fruiting peduncles suberect. Flowering July. Sandy flats, NW (Bokkeveld Mountains).

Romulea diversiformis M.P. de Vos

Plants 8–20 cm high; corm rounded at base, with curved acuminate teeth. Leaves 6–10, basal, narrowly four-grooved, 0.5–1.5 mm diam. Flowers yellow, tepals dimorphic, the outer broader, 18–28 mm long, filaments 4.5–6 mm long, anthers 5–7.5 mm long; bracts with wide membranous margins and apices, inner bracts with wide membranous margins. Fruiting peduncles bent. Flowering August–September. Moist or waterlogged dolerite and clay, RV (Hantamsberg and Roggeveld Escarpment).

Romulea diversiformis

Romulea elliptica M.P. de Vos

Plants 15–30 cm high, stem to 16 cm high; corm with an oblique basal ridge. Leaves three or four, lower two basal, narrowly four-grooved, 1–1.5 mm diam. Flowers yellow with dark streaks in the cup, tepals 18–27 mm long, elliptical, filaments 6–7 mm long, anthers 4–6 mm long; bracts with hardly visible membranous margins, inner bracts submembranous below with narrow, white, membranous margins. Fruiting peduncles erect or suberect. Flowering August. Sandy flats, SW (Vredenburg).

Romulea eximia M.P. de Vos

Plants mostly 8–15 cm high, rarely as high as 25 cm; corm pointed at base, with straight acuminate teeth. Leaves three to eight, basal, narrowly or broadly four-grooved, 1–3 mm diam. Flowers old rose or red, with dark blotches around the greenish or pale yellow cup, tepals 33–40 mm long, oblanceolate, filaments 9–12 mm long, anthers 7–12 mm long; bracts with narrow, hardly visible membranous margins, inner bracts submembra-

Romulea eximia

Romulea flava, yellow form

Romulea flava, white form

nous with wide membranous margins. Fruiting peduncles remaining erect or slightly spreading. Flowering August–September. Sandy flats, SW (Vredenburg to Melkbos).

Romulea fibrosa M. P. de Vos
Plants to 35 cm high, stem to 32 cm high; corm with an oblique basal ridge of fibril clusters, usually with fibrous neck and remains of tunics. Leaves two to six, lowest two basal, narrowly four-grooved, sometimes minutely hairy, 0.5–1 mm diam. Flowers magenta to pink, with diffuse purple markings around a yellow cup, tepals 16–25 mm long, oblanceolate, filaments 5–8 mm long, anthers 4–6 mm long; bracts submembranous or greenish in the center with membranous, usually rusty red margins; inner bracts with wide, colorless or rusty red, membranous margins. Fruiting peduncles suberect. Flowering October–December. High elevations on sandstone, KM, LB, SE (Langeberg to Great Winterhoek Mountains).

Romulea flava (Lamarck) M. P. de Vos
Plants mostly 10–15 cm high; corm with an oblique basal ridge. Leaves three or four, lower one basal, often wider and clasping below, narrowly or widely four-grooved, sometimes minutely hairy, 1–4 mm diam. Flowers white or yellow, rarely blue or pinkish, with a yellow cup, sometimes scented, tepals 10–30 mm long, oblanceolate, filaments 4–7 mm long, anthers 3–7 mm long; bracts with narrow or scarcely visible membranous margins, inner bracts membranous or submembranous, often streaked. Fruiting peduncles recurved, later erect. Flowering June–September. Sandy and clay soils, fynbos or renosterveld, NW, SW, AP, LB, SE (Bokkeveld Mountains to Humansdorp).

Romulea flexuosa Klatt
Plants mostly 5–15 cm high; corm with an oblique basal ridge. Leaves three to five, lower two basal, narrowly four-grooved, 0.5 mm diam. Flowers white with a yellow to buff cup, lightly scented, tepals 25–35 mm long, elliptical, filaments 6–7 mm long, anthers sagittate, 12–15 mm long with attenuate connectives 2.5–6 mm long; bracts

with narrow membranous margins, inner bracts with wide membranous margins. Fruiting peduncles curved. Flowering May–July. Sandstone rocks in fynbos, NW, SW (Bokkeveld to Hottentots Holland Mountains).

Romulea gigantea Béguinot
Plants 20–50 cm high, stem 5–20 cm high; corm with a high, oblique basal ridge, the fibrils sharply bent over. Leaves four to six, lower two basal, narrowly four-grooved, 1–3 mm diam. Flowers white, lilac, or blue, with greenish yellow cup, tepals 10–15 mm long, elliptical, filaments 3–7 mm long, anthers 3–4 mm long; bracts with hardly visible membranous margins, inner bracts with wide, brown-edged, membranous margins. Fruiting peduncles curved, later erect. Flowering September–October. Moist places, SW, LB, SE (Kleinmond to Port Alfred).

Romulea gracillima Baker
Plants 6–25 cm high, stem sometimes branched above ground; corms symmetrical, bell-shaped, with a circular rim of fibers. Leaves two to five, basal and usually cauline, narrowly four-grooved, 0.5–1 mm diam. Flowers pale pink, sometimes with red lines in the yellow cup, tepals 12–18 mm long, oblanceolate, filaments 3–5 mm long, anthers 2–4 mm long; bracts without visible membranous margins, inner bracts with wide membranous margins. Fruiting peduncles suberect. Flowering August–September. Sandstone slopes, SW, AP (Cape Peninsula to Agulhas flats).

Romulea hallii M. P. de Vos
Plants 8–13 cm high; corm rounded at base, with curved acuminate teeth. Leaves three to five, spreading, somewhat swollen, widely four-grooved, 2–3 mm diam. Flowers pale wisteria blue with violet and black blotches around the yellow cup, tepals 15–22 mm long, obovate-cuneate, filaments 5–6 mm long, anthers 4–5 mm long; bracts with a triangular green lower half and wide, brown-speckled, membranous margins and apices, inner bracts with wide membranous margins. Fruiting peduncles strongly recurved or later flexuous. Flowering May–July. Clay flats, RV (Sutherland).

Romulea hantamensis (Diels) Goldblatt
Plants 7–15 cm high; corm pointed at base, with straight acuminate teeth. Leaves 3–10, narrowly four-grooved, 1–1.5 mm diam. Flowers salverform, magenta with purple veining, perianth tube 35–70 mm long, tepals 10–14 mm long, elliptical, filaments 3 mm long, smooth, anthers 3–5 mm long; bracts with narrow membranous margins, inner bracts with wider membranous margins. Fruiting peduncles suberect. Flowering August–September. Damp dolerite flats, RV (Hantamsberg). Page 340.

Romulea flexuosa

Romulea hallii

Romulea hantamensis

Romulea hirsuta

Romulea hirta; see also page 22

Romulea komsbergensis

Romulea hirsuta (Steudel ex Klatt) Baker
Plants mostly 6–12 cm high, stem often branched above ground; corms symmetrical, bell-shaped, with a circular rim of fibers. Leaves two to six, basal and usually cauline, narrowly or widely four-grooved, sometimes minutely hairy, 0.5–4 mm diam. Flowers pink to rose or coppery orange, often with dark marks around the yellow cup, tepals 15–35 mm long, oblanceolate, filaments 4–8 mm long, anthers 3–7 mm long; bracts without visible membranous margins, inner bracts with narrow or wide membranous margins. Fruiting peduncles suberect or somewhat spreading. Flowering August–September. Sandstone or clay slopes and flats, NW, SW (Clanwilliam to Elim).

Romulea hirta Schlechter
Plants mostly 5–15 cm high; corm rounded at base, with curved acuminate teeth. Leaves three to six, basal, suberect or curved, four-winged, H-shaped in cross section with two broad lateral grooves, the wings sometimes hairy or crisped, 2–5 mm diam. Flowers pale yellow, sometimes with obscure chestnut blotches at the edge of the cup, tepals 12–25 mm long, elliptical, filaments 5–6 mm long, anthers 3–5 mm long; bracts with narrow, usually brown-spotted, membranous margins, inner bracts with brownish membranous margins. Fruiting peduncles recurved or suberect. Flowering July–September. Damp dolerite and clay flats, RV, NW (Bokkeveld Mountains and Calvinia to Sutherland, and northern Cedarberg Mountains).

Romulea jugicola M. P. de Vos
Plants c. 30 cm high, stem mostly 4–12 cm high, often hairy on the angles; corm with an oblique basal ridge of fibril clusters. Leaves two to four, lowest one basal, narrowly or widely four-grooved, conspicuously hairy, c. 1 mm diam. Flowers orange with yellow cup, tepals 18–30 mm long, elliptical, filaments 6–7 mm long, anthers 4–6 mm long; bracts with narrow membranous margins, inner bracts with brown-speckled membranous margins. Fruiting peduncles spreading. Flowering August. Clay soils in renosterveld, SW, KM, SE (Potberg, Little Karoo mountains, and near George).

Romulea komsbergensis M. P. de Vos
Plants mostly 8–12 cm high, rarely as high as 30 cm; corm rounded at base, with curved acuminate teeth. Leaves five to eight, basal, narrowly four-grooved, c. 1 mm diam. Flowers magenta with a narrow blue band around the yellow cup, which is brown at the base, tepals 15–28 mm long, obovate, filaments 4–5 mm long, anthers 3–5 mm long, pollen brown or rust colored; bracts submembranous below with wide membranous margins and apices, inner bracts with wide membranous margins. Fruiting peduncles recurved and later coiled. Flowering August–September. Damp loamy flats, RV (Roggeveld Escarpment).

Romulea leipoldtii Marais
Plants 15–30 cm high, stem 5–30 cm high; corm with an oblique basal ridge. Leaves four to six, lower two basal, narrowly four-grooved, c. 1 mm diam. Flowers cream with yellow cup and lower part of the tepals, sweetly scented, tepals 18–35 mm long, elliptical, filaments 5–8 mm long, anthers 5–8 mm long; bracts with hardly visible membranous margins, inner bracts with wide membranous margins. Fruiting peduncles at first bent, later erect. Flowering September–October. Damp sandy sites, NW, SW (Bokkeveld Mountains to Malmesbury).

Romulea lilacina J. C. Manning & Goldblatt
Plants 2–6 cm high, stem subterranean; corm rounded at the base, with curved acuminate teeth. Leaf single, narrowly four-grooved, flushed maroon, sticky, c. 0.5 mm diam. Flowers pale lilac with yellow at the base of the cup, tepals 16–17 mm long, elliptical, filaments 8–9 mm long, anthers 3.5–4 mm long; bracts with narrow membranous margins, sticky, inner bracts submembranous with wide, colorless, membranous margins. Fruiting peduncles recurved. Flowering May–June. Deep sandy soils in washes, NW (Cold Bokkeveld at Katbakkies).

Romulea longipes Schlechter
Plants 15–50 cm high, stem to 35 cm high; corm with an oblique basal ridge of fibril clusters. Leaves three to five, lowest two basal, narrowly four-grooved, 0.5–1 mm diam. Flowers cream to apricot, with small markings

Romulea luteoflora

Romulea membranacea

around the yellow cup, filaments 3–8 mm long, anthers 5–7 mm long; bracts with narrow membranous margins, inner bracts with wide, usually brownish membranous margins. Fruiting peduncles erect or somewhat spreading. Flowering July–November. Sandy flats, SE (Port Elizabeth to East London).

Romulea luteoflora (M. P. de Vos) M. P. de Vos
Plants 10–40 cm high; corm rounded at base, with curved acuminate teeth. Leaves two to eight, basal, narrowly or widely four-grooved, 1–2 mm diam. Flowers yellow with dark lines or blotches around the cup, tepals 18–35 mm long, obovate, filaments 4–7 mm long, anthers 6–9 mm long; bracts with narrow membranous margins and prominent membranous tip, inner bracts with wide, colorless or brownish, membranous margins. Fruiting peduncles recurved and later coiled. Flowering July–September. Loamy soils, RV, NW, KM, LB (Kamiesberg and Cedarberg Mountains to Riversdale, western Karoo and Lesotho).

Romulea malaniae M. P. de Vos
Plants 12–25 cm high; corm rounded at base, with curved acuminate teeth. Leaves one to three, sometimes as many as five, basal, narrowly grooved, c. 1 mm diam. Flowers on sharply bent peduncles, pale yellow, tepals 8–20 mm long, oblanceolate, filaments 4–5 mm long, anthers 3–4 mm long; bracts submembranous or green in the center in the upper half with membranous margins, inner bracts with wide membranous margins. Fruiting peduncles sharply recurved and later coiled. Flowering August. Sandstone outcrops, NW (Matroosberg to Koo).

Romulea membranacea M. P. de Vos
Plants 7–12 cm high; corm pointed at base, with straight acuminate teeth. Leaves three to eight, basal, narrowly four-grooved, 0.5 mm diam. Flowers deep yellow with dark lines in the cup, tepals 15–25 mm long, oblanceolate, filaments 5–6 mm long, anthers 3–4 mm long; bracts submembranous with wide, brown-speckled, membranous margins, inner bracts with wide, brown-

speckled, membranous margins. Fruiting peduncles strongly recurved. Flowering July–August. Sandy flats, RV, NW (western Karoo and Bokkeveld Escarpment).

Romulea minutiflora Klatt
Plants 6–20 cm high; corm obliquely flattened with a spathulate basal ridge. Leaves several, basal, narrowly four-grooved, 0.5–1.5 mm diam. Flowers pale mauve with a yellowish cup, tepals 4–9 mm long, elliptical, filaments 2–4 mm long, anthers 1.5–2 mm long; bracts with narrow, often brown-speckled, membranous margins, inner bracts membranous or submembranous. Fruiting peduncles curved, later erect. Flowering July–September. Flats, RV, NW, SW, AP, KM, LB, SE (widespread, Bokkeveld Mountains to Grahamstown).

Romulea monadelpha (Sweet) Baker
Plants mostly 10–18 cm high, rarely as high as 30 cm; corm rounded at base, with curved acuminate teeth. Leaves three to five, basal, filiform, four-grooved, 1–2 mm diam. Flowers dark red with black and silvery blotches in the cup, tepals 25–40 mm long, obovate, filaments oblong, joined into a stout column, 3–4 mm long, usually smooth, anthers 10–15 mm long; bracts usually keeled above, with narrow, usually brown, membranous margins; inner bracts two-keeled with usually brown membranous margins. Fruiting peduncles curved. Flowering August–September. Damp dolerite flats and outcrops, RV (Bokkeveld and Roggeveld Escarpments).

Romulea monadelpha

Romulea montana Schlechter ex Béguinot
Plants 8–30 cm high, stem mostly 8–10 cm high; corm with a wide oblique basal ridge. Leaves four to six, lower two basal, narrowly four-grooved, 0.5–1 mm diam. Flowers yellow with dark streaks or blotches in the throat, tepals 15–35 mm long, elliptical, filaments 5–6 mm long, anthers 4–8 mm long; bracts with hardly visible membranous margins, inner bracts with wide, brownish, membranous margins. Fruiting peduncles widely spreading. Flowering July–September. Sandstone outcrops, NW (Bokkeveld to Cedarberg Mountains).

Romulea montana

Romulea monticola

Romulea monticola M. P. de Vos
Plants 10–25 cm high; corm rounded at base, with curved acuminate teeth. Leaves three to six, basal, narrowly four-grooved, c. 1 mm diam. Flowers yellow with darker veins in the throat, tepals 18–27 mm long, elliptical, filaments 4–5 mm long, anthers 3–5 mm long; bracts submembranous, often purplish with narrow, brownish, membranous margins, inner bracts with wide, brown, membranous margins. Fruiting peduncles suberect or curved. Flowering June–September. Sandy loam in fynbos, NW (Bokkeveld Mountains to Gifberg).

Romulea multifida M. P. de Vos
Plants 10–20 cm high; corm rounded at base, with curved acuminate teeth. Leaves two or three, basal, narrowly four-grooved, 0.5–1 mm diam. Flowers magenta with a narrow blue band and dark blotches around the yellow cup, tepals 14–20 mm long, obovate-cuneate, filaments 5–6 mm long, anthers 3–5 mm long; style highly branched with more than six stigmas; bracts submembranous with wide membranous margins and apices, inner bracts with wide membranous margins. Fruiting peduncles recurved and later coiled. Flowering August. Clay flats, RV (Sutherland).

Romulea multisulcata M. P. de Vos
Plants 30–50 cm high, stem 6–25 cm high; corm with an oblique basal ridge. Leaves three or four, lowermost two basal, narrowly six- to eight-grooved, 1–2 mm diam. Flowers yellow or white with yellow cup and lower part of the tepals, tepals obovate, 15–25 mm long, filaments 4–6 mm long, anthers 6–8 mm long; bracts with narrow membranous margins, inner bracts with wide membranous margins. Fruiting peduncles widely spreading. Flowering August–September. Seasonal pools, NW (Bokkeveld Mountains, Gifberg flats, and Namaqualand at Hondeklip Bay).

Romulea obscura Klatt
Plants mostly 6–15 cm high; corm rounded at base, with curved acuminate teeth. Leaves three to six, basal or some cauline, narrowly four-grooved, 0.5–1 mm diam. Flowers yellow or apricot to red, often with dark blotches

Romulea monticola

Romulea multisulcata

around the greenish to yellow cup, tepals 10–40 mm long, oblanceolate, filaments 3–8 mm long, anthers 3–9 mm long; bracts with very narrow membranous margins, inner bracts with wide, colorless or brownish margins. Fruiting peduncles widely spreading from the base. Flowering August–October. Sandy flats, NW, SW, AP (Clanwilliam to Agulhas).

Romulea pratensis M. P. de Vos
Plants 12–25 cm high; corm with a high, oblique basal ridge, the fibrils sharply bent over. Leaves five to eight, basal, narrowly four-grooved, 1–2 mm diam. Flowers white, lilac, or rose, with greenish yellow cup, tepals 8–15 mm long, elliptical, filaments 3–4 mm long, anthers 3–4 mm long; bracts usually submembranous in the lower half with hardly visible membranous margins, inner bracts with wide membranous margins. Fruiting peduncles curved, later erect. Flowering July–September. Grassland, SE (Avontuur to Alexandria).

Romulea rosea (Linnaeus) Ecklon
Plants mostly 6–15 cm high, rarely as high as 60 cm; corm rounded at base, with curved acuminate teeth. Leaves three to six, basal, narrowly four-grooved, 0.5–2 mm diam. Flowers pink to magenta or white, often with a purplish zone around the yellow cup, tepals 10–38 mm long, oblanceolate, filaments 4–6 mm long, anthers 3–10 mm long; bracts with narrow membranous margins, inner bracts with wide, brownish, membranous margins. Fruiting peduncles curved at first, later erect. Flowering July–October. Sandy and clay slopes and flats, NW, SW, AP, KM, LB, SE (Bokkeveld Mountains to Port Elizabeth).

Romulea sabulosa Schlechter ex Béguinot
Plants 12–18(–40) cm high; corm rounded at base, with curved acuminate teeth. Leaves three to five, basal, filiform, four-grooved, c. 1 mm diam. Flowers dark red, rarely pink, with black blotches within a creamy green cup, tepals 25–35 mm long, obovate-cuneate, filaments 3–5 mm long, anthers 8–12 mm long; bracts usually keeled above, with narrow, usually brown membranous margins, inner bracts two-keeled with usually brown membranous margins. Fruiting peduncles suberect.

Romulea obscura

Romulea rosea

Romulea sabulosa; see also pages 22, 24

Romulea saldanhensis

Flowering July–September. Clay slopes in renosterveld, NW (Bokkeveld Escarpment).

Romulea saldanhensis M. P. de Vos
Plants 20–60 cm high, stem 5–18(–35) cm high; corm with an oblique basal ridge. Leaves three to six, lower one basal, narrowly four-grooved, sheathing below, 1–2 mm diam. Flowers orange-yellow with dark lines in the cup, tepals 20–30 mm long, oblanceolate, filaments 5–7 mm long, anthers 5–7 mm long; bracts with hardly visible membranous margins, inner bracts submembranous with wide membranous margins. Fruiting peduncles sharply curved, later erect. Flowering August–September. Wet granitic flats, mainly coastal, SW (Vredenburg to Darling).

Romulea sanguinalis M. P. de Vos
Plants 15–35 cm high, stem branched above ground; corm almost bell-shaped, with incomplete basal fringe of fibril clusters. Leaves three, basal and cauline, narrowly four-grooved, c. 0.7 mm diam. Flowers uniformly red, tepals 22–35 mm long, obovate-cuneate, filaments c. 5 mm long, smooth, anthers 8–10 mm long; bracts with scarcely visible membranous margins, inner bracts with wide membranous margins. Flowering August. Rocky flats, NW (Bokkeveld Mountains near Botterkloof).

Romulea saxatilis M. P. de Vos
Plants 10–40 cm high, stem very slender and wiry, 10–25 cm high; corm with an oblique basal ridge. Leaves three or four, lower two basal, narrowly four-grooved, c. 0.5 mm diam. Flowers magenta-pink with yellow cup, tepals 9–22 mm long, elliptical, filaments swollen in the middle, 3–4 mm long, anthers 3–4 mm long; bracts with narrow membranous margins, inner bracts with wide membranous margins. Fruiting peduncles erect or slightly spreading. Flowering September–October. Sandstone rocks, NW (Cedarberg Mountains to Ceres).

Romulea schlechteri Béguinot
Plants 8–30 cm high, stem 2–30 cm high; corm with an oblique basal ridge. Leaves three to six, lower two basal, narrowly four-grooved, sometimes minutely hairy, 0.5–

1.5 mm diam. Flowers lilac or mauve to white, with deep yellow cup, scented of honey and coconut, tepals 12–40 mm long, elliptical, filaments 4–10 mm long, anthers 4–9 mm long; bracts with hardly visible membranous margins, inner bracts with wide white membranous margins. Fruiting peduncles erect or suberect. Flowering July–September. Sandy soils, often along streams or in seasonally wet places, NW, SW (Bokkeveld Mountains to Caledon).

Romulea setifolia N. E. Brown

Plants 5–25 cm high, stem sometimes elongated; corm with an oblique basal ridge of fibril clusters. Leaves three to six, mostly basal, narrowly four-grooved, 0.5–1.5 mm diam. Flowers yellow to apricot, sometimes with dark blotches in the throat, tepals 8–35 mm long, elliptical, filaments 4–6 mm long, anthers 2–7 mm long; bracts with narrow membranous margins, inner bracts with membranous, rarely brown-edged margins. Fruiting peduncles remaining suberect. Flowering July–September. Sandy flats, RV, NW, SW, AP, KM, LB, SE (Bokkeveld Mountains and western Karoo to Port Elizabeth).

Romulea sinispinosensis M. P. de Vos

Plants 12–20 cm high; corm obliquely flattened with a spathulate basal ridge. Leaves several, basal, narrowly four-grooved, c. 1 mm diam. Flowers cream to white, with yellowish green cup, tepals 10–12 mm long, elliptical, filaments 3–4 mm long, anthers 3–4 mm long; bracts with narrow membranous margins, inner bracts membranous or submembranous. Fruiting peduncles curved, later erect. Flowering August. Sandy slopes, NW (Doringbaai to Sauer).

Romulea sladenii M. P. de Vos

Plants 7–15(–30) cm high, stem branched above ground; corms symmetrical, bell-shaped, with a wide circular rim of fibers. Leaves three to five, basal and cauline, narrowly four-grooved, 0.5–1 mm diam. Flowers white with a yellow cup, tepals 15–25 mm long, elliptical, filaments 5–7 mm long, anthers 4–6 mm long; bracts without visible membranous margins, inner bracts with wider membranous margins. Fruiting peduncles sharply spreading.

Romulea schlechteri

Romulea sladenii

Romulea sphaerocarpa

Romulea stellata

Flowering August–September. Rocky sandstone flats, NW (Gifberg).

Romulea sphaerocarpa M. P. de Vos
Plants 15–30 cm high; corm obliquely flattened with a fan-shaped basal ridge. Leaf single, sometimes two leaves, basal, sticky, narrowly four-grooved, c. 1 mm diam. Flowers usually solitary, yellow with brown streaks in the cup, tepals 15–25 mm long, elliptical, filaments 5–7 mm long, anthers 6–8 mm long; bracts with narrow membranous margins, sticky, inner bracts submembranous with wide membranous margins. Fruiting peduncles curved. Flowering June. Sandstone outcrops, NW, KM (Swartruggens to Witteberg).

Romulea stellata M. P. de Vos
Plants 3–5 cm high; corm with an oblique basal ridge. Leaves one or two, basal, narrowly four-grooved, 0.5 mm diam. Flowers salverform, violet or occasionally white, with yellow throat, perianth tube 11–17 mm long, tepals 7–11 mm, elliptical, filaments smooth, 2–3.5 mm, anthers 2–3 mm long; bracts submembranous, inner bracts with narrow membranous margins. Fruiting peduncle short, suberect. Flowering May–July. Sandstone pavement, NW (Gifberg to northern Cedarberg Mountains).

Romulea subfistulosa M. P. de Vos
Plants 10–25 cm high; corm rounded at base, with curved acuminate teeth. Leaves four to nine, basal, curved, somewhat spongy, broadly four-grooved and almost winged, 2–5 mm diam. Flowers pink with dark blotches at the edge of a yellow cup, tepals 25–50 mm long, obovate, filaments 4–6 mm long, anthers 8–11 mm long; bracts keeled above with narrow membranous margins, inner bracts two-keeled, with colorless or speckled membranous margins. Fruiting peduncles recurved at first, later suberect. Flowering August–October. Dolerite flats, RV (Calvinia to Roggeveld Escarpment).

Romulea sulphurea Béguinot
Plants 5–20 cm high, stem to 15 cm high; corm with an oblique basal ridge. Leaves three to five, lower two basal,

narrowly four-grooved, 0.5 mm diam. Flowers orange-yellow with dark marks in the cup, sweetly scented, tepals 12–20 mm long, elliptical, filaments 6–9 mm long, hairy to the top, anthers 2.5–3 mm long; bracts with narrow membranous margins, inner bracts with wide membranous margins. Flowering July–August. Sandstone pavement, NW (Pakhuis Mountains).

Romulea syringodeoflora M. P. de Vos
Plants 12–20 cm high; corm rounded at base, with curved acuminate teeth. Leaves about five, basal, curved, sparsely hairy, narrowly or widely four-grooved, 1.5–2.5 mm diam. Flowers salverform, pink to purple, tube 15–20 mm long, tepals 10–17 mm long, elliptical, filaments 4–5 mm long, anthers 4–6 mm long; bracts with narrow white membranous margins, inner bracts with white membranous margins. Flowering September–October. Shale flats and slopes, RV (Sutherland).

Romulea tabularis Ecklon ex Béguinot
Plants 10–35(–60) cm high, stem 1–30 cm high; corm with an oblique basal ridge. Leaves three to five, lower one or two basal, narrowly four-grooved, 1–2 mm diam. Flowers blue, rarely white, with yellow cup and usually lower half of the tepals, sometimes fragrant, tepals 10–28 mm long, elliptical, filaments 3–6 mm long, anthers 3–6 mm long; bracts with hardly visible membranous margins, inner bracts submembranous with wide brown-marked membranous margins. Fruiting peduncles arching. Later erect. Flowering July–October. Moist sandy or limestone flats, often in seasonal pools, NW, SW, AP (southern Namaqualand to Agulhas). Page 350.

Romulea tetragona M. P. de Vos
Plants 8–30 cm high; corm with an oblique basal ridge. Leaves four to six, basal, four-winged, hairy, 1.5–7 mm diam. Flowers on hairy peduncles, rose to lilac or pink with dark bands around the yellowish, violet, or brownish cup, tepals 12–28 mm long, obovate, filaments 3–4 mm long, anthers 2–6 mm long; bracts with narrow membranous margins and broader membranous apices, hairy on the lower part, inner bracts with wide membra-

Romulea subfistulosa

Romulea sulphurea

Romulea tabularis

Romulea tetragona

Romulea tortuosa

Romulea toximontana

nous margins. Fruiting peduncles hairy, curved, later straightening. Flowering August–September. Clay soils, RV, NW, KM (western Karoo and Cold Bokkeveld to Tweedside).

Romulea tortilis Baker
Plants 6–12 cm high, stem sometimes branched above ground; corms symmetrical, bell-shaped, with a circular rim of fibers. Leaves two to five, basal and usually cauline, tightly sinuous, narrowly four-grooved, sometimes minutely hairy, 0.5–1 mm diam. Flowers old rose with dark red blotches around the yellow cup, tepals 15–25 mm long, oblanceolate, filaments 5–6 mm long, anthers 3.5–5 mm long; bracts without visible membranous margins, inner bracts with wider membranous margins. Flowering July–September. Sandstone slopes, NW (Clanwilliam to Piketberg).

Romulea tortuosa (Lichtenstein ex Roemer & Schultes) Baker
Plants 5–10(–25) cm high; corm obliquely flattened with a wide fan-like basal ridge. Leaves several, usually flexuous or twisted, narrowly four-grooved beneath and channeled almost throughout, 0.5–1 mm diam. Flowers yellow with or without black marks or blotches in the throat, sweetly scented, tepals 10–40 mm long, oblanceolate, filaments 3–10 mm long, anthers 3–10 mm long; bracts and inner bracts membranous or submembranous. Fruiting peduncles curved or coiled. Flowering June–September. Sandstone and clay soils, RV, NW, SW (Kamiesberg, western Karoo to Hex River Pass, and near Worcester).

Romulea toximontana M. P. de Vos
Plants 10–25 cm high, stem to 10 cm high; corm obliquely flattened with a wide fan-shaped basal ridge. Leaves three to five, lower two basal, narrowly four-grooved, sometimes minutely hairy, c. 1 mm diam. Flowers cream with yellow cup, tepals 13–22 mm long, elliptical, filaments 3–5 mm long, anthers 4–6 mm long; bracts with narrow membranous margins, inner bracts with wide, brown-edged, membranous margins. Fruiting peduncles widely spreading. Flowering August. Sandy soils, NW (Bokkeveld Mountains to Gifberg).

Romulea triflora (Burman fil.) N. E. Brown
Plants 10–30 cm high, stem branched above ground; corms symmetrical, bell-shaped, with a circular rim of fibers. Leaves two to six, basal and cauline, narrowly four-grooved, 0.5–1 mm diam. Flowers yellow or white with or without darker zones or markings around the yellow cup, tepals 14–30 mm long, oblanceolate, filaments 4–5 mm long, anthers 4–7 mm long; bracts without visible membranous margins, inner bracts with wider membranous margins. Fruiting peduncles suberect or somewhat spreading. Flowering August–October. Sandstone slopes, mostly in seasonally moist sites, NW, SW (Citrusdal to Stanford).

Romulea unifolia M. P. de Vos
Plants 15–30 cm high; corm rounded at base, with curved acuminate teeth. Leaf single, sometimes two leaves, basal, curved, somewhat spongy, broadly four-grooved, 2–4 mm diam. Flowers orange-red with black

Romulea unifolia

and yellow blotches within the cup, tepals 28–45 mm long, obovate-cuneate, filaments 5–6 mm long, anthers 9–12 mm long; bracts keeled with narrow, white, membranous margins, inner bracts two-keeled with membranous margins. Fruiting peduncles straight. Flowering August–September. Dolerite flats, RV (Calvinia and northern Roggeveld Escarpment).

Romulea vinacea M. P. de Vos
Plants 7–25 cm high, stem 2–10 cm high; corm with an oblique basal ridge. Leaves three or four, lower two basal, narrowly four-grooved, often minutely hairy, c. 1 mm diam. Flowers blue-violet with cream and yellow cup, outer tepals shiny and wine colored on reverse, tepals 14–28 mm long, elliptical, filaments 6–9 mm long, anthers 4–6 mm long; bracts with hardly visible membranous margins, inner bracts with wide membranous margins. Fruiting peduncles suberect. Flowering August. Sandy soils, NW (Pakhuis Pass).

Romulea viridibracteata M. P. de Vos
Plants 10–30 cm high; corm rounded at base, with curved acuminate teeth. Leaves three to five, basal, filiform, narrowly four-grooved, 1–2 mm diam. Flowers yellow with dark brown markings at the edge of the cup, tepals 20–35 mm long, obovate, filaments 4–5 mm long, anthers 6–9 mm long; bracts usually keeled above with narrow, often brown, membranous margins, inner bracts two-keeled with colorless or brown-dotted membranous margins. Fruiting peduncles at first spreading, later suberect. Flowering August–September. Sandstone slopes, NW (Bokkeveld Mountains to Pakhuis Pass).

Romulea vlokii M. P. de Vos
Plants 25–35 cm high; corm pointed at base, with straight acuminate teeth. Leaves three to five, narrowly four-grooved. Flowers pink with dark blotches around the orange-yellow cup, tepals 32–40 mm long, oblanceolate, filaments 4–5 mm long, anthers c. 7 mm long; bracts with distinct brown-spotted membranous margins and conspicuous membranous apices, inner bracts with wide membranous margins. Flowering July–August. Wet sands, KM (Kammanassie Mountains).

Scadoxus

COMMON NAME blood lily, FAMILY Amaryllidaceae. Deciduous perennials. ROOTSTOCK predominantly an elongated rhizome or with a bulbous part above. LEAVES as many as 10, dry or green at flowering, narrowed into a petiole-like base, often sheathing to form a false stem, with or without red spotting, the blade thin textured with a prominent midrib. INFLORESCENCE a many-flowered compact or spherical umbel on a fleshy, stout, slightly compressed scape; spathe bracts four or more, showy or withering early. FLOWERS actinomorphic, salver-shaped and spreading or narrowly funnel-shaped and compact, red to orange, the perianth tube short to long, the tepals erect or spreading, as long as or longer than the tube. STAMENS inserted in throat, slightly longer than the tepals, the anthers dorsifixed. OVARY with one or few ovules per locule; STYLE straight, as long as the stamens, the stigma undivided. FRUIT fleshy, ovoid to globose, red-skinned with yellow pulp. SEEDS ovoid, 5–10 mm wide, ivory colored, the embryo green. Basic chromosome number $x = 9$. Widespread in tropical Africa; 9 spp., 3 in southern Africa, mainly in the relatively well watered areas of the summer-rainfall region, 2 in the Cape.

Scadoxus was long regarded as a subgenus of *Haemanthus* but because of important differences in the rootstock, foliage, and number of chromosomes, it is now treated as a distinct genus. Unlike most species of *Haemanthus*, species of *Scadoxus* are well suited to shady conditions, and this has made them popular horticultural subjects. The inflorescence is attractive at all stages of growth, beginning with the richly colored spathe bracts and the dramatically spotted scape, as it pushes through the ground, followed by the dense aggregations of scarlet flowers. Finally, the clusters of berries turn crimson, and in *S. membranaceus* and *S. puniceus* they appear to glow in the cup formed by the broad, contrasting bracts.

The brush-like inflorescences of species like *Scadoxus puniceus* are probably pollinated mainly by bees, but the brilliant red flowers of the eastern southern African *S. multiflorus* Rafinesque seem to be adapted to pollination by large butterflies, especially swallowtails. The nodding inflorescence of the tropical *S. nutans* (Friis & I. N. Björnstad) Friis & Nordal is almost certainly an adaptation to bird pollination.

Propagation is by seed and offsets, which can be removed after the flowering period. Unlike most species of *Haemanthus*, *Scadoxus* favors semishade and can be expected to flower from the third season onward.

FURTHER READING. Studies of the taxonomy of *Scadoxus* were published by Bjørnstad and Friis (1974). The separation of *Scadoxus* from *Haemanthus* was formalized by Friis and Nordal (1976).

Scadoxus membranaceus (Baker) Friis & Nordal

Plants to 40 cm high. Leaves two to six, dry or green at flowering, spreading, the petiole-like bases not sheathing, spotted with red, the blades lanceolate, 30–130 mm wide. Umbel compact, obconical, on a scape spotted with red toward the base, spathe bracts four or five, suberect, broad, blunt, and of equal size, longer than the flowers, waxy, red to green, flowers 20–25 mm long, greenish to pink, with a tube 2.5–7 mm long, stamens and style slightly exserted. Flowering January–March. Coastal sand, SE (Port Elizabeth to KwaZulu-Natal).

Scadoxus puniceus (Linnaeus) Friis & Nordal

Plants to 75 cm high. Leaves two to seven, dry or green at flowering, the petiole-like bases sheathing to form a long false stem surrounded by spotted basal sheaths, the blades spreading, lanceolate to ovate, 50–150 mm wide. Umbel dense, obconical to hemispherical, on a basally spotted scape, spathe bracts 5–8(–11), suberect, of variable shape, as long as or longer than the flowers, green to red, flowers 20–35 mm long, yellow-green to red, with a tube 3–12 mm long, stamens and style slightly exserted. Flowering September–January. Coast and river valleys, in subtropical thicket, AP, SE (Bredasdorp to tropical Africa).

Scilla

COMMON NAME squill, FAMILY Hyacinthaceae. Deciduous perennials. ROOTSTOCK a globose bulb, the tunics sometimes fibrous above, rarely loose. LEAVES two to several, linear to ovate, sometimes hairy, suberect or spreading, sometimes with reddish markings toward the base but never spotted. INFLORESCENCE a few- to many-flowered raceme, rarely branched, sometimes congested and subcorymbose, the pedicels mostly long; bracts usually small, membranous, often auriculate, sometimes with an inner bracteole. FLOWERS cup- or bell-shaped, the tepals spreading or more erect and recurved above, united at the base, blue to purple, rarely white to pink, usually unscented. STAMENS with filaments joined to the base of the tepals, free or united at the base, linear-lanceolate. OVARY obovoid to subglobose with two to several ovules per locule; STYLE slender, usually shorter than the perianth. FRUIT an ovoid to obovoid capsule. SEEDS few per locule, subglobose, black. Basic chromosome numbers $x = 4$–10. Africa and Eurasia to China, mostly Northern Hemisphere; c. 40 spp., 1 in the Cape.

Concentrated in the northern temperate zone, the genus *Scilla* has several European segregates distin-

Scadoxus puniceus

guished by small floral differences that may be more functional than fundamental. The exact status of the relationship between the European and southern African members is only now becoming clear. In southern Africa, most of the species once included in *Scilla* have been transferred to the genus *Ledebouria*, which is distinguished by its often spotted leaves, typically several inflorescences per plant, and stalked ovary containing two paired ovules in each locule. The remaining four or five species are also not related to the true scillas and in more recent treatments are accommodated in three separate genera. A single species, *S. plumbea*, occurs in the winter-rainfall region, where it is confined to a small area of the Cape Fold Mountains. It grows on wet sandstone slopes and flowers in the summer. Other southern African species are typically found in rocky grassland or on damp rock pavement in the summer-rainfall region. The flowers of *S. plumbea* are visited by bees of the genus *Amegilla* (Apidae: Anthophorinae) and also by smaller pollen-collecting bees of the family Halictidae.

Blue flowers are uncommon in the family Hyacinthaceae and are largely characteristic of *Scilla* and related genera but occur also in several species of *Lachenalia*. The flowers of *S. plumbea* are exceptionally vividly colored and the tall spikes highly attractive, but the species is scarcely known in cultivation. Its sandstone habitat suggests that it may not be easy to grow.

FURTHER READING. The South African species of *Scilla* were revised by Jessop (1970), and *S. plumbea* was separately treated by Lewis (1947), along with a fine illustration.

Scilla plumbea Lindley

Plants 20–40 cm high. Leaves suberect, linear, fleshy, deeply channeled. Flowers on spreading pedicels 10–15 mm long, purple-blue, unscented, tepals reflexed above, 8–12 × 2–3 mm, stamens well exserted, 11–13 mm long. Flowering December–January. Sandstone slopes in seeps, SW (Bain's Kloof Mountains).

Sparaxis

COMMON NAMES bluebonnets, Cape buttercup, or harlequin flower (depending on species), FAMILY Iridaceae. Small deciduous perennials. ROOTSTOCK a globose to conical corm, rooting from the base, the tunics pale, composed of fine to coarse fibers. LEAVES several, unifacial, soft textured, mostly basal and lanceolate, usually obtuse; flowering stems firm, erect, simple or if branched then from either above or below the ground. INFLORESCENCE a spike; bracts dry, crinkled, translucent, irregularly streaked with brown markings, and often lacerate; the outer usually tricuspidate, the inner smaller but often as long as the outer, bicuspidate. FLOWERS often large, variously colored, actinomorphic and rotate or zygomorphic and bilabiate; perianth tube either funnel-shaped, the cylindrical lower part usually short, or cylindrical and sharply bent below the apex; tepals subequal and spreading or the uppermost largest and then erect or hooded and the lower three smaller. STAMENS either

Scilla plumbea

erect and symmetrically disposed, or unilateral and spreading or arcuate; anthers straight or twisted. OVARY globose, style branches either short with expanded apex, or long and filiform, erect or arched behind the stamens. FRUIT a barrel-shaped, cartilaginous capsule, showing the outline of the seeds. SEEDS globose, smooth, and shiny. Basic chromosome number $x = 10$. Southwestern Cape and the western Karoo; mainly on clay soils in renosterveld, less often in coastal sandveld; 15 spp.

The unusual dry, crinkled bracts of *Sparaxis* recall those of *Dierama* but differences in leaf anatomy and morphology make a close relationship seem unlikely; *Sparaxis* may be most closely related to *Tritonia*. The short-tubed, zygomorphically flowered species are pollinated by bees whereas the long-tubed species are pollinated by long-proboscid flies of the genus *Prosoeca* (Nemestrinidae). The actinomorphic, orange- and pink-flowered species with short tubes are pollinated by a combination of monkey beetles (Scarabaeidae: Hopliini) and the short-proboscid fly, *Philoliche angulata* (Tabanidae).

Species of *Sparaxis* have been cultivated for more than 200 years and the harlequin sparaxis, *S. tricolor*, was actually first described in 1792 from plants grown in Holland. Even before that, the more common *S. grandiflora* was grown in Britain, Holland, Austria, and France. Horticultural interest in the genus has been sporadic, however, and these charming plants, so easy to grow and so free-flowering, are far less well known than they deserve. Hybrids were first raised in the 1820s in the garden of a wealthy businessman in Cape Town, perhaps by the accidental crossing of wild species by insects, and have been in the horticultural trade for many years. They have brightly colored orange, scarlet, or pink flowers strongly marked with contrasting yellow and dark purple to black centers. They will grow in any fertile garden soil and thrive outdoors in areas of Mediterranean climate, and even in areas of summer rainfall and relatively mild winters. They are displayed to advantage in the rock garden, when massed in borders and tubs, and alone or mixed with annuals and later-flowering bulbs. All three of the parental species of the hybrids, *S. elegans*, *S. pillansii*, and *S. tricolor*, are restricted to the Bokkeveld Mountains and are as attractive as the hybrids.

Other species have received less attention but the white-flowered *Sparaxis bulbifera* clearly has potential, for it grows easily and has large creamy flowers with loosely cupped tepals and branched stems. The ample production of bulblets makes it easy to increase stocks. One of few species native to sandy, waterlogged soils, it can be used in damp corners of the garden. *Sparaxis grandiflora* has the largest flowers in the genus and has forms with white, bright yellow, or plum red tepals. The yellow form (subsp. *acutiloba*) is available and very attractive, but we have never seen the plum form (subsp. *grandiflora*) in cultivation. Species of the former genus *Synnotia*, now included in *Sparaxis*, have zygomorphic flowers, and several have *Gladiolus*-like bilabiate flowers. Two of these, *S. caryophyllacea* and *S. galeata*, have a strong pleasant scent and grow as readily as the more common sparaxis. *Sparaxis auriculata*, described only in 1999, has tall stems, to 0.6 m high, bearing large yellow and violet flowers.

FURTHER READING. *Sparaxis* was expanded by Goldblatt (1992) to include the species previously referred to *Synnotia*, and the earlier revisions by Lewis (1956) and Goldblatt (1969) have been superseded by a complete account by Goldblatt (1999) that includes the new species described by Goldblatt and Manning (1999). The diverse methods of pollination biology in the genus and their influence on flower form and speciation were examined by Goldblatt et al. (2000).

Sparaxis auriculata Goldblatt & J. C. Manning

Plants to 60 cm high; corm narrowly conical with tunics of medium-textured fibers. Leaves lanceolate, acute, the sheaths liberally speckled with dark spots, the blades with a prominent submarginal vein. Flowers mostly five to seven per spike, zygomorphic and bilabiate, c. 42 mm long, violet and yellow, lightly fragrant, tube c. 18 mm long, dorsal tepal suberect, c. 25 mm long, style branches slender, overtopping the anthers; bracts with prominent cusps. Flowering August, early September. Rocky sandstone slopes, often in light shade, NW (Gifberg). Page 356.

Sparaxis bulbifera (Linnaeus) Ker Gawler

Plants 15–45 cm high; corm globose with finely fibrous tunics, the stem bearing numerous axillary cormels after

Sparaxis auriculata

Sparaxis bulbifera; see also page 20

blooming. Leaves lanceolate, obtuse. Flowers two to five per spike, subactinomorphic with rotate perianth and unilateral stamens and style, 40–45 mm diam., white to cream with pale yellow center, rarely with a blackish spot at tepal base, rarely purplish on reverse, unscented, tube c. 15 mm long, tepals subequal, ovate-oblong, lightly cupped, 24–28 × c. 12 mm, stamens and style unilateral but stamens not contiguous, style branches slender; bracts with long, dark cusps. Flowering September–October. Wet sandy or limestone flats, SW, AP (Darling to Agulhas).

Sparaxis caryophyllacea Goldblatt

Plants 8–20 cm high; corm globose with tunics of coarse fibers. Leaves several, mostly prostrate, darkly speckled basally, lanceolate to oblong, obtuse. Flowers two to four per spike, zygomorphic and bilabiate, 36–40 mm long, yellow and white, flushed mauve on the outside, the throat darkly streaked, sweetly violet scented, perianth tube 18–20 mm long, dorsal tepal hooded, c. 20 mm long, style branches slender; bracts with short cusps. Flowering August to early September. Dry sandstone slopes, NW (Nardouw Mountains).

Sparaxis elegans (Sweet) Goldblatt

Plants 9–20 cm high; corm globose with tunics of fine fibers. Leaves lanceolate, obtuse. Flowers mostly two to four per spike, actinomorphic, 40–50 mm diam., salmon, rarely white, with purple and yellow center, unscented, tube c. 8 mm long, blocked below by the style, tepals 18–22 × c. 15 mm, stamens and style central, anthers sigmoid, style short, spathulate; bracts obscurely toothed. Late August–September. Clay flats, NW (Bokkeveld Escarpment and western Karoo).

Sparaxis fragrans (Jacquin) Ker Gawler

Plants 10–25 cm high; corm globose with tunics of fine fibers. Leaves linear or narrowly sword-shaped. Flowers mostly two to four per spike, actinomorphic, 30–35 mm diam., yellow to buff, often mauve on reverse, sour scented, tube c. 7 mm long, the lower part blocked by the style, tepals subequal, spreading, oblong, 18–22 × c. 8 mm, stamens and style central, style branches long and slender; bract cusps long, dark brown, the edges irregularly serrated. Flowering mid-August into September. Clay slopes in renosterveld, SW (Caledon district from Bot River to Napier).

Sparaxis galeata Ker Gawler
Plants 12–35 cm high; corm globose with tunics of fine fibers, densely matted and forming a neck. Leaves several, often prostrate and speckled basally, lanceolate, obtuse, margins rarely thickened. Flowers four to seven per spike, zygomorphic and bilabiate, c. 35 mm long, cream and yellow with mauve markings, usually intensely sweetly scented of freesia, tube c. 15 mm long; dorsal tepal largest, c. 20 mm long, erect or flexed backward, style dividing opposite the lower half of the anthers, the branches slender, c. 4 mm long; bracts with short cusps. Flowering July–September. Dry clay slopes in renosterveld, RV, NW (Vanrhyn's Pass and Calvinia to lower Olifants River Valley).

Sparaxis grandiflora (D. Delaroche) Ker Gawler
Plants 10–25 cm high; corm globose with tunics of fine fibers. Leaves sometimes prostrate, lanceolate, obtuse. Flowers mostly three to five per spike, subactinomorphic with rotate perianth and unilateral stamens and style, white, cream, yellow, or mauve to reddish purple, pale forms often with a blackish spot at the base of each tepal, unscented, tube 10–14 mm long, the slender part blocked by the style; tepals subequal, spreading or lightly cupped, oblong to spathulate, 24–30 × 12–16 mm, stamens and style unilateral but stamens not contiguous, style branches slender; bracts with long, dark cusps. Flowering August–September. Clay flats and slopes in renosterveld, NW, SW (Clanwilliam to Bredasdorp).

Four subspecies are recognized: subspecies *acutiloba* Goldblatt with bright yellow flowers, tepals more or less acute, NW (Olifants River Valley), subspecies *fimbriata* (Lamarck) Goldblatt with cream to white flowers, tepals rounded at the tips, SW (Gouda to Cape Peninsula), subspecies *grandiflora* with deep plum red flowers, tepals rounded at the tips, NW (Tulbagh Valley), and subspecies *violacea* (Ecklon) Goldblatt with cream to violet flowers, tepals markedly spathulate, SW (Bot River to Bredasdorp).

Sparaxis elegans

Sparaxis fragrans

Sparaxis grandiflora subsp. *acutiloba*

Sparaxis grandiflora subsp. *fimbriata*

Sparaxis grandiflora subsp. *grandiflora* with *Geissorhiza aspera*

Sparaxis grandiflora subsp. *violacea*

Sparaxis maculosa Goldblatt
Plants 10–20 cm high; corm globose with tunics of fine, matted fibers. Leaves several, lanceolate-falcate. Flowers one to three per spike, actinomorphic, 55–60 mm diam., yellow with a dark maroon-black center, unscented, tube c. 7 mm long, the slender part blocked by the style, tepals outspread, oblong, 27–35 × 8–10 mm, stamens and style central, style branches long and slender; bracts with long cusps, the edges lightly serrated. Flowering September. Clay slopes in renosterveld, SW (Villiersdorp, Doring River Valley).

Sparaxis metelerkampiae L. Bolus
Plants 15–30 cm high; corm globose with tunics of fairly coarse fibers. Leaves several, rarely prostrate, lanceolate, obtuse to acute. Flowers two to five per spike, zygomorphic and bilabiate, 45–55 mm long, violet marked with white, unscented, tube elongate, sharply bent, 35–40 mm long, dorsal tepal erect, 14–17 mm long, style branches short; bracts with long brown cusps. Flowering August–September. Rocky sandstone slopes, NW (Bokkeveld Mountains to Piekeniers Kloof).

Sparaxis parviflora (G. J. Lewis) Goldblatt
Plants 15–30 cm high; corm globose with tunics of fine fibers. Leaves several, linear to sword-shaped. Flowers mostly two to four per spike, zygomorphic and bilabiate, 15–18 mm long, cream and yellow, flushed with purple, with a light spicy-sweet scent, tube to 9 mm long, dorsal tepal hooded, c. 9 mm long, style slender; bracts with short cusps. Flowering August–September. Granite slopes and rocks, SW (Saldanha to Darling).

Sparaxis pillansii L. Bolus
Plants to 40 cm high; corm globose with tunics of fine fibers. Leaves several, sword-shaped. Flowers mostly three to five per spike, actinomorphic, 30–35 mm diam., light rose red, the center yellow, edged with dark maroon, unscented, tube c. 8 mm long, blocked below by the style, tepals ovate, 22–29 × c. 10 mm, stamens and style central, style branches short, spathulate; bracts obscurely toothed. Flowering September to early October. Shale

Sparaxis metelerkampiae

Sparaxis parviflora

Sparaxis pillansii; see also page 11

Sparaxis roxburghii

Sparaxis tricolor; see also page 2

Sparaxis villosa

and heavy doleritic clay in waterlogged depressions, RV (Bokkeveld Plateau to Calvinia).

Sparaxis roxburghii (Baker) Goldblatt

Plants 28–45 cm high; corm conical with tunics of fine, often matted fibers forming a neck. Leaves several, sword-shaped, speckled on the sheaths. Flowers mostly four to six per spike, zygomorphic and bilabiate, 42–55 mm long, mauve to lilac, with yellow on the lower tepals, unscented, tube elongate, cylindrical, 20–30 mm long, dorsal tepal erect, 22–28 mm long, style branches slender; bracts with short cusps. Flowering late August to mid-September. Rocky sandstone slopes, NW (Olifants River Valley between Clanwilliam and Citrusdal).

Sparaxis tricolor (Schneevoogt) Ker Gawler

Plants 12–30 cm high; corm globose with tunics of fine fibers. Leaves several, lanceolate. Flowers two to five per spike, actinomorphic, 40–50 mm diam., orange-scarlet, the center yellow, broadly edged with reddish black, unscented, tube c. 8 mm long, tepals ovate, 25–30 × c. 10 mm, stamens and style central, style branches short, spathulate; bracts obscurely toothed. Flowering September–October. Damp clay and stony soils in renosterveld, NW (Bokkeveld Escarpment).

Sparaxis variegata (Sweet) Goldblatt

Plants mostly 15–30 cm high; corm globose with tunics of coarse fibers. Leaves several, often inclined toward the ground, oblong-lanceolate, obtuse. Flowers three to eight per spike, zygomorphic and bilabiate, 45–50 mm long, violet with yellow on the lower tepals, unscented, tube elongate, sharply bent, 30–32 mm long, dorsal tepal inclined to hooded, 25–30 mm long, style branches slender; bracts with short cusps. Flowering August–September. Rocky sandstone slopes, NW (Olifants River Valley, Clanwilliam to Klawer).

Sparaxis villosa (Burman fil.) Goldblatt

Plants 12–35 cm high; corm globose with tunics of fairly coarse fibers. Leaves several, sword-shaped, often obtuse. Flowers mostly two to four per spike, zygomorphic and bilabiate, 28–32 mm long, cream to yellow with violet-flushed dorsal tepal, throat streaked with dark purple, unscented, tube mostly 14–16 mm long, dorsal tepal hooded, 14–16 mm long, style branches slender, short; bracts with short cusps. Flowering mid-August into September. Clay and granite slopes, NW, SW (Citrusdal to Cape Peninsula).

Spiloxene

COMMON NAME Cape star, FAMILY Hypoxidaceae. Small deciduous perennials. ROOTSTOCK a corm covered with hard, netted fibers or firm, twisted roots, rarely smooth. LEAVES as many as 12, rarely dry at flowering, linear to ovate, sheathing at the base, smooth or the margin occasionally minutely toothed. INFLORESCENCE of one to six flowers, each subtended by one or two linear or leaf-like bracts on a short to long or occasionally subterranean scape. FLOWERS star- to funnel-shaped, orange, yellow, or white, rarely pink, occasionally with a dark center, green, red, or pink on the reverse, the pedicel long or rarely reduced, the tepals six, rarely five or four, free to the ovary or arising from a solid neck above the ovary, narrowly ovate, outspread to reflexed. STAMENS six, rarely five, four, or two, inserted at the base the tepals and style, suberect, filaments short, attached to the base of the long anthers. OVARY three-locular, rarely two- or one-locular through the incomplete fusion of the ovary septa; ovules many, axile or apparently parietal; STYLE short, the three stigma lobes broad, papillate on the inner surface and margins. FRUIT a cylindrical to top-shaped capsule, opening by means of an apical lid and then sometimes splitting longitudinally. SEEDS subglobose or rarely J-shaped, black and shiny, minutely tuberculate with a conspicuous raphe and hilum. Basic chromosome number x unknown. Mainly southern Africa, c. 25 spp. mostly in the winter-rainfall region (16 in the Cape), and 4 in Australia and New Zealand.

The genus *Spiloxene* was separated from *Hypoxis* in 1914, when it came to be known as *Ianthe*. The name *Ianthe*, however, had already been used for a plant in the family Scrophulariaceae, and to correct the error the name *Spiloxene* was substituted in 1932. The nomenclatural change to *Spiloxene* has only been formalized for the southern African species, and four species still remain under *Hypoxis* section *Ianthe* in the *Flora of Australia*. The morphological and preliminary molecular data indicate that the Australian species are closely allied to the southern African *Spiloxene* species, suggesting that they should be transferred to the genus.

Most species of *Spiloxene* are visited by a variety of insects, particularly pollen-collecting bees, but the dark-eyed forms of *S. capensis* are probably adapted to pollination by monkey beetles (Scarabaeidae: Hopliini).

Cape stars favor moist places, and where conditions are suitable, populations of two or more species often co-occur. Several Western Cape species are strikingly beautiful, most notably the highly variable *Spiloxene capensis*. Many of its forms have flowers with brilliant centers, ranging from brown to metallic green and black, on white, cream, yellow, or occasionally pink tepals. As in many other representatives of the genus *Spiloxene*, the outer tepals are backed with bold red or green stripes and bands. The flowers of the sun-loving species close each night and open before noon on warm, sunny days. In the less attractively marked shade-loving species, however, the flowers remain open all day. The flowers of both kinds generally last a few days. The peacock colors of *S. capensis* make it a deserving choice for the enthusiast.

FURTHER READING. A key and descriptions of *Spiloxene* species in the Cape were published by Baker (1896), and Henderson (1987) dealt with the allied species in Australia. Garside (1936) formalized the transfer of southern African species from *Ianthe* to *Spiloxene*.

Spiloxene alba (Thunberg) Fourcade
Plants 5–15 cm high, forming clumps; corm loosely fibrous above, otherwise smooth. Leaves two to five, erect, succulent, shorter than the inflorescence but elongating after flowering, linear, c. 3 mm wide, triangular in cross section, surrounded by bladeless basal sheaths, margins sometimes minutely toothed near apex. Flowers two per scape, sometimes one, tepals 10–20 mm long, spreading from a neck 3–30 mm long, white, rarely cream or yellow, with pink reverse; bracts two, green, firm, clasping the pedicels toward the base, ovary longer than the tepals, narrowly cylindrical. Flowering April–June. Marshes and damp flats, NW, SW (Ceres to Breede River Valley, Malmesbury to Hermanus).

Spiloxene aquatica (Linnaeus fil.) Fourcade
Plants 20–45 cm high, solitary; corm smooth or loosely fibrous above. Leaves two to five, erect, succulent, exceeding the inflorescence, linear, c. 3 mm wide, somewhat triangular in cross section, lacking bladeless sheaths, margins smooth. Flowers two to seven per scape, tepals 8–35 mm long, white with green reverse, often scented; bracts two or more, green, clasping the pedicels toward the base, ovary as long as or longer than the tepals, narrowly cylindrical. Flowering June–November. Seasonal pools and streams, NW, SW, AP, LB (Namaqualand to Cape Peninsula and Swellendam).

Spiloxene canaliculata Garside
Plants 10–35 cm; corm with a cap of short hard bristles. Leaves two to five, recurved, 2–4 mm wide, U-shaped in cross section, tough, without a keel, margins with minute teeth when young. Flowers one per scape, tepals 25–45 mm long, orange to yellow with a dark purple, noniridescent center, reverse with reddish stripes; bract single, long, green, tightly sheathing the pedicel, ovary shorter than the tepals, expanding upward. Seeds J-shaped. Flowering July–November. Seasonally wet flats in heavy soils, SW (Darling to Cape Peninsula).

Spiloxene capensis (Linnaeus) Garside
Plants 10–35 cm high; corm with a cap of short fine bristles. Leaves two to eight, linear, 3–15 mm wide, V-shaped in cross section, distinctly keeled, margins often thickened, usually with minute recurved teeth. Flowers one per scape, tepals 15–35 mm long, white, cream, or yellow, rarely pink, unspotted or with an iridescent or noniridescent dark center, greenish on reverse, usually lined with red; bract single, long, green, tightly sheathing the pedicel, ovary as long as or shorter than the tepals, expanding upward. Flowering July–October. Seasonally wet flats, RV, NW, SW, AP, KM, LB (western Karoo to Cape Peninsula, and Little Karoo).

Spiloxene alba

Spiloxene aquatica

Spiloxene canaliculata

Spiloxene capensis, white form

Spiloxene capensis, yellow form

Spiloxene curculigoides (Colin Paterson-Jones)

Spiloxene flaccida

Spiloxene curculigoides (Bolus) Garside

Plants 5–20 cm high; corm with a prominent neck of hard, straight, tightly clustered, light brown fibers. Leaves three, sometimes as many as five, erect, 1–2 mm wide, somewhat leathery, base usually surrounded by a long sheath, margins smooth. Flowers one per scape, tepals 10–20 cm long, yellow with green reverse; bract single, green, tightly sheathing the pedicel, ovary oblong, shorter than the tepals. Flowering April–August. Seasonally damp areas in sand or among rocks, SW, AP (Tulbagh to Cape Peninsula and Bredasdorp).

Spiloxene flaccida (Nel) Garside

Plants 5–25 cm high; corm covered with firm, branched, dark fibers with outwardly curved tips. Leaves three to six, sometimes as many as nine, 1–4 mm wide, soft, V-shaped in cross section, margins smooth. Flowers two per scape, tepals 5–20 mm long, yellow with green backs; bracts two, lanceolate, three- to five-veined, clasping the pedicels at the base, pale green with translucent margins, usually drying brown, ovary usually less than half as long as the tepals, widening upward. Flowering July–September. Damp flats and slopes, SW, AP, LB, SE (Cape Peninsula to Humansdorp).

Spiloxene minuta (Linnaeus) Fourcade

Plants 1–7 cm high; corms woody with a broad flat base. Leaves usually three, linear, 1–2 mm wide, firm, channeled, margins smooth. Flowers two per scape, tepals 4–6 mm long, white with green reverse, often scented; bracts two, narrowly lanceolate, clasping the pedicels at the base, pale green, ovary much shorter than the tepals, expanding upward. Flowering April–June. Damp flats in heavy soils, NW, SW (Clanwilliam to Cape Peninsula and Gordon's Bay).

Spiloxene monophylla (Schlechter) Garside

Plants 2–10 cm high, scape often subterranean; corm covered with fine, branched fibers. Leaf single, spreading, 1.5 mm wide, firm, shallowly channeled, margins smooth. Flowers one per scape, tepals 10–25 mm long, yellow with pale green reverse, much longer than the stamens and style; bract single, lanceolate, green to whitish, clasping the pedicel toward base, ovary much shorter than the tepals, expanding upward. Flowering December–April, especially after fire. Sandstone slopes, SW (Kogelberg to Elim).

Spiloxene ovata (Linnaeus fil.) Garside

Plants 4–22 cm high; corm covered with hard, twisted roots. Leaves three to seven, linear to lanceolate, recurved to suberect, 2–20 mm wide, channeled, midrib usually prominent, margins often thickened and papillate. Flowers one per scape, tepals 4–20 mm long, white, yellow, or orange, with red to green reverse; bract one, linear, spreading, ovary shorter than the tepals, expanding upward. Flowering June–October. Seasonally wet rocks and depressions in clay or sandy soils, NW, SW, LB (Namaqualand to Cape Peninsula, Worcester to Heidelberg).

Spiloxene schlechteri (Bolus) Garside

Plants 5–15 cm high; corm enclosed by rigid, dark brown fibers, fibers netted above but parallel toward the base. Leaves three to seven, linear, erect to recurved, firm, 1–5 mm wide, almost round or U-shaped in cross section, margins sometimes with minute multicellular teeth. Flowers one or two per scape, tepals 5–15 mm long, yellow with reddish brown reverse; bracts two, one sometimes hardly visible, lanceolate, green, firm, clasping the pedicels, ovary somewhat shorter than the tepals, expanding evenly upward. Flowering June–August. Marshy flats on the coast and inland, NW, SW (Nieuwoudtville to Cape Peninsula and Worcester).

Spiloxene serrata (Thunberg) Garside

Plants 6–30 cm high; corm finely fibrous, sometimes covered with twisted roots. Leaves 5–15, erect to recurved, 1–3 mm wide, channeled, without a keel, leathery, margins usually with scattered minute, recurved teeth. Flowers one per scape, rarely two, tepals 10–30 mm long, white, yellow, or orange, with green reverse; bracts two, linear, spreading, ovary slightly shorter than the tepals, expanding upward. Flowering May–September. Inland

Spiloxene monophylla (Colin Paterson-Jones)

Spiloxene ovata

Spiloxene serrata

and coastal flats in sand or heavy clay, usually in seasonally damp sites RV, NW, SW (Namaqualand and Roggeveld Escarpment to Cape Peninsula and Worcester).

Spiloxene trifurcillata (Nel) Fourcade

Plants 3–10 cm high; corm covered with fine, netted, dark fibers. Leaves three to seven, 1–4 mm wide, V-shaped in cross section, midrib prominent, base surrounded by dark papery sheaths, margins smooth. Flowers two per scape, tepals 5–7 mm long, yellow or rarely white; bracts two, linear-lanceolate, one- to three-veined, membranous, clasping the pedicel at base, ovary shorter than the tepals, expanding upward. Flowering March–May. Seasonally damp flats and slopes, SE (Humansdorp to Port Elizabeth, Eastern Cape).

Spiloxene umbraticola (Schlechter) Garside

Plants 6–23 cm high; corms softly fibrous to smooth. Leaves two to six, recurved, 2–8 mm wide, V-shaped in cross section, keeled, margins often thickened and minutely papillate. Flowers two per scape, tepals 7–13 mm long, yellow or rarely white, with green reverse; bracts two, soft, green, clasping the pedicel, ovary cylindrical, as long as or longer than the tepals. Shaded damp slopes and rock crevices, NW (Bokkeveld Mountains to Citrusdal).

Spiloxene sp. 1

Delicate plants 5–30 cm high, forming dense mats; corm softly fibrous. Leaves two to five, suberect, 1–2 mm wide, channeled, soft, pale green. Flowers two per scape, rarely one, tepals four, sometimes as many as six, 2–6 mm long, spreading to reflexed from a short neck, yellow, cream, or white, often with dark tips; bracts two, pale green, clasping the pedicel at base, ovary club-shaped, as long as or longer than the tepals. Moist sand and deep shade beneath overhanging rocks, NW (Bokkeveld Escarpment to Cedarberg Mountains).

Spiloxene sp. 2

Plants 3–15 cm high; corm covered with firm, netted fibers. Leaves 3–11, suberect to recurved, 1–7 mm wide, firm, semiterete to channeled, margins often minutely toothed. Flowers one per scape, sessile, tepals arising from a narrow neck 20–70 mm long, expanding into a short cup above, 10–30 mm long, white with a yellow throat and pink to maroon reverse; bract one, linear-lanceolate, membranous, exceeding the slender subterranean ovary. Flowering June–September. Open, seasonally wet clay flats and slopes, RV, NW (Ceres and Roggeveld Escarpment).

Spiloxene sp. 3

Plant 3–10 cm high; corm covered with firm, dark, branched fibers. Leaves two to five, suberect, 1–2 mm wide, firm, channeled, base surrounded by dark leathery sheaths, margins smooth. Flowers one per scape, tepals 4–8 mm long, yellow; bract one, linear, minute; ovary shorter than the tepals, expanding upward. Flowering May–June. Shallow, poorly drained soils on rocky slopes, KM (Little Karoo, Montagu to Barrydale).

Strumaria

COMMON NAME Cape snowflake, FAMILY Amaryllidaceae. Deciduous perennials, often small. ROOTSTOCK a bulb with parchment to felt-like outer tunics that produce extensible threads when torn. LEAVES two to six, opposite, sometimes arranged in a spreading fan, dry or emerging at flowering, erect to prostrate, linear to elliptical, smooth or hairy, sometimes sticky. INFLORESCENCE a widely spreading or clustered, often nodding umbel, 2- to 30-flowered on a slender scape; spathe bracts two, rapidly withering. FLOWERS actinomorphic, funnel- to star-shaped, pink, white, or sometimes lemon yellow, often with an outer dark central stripe, the pedicels lax or rigid, equal to or much longer than the flowers, the tepals free or forming a short tube, spreading to outspread, with margins sometimes crisped. STAMENS spreading, the filaments joined to the style at their base or for as much as half their length, sometimes thickened and toothed, the anthers dorsifixed to subcentrifixed. OVARY with as many as nine ovules per locule; STYLE thickened toward the base, three-winged, ovoid, discoid, or depressed-conical, slender above, the stigma trifid. FRUIT a small, thin-walled capsule. SEEDS fleshy, ovoid, reddish green, 2–5 mm diam. Basic chromosome number $x = 10$. Southern Africa, extending from the mountains of southern Namibia, through Namaqualand and the Cape to the eastern Free State and Lesotho; 24 spp., 15 in the Cape.

Among southern African Amaryllidaceae, *Strumaria* is second only to *Cyrtanthus* in terms of the natural rarity of many of the species. Of the 24 species, 11 are rare, 3 vulnerable, and 2 endangered. Many of the rarer species of *Strumaria* are found on the periphery of the winter-rainfall region of southern Africa, notably southern Namibia and the Richtersveld. This contrasts with the widespread distribution ranges of species in the closely related genus *Hessea*, which does not extend as far eastward as *Strumaria*. Preliminary work suggests that *Hessea* species require cross-fertilization whereas *Strumaria* species are capable of self-fertilization. This flexibility in breeding behavior in *Strumaria* may have favored the evolution and establishment of narrowly distributed species in ecologically marginal areas.

Molecular studies of Amaryllidaceae tribe Amaryllideae, to which *Strumaria* belongs, show that *Carpolyza*, with a single species, clearly falls within the genus *Strumaria* and is closely related to *S. tenella*. *Strumaria* is highly suited to pot culture. In cultivation, plants flower well and produce abundant seed. Flowers can be expected from their third season onward. The large, pink-flowered species such as *S. salteri* are particularly attractive.

FURTHER READING. *Strumaria* was revised in a well-illustrated account by Snijman (1994). An earlier treatment by D. and U. Müller-Doblies (1985) split the genus into four small genera.

Strumaria chaplinii (W. F. Barker) Snijman

Plants to 20 cm high; bulb whitish inside. Leaves two, dry at flowering, prostrate, elliptical to oblong, 5–10 mm wide, the upper surface covered with long, soft, erect hairs. Flowers 4–14 on long, spreading pedicels, star-shaped, 10–12 mm diam., tepals flat, white with red or green midribs, scentless, stamens slightly shorter than the tepals, filaments bulbous at base, attached to the style base, style expanding evenly to a broad base. Flowering March–April. Granite outcrops, SW (Saldanha Bay). Page 368.

Strumaria discifera Marloth ex Snijman

Plants to c. 20 cm high; bulbs solitary or in large clumps, white to pale mauve inside. Leaves two, sometimes three, usually dry at flowering, suberect to prostrate, 3–10 mm wide, softly hairy on the upper surface or both surfaces, rarely smooth. Flowers (2–)5–16 on long, spreading pedicels, star-shaped, 8–14 mm diam., with channeled tepals, glistening white with pink or greenish midribs, often scented, stamens about equal to the tepals, filaments attached to the style base, style abruptly expanded into a bulbous or thick disk-like base, often with a prominent rim, slender above. Flowering March–May. Heavy soils on flats, RV, NW (Knersvlakte, Bokkeveld Plateau and Roggeveld Escarpment).

Two subspecies are recognized: subspecies *bulbifera* Snijman, plants clumped, flowers with the stylar swelling topped by a frilly rim, dolerite ridges, NW (Nieuwoudtville), and subspecies *discifera*, plants solitary, flowers with the stylar swelling smooth above, clay flats, RV, NW (Knersvlakte, Bokkeveld Plateau, and Roggeveld Escarpment).

Strumaria gemmata Ker Gawler

Plants to 30 cm high; bulb yellowish inside. Leaves two, usually dry at flowering, recurved to prostrate, elliptical to strap-shaped, 5–25 mm wide, softly hairy or rarely smooth. Flowers (2–)6–14 on long, spreading pedicels, star-shaped, 8–16 mm diam., scentless, tepals with a thick midrib and crisped margins, pale lemon or occasionally cream, the upper surface bearing a shiny translucent swelling at the base, stamens about equal to the tepals, the filaments attached to the style base, style tapering evenly from a broad base. Flowering February–May. Stony slopes or flats in clay or limestone, AP, KM, LB, SE (Bredasdorp to Ladismith and Port Elizabeth, Great Karoo).

Strumaria karooica (W. F. Barker) Snijman

Plants to 20 cm high; bulb yellowish inside. Leaves two, dry at flowering, usually prostrate, rarely suberect, more or less elliptical, 15–20 mm wide, smooth or the undersurface sparsely hairy, minutely fringed. Flowers 4–16 on long, spreading pedicels, star-shaped, 12–16 mm diam., scentless, tepals pale pink with dark red midribs and somewhat undulate margins, stamens about equal to the tepals, the filaments attached to the style base, style expanding evenly to the slightly enlarged base. Flowering March–April. Flats in heavy soil, usually near rocks, RV (Roggeveld Escarpment to Matjiesfontein).

Strumaria chaplinii

Strumaria discifera subsp. *discifera* (Colin Paterson-Jones)

Strumaria karoopoortensis (D. & U. Müller-Doblies) Snijman

Plants to 20 cm high; bulb yellowish inside. Leaves two, sometimes three, dry at flowering, recurved, flaccid, broadly strap-shaped, 20–50 mm wide, smooth or sparsely fringed, grayish green. Flowers 11–16 on long, spreading pedicels, star-shaped, 20–28 mm diam., scentless, tepals shortly clawed at the base, the margins folded together near the apex, white with deep pink midribs, later turning deep pink, stamens equal to the tepals, distinctly bulbous at the base, attached to the style base, style expanding evenly to the broad base. Flowering March. Rock crevices in shale, RV, KM (southern Tanqua Karoo to Anysberg).

Strumaria leipoldtii (L. Bolus) Snijman

Plants to 15 cm high; bulb whitish inside. Leaves two, sometimes three, dry at flowering, broadly oval to strap-shaped, 17–35 mm wide, smooth with a long, soft, dense fringe. Flowers 8–15 on long, spreading pedicels, star-shaped, 10–20 mm diam., white with green or pink midribs, scentless, stamens slightly shorter than the tepals, the filaments bulbous at the base, attached to the swollen style base, style evenly enlarged in the basal third. Flowering March–April. Sandstone rock ledges in loamy soils, NW (Lambert's Bay to Olifants River Valley).

Strumaria perryae Snijman

Plants to 20 cm high; bulb whitish inside. Leaves two, dry at flowering, recurved, narrowly strap-shaped, 2.5–5 mm wide, softly hairy. Flowers 3–11, more or less ascending, widely funnel-shaped, 10–17 mm long, pale pink with deep pink central bands, scentless, stamens slightly longer than the tepals, joined to the style base as much as 3.5 mm, style stout and three-angled toward the base. Flowering May. Shale flats, RV (Bokkeveld Escarpment).

Strumaria picta W. F. Barker

Plants to 30 cm high; bulb cream inside. Leaves two, dry at flowering, spreading, strap-shaped, 12–30 mm wide, grayish green, the edges sometimes rolled back, minutely fringed. Flowers 5–11, somewhat ascending, on mi-

Strumaria gemmata

Strumaria leipoldtii (Colin Paterson-Jones)

Strumaria picta (Colin Paterson-Jones)

nutely hairy pedicels, widely bell-shaped, 12–18.5 mm long, white with reddish brown central bands on the outer surface, scented of spice, stamens shorter than the tepals, the filaments broad with an inner ridge in the lower half, attached to the style base, style narrowly ovoid and six-grooved in the lower two-thirds. Flowering May–June. Flats and lower slopes in shale soils, RV (Bokkeveld Plateau).

Strumaria salteri (Colin Paterson-Jones)

Strumaria spiralis

Strumaria pubescens W. F. Barker
Plants to 20 cm high; bulb yellowish inside. Leaves two, sometimes three, dry at flowering, spreading, strap-shaped, 10–27 mm wide, pale green, the upper surface usually softly hairy, at least on the margins. Flowers 4–30, more or less ascending, funnel-shaped, 10–20 mm long, delicate pink with darker pink outer bands, scented, stamens about half as long as the tepals, shortly united to the style base as much as 2.5 mm, style stout and three-angled near the base. Flowering February–March. Shale rock ledges, RV (Roggeveld Escarpment to Matjiesfontein).

Strumaria salteri W. F. Barker
Striking plants to 25 cm high; bulb whitish inside. Leaves two, sometimes three, dry at flowering, prostrate, strap-shaped to elliptical, 13–28 mm wide, dark green above, smooth, the margins minutely fringed. Flowers 5–14, spreading, widely funnel-shaped, 15–29 mm long, glistening pink with reddish pink central bands, scentless, stamens as long as or longer than the tepals, joined to the style base as much as 3.5 mm, style stout and three-angled toward the base. Flowering May. Sandstone rock crevices, NW (Nardouw to Pakhuis Mountains and Olifants River Valley).

Strumaria spiralis (L'Héritier) Aiton
Plants 4–15(–27) cm high, scape wiry and coiled in lower part; bulb small, globose with a slender neck to 7.5 cm long. Leaves four to six, spreading, sometimes curled, filiform, c. 1 mm wide, shiny green. Flowers one to four, white to pale pink, often with a greenish center, perianth tube 3–4 mm long, tepals 7–14 mm long. Flowering May–August. Seasonally wet flats and rock crevices in a variety of soils, SW, AP, KM, LB (Cape Peninsula to Riversdale and Oudtshoorn).

Strumaria tenella (Linnaeus fil.) Snijman
Small plants, at most 15 cm high; bulb whitish inside. Leaves three to six, often one to three produced at a time, green at flowering, linear, c. 0.7 mm wide, smooth. Flow-

ers 2–14 on long, spreading pedicels, star-shaped, 6–12 mm diam., white to delicate pink, often lined with darker pink, scented, stamens equal to the tepals, joined to the base of the swollen style, style abruptly dilated in the lower half into a six-sided swelling. Flowering April–July. Seasonally damp loamy flats, RV, NW, SW, LB (Bokkeveld and Roggeveld Escarpments, Vredenburg to Cape Peninsula and Riviersonderend, Free State).

Two subspecies are recognized: subspecies *orientalis* Snijman with white flowers, tepals 2–3 mm wide, stylar swelling dome-shaped, flowering February–March, dolerite outcrops (Free State), and subspecies *tenella* with white to pink flowers, tepals 1.5–2 mm wide, stylar swelling indented, flowering April–July, sometimes as late as August, seasonally damp flats, RV, NW, SW, LB (Bokkeveld and Roggeveld Escarpments to Riviersonderend).

Strumaria truncata Jacquin

Plants to 30 cm high; bulb whitish inside. Leaves two to six in a suberect fan, strap-shaped, (3–)7–16(–20) mm wide, twisted one to three times or rarely plane, smooth, the single basal sheath, sometimes two, exposed, inflated and reddish when fresh. Flowers 3–26, usually hanging to one side, rarely evenly spreading, funnel-shaped, 7–13(–16) mm long, white or pale to deep pink, scented, tepals united into a basal tube to 7(–10) mm long, stamens longer than the tepals, the outer filaments joined to the sharp angles of the style base, style three-winged near the base, the wings sometimes extending up the style 9 mm. Flowering April–June. Stony or loamy flats, RV, NW (Namaqualand to Bokkeveld Escarpment and western Karoo).

Strumaria unguiculata (W. F. Barker) Snijman

Plants to 30 cm high; bulb whitish inside. Leaves two, sometimes three, usually dry at flowering, suberect to recurved, elliptical to lanceolate, (15–)30–60 mm wide, abruptly narrowed at the base, light green, thin textured, the margins sometimes undulate. Flowers 7–24, spreading on long pedicels, shallowly cup-shaped, 15–20 mm diam., glistening white with red midribs, scented of spice, tepals clawed at the base, forming conspicuous windows

Strumaria tenella subsp. *tenella*

Strumaria truncata

Strumaria unguiculata (Colin Paterson-Jones)

between adjacent tepals, the edges more or less folded toward the apex, stamens as long as the tepals, slightly bulbous at the base, attached to the style base, style expanding evenly to a broad base. Flowering May. Loamy, stony soils, NW (Botterkloof valley).

Strumaria watermeyeri L. Bolus

Plants to 15 cm high; bulb whitish inside. Leaves two, sometimes three, dry at flowering, prostrate, elliptical to lanceolate, 8–17 mm wide, leathery, the upper surface dark green, the edges pustulate and sticky, often covered with sand. Flowers 4–11, suberect or curved to one side, funnel-shaped, 7–23 mm long, delicate pink, usually banded with darker pink, scentless, stamens equal to or longer than the tepals, joined to the style base 0.5–4 mm, style stout and three-angled toward the base. Flowering April–May. Shallow soil on sandstone pavement, NW (Bokkeveld Mountains).

Two subspecies are recognized: subspecies *botterkloofensis* (D. & U. Müller-Doblies) Snijman with widely funnel-shaped flowers, tepals 7–11 mm long, joined to the filaments for 0.5–1 mm, sandstone pavement (Botterkloof Pass), and subspecies *watermeyeri* with funnel-shaped flowers, tepals 14–23 mm long, joined to the filaments for 2.5–8 mm, sandstone pavement (Bokkeveld Mountains).

Syringodea

COMMON NAME Cape crocus, FAMILY Iridaceae. Deciduous perennials, the stem short and subterranean. ROOTSTOCK an asymmetric, top-shaped or compressed corm with a circular to crescent-shaped basal ridge, with papery or woody tunics. LEAVES one to several, bifacial below or throughout, linear to lanceolate and flat or channeled or terete above, the margins sometimes hairy basally. INFLORESCENCE condensed, of solitary flowers; bracts membranous, the margins united below, the inner usually notched apically. FLOWERS actinomorphic, star- or cup-shaped, the tepals united below into a long slender tube, blue to mauve or white, unscented. STAMENS inserted near the top of the tube, erect and symmetrically disposed. OVARY subterranean, with several ovules per locule; STYLE slender, three-branched, the branches oblanceolate, channeled, rarely fringed at the tips. FRUIT usually a top-shaped loculicidal and septicidal capsule splitting into six valves above when wet (hydrochastic) or rarely an ellipsoidal loculicidal capsule splitting into three valves when dry (xerochastic). SEEDS several per locule, subglobose or weakly angled. Basic chromosome number $x = 6$, rarely 11. South Africa; c. 8 spp., 4 in the Cape.

The small genus *Syringodea* seems to be most closely related to the Eurasian genus *Crocus*, with which it shares a stemless habit and long-tubed, actinomorphic flowers with the bracts entirely membranous and tubular below, but also channeled, bifacial leaves and, less obviously, spherical, inaperturate pollen. Species of *Syringodea* may also be easily confused with long-tubed species of *Romulea*, but that genus usually has grooved leaves round or oval in cross section, a partly aerial stem, divided style branches, and aperturate pollen. The three genera share flowers that are particularly responsive to temperature, opening only on warm days. The species of *Syringodea* are equally divided between the summer- and winter-rainfall zones of southern Africa and are typically found in the arid fringes of the Great Karoo. Although most species are found on stony clay soils, *S. unifolia* favors dolerite flats whereas *S. derustensis* and *S. saxatilis*, both very localized endemics from the Little Karoo, are restricted to the tops of low hills, where they grow in open patches among quartzitic stones. *Syringodea longituba* is sometimes found on sandy soils and sandstone pavement.

Although the unscented, bluish flowers of *Syringodea* produce minute quantities of nectar, this does not reach to near the top of the tube, which is more or less occluded by the style and serves to lift the flower above the ground. Produced in early winter when the range of pollinators is limited, the flowers of *Syringodea* are pollinated predominantly by honeybees collecting pollen but may also be visited by butterflies.

Like a small-flowered crocus, syringodeas make a fleeting appearance in the autumn or early winter, at a time when few other bulbs are in flower. *Syringodea saxatilis* and *S. unifolia* have fairly large flowers, and could easily be treated in the garden or planter just as crocuses are in the Northern Hemisphere. Syringodeas are not as cold hardy as spring crocuses but tolerate frost. It is difficult to obtain seeds or corms. At Kirstenbosch botanical garden, several species have been grown successfully for many years.

FURTHER READING. *Syringodea* was thoroughly revised by De Vos (1974, 1983b).

Syringodea derustensis M. P. de Vos

Plants 5–8 cm high; corm top-shaped with an oblique basal ridge. Leaves three to five, lanceolate or oblong, spreading, mostly or entirely bifacial, the margins minutely hairy toward the base, flattened or lightly channeled, 30–60 × 3–6 mm. Flowers violet, rarely white, 30–40 mm diam., tube 25–35 mm long. Capsule top-shaped, six-valved, opening when wet. Flowering May–June. Stony hills in washes among quartzite, KM (Little Karoo at Dysseldorp and De Rust).

Syringodea longituba (Klatt) Kuntze

Plants 4–10 cm high; corm top-shaped with an oblique basal ridge. Leaves five to eight, filiform with a dorsal groove, often twisted, 15–60 × 0.8–1.5(–2) mm. Flowers blue-violet with a white or yellow center, (15–)20–25 mm diam., tube (15–)20–30 mm long. Capsule top-shaped, six-valved, opening when wet. Flowering April–June. Sandstone and shale flats and slopes, RV, NW, SW,

Syringodea derustensis, different color forms

Syringodea longituba

KM, LB (Namaqualand, western and Little Karoo, Caledon to Potberg).

Syringodea saxatilis M. P. de Vos

Plants 4–8 cm high; corm top-shaped with an oblique basal ridge. Leaf single, falcate, mostly channeled, with minutely hairy margins but terete and fleshy apically, 50–120 × 1.5–2.5 mm. Flowers lilac to violet, 20–40 mm diam., tube 15–20 mm long. Capsule top-shaped, six-valved, opening when wet. Flowering May–June. Stony hills in washes among quartzite, KM (Ladismith).

Syringodea saxatilis

Syringodea unifolia

Syringodea unifolia Goldblatt

Plants 5–12 cm high; corm vertically flattened, almost lens-shaped, with a fan-shaped basal ridge. Leaf single, falcate, channeled but terete and fleshy apically, 50–150 × 1.5–3.5 mm. Flowers blue-violet, rarely white, often with a yellow center, 40–60 mm diam., tube 30–40(–50) mm long. Capsule three-angled and ellipsoidal, three-valved, opening when dry. Flowering May–June. Clay flats, RV, NW (western Karoo to Keeromsberg).

Thereianthus

COMMON NAME summer pipes, FAMILY Iridaceae. Small deciduous perennials. ROOTSTOCK a globose corm, rooting from the base, axillary in origin, the tunics composed of fine to coarse fibers. LEAVES few, unifacial or terete, the lowermost longest and arising on stem above the corm, firm textured; flowering stems firm, erect, simple or if branched then from either above or below the ground. INFLORESCENCE a spike with flowers spirally arranged or more or less two-ranked when crowded; bracts firm textured, short, lax or overlapping, green below, apices dry and brown, or entirely dry. FLOWERS blue or purple to white, zygomorphic with unilateral stamens, lower three tepals with darker markings in the lower half, scentless, with or without nectar; perianth tube short to elongate, funnel-shaped or cylindrical to filiform; tepals subequal, spreading or the dorsal largest. STAMENS unilateral and arcuate or symmetrically arranged and the style central. STYLE filiform, mostly dividing opposite the anthers, the branches each deeply divided and recurved. FRUIT a woody, ellipsoidal to fusiform capsule. SEEDS angular-elongate with a chalazal crest or spindle-shaped with a long persistent funicle in 1 sp., smooth or rugose. Basic chromosome number $x = 10$. Southwestern Cape, mostly in sandstone soils; 8 spp.

Unusual in blooming during the hot summer months in an area of winter rainfall, *Thereianthus* is poorly known, even to the specialist. It is related to *Micranthus* but lacks the largely membranous bracts and distinctly two-ranked spike of that genus. The short-tubed and nectarless flowers of *T. racemosus* appear to be pollinated by monkey beetles (Scarabaeidae: Hopliini), as do those of *T.*

ixioides, which has a filiform perianth tube but does secrete nectar. Long-tubed *T. longicollis* is probably pollinated by long-proboscid horseflies (Tabanidae). The remaining species are probably pollinated by a range of insects, including bees and butterflies.

Although not cultivated at all, species of *Thereianthus* are mostly very drought-tolerant plants that will probably grow well in dry, rough parts of the garden where they require minimal care. In the wild, the species flower late in the season, seldom before October and more often in November and even December, at a time when few Cape bulbs are in bloom. *Thereianthus juncifolius* is a plant of wet habitats, and we have seen it looking well along streambanks in the Cape mountains. The flowers of all *Thereianthus* species last well in the wild in hot, dry conditions, and this characteristic may make them useful in the rock garden in dry parts of the world. *Thereianthus spicatus* is probably the species with the most attractive flowers.

FURTHER READING. *Thereianthus* was revised by Lewis (1941). A brief, more up-to-date account appears in *Cape Plants* (Goldblatt & Manning 2000a).

Thereianthus bracteolatus (Lamarck) G. J. Lewis

Plants 15–25 cm high; corm globose with coarsely fibrous tunics. Leaves terete without prominent veins. Flowers in a dense spike, facing to the side, deep blue to purple, rarely white, perianth tube cylindrical to narrowly funnel-shaped, 10–12 mm long, tepals c. 15 mm long, prominently three- to six-veined, filaments well exserted and 8–10 mm long, erect, lying above the lower tepal; bracts 7–15 mm long. Flowering November–January, mainly after fire. Dry sandstone slopes, NW, SW (Cold Bokkeveld to Bredasdorp).

Thereianthus ixioides G. J. Lewis

Plants 25–45 cm high; corm globose with coarsely fibrous tunics. Leaves linear with thickened veins. Flowers in a fairly dense spike, white with violet markings in the center, perianth tube straight and filiform, 8–10 mm long, tepals subequal, 10–12 mm long; bracts 7–15 mm long. Flowering October–November. Sandstone mountain slopes, SW (Bain's Kloof to Du Toit's Kloof).

Thereianthus juncifolius (Baker) G. J. Lewis

Plants 30–40 cm high; corm globose with fairly fine, fibrous tunics. Leaves round to oval in cross section, slender. Flowers in a lax spike, blue to mauve, white in the throat, perianth tube slender, 12–20 mm long, tepals subequal, c. 10 mm long, stamens erect, unilateral; bracts 3–5 mm long. Flowering November–March. Mountain seeps, marshes, and streambanks in sandstone, NW, SW (Cold Bokkeveld to the Riviersonderend Mountains and Hermanus). Page 376.

Thereianthus longicollis (Baker) G. J. Lewis

Plants 20–30 cm high; corm globose with coarsely fibrous tunics. Leaves linear with prominent veins. Flowers in a fairly dense spike, pale lilac, rarely white, with pur-

Thereianthus bracteolatus

Thereianthus ixioides

Thereianthus juncifolius

Thereianthus minutus

Thereianthus spicatus

ple markings on the lower tepals, perianth tube 25–45 mm long, tepals subequal, c. 13 mm long, about at least twice as long as the tube; bracts 12–18 mm long. Flowering November–January. Sandstone slopes, NW, SW (Porterville Mountains to Tulbagh Falls).

Thereianthus minutus (Klatt) G. J. Lewis

Plants 10–20 cm high; corm globose with tunics of fine, matted fibers. Leaves sword-shaped to falcate, leathery but with a definite midrib. Flowers in a fairly lax spike but bracts just overlapping, bright pinkish purple, perianth tube elongate, 20–30 mm long, tepals subequal, spreading, c. 10 mm long, mostly above twice as long as the tube, stamens erect, unilateral; bracts 5–10 mm long. Flowering November–January. Seeps and wet sandstone rocks, NW, SW (Cold Bokkeveld to Du Toit's Kloof Mountains).

Thereianthus racemosus (Klatt) G. J. Lewis

Plants 15–30 cm high; corm globose with coarsely fibrous tunics. Leaves linear to sword-shaped, with a definite midrib. Flowers in a dense spike, pale blue with dark markings on the lower tepals, perianth tube 1–2 mm long, included in the bracts, tepals c. 8 mm long; bracts 3–5 mm long. Flowering October–December. Rocky sandstone slopes, NW (Grootwinterhoek Mountains and Piketberg).

Thereianthus spicatus (Linnaeus) G. J. Lewis
Plants 20–30 cm high; corm globose with coarsely fibrous tunics. Leaves linear with prominent veins or terete. Flowers in a fairly dense spike, pale blue to mauve, with darker markings on the lower three tepals, perianth tube 12–16(–20) mm long, usually slightly curved near the apex, tepals c. 15 mm long, not prominently veined; stamens erect, unilateral, filaments c. 4 mm long; bracts 9–18 mm long. Flowering October–November, especially after fire. Sandstone slopes, SW (Elandskloof Mountains to Kleinmond).

Thereianthus sp. 1
Plants 25–35 mm high; corm unknown. Leaves linear with a few prominent veins. Flowers few in a dense spike, dark violet, perianth tube c. 25 mm long, tepals c. 10 mm long, filaments c. 4 mm long, erect; bracts 6–8 mm long. Flowering mainly February. Steep, south-facing slopes at high elevations, SW (Riviersonderend Mountains).

Tritonia
COMMON NAME tritonia, FAMILY Iridaceae. Small deciduous perennials. ROOTSTOCK a globose corm, rooting from the base, basal in origin, the tunics pale, composed of fine to coarse fibers. LEAVES several, unifacial with a definite midrib, mostly basal and often forming a two-ranked fan, blades plane and linear to sword-shaped or round or oval in cross section, sometimes the margins undulate to crisped, rolled inward, or winged, thus H-shaped in cross section, cauline leaves few and reduced; stem firm, erect, simple, or branched, then from either above or below the ground, sometimes very short and more or less subterranean. INFLORESCENCE usually a secund spike, the flowers sometimes two-ranked or spirally arranged, rarely with one flower per branch; bracts small to medium, green and firm, or membranous to scarious, outer usually three-cusped, inner about as long as or slightly smaller than outer and two-toothed or notched apically. FLOWERS zygomorphic and funnel-shaped to salverform or rarely actinomorphic and rotate, mostly orange to yellow, rarely red, pink, or cream to white, often the veins darker, lower tepals sometimes with contrasting markings, occasionally sweetly scented; perianth tube funnel-shaped or cylindrical, short or elongate; tepals subequal to unequal, then the dorsal usually largest, the lower tepals often with a tooth-like callus or ridge in the lower midline. STAMENS unilateral and arcuate, sometimes loosely spreading, or symmetrically disposed and erect; anthers sometimes included in the tube. STYLE exserted or included, arcuate or central, branches slightly flattened and expanded apically and recurved. FRUIT a globose to ellipsoidal, cartilaginous capsule. SEEDS globose, flattened at the chalazal end, usually smooth, raphal vascular trace excluded. Basic chromosome number $x = 11$ or 10. Mostly in the winter-rainfall region of southern Africa but extending from the southwestern Cape to Tanzania, occurring in a variety of habitats, grassland in areas of summer rainfall, and in renosterveld, karroid scrub, or fynbos in areas of winter rainfall; 28 spp., 18 in the Cape.

Although *Tritonia* is sometimes difficult to distinguish from *Ixia*, differences in leaf anatomy suggest that the two genera are not immediately related. It is likely that *Tritonia* is most closely related to *Crocosmia*, which is similar in its leaf anatomy, chromosome number, and orange flowers in the ancestral species. Flowers are mostly pollinated by long-tongued bees, but the long-tubed species such as *T. cooperi* and *T. crispa*, which have cream flowers with reddish markings, are pollinated by long-proboscid flies, including *Philoliche* (Tabanidae) and *Moegistorhynchus* (Nemestrinidae). Species with a bowl-shaped actinomorphic perianth are pollinated by monkey beetles (Scarabaeidae: Hopliini).

Two species, *Tritonia crocata* and *T. squalida*, are widely known and available in the horticultural trade. Like the commonly cultivated *Sparaxis tricolor* and its hybrids, they have brilliantly colored flowers with an actinomorphic perianth. These two species and the related *T. deusta* are excellent subjects for the rock garden. They are not fussy about soil conditions and are drought resistant. In the wild, they grow on dry flats and slopes, flowering when the soil has all but dried completely. *Tritonia squalida*, despite its name, has beautiful pink flowers; although it grows on limestone outcrops in the wild, it is successfully grown in a rich peaty mix.

Unfortunately, other species, although lovely in the wild, are more difficult to maintain in cultivation. *Tritonia watermeyeri*, with bright orange flowers and attractively crisped leaves, is such a species. It is native to dry valleys of the Little Karoo where plants receive less than 250 mm (10 inches) of rain a year. In cultivation, the corms have a tendency to rot and require a well-drained soil. Desert areas would be the ideal situation to grow it in the open ground. Another desert species, *T. karooica*, has large, wonderfully fragrant flowers. We have no personal experience growing that species but the few who have tried it find it easier to deal with than *T. watermeyeri*. In general, Cape species of *Tritonia* tend to flower later than other Cape bulbs. After flowering, it is best to dry the plants quickly, then lift the corms unless their space is to be left undisturbed, and dry for the next 6 months.

FURTHER READING. *Tritonia* was thoroughly revised by De Vos (1982, 1983a, 1999b).

Tritonia bakeri Klatt

Plants mostly 40–60 cm high; corm depressed-globose with tunics of fine, netted fibers. Leaves linear and subterete, rigid, 1–3 mm wide. Flowers in a lax, two-ranked spike, long-tubed, perianth nearly actinomorphic but stamens unilateral, pale yellow or cream to pale mauve, perianth tube mostly 30–50 mm long, tepals spreading, 15–25 mm long; bracts membranous, dry and speckled brown above. Flowering October–December. Rocky sandstone slopes KM, LB, SE (Little Karoo to Long Kloof at Avontuur).

Tritonia chrysantha Fourcade

Plants 15–40 cm high; corm globose with tunics of medium-textured fibers, often thickened below. Leaves sword-shaped, 4–10 mm wide. Flowers in a two-ranked spike, long-tubed, bright yellow, perianth tube 20–28 mm long, tepals 8–15 mm long, the dorsal erect and largest, the lower tepals each with a large median tooth; bracts membranous, short. Flowering August–October. Dry karroid slopes, KM, SE (Oudtshoorn to Somerset East and Grahamstown).

Tritonia cooperi (Baker) Klatt

Plants 40–60 cm high; corm globose with tunics of fairly fine, matted fibers. Leaves narrowly sword-shaped with the margins raised into broad wings, thus H-shaped in cross section. Flowers in a horizontally flexed, secund spike, white to cream, fading pink, with red markings, perianth tube 30–55 mm long, tepals spreading, 14–24 mm long; bracts green, drying above, with dark brown margins. Flowering November–December. Rocky sandstone soils, SW, LB (Du Toit's Kloof to Langeberg Mountains at Riversdale).

Tritonia crispa

Tritonia crispa (Linnaeus fil.) Ker Gawler
Plants 18–35 cm high; corm conical with tunics of fairly fine fibers. Leaves sword-shaped to linear, with undulate and strongly crisped margins. Flowers in a dense, horizontally flexed, secund spike, cream with red markings, pink on the outside, perianth tube elongate, 40–60 mm long, tepals spreading, 12–20 mm long; bracts green and leathery with dark brown margins, small, obtuse. Flowering October–December. Rocky sandstone slopes in fynbos, NW, SW (Bokkeveld Mountains to Grabouw).

Tritonia crocata (Linnaeus) Ker Gawler
Plants 25–50 cm high; corm depressed-globose with tunics of fairly fine fibers. Leaves sword-shaped, 5–10 mm wide. Flowers in inclined, secund spikes, almost actinomorphic, rotate, with stamens and style randomly twisted and spreading, orange to reddish, perianth tube 10–15 mm long, widely funnel-shaped, tepals 20–25 mm long, subspathulate, the margins more or less transparent below; bracts usually dry and brownish, short. Flowering September–November. Stony clay slopes in renosterveld, AP, LB, SE (Swellendam to Humansdorp).

Tritonia deusta (Aiton) Ker Gawler
Plants 15–25 cm high; corm globose with tunics of fairly fine fibers. Leaves sword-shaped, 4–8 mm wide. Flowers in inclined, secund spikes, perianth almost actinomorphic, rotate, with stamens and style randomly twisted and spreading, orange with a yellow, star-shaped center, often with dark marks on the outer tepals, perianth tube 10–12 mm long, widely funnel-shaped, tepals 18–25 mm long; bracts usually dry and brown, short. Flowering September–October. Clay or granite slopes in renosterveld, SW, AP, LB (Cape Peninsula to Riversdale).

Tritonia dubia Ecklon ex Klatt
Plants 12–25 cm high; corm globose with tunics of fairly fine, netted fibers. Leaves lanceolate-falcate, 3–8 mm wide. Flowers spirally arranged in dense spikes, actinomorphic, rotate, pink to orange with dark veins, stamens central around the erect style, perianth tube 6–10 mm long; tepals 12–20 mm long; bracts dry and papery.

Tritonia crocata

Tritonia deusta

Flowering August–September. Clay slopes in renosterveld and open bush, SE (Humansdorp to Port Elizabeth).

Tritonia flabellifolia (D. Delaroche) G. J. Lewis
Plants 25–50 cm high; corm depressed-globose with tunics of fairly fine, netted fibers. Leaves sword-shaped to linear, 2–10 mm wide. Flowers in a secund spike, cream with red streaks on the lower tepals, perianth tube elongate, 40–60 mm long, tepals unequal, the dorsal largest, 16–25 mm long; bracts large, dry, rust colored above and attenuate. Flowering mainly October–November. Rocky sandstone and shale slopes in renosterveld or fynbos, SW, KM, LB (Villiersdorp to Albertinia and Little Karoo).

Tritonia florentiae (Marloth) Goldblatt
Plants 7–12 cm high, the stem subterranean or short and concealed by the bracts; corm globose with tunics of fine, netted fibers. Leaves lanceolate-falcate in a dense fan, 3–6 mm wide. Flowers few in a crowded spike, bright yellow, perianth tube 15–24 mm long, tepals 15–25 mm long, the dorsal lightly hooded and largest, the lower three each with a large, triangular, crisped median tooth; bracts papery and thin with brown streaks, fairly long. Flowering May–July. Dry stony clay flats, RV (Tanqua Karoo to Prince Albert and Beaufort West).

Tritonia karooica M. P. de Vos
Plants 10–18 cm high; corm globose with tunics of medium-textured fibers. Leaves lanceolate-falcate in a dense fan, 3–6 mm wide. Flowers few in a weakly two-ranked spike, yellow flushed with orange, the tepals darkly veined, heavily scented, perianth tube 25–32 mm long, tepals 12–18 mm long, lightly recurved in the upper half, the lower three each with a thickened median ridge; bracts papery with brown veins, fairly long. Flowering August–September. Dry stony clay flats, RV (Middelpos and Calvinia, and through the Great Karoo and eastern Namaqualand).

Tritonia lancea (Thunberg) N. E. Brown
Plants 10–25 cm high; corm globose with tunics of fine, matted fibers. Leaves sword-shaped, leathery, 2–8 mm wide, the margins rolled inward on one side, tapering to

Tritonia flabellifolia

Tritonia florentiae

a narrow, petiole-like base. Flowers in a horizontally flexed, secund spike, white with red streaks on the lower tepals, perianth tube elongate, 20–25 mm long, tepals subequal, 12–18 mm long; bracts membranous with dark brown margins, short, obtuse. Flowering August–September. Sandstone slopes, NW (Piketberg).

Tritonia laxifolia Bentham ex Baker
Plants 20–40 cm high; corm globose with tunics of fairly fine fibers. Leaves sword-shaped, 5–10 mm wide. Flowers in a secund spike, bilabiate, reddish to orange, perianth tube 12–16 mm long, tepals 12–15 mm long, the dorsal tepal erect and largest, the lower tepals each with a yellow, median, tooth-like callus. Flowering March–May. Grassy slopes, SE (Uitenhage to Tanzania).

Tritonia lineata (Salisbury) Ker Gawler
Plants to 60 cm high; corm globose with tunics of fairly finely netted fibers. Leaves sword-shaped to lanceolate, with a prominent vein near each margin, 5–10 mm wide. Flowers in a secund spike, weakly bilabiate, cream or yellow, with dark veins, perianth tube 10–15 mm long, tepals 15–20 mm long, the dorsal tepal erect and largest, the lower three often with a thickened median ridge; bracts membranous, fairly short. Flowering August–November. Grassland, KM, SE (Swartberg Mountains and Jeffrey's Bay to Mpumalanga).

Tritonia pallida Ker Gawler
Plants mostly 20–50 cm high; corm globose with tunics of fine, netted fibers. Leaves sword-shaped, 8–15 mm wide. Flowers in a two-ranked spike, cream or pink to pale lilac, perianth tube 25–65 mm long, tepals 10–20 mm long, the dorsal largest, the lower tepals each often with a yellowish green median ridge; bracts fairly short, dry and straw colored, the tips membranous. Flowering September–October. Sandstone and clay slopes, NW, KM (Langeberg foothills at Robertson to Oudtshoorn).

Tritonia parvula N. E. Brown
Plants 10–25 cm high; corm globose with tunics of coarse, netted fibers. Leaves linear, 1–4 mm wide. Flowers in a secund spike, bilabiate, reddish to orange, peri-

Tritonia karooica

Tritonia pallida

anth tube 6–12 mm long, tepals 9–12 mm long, the dorsal tepal largest, erect, the lower tepals each with a tooth-like, yellow callus; bracts membranous, straw colored with brown veins, short. Flowering September–November. Stony sandstone soils, KM, LB, SE (Riversdale to Willowmore).

Tritonia securigera (Aiton) Ker Gawler
Plants 15–40 cm high; corm globose with tunics of fairly fine fibers. Leaves sword-shaped to linear, mostly shorter than the spike, 4–10 mm wide. Flowers in a secund spike, bilabiate, reddish to orange, perianth tube 12–20 mm long, tepals unequal, 12–20 mm long, the dorsal tepal largest, erect, the lower tepals each with a large, median, tooth-like yellow callus; bracts papery, short. Flowering September–November. Clay slopes, KM, LB, SE (Riversdale to Graaf Reinet).

Tritonia squalida (Aiton) Ker Gawler
Plants 25–40 cm high; corm depressed-globose with tunics of fairly fine, netted fibers. Leaves sword-shaped, 4–10 mm wide. Flowers in inclined, secund spikes, perianth almost actinomorphic, rotate, with stamens and style randomly twisted and spreading, pink to purple with darker veins, perianth tube 8–15 mm long, widely funnel-shaped, tepals 20–28 mm long, more or less spathulate, lower margins transparent; bracts dry and brown, short. Flowering September–October. Limestone outcrops and calcareous sands, AP, LB (Riversdale to Albertinia).

Tritonia watermeyeri L. Bolus
Plants 15–30 cm high; corm globose with tunics of fairly fine to coarse fibers. Leaves linear, twisted and tightly undulate to crisped along the margins, 3–8 mm wide. Flowers in a secund spike, bilabiate, reddish to orange, perianth tube 3–7 mm long, tepals 15–22 mm long, the dorsal hooded and largest, the lower tepals each with a large, median, yellow, tooth-like callus; bracts membranous, speckled brown above. Flowering August–September. Stony clay flats and lower slopes in succulent karoo, KM (Little Karoo from Montagu to Barrydale).

Tritoniopsis

COMMON NAME mountain pipes, FAMILY Iridaceae. Deciduous or evergreen perennials. ROOTSTOCK a globose corm, axillary in origin and rooting from the base, the tunics composed of medium-textured to coarse, often matted fibers. LEAVES several, unifacial, soft textured, the basal longest, decreasing in size above, the blades plane, sometimes pseudopetiolate and abruptly expanded above the base, with more than one main vein unless very narrow, often partly or entirely dry at flowering; stem branched or simple, leafy below or with dry scales at the nodes. INFLORESCENCE a lax or dense spike, the flowers mostly spirally arranged; bracts leathery or dry and brown at flowering time, inner as long as or usually longer than outer, entire. FLOWERS usually zygomorphic and bilabiate, the tube sometimes elongate, rarely actinomorphic, usually pink to purple or red, sometimes white, yellow, brown or cream, lower tepals usually with darker or lighter markings, sometimes scented, with nectar from septal nectaries; perianth tube short to long, cylindrical, funnel-shaped, or narrow below and broadly

Tritonia squalida

tubular above; tepals subequal, or unequal then bilabiate, sometimes markedly clawed. STAMENS unilateral and arcuate or horizontal, rarely symmetrically disposed and erect; filaments arising in the mouth of the tube or at the base of wider part, diverging after anther dehiscence; anthers blunt or short- to long-apiculate. STYLE filiform, the branches short and recurved, sometimes emarginate or shortly bilobed. FRUIT an ovoid to globose capsule, leathery, often somewhat to much inflated. SEEDS angled, with a chalazal crest, often winged on the angles and coat somewhat spongy and irregularly sculpted. Basic chromosome number $x = 16, 15$, and possibly 17. Mainly southwestern Cape, extending from the Bokkeveld Escarpment to the Transkei, most often in sandstone soils in fynbos; 24 spp.

Tritoniopsis is taxonomically isolated in the family Iridaceae and is readily distinguished by the short, firm-textured floral bracts with the inner bract longer than the outer, and the characteristic leaves, which have more than one main vein, thus lacking a definite midrib. The genus is characteristic of sandstone soils although some species, especially *T. antholyza*, are more tolerant of clay substrates. Most of the species are summer flowering, at which time the leaves are usually dry and withered. Flowering is generally stimulated by fire, especially in *T. parviflora*, which does not flower in the wild unless the vegetation has been burned the previous season. All the species have a deeply buried corm covered with tough fibrous tunics.

The flowers of *Tritoniopsis* are adapted for pollination by a variety of agents. The short-tubed species are mostly pollinated by bees whereas the long-tubed species are specialized for a range of other pollinators. The long-tubed, pink-flowered species are pollinated by long-proboscid flies, but the single species with long-tubed, fragrant, cream flowers, *T. nervosa*, is adapted to moth pollination. *Tritoniopsis lesliei*, which has brilliant red, actinomorphic flowers with a long, slender perianth tube, is probably pollinated by the butterfly *Aeropetes*. Other red-flowered species have zygomorphic flowers and are mainly pollinated by sunbirds but in some instances also by *Aeropetes*. The light, spongy seeds with winged angles appear to be adapted for dispersal by wind.

Despite their often large and attractive flowers, species of *Tritoniopsis* have not attracted horticultural attention. Species like *T. caffra* and *T. burchellii*, which produce bright red flowers in long spikes, are especially striking. Moreover, they bloom in the summer when few Cape bulbs flower. The white-flowered *T. nervosa* and pink-flowered *T. revoluta* are equally attractive, the former producing a fine perfume. It is possible that *Tritoniopsis*, like other genera adapted to the nutrient-poor sandstone soils of the Cape, is difficult to grow in cultivation. Nevertheless, some species are so striking that they should be tried. They are too large for containers and seem ideal for the rock garden.

FURTHER READING. *Tritoniopsis* was expanded by Goldblatt (1990) to include the red-flowered and mostly bird-pollinated taxa previously referred to *Anapalina*. Revisions of all the species were published by Lewis (1959b, 1960) but several additional species have since been described by Manning and Goldblatt (2001b), and one reduced to synonymy (Goldblatt and Manning 2000a).

Tritoniopsis antholyza (Poiret) Goldblatt

Plants to 90 cm high, stem unbranched; corm depressed-globose with tunics of coarse fibers usually extending upward in a neck. Leaves lanceolate to linear, three- to six-veined. Flowers crowded in a dense, more or less two-ranked spike, tubular, salmon pink to red, perianth tube 25–30 cm long, tepals unequal, the dorsal largest, arising below the lower, 22–30 mm long, lower tepals often with dark streaks, filaments 32–40 mm long; bracts green or becoming dry. Flowering mostly November–April. Rocky sandstone slopes, NW, SW, AP, KM, LB, SE (Bokkeveld Mountains to Port Elizabeth). Page 384.

Tritoniopsis bicolor J. C. Manning & Goldblatt

Plants 20–60 cm high; corm globose with tunics of fine-textured fibers. Leaves narrowly lanceolate, one- to three-veined, abruptly narrowed into a semiterete false petiole. Flowers in a dense spike, yellow with brown to maroon markings, sweetly spicy scented, perianth tube 2–5 mm long, tepals subequal, the dorsal larger, 14–16 mm long, filaments 6–7 mm long; bracts green below, dry above. Capsules globose, inflated, to 3 cm diam. Flowering De-

Tritoniopsis antholyza

Tritoniopsis bicolor

Tritoniopsis burchellii

Tritoniopsis caffra

cember. Seasonally waterlogged plateaus, SW (Bredasdorp Mountains).

Tritoniopsis burchellii (N. E. Brown) Goldblatt
Plants 50–90 cm high; corm depressed-globose with tunics of coarse fibers. Leaves linear, three-veined, with a long, terete, false petiole, usually dry at flowering, upper leaves filiform, dry and brown. Flowers in a dense spike, tubular, scarlet, perianth tube 30–40 mm long, tepals unequal, the upper three larger, 20–25 mm long, filaments 30–37 mm long; bracts dry. Flowering February–April. Rocky sandstone slopes, 200–600 m, NW, SW, AP, LB (Riebeek Kasteel to Albertinia).

Tritoniopsis caffra (Ker Gawler ex Baker) Goldblatt
Plants 20–80 cm high; corm depressed-globose with tunics of coarse fibers. Leaves sword-shaped to linear, two- to four-veined. Flowers in a fairly lax spike, red, perianth tube 20–30 mm long, tepals unequal, dorsal largest, elongate-spathulate, 26–33 mm long, arising 6–8 mm beyond the lower, filaments 33–38 mm long; bracts green. Flowering September–December. Sandstone slopes, LB, SE (Heidelberg to East London).

Tritoniopsis caledonensis (R. C. Foster) G. J. Lewis
Plants 30–55 cm high; corm globose with tunics of medium-textured fibers. Leaves linear, one- or two-veined, 1–3 mm wide. Flowers in a dense spike, yellowish with mauve nectar guides, fragrant, 12–15 mm long, perianth tube c. 3 mm long, tepals unequal, the dorsal largest, c. 10 mm long, filaments 3–5 mm long; bracts green below, dry above. Flowering November. Rocky sandstone slopes, SW (Houw Hoek to Shaw's Mountains).

Tritoniopsis dodii (G. J. Lewis) G. J. Lewis
Plants 15–30 cm high, stems unbranched; corm globose with tunics of medium-textured fibers. Leaves linear to lanceolate, one- to three-veined. Flowers in a dense spike, pink with darker pink nectar guides, acridly scented, perianth tube 5–8 mm long, tepals unequal, the dorsal largest, 20–23 mm long, anthers shortly apiculate, filaments 12–14 mm long; bracts short, obtuse, usually dry

Tritoniopsis caledonensis

Tritoniopsis dodii

and rigid. Flowering February–April. Sandstone slopes, SW, AP (Cape Peninsula to Agulhas flats).

Tritoniopsis elongata (L. Bolus) G. J. Lewis
Plants 40–60 cm high, stems usually slender and branched; corm globose with tunics of medium-textured fibers. Leaves linear to lanceolate, three- or four-veined. Flowers in a long, lax spike, dull pink with darker veins, perianth tube 6–8 mm long, tepals unequal, the dorsal largest, 20–25 mm long, anthers shortly apiculate, filaments 13–16 mm long; bracts short, apiculate, usually green. Flowering March–April. Sandy loam at low elevations, SW (Elandsberg Mountains to Caledon).

Tritoniopsis flava J. C. Manning & Goldblatt
Plants 50–60 cm high, unbranched; corm globose with tunics of medium-textured fibers. Leaves narrowly lanceolate, two- or three-veined, narrowed into a flattened false petiole. Flowers in a dense spike, yellow, perianth tube 4–5 mm long, tepals subequal, the dorsal larger, 15–16 mm long, filaments 10 mm long; bracts green below, dry above. Flowering December. Seasonally waterlogged streamsides and seeps, SW (Kogelberg).

Tritoniopsis flexuosa (Linnaeus fil.) G. J. Lewis
Plants 15–30 cm high, stem unbranched; corm globose with tunics of coarse fibers. Leaves ovate, prominently two-veined, with a long, terete, false petiole, margins undulate. Flowers in a fairly dense spike, pale pink, the lower tepals with a darker pink median streak, perianth tube 35–40 mm long, tepals unequal, the dorsal largest, 25–30 mm long, filaments c. 15 mm long, anthers long-apiculate; bracts dry, 25–35 mm long. Flowering January–February. Clay slopes in renosterveld, SW, AP (Shaw's Mountains to Bredasdorp).

Tritoniopsis intermedia (Baker) Goldblatt
Plants 20–40 cm high; corm depressed-globose with tunics of coarse fibers. Leaves sword-shaped to linear, two- to four-veined, shorter than the stem. Flowers in a fairly dense spike, tubular, salmon to reddish, the lower tepals with purple-black markings, perianth tube 25–30 mm long, tepals unequal, the dorsal largest, 25–30 mm long,

Tritoniopsis elongata

Tritoniopsis flexuosa

arising 3–5 mm beyond the lower, filaments 40–45 mm long; bracts 9–18 mm long. Flowering September–December. Rocky sandstone slopes, SE (Uniondale to Port Elizabeth).

Tritoniopsis lata (L. Bolus) G. J. Lewis
Plants 15–30 cm high, stems usually unbranched; corm globose with tunics of medium-textured fibers. Leaves linear to lanceolate, one- to three-veined. Flowers in a lax spike, deep pink with dark markings, perianth tube 7–10 mm long, tepals unequal, the dorsal largest, 23–33 mm long, anthers shortly apiculate, filaments 17–20 mm long; bracts short, usually green. Flowering February–May. Sandstone mountain slopes, SW (Bain's Kloof to Hermanus).

Tritoniopsis latifolia G. J. Lewis
Plants 15–30 cm high, stems unbranched; corm globose with tunics of coarse fibers. Leaves lanceolate, four- to six-veined, to 30(–40) mm wide. Flowers in a fairly dense spike, pale pink to cream with darker markings, perianth tube 8–10 mm long, tepals unequal, the dorsal largest, 20–25 mm long, anthers shortly apiculate, filaments 12–14 mm long; bracts short, usually dry. Flowering December–January. Rocky sandstone slopes, NW (northern Cedarberg Mountains).

Tritoniopsis lesliei L. Bolus
Plants 35–65 cm high, stems usually branched; corm globose with tunics of coarse fibers. Leaves linear, one- or two-veined. Flowers in a lax spike, actinomorphic, bright red, perianth tube elongate, 20–25 mm long, tepals 18–28 mm long, filaments 16–20 mm long; bracts more or less dry. Flowering February–April. Rocky sandstone slopes in seeps and along streams, NW (Skurfdeberg, Ceres district).

Tritoniopsis nemorosa (E. Meyer ex Klatt) G. J. Lewis
Plants 1–1.5 m high, stems often branched; corm globose with tunics of coarse fibers. Leaves sword-shaped, five- to seven-veined. Flowers in a lax spike, yellow with brown markings, perianth tube c. 8 mm long, tepals unequal, the dorsal largest, c. 25 mm long, filaments 12–15

Tritoniopsis lata

Tritoniopsis lesliei

mm long, anthers shortly biapiculate; bracts green or becoming dry. Flowering November–January. Rocky slopes in fynbos, NW (Cedarberg Mountains to Elandskloof).

Tritoniopsis nervosa (Baker) G. J. Lewis

Plants 50–100 cm high; corm globose with tunics of medium-textured fibers. Leaves sword-shaped, two- or three-veined. Flowers in a lax spike, cream or white, sweetly fragrant, perianth tube elongate, 30–40 mm long, tepals subequal, 9–13 mm long, filaments 5–6 mm long; bracts dry, short. Flowering December–January. Rocky mountain slopes, NW (Pakhuis Mountains to Ceres).

Tritoniopsis parviflora (Jacquin) G. J. Lewis

Plants 15–40 cm high; corm globose with tunics of medium-textured fibers. Leaves linear, one- or two-veined, narrowed into a flattened false petiole. Flowers in a dense spike, yellow with brown to maroon markings, sweetly spicy scented, perianth tube 3–5 mm long, tepals subequal, the dorsal larger, 14–20 mm long, filaments 12–14 mm long; bracts green below, dry above. Capsules globose, inflated, to 4 cm diam. Flowering November–January. Rocky sandstone slopes, NW, SW, AP (Citrusdal to Agulhas).

Tritoniopsis pulchella G. J. Lewis

Plants 15–30 cm high, stems usually slender and branched; corm globose with tunics of medium-textured fibers. Leaves linear to lanceolate, one- to three-veined. Flowers in a lax spike, deep pink with dark markings, perianth tube 15–20 mm long, tepals unequal, more or less truncate, the upper three larger, 23–25 mm long, anthers shortly apiculate, filaments 17–25 mm long; bracts short, usually green. Flowering December–February. Sandstone slopes, SW (Bain's Kloof to Bot River).

Tritoniopsis pulchra (Baker) Goldblatt

Plants 25–60 cm high; corm globose with tunics of coarse fibers. Leaves linear to lanceolate, two- or three-veined. Flowers in a dense spike, dark rose, perianth tube 30–33 mm long, tepals nearly equal, the dorsal 15–19 mm long, filaments 20–23 mm long; bracts dry. Flowering February–June. Rocky sandstone slopes, SW, AP (Hottentots Holland Mountains to the Agulhas coast).

Tritoniopsis ramosa (Ecklon ex Klatt) G. J. Lewis

Plants 15–30 cm high, stems usually slender and branched; corm globose with tunics of medium-textured reddish fibers. Leaves linear to lanceolate, one- to three-veined. Flowers in a lax spike, deep pink with dark markings, perianth tube 7–20 mm long, tepals unequal, the dorsal largest, 21–28 mm long, filaments 15–18 mm long; bracts short, usually green. Flowering January–April. Sandstone slopes, NW, SW, LB, SE (Cedarberg to Humansdorp). Page 390.

Tritoniopsis revoluta (Burman fil.) Goldblatt

Plants 25–40 cm high; corm globose with tunics of medium-textured fibers. Leaves sword-shaped, three- to five-veined. Flowers in a dense spike, pink with a dark pink streak on the lower tepals, perianth tube elongate, (20–)40–70 mm long, tepals unequal, the dorsal longest,

Tritoniopsis nemorosa

Tritoniopsis nervosa

Tritoniopsis parviflora

Tritoniopsis pulchella

Tritoniopsis pulchra

Tritoniopsis ramosa

Tritoniopsis revoluta

Tritoniopsis toximontana

Tritoniopsis triticea

40–70 mm long, filaments 15–20 mm long, anthers long-apiculate; bracts large, brown, 20–50 mm long. Flowering March–May. Stony soils, coastal to 1000 m, AP, KM, LB (Potberg, Langeberg, and Swartberg Mountains).

Tritoniopsis toximontana J. C. Manning & Goldblatt
Plants 50–65 cm high, stem unbranched; corm globose with tunics of reddish brown, matted fibers forming a neck. Leaves sword-shaped, prominently three-veined, with a long, terete, false petiole. Flowers in a fairly lax spike, pale pink, the lower tepals with a darker pink median streak, perianth tube c. 20 mm long, tepals unequal, the dorsal slightly larger and hooded, c. 24 mm long, filaments 13–15 mm long, anthers long-apiculate; bracts dry, 12–16 mm long. Flowering January–February. Rocky sandstone slopes, NW (Gifberg Mountains).

Tritoniopsis triticea (Burman fil.) Goldblatt
Plants 50–90 cm high; corm depressed-globose with tunics of coarse fibers. Leaves linear, three-veined, with a long, terete, false petiole, usually dry at flowering time, upper leaves filiform, dry and brown. Flowers in a dense spike, scarlet, perianth tube 25–30 mm long, tepals unequal, the dorsal slightly larger, to 15 mm long, filaments 20–23 mm long; bracts dry. Flowering mainly February–April. Rocky granite and sandstone slopes, NW, SW, LB (Cape Peninsula and Porterville Mountains to Mossel Bay).

Tritoniopsis unguicularis (Lamarck) G. J. Lewis
Plants 20–55 cm high; corm globose with tunics of medium-textured fibers. Leaves linear-lanceolate, one- to three-veined, 1–5 mm wide. Flowers in a fairly dense spike, 12–15 mm long, cream to yellowish with faint mauve nectar guides, faintly scented, perianth tube c. 3 mm long, tepals subequal, 10–13 mm long, filaments 5–7 mm long; bracts more or less dry. Flowering December–March. Rocky sandstone slopes, SW (Cape Peninsula to Elim).

Tritoniopsis williamsiana Goldblatt
Plants to 1.3 m high; corm depressed-globose with tunics of medium-textured fibers, not forming a neck.

Tritoniopsis unguicularis

Tritoniopsis williamsiana

Leaves sword-shaped to linear, two- to four-veined. Flowers in a fairly lax spike, scarlet-red, perianth tube 20–30 mm long, tepals unequal, the dorsal largest, elongate-spathulate, 16–18 mm long, arising 2–3 mm beyond the lower, filaments c. 28 mm long; bracts dry. Capsules small and warty, to 10 mm long, seeds flattened. Flowering December–January. Marshes on peaty sandstone slopes, SW (Hermanus Mountains).

Tulbaghia

COMMON NAME wild garlic, FAMILY Alliaceae. Deciduous or evergreen perennials, usually with an onion or garlic smell when bruised. ROOTSTOCK a bulb or short rhizome. LEAVES several, strap-like, usually present at flowering. INFLORESCENCE an umbel on a naked peduncle, the peduncle often mottled gray or purple, the umbel subtended by two large bracts united along the margins in bud, the pedicels elongating in fruit. FLOWERS more or less nodding but erect in fruit, somewhat tubular or trumpet-shaped, often scented at night, the tepals united about half their length into a cylindrical tube surmounted by a corona of three or more free scales, sometimes united into a fleshy ring, white to purplish or green, the corona sometimes orange or brown. STAMENS in two series in the upper part of the tube or rarely the upper series on the corona, anthers sessile. OVARY ovoid; STYLE short with a knob-like stigma. FRUIT an obovoid or top-shaped capsule, three-lobed and indented above. SEEDS few per locule, wedge-shaped, black. Basic chromosome number $x = 6$. Southern Africa and southern tropical Africa; 20 spp., 4 in the Cape.

The genus *Tulbaghia* is the only unequivocally African member of the family Alliaceae. The flowers are notable for the curious corona surrounding the mouth of the tube, a development of the perianth found also in a few American genera of the family and in several genera in Amaryllidaceae. The corona comprises several fleshy scales, which may be united to form a complete ring, and often differs from the tepals in color. The flowers themselves may be scented, usually only in the evening, either of cloves or more sweetly, but this is easily overpowered by the smell of garlic if the tissues are damaged. The species typically occur on rocky outcrops or stony flats.

Most of the species of *Tulbaghia* are adapted for moth pollination and have dull flowers that become sweetly scented in the evening. The two mauve-flowered species, *T. violacea* and the eastern southern African *T. simmleri* Palisot de Beauvois, are scented during the day also, and pollination by butterflies or bees seems likely.

Only the two mauve-flowered species, *Tulbaghia violacea* and *T. simmleri* (the latter long known as *T. fragrans* I. Verdoorn), enjoy any popularity in cultivation and in South African gardens. *Tulbaghia violacea* is a very popular plant, especially in commercial plantings where it thrives with minimal attention. It is also less strongly winter growing than many other Cape bulbs and will tolerate almost year-round watering. The species are very easy to grow, are drought and disease resistant, and multiply rapidly. Their main requirement is good lighting if they are to flower well and not become lanky and etiolated.

Tulbaghia alliacea

FURTHER READING. *Tulbaghia* was reviewed by both Vosa (1975) and Burbidge (1978), and more recently again by Vosa (2000).

Tulbaghia alliacea Linnaeus fil.
Plants 15–30 cm high, strongly aromatic. Leaves absent or emergent at flowering, spreading, linear. Flowers 6–10 on pedicels to 20 mm long, brownish to green, with an orange corona, scented of coconut and honey at night, tube c. 6 mm long, tepals 2–4 mm long, corona cylindrical, fleshy, obscurely crenate, 6–8 mm long, upper anthers inserted on the corona. Flowering March–May. Widespread on clay or gravelly flats, RV, NW, SW, SE (Clanwilliam to Cape Peninsula to Swellendam, throughout southern Africa).

Tulbaghia capensis Linnaeus
Plants 15–35 cm high, strongly aromatic. Leaves spreading, linear. Flowers (4–)6–10 on pedicels to 20 mm long, brownish to purplish and green, with an orange corona, sweetly scented at night, tube c. 7 mm long, tepals 2–4 mm long, corona to 5 mm long, trisect with each lobe deeply bifid, upper anthers inserted at the base of the corona. Flowering April–October. Rocky slopes, SW, AP, LB, SE (Namaqualand, Cape Peninsula to Long Kloof).

Tulbaghia dregeana Kunth
Plants 15–25 cm high, strongly aromatic. Leaves spreading, linear. Flowers five to nine on pedicels 8–10 mm long, cream to greenish yellow, with cream or brown corona, sweetly scented or musk scented at night, tube to 9 mm long, tepals 4–4.5 mm long, corona annular, fleshy, obscurely crenate, 2 mm long, upper anthers inserted at the base of the corona. Flowering May–October. Stony soils, RV, NW, SW (Namaqualand and western Karoo to Worcester, Cape Peninsula to Stanford).

Tulbaghia violacea Harvey
Plants 20–35 cm high, strongly aromatic. Leaves suberect, linear, glaucous. Flowers six to nine on pedicels 10–18 mm long, mauve, lightly scented, tube 6–13 mm long, tepals 6–12 mm long, corona trisect, 1.5–2.5 mm long, upper anthers inserted below the corona. Flower-

Tulbaghia dregeana

Tulbaghia violacea

ing November–April. Forest margins and stream banks, KM, SE (Ladismith, Knysna to KwaZulu-Natal).

Veltheimia

COMMON NAME sand lily, FAMILY Hyacinthaceae. Deciduous or almost evergreen perennials. ROOTSTOCK a pear-shaped or globose, often large bulb, entirely fleshy or with pale, papery or membranous outer tunics lightly barred above. LEAVES few to several, lanceolate to oblanceolate or narrowly oblong, undulate or sometimes almost crisped, suberect. INFLORESCENCE a dense, ovoid or subcylindrical, many-flowered raceme, the peduncle usually mottled purple; bracts pale and soft, lanceolate-attenuate. FLOWERS spreading or more or less nodding, tubular and usually gently curved, the tepals united for most of their length, with small ovate lobes, white to greenish but more or less deeply flushed and spotted with dull red or pink on the tube, unscented. STAMENS with slender and terete filaments joined to the tepals for half their length and obliquely inserted at about the middle of the tube, the upper filaments or at least the uppermost progressively shorter and inserted slightly lower down the tube, the anthers just included or shortly exserted. OVARY narrowly ellipsoidal and six-ribbed with two axile ovules per locule; STYLE slender, longer than the ovary, slightly declinate, recurved at the tip, reaching to the mouth of the tube. FRUIT a large, three-winged, papery capsule. SEEDS two per locule, pear-shaped, black, smooth or finely wrinkled. Basic chromosome number $x = 10$. Western and southern South Africa; 2 spp.

Among the larger and more striking members of the family Hyacinthaceae in the Cape flora, the two species of *Veltheimia* take readily to cultivation. The attractive glossy or glaucous leaves are accompanied by bold *Aloe*-like racemes of pink to dull red flowers and, later, by large papery capsules unique in the family. The genus is closely but not immediately related to *Lachenalia*, with which it shares obliquely inserted filaments, a style inflexed at the tip, and pear-shaped seeds with a prominent strophiole (arillode). It differs substantially from *Lachenalia*, however, in several details apart from foliage and stature. These differences include the almost complete union of both tepal whorls, the insertion of the filaments halfway up the tube, and the large papery capsules with only two ovules per locule. The resemblance between the inflorescence of *Veltheimia* and that of *Kniphofia* or *Aloe* is a striking example of convergent evolution in different families for sunbird pollination. The tubular pinkish flowers are visited by several species, including the lesser double-collared sunbird.

The two species of *Veltheimia* are very similar and replace one another along a geographic-climatic axis. Both are attractive and easy to cultivate, but whereas *V. bracteata* is best grown in light shade and will thrive under small trees, *V. capensis* requires full sun to flower well, and in shaded conditions the leaves become flaccid and lose their attractively crisped margins. The western *V. capensis* is adapted to a dry winter and is strictly deciduous, flowering in autumn and early winter after the first rains and

Veltheimia bracteata

often before the dull bluish gray leaves have fully expanded. The eastern *V. bracteata*, however, is more or less evergreen, although it will benefit from reduced watering during the summer, and flowers in spring when the glossy deep green leaves are fully developed. Both species can also be grown in pots.

FURTHER READING. The differences between the species of *Veltheimia* were reviewed by Marais (1972). Both species have been separately treated, along with fine illustrations, by Obermeyer (1961) and Batten (1986).

Veltheimia bracteata Harvey ex Baker
Plants 20–40 cm high, more or less evergreen or briefly deciduous; bulb tunics fleshy. Leaves glossy green, lanceolate to oblanceolate. Flowers spreading to nodding, pink or pale yellow, finely speckled with red, tube 20–35 mm long, tepals ovate, c. 3 mm long; bracts 10–30 mm long. Capsules inflated, ellipsoidal, three-winged. Flowering August–September. Coastal scrub, SE (Humansdorp to Eastern Cape).

Veltheimia capensis (Linnaeus) De Candolle
Plants 20–40 cm high, deciduous; outer bulb tunics papery. Leaves grayish or glaucous, lanceolate to oblong, sometimes narrowly oblong and strongly crisped. Flowers and capsules as in *V. bracteata* but bracts 10–15 mm long. Flowering April–July. Rocky slopes, NW, SW, AP, KM (Namaqualand and western Karoo to Darling, Potberg, and Little Karoo).

Wachendorfia

COMMON NAME butterfly lily, FAMILY Haemodoraceae. Deciduous or evergreen perennials. ROOTSTOCK a short rhizome with bright red flesh, covered with papery tunics. LEAVES several, unifacial, lanceolate, pleated, hairless or hairy, more or less narrowed below into a false petiole. INFLORESCENCE a lax or dense, many-flowered paniculate cyme, the axis hairy below and glandular hairy above; bracts green and leaf-like or dry, erect or recurved, usually hairy. FLOWERS zygomorphic, the lower three tepals free and spreading, without spurs but the upper three closer together and united at the base with two open, spur-like nectaries at the base of each tepal, outer tepals hairy on the outer surface, yellow to orange with pale and dark markings at the base of the upper tepals, usually unscented, each lasting just a day. STAMENS three, inserted at the base of the inner tepals, slender, declinate, the lower flexed sharply sideways opposite the style. OVARY superior, ovoid with one ovule per locule, hairy; STYLE slender, bent sideways (left or right in any single plant). FRUIT a three-lobed, loculicidal capsule, usually glandular hairy. SEEDS one per locule, globose or ovoid, densely hairy. Basic chromosome number $x = 15$. Winter-rainfall South Africa; 4 spp.

Restricted to the winter-rainfall region of South Africa, the species of *Wachendorfia* are usually associated with sandy or well-drained soils derived from sandstone or granite, but *W. thyrsiflora* favors streamsides or marshes on sandstone or shale. All the species flower best when not overgrown; *W. paniculata* is particularly prominent after a

Veltheimia capensis

Wachendorfia brachyandra

Wachendorfia multiflora

burn, when plants can cover the blackened slopes in their thousands. The genus is closely allied to the forest-loving, summer-rainfall species *Barberetta aurea,* with which it shares soft, more or less pleated leaves and zygomorphic, orange flowers with a secondarily superior ovary.

The flowers of *Wachendorfia* are rather similar in appearance in all the species, and although short-lived, each lasts most of the day and is replaced early each morning. Thus the plants are never without open flowers during the flowering season. In most species the flowers wither in the late afternoon, but in *W. brachyandra* they do not last much beyond midday. That species is also distinctive in its very short stamens and is adapted primarily to pollination by honeybees. The remaining species are also visited by long-tongued bees of the genera *Amegilla, Anthophora,* and *Xylocopa* (Apidae: Anthophorinae and Xylocopinae) and sometimes by long-proboscid flies (Tabanidae).

Wachendorfia thyrsiflora is particularly handsome and is extensively grown as a streamside planting at Kirstenbosch botanical garden, where it provides a magnificent show in late spring and early summer. This species is highly recommended for seasonally waterlogged soils but can also be grown in more conventional borders. Its tall, golden flowered inflorescences combine well with the white chalices of another moisture-loving favorite in the Cape, *Zantedeschia aethiopica.* The other species, although less spectacular, are also worth attention, particularly *W. paniculata,* which thrives in dry, rocky conditions.

FURTHER READING. *Wachendorfia* was monographed by Helme and Linder (1992); a nomenclatural correction was made by Goldblatt and Manning (2000a).

Wachendorfia brachyandra W. F. Barker

Plants 20–65 cm high, deciduous. Leaves hairless, linear to lanceolate, usually shorter than the stem, to 35 mm wide. Flowers in a lax panicle, pale apricot-yellow, tepals 12–20 × 4–14 mm, stamens and style half as long as the tepals, clustered; bracts mostly papery, recurved above. Flowering August–December. Damp sandstone or granite, SW (Gouda to Cape Peninsula and Kogelberg).

Wachendorfia multiflora (Klatt) J. C. Manning & Goldblatt
Plants 10–30 cm high, deciduous. Leaves softly hairy, linear to lanceolate, usually sickle-shaped and longer than the stem, to 25 mm wide. Flowers in a short dense panicle, dull yellow to brownish purple, tepals 15–25 × 3–6 mm, stamens and style two-thirds as long as the tepals, spreading; bracts leaf-like, green, erect, often longer than the flowers. Flowering August–September. Sandstone and granitic soils, NW, SW, KM (Namaqualand to Cape Peninsula and Robertson).

Wachendorfia paniculata Burman
Plants mostly 20–70 cm high, deciduous. Leaves usually hairy, linear to lanceolate, usually shorter than the stem, 5–35 mm wide. Flowers in a lax to dense panicle, pale yellow to bright apricot, lightly scented, tepals 13–31 × 4–16 mm, stamens and style two-thirds to three-quarters as long as the tepals, spreading; bracts papery or somewhat membranous, usually recurved. Flowering mainly August–November. Mainly sandstone soils, NW, SW, AP, KM, LB, SE (Bokkeveld Mountains to Port Elizabeth).

Wachendorfia paniculata

Wachendorfia thyrsiflora Burman
Plants 1–2(–2.5) m high, evergreen. Leaves hairless, lanceolate, usually shorter than the stem, to 80 mm wide. Flowers in a crowded cylindrical panicle, golden yellow, tepals 12–28 × 8–14 mm, stamens and style three-quarters as long as the tepals, spreading; bracts papery, recurved. Flowering September–December. Permanent marshes and streams, NW, SW, AP, LB, SE (Clanwilliam to Humansdorp).

Walleria

COMMON NAME potato lily, FAMILY Tecophilaeaceae. Deciduous, twining or scrambling perennials. ROOTSTOCK a deep-seated corm without evident tunics. LEAVES several, scattered along the stem, sessile or clasping the stem, ovate to linear-lanceolate, hairless or scabrid to prickly on the midrib beneath, sometimes attenuate and drawn into a tendril, producing threads

Wachendorfia thyrsiflora; see also page 32

when torn. INFLORESCENCE of mostly solitary flowers in the lower axils, borne on slender, sometimes recurved, smooth, scabrid, or prickly pedicels; inner bracts inserted well along the pedicels, rarely subtending a second flower. FLOWERS actinomorphic, often nodding, star-shaped, the tepals spreading, shortly united at the base, blue to mauve or white, scented in at least 1 sp. STAMENS inserted at the mouth of the short tube, on short filaments, narrow, usually united at the attenuated tips into a cone, dehiscing by an inward-facing subapical slit-like pore. OVARY almost superior, ovoid, with about eight ovules per locule; STYLE slender. FRUIT a nodding, ovoid, loculicidal capsule with small apical bosses on each locule. SEEDS four or five per locule, ovoid, conspicuously papillate, at least in the upper part, the papillae with an apical tuft of minute hairs, sometimes the uppermost papillae large and sausage-like, forming an apical mop, brown. Basic chromosome number $x = 12$. Southern and tropical Africa; 3 spp., 1 in the Cape.

Mostly tropical African in distribution, *Walleria* is unique in the family Tecophilaeaceae in its leafy stems and highly unusual, papillate seeds, which lack phytomelan in the coat. The single winter-rainfall species, *W. gracilis,* is restricted to the northwestern coast of South Africa. It is closely related to *W. nutans* Kirk from central and southern central Africa north of the Karoo, but the white flowers (often purplish toward the center) with lilac-tipped anthers, the modified, tendriled leaves, and twining habit are distinctive. In habit and leaf it recalls a miniature *Gloriosa* although the latter does not have prickles. *Walleria gracilis* was first collected in fruit in 1686 during the expedition to the copper deposits in Namaqualand led by the Dutch governor of the Cape, Simon van der Stel, and has been collected only sporadically since then. Although apparently centered in a small area along the lower reaches of the Olifants River Valley near the town of Klawer, where it grows in deep sandy soil among outcrops of sandstone, the species has been collected once from the Richtersveld, some 240 km (150 miles) to the north.

The nodding flowers, similar to those of the potato (*Solanum tuberosum*) are typical of buzz-pollinated species (discussed under *Cyanella*) and are likely to be visited by solitary bees (Apidae: Anthophorinae). Its climbing habit and curious, tendriled leaves make *Walleria gracilis* an interesting subject for pot culture. The distinctively shaped purple and white flowers are attractive in both appearance and scent.

FURTHER READING. *Walleria* was revised by Carter (1962). Two of the species were separately treated, along with fine, color illustrations, by Dyer (1960) and Manning et al. (2001).

Walleria gracilis (Salisbury) S. Carter

Plants to 30 cm high, stems prickly below. Leaves narrowly lanceolate, clasping the stem at the base, tapering into tendrils, the midribs with hooked prickles beneath. Flowers axillary, nodding, white with a purple center, rose scented, anthers yellow below and purple above with gray tips, tepals recurved, 10–15 × 2.5–3 mm, filaments 0.5–1 mm long, anthers 5–6 mm long. Flowering June–July. Low, dry, rocky outcrops in scrub, NW (Richtersveld and Gifberg to Pakhuis Mountains).

Walleria gracilis

Watsonia

COMMON NAME watsonia, FAMILY Iridaceae. Small to large, deciduous or sometimes evergreen perennials. ROOTSTOCK a depressed-globose corm, axillary in origin and rooting from below, with tunics of medium-textured to coarse fibers. LEAVES several, unifacial with a definite midrib, leathery and fibrotic, mostly basal, plane, margins and midribs often thickened and prominent, stem leaves smaller than the basal and progressively reduced above; flowering stem usually branched. INFLORESCENCE a simple or branched, two-ranked spike, the bracts firm textured, green or partly to completely dry at anthesis, the inner smaller, as long as or longer than the outer, usually forked apically. FLOWERS zygomorphic, actinomorphic in 1 sp., pink, orange, or red, rarely cream to pale yellow, occasionally with contrasting markings on lower tepals, scentless; perianth tube slightly to strongly curved, the lower part narrow and cylindrical, the upper part flared or broad and cylindrical; tepals subequal. STAMENS unilateral and arcuate or declinate, symmetrically arranged around the style in 1 sp. STYLE filiform, the branches each forked half their length and recurved. FRUIT a globose to oblong to spindle-shaped capsule, mostly more or less woody. SEEDS large, angular or compressed and winged at one or both ends, matte. Basic chromosome number $x = 9$. Southern Africa, centered in the southwestern Cape but extending into Namaqualand in the north and well represented in summer-rainfall southern Africa, especially southern KwaZulu-Natal and the escarpment of Mpumalanga and Swaziland; 52 spp., 33 in the Cape.

The genus *Watsonia* is distinguished by a strongly two-ranked inflorescence of usually pink to red flowers in which the three style branches are each deeply divided. It appears to be most closely allied to *Micranthus* and *Thereianthus*. Species of *Watsonia* exhibit a wide range of floral forms, which are correlated with their pollination biology. Those with pink or yellow, short-tubed flowers produce small quantities of nectar and are pollinated by bees whereas those with a red perianth and long, dimorphic, cylindrical tube produce ample nectar and are pollinated by sunbirds. A few species have pink flowers with a long perianth tube and are mostly pollinated by long-proboscid flies.

Most species of *Watsonia* have tall, elegant spikes with numerous flowers that last several days. Their potential as bedding plants is largely overlooked except to some extent in Cape Town, where they are a prominent feature of some roadside plantings. Likewise, their value as a cut flower is only beginning to be appreciated. Watsonias planted together with *Agapanthus* are a perfect combination for large areas, the two plants providing successive waves of color for several months. Mixed plantings of several varieties of *Watsonia* alone will flower year after year in the spring and if mixed judiciously a display can be achieved throughout the spring, from October to December. After this, they should be mowed back. Interplanting species of *Watsonia* with *Amaryllis*, which flower in the autumn, in combination with deciduous *Agapanthus*, which flower in the summer, will provide colorful displays more than half the year. The roadside plantings in Cape Town persist for years with this mix of species, requiring only a seasonal mowing and occasional watering and feeding. The plantings of watsonias at Kirstenbosch botanical garden, where several species have been grown for years, are one of its glories. In late spring, tall *W. marginata* forms huge mauve or pink banks in front of shrubberies just coming into leaf. The scimitar-shaped leaves of silvery gray remain an elegant accent after the spring displays have faded; even their reddish fruiting stalks and capsules are attractive. Almost all the species have the potential to make good displays. The pink- or purple-flowered *W. knysnana* blooms in November, and orange to scarlet *W. pillansii* in December. Another fine plant is the floriferous smaller form of *W. meriana*, not the rather untidy cultivar, 'Bulbillifera', that has far too few flowers for its bulk, produces bulblets, and becomes bothersome. Unlike *W. knysnana* and *W. pillansii*, it is fully deciduous and dies back after flowering. The dwarf species, *W. laccata*, for example, which has pink, purple, and bright orange forms, are good for the bulb border or rock garden; *W. laccata* is also an excellent pot subject. Other dwarf species such as *W. humilis* and *W. stenosiphon* should also be given attention. For an unusual specimen planting that will create immediate interest, *W. vanderspuyiae* is recommended. Plants have broad *Iris*-like leaves more than 10 cm wide, and the stems grow to 2 m before producing spikes of dark red, *Fuchsia*-like flowers. It is easy to grow and will even flower in a pot, though it looks misplaced in any container. Experience in areas of alternative climate shows that Cape watsonias thrive under summer rainfall and mild winter frost. A range of cultivars is available but the species are much more varied.

FURTHER READING. *Watsonia* was thoroughly revised by Goldblatt (1989b) in a well-illustrated monograph.

Watsonia aletroides (Burman fil.) Ker Gawler

Plants to 45 cm high. Leaves sword-shaped, 3–10 mm wide. Flowers mostly in an unbranched spike, red, rarely pinkish or mauve, nodding, perianth tube elongate and recurved, 35–42 mm long, tepals c. 10 mm long, barely spreading, stamens declinate; bracts 11–24 mm long, clasping the stem. Capsules spindle-shaped, tapering to a narrow tip. Flowering September–October. Clay slopes, mainly renosterveld, SW, AP, LB, SE (Caledon to Knysna).

Watsonia amabilis Goldblatt

Plants mostly 15–30 cm high. Leaves sword-shaped with lightly thickened margins, 5–20 mm wide. Flowers in a short spike, pink with dark markings in the throat, perianth tube 16–26 mm long, flared above, tepals 19–25 mm long, stamens declinate; bracts 12–20 mm long. Flowering October–November. Granite slopes in renosterveld, SW (Paarl to Sir Lowry's Pass).

Watsonia angusta Ker Gawler

Plants to 1.2 m high. Leaves sword-shaped, often with a waxy bloom, 12–20 mm wide. Flowers in an elongate, usually branched spike, scarlet, perianth tube 36–44 mm long, tubular above, tepals 19–25 mm long, stamens arcuate; bracts mostly 9–14 mm long. Capsules narrowly spindle-shaped, tapering to a narrow tip. Flowering mainly November–January. Montane marshes and streambanks in fynbos, NW, SW, AP, LB, SE (Cedarberg Mountains to southern KwaZulu-Natal).

Watsonia borbonica (Pourret) Goldblatt

Plants 50–200 cm high, stems usually several-branched,

Watsonia aletroides

Watsonia angusta

often purple. Leaves sword-shaped, glossy, mostly 15–40 mm wide. Flowers in elongate branched spikes, purple-pink, rarely white, perianth tube 20–30 mm long, flared above, tepals mostly 30–35 mm long, stamens declinate or arcuate; bracts 10–18 mm long. Capsules obovoid to oblong, often widest near the tip. Flowering October–January. Mainly rocky sandstone slopes, also granite and clay, 100–1500 m, NW, SW (Tulbagh to Bredasdorp).

Watsonia coccinea Herbert ex Baker
Plants 14–40 cm high. Leaves sword-shaped, 3–8 mm wide. Flowers in a few-flowered spike, purple, pink, or scarlet, perianth tube elongate, 38–45 mm long, tubular above, tepals 16–23 mm long, stamens arcuate; bracts 20–25 mm long. Capsules oblong. Flowering August–November. Sandstone flats and plateaus, SW, AP (Malmesbury to Bredasdorp).

Watsonia distans L. Bolus
Plants 15–35 cm high, slender. Leaves sword-shaped, margins lightly thickened, 3–6 mm wide. Flowers in few-flowered spikes, deep pink, perianth tube 16–22 mm long, narrowly flared above, tepals 15–20 mm long, stamens arcuate; bracts 10–13 mm long. Flowering November–December. Mountain marshes, SW (Franschhoek to Kleinmond).

Watsonia dubia Ecklon ex Klatt
Plants 25–40 cm high. Leaves sword-shaped with lightly thickened margins, 3–12 mm wide. Flowers in a few-flowered spike, tepals with a dark streak in the lower midline, pink, perianth tube elongate and slender, 32–40 mm long, flared near the apex, tepals 24–30 mm long, stamens declinate; bracts mostly 30–50 mm long, becoming dry and lacerated. Capsules oblong. Flowering October–November. Granite and clay slopes in renosterveld, NW, SW (Citrusdal to Wellington).

Watsonia elsiae Goldblatt
Plants 40–65 cm high. Leaves sword-shaped, margins strongly thickened, 7–12 mm wide. Flowers in elongate spikes, scarlet, perianth tube 22–35 mm long, tubular

Watsonia borbonica

Watsonia coccinea

above, the tube often slightly nodding, tepals 13–16 mm long, stamens included in the tube; bracts mostly 8–12 mm long. Capsules ovoid. Flowering mainly November–December. Stony sandstone slopes, SE (Uniondale to Joubertina).

Watsonia fourcadei

Watsonia emiliae L. Bolus
Plants 40–60 cm high. Leaves sword-shaped, margins moderately thickened, 4–5 mm wide. Flowers in few-flowered, usually branched spikes, pale pink, perianth tube 16–20 mm long, flared above, tepals 16–20 mm long, stamens arcuate; bracts 12–15 mm long. Capsules ovoid. Flowering November–December. Rocky sandstone slopes, KM, LB (Swartberg and Langeberg Mountains at Riversdale).

Watsonia fergusoniae L. Bolus
Plants to 80 cm high. Leaves sword-shaped, mostly 4–12 mm wide. Flowers in an elongate spike, bright orange-red, perianth tube elongate, 36–50 mm long, tepals 20–25 mm long, stamens arcuate; bracts mostly 20–27 mm long. Capsules oblong-cylindrical. Flowering October–November. Limestone outcrops, AP (Agulhas to Albertinia).

Watsonia fourcadei J. W. Mathews & L. Bolus
Plants to 2 m high. Leaves sword-shaped, 15–40 mm wide. Flowers in elongate spikes, mostly orange to red, rarely pink or purple, perianth tube elongate, 42–55 mm long, tubular above, tepals 24–33 mm long, stamens arcuate; bracts 10–20 mm long. Capsules tapering above. Flowering November–January. Rocky sandstone slopes, NW, SW, LB, SE (Cedarberg to Great Winterhoek Mountains).

Watsonia galpinii L. Bolus
Plants to 1.5 m high. Leaves linear to sword-shaped, 10–20 mm wide. Flowers in fairly dense spikes, dark red, perianth tube 14–20 mm long, tubular to flared above, tepals 15–20 mm long, stamens arcuate; bracts 6–12 mm long. Capsules obovoid. Flowering December–May. Streamsides, KM, SE (Swartberg and Outeniqua Mountains).

Watsonia humilis Miller
Plants 15–40 cm high. Leaves sword-shaped, 8–14 mm wide. Flowers in a few-flowered, mostly unbranched spike, pale pink to white, perianth tube elongate, 30–45 mm long, tubular above, tepals 15–22 mm long, stamens

arcuate; bracts overlapping and keeled in the midline, mostly 20–30 mm long. Capsules oblong. Flowering September–November. Sandstone or granite flats, SW (Malmesbury to Gordon's Bay).

Watsonia hysterantha J.W. Mathews & L. Bolus
Plants 50–90 cm high with fairly slender stems. Leaves dry at flowering, linear with moderately thickened margins, 4–10 mm wide. Flowers in an elongate, mostly unbranched spike, red, perianth tube elongate, 38–44 mm long, tubular above, tepals 25–30 mm long, stamens arcuate; bracts 15–24 mm long. Capsules ovoid. Flowering April–July. Coastal granite outcrops SW (Saldanha to Langebaan).

Watsonia knysnana L. Bolus
Plants to 1.6 m high, robust. Leaves sword-shaped, 8–24 mm wide. Flowers mostly pink to purple, perianth tube elongate, 30–40 mm long, tubular above, tepals mostly 19–22 mm long, stamens arcuate; bracts 14–22 mm long. Capsules obovoid. Flowering November–January. Sandstone slopes in fynbos, LB, SE (Mossel Bay to East London).

Watsonia laccata (Jacquin) Ker Gawler
Plants 30–40 cm high. Leaves sword-shaped with lightly thickened margins, mostly 6–15 mm wide. Flowers in a short spike, pink to purple, orange, or white and then rarely with pink keels, perianth tube 18–22 mm long, flared above, tepals 14–16 mm long, stamens declinate; bracts 10–20 mm long, clasping the stem. Capsules spindle-shaped, tapering to a narrow tip. Flowering September–November. Sandstone slopes in fynbos, NW, SW, AP, SE (Kleinmond to Humansdorp).

Watsonia marginata (Linnaeus fil.) Ker Gawler
Plants 50–200 cm high. Leaves broad, 20–50 mm wide, with heavily thickened margins and midribs. Flowers actinomorphic, pink, rarely white or purple, perianth tube 12–20 mm long, flared above, tepals 15–22 mm long, stamens symmetrically arranged around a central style; bracts 10–18 mm long. Capsules globose, with angled seeds. Flowering September–December. Sandy and

Watsonia hysterantha

Watsonia marginata

granitic soils, often damper sites, NW, SW (Bokkeveld Mountains to Hermanus).

Watsonia marlothii L. Bolus

Plants 60–120 cm high. Leaves sword-shaped with heavily thickened margins and midrib, 9–12 mm wide. Flowers in elongate spikes, mainly red to pink, perianth tube elongate, 24–30 mm long, tubular above, tepals 12–16 mm long, stamens arcuate; bracts 9–12 mm long. Capsules globose. Flowering mainly November–January. Rocky sandstone slopes, KM (Swartberg Mountains).

Watsonia meriana (Linnaeus) Miller

Plants 60–200 cm high, sometimes with cormels at the nodes. Leaves sword-shaped, the margins usually strongly thickened, mostly 20–35 mm wide. Flowers in an elongate spike, red to orange, pink or mauve, perianth tube elongate, 42–50 mm long, tubular above, tepals 21–26 mm long, stamens arcuate; bracts mostly 24–30 mm long. Capsules oblong. Flowering September–November. Sandy or granitic soils, often marshes and streambanks, NW, SW, AP (Namaqualand to Bredasdorp).

Watsonia minima Goldblatt

Plants 10–45 cm high. Leaves few, narrowly sword-shaped, 2–5 mm wide. Flowers in few-flowered spikes, orange-red, perianth tube elongate, 16–20 mm long, tubular above, tepals 13–15 mm long, stamens arcuate; bracts 8–14 mm long. Capsules obovoid-truncate. Flowering November–December. Marshes and waterlogged, stony, sandstone slopes, SW (Riviersonderend Mountains).

Watsonia paucifolia Goldblatt

Plants 20–45 cm high. Leaves few, nearly linear, margins lightly thickened, 3–10 mm long. Flowers in a few-flowered spike, pink, perianth tube elongate, 22–30 mm long, narrowly tubular above, tepals 14–16 mm long, stamens arcuate; bracts 10–18 mm long. Capsules ovoid. Flowering November–January. Rocky sandstone slopes, 500–1200 m, NW, SW (Tulbagh Mountains to Greyton).

Watsonia meriana

Watsonia paucifolia

Watsonia pillansii L. Bolus

Plants 50–120 cm high. Leaves sword-shaped, mostly 10–18 mm wide. Flowers in an elongate spike, scarlet to orange, perianth tube elongate, 35–50 mm long, tubular above, tepals 20–26 mm long, stamens arcuate; bracts 20–33 mm long. Capsules obovoid. Flowering November–January. Sandy soils, mostly at low elevations, SE (George to central KwaZulu-Natal).

Watsonia rogersii L. Bolus

Plants (20–)30–50 cm high, stems sometimes branched. Leaves narrowly sword-shaped, 5–10 mm wide. Flowers in lax, sometimes branched spikes, purple-pink, perianth tube 20–25 mm long, flared above, tepals mostly 22–25 mm long, stamens declinate; bracts 9–16 mm long. Capsules elongate to ovoid. Flowering October–December. Mainly rocky sandstone slopes at low elevations, also granite and clay, SW (Paarl to Hermanus).

Watsonia schlechteri L. Bolus

Plants 40–100 cm high. Leaves sword-shaped with strongly thickened margins, 6–15 mm wide. Flowers in an elongate spike, scarlet, perianth tube elongate, 40–50 mm long, tubular above, tepals 20–24 mm long, stamens arcuate; bracts 18–30 mm long. Capsules obovoid. Flowering November–February, mainly after fire. Rocky sandstone slopes in fynbos, NW, SW, AP, KM, LB, SE (Citrusdal to Kouga Mountains). Page 406.

Watsonia spectabilis Schinz

Plants 25–50 cm high. Leaves linear to sword-shaped, 3–10 mm wide. Flowers in a few-flowered spike, large, scarlet, perianth tube elongate, 38–46 mm long, tubular above, tepals c. 35 mm long, the lowermost tepals recurved, stamens arcuate; bracts 20–40 mm long. Capsules obovoid to globose. Flowering August–November. Sandy flats and plateaus, often near water, NW, SW, AP (Bokkeveld Mountains to Potberg). Page 406.

Watsonia stenosiphon L. Bolus

Plants mostly 20–35 cm high, slender. Leaves linear to sword-shaped, margins slightly thickened, 5–12 mm wide. Flowers in an elongate unbranched spike, bright

Watsonia pillansii

Watsonia rogersii

Watsonia schlechteri

Watsonia spectabilis

Watsonia stokoei; see also page 17

Watsonia tabularis

orange, perianth tube elongate, 27–34 mm long, slender throughout, tepals 17–20 mm long, stamens arcuate; bracts 15–22 mm long. Capsules cylindrical. Flowering September–October. Sandy coastal flats, SW (Hermanus to Potberg).

Watsonia stokoei L. Bolus
Plants to 1 m high. Leaves sword-shaped, 8–15 mm wide. Flowers in a lax spike, small, red to orange, rarely purplish, perianth tube elongate, 22–32 mm long, tubular above, tepals 12–15 mm long, stamens arcuate; bracts mostly 12–16 mm long. Capsules obovoid. Flowering November–January. Sandstone soils in seeps and marshes, NW (Gifberg to Grootwinterhoek Mountains).

Watsonia strictiflora Ker Gawler
Plants 25–45 cm high. Leaves sword-shaped with moderately thickened margins, 8–16 mm wide. Flowers in few-flowered spikes, pink with dark markings in the throat, perianth tube elongate, 30–45 mm long, flared above, tepals 22–25 mm long, stamens declinate. Capsules ovoid to oblong. Flowering November–December. Mainly sandstone outcrops, SW (Durbanville to Klapmuts).

Watsonia tabularis J. W. Mathews & L. Bolus
Plants to 1.5 m high. Leaves sword-shaped, 20–35 mm wide, the cauline leaves inflated. Flowers in an elongate branched spike, orange or pink, perianth tube elongate, 40–50 mm long, tepals 20–26 mm long, stamens arcuate; bracts 10–15 mm long. Capsules oblong-truncate. Flowering November–December. Rocky sandstone soils, 50–400 m, SW (Cape Peninsula).

Watsonia vanderspuyiae L. Bolus
Plants 1–2 m high, robust. Leaves lanceolate, unusually broad with heavily thickened margins, 33–85 mm wide. Flowers in an elongate branched spike, dark red, perianth tube elongate, c. 50 mm long, tubular above, tepals 25–35 mm long, stamens arcuate; bracts 25–45 mm long. Capsules oblong. Flowering September–November. Sandstone outcrops, NW (Cedarberg Mountains to Ceres and Piketberg).

Watsonia versfeldii J. W. Mathews & L. Bolus
Plants 1.2–2 m high, robust. Leaves sword-shaped, 25–40 mm wide. Flowers in an elongate branched spike, pink-purple, perianth tube elongate, 35–50 mm long, tubular above, tepals 33–46 mm long, stamens arcuate; bracts 15–26 mm long. Capsules oblong-conical. Flowering October–November. Sandstone slopes, NW (Piketberg and Porterville Mountains).

Watsonia wilmaniae J. W. Mathews & L. Bolus
Plants 80–150 cm high. Leaves sword-shaped, 16–30 mm wide. Flowers in a branched spike, orange, red, or purple, perianth tube elongate, slender, 30–35 mm long, tubular above, tepals 18–22 mm long, stamens arcuate; bracts 7–12 mm long. Capsules obovoid. Flowering November–January. Rocky sandstone soils, often wet sites, KM, SE (Ladismith to Knysna).

Watsonia zeyheri

Watsonia zeyheri L. Bolus

Plants 50–120 cm high. Leaves sword-shaped, 12–18 mm wide. Flowers in an elongate spike, bright orange, perianth tube elongate, 32–38 mm long, tubular above, tepals 20–22 mm long, stamens arcuate; bracts 14–18 mm long. Capsules spindle-shaped, tapering above. Flowering November–January. Marshes on sandstone, coastal to 100 m, SW, AP (Cape Peninsula to Agulhas coast). Page 407.

Whiteheadia

COMMON NAME pagoda lily, FAMILY Hyacinthaceae. Deciduous perennial. ROOTSTOCK a globose bulb with pale, papery or thinly leathery outer tunics lightly barred above. LEAVES two, prostrate, oblong to broadly elliptical, subsucculent and fragile, the veins depressed. INFLORESCENCE a many-flowered conical spike, bearing a crown of green, leafy bracts, elongating in fruit; bracts large and green, ovate acuminate, subsucculent and fragile, more or less clasping below. FLOWERS subsessile, cup-shaped, the tepals shortly united at the base into a shallow cup, pale whitish green, sour smelling. STAMENS with firm filaments, broadened below and united into a shallow cup inserted at the mouth of the perianth tube, slender and slightly incurved above. OVARY obtriangular, three-angled and conspicuously shouldered above, with several ovules per locule; STYLE to about as long as the ovary, tapering and slightly curved, the stigma minute. FRUIT an inflated, ovoid or obtriangular, three-winged papery capsule, style persistent. SEEDS several per locule, subglobose, black. Basic chromosome number x unknown. Southern Namibia to Western Cape; 1 sp.

Whiteheadia, with a single species, is restricted to the more arid parts of the southern African winter-rainfall region. The subsucculent, fragile plants are always found in sheltered rocky sites that are locally moist and offer shade and protection from the sun. Resembling *Eucomis* somewhat in the crown of leafy bracts that terminate the inflorescence, *Whiteheadia* is closely related to *Massonia* and is most obviously separated from that genus by the elongate, spike-like inflorescence, which bears subsessile flowers in the axils of green, subsucculent bracts. In *Massonia* the inflorescence axis is much contracted, subcorymbose, and not exserted much above the leaves, and the flowers are more or less distinctly pedicellate in the axils of membranous bracts. Circumstantial evidence suggests that the shallow, whitish or greenish flowers of *Whiteheadia*, with their sour smell, are visited by rodents for the nectar contained in their shallow bowl.

FURTHER READING. *Whiteheadia* was revised by U. and D. Müller-Doblies (1997) but the circumscriptions of the genera in their treatment are controversial. The species *W. bifolia* was treated separately, along with a fine, color illustration, by Obermeyer (1965).

Whiteheadia bifolia (Jacquin) Baker

Plants 8–15 cm high. Leaves subsucculent, fragile, 8–40 × 6–25 cm; bracts ovate, 16–40 × 12–20 mm. Flowers subsessile in a dense conical spike to 15 cm long, sour smelling, pedicels short and stout, 3–4 mm long, tepals whitish or greenish, 10–15 mm long, united below for 4–7 mm, filaments 7–9 mm long, broadened below and united into a shallow cup 2 mm deep, style 1–3 mm long.

Whiteheadia bifolia

Capsule inflated, obtriangular, three-winged. Flowering June–August. Mostly in the lee of rocks, NW (southwestern Namibia to Pakhuis Pass).

Wurmbea

COMMON NAME spider lily, FAMILY Colchicaceae. Deciduous perennials. ROOTSTOCK an ovoid to subglobose corm covered with dark, leathery or papery tunics. LEAVES two to four, scattered along the stem, filiform to ovate, clasping below. INFLORESCENCE a bractless spike-like scorpioid cyme. FLOWERS one to many, sessile, star- or trumpet-shaped, the tepals united into a short or long tube, suberect to reflexed above with a pouch-like nectary at the base of the free part, persistent and reflexed in fruit, white, cream, or yellowish to red or brown, with or without darker margins or tips, often with dark nectaries, often fetid smelling. STAMENS arising at or beyond the mouth of the tube. OVARY cylindrical and deeply lobed with several ovules per locule; STYLES three, slender or short and hook-like, subterminal on each lobe. FRUIT an ovoid to oblong septicidal or less commonly loculicidal capsule. SEEDS several per locule, globose or subglobose, brown or black. Basic chromosome number $x = 11$ or 10. Sub-Saharan Africa and Australia; 38 spp., 13 in the Cape.

The species of *Wurmbea* are almost equally divided between Africa and Australia. The African species are concentrated in the winter-rainfall region with a second center of diversity in the Drakensberg Mountains of KwaZulu-Natal and the Eastern Cape. Only a single species extends to any extent into tropical Africa, where it is confined to montane habitats. Both primitive and more specialized species occur in the Cape Floral Region, and the genus is thought to have had an origin in the temperate Southern Hemisphere. Some of the Australian species are unusual in having the flowers functionally unisexual. Speciation seems to be mainly geographic without a change in pollinators, and several instances of naturally occurring hybridization are known. The small, cream to brown flowers are more or less fetid smelling and mostly adapted to pollination by various carrion flies or houseflies.

Long-lasting and appealing when massed, the spires of small, creamy flowers of most species of *Wurmbea* are unfortunately unattractively scented. The two maroon-flowered species, *W. marginata* and *W. recurva*, are among the few almost black-flowered bulbs, and their bright yellow anthers contrast particularly well against the dark tepals. The species should be grown in pots where their individuality can best be appreciated.

FURTHER READING. The Cape species of *Wurmbea* were revised by Nordenstam (1986).

Wurmbea capensis Thunberg
Plants 5–10 cm high. Leaves linear, attenuate. Flowers two to seven in a spike 1–2.8 × 0.5–1 cm, cream with brown speckles, margins and nectaries, tube 4–5.5 mm long, tepals 2–3.5 mm long, suberect, filaments 1.2–1.5 mm long, anthers 0.5–0.7 mm long, styles short and hooked. Flowering August–September. Stony slopes, NW, SW (Clanwilliam to Stellenbosch).

Wurmbea compacta B. Nordenstam
Plants 5–18 cm high. Leaves linear-lanceolate, falcate. Flowers many in a dense spike 1.5–5 × 1–1.5 cm, pink with darker margins, tube 2–5 mm long, tepals 2.5–4 mm long, suberect, filaments 3–4 mm long, anthers 0.8–1 mm long. Flowering June–July. Stony slopes, KM (Montagu).

Wurmbea dolichantha B. Nordenstam
Plants 10–30 cm high. Leaves lanceolate. Flowers many in a spike (3–)5–15 × (2.5–)3–5 cm, white or cream with purple nectaries, fetid smelling, tube 8–17 mm long, tepals spreading, 6–7 mm long, filaments 2–3 mm long, anthers 1.2–1.5 mm long. Flowering September–October. Sand, clay, NW (Bokkeveld Escarpment to Piketberg). Page 410.

Wurmbea elongata B. Nordenstam
Plants 7–20 cm high. Leaves linear. Flowers many in a spike 3–12 × 1 cm, greenish white to cream, sometimes with dark margins, honey scented, tube 1.5–2.5 mm long, tepals spreading, 4–5 mm long, filaments 2–3 mm long, anthers 0.8–1 mm long. Flowering September–October. Rocky sandstone slopes, NW (Cedarberg Mountains to Piketberg).

Wurmbea dolichantha

Wurmbea inusta

Wurmbea marginata

Wurmbea recurva

Wurmbea hiemalis B. Nordenstam
Plants 4–15 cm high. Leaves linear. Flowers few to many in a spike 1–8 × 1–1.5 cm, white with purple or black margins, tube 2–4 mm long, tepals spreading, 2.5–5 mm long, filaments 1.3–1.7 mm long, anthers c. 0.5 mm long. Flowering May–August. Damp sandy slopes, SW (Cape Peninsula).

Wurmbea inusta (Baker) B. Nordenstam
Plants 5–20 cm high. Leaves linear. Flowers few to many in a spike 2–10 × 1.5–2 cm, greenish or cream with purple margins and bands above the nectaries, fragrant, tube 4.5–7 mm long, tepals spreading, 4–7 mm long, filaments 1.5–2 mm long, anthers c. 0.8 mm long. Flowering September–November. Damp gravelly flats, NW, SW (Tulbagh to Bredasdorp).

Wurmbea marginata (Desroussaux) B. Nordenstam
Plants 60–22 cm high. Leaves lanceolate. Flowers in a dense spike 3–4 × 1.2–2.5 cm, red or purple with darker margins, foul smelling, tube 1.2–3 mm long, tepals spreading, 6–11 mm long, filaments 1.5–2.2 mm long, anthers 1–1.5 mm long. Flowering September–October. Mostly clay or loam in renosterveld, SW, AP, LB (Hopefield to Albertinia).

Wurmbea minima B. Nordenstam
Plants 2–5 cm high. Leaves lanceolate. Flowers one to seven in a spike to 2 × c. 1 cm, white, tube vestigial, tepals spreading, clawed below, 4.5–5.5 mm long, filaments 2–3 mm long, anthers c. 1 mm long. Flowering October. Moist shallow soils, NW (Cedarberg to Porterville Mountains).

Wurmbea monopetala (Linnaeus fil.) B. Nordenstam
Plants 5–25 cm high. Leaves narrowly lanceolate. Flowers often in a lax spike 1.5–10 × 1–2 cm, greenish or cream with dark margins in the upper two-thirds, tube 2–3.5 mm long, tepals suberect, well separated at the bases, 5–6 mm long, filaments 0.5–0.8 mm long, anthers 0.5–0.8 mm long. Flowering August–November. Sandstone and granite slopes, NW, SW (Pikeberg to Caledon).

Wurmbea recurva B. Nordenstam
Plants 5–20 cm high. Leaves narrowly lanceolate. Flowers several to many in a spike (2–)4–12 × 0.6–1 cm, red to purplish brown, honey scented, tube 2–3 mm long, tepals recurved, 3–4.5 mm long, filaments 0.7–1.3 mm long, anthers 0.6–1.2 mm long. Flowering September–October. Damp gravelly slopes in renosterveld, NW, SW (Tulbagh to Somerset West).

Wurmbea robusta B. Nordenstam
Plants 15–25 cm high. Leaves lanceolate. Flowers in a dense spike 3–13 × 1.5–2 cm, white with purple margins, tube 3–5 mm long, tepals 4.5–7.5 mm long, filaments 4–6 mm long, anthers 1.2–1.5 mm long. Flowering July–September. Clay and granite slopes in renosterveld, NW, SW (Mooreesburg to Malmesbury).

Wurmbea spicata (Burman fil.) Durand & Schinz
Plants 5–20 cm high. Leaves narrowly lanceolate. Flowers usually in a dense spike 1.5–10 × 1.5–2.5 cm, white to cream, sometimes with dark margins, tube 3–6 mm

Wurmbea spicata

long, tepals more or less spreading, 4–7.5 mm long, filaments 1.5–3.5 mm long, anthers 0.8–1.2 mm long. Flowering August–November. Mostly clay and granite slopes in renosterveld, NW, SW, AP, KM, LB (Bokkeveld Mountains to Swellendam).

Wurmbea variabilis B. Nordenstam
Plants 5–20 cm high, often clumped. Leaves ovate-lanceolate. Flowers few to many in a spike 2–12 × (1–)1.5–3 cm, greenish or cream with purple nectaries and sometimes margins, fetid smelling, tube 3–6(–8) mm long, tepals 6–12 mm long, filaments 3–5 mm long, anthers 0.8–1.5 mm long. Flowering August–October. Sandy slopes, RV, NW, SW, KM, LB, SE (western Karoo and Clanwilliam to Port Elizabeth).

Xenoscapa

COMMON NAME fairy pipes, FAMILY Iridaceae. Dwarf deciduous perennial. ROOTSTOCK a small globose corm rooting from below, basal in origin, tunics of fine fibers. LEAVES few, lower two or three forming cataphylls, foliage leaves two or three, unifacial, with a definite midrib, prostrate, soft textured; stem short or long, erect, terete, often with one to three short branches. INFLORESCENCE with flowers solitary on the main axis and on each branch; bracts green, leathery, inner often slightly longer, or slightly shorter than outer, often notched apically. FLOWERS zygomorphic, tubular, whitish or pink, sometimes with contrasting markings on lower tepals, sometimes sweetly scented; perianth tube cylindrical and elongate; tepals subequal, spreading or the dorsal erect, slightly larger, and cucullate. STAMENS unilateral and arcuate. STYLE filiform, the branches short, deeply divided and recurved. FRUIT an oblong to cylindrical, cartilaginous capsule. SEEDS angular, with a chalazal crest, the surface rough. Basic chromosome number $x = 11$. Winter-rainfall southern Africa; 2 spp., 1 in the Cape.

Xenoscapa comprises one widespread species of the winter-rainfall region, extending from southwestern Namibia and Namaqualand to the Little Karoo, and a local endemic of central Namaqualand. The relationships of the genus are uncertain. *Xenoscapa uliginosa* Goldblatt

Wurmbea variabilis

Xenoscapa fistulosa

& J. C. Manning, the Namaqualand endemic, has flowers adapted for pollination by the long-proboscid fly *Prosoeca peringueyi* (Nemestrinidae), whereas we infer moth pollination for *X. fistulosa*, which has whitish,fragrant flowers with a relatively long perianth tube.

The tiny-flowered *Xenoscapa fistulosa* is so small that it must be grown as a pot plant. Plants have two leaves to 2.5 cm long, spreading horizontally, and an erect, branched stem. The corms, the size of a small pea, lie just below the surface or, indeed, right on the surface when plants grow on rock. In the wild, plants grow in sheltered sites, under shrubs and on cooler, wetter south-facing slopes.

FURTHER READING. Initially included in the genus *Anomatheca* by Goldblatt (1972b), *Xenoscapa fistulosa* was later transferred to its own genus along with a newly discovered species, *X. uliginosa* of Namaqualand, by Goldblatt and Manning (1995c).

Xenoscapa fistulosa (Sprengel ex Klatt) Goldblatt & J. C. Manning

Plants 3–20 cm high, usually with one or two branches. Leaves ovate, prostrate, soft textured. Flowers solitary on the main axis and on each branch, small, white, fragrant, perianth tube 15–30 mm long, tepals unequal, the dorsal largest, boat-shaped, c. 7 mm long. Flowering August–October. Damp clay soil, rarely on granite, often in shady places, RV, NW, SW, KM (southern Namibia to Cape Peninsula and Little Karoo).

Zantedeschia

COMMON NAMES arum lily, calla lily, pig lily, FAMILY Araceae. Deciduous or evergreen perennials. ROOTSTOCK a fleshy rhizome. LEAVES several, petiolate, the petioles long, spongy, sometimes mottled with purple below, shortly clasping to form a short neck, the blades narrowly elliptical to lanceolate or sagittate, sometimes spotted with white. INFLORESCENCE a spike on a stout, naked peduncle surmounted by a large, petaloid spathe enclosing the flowers, the spathe white to pink or yellow, sometimes black or purple at the base within. FLOWERS minute, unisexual, crowded on a slender spike-like spadix, the upper male, the lower female, without a perianth, usually unscented. STAMENS sessile. OVARY subglobose with one to eight ovules per locule; STYLE short. FRUIT a fleshy berry, green or orange when ripe. SEEDS one to few per locule, subglobose or ovoid, leathery, grayish. Basic chromosome number $x = 7$, possibly. Southern Africa; 8 spp., 2 in the Cape.

The small, southern temperate African genus *Zantedeschia* contains some of the most attractive species in the large, predominantly tropical family Araceae. Most species are deciduous and die back over the dry season, but *Z. aethiopica* will remain green throughout the year as long as some moisture remains. The long-lasting, elegant inflorescences are sought as cut flowers. Several brilliantly colored forms of the eastern southern African species have been developed in the Netherlands. Popularly but inappropriately known as arums on account of their resemblance to the European genus *Arum*, they lack the offensive odors typical of that genus; only *Z. odorata* from Nieuwoudtville has more than a faint fragrance. The rhizomes, although highly unpalatable to humans, are relished by porcupines, and *Z. aethiopica* is known locally as the pig lily in allusion to this, porcupines rejoicing in the highly descriptive Afrikaans name, *ystervark*, iron pig. *Zantedeschia* is probably pollinated by a variety of small insects.

Much prized as a cut flower on account of its elegance and longevity, *Zantedeschia aethiopica* is a common plant of ditches and damp places in the Western Cape. One of the first introductions into Europe from the Cape, the species was in cultivation in the Jardin des Plantes, Paris, by 1644. The species was among many bulbous plants sent to Holland by the governor of the Cape of Good Hope, Simon van der Stel, in the late 17th century. Described as the *Morelandse kalfsvoet* (calf's foot from the land of the Moors) because of their appearance, the rhizomes are rich in needle-like calcium oxalate crystals, which irritate and inflame the mouth if eaten. Cooking neutralizes this effect, and boiled rhizomes, mixed with honey or syrup, were traditionally taken in the Cape for ailments of the throat. At least some early settlers at the Cape, however, are known to have served unsuspecting newcomers the fresh rhizomes of *Z. aethiopica* as edible roots, much like radish, in rude anticipation of the burning and inflammation to follow. This stately species has become prized as a cut flower in Europe and North America as its earlier association with funerals has faded. Large bunches of the flowering spikes are still sold in the streets of Cape Town by local flower-pickers in the spring, and the species is easily grown in gardens or pots. The dark, arrow-shaped leaves are almost as elegant as the flower spikes. Plants thrive in shade as well as sun. They tolerate water throughout the year and are thus particularly useful in gardens.

FURTHER READING. The revision of *Zantedeschia* by Letty (1973) is sumptuously illustrated but should be augmented by the subsequent publications by Perry (1989) and Singh et al. (1995), which detail new discoveries.

Zantedeschia aethiopica (Linnaeus) Sprengel

Plants 60–100 cm high, more or less evergreen. Leaves ar-

Zantedeschia odorata

Zantedeschia aethiopica; see also page 32

row-shaped on long, spongy petioles. Flowers minute, faintly scented, spadix 50–75 × 5–7 mm, surrounded by a large, white, funnel-shaped spathe. Berries soft and orange when ripe, peduncle erect in fruit. Flowering June–December. Sandy or rocky places, usually seasonally damp, NW, SW, AP, LB, SE (Richtersveld, Kamiesberg, and Bokkeveld Mountains to Northern Province).

Zantedeschia odorata P.L. Perry

Plants to 75 cm high, deciduous. Leaves arrow-shaped on long, spongy petioles. Flowers minute, strongly freesia scented, spadix 25–35 × 5–10 mm, surrounded by a large, white, weakly flaring spathe. Berries firm and green when ripe, peduncle recurved in fruit. Flowering July–August. Dolerite outcrops, seasonally moist, RV (Bokkeveld Plateau near Nieuwoudtville).

KEYS TO SPECIES

About three-quarters of the 79 genera included in *The Color Encyclopedia of Cape Bulbs* include descriptions of more than one species, and the species may be identified by using the following keys.

Agapanthus

1 Flowers nodding, tubular, the tepals cohering .... *A. walshii*
1' Flowers spreading, broadly funnel-shaped, the tepals spreading 2
2 Smaller plants, mostly to 50 cm high; flowers deep blue, thick in texture; stamens shorter than the tepals .... *A. africanus*
2' Larger plants, mostly more than 80 cm high; flowers paler blue, thin in texture; stamens mostly as long as the tepals .... *A. praecox*

Albuca

Subgenera of *Albuca*

1 Inner tepals with a hinged fleshy flap at the tips; flowers always nodding; outer anthers lacking .... subgenus *Albuca*
1' Inner tepals more or less cupped or hooded at the tips but not hinged; outer anthers well developed, reduced or lacking 2
2 Inner tepals with the tips not developed into a fleshy knob above the concave tip; flowers erect or nodding .... subgenus *Falconera*
2' Inner tepals with the tips developed into a fleshy knob above the concave tip which is often bright yellow; flowers erect .... subgenus *Mitropetalum*

Albuca Subgenus *Albuca*

1 Leaves hairy or glandular hairy, at least on the margins and often twisted or coiled 2
1' Leaves hairless, never twisted or coiled 6
2 Leaves oblong, flat or twisted, margins minutely hairy 3
2' Leaves semiterete, often coiled at the tips, hairy or glandular hairy on the lower surface 4
3 Leaves several, not clasping, narrowly oblong, often corkscrew twisted .... *A. ciliaris*
3' Leaves few, clasping below, oblong but cupped and boat-shaped at the tips .... *A. navicula*
4 Hairs eglandular .... *A. namaquensis*
4' Hairs glandular 5
5 Leaves relatively short and obtuse with more or less sessile glands; peduncle smooth .... *A. hallii*
5' Leaves tapering and slender with stalked glands; peduncle glandular hairy .... *A. spiralis*
6 Flowers white and green; outer, sterile filaments oblanceolate; large plants with fruits on long, spreading pedicels abruptly curved upward and erect at the tips .... *A. maxima*
6' Flowers yellowish and green 7
7 Bulb scales more or less fibrous above 8
7' Bulb scales not fibrous above 10
8 Leaf sheaths distinctly warty basally .... *A. cooperi*
8' Leaf sheaths smooth 9
9 Flowers larger, 1.5–2 cm long; style about as long as the ovary .... *A. acuminata*
9' Flowers small, to 1 cm long; style about half as long as the ovary .... *A. massonii*
10 Leaves not clasping below, usually terete above; racemes nodding in bud .... *A. juncifolia*
10' Leaves more or less clasping below, longitudinally rolled throughout; racemes erect 11
11 Bulb flattened and fragmenting into wedges ...... *A. paradoxa*
11' Bulb subglobose and not segmented 12
12 Plants slender with 1–3 leaves; seeds sharply papillate .... *A. echinosperma*
12' Plants more robust with several leaves; seeds smooth .... *A. flaccida*

Albuca Subgenus *Falconera*

1 Flowers erect; outer stamens sterile .... *A. decipiens*
1' Flowers nodding 2
2 Leaves and peduncle base glandular hairy 3
2' Leaves and peduncle hairless 4
3 Leaves few, clasping below; peduncle glandular hairy throughout; outer stamens sterile .... *A. foetida*
3' Leaves several, not clasping below; peduncle smooth above; outer stamens fertile; bulb often pinkish .... *A. viscosa*
4 Outer stamens sterile, the anthers lacking .... *A. goswinii*
4' Outer stamens fertile, the anthers usually reduced but present 5
5 Leaves clasping below with papery to fibrous, often warty sheaths; ovary with diverging septal ridges; style triquetrous with cells approximately isodiametric .... *A. papyracea*
5' Leaves scarcely clasping below, withered at flowering; septal ridges not diverging; style terete with cells fusiform 6
6 Stout plants to 2 m with the leaves withered at flowering; racemes erect in bud; flowers 25–35 mm long, mostly yellow, outer tepals scarcely flaring, not scented; style twice as long as the ovary .... *A. clanwilliamigloria*
6' Smaller plants; racemes nodding in bud; flowers 15–25 mm long with conspicuous green keels, outer tepals flaring, scented; style 1.5 times as long as the ovary .... *A. fragrans*

Albuca Subgenus *Mitropetalum*

1 Plants glandular hairy; outer stamens sterile ..... *A. glandulosa*
1' Plants hairless; outer stamens fertile 2
2 Bulb usually above ground, the scales appearing to overlap partially like roof tiles, firm, green, abruptly truncate 3
2' Bulb more or less underground, the scales not as above 4
3 Bulb scales lightly fibrous above; flowers 25–40 mm long, the outer tepals spreading or recurved; large, clump-forming plants with inclined racemes .... *A. batteniana*
3' Bulb scales not fibrous above; flowers 10–20 mm long, the outer tepals suberect; solitary plants with long, drooping racemes .... *A. cremnophila*
4 Bulb scales coarsely fibrous above 5
4' Bulb scales not fibrous 6
5 Fibrous neck without woody rings; leaf margins transparent and often minutely hairy .... *A. setosa*
5' Fibrous neck with woody rings; leaf margins not transparent or hairy .... *A. exuviata*
6 Leaves flat, oblong, with transparent margins ... *A. schoenlandii*
6' Leaves channeled, tapering, without transparent margins 7
7 Leaves clasping below, green at flowering; raceme inclined, often subsecund; bulb scales often bluish .... *A. aurea*
7' Leaves not clasping below, withered at flowering; inflorescence never subsecund .... *A. longipes*

Androcymbium

1 Tepals flat, not eared or cupped above the claws, the blades ovate-acuminate; leaves and subtending bracts similar, linear-attenuate, the flowers exposed; filaments very short, 0.5–1 mm long with a cushion-like swelling at the base .... *A. dregei*
1' Tepals eared and cupped above the claw; filaments longer, 4–12 mm 2
2 Bracts grading gradually into the leaves, like the leaves in shape, color, and margins 3
2' Bracts more or less abruptly differentiated from the leaves, differing in shape and often color, the margins and keel usually ciliolate 6
3 Leaves in 3 ranks, often conspicuously striate; bracts smaller than the flowers, spreading and exposing them 4
3' Leaves in 2 ranks; bracts larger than the flowers, erect and concealing them 5
4 Leaves ovate-lanceolate, acute .... *A. cuspidatum*
4' Leaves lanceolate-attenuate, aristate .... *A. hughocymbion*
5 Tepal claws longer than the blades, 10–35 mm long .... *A. longipes*
5' Tepal claws about as long as the blades, 5–8 mm long .... *A. eucomoides*
6 Stamens much longer than the tepal blades, conspicuously exserted 7
6' Stamens about as long as the tepal blades or shorter, rarely slightly longer 9
7 Leaves narrowly lanceolate, the margins crisped and bristly .... *A. crispum*
7' Leaves ovate-lanceolate, the margins not crisped, rarely ciliolate 8
8 Bracts mostly white or with green tips .... *A. burchellii*
8' Bracts wine red with green bases .... *A. latifolium*
9 Bracts white or cream, conspicuously longitudinally striped with green; plants usually with a well-developed stem 10
9' Bracts white or green but not conspicuously longitudinally striped with green; plants stemless 11
10 Tepal blades deeply cupped or almost tubular below, abruptly tapering above, shorter than the filaments; filaments 8–10 mm long .... *A. melanthioides*
10' Tepal blades channeled and eared below but not deeply cupped, linear channeled above, longer than the filaments; filaments 4–5 mm long .... *A. orienticapense*
11 Leaves linear-lanceolate, often coiled at the tips, more or less erect; filaments slightly longer than the tepal blades .... *A. volutare*
11' Leaves lanceolate, spreading or prostrate; filaments shorter than the tepal blades 12

12 Bracts ovate, acute to apiculate, whitish or green above and white below; tepal blades attenuate, more or less deeply cupped or tubular below; leaves often ciliolate ..... *A. capense*

12′ Bracts oblong, obtuse, green above flushed red below; tepal blades narrowly oblong, conspicuously eared below; leaves never ciliolate .... *A.* sp. 1

Apodolirion

1 Leaf single, spreading to prostrate, usually more than 4 mm wide .... *A. lanceolatum*

1′ Leaves 2 or more, recurved to suberect, usually less than 4 mm wide 2

2 Leaves straight, margins smooth; tepals 4–6 mm wide .... *A. cedarbergense*

2′ Leaves twisted, margins papillate; tepals 8–10 mm wide .... *A. macowanii*

Aristea

Subgenera of *Aristea*

1 Capsules ovoid to oblong or cylindrical, sometimes prominently 3-lobed .... subgenus *Eucapsulares*

1′ Capsules with 3 narrow wings .... subgenus *Aristea*

Aristea Subgenus *Aristea*

1 Plants mostly small, mostly less than 25 cm high; style 3-lobed apically and fringed; stems dichotomously branched, rarely unbranched (section Aristea) 2

1′ Plants mostly large, mostly more than 40 cm, often exceeding 1 m high; style minutely 3-notched to minutely 3-lobed; stem variously branched but seldom dichotomously, or simple with lateral flower clusters sessile (section Racemosae) 8

2 Spathes and bracts regularly fringed 3

2′ Spathes and bracts unbroken or irregularly torn 4

3 Bracts and spathes fringed more than half their length, the lacerate part usually uniformly colored .... *A. africana*

3′ Bracts and spathes fringed less than a third their length, the tips usually rust colored .... *A. recisa*

4 Flowering stems and flowers nodding .... *A. singularis*

4′ Flowering stems and flowers erect 5

5 Spathes and bracts with a broad green to brown keel and margins membranous and translucent; plants mostly forming cushions and never more than 30 cm high 6

5′ Spathes and bracts silvery translucent entirely or with a narrow dark keel; plants not forming large cushions and usually at least 20 cm high 7

6 Plants forming small cushions; stems dichotomously branched repeatedly, weakly 2-angled below the flower clusters .... *A. dichotoma*

6′ Plants not normally forming cushions; stems simple or single- to few-branched, 2-winged below the flower clusters ... . *A. glauca*

7 Plants 15–30 cm high; bracts with fairly broad, green keels, folded in the midline; leaves mostly 2–3 mm wide, firm to rigid .... *A. oligocephala*

7′ Plants 50–100 cm high; bracts narrow with dark keels, not folded in the midline; leaves mostly 4–9 mm wide and relatively soft textured .... *A. palustris*

8 Leaves round to elliptical in cross section, 1–3 mm wide, without distinct margins; capsules oblong in outline, at least twice as long as wide 9

8′ Leaves more or less plane or slightly elliptical in cross section, the larger basal leaves at least 3 mm wide, usually 4–15(–25) mm wide, with visible margins often sharply angled and translucent; capsules broadly ovate to oblong, about as long to more than twice as long as wide 12

9 Leaves elliptical in cross section, sometimes almost plane, usually 2–5 mm diam., occasionally less 10

9′ Leaves round to elliptical in cross section and less than 2 mm diam. at the widest; binate rhipidia either not sub-tended by a prominent bract, or if bract present usually dry and not keeled above but lightly folded in the midline below 11

10 Plants mostly 40–60 cm high; flower clusters subtended by a prominent green bract, this keeled above and often folded in the midline below, and at least the lower subtending bracts exceeding the spathes and floral bracts .... *A. juncifolia*

10′ Plants robust, usually 80–130 cm high; bracts subtending the flower clusters and branches of the compound inflorescence narrowly lanceolate .... *A. rigidifolia*

11 Plants robust or short and slender, sometimes growing in clumps; the lower flower clusters sometimes subtended by large, evidently dry bracts; flower clusters (1–)3–8, the lateral all (or mostly) sessile; spathes and floral bracts rust colored with narrow to broad transparent margins, 10–15 mm long; capsules mostly 10–14 mm long .... *A. racemosa*

11′ Plants slender, solitary; flower cluster usually 1, occasionally 2, the lateral sessile; spathes and floral bracts green, drying blackish, with narrow transparent margins, 15–24 mm long; capsules 18–25(–30) mm long .... *A. zeyheri*

12 Spathes and floral bracts broadly ovate or obovate and lightly hispid 13

12′ Spathes and floral bracts either lanceolate and acute to acuminate or ovate but always smooth 15

13 Plants 20-40 cm high; lower leaves 2-3 mm wide; flowering stems dichotomously branched and all flower clusters stalked .... *A. rupicola*
13' Plants taller, (50-)80-150 cm high; lower leaves (3-)4-12 mm wide; flowering stems branched in racemose pattern and flower clusters at the upper stem usually sessile 14
14 Lower leaves (8-)12-25 mm wide; capsules 20-30 mm long .... *A. bakeri*
14' Lower leaves (3-)4-6 mm wide; capsules 7-10 mm long .... *A. bracteata*
15 Spathes and floral bracts lanceolate and acuminate, dark green to brown in the center with wide transparent margins; capsules 8-12 mm long, slightly longer to almost twice as long as wide; inflorescence mostly secund 16
15' Spathes and floral bracts lanceolate and acute to ovate, with or without fringed margins; capsules 14-20 mm long, at least twice to about 3 times as long as wide; inflorescence not normally secund, flowers usually upright 17
16 Inflorescence a congested cylindrical compound panicle, the flower clusters overlapping and largely or completely concealing the main axis; stamens equal .... *A. capitata*
16' Inflorescence a lax panicle the lower branches long and diverging, the flower clusters widely spaced along the branches; stamens unequal, the lower (anterior) filament c. 2 mm longer than the upper two .... *A. inaequalis*
17 Leaves 8-20 mm wide .... *A. bakeri*
17' Leaves 3-6 mm wide 18
18 Spathe and floral bract margins fringed and the margins rust brown; stem compressed and 2-winged; plants small, seldom exceeding 28 cm .... *A. fimbriata*
18' Spathe and floral bract margins entire or irregularly lacerate (usually so with age); stems more or less terete to lightly compressed; plants large, mostly 35-60 cm .... *A.* sp. 1

Aristea Subgenus *Eucapsulares*

1 Stems unbranched, sometimes with sessile lateral inflorescences 2
1' Stems usually branched, if unbranched then broadly 2-winged and leafless except for a short leaf immediately below the flower clusters 9
2 Perianth uniformly dark blue; tepals subequal 3
2' Perianth pale blue, white, or lilac, often with contrasting markings on the tepals, or the inner tepals differing from the outer 4
3 Plants growing in tufts, leaves linear, mostly 2-4 mm wide; ovary sharply 3-angled .... *A. pauciflora*
3' Plants not markedly tufted, leaves linear to sword-shaped, mostly more than 3 mm wide; ovary 3-lobed .... *A. pusilla*
4 Stems broadly winged above the first flower cluster, or uppermost leaf if lateral flower clusters lacking; filaments mostly longer than the anthers and 14-18 mm long, rarely only 8-10 mm long; flowers facing to the side .... *A. spiralis*
4' Stems not broadly winged above the first flower cluster or uppermost leaf; filaments short, as long as or not much longer than the anthers, 3-6.5 mm long; flowers either facing to the side or upright 5
5 Outer tepals about the same size or slightly smaller than the inner and similarly colored 6
5' Outer tepals differentiated from the inner, smaller, and each either with a dark basal or distal marking or with a pair of large transparent windows in the lower half 7
6 Tepals cream or lilac to light mauve but dark purple or greenish black at the base, the center of the flower thus with a dark central eye .... *A. cantharophila*
6' Tepals pale to deep blue, paler in the center; flowers facing sideways .... *A. simplex*
7 Outer tepals brownish black or blue-black in the upper halves and nearly symmetric about the midline; inner tepals about twice as long as the outer .... *A. lugens*
7' Outer tepals the same color as the inner tepals in the upper halves and asymmetric about the midline; inner tepals slightly longer than the outer, not twice as long 8
8 Outer tepals each with a large, dark bronze-brown mark near the base; leaves terete or linear, c. 1 mm diam. .... *A. teretifolia*
8' Outer tepals not darkly colored below but each with paired translucent windows of membranous tissue above the base; leaves linear, (2-)3-5.5 mm wide .... *A. biflora*
9 Stem broadly 2-winged; leaves basal or one inserted at the stem apex; stem consisting of one long internode with 1-2 closely set flower clusters 10
9' Stem rounded to lightly compressed or sometimes weakly angled to winged, leaves basal and inserted along the stem 11
10 Capsules ovoid; bracts green or dry and grayish .... *A. abyssinica*
10' Capsules cylindrical; bracts rusty brown .... *A. anceps*
11 Capsules cylindrical and fairly deeply 3-lobed 12
11' Capsules ovoid, shallowly or not at all 3-lobed 13
12 Capsules (10-)12-20 mm long, dehiscent .... *A. ecklonii*
12' Capsules 35-50 mm long, indehiscent, decaying on the plant to release the seeds .... *A. ensifolia*
13 Flowering stems repeatedly branched, flower clusters stalked, subtended by green or dry, translucent spathes and bracts; leaves 15-25 mm wide, coarsely fibrotic .... *A. latifolia*
13' Flowering stems simple or 1- or 2-branched, flower clusters mostly sessile, subtended by dry, rust-colored spathes and bracts; leaves 5-9 mm wide, not noticeably fibrotic .... *A. schizolaena*

Babiana

Groups of Babiana

1 Inner bracts divided half their length or less 2
1' Inner bracts divided more than three-quarters their length 5
2 Flowers red, the upper tepal 2–3 times as long as the lower, filaments 35–60 mm long . . . . *Ringens* group
2' Flowers blue to mauve or yellowish, the upper tepal at most slightly longer than the lower, filaments 6–20 mm long 3
3 Bracts 8–10 mm long; tepals clawed, the upper arched, often curving backward with age, and the lower united at the base . . . . *Sinuata* group
3' Bracts 13–50 mm long; tepals rarely clawed, the upper weakly or not arched and the lower free or united at the base 4
4 Perianth tube longer than the upper tepals, 35–85 mm long, the lower tepals free to the base; flowers mauve to purple with white or red markings . . . . *Sambucina* group
4' Perianth tube usually shorter than the upper tepals, 12–35 (–50) mm long, if longer then the lower tepals shortly joined and the flowers yellow or mauve with yellow markings . . . . *Nana* group
5 Bracts and inner bracts wholly papery, brown or pale with brown flecks . . . . *Scariosa* group
5' Bracts and inner bracts partly or entirely green, rarely brown but then not papery 6
6 Flowers strictly actinomorphic with the stamens symmetrically arranged in the center of the flower and the anthers yellow or mauve . . . . *Villosula* group
6' Flowers actinomorphic or weakly to strongly zygomorphic with the stamens arcuate or symmetrically arranged in the center of the flowers but then the anthers purple to black . . . *Disticha* group

Babiana Group Disticha

1 Tepals equal or subequal, the dorsal at most slightly longer than and not widely separated from the upper lateral tepals, the lower three tepals not joined together at the base; anthers often purple to black 2
1' Tepals unequal, the dorsal mostly longer than and well-separated from the upper lateral tepals, the lower three tepals usually joined together at the base and the flowers thus distinctly two-lipped; anthers yellow to mauve 10
2 Perianth perfectly actinomorphic with all tepals either unmarked or similarly marked 3
2' Perianth slightly zygomorphic with only the lower 3 tepals marked 6
3 Flowers bicolored, deep blue with a red cup 4
3' Flowers uniformly colored 5
4 Stamens slightly arched and facing the stem apex; style branching opposite the middle of the anthers, the stigmas broad and glossy . . . . *B. rubrocyanea*
4' Stamens erect and symmetrical; style branching below the anthers, the stigmas slender . . . . *B. regia*
5 Stems arched above; flowers dark red to purplish red; tepals ovate . . . . *B. villosa*
5' Stems erect; flowers blue to pink; tepals narrowed and clawed below . . . . *B. melanops*
6 Stems strongly inclined and decurved at the tips in bud, inflorescence subsecund and the flowers inverted to face the stem apex, dark blue or violet; perianth tube filiform, 11–20 mm long . . . . *B. angustifolia*
6' Stems erect, inflorescence not subsecund nor the flowers inverted, mauve or purple; perianth tube slender but not filiform 7
7 Leaves lanceolate, soft textured; inflorescence usually branched, the flowers not crowded at the stem apex . . . . *B. disticha*
7' Leaves linear-lanceolate, firm textured; inflorescence usually unbranched, the flowers crowded at the stem apex 8
8 Perianth tube shorter to as long as the tepals, 10–16 mm long . . . . *B. stricta*
8' Perianth tube longer than the tepals, 18–28 mm long 9
9 Flowers purplish pink; anthers arrow-shaped with broadened connective, 2–4 mm wide; stigmas usually exceeding the anthers . . . . *B. purpurea*
9' Flowers white to mauve or blue; anthers narrowly oblong; stigmas shorter than the anthers . . . . *B. patersoniae*
10 Ovary densely hairy or silky 11
10' Ovary hairless or thinly hairy, sometimes only on the ribs 16
11 Perianth tube much longer than the tepals, 35–45 mm long; flowers purple with white markings . . . . *B. ecklonii*
11' Perianth tube shorter than the tepals or much longer; flowers yellow or mauve with yellow markings 12
12 Bracts and flowers small, the bracts to 10 mm long and the flowers usually 25–30 mm long . . . . *B. lineolata*
12' Bracts and flowers larger than above, the bracts rarely less than 15 mm long and the flowers 35 mm long or more 13
13 Leaf margins slightly thickened and raised . . . . . . *B. klaverensis*
13' Leaf margins not thickened and raised 14
14 Flowers blue to mauve with yellow markings on the lower tepals, weakly scented; perianth tube 15–25 mm long . . . . *B. mucronata*
14' Flowers pale yellow, rarely light mauve, the lower tepals deep yellow, highly fragrant 15
15 Perianth tube 10–14(–15) mm long . . . . *B. odorata*
15' Perianth tube 32–38 mm long . . . . *B. noctiflora*
16 Bracts tricuspidate with the central cusp attenuate, mostly more or less lacerated at flowering; flowers twisted to face the stem apex; anthers yellow . . . . *B. secunda*
16' Bracts not tricuspidate nor lacerate at flowering; flowers not twisted; anthers lilac or mauve 17

17 Perianth tube longer than the tepals . . . . *B. fourcadei*
17′ Perianth tube shorter than the tepals 18
18 Corm tunics of netted fibers, the neck thin and sparse or lacking 19
18′ Corm tunics of more or less matted fibers not obviously netted, the neck well developed and enclosing the stem below ground 20
19 Leaf blade arising very obliquely, not pleated . . . . *B. obliqua*
19′ Leaf blade not arising very obliquely, usually pleated . . . . *B. ambigua*
20 Stamens unequal in length, filaments 7–10 mm long; stigmas large, flattened spherical; bracts with conspicuous rusty tips . . . . *B. montana*
20′ Stamens equal, filaments 12–18 mm long; stigmas small, spathulate and the margins folded together; bracts with or without rusty tips 21
21 Bracts bifid or irregularly lacerate and usually rusty at the tips; inner tepals widest at or near the apices; juvenile leaves not curled at the apices . . . . *B. patula*
21′ Bracts acute and not noticeably rusty at the tips; inner tepals widest near the middle; juvenile leaves curling at the tips . . . . *B. scabrifolia*

Babiana Group *Nana*

1 Flowers actinomorphic, yellow or creamy yellow with a purplish center; stamens erect, symmetrically arranged; tepals obovate, 30–50 mm long . . . . *B. pygmaea*
1′ Flowers zygomorphic, mauve to blue; stamens arched, unilateral; tepals lanceolate 2
2 Perianth tube 25–50 mm long 3
2′ Perianth tube 12–25 mm long 4
3 Leaves oblong-lanceolate, subacute, soft textured, and weakly pleated; flowers violet, the lower tepals yellow and distinctly marked . . . . *B. pauciflora*
3′ Leaves linear-lanceolate, acute, firm textured, and distinctly pleated; flowers yellow or flushed lilac, not distinctly marked . . . . *B. vanzyliae*
4 Leaves conspicuously undulate or crisped . . . . *B. crispa*
4′ Leaves at most slightly undulate 5
5 Lower lateral tepals distinctly eared near the base . . . . *B. auriculata*
5′ Lower tepals not eared 6
6 Leaves very firm, closely pleated and somewhat pungent, velvety . . . . *B. cedarbergensis*
6′ Leaves softer, weakly pleated, softly hairy 7
7 Corm tunics not forming a neck or rarely with a short and sparse neck that does not enclose the whole stem below ground; leaves usually short, obliquely ovate to oblong-lanceolate; perianth tube 12–17 mm long; lower tepals free . . . . *B. nana*

7′ Corm tunics forming a well-developed neck enclosing the stem below ground; leaves lanceolate; perianth tube 20–22 mm long; lower tepals united below . . . . *B. minuta*

Babiana Group *Ringens*

1 Upper tepal 25–50 mm long, tubular below; main axis of the spike sterile, the flowers restricted to a single side branch near the ground; leaves hairless . . . . *B. ringens*
1′ Upper tepal 15–20 mm long, not tubular below; main axis fertile with several side branches borne well above the ground; leaves finely velvety . . . . *B. thunbergii*

Babiana Group *Sambucina*

1 Ovary hairy or silky; style branches 11–13 mm long; stamens slightly spreading . . . . *B. geniculata*
1′ Ovary hairless or minutely hairy on the ribs only; style branches 4–5 mm long; stamens parallel 2
2 Leaves more or less truncate with the apex uneven or toothed . . . 3
2′ Leaves acute 4
3 Perianth tube funnel-shaped, widening toward the throat, filaments c. 15 mm long, arcuate, well exserted from the tube . . . . *B. cuneifolia*
3′ Perianth tube cylindrical throughout, filaments c. 7 mm long, erect, shortly exserted from the tube . . . . *B. flabellifolia*
4 Flowers white or cream to pinkish with small red markings on the lower tepals; perianth tube often more than twice as long as the lobes; tepals somewhat clawed below . . . . *B. tubulosa*
4′ Flowers blue to violet or white but then without red markings; perianth tube to about twice as long as the lobes; tepals not clawed 5
5 Perianth tube narrowly cylindrical to the top with a slight curve shortly below the throat and slightly widened from there up, usually about twice as long as the lobes; flowers unscented . . . . *B. framesii*
5′ Perianth tube evenly and slightly widened from base to throat, straight, usually less than twice as long as the lobes; flowers scented 6
6 Flowers lilac to violet; perianth tube 35–50 mm . . . *B. sambucina*
6′ Flowers white or rarely with a faint lilac tinge; perianth tube 60–65 mm . . . . *B. virginea*

Babiana Group *Scariosa*

1 Plants stemless, the flowers clustered at ground level; flowers actinomorphic, deep blue; perianth tube filiform . . . *B. papyracea*
1′ Plants with well-developed stems; flowers zygomorphic, mauve to cream; perianth tube cylindrical or funnel-shaped 2
2 Perianth tube shorter than the tepals, c. 20 mm long; flowers mauve with yellow lower tepals . . . . *B. scariosa*
2′ Perianth tube longer than the tepals, 35–45 mm long; flowers cream or lilac with red markings . . . . *B. spathacea*

Babiana Group *Sinuata*

1 Flowers yellow; bracts 6-8 mm long; ovary hairy; leaves not distinctly coiled or undulate . . . . *B. unguiculata*
1' Flowers blue; bracts 8-10 mm long; ovary hairless; leaves distinctly coiled or undulate 2
2 Anthers cohering; leaves undulate and twisted . . . . *B. sinuata*
2' Anthers free; leaves coiled above . . . . *B. fimbriata*

Babiana Group *Villosula*

1 Bracts entirely green . . . . *B. foliosa*
1' Bracts brown and scarious at the apices 2
2 Filaments 8-10 mm long, the anthers well exserted from the perianth tube; pollen cream; flowers with a darker center . . . . *B. leipoldtii*
2' Filaments 5-8 mm long, the anthers incompletely exserted from the perianth tube; pollen mauve; flowers concolorous or with a white center 3
3 Flowers mauve to white; tepals oblong to obovate, 6-13 mm wide; style dividing opposite the anthers . . . . *B. villosula*
3' Flowers rosy pink; tepals obovate to rounded, 14-20 mm wide; style dividing below the anthers . . . . *B. blanda*

Bobartia

1 Leaves plane or elliptical in cross section 2
1' Leaves round in cross section 5
2 Individual flower clusters solitary at branch tips; nodes sticky 3
2' Individual flower clusters solitary to many in a flattened compound head; nodes not sticky 4
3 Flowers blue to mauve; individual flower clusters in an open panicle . . . . *B. lilacina*
3' Flowers yellow; individual flower clusters in a panicle at the end of the flowering stalk . . . . *B. paniculata*
4 Stem flattened or subterete; flower clusters more than 5 . . . . *B. gladiata*
4' Stem rounded; flower clusters mostly 1-3 . . . . *B. filiformis*
5 Flower clusters enclosed by dry, fibrotic, brown or gray spathes 6
5' Flower clusters enclosed by firm, green (to purplish) spathes 10
6 Plants to 40 cm high; flowers clusters 3-7 per stalk . . . *B. parva*
6' Plants more than 50 cm high; flowers clusters more than 12 . . . 7
7 Ovary and capsules distinctly warty . . . . *B. robusta*
7' Ovary and capsules smooth or lightly warty 8
8 Flowers with a short perianth tube . . . . *B. macrospatha*
8' Flowers with the tepals free to the base 9
9 Flowers clusters in distinct fascicles within a loose head; bracts straw colored . . . . *B. fasciculata*
9' Flowers clusters not grouped in distinct fascicles within the head; bracts brownish red . . . . *B. rufa*

10 Ovary and capsules distinctly warty . . . . *B. aphylla*
10' Ovary and capsules smooth or rarely slightly roughened 11
11 Leaves much longer than the stem, flexible and trailing above . . . . *B. indica*
11' Leaves about as long as the stem, more or less straight and erect 12
12 Capsules globose with conspicuous valves . . . . *B. orientalis*
12' Capsules ovoid to obovoid 13
13 Flower clusters in a small head borne on a short stalk above the subtending leaf; capsules obovoid to oblong . . . . *B. macrocarpa*
13' Flower clusters in a small head borne immediately above the subtending leaf; capsules ovoid . . . . *B. longicyma*

Boophone

1 Tepals pink to red, distinctly recurved; spathe bracts becoming reflexed before the flowers open fully . . . . *B. disticha*
1' Tepals cream to lemon colored, tinged with pink in older flowers, erect to slightly spreading; spathe bracts usually remaining upright when the flowers open fully . . . . *B. haemanthoides*

Brunsvigia

1 Flowers pink or red; tepals widely flared from the base; pedicels straight during flowering 2
1' Flowers red; tepals closely overlapping, rolling back strongly from the apex, the 3 upper more so than the 3 lower; pedicels curved near the ovary during flowering 7
2 Flowers more or less actinomorphic; stamens and style central, nearly straight 3
2' Flowers zygomorphic; stamens and style deflexed downward, upturned toward the tips 4
3 Flowers usually brilliant red; perianth tube 5-10 mm long; stamens 30-45 mm long . . . . *B. marginata*
3' Flowers usually bright pink; perianth tube 2-5 mm long; stamens 10-16 mm long . . . . *B. elandsmontana*
4 Tepals oblong, more or less free to the base, not joined into a distinct perianth tube; stamens arranged in a loose cluster in 2 whorls of different lengths 5
4' Tepals tapering in the lower third, joined into a perianth tube at least 2 mm long; stamens approximately equal, arranged in a tight cluster 6
5 Leaves at most 4 cm wide; flowers fewer than 20; pedicels shorter than 2.5 cm; at least 5 tepals flared upward; capsule small, rounded, soft, ribs inconspicuous . . . . *B. comptonii*
5' Leaves more than 5 cm wide; flowers usually many more than 20; pedicels longer than 3 cm; all tepals more or less evenly spreading; capsule 3-angled, the angles strongly ribbed . . . . *B. bosmaniae*

6 Flowers fewer than 30; capsules rounded at the apex, softly papery, lightly ribbed .... *B. striata*
6' Flowers mostly more than 30; capsules indented at the apex, walls papery with conspicuously thickened ribs ..... *B. gregaria*
7 Bulb tunics brittle; leaves at most 8, pressed flat on the ground, the upper surface dark green, the lower surface light green; capsules 3-angled, tapering toward the pedicel .... *B. orientalis*
7' Bulb tunics parchment-like; leaves at least 8, suberect, grayish; capsules more or less cylindrical 8
8 Bulb deep-seated; leaves suberect, twisted toward the apex; perianth tube 1.5–2.5 cm long .... *B. litoralis*
8' Bulb usually exposed; leaves spreading, not twisted; perianth tube to 1.5 cm long .... *B. josephinae*

Bulbinella

1 Leaves equal or subequal in length; plants mostly less than 50 cm high 2
1' Leaves diminishing in size toward the center or leaf single; plants mostly more than 50 cm high 6
2 Sheathing fibers papery, 1–2 mm wide, shiny brown or silvery .... *B. chartacea*
2' Sheathing fibers not papery, less than 0.5 mm wide, dull brown or gray 3
3 Inner membranous cataphyll protruding above the brown fibrous sheath; flowers yellow .... *B. divaginata*
3' Inner membranous cataphyll not protruding above the fibrous sheath 4
4 Leaves 4–7, scarcely developed at flowering, the margins seldom toothed .... *B. trinervis*
4' Leaves more than 7, well developed at flowering, the margins toothed 5
5 Sheathing fibers soft, fine, and straight to slightly netted; leaves to 1.5 mm wide .... *B. triquetra*
5' Sheathing fibers regularly and compactly netted; leaves 2–3 mm wide .... *B. elegans*
6 Roots cylindrical, orange-yellow; leaves broad, to 65 mm wide, bright green and somewhat fleshy 7
6' Roots wiry below but swollen above, white; leaves narrow, to 9 mm wide, dark green to grayish, somewhat leathery 9
7 Leaf blades flat; raceme long and slender; flowers cream .... *B. elata*
7' Leaf blades channeled; racemes broadly conical 8
8 Largest leaves 10–30 mm wide; raceme to 55 mm diam.; flowers bright yellow or cream .... *B. nutans*
8' Largest leaves 20–65 mm wide; raceme to 40 mm diam.; flowers deep yellow or orange .... *B. latifolia*
9 Leaves 1–4, not sheathing at the base; flowers yellow 10
9' Leaves 5–14, sheathing below; flowers white to cream 11
10 Leaf 1(2), semiterete .... *B. potbergensis*
10' Leaves 2–3(4), channeled .... *B. punctulata*
11 Leaf margins finely or roughly hairy 12
11' Leaf margins smooth or with a few wispy hairs 13
12 Leaf margins finely hairy; raceme narrowly cylindrical and pointed, c. 20 mm diam.; flowers off-white .... *B. barkerae*
12' Leaf margins roughly hairy; raceme broadly cylindrical and blunt, c. 30 mm diam.; flowers buff to ivory ...... *B. eburniflora*
13 Raceme narrowly conical, c. 30 mm diam.; flowers white with pink midveins; capsules and seeds 5 mm long ... *B. caudafelis*
13' Raceme narrowly cylindrical, c. 15 mm diam.; flowers white; capsules to 3.5 mm long and seeds to 2.5 mm long .... *B. graminifolia*

Chasmanthe

1 Tepals arising at the same level; lateral tepals 5–8 mm long .... *C. bicolor*
1' Dorsal tepal arising 3–7 mm beyond the others; lateral tepals (7–)10–20 mm long 2
2 Spike secund or subsecund, flexed at the base and inclined to horizontal; perianth tube abruptly expanded at the top of the slender part .... *C. aethiopica*
2' Spike 2-ranked, upright, often branched; perianth tube gradually expanding from the lower slender part to the wider upper part...................................... *C. floribunda*

Crinum

1 Leaves to 2.5 cm broad; pedicels to 2.5 cm long; perianth tube 3–10 cm long; anthers black .... *C. lineare*
1' Leaves to 5 cm broad; pedicels to 5 cm long; perianth tube 2–4 cm long; anthers cream .... *C. variabile*

Crossyne

1 Flowers yellow, strongly zygomorphic, the stamens and style curved downward when mature .... *C. flava*
1' Flowers dark brownish maroon to dusky pink, actinomorphic, only the style curved to one side when mature .... *C. guttata*

Cyanella

1 Flowers with 3 lower and 3 upper stamens, not enantiostylous, mauve with maroon center .... *C. orchidiformis*
1' Flowers with a single lower and 5 upper stamens, more or less enantiostylous, uniformly colored 2
2 Flowers solitary, usually on pedicels more than 10 cm long; leaves filiform and terete .... *C. alba*
2' Flowers several in racemose inflorescences, on pedicels less than 8 cm long; leaves linear to oblong-lanceolate 3

3 Filaments free to the base, anthers with conspicuous sterile spathulate tips; pedicels suberect; flowers yellow or pink . . . . *C. lutea*
3′ Filaments united below into a short tube; pedicels spreading at c. 90° 4
4 Raceme sparsely branched, few-flowered; pedicels to 20 mm long; flowers orange . . . . *C. aquatica*
4′ Raceme much branched, many-flowered; pedicels more than 20 mm long; flowers blue to mauve or white . . . . *C. hyacinthoides*

Cyrtanthus

1 Large plants; bulbs more than 6 cm diam.; leaves broader than 2 cm, twisted; flowers nodding 2
1′ Less robust plants; bulbs less than 6 cm diam.; leaves narrower than 1.5 cm, if wider then not twisted; flowers erect, spreading to nodding 3
2 Flowers tubular, pink to red . . . . *C. carneus*
2′ Flowers funnel-shaped, yellow to orange with green tips . . . . *C. obliquus*
3 Perianth tubular to slightly flared above the base; throat at most 10 mm wide; tepals less than 25 mm long, if longer then the tepals bilabiate and the stamens and style arched against the upper tepals 4
3′ Perianth tube narrow at base, flaring distinctly to a wide, open throat at least 10 mm wide; tepals more than 25 mm long, regularly arranged, if tepals shorter and throat slightly narrower then the stamens and style curved downward against the lower tepal 17
4 Perianth tubular, widening evenly from base to throat 5
4′ Perianth tunnel-shaped, the tube narrow at the base, somewhat dilated in the upper two-thirds 13
5 Flowers dark red to maroon, sweetly scented . . . . *C. odorus*
5′ Flowers variously colored, if sweetly scented then yellow, cream, or white 6
6 Flowers bright red to coral red, sometimes with an orange throat 7
6′ Flowers yellow, cream, or white 11
7 Tepal arrangement regular 8
7′ Tepal arrangement bilabiate 9
8 Leaves shiny green, more than 6 mm wide; flowers nodding, firm; style longer than the perianth . . . . *C. angustifolius*
8′ Leaves grayish green, less than 6 mm wide; flowers spreading, not fleshy; style shorter than the perianth . . . . *C. collinus*
9 Leaves 10–20 mm wide, almost plane, without a prominent midrib, the base slightly narrow and flat in cross section; 4 upper tepals hooded; style strongly curved apically . . . . *C. labiatus*
9′ Leaves less than 5 mm wide, deeply channeled, with a prominent midrib, the base narrow and triangular in cross section; 3 upper tepals hooded; style slightly curved apically 10
10 Leaves thick, striate beneath, the veins minutely papillate; 5 stamens arched against the upper lip . . . . *C. fergusoniae*
10′ Leaves thin textured, smooth, only the midrib prominent; 3 stamens arched against the upper lip . . . . *C. inaequalis*
11 Flowers unscented, weakly bilabiate . . . . *C. leptosiphon*
11′ Flowers scented, not bilabiate 12
12 Tepals more than 7 mm wide and 13 mm long . . . . *C. leucanthus*
12′ Tepals less than 5 mm wide and 10 mm long . . . *C. ochroleucus*
13 Style included in the perianth tube below the filament insertion . . . . *C. wellandii*
13′ Style exserted from the perianth tube, level with or exserted beyond the stamens 14
14 Stamens inserted near the base of the perianth tube; stigma minutely trifid . . . . *C. ventricosus*
14′ Stamens inserted at or just below the perianth throat; stigma 3-branched 15
15 Leaves spirally twisted . . . . *C. spiralis*
15′ Leaves spreading, without spirals 16
16 Perianth ribbed and often fluted toward the base; style curved strongly downward toward lower tepal . . . . *C. staadensis*
16′ Perianth not ribbed toward base; style arched against upper tepal . . . . *C. collinus*
17 Flowers bright red, rarely pink or white; stamens slightly shorter than or as long as the tepals, reaching the same height 18
17′ Flowers cream, pale lemon, salmon, or pink; stamens reaching less than halfway up the tepals, in 2 series 21
18 Leaves firm; blade abruptly narrowed to the base; stigma distinctly 3-branched . . . . *C. flammosus*
18′ Leaves firm to soft, linear or strap-shaped; blade only slightly narrowed to the base; stigma minutely 3-lobed 19
19 Flower 1, rarely 2, almost sessile; pedicel less than 5 mm long . . . . *C. guthrieae*
19′ Flowers as many as 5 or more, rarely 1–2, distinctly pedicellate; pedicel at least 15 mm long 20
20 Tepals narrow, less than 12 mm wide . . . . *C. montanus*
20′ Tepals broad, at least 20 mm wide . . . . *C. elatus*
21 Perianth with contrasting scarlet stripes leading down the throat from between the tepals; tepal backs not marked . . . . *C.* sp. 1
21′ Perianth with contrasting pink, yellow or green central stripes on the tepal backs 22
22 Leaves mostly green at flowering; flowers cream to pale lemon colored; tube abruptly inflated in the upper region; stamens and style declinate to lowest tepal but set apart from each other . . . . *C. loddigesianus*
22′ Leaves dry at flowering; flowers pink; tube expanding evenly to the throat; stamens and style tightly clustered against lowest tepal . . . . *C. debilis*

Daubenya

1 Flowers strongly dimorphic, the lower (outer) strongly bilabiate with the lower tepals much enlarged .... *D. aurea*
1' Flowers all similar and actinomorphic 2
2 Filaments free or united below into a short collar to 3 mm long 3
2' Filaments united below into a narrowly cylindrical tube 7–15 mm long 4
3 Inflorescence conical and topped with a coma of conspicuous bracts; perianth tube compressed-cylindrical, 2–3 mm diam.; filaments uniformly orange to red .... *D. marginata*
3' Inflorescence globular, without a conspicuous coma; perianth tube cylindrical, 1.5–2 mm diam.; filaments reddish with the basal collar purple .... *D. zeyheri*
4 Tepals united above the filament insertion into a tubular collar with minute free lobes 1.5–3 mm long .... *D. stylosa*
4' Tepals free above the filament insertion, oblong to linear, 6–13 mm long 5
5 Flowers yellow; tepals oblong, 10–13 mm long; the staminal tube occluded at the mouth by a perforated disk .... *D. capensis*
5' Flowers white flushed lilac or pink; tepals linear, 6–8 mm long; the staminal tube without a perforated disk in the mouth .... *D. alba*

Dilatris

1 Inflorescence axis covered with reddish glandular hairs; flowers yellow, nodding in bud; tepals linear-oblanceolate ... *D. viscosa*
1' Inflorescence axis covered with whitish nonglandular hairs; flowers mauve, erect in bud; tepals ovate-lanceolate 2
2 Inflorescence often paniculate or corymbose; stamens well exserted, much longer than the tepals; large anther 2.5–3 mm long, 3–4 times as long as the smaller .... *D. ixioides*
2' Inflorescence corymbose or umbellate; stamens included or scarcely exserted, shorter than to slightly longer than the tepals; large anther 1.5–2.5 mm long, to 2.5 times as long as the smaller 3
3 Longer stamens about as long as the tepals; large anther more than twice as long as the smaller; tepals lanceolate .... *D. corymbosa*
3' Longer stamens much shorter than the tepals; large anther c. 1.5 times as long as the smaller; tepals ovate-cucullate .... *D. pillansii*

Dipcadi

1 Outer tepals longer than the inner and with short to long tail-like appendages, at least present as short teeth in bud 2
1' Outer tepals about as long as the inner and not tailed 3

2 Leaves crisped-undulate and often spirally twisted, more or less coarsely hairy .... *D. crispum*
2' Leaves straight, smooth, and hairless .... *D. viride*
3 Leaves 2–3(4), smooth and hairless; flowers 12–20 mm long ... . *D. brevifolium*
3' Leaves c. 6, crisped with hairy margins; flowers (16–)20–28 mm long .... *D. ciliare*

Drimia

Groups of *Drimia*

1 Raceme branched, persistent; pedicels erect or deflexed in fruit .... *Schizobasis* group: *D. intricata*
1' Raceme simple, deciduous; pedicels erect or spreading in fruit 2
2 Anthers subsessile or filaments to 2.5 mm long, often included in perianth; flowers mostly nodding, often urn-shaped 3
2' Anthers exserted and filaments longer than 2.5 mm 4
3 Flowers 1–2, cylindrical; anthers subsessile, inserted in middle of perianth tube, opening by longitudinal slits .... *Litanthus* group: *D. uniflora*
3' Flowers several, urn- or cup-shaped; anthers connivent over ovary, inserted near base of perianth tube, opening by pores or by longitudinal slits .... *Rhadamanthus* group
4 Raceme erect, firm; perianth tubular below, tepals united about a third of their length, recurved above; stamens usually connivent around style; capsules large, c. 10 mm long, conspicuously 3-angled or 3-winged .... *Drimia* group
4' Raceme usually flexuous or wiry; flowers bell- or star-shaped, tepals free or shortly united below, spreading or recurved; stamens erect or spreading, rarely connivent around style; capsules smaller, obscurely 3-lobed 5
5 Leaf bases enclosed in an elongated, transversely ridged, and banded sheath; tepals free; stamens clustered around ovary, with basifixed anthers; style declinate .... *Tenicroa* group
5' Leaf bases without an elongate, banded sheath; tepals free or united below; anthers usually dorsifixed; style straight or declinate .... *Urginea* group

Drimia Group *Drimia*

1 Flowers irregularly clustered in an elongate raceme 1–2 m high, white to yellowish; anthers green, 3–8 mm long before dehiscence; leaves large, c. 10 cm broad .... *D. capensis*
1' Flowers in a lax raceme to 50 cm high, often silvery brown; anthers mauve to dark purple, 1–3 mm long before dehiscence; leaves smaller, to 2 cm broad 2
2 Leaves present at flowering, stiff and knitting needle-like .... *D. media*
2' Leaves dry and withered at flowering, soft and narrowly oblanceolate 3

3   Bulbs exposed, with loose scales .... *D. haworthioides*
3′ Bulbs subterranean, with cohering scales 4
4   Flowering peduncle 30–100 cm high, 3–4 mm diam., many-flowered; capsules longer than broad .... *D. elata*
4′ Flowering peduncle 6–15 cm high, 1–2 mm diam., few-flowered; capsules as broad as long .... *D. pusilla*

Drimia Group *Rhadamanthus*

1   Flowers white, star-shaped or shallowly cup-shaped, not nodding; filaments very short, to 0.5 mm long 2
1′ Flowers pinkish to brownish, subglobose or urn-shaped, nodding; filaments longer, 0.8–1.5 mm long 3
2   Tepals all alike, flat .... *D. albiflora*
2′ Tepals dissimilar, the inner longitudinally rolled and incurved ... *D. involuta*
3   Anthers rounded and smooth at the base 4
3′ Anthers apiculate, shortly tailed or barbed at the base 5
4   Anthers dehiscing by longitudinal slits almost to the base; leaves oblong-obovate, 7–9 mm wide .... *D. karooica*
4′ Anthers dehiscing by apical pores; leaves subterete, 2–3 mm wide .... *D. convallarioides*
5   Anther thecae diverging and barbed below; filaments papillate-hairy; leaves 2, elliptical to ovate, short-velvety above .... *D. platyphylla*
5′ Anther thecae parallel and apiculate or tailed below; filaments smooth; leaves 2 to several, linear, hairless 6
6   Bulb scales closely overlapping; scape and ovary minutely hairy .... *D. uranthera*
6′ Bulb scales loosely overlapping with separate tips; scape and ovary smooth .... *D. arenicola*

Drimia Group *Tenicroa*

1   Leaves firm, leathery, stiffly erect, one to many, usually about as long as the raceme 2
1′ Leaves softer, subsucculent, flexuous or coiled, many, distinctly shorter than the raceme 3
2   Leaves 1–4, (2–)3–4 mm diam. .... *D. exuviata*
2′ Leaves one to many, 0.5–2 mm diam. .... *D. filifolia*
3   Leaves c. 0.5 mm diam. .... *D. multifolia*
3′ Leaves 1–1.5 mm diam. .... *D. fragrans*

Drimia Group *Urginea*

1   Flowers crowded in head-like or corymbose racemes; pedicels of open flowers longer than the raceme above them 2
1′ Flowers in elongate racemes; pedicels of open flowers shorter than the raceme above them 6
2   Leaves soft, lanceolate to elliptical .... *D. physodes*
2′ Leaves firm, oblong to linear or terete 3
3   Leaves elliptical, hairy beneath .... *D.* sp. 1
3′ Leaves lanceolate, smooth 4
4   Leaves terete, filiform; peduncle hairy below .... *D. minor*
4′ Leaves broader; peduncle smooth and hairless 5
5   Leaves leathery, prostrate, with thick cartilaginous margins ... *D. marginata*
5′ Leaves fleshy, falcate, margins not thickened .... *D. virens*
6   Peduncle and pedicels wiry; pedicels 10–20 mm long; flowers nodding in bud 7
6′ Peduncles and pedicels not wiry; pedicels to 10 mm long; flowers ascending in bud 8
7   Leaves 2–3, terete, fibrotic and striate, erect, c. 1.5 mm diam. .... *D. sclerophylla*
7′ Leaves 3–5, elliptical to oblanceolate, prostrate, to 12 mm wide .... *D. ciliata*
8   Leaf bases persistent, surrounding the base of the peduncle, papery, and banded .... *D.* sp. 2
8′ Leaf bases not persistent and papery 9
9   Flowers nodding, 8 mm long; tepals almost free, narrowly oblong, recurved at anthesis .... *D. revoluta*
9′ Flowers ascending or spreading, 4–5 mm long; tepals united below, ovate, spreading at anthesis 10
10 Leaves 1(–2), dry at flowering .... *D. dregei*
10′ Leaves 2–5, emergent at flowering .... *D. salteri*

Empodium

1   Flowers with the neck above the ovary exceeding 2 cm long; anthers suberect 2
1′ Flowers with the neck above the ovary shorter than 2 cm long; anthers spreading, often curved outward 3
2   Flowers coinciding with the leaves; leaves longer than the inflorescence; neck above the ovary smooth .... *E. gloriosum*
2′ Flowers appearing in advance of the leaves or if coinciding then the leaves shorter than the inflorescence; neck above the ovary hispid .... *E. plicatum*
3   Flowers appearing mostly in advance of the leaves or if coinciding then the leaves shorter than the inflorescence; anthers bearing sterile apical appendages .... *E. flexile*
3′ Flowers coinciding with the leaves, the leaves usually longer than the inflorescence; anthers without apical appendages ... 4
4   Leaves lanceolate, 10–20 mm wide, the basal sheaths dark brown for their entire length; flowers carried 10 cm or more above the ground .... *E. veratrifolium*
4′ Leaves ovate-lanceolate, 15–60 mm wide, the basal sheaths pale with dark brown tips; flowers carried less than 5 cm above the ground .... *E. namaquensis*

Eriospermum

Subgenera of *Eriospermum*

1   Tepals clearly dimorphic; tuber irregularly shaped with lateral

to basal growing point, flesh white or pink ....
.... subgenus *Eriospermum*

1' Tepals equal or subequal; tuber subglobose with apical growing point to irregularly shaped with lateral growing point, flesh white, yellow, or pink 2

2 Filaments oblong or ovate, rarely narrower, erect around the ovary; tepals obovate; style usually shorter than the ovary; inflorescence usually narrow, subspicate ....
.... subgenus *Cyathiflorum*

2' Filaments more or less filiform, mostly suberect or spreading; tepals oblanceolate; style usually longer than the ovary; inflorescence various .... subgenus *Ligulatum*

Eriospermum Subgenus *Cyathiflorum*

1 Flowers bowl- or cup-shaped with the tepals not opening out flat 2

1' Flowers star-shaped with the tepals opening out flat or reflexed 4

2 Inflorescence few-flowered, often secund; filaments filiform to narrowly oblong; leaf small, 20–90 × 10–25 mm, narrowly lanceolate to elliptical .... *E. cernuum*

2' Inflorescence many-flowered, not secund; filaments broadly ovate-obovate; leaf larger, 60–150 × 70–85 mm, ovate to heart-shaped 3

3 Tuber spreading with thick, branched rhizomes; inflorescence subspicate, pedicels to 3 mm long; leaf leathery ....
.... *E. rhizomatum*

3' Tuber solitary; inflorescence racemose, pedicels to 12 mm long; leaf and peduncular bract pilose .... *E. brevipes*

4 Leaf prostrate, broadly ovate to round or heart-shaped; leaf sheath not exserted above ground level 5

4' Leaf erect, elliptical to lanceolate; leaf-sheath exserted above ground level 7

5 Peduncle to 30 mm long; inflorescence compact ....
.... *E. breviscapum*

5' Peduncle 60–300 mm long; inflorescence elongate 6

6 Leaf closely pressed to the ground, round to heart-shaped, fleshy, light green; filaments oblong-obovate .... *E. zeyheri*

6' Leaf prostrate but not pressed to the ground, broadly ovate to heart-shaped, thin, leathery, dark green, often purple beneath; filaments ovate-lanceolate .... *E. porphyrium*

7 Leaf base and petiole sparsely hairy; raceme subspicate, pedicels to 3 mm long; flowers to 6.5 mm diam. ..... *E. bruynsii*

7' Leaf hairless; flowers 9–21 mm diam. 8

8 Peduncular bract densely hairy .... *E. aequilibre*

8' Peduncular bract hairless 9

9 Leaf softer, somewhat undulate; pedicels 2–7 mm long; flowers c. 12 mm diam. .... *E. bayeri*

9' Leaf firm, leathery; raceme subcorymbose to broadly cylindrical, pedicels to 40 mm long 10

10 Flowers large, c. 21 mm diam.; filaments ovate .... *E. crispum*

10' Flowers smaller, to 11 mm diam.; filaments oblong, bifid at the apex and overtopping the anthers .... *E. bifidum*

Eriospermum Subgenus *Eriospermum*

1 Tuber flesh white, rarely pale pink; flowers urn-shaped to bell-shaped; tepals more or less erect and attenuate; buds pointed 2

1' Tuber flesh pink or red, rarely white; flowers with the outer tepals spreading; tepals not conspicuously attenuate; buds rounded 4

2 Leaf ovate, thin; flowers racemose; pedicels to 25 mm long ...
.... *E. subtile*

2' Leaf oblong-linear; flowers subspicate; pedicels to 8 mm long 3

3 Tuber flesh white; leaf narrowly lanceolate, sheath straight; flowers pale yellow .... *E. exile*

3' Tuber flesh pale pink; leaf linear, sheath coiled; flowers white ..
.... *E. exigium*

4 Leaf with one or more outgrowths (enations) 5

4' Leaf without outgrowths 11

5 Leaf and outgrowths (enations) hairless and terete 6

5' Leaf and or outgrowths hairy or hairless, then flat 7

6 Leaf sheath fibrous, light brown; outgrowths scarcely 1 mm diam., dark, shiny green; raceme cylindrical, pedicels to 2.5 mm long .... *E. flabellatum*

6' Leaf sheath papery, white; outgrowths 1–2 mm diam., glaucous; raceme spicate .... *E. bowieanum*

7 Outgrowths (enations) simple, terete; flowers in a lax raceme on a slender peduncle; pedicels wiry, to 30 mm long 8

7' Outgrowths mostly branched but flat if simple; flowers crowded in a compact raceme on a short peduncle; pedicels to 10 mm long 9

8 Outgrowths numerous, 2.5 mm long, each with an apical tuft of hairs; petiole and leaf sheath hairless .... *E. erinum*

8' Outgrowths few to many, to 60 mm long, almost hairless or hairy; petiole and leaf sheath hairy .... *E. proliferum*

9 Leaf blade as long as or longer than the outgrowths; outgrowths simple or branched, flat .... *E. alcicorne*

9' Leaf blade much shorter than the outgrowths; outgrowths terete 10

10 Hairs in stellate clusters .... *E. dregei*

10' Hairs simple .... *E. cervicorne*

11 Leaf erect, elliptical to lanceolate, or if ovate then sheath exserted 12

11' Leaf prostrate to suberect, ovate and heart-shaped, sheath barely exserted 18

12 Leaf oblong-linear, softly hairy on both surfaces ... *E. villosum*

12' Leaf hairless, very sparsely hairy, or woolly beneath only ... 13

13 Leaf white woolly beneath .... *E. glaciale*

13' Leaf hairless or sparsely hairy 14
14 Leaf blade broadly lanceolate to ovate, less than twice as long as wide 15
14' Leaf blade linear-lanceolate, more than twice as long as wide 17
15 Leaf leathery, margin red and lightly crisped ... *E. lanceifolium*
15' Leaf thin textured 16
16 Leaf sheath glabrous .... *E. dissitiflorum*
16' Leaf sheath finely hairy .... *E. orthophyllum*
17 Leaf hairless; pedicels to 80 mm long ...... *E. laxiracemosum*
17' Leaf sparsely hairy; pedicels to 45 mm long .. *E. graminifolium*
18 Leaf with the margin minutely hairy 19
18' Leaf hairless or hairy but then hairs not restricted to the margin 20
19 Leaf margin minutely hairy with the hairs often in bunches; tepals scarcely joined below, inner erect .... *E. marginatum*
19' Leaf margin with a collar of curly hairs; tepals joined below into a tube 2 mm long, inner recurved above .... *E. lanimarginatum*
20 Leaf prostrate, small, to 25 × 26 mm; pedicels to 17 mm long 21
20' Leaf suberect, larger 22
21 Leaf pustulate-hairy; plants solitary ..... *E. minutipustulatum*
21' Leaf margin minutely hairy; plants clumped, stoloniferous .... *E. vermiforme*
22 Inflorescence subspicate, pedicels to 9 mm long; flowers to 14 mm diam. .... *E. cordiforme*
22' Inflorescence racemose, pedicels longer 23
23 Leaf pustulate-hairy .... *E. pustulatum*
23' Leaf hairless or hairy but then hairs not on pustules 24
24 Leaf hairless or almost hairless above but densely woolly beneath 25
24' Leaf hairless or more or less equally hairy on both surfaces ... 26
25 Upper leaf surface dull green, slightly rugose; pedicels to 40 mm long; flowers larger, to 12 mm diam.; filaments narrowly triangular .... *E. lanuginosum*
25' Upper leaf surface bright shiny green; pedicels 9–15 mm long; flowers small, to 7 mm diam.; filaments dimorphic, outer ovate .... *E. subincanum*
26 Hairs pressed to the leaf surface, silvery or golden .... *E. pubescens*
26' Hairs not pressed to the surface or leaves hairless 27
27 Tuber flesh pink; pedicels 25–30 mm long; filaments narrowly triangular .... *E. nanum*
27' Tuber flesh maroon; pedicels 30–60 mm long; filaments ovate .... *E. capense*

Eriospermum Subgenus *Ligulatum*
1 Leaf terete, needle-like; peduncle and pedicels persistent and photosynthetic; tuber globose, growing point apical 2
1' Leaf flat 4

2 Peduncle firm and glaucous, straight or slightly kinked; flowers tinged pinkish .... *E. aphyllum*
2' Peduncle wiry, spirally coiled below; flowers white or yellow ... 3
3 Inflorescence corymbose, broader than long; flowers white or yellow; tuber 10–12 mm diam., flesh white .... *E. spirale*
3' Inflorescence laxly racemose, longer than broad; flowers yellow; tuber 20–40 mm diam., flesh pale pink ...... *E. flavum*
4 Flowers yellow 5
4' Flowers white 7
5 Inflorescence subcorymbose; tubers often rhizomatous and forming chains; leaf elliptical .... *E. macgregorianum*
5' Inflorescence racemose; tubers never rhizomatous 6
6 Tuber globose with apical growing point; leaf elliptical, hairless, interspersed with dead brown leaves of previous seasons .... *E. schlechteri*
6' Tuber pear-shaped with basal growing pint; leaf heart-shaped, the margins minutely hairy .... *E. ciliatum*
7 Inflorescence lax with pedicels to 55 mm long 8
7' Inflorescence compact with pedicels to 15 mm long 9
8 Petiole abruptly inflated, red, persisting around the base of the plant as distinctive ring-like collars ..... *E. patentiflorum*
8' Petiole not as above .... *E. arenosum*
9 Tuber globose with apical growing point 10
9' Tuber irregularly shaped with basal to lateral growing point ... 11
10 Leaf elliptical to heart-shaped; raceme narrowly cylindrical with as many as 70 flowers .... *E. parvifolium*
10' Leaf narrowly elliptical to oblong-lanceolate; raceme narrowly conical with as many as 40 flowers .... *E. pumilum*
11 Leaf with a mop of feathery, hairy outgrowths (enations); flowers large, to 17 mm diam., scented .... *E. paradoxum*
11' Leaf without outgrowths 12
12 Leaf erect, elliptical, hairless, rugose, small, to 16 mm long; raceme lax with 2–4 flowers .... *E. inconspicuum*
12' Leaf suberect, ovate, usually finely hairy, larger, 25–100 mm long; raceme with 15–40 flowers .... *E. dielsianum*

Eucomis

1 Leaves broadly oblanceolate, striate, usually prostrate; terminal bracts deflexed over the inflorescence axis and slightly shorter than it; pedicels to 2 mm long at flowering; winter growing .... *E. regia*
1' Leaves elliptical to lanceolate, suberect; terminal bracts suberect or spreading and mostly much shorter than the inflorescence axis; pedicels 3–30 mm long at flowering; summer growing 2
2 Pedicels to 10 mm long at flowering; leaves not speckled .... *E. autumnalis*
2' Pedicels 15–30 mm long at flowering; leaves speckled with purple beneath .... *E. comosa*

Ferraria

1. Anther lobes parallel; ovary spindle-shaped, without a sterile beak 2
1'. Anther lobes diverging from the apex, or initially parallel, later slightly diverging near the base; ovary with a prominent sterile beak at last 8 mm long 4
2. Stem slender with internodes partly exposed; leaves linear with blades usually less than 5 mm wide .... *F. densepunctulata*
2'. Stem stout, mostly covered by leaf bases; leaves sword-shaped to falcate, more than 5 mm wide 3
3. Leaves with a thickened zone in the middle and a strong pseudomidrib, 2-ranked .... *F. crispa*
3'. Leaves with numerous veins of equal size and without a pseudomidrib, often spirally 2-ranked .... *F. foliosa*
4. Margins of at least some leaves crisped; tepals attenuate with the tips twisted .... *F. uncinata*
4'. Margins smooth; tepals acute the tips not markedly twisted ... 5
5. Stem partly exposed, blades more or less linear, longer than the sheaths; leaf and stem bases speckled white on purple .... *F. ferrariola*
5'. Stem densely leafy, covered by leaf bases, blades sword-shaped, shorter or longer than the sheaths; leaf and stem bases uniformly colored 6
6. Outer tepals 10–20 mm wide; perianth cup bell-shaped, 13–20 mm wide at the rim .... *F. divaricata*
6'. Outer tepals less than 10 mm wide; perianth cup funnel-shaped, 6–10 mm wide at the rim .... *F. kamiesbergensis*

Freesia

1. Flowers with a tapering or uniformly cylindrical perianth tube 2
1'. Flowers with a widely funnel-shaped perianth tube 3
2. Stem flattened and 2-winged; flowers green or turning dull purple, with a tapering tube; spike inclined .... *F. viridis*
2'. Stem terete; flowers pink with white and dark pink markings and a cylindrical perianth tube; spike more or less horizontal ... . *F. verrucosa*
3. Bracts green-membranous to dry, often with brown tips 4
3'. Bracts firm and leathery, green throughout 7
4. Flowers mostly 50–65 mm long; leaves obtuse or subobtuse ... . *F. speciosa*
4'. Flowers mostly 30–45 mm long; leaves acute to more or less obtuse 5
5. Bracts membranous, not dark at the tips; flowers mostly greenish cream with cream to bright yellow markings; spicy scented .... *F. refracta*
5'. Bracts membranous, dark at the tips; flowers mostly cream to yellow, rarely pink; sweetly scented 6

6. Leaves mostly acute, usually less than half as long as the stem; inner bracts c. 2 mm wide, dividing into obtuse, dark brown tips .... *F. corymbosa*
6'. Leaves obtuse to subobtuse, mostly two-thirds as long as the stem; inner bracts dividing into acute tips, barely tipped with brown .... *F. occidentalis*
7. Leaves prostrate unless growing in the shade of shrubs, then ascending; leaf apices obtuse 8
7'. Leaves erect or suberect; leaf apices more or less acute 9
8. Plants mostly less than 10 cm high and rarely branched; stem mostly prostrate; flowering mainly May–June .... *F. caryophyllacea*
8'. Plants usually 12–20 cm high and often branched; stem prostrate near the base, then erect; flowering mainly July–Aug. .... *F. fergusoniae*
9. Flowers relatively small, mostly 30–40 mm long; slender part of the perianth tube 12–15 mm long, about as long as the upper part; dorsal tepal c. 11 × 5–7 mm .... *F. sparrmannii*
9'. Flowers mostly 35–50 mm long; slender part of the perianth tube 6–8 mm long, significantly shorter than the upper part; dorsal tepal 15–18 × 8–12 mm 10
10. Tepals subequal, the lower 3 unmarked or only the lowermost with a yellow mark .... *F. alba*
10'. Tepals unequal, the lower 3 each with a yellow mark 11
11. Flowers predominantly white; bracts tricuspidate .... *F. fucata*
11'. Flowers predominantly yellow; bracts not tricuspidate .... *F. leichtlinii*

Geissorhiza

Subgenera of *Geissorhiza*

1. Plants with concentric corm tunics, old tunics completely enclosed by new ones and layers splitting vertically from base to apex, tunics usually brown or tunics more or less fibrous; stamens always equal in length .... subgenus *Weihea*
1'. Plants with overlapping corm tunics, old tunics pushed upward and fragmenting into segments from the base and broken to the apex, usually blackish; stamens equal or unequal with one filament shorter than the other two ...... subgenus *Geissorhiza*

Geissorhiza Subgenus *Geissorhiza*

1. Stem minutely hairy, puberulous or pilose 2
1'. Stem smooth 16
2. Flowers zygomorphic, stamens and style unilateral and declinate 3
2'. Flowers actinomorphic, stamens and style symmetrically disposed 5
3. Flowers white with reddish to brown center .... *G. tulbaghensis*
3'. Flowers dark blue-violet, sometimes red or pale in the center ... 4
4. Flowers glossy, deep blue-violet, anthers brown; filaments

      c. 5 mm long .... *G. splendidissima*
4' Flowers dark blue, sometimes red or pale in the center; filaments 6–8 mm long .... *G. monanthos*
5 One stamen at least 0.5 mm shorter than the other 2 6
5' Stamens equal 12
6 Leaves plane with margins and midrib lightly thickened 7
6' Leaves more or less ridged with the margins significantly thickened and raised 8
7 Tepals 11–16 mm long; short filament as much as 2 mm shorter than the long filaments .... *G. aspera*
7' Tepals 18–23 mm long; short filament at least 4 mm shorter than the long filaments .... *G. inaequalis*
8 Flowering stem with a short, membranous, scale-like bract in the upper third 9
8' Flowering stem bearing 3 foliage leaves and without a scale-like bract in the upper third 10
9 Tepals 8–9 mm long; anthers c. 2.5 mm long .... *G. scopulosa*
9' Tepals 10–22 mm long; anthers 4–6 mm long ... *G. heterostyla*
10 Flowers pink; perianth tube 15–17 mm long ..... *G. silenoides*
10' Flowers blue or pale mauve, white, or pale pink; perianth tube 1.5–2 mm long 11
11 Leaves conspicuously hairy along the margin edges; flowers pale mauve, whitish, or pale pink .... *G. leipoldtii*
11' Leaves smooth or minutely hairy along the margin edges; flowers blue .... *G. arenicola*
12 Leaves plane with margins and midrib no more than lightly thickened; tepals 9–15 mm long .... *G. aspera*
12' Leaves with the margins significantly thickened and raised, the margin edges raised at right angles to the blade surface ... 13
13 Margin edges hispid 14
13' Margin edges smooth, not hispid 15
14 Flowers small with the tepals 6–8 mm long; anthers c. 2.5 mm long .... *G. erubescens*
14' Flowers larger, tepals (13–)15–28 mm long; anthers (3–)6–8 mm long .... *G. leipoldtii*
15 Flowers small, the tepals 6–7 mm long; leaves c. 1 mm wide .... *G. ciliatula*
15' Flowers medium-sized, the tepals 7–10 mm long; leaves 1.5–3.5 mm wide .... *G. intermedia*
16 Stamens unequal, one at least 0.5 mm and usually more than 2 mm shorter than the other 2; leaf margins lightly to moderately thickened but never raised into wings extended at right angles to the surface 17
16' Stamens equal in length; leaf margins either only lightly to moderately thickened or raised into wings held at right angles to the surface and minutely hairy to hispid along the edges 27
17 Flowers small, the tepals 7–11 mm long 18
17' Flowers moderate in size to large, the tepals (12–)14–30 mm long 20

18 Stem inclined to trailing, usually 1-branched, occasionally 2-branched; flowers white .... *G. bryicola*
18' Stem erect, simple or usually 2- or 3-branched; flowers white or blue to violet 19
19 Flowers blue to violet .... *G. ramosa*
19' Flowers white .... *G. minuta*
20 Flowers creamy yellow, sometimes with a dark center 21
20' Flowers blue, purple, mauve, or pink 22
21 Flower uniformly creamy yellow; tepals 18–28 mm long; stamens symmetrically arranged, the longer filaments 7–9 mm long .... *G. louisabolusiae*
21' Flower pale yellow with a blackish center; tepals 22–30 mm long; stamens unilateral and declinate, the longer filaments 15–20 mm long .... *G. barkerae*
22 Perianth tube short, to 3 mm long .... *G. tabularis*
22' Perianth tube at least 4 mm long and as much as 25 mm long 23
23 Leaf blades plane .... *G. pseudinaequalis*
23' Leaf blades with the margins and midrib moderately to heavily thickened 24
24 Perianth tube 4–6 mm long .... *G. burchellii*
24' Perianth tube 10–25 mm long 25
25 Tepals 12–15 mm long .... *G. rupicola*
25' Tepals 22–30 mm long 26
26 Perianth tube 10–18 mm long; anthers and pollen yellow .... *G. grandiflora*
26' Perianth tube 22–25 mm long; anthers purple and pollen pinkish .... *G. callista*
27 Leaf blades minutely to velvety hairy on the veins and margins; bracts more or less dry and rust colored distally at anthesis 28
27' Leaf blades not visibly hairy or minutely hairy; bracts remaining green or dry and pale distally 30
28 Leaf blades with the margins and midribs raised and winged, minutely hairy to pubescent on the edges; stem without a scale like-bract in the upper half .... *G. inflexa*
28' Leaf blades more or less ribbed and velvety; stem with 1–2 scale-like bracts in the upper half 29
29 Flowers cream, the outer tepals flushed reddish on the reverse; tepals c. 10 mm long .... *G. divaricata*
29' Flowers blue to mauve; tepals 12–17 mm long .... *G. subrigida*
30 Leaf blades of the lower two leaves linear or terete, the margins and midrib moderately to heavily thickened, the grooves between the raised parts sometimes very narrow ... 31
30' Leaf blades of the lower two leaves several-ribbed 33
31 Foliage leaves 2, the upper of these sheathing the lower half of the stem and with a short free blade; stem bearing a short, membranous, scale-like bract in the upper half .... *G. scillaris*
31' Foliage leaves 3, sometimes the lowermost lost by flowering time; stem without a scale-like bract in the upper half 32

32 Leaf blades terete with 4 hair-like longitudinal grooves .... *G. brehmii*
32' Leaf blades with the midrib and margins separated by wide grooves .... *G. similis*
33 Flowers shades of white to pale yellow, sometimes with a dark central mark 34
33' Flowers shades of blue-violet with a red center 36
34 Tepals mostly 11–25 mm long and perianth tube mostly 4–8 mm long; tepals often flushed reddish on the reverse, often without a dark center .... *G. imbricata*
34' Tepals mostly 10–16 mm long and perianth tube 2–4 mm long; tepals seldom flushed red on the reverse and with a dark center 35
35 Spikes mostly with 2–3 flowers, rarely more; perianth cream to yellow with a dark brown to purplish center ... *G. purpureolutea*
35' Spikes mostly with at least 5 flowers; perianth uniformly white or cream .... *G. sulphurascens*
36 Stamens and style unilateral and declinate; style branches linear-filiform; the red center of the flower edged in white .... *G. radians*
36' Stamens and style symmetrically arranged; style branches ovate-spathulate, about 2–3 × 2 mm; the red center of the flower not edged in white 37
37 Perianth tube to 2.5 mm long; anthers arching inward, borne above the style branches .... *G. mathewsii*
37' Perianth tube 6–9 mm long; anthers erect, borne below the style branches .... *G. eurystigma*

Geissorhiza Subgenus *Weihea*

1 Stamens and style included in the lower half of the perianth tube 2
1' Stamens and style, or at least the style branches, exserted from the perianth tube 3
2 Leaves plane, 3–5 mm wide; flowers white ... *G. esterhuyseniae*
2' Leaves with margins and midrib heavily thickened, 1.5–2 mm wide; flowers pink with dark markings at the bases of the tepals .... *G. cedarmontana*
3 Leaf single and stem with a scale-like, membranous bract in the upper half .... *G. unifolia*
3' Leaves 2 or more in addition to scale-like bracts in the upper half of the stem 4
4 Leaf blades spirally twisted; flowering stems each with a single flower; style usually dividing opposite the base of the anthers 5
4' Leaf blades more or less straight; flowering stems usually with more than one flower; style dividing at or beyond the anthers ... 6
5 Flowers yellow; perianth tube c. 3 mm long ...... *G. corrugata*
5' Flowers mauve; perianth tube 4–5 mm long .... *G. spiralis*
6 Corm tunics entirely of fibrous layers or softly membranous, becoming fibrous with age 7

6' Corm tunics firm, papery to woody in texture, often drawn into bristles above 11
7 Perianth tube 2–4 mm long; tepals less than 14 mm long 8
7' Perianth tube 4.5–18 mm long 10
8 Flowers white to pale mauve-pink .... *G. umbrosa*
8' Flowers deep blue to mauve or violet 9
9 Perianth tube 4–6 mm long; perianth pale in the throat .... *G. cataractarum*
9' Perianth tube 2–3 mm long; perianth uniformly colored .... *G. alticola*
10 Tepals 17–22 mm long, pink to pink-purple; perianth tube 10–18 mm long, well exserted from the bracts .... *G. nubigena*
10' Tepals 12–18 mm long, violet; perianth tube 5–8(–10) mm long, not or barely exserted from the bracts .... *G. hesperanthoides*
11 Leaves not plane, either strongly ridged, or the margins and midrib heavily thickened, or blade terete with 4 narrow longitudinal grooves 12
11' Leaves plane or nearly so, the margins and midribs only lightly raised 30
12 Flowers moderate in size to large, mostly whitish or cream to pink, usually darker pink on the reverse; stamens unilateral and declinate; bracts acute (Engysiphon group) 13
12' Flowers small to moderate in size, mostly shades of cream to yellow, or deep pink, whitish flushed pink in 1 sp.; stamens symmetrically arranged; bracts obtuse 21
13 Leaves not sticky, the blades either plane with the margins and midrib lightly thickened or terete with 4 hairline grooves; stems branched or unbranched but flowers always one per branch 14
13' Leaves, sometimes only the sheaths, sticky, the blades always with the margins strongly thickened or raised but if 4-grooved then the grooves clearly visible 15
14 Leaves linear, the margins and midrib lightly thickened; perianth tube 9–13 mm long; plants of waterfalls and wet, shady rocks .... *G. uliginosa*
14' Leaves terete with hairline longitudinal grooves; perianth tube 12–20 mm long; tepals 20–30 mm long; plants of exposed rock outcrops only seasonally moist ...... *G. fourcadei*
15 Leaf blades with the margins raised and winged but the midrib hardly thickened, thus appearing H-shaped in cross section, the marginal wings often curving inward, the blade appearing terete 16
15' Leaf blades terete to linear or falcate, with both midrib and margins thickened and winged but visibly with 2 narrow grooves on each surface 18
16 Tepals linear or narrowly lanceolate, usually uniformly white ... . *G. tenella*
16' Tepals oblong to obovate, usually whitish flushed with pink or uniformly pink 17

17 Perianth tube 15–30 mm long; spike borne on a well-developed stem, mostly 2- to 4-flowered .... *G. bonaspei*
17′ Perianth tube 40–80 mm long; spike borne on a disproportionately short stem, sometimes the spike virtually at ground level, often with more than 4 flowers and as many as 15 ... *G. exscapa*
18 Perianth tube c. 8 mm long, included in the bracts and about a third as long as the tepals .... *G. brevituba*
18′ Perianth tube 20–50 mm long, reaching at least to the bract apices or exceeding the bracts and about as long as or longer than the tepals 19
19 Tepals 17–27 mm long, white or barely flushed with pink .... *G. longifolia*
19′ Tepals 28–40 mm long, pink or cream, becoming flushed with pink with age 20
20 Tepals slightly longer than the perianth tube, 9–15 mm wide .... *G. schinzii*
20′ Tepals shorter than the perianth tube, 7–10 mm wide .... *G. confusa*
21 Leaf blade terete with hairline longitudinal grooves 22
21′ Leaf blade linear to falcate with 2 visible longitudinal grooves on each surface 24
22 Perianth tube elongate, 40–80 mm long .... *G. stenosiphon*
22′ Perianth tube short, 2–5 mm long 23
23 Flower fairly large, pale to golden yellow, tepals remaining cupped when fully open, 15–22 mm long; perianth tube 3–5 mm long .... *G. furva*
23′ Flower small, cream to yellow, tepals outspread when fully open, 8–14 mm long; perianth tube 2–3 mm long .... *G. juncea*
24 Flowers mauve, blue, or purple 25
24′ Flowers white to cream or yellow 26
25 Perianth tube 3–6 mm long; spike 4- to 10-flowered .... *G. purpurascens*
25′ Perianth tube 7–8 mm long; spike 1- to 4-flowered ... *G. lithicola*
26 Flowers small, the tepals 7–9 mm long and stem smooth or 8–10 mm long and stem minutely hairy 27
26′ Flowers moderate in size, the tepals 10–22 mm long; stem smooth 28
27 Stem smooth .... *G. pappei*
27′ Stem minutely hairy in the upper half .... *G. intermedia*
28 Bracts not normally sticky; perianth tube 9–11 mm long; flowers with a dark center .... *G. darlingensis*
28′ Bracts sticky and usually with sand adhering; perianth tube 3–6 mm long; flowers uniformly colored inside 29
29 Flowers whitish to cream, the outer tepals usually flushed reddish on the reverse; tepals 10–15 mm long and perianth tube 3–4 mm long .... *G. hispidula*
29′ Flowers pale yellow; tepals 16–26 mm long, not normally flushed red on the reverse, and perianth tube 5–6 mm long .... *G. humilis*
30 Flowers zygomorphic with the stamens and style unilateral and declinate 31
30′ Flowers actinomorphic with stamens symmetrically arranged 33
31 Flowers purple; tepals 12–15 mm long .... *G. karooica*
31′ Flowers pink with darker markings; tepals 22–32 mm long ... 32
32 Stems and leaves trailing; leaf blades soft textured; perianth tube 10–13 mm long .... *G. outeniquensis*
32′ Stems and leaves erect; leaf blades firm textured; perianth tube 8–10 mm long .... *G. roseoalba*
33 Leaves linear to narrowly sword-shaped, mostly 1–2(–4) mm wide, hairy or smooth; stems sometimes with only 1–2 flowers 34
33′ Leaves sword-shaped, lanceolate or ovate, (2–)3–10 mm wide, hairless except sometimes on the margins; stems with 3 flowers or more 41
34 Flowers with perianth tube 6–8 mm long, usually exserted from the bracts; perianth white to cream, rarely pale yellow ... 35
34′ Flowers with perianth tube 2–5 mm long, included in the bracts; perianth white, yellow or lilac 36
35 Plants usually more than 12 cm high; stem usually branched dichotomously .... *G. geminata*
35′ Plants 4–8 cm high; stem rarely branched, never dichotomously .... *G. setacea*
36 Flowers blue; leaf sheaths, some times the proximal parts of the blades and the margins minutely hairy to pubescent .... *G. pusilla*
36′ Flowers white to lilac; leaf sheaths and blades smooth 37
37 Flowers yellow; corms pointed at base or bell-shaped with a flat base 38
37′ Flowers white or lilac; corms pointed at base 39
38 Flowers rotate when fully open; tepals 6–12(–18) mm long; perianth tube 2–3 mm long .... *G. ornithogaloides*
38′ Flowers cup-shaped; tepals 13–25 mm long; perianth tube c. 4 mm long .... *G. malmesburiensis*
39 Flowers tiny, tepals 3–6 mm long; perianth tube 1–2.5 mm long .... *G. nana*
39′ Flower somewhat larger, tepals 6–12 mm long; perianth tube 2–5 mm long 40
40 Perianth tube 2–3 mm long; leaves soft textured, spreading or prostrate .... *G. delicatula*
40′ Perianth tube 3–5 mm long; leaves firm, ascending to erect ... . *G. bracteata*
41 Leaves held more or less erect 42
41′ Leaves prostrate or inclined toward the ground 46
42 Perianth tube 8–10 mm long; flowers pale pink ...... *G. elsiae*
42′ Perianth tube 2–6 mm long; flowers white, pink, or violet 43
43 Plants branching only at the base; flowering stems mostly with 1–2 flowers, rarely 3 .... *G. bracteata*
43′ Plants branching above ground level, or unbranched; flowering stems usually with at least 3 flowers and as many as 7 44

44 Leaves half to two-thirds as long as the spike; flowers white or violet, with tepals mostly 8–11 mm long, sometimes longer .... *G. inconspicua*
44' Leaves less than a third as long as the spike; flowers pink, with tepals 13–17 mm long 45
45 Perianth tube 4–5 mm long; style branches c. 3 mm long .... *G. foliosa*
45' Perianth tube c. 2 mm long; style branches 4–5 mm long .... *G. nigromontana*
46 Perianth tube 10–30 mm long, as long as or longer than the tepals; leaves usually broadly ovate and minutely pubescent along the margins .... *G. ovata*
46' Perianth tube 2–8 mm long; leaves narrowly ovate to lanceolate, usually hairless 47
47 Leaves firm textured; cormels never produced in the aerial leaf axils .... *G. parva*
47' Leaves soft textured, often flaccid; cormels borne in the aerial leaf axils 48
48 Flowers solitary on each flowering stem, lilac ...... *G. delicatula*
48' Flowers usually more than one per flowering stem, white to pale yellow 49
49 Stem either without or with only one cauline leaf; flowers fertile, capsules developing rapidly after flowering ... *G. ovalifolia*
49' Stem bearing 2 leaves or more above ground level; flowers sterile, and cormels produced in the bract axils in place of capsules after flowering .... *G. bolusii*

Gethyllis

Groups of *Gethyllis*

1 Flowers often cup-shaped; stamens spreading; filaments more or less stout, often divided; anthers 6 to numerous; style erect, central, approximately as long as the fresh stamens; stigma narrowly trifid .... *Afra* group
1' Flowers with outspread to recurved tepals; stamens erect; filaments filiform, undivided; anthers 6; style curved sideways, distinctly longer than the fresh stamens; stigma broadly trilobed .... *Villosa* group

Gethyllis Group *Afra*

1 Leaves 1–2 at maturity; blades opposite, plane ... *G. gregoriana*
1' Leaves at least 4 at maturity; blades twisted or spiraled 2
2 Leaves often green at flowering; flower with 6 anthers .... *G. kaapensis*
2' Leaves dry at flowering; flower with at least 9 anthers 3
3 Leaves hemiterete; flower with 12 anthers; filaments consistently in pairs .... *G. campanulata*
3' Leaves channeled; flower usually with more than 12 anthers, if less then the filaments seldom in definite pairs 4
4 Leaves with a fringe of rigid upturned hairs .... *G. ciliaris*
4' Leaves smooth to sparsely covered or fringed with soft hairs ... 5
5 Leaf sheaths usually entirely hidden by fibrous tunics; leaves leathery; flowers with 9–18 anthers; filaments varying from 1 to 3 in each cluster .... *G. afra*
5' Leaf sheaths protruding well beyond the fibrous tunics or rarely entirely free of dry tunics; leaves somewhat succulent, gray-green; flowers with 20 or more anthers; filaments varying from 3 to 6 in each cluster 6
6 Leaf sheaths 2, often exserted well above ground; leaves 1.5–4 mm wide, smooth .... *G. britteniana*
6' Leaf sheath 1, entirely subterranean or slightly exserted; leaves 8–12 mm wide, smooth to sparsely hairy ..... *G. latifolia*

Gethyllis Group *Villosa*

1 Leaves surrounded by prominent, spotted basal sheaths with the upper edge distinctly fringed .... *G. verticillata*
1' Leaves surrounded by inconspicuous basal sheaths without spots or a fringe 2
2 Leaves smooth or more or less covered with simple hairs 3
2' Leaves covered with compound T- or star-shaped hairs 10
3 Leaves spreading to suberect, more or less spiraled 4
3' Leaves more or less prostrate, not spiraled 8
4 Base of anthers sagittate, the lobes somewhat diverging and 0.8–1.5 mm long .... *G. transkarooica*
4' Base of anthers round, the lobes short and parallel 5
5 Leaves with short, rather rigid hairs in rows near the margin .... *G. fimbriatula*
5' Leaves softly hairy or smooth 6
6 Leaves softly hairy on both surfaces .... *G. lanuginosa*
6' Leaves smooth, rarely sparsely fringed 7
7 Bulbs forming clumps; leaves tightly coiled, subsucculent, smooth .... *G. linearis*
7' Bulbs solitary; leaves twisted, leathery, smooth to sparsely fringed .... *G. spiralis*
8 Leaf margin fringed with spreading clusters of short, straw-colored bristles .... *G. pectinata*
8' Leaf margin without hairs or bristles 9
9 Leaf margin reddish or straw colored, raised and often minutely crisped .... *G. lata*
9' Leaf margin green, not raised .... *G. roggeveldensis*
10 Hairs on leaves scale-like, the arms parallel and attached to a dark center .... *G. verrucosa*
10' Hairs on leaves soft and star-like, the arms radiating from a colorless center 11
11 Leaves more or less elliptical, plane .... *G. barkerae*
11' Leaves narrowly lanceolate, more or less loosely spiraled .... *G. villosa*

Gladiolus

In the keys to *Gladiolus*, observations and measurements should be made according to the following notes:

- Measure perianth length from the top of the ovary to the apex of the dorsal tepal of a mature flower.
- Measure perianth tube length from the top of ovary to the first point of separation of any tepal (usually the dorsal).
- Measure lower tepals from the apices to the point of fusion with each other.
- For leaf number, exclude basal sheathing cataphylls but include both fully developed long-bladed foliage leaves and partly and entirely sheathing (bladeless) leaves present on the flowering stem.
- Terete leaves usually have 4 longitudinal grooves but are described as terete whether 4-grooved or solidly terete.
- For bract length, measure the outer bracts in the middle of the spike.
- For leaf width, choose a well-developed, preferably basal leaf, and measure near the midline of the blade.

Sections of *Gladiolus*

1. Leaves sword-shaped to lanceolate, usually at least 4 mm wide, often with well-developed secondary veins, sometimes the secondary veins fine and closely set; flowers mostly slightly bilabiate with the lower tepals not narrow and clawed below 2
1'. Leaves linear, usually less than 5 mm wide, usually without well-developed secondary veins, rarely broader but then without a well-developed midrib; flowers usually strongly bilabiate with the lower tepals narrow and clawed 3
2. Leaves in a 2-ranked fan, smooth, rarely minutely puberulous ... . section *Blandus*
2'. Leaves usually superposed, sheaths and sometimes blades with long hairs; leaf blades of the flowering stem often reduced; corm tunics consisting of flattened, parallel vertical fibers, often dark brown .... section *Linearifolius*
3. Leaves occasionally 2, usually 3–4, superposed (inserted serially up the stem); spike usually strongly flexuous; stems never branched; nectar guides when present usually consisting of fine dark longitudinal streaks and spots over a pale area or transverse bands of pale color; capsule almost always ellipsoidal to ovoid with acute apices; flowers often fragrant except when red or long-tubed and pink .... section *Homoglossum*
3'. Leaves usually several, at least 3 basal 4
4. Leaf margins usually unthickened and the blades plane, slightly raised in the midline, rarely ridged and corrugate; corm tunics membranous, papery, woody, or fibrous, not accumulating in a neck; spike drooping in bud; flowers frequently fragrant, except red-flowered species; capsules usually ellipsoidal and pointed above, sometimes obovate and deeply 3-lobed ... section *Hebea*
4'. Leaf margins and midribs usually heavily thickened and the blades cross-shaped, oval or round in cross section, rarely plane and lightly ridged; corm tunics coarsely fibrous, often accumulating in a neck around the base of the stem; flowers rarely lightly fragrant; capsules usually oblong, slightly 3-lobed above .... section *Heterocolon*

Gladiolus Section *Blandus*

1. Flowers carmine to red, sometimes with white median streaks or spots on the lower tepals 2
1'. Flowers various colors except carmine to red and with various markings on the lower tepals 6
2. Flowers more or less of one color; tepals broadly obovate, widest in the upper third, obtuse, 27–30 mm long; filaments c. 20 mm long .... *G. insolens*
2'. Flowers with white markings on the lower tepals; tepals more or less lanceolate, usually acute, 35–67 mm long; filaments 21–50 mm long 3
3. Leaves with blades reduced or absent at flowering time 4
3'. Leaf blades well developed at flowering time 5
4. Flowers large, the dorsal tepal 53–58 mm long and tube 35–45 mm long; filaments 30–42 mm long, exserted 20–32 mm from the tube; lower 3 tepals smaller than the dorsal; anthers dark purplish, or yellow with purple lines ... *G. stefaniae*
4'. Flowers medium-sized, dorsal tepal 35–45 mm long, tube 30–35 mm long; filaments 21–26 mm long and exserted 10–15 mm from the tube; lower tepals hardly smaller than the dorsal; anthers yellow .... *G. carmineus*
5. Stems erect or inclined; corm vestigial, producing rhizome-like stolons; Outeniqua Mountains, flowering mostly Mar.–May .... *G. sempervirens*
5'. Stems inclined to drooping; corm small but developed, without stolons; southwestern Cape, flowering Dec.–Jan. .... *G. cardinalis*
6. Leaves somewhat succulent, without evident veins and margins unthickened; tepals subequal, blue-mauve, the lower or all the tepals with a white median streak edged with dark red; strand plants growing above the high tide zone in deep sand .... *G. gueinzii*
6'. Leaves not succulent, the margins usually prominent and secondary veins usually evident, often conspicuous; flowers white to cream, greenish cream, or pink to mauve or salmon-orange, the lower tepals with spade-, diamond-, or spear-shaped markings, or a single median streak, rarely without markings, in red to purple or pale color outlined in dark color ... 7
7. Leaves in a tight 2-ranked fan; leaf blades firm textured with strongly thickened margins and midribs; corm tunics of dense,

matted, coarse fibers, often interspersed with stiffly papery fragments, always accumulating with the remains of the leaf bases in a coarse fibrous neck around the underground part of the stem 8

7' Leaves in a loose 2-ranked fan or superposed; leaf blades soft textured with margins often lightly thickened; corm tunics of medium-textured fibers not accumulating markedly and not extending upward in a neck 11

8 Perianth tube 18–21 mm long; filaments 12–14 mm long; tepals acute, the lower laterals with spear-shaped yellow markings outlined in dark color; base of the plant heavily marked with raised white speckles .... *G. rudis*

8' Perianth tube 22–70 mm long; filaments 14–37 mm long; tepals more or less obtuse to retuse, the lower tepals each with a dark median streak; base of the plant lightly marked but not textured with white or green speckles 9

9 Perianth tube 22–35(–55) mm long; lower tepals three-fourths to as long as the dorsal .... *G. grandiflorus*

9' Perianth tube 40–70 mm long, if less than 50 mm then lower tepals half to three-quarters as long as the dorsal 10

10 Filaments 35–37 mm long; flowers salmon to orange-red; perianth tube slender and cylindrical in the lower 20–35 mm, wide and cylindrical above .... *G. miniatus*

10' Filaments 20–23 mm long; flowers cream to yellow or greenish; perianth tube slender below for 20–55 mm, flared above .... *G. floribundus*

11 Corms scarcely developed, without accumulated tunics; robust plants with inclined to drooping stems growing on wet rocks and cliffs 12

11' Corms well developed, with or without accumulated tunics ... 13

12 Spike usually with 15–20 flowers; lower tepals less than half as long as the dorsal; perianth tube 45–50 mm long, completely enclosed in the bracts .... *G. buckerveldii*

12' Spike with fewer than 15 flowers; lower tepals two-thirds to nearly as long as the dorsal; perianth tube (25–)34–40 mm long, exceeding the bracts .... *G. aquamontanus*

13 Perianth tube (45–)50–110 mm long; flowers cream to yellowish or salmon or lilac, with red to purple markings 14

13' Perianth tube (15–)20–50 mm long; flowers pale to deep pink to mauve, purple, or rarely white 16

14 Tepals attenuate and strongly undulate; lower tepals slightly shorter than the upper .... *G. undulatus*

14' Tepals obtuse to acute not attenuate and weakly undulate; lower tepals usually about two-thirds as long as the upper ... 15

15 Leaves 4–5; flowers cream to yellowish, with prominent spear-shaped markings outlined in red on the lower tepals; flowering Oct.–Nov.; Western Cape mountains and flats ..... *G. angustus*

15' Leaves 3; flowers salmon with red linear markings on the lower tepals; flowering Mar.–Apr.; southern Cape, Swellendam to Albertinia .... *G. bilineatus*

16 Flowers large, dorsal tepal 40–55 mm long; occurring east of Uniondale and Plettenberg Bay .... *G. geardii*

16' Flowers smaller, dorsal tepal 18–40(–50) mm long; occurring west of Knysna 17

17 Leaf blades with 2 prominent veins on at least some of the leaves; corm tunics of fine, more or less netted fibers; flowering mid-Nov. to Jan. 18

17' Leaf blades either with only the midrib and margins thickened or at least one other pair of veins prominent 19

18 Flowers 48–60 mm long; floral bracts 25–33 mm long; markings on the lower tepals triangular in the middle and large dark spots toward the base and in the throat .... *G. crispulatus*

18' Flowers 33–46 mm long; floral bracts 13–25 mm long; markings on the lower tepal spear-shaped, white to yellow in the center surrounded by dark pink to purple .... *G. oreocharis*

19 Leaves narrow, 1.5–3 mm wide; flowers 1–2(3) per spike; corm tunics weakly developed, membranous, not accumulating .... *G. pappei*

19' Leaves (2–)6–20 mm wide; flowers usually at least 5 per spike; corm tunics usually accumulating, fibrous or firm-papery 20

20 Floral bracts 13–16 mm long; perianth tube 18–20 mm long; lower tepals narrowed below into claws .... *G. phoenix*

20' Floral bracts 35–45(–65) mm long; perianth tube (15–)25–45 mm long; lower tepals not abruptly narrowed below .... *G. carneus*

Gladiolus Section *Hebea*

1 Flowers zygomorphic with the upper lateral and lower median tepals (the outer whorl) heart-shaped at the base with a short claw and the filaments long and strongly arched, sometimes shorter but then sparsely pilose; sutures between the tepals forming iridescent papillate ridges 2

1' Flowers actinomorphic or zygomorphic with the upper lateral tepals obscurely or not at all heart-shaped with a short claw at the base and the filaments short to long, horizontal, ascending, or strongly arched but then never sparsely pilose; sutures between the tepals never forming iridescent papillate ridges ... 10

2 Flowers scarlet to orange or pink; stems angled or lightly winged; floral bracts folded on the midline or strongly keeled ... 3

2' Flowers purple, green, gray, pale yellow, or brownish, occasionally pale pink but then veined with dark color; stems terete; floral bracts not folded or keeled 6

3 Leaf blades plane, the midrib and other veins barely evident and not raised; stamens and style lightly pilose or smooth above 4

3' Leaf blades ribbed, at least the midrib and usually several other veins thickened and raised, the blade thus corrugate; stamens and style lightly pilose 5

4   Dorsal tepals strongly hooded and concave; stamens and style hairless above; upper lateral tepals weakly spreading above, the limbs virtually sessile, often colored yellow with orange margins on the reverse .... *G. speciosus*

4′ Dorsal tepals more or less plane, inclined, or more or less erect; upper lateral tepals spreading, with claws 3–4 mm long, uniformly salmon-orange on the reverse ..... *G. pulcherrimus*

5   Flowers predominantly salmon pink to brick red, the lower laterals with small yellow marks broadly edged distally with reddish black; filaments c. 15 mm long .... *G. meliusculus*

5′ Flowers predominantly orange to scarlet; filaments 20–26 mm long .... *G. alatus*

6   Blade of the basal leaf plane 7

6′ Blade of the basal leaf ridged (thus corrugate) or with the margins and sometimes other veins thickened and raised, then sometimes terete 8

7   Dorsal tepal narrow with sides parallel, arched in a semicircle; corm tunics firm textured to hard and coarsely fibrous and the corm producing small cormels around the base .... *G. orchidiflorus*

7′ Dorsal tepal fairly broad, lanceolate and erect; corm tunics of soft-textured layers and the corm producing stolons, each with a fairly large terminal cormel .... *G. uysiae*

8   Dorsal tepal hooded and horizontal, partially translucent; leaf blade with several ridges of equal size ..... *G. watermeyeri*

8′ Dorsal tepal erect to slightly inclined, not translucent; leaf blade with a prominent central vein, secondary veins also sometimes thickened, but not uniformly corrugate 9

9   Leaf bases overlapping, the stem visible only above the sheathing part of the uppermost leaf; corms with dark, firm-textured, almost woody tunics; Knersvlakte, western Karoo, and Cold Bokkeveld .... *G. ceresianus*

9′ Leaf bases not overlapping, the stem visible below the uppermost leaf; corms with soft-textured almost membranous tunics; Breede River Valley and southern Cape east of Bot River to the Long Kloof .... *G. virescens*

10 Flowers carmine to red, sometimes the lower tepals much reduced and with yellow and or green markings 11

10′ Flowers variously colored but not carmine to red 13

11 Dorsal and upper lateral tepals nearly equal in size, lanceolate; upper part of the perianth tube 20–23 mm long; southern Cape .... *G. vandermerwei*

11′ Dorsal tepal about twice as long as the upper laterals or longer, spathulate; upper part of the perianth tube 2–10 mm long ... 12

12 Lower median tepal shorter than the lower laterals, the limb curving inward; spike inclined sometimes nearly horizontal; Cape coast from Saldanha to Knysna .... *G. cunonius*

12′ Lower median tepal more than twice as wide as the lower laterals, the limb directed downward; spike stiffly erect; western Karoo .... *G. splendens*

13 Corm tunics hard, woody, and somewhat gnarled or membranous but then leaf sheaths hairy 14

13′ Corms tunics never hard and woody, either leathery, fibrous, or membranous 18

14 Uppermost cataphyll purple mottled with white above the ground .... *G. viridiflorus*

14′ Uppermost cataphyll not mottled 15

15 Corm tunics softly membranous, not accumulating with age; sheaths and blades of the lower leaves shortly hairy; capsules ellipsoidal, acute at apex .... *G. arcuatus*

15′ Corm tunics hard, woody, and gnarled, accumulating with age; leaf sheaths not hairy; capsules ovoid to globose, 3-lobed and retuse above 16

16 Perianth tube cylindrical, 35–40 mm long; filaments c. 8 mm long; flowers cream .... *G. lapeirousioides*

16′ Perianth tube obliquely funnel-shaped, 12–18 mm long; filaments 11–25 mm long 17

17 Lower tepals with a conspicuous sharp bend at the base of the limbs and the upper edges of the claws with broad auriculate lobes; upper lateral tepals twisted to lie partly above the dorsal .... *G. venustus*

17′ Lower tepals with a more or less sharp bend at the base of the limb and the upper edges of the claws not or only weakly auriculate; perianth windowed in profile (gaping between the dorsal and upper lateral tepals) .... *G. scullyi*

18 Leaves lanceolate to sword-shaped or nearly linear but usually at least 3 mm wide; perianth not windowed in profile; flowers with the upper lateral tepals twisted to overlap the dorsal tepal, the lower lateral tepals strongly involute below and conspicuously shorter than the lower median tepal .... *G. involutus*

18′ Leaves linear, 1–2 mm wide, or round to oval in cross section ... 19

19 Flowers actinomorphic, perianth stellate; filaments symmetrically disposed .... *G. stellatus*

19′ Flowers zygomorphic, perianth bilabiate; filaments unilateral 20

20 Perianth tube 28–50 mm long, at least 1.5 times as long as the dorsal tepal; flowers white or cream ..... *G. leptosiphon*

20′ Perianth tube 9–28(–35) mm long, less than 1.5 times as long as the dorsal tepal 21

21 Tepals subequal and lanceolate-acuminate; perianth tube 16–30 mm long; filaments 6–10 mm long and included in the tube, rarely exserted as much as 2 mm; flowers yellowish green, often flushed brown to purple on the reverse, the lower tepals unmarked .... *G. acuminatus*

21′ Plants not as above 22

22 In profile, the perianth windowed (gaping between dorsal and upper lateral tepals); flowers usually sweetly scented .. 23

22′ In profile, the perianth not windowed; flowers usually unscented, rarely lightly fragrant 24

23 Perianth tube 22–28(–35) mm long; dorsal tepal 28–30 mm long . . . . G. uitenhagensis
23′ Perianth tube 9–15 mm long; dorsal tepal 16–33 mm long . . . . G. permeabilis
24 Lower tepals linear, involute, marked with a broad green transverse band edged with pink; upper lateral tepals 25–28 mm long, attenuate, much longer than the dorsal tepal . . . . G. involutus
24′ Lower tepals lanceolate, mostly unmarked; upper lateral tepals 15–23 mm long, acute or obtuse, slightly shorter than the dorsal tepal . . . . G. wilsonii

Gladiolus Section Heterocolon

1 Leaf blades X-shaped in cross section; flowers pale bluish . . . . G. marlothii
1′ Leaf blade plane; flowers pink with the lower tepals marked with pale green . . . . G. mostertiae

Gladiolus Section Homoglossum

1 Plants with only 3 leaves, including partly to entirely sheathing upper leaves, and the lowermost leaf longest and with a well-developed blade, the blade terete but X-shaped in cross section, or at least with margins and the midrib heavily thickened; corm tunics often cartilaginous or more or less woody layers, with age these becoming regularly notched below into claw-like segments or coarsely fibrous 2
1′ Plants with 2 to many leaves, if only 3 either the blade of the lowermost vestigial (much shorter than the sheathing part, or lacking) or the blade well developed with the midrib and margins not or only lightly thickened; corm tunics various, woody to more or less membranous, sometimes coarsely to finely fibrous 16
2 Floral bracts 14–30 mm long or if longer then perianth tube less than 25 mm long; perianth tube short to long, usually shorter than the bracts but if longer then flowers pink with reddish markings on the lower tepals 3
2′ Bracts (25–)30–80(–115) mm long; perianth tube always fairly long, at least 25 mm and often about as long as the bracts or as much as twice as long 7
3 Perianth either almost actinomorphic, the tepals subequal, or zygomorphic but then yellow; tepal markings when present confined to the tepal bases . . . . G. trichonemifolius
3′ Perianth zygomorphic and white to pink or purple; tepal markings more or less in the middle of the lower tepals 4
4 Flowers blue to grayish or cream, the lower lateral tepals marked with a transverse band of yellow outlined with dark blue; perianth tube sharply bent, short, 10–12(–15) mm long to half as long as the dorsal tepal; the stem base always with a well-developed fibrous neck . . . . G. patersoniae
4′ Flowers whitish to pale pink, mauve, or purple, the lower lateral tepals with a median streak or diamond-shaped mark in red or yellow outlined in dark blue to purple; perianth tube usually curved, 11–55 mm long, at least half as long to 3 times as long as the dorsal tepal; the stem base with or without a well-developed fibrous neck 5
5 Flowers pale pink to whitish with red median streaks on the lower tepals; Swartberg Mountains . . . . G. nigromontanus
5′ Flowers mauve, purple, or pink to white with diamond-shaped or transverse markings on the lower tepals; Cedarberg to Langeberg Mountains 6
6 Perianth tube mostly 12–18(–30) mm long; flowers bell- to trumpet-shaped, the dorsal tepal ascending to hooded; filaments 12–18 mm long; the uppermost, third, leaf often reduced to a short scale; flowering mainly Sept.–Nov., rarely Dec. . . . . G. inflatus
6′ Perianth tube (25–)35–52 mm long; flowers salverform, the tepals spreading more or less at right angles to the tube; filaments 7–8 mm long; the upper, third, leaf short but not scale-like; flowering Dec.–Jan. . . . . G. cylindraceus
7 Flowers white, cream, brown, to dull purple or dull reddish orange; perianth tube widening gradually from base to apex; often sweetly scented in the evening 8
7′ Flowers red to deep orange, the tepals sometimes marked with yellow or green; perianth tube narrow and cylindrical below, abruptly widened into a long cylindrical horizontal upper part 11
8 Flower mostly white to cream, sometimes streaked or spotted with brown; leaves oval, round, or X-shaped in cross section . . . 10
8′ Flowers mainly brown, dull purplish green, or reddish orange; leaf blade oval in cross section with the margins and midribs heavily thickened and with 2 narrow grooves on each surface . . . 9
9 Bracts long and attenuate; tepals long and attenuate, (31–)40–45 mm; perianth tube 40–53 mm long . . . . G. liliaceus
9′ Bracts short and not normally attenuate; tepals obtuse to acute, the upper 22–30 mm long; perianth tube 25–36 mm long . . . . G. hyalinus
10 Perianth tube as much as 1.5 times as long as the bracts; filaments (15–)18–25 mm long; winter-rainfall zone, Bokkeveld Mountains to Port Elizabeth . . . . G. tristis
10′ Perianth tube 1.3 to c. 3 times as long as the bracts; filaments 5–13 mm long; winter- and summer-rainfall zones, Oudtshoorn to Northern Province . . . . G. longicollis
11 The upper lateral tepals about as long to slightly longer than the dorsal; leaf blades oblong to oval in cross section, the margins and midribs thickened; corm tunics hard and more or less woody in texture, decaying into vertical segments from below 12
11′ The upper lateral tepals somewhat shorter to less than half as long as the dorsal; leaf blades X-shaped in cross section, the margins and edges of the midribs thickened; corm tunics

cartilaginous to fairly soft in texture, decaying with age into fine vertical fibers 13

12 Upper and lower lateral tepals lanceolate, more than twice as long as wide; blade of the lowermost leaf linear (oblong in cross section), (1.5-)3-5 mm at the widest; Breede River Valley west of Worcester and west of the Hottentots Holland–Porterville Mountain axis .... *G. watsonius*

12' Upper and lower lateral tepals ovate, as much as twice as long as wide; blade of the lowermost leaf oval in cross section, 1-2 mm at the widest; east of the Hottentots Holland Mountains and Breede River Valley east of Robertson .... *G. teretifolius*

13 Tepals lanceolate, the upper laterals more than twice as long as wide; flowers with the lower tepals uniformly red or orange toward the base; Cold Bokkeveld and Ceres district .... *G. quadrangularis*

13' Tepals ovate to elliptical, the upper laterals less than twice as long as wide; flower with the lower tepals with yellow to greenish markings; Caledon to Grahamstown 14

14 Dorsal tepal horizontal, concave, and 2-3 times as long as the upper laterals; lower tepals mostly dark green to reddish black, the median shorter than the laterals, 3-6 mm long .... *G. abbreviatus*

14' Dorsal tepal erect to lightly inclined and less than 1.5 times as long as the upper laterals; lower tepals mostly yellow, the lower median about as long as or slightly longer than the laterals, 9-22 mm long 15

15 Flowers large, the dorsal tepal 25-40 mm long; filaments 32-45 mm long; flowers mostly orange with the reverse of the upper part of the tube with dark red longitudinal streaks below the upper lateral tepal sinuses .... *G. huttonii*

15' Flowers smaller, the dorsal tepal 15-20 mm long; filaments 26-32 mm long; flower dull red or greenish, the upper tepals with red to gray veining, the tube without red streaks .... *G. fourcadei*

16 Leaf sheaths and sometimes the blades hairy 17

16' Leaf sheaths and blades hairless or minutely scabrid 18

17 Leaf blades X-shaped in section; flowers greenish to pale yellow without strongly developed dark markings on the lower tepals .... *G. sufflavus*

17' Leaf blades with 1-2 raised veins, the margins not thickened; flowers yellow with brown to reddish transverse markings on the lower tepals .... *G. pritzelii*

18 Leaf blades vestigial, lacking or less than 10 mm long 19

18' Leaf blades usually well developed to fairly short but always present 23

19 Perianth tubular, the tube (22-)30-60 mm long; Langeberg foothills .... *G. engysiphon*

19' Perianth funnel-shaped, the tube 6.5-20 mm long 20

20 Leaves 2, the lowermost sheathing the lower two-thirds of the stem .... *G. vaginatus*

20' Leaves 2-4, all rather short 21

21 Corm tunics fibrous; flowers lacking a strong scent; leaves of nonflowering plants hairy .... *G. subcaeruleus*

21' Corm tunics very soft in texture, membranous, and not accumulating; flowers usually with a strong sweet scent; leaves of nonflowering plants hairless 22

22 Flowers mauve or pink; flowering Feb.–May; leaf on nonflowering plants solitary; lower tepals joined to the upper laterals for 2-5 mm .... *G. martleyi*

22' Flowers cream, yellow, or pale lilac; mostly flowering Dec.–Jan.; leaves of nonflowering plants 2-3; lower tepals not united basally with the upper laterals .... *G. jonquilliodorus*

23 Leaves linear, smooth, neither the midribs nor margins thickened 24

23' Leaves with either the margins or midribs raised or both 29

24 Perianth tube shorter than the bracts, 11-17 mm long; flowers pale blue to brown; filaments 10-15 mm long 25

24' Perianth tube slightly shorter than the bracts to twice as long, 23-48 mm; flowers red, pink, brownish, or cream to yellow ... 26

25 Leaves 4 .... *G. mutabilis*

25' Leaves 3 .... *G. exilis*

26 Perianth tube slender below, abruptly expanded above into a wide cylindrical upper part; flowers cream, pink, or red; filaments 25-40 mm long 27

26' Perianth tube gradually expanded from base to apex; flowers cream to yellowish or brown to dull lilac, scented; filaments 12-16 mm long 28

27 Leaves usually 4, rarely 3; flowers predominantly red, yellow in the throat .... *G. priorii*

27' Leaves 3; flowers yellow, or pale to deep pink but not yellow in the throat, the lower tepals often darkly speckled below .... *G. meridionalis*

28 Flowers cream or white; perianth tube 37-65 mm long, well exserted from the bracts .... *G. albens*

28' Flowers dull yellow to lilac conspicuously mottled with brown to purple; perianth tube 23-37(-48) mm long, not or barely exserted from the bracts .... *G. maculatus*

29 Lower leaf blade with the margins raised into wings extended at right angles to the blade surface, H-shaped in cross section 30

29' Lower leaf blade with the margins unthickened or thickened but not raised into wings extending at right angles to the surface or the leaves reduced and clasping 32

30 Perianth tube slightly shorter to about as long as the bracts, 27-36 mm long; tepals attenuate and recurved, mostly cream to pale pink or grayish .... *G. recurvus*

30' Perianth tube shorter than the bracts, 12-18 mm long; tepals not attenuate and recurved, mostly blue, occasionally pink or yellowish to light brown 31

31 Leaves soft and broad with the flanges at right angles to the blade; lower tepals rounded and marked with discrete spots; flowers (4–)8–14 per spike .... *G. caeruleus*
31′ Leaves firm and narrow with the flanges arching over and almost concealing the blade; lower tepals more or less acute and marked with streaks; flowers 2–7 per spike ..... *G. gracilis*
32 Uppermost cataphyll purple mottled with white above the ground 33
32′ Uppermost cataphyll uniformly colored above the ground or flushed with darker color but not distinctly mottled 36
33 Perianth actinomorphic or nearly so, flowers stellate with tepals spreading .... *G. quadrangulus*
33′ Perianth zygomorphic and usually more or less bilabiate, with an arched dorsal tepal and smaller lower tepals 34
34 Flowers inflated and bell-like, blue, the lower tepals each with a transverse or median white or yellow marking; leaves usually 4, occasionally 3; corm tunics firm textured to almost woody and broken into narrow vertical strips .... *G. rogersii*
34′ Flowers funnel-shaped, blue, pink, yellow, or grayish, the lower tepals each pale to deep yellow and lightly streaked with longitudinal lines or dots; leaves 3, rarely 4; corm tunics soft textured, irregularly fragmented or somewhat fibrous 35
35 Flowers larger, 37–54 mm long; perianth tube 13–16 mm long; flowering mainly late July–Sept. .... *G. carinatus*
35′ Flowers smaller, 22–36 mm long; perianth tube 6–10 mm long; flowering May–mid-July .... *G. griseus*
36 Flowers white to pink or pale blue-mauve with purple to red spots, streaks, or diamond-shaped markings on the lower tepals; leaf blades linear and usually with thickened margins 37
36′ Flowers blue, yellow, or orange to salmon or scarlet 43
37 Corm tunics membranous or firm-papery to leathery and becoming fibrous with age 38
37′ Corm tunics woody, splitting below into regular segments ... 39
38 Flower whitish to pale pink, the lower 3 tepals feathered with deep red below; corm tunics leathery to firmly papery, becoming coarsely fibrous with age; perianth tube 36–44 mm long .... *G. roseovenosus*
38′ Flower deep pink, the lower tepals each with an elongate pale median mark edged in darker pink; corm tunics soft textured, membranous, not accumulating; perianth tube 18–20 mm long .... *G. ornatus*
39 Perianth tube 35–40 mm long, usually c. 1.5 times as long as the bracts; floral bracts with a smooth surface, not ridged ... . *G. vigilans*
39′ Perianth tube 10–24 mm long, slightly shorter to c. 1.5 times as long as the bracts 40
40 Leaves usually 3, rarely 4; floral bracts smooth, not ridged; dorsal tepal 25–30 mm long; flowers whitish to pale pink with large red spots unevenly spread across the lower half of the lower tepals .... *G. variegatus*
40′ Leaves 4; floral bracts ridged above the veins 41
41 Filaments 4–10 mm long; dorsal tepal 17–27 mm long; flowers white or pale pink with red markings on the lower tepals .... *G. debilis*
41′ Filaments 12–16 mm long; dorsal tepal 28–44 mm long; flowers pale to deep pink or blue-mauve with red or yellow markings on the lower tepals 42
42 Perianth tube narrowly funnel-shaped to cylindrical, 22–27 mm long; lower tepals with darker V-shaped transverse markings .... *G. virgatus*
42′ Perianth tube obliquely funnel-shaped, 13–24 mm long; lower tepals cream to yellow with dark longitudinal lines and spots .... *G. blommesteinii*
43 Flowers yellow or orange to salmon or scarlet 44
43′ Flowers blue 46
44 Flower more or less actinomorphic, orange; perianth tube 2.4–4 mm long .... *G. brevitubus*
44′ Flower zygomorphic, bilabiate, never orange, salmon or scarlet; perianth tube at least 8 mm long 45
45 Flowers buttercup yellow; upper tepals narrowly elliptical, tapering to long-attenuate, acute tips; lower tepals marked with fine lines and dots; perianth tube 11–14 mm long .... *G. comptonii*
45′ Flowers creamy yellow; upper tepals ovate; lower tepals with paired narrow reddish streaks in the lower third; perianth tube c. 8 mm long .... *G. delpierrei*
46 Leaves 3 47
46′ Leaves 4, rarely 5; flowers with transverse or lateral yellow to white markings 48
47 Flowers irregularly mottled with purple, without transverse yellow to white markings on the lower tepals .... *G. inflexus*
47′ Flowers with transverse yellow markings on the lower tepals, not irregularly mottled with purple .... *G. taubertianus*
48 Upper tepals narrowly elliptical with long-attenuate acute apices; lower tepals marked with fine lines and dots 49
48′ Tepals lanceolate to ovate, obtuse to acute, not attenuate ... 50
49 Leaf blade with the midrib winged only on one side, the blade thus triangular in cross section; tepals pale blue, streaked, speckled, and feathered with violet, the lower tepals white to yellow below and more strongly marked than the upper; northwestern Cape .... *G. violaceolineatus*
49′ Leaf blades identical on both surfaces; tepals violet, the lower tepals pale yellow in the lower two-thirds and finely feathered with dark violet; Riviersonderend Mountains ..... *G. atropictus*
50 Flowers 1–2 per spike; floral bracts ridged and attenuate, mostly 30–50 mm long .... *G. bullatus*
50′ Flowers usually 3 per spike or more; bracts smooth and not attenuate, 15–22 mm long .... *G. rogersii*

Gladiolus Section *Linearifolius*

1. Leaves entirely sheathing, lacking blades 2
1′. Leaf blades well developed, usually at least the lowermost as long as the sheaths or much longer, narrowly lanceolate to linear 6
2. Flowers red to orange-red 3
2′. Flowers pink, mauve, white, or cream to yellow, greenish, or brownish 4
3. Flowers with the tepals cupped, laxly spaced on an erect stem; filaments c. 20 mm long, exserted c. 10 mm from the tube; Riviersonderend Mountains .... *G. stokoei*
3′. Flowers with the tepals spreading at right angles to the tube, crowded apically on an inclined stem; filaments 8–10 mm long, included in the perianth tube; Hottentots Holland Mountains .... *G. nerineoides*
4. Perianth tube 11–13 mm long .... *G. brevifolius*
4′. Perianth tube cylindrical, expanded only near the apex, 22–45 mm long 5
5. Flowers yellow mottled brownish or plain yellow, strongly scented; perianth tube 32–45 mm long; Riviersonderend and Langeberg Mountains and coastal foothills .... *G. emiliae*
5′. Flowers cream to pale pink or apricot, the lower tepals each with a reddish to yellow median streak, unscented; perianth tube 22–30 mm long; Cape Peninsula .... *G. monticola*
6. Flowers yellow to orange or scarlet; perianth tube longer than the bracts, slender and cylindrical below and abruptly expanded into a flared or broad cylindrical upper part 7
6′. Flowers pink, cream, purple, or dull red to brownish; upper part of perianth tube gradually expanded and flared toward the mouth 9
7. Flowers clear yellow; upper part of the perianth tube flared; filaments 9–12 mm long .... *G. aureus*
7′. Flowers scarlet to orange, rarely entirely yellow; upper part of the perianth tube wide and cylindrical; filaments 28–32 mm long 8
8. Leaves hairy; tepals subequal, broadly ovate ..... *G. bonaspei*
8′. Leaves minutely scabrid; tepals unequal, the lower 3 smaller and elliptical .... *G. overbergensis*
9. Flowers brownish purple or dull pink to dull reddish brown, the lower tepals yellowish and mottled with brown; flowering Apr.–June, occasionally to mid-July .... *G. guthriei*
9′. Flowers cream to pink or purple, the lower tepals streaked with dark red to purple; flowering mostly July–Oct., occasionally June 10
10. Perianth tube cylindrical for most of its length, expanded in the upper fifth; tepals lanceolate and acute, the margins not crisped, the lower tepals each with a median white spear-shaped marking edged with red .... *G. rhodanthus*
10′. Perianth tube obliquely funnel-shaped, expanded in the upper half; tepals ovate and obtuse, the margins usually crisped, the lower tepals irregularly streaked and spotted ... 11
11. Flowers 34–58(–75) mm long, the dorsal tepal 19–27(–35) mm long; unscented or occasionally lightly sweetly scented; leaves with the margins and midribs lightly, or occasionally moderately thickened .... *G. hirsutus*
11′. Flowers large, (67–)75–85 mm long, the dorsal tepal 37–45 mm long; usually strongly scented of cloves; leaves with the margins and midribs strongly thickened ... *G. caryophyllaceus*

Haemanthus

1. Leaves green at flowering; bulbs often turning green if exposed to light; scape green; bracts and flowers white ...... *H. albiflos*
1′. Leaves dry at flowering; bulbs often flushed with pink if exposed to light; scape, bracts, and flowers pink or red, rarely white ... 2
2. Leaves in mature plants solitary; both surfaces sticky and rough, often collecting wind-blown sand; scape rough .... *H. nortieri*
2′. Leaves in mature plants 2, rarely 3; the upper surface sometimes rough but never sticky nor collecting wind-blown sand; scape smooth or hairy 3
3. Leaves with undulate edges, with a broad midrib beneath; flowers with pedicels less than 5 mm long .... *H. crispus*
3′. Leaves with plane edges, without a midrib beneath; flowers with pedicels mostly longer than 5 mm 4
4. Leaves entirely smooth 5
4′. Leaves hairy or at least shortly fringed 8
5. Leaves twisted at least once .... *H. pumilio*
5′. Leaves straight 6
6. Leaves barred with red near the base beneath; bracts and flowers red, rarely pink; tepals 3–4.5 mm wide .... *H. canaliculatus*
6′. Leaves without barring beneath; bracts and flowers pink or whitish; tepals less than 3 mm wide 7
7. Leaf blades channeled, dull grayish green .... *H. tristis*
7′. Leaf blades flat, shiny green .... *H. amarylloides*
8. Leaves with a red, rarely opaque, cartilaginous margin, bearing a short, recurved, firm fringe .... *H. sanguineus*
8′. Leaves densely or sparsely covered with short or long, soft, white, straight hairs, sometimes on the margin only 9
9. Leaf whitish with maroon or dark green bars toward the base beneath, margins flat; bracts and flowers pink, spreading apart .... *H. barkerae*
9′. Leaf green with maroon or dark green bars beneath, if whitish then the margins rolled back; bracts and flowers red, usually suberect 10
10. Leaves tongue-shaped, usually broader than 85 mm, recurved or rarely prostrate; bracts surrounding the flowers 6–9, the apex blunt or slightly acute .... *H. coccineus*
10′. Leaves strap-shaped, usually narrower than 45 mm, prostrate; bracts surrounding the flowers 4–6, broad above, the apex bearing a distinct point .... *H. pubescens*

Hesperantha

1. Flowers with the perianth tube curved at the apex and thus facing to the side or nodding; outer floral bracts with the margins united around the axis in the lower part, sometimes only near the base; corm bell-shaped with a flat or oblique base, the tunics often forming scalloped, concave segments 2
1′. Flowers with the perianth tube straight, rarely curved at the apex and facing to the side or half-nodding; outer floral bracts with the margins free to the base; corm tunics asymmetric or symmetric and with a round or flat base but never with the tunic layers forming scalloped sections 7
2. Flowers deep pink; stamens and style branches included in the perianth tube .... *H. elsiae*
2′. Flowers white to cream or pale pink; stamens and style branches exserted 3
3. Bract margins united only basally; perianth tube 6–8 mm long .... *H. brevifolia*
3′. Bract margins united at least 2 mm 4
4. Flowers large with tepals 16–25 mm long and tube 15–25 mm long; perianth pale pink with darker veins .... *H. muirii*
4′. Flowers smaller with tepals 10–17 mm long and tube 5–12 mm long; perianth white or cream 5
5. Leaves terete .... *H. juncifolia*
5′. Leaves plane, often somewhat thicker in the middle and occasionally weakly cross-shaped 6
6. Bracts usually united around stem about half their length; spike straight with the bracts parallel to the axis; plants mostly 20–60 cm high with (1–)5–15 flowers per spike ..... *H. radiata*
6′. Bracts usually united around stem about a third of their length; spike flexuous with the bracts diverging from the axis; plants short, mostly 5–10 cm, with 1–5 flowers per spike ... *H. marlothii*
7. Plants stemless or stem extending barely above the ground but sheathed by the leaf bases 8
7′. Plants with an aerial stem 11
8. Flowers small, tepals 8–10(–12) mm long .... *H. hantamensis*
8′. Flowers larger, tepals 13–25 mm long 9
9. Perianth tube elongate, 30–45 mm long; tepals with dark blotches toward the base .... *H. luticola*
9′. Perianth tube less than 30 mm long, mostly 18–28 mm; tepals uniformly colored within 10
10. Flowers yellow, closed during the day, opening at sunset .... *H. flava*
10′. Flowers pink, open during the day, closing at night ... *H. humilis*
11. Leaves pilose to ciliate-scabrid, sometimes hairs visible only microscopically 12
11′. Leaves and stems smooth 15
12. Leaves hollow and with minute longitudinal grooves; finely ciliate-scabrid along the groove edges 13
12′. Leaf blade flat or the margins and midrib raised; pilose along the margins and veins 14
13. Leaves more or less round in cross section; flowers white to cream, nocturnal, opening in the late afternoon, closing during the night .... *H. teretifolia*
13′. Leaves oval in cross section; flowers pink, mauve, or purple, open in the day, closing in the early afternoon ..... *H. ciliolata*
14. Leaves sword-shaped to oblong; scale-like leaf below spike mostly 12–20 mm long, often pilose .... *H. pseudopilosa*
14′. Leaves linear to narrowly sword-shaped; scale-like leaf below the spike 3–5(–10) mm long .... *H. pilosa*
15. Perianth tube curved outward near the top, flowers half-nodding .... *H. bachmannii*
15′. Perianth tube straight throughout, flowers facing upward ... 16
16. Corms triangular to bell-shaped in outline, with a horizontal or oblique flat base 17
16′. Corms rounded, often more or less asymmetric, often with one side somewhat flattened 22
17. Corm base usually with prominent radiating spines or the margins toothed; flowers mostly pink to reddish purple, rarely yellow .... *H. pauciflora*
17′. Corm base with small teeth or scarcely serrated but without prominent spines; flowers white to yellow 18
18. Style dividing at or below the middle of the perianth tube; style branches and sometimes the anthers partly or completely included in the perianth tube 19
18′. Filaments partly and anthers and style branches fully exserted 20
19. Flowers 20–25 mm diam. with tepals 10–12 mm long; stamens and style branches fully included in the perianth tube .... *H. cedarmontana*
19′. Flowers c. 18 mm diam. with tepals 9–10 mm long; anthers exserted but style branches reaching only to the mouth of the tube .... *H. saldanhae*
20. Flowers small on a straight secund spike; perianth tube slightly curved, 4–6 mm long; tepals 4–7 mm long; leaves either plane and sometimes with crisped margins, or oval in cross section; seeds with sharp angles (minute wings) and seed coat of whitish spongy cells .... *H. spicata*
20′. Flowers medium to large, on a straight or flexuous, not obviously secund spike; perianth tube straight, (5–)7–14 mm long; tepals 6–18 mm long; leaves plane with straight margins; seeds globose or the sides lightly flattened by pressure, seed coat dark brown 21
21. Plants with 3 basal leaves only; perianth tube 12–16 mm long; tepals 6–10 mm long, always shorter than the tube; flowers pale yellow .... *H. sufflava*
21′. Plants with 2 basal leaves or more, usually one subbasal or cauline and largely sheathing; perianth tube 5–9 mm long; tepals (9–)12–18 mm long, usually longer than the tube; flowers white, cream, or yellow .... *H. falcata*
22. Flowers pink, mauve, or purple 23

22' Flowers white, cream, or yellow 26
23 Perianth tube elongate, exceeding the tepals and 20-35 mm long 24
23' Perianth tube 7-12 mm long, usually shorter than to about as long as the tepals 25
24 Leaves linear, 2-3 mm wide; tube 25-30 mm long and filaments 8-10 mm long .... *H. oligantha*
24' Leaves sword-shaped, 7-10 mm wide; tube c. 20 mm long and filaments c. 2 mm long .... *H. purpurea*
25 Basal leaves sword-shaped, sometimes linear, 2-4 mm wide, margins and often the midrib much thickened; stem lacking a scale-like leaf in the upper part of the stem .... *H. fibrosa*
25' Basal leaves ovate, 12-20 × 4-8 mm, margins and midrib hardly thickened; stem with a short scale-like leaf in the upper part of the stem .... *H. truncatula*
26 Perianth tube mostly 16-20 long, as long as to slightly longer than the tepals .... *H. pallescens*
26' Perianth tube 2-12 mm long, shorter than to rarely about as long as the tepals 27
27 Plants consistently with 2 basal leaves and a third entirely sheathing leaf sheathing the lower half of the stem .... *H. quadrangula*
27' Plants mostly with 4 leaves, sometimes the uppermost more or less scale-like 28
28 Flowers bright yellow 29
28' Flowers white, sometimes cream 31
29 Tepals 10-17 mm long; anthers c. 7 mm long .... *H. acuta*
29' Tepals 20-35 mm long; anthers 9-15 mm long 30
30 Plants to 6 cm tall, almost stemless; flowers moderate in size, the tepals c. 20 mm long, uniformly yellow .... *H. karooica*
30' Plants 12-18 cm tall; flowers large, the tepals 25-35 cm long, often but not invariably marked with dark chocolate brown .... *H. vaginata*
31 Leaves elliptical in cross section and hollow, without a thickened midrib .... *H. rivulicola*
31' Leaves more or less parallel-sided in cross section, not hollow, and with midrib lightly thickened 32
32 Corm tunics more or less overlapping or concentric but corms relatively large, mostly 10-14 mm diam. .... *H. cucullata*
32' Corm tunics concentric and corms fairly small, mostly 3-8 mm diam. 33
33 Stem with a short sheathing leaf in the upper half .... *H. acuta*
33' Stem without a short sheathing leaf in the upper half 34
34 Leaves (3)4-5, the lower 3 basal, linear to sword-shaped and acute, always erect; perianth tube 8-10 mm long; flowers cream, rarely white; western coast north of Cape Town, mostly on granite rocks .... *H. erecta*
34' Leaves (3)4, the lower 2 basal, oblong and obtuse, normally prostrate; perianth tube c. 12 mm long; flowers white; mountain habitats in rocky sandstone soil .... *H. montigena*

Hessea

1 Filaments each with an inwardly curved fleshy hook and minute papillae in the lower third of the inner surface 2
1' Filaments smooth without hooks or papillae 3
2 Bulb 20-25 mm diam.; leaf blades 2-5 mm wide, straight; pedicels 40-80 mm long, rigid; tepals 6-8 mm long .... *H. mathewsii*
2' Bulb 10-20 mm diam.; leaf blades 1-2 mm wide, spirally twisted apically; pedicels 20-50 mm long, wiry; tepals 4-6 mm long .... *H. pulcherrima*
3 Flowers with distinctly crisped tepals 4
3' Flowers with tepals smooth or slightly undulate toward the base 6
4 Flowers spreading to one side; apex of outer tepals with a short stout point .... *H. cinnamomea*
4' Flowers equally spreading; apex of outer tepals not prominently pointed 5
5 Tepals 6-8 mm long; stamens two-thirds to as long as the tepals .... *H. undosa*
5' Tepals 10-25 mm long; stamens less than two-thirds as long as the tepals .... *H. monticola*
6 Bulbs to 40 mm diam. with thick felt-like tunics and stout neck; basal sheath exserted above ground, brownish red when fresh .... *H. breviflora*
6' Bulbs to 25 mm diam. with thin tunics and slender neck; basal sheath not exserted above ground 7
7 Bulbs 10-15 mm diam.; leaves to 1 mm wide; flowers glistening; filament tube 2 mm long, narrowing upward, filaments spreading horizontally from the tube .... *H. pusilla*
7' Bulbs 15-25 mm diam.; leaves 1-7 mm wide; flowers not glistening; filament tube less than 1.5 mm long, widening upward, filaments spreading upward from the tube ... *H. stellaris*

Hypoxis

1 Flowers with tepals less than 10 mm long 2
1' Flowers with tepals more than 10 mm long 4
2 Leaves with several parallel thickened veins .... *H. argentea*
2' Leaves without thickened veins or at most the midrib and margin raised 3
3 Leaves without a prominent midrib, margin not thickened, both surfaces softly shaggy .... *H. floccosa*
3' Leaves with a prominent midrib, margin occasionally thickened, only the midrib and margin hairy .... *H. angustifolia*
4 Leaf surfaces discolorous, the upper surface green, the lower surface silver-white and felt-like .... *H. stellipilis*
4' Leaf surfaces more or less the same color 5
5 Leaves distinctly longer than the inflorescence, hairless when mature .... *H. longifolia*

Ixia

Subgenera of *Ixia*

1. Perianth tube hollow, cylindrical to funnel-shaped; filaments inserted within the tube and often decurrent .... subgenus *Morphixia*
1'. Perianth tube filiform, tightly enveloping the style and thus blocked by it; filaments inserted at the base of the tepals, often contiguous or united to close the mouth of the tube .... subgenus *Ixia*

Ixia* Subgenus *Ixia

1. Flowers pale to deep pink; anthers short, bilobed, sometimes nodding, dehiscing normally or incompletely from the base, pollen not exposed on the open anther sacs 2
1'. Flowers variously colored, occasionally pink, then usually darkly pigmented in the center; anthers oblong to linear, not bilobed, dehiscing longitudinally and pollen exposed 11
2. Leaf margins crisped or strongly undulate .... *I. erubescens*
2'. Leaf margins straight, rarely lightly undulate, but then anthers unilateral and pendent 3
3. Leaves linear-filiform, rarely more than 1.5 mm wide .... *I. micrandra*
3'. Leaves linear to sword-shaped or lanceolate, 2–10 mm wide ... 4
4. Perianth tube very short, c. 1.5 mm long; flowers pale pink or mauve .... *I. brevituba*
4'. Perianth tube 3–6 mm long; flowers mostly deep pink, sometimes pale pink 5
5. Anthers almost spherical to broadly oblong, 2–3 mm long, as wide or almost as wide as long 6
5'. Anthers oblong, more than twice as long as wide, 3–5 mm long 7
6. Leaves 2, the uppermost sheathing for most of its length; lower leaf blades lanceolate, firm textured, with 3 prominent hyaline veins .... *I. trinervata*
6'. Leaves 3–4; leaf blades lanceolate with strongly thickened margins, spirally twisted and often dry at flowering ... *I. stricta*
7. Anthers erect or suberect, symmetrically disposed 8
7'. Anthers asymmetrically disposed, unilateral, erect or all nodding 9
8. Corm mostly with a fibrous neck; leaves linear, 2–4 mm wide; bracts 4–5 mm long .... *I. curvata*
8'. Corm without a fibrous neck; leaves lanceolate, 6–10 mm wide; bracts 7–9 mm long .... *I. trifolia*
9. Filaments bent at right angles in the upper third, flat and widening above; plants 50–100 cm high .... *I. collina*
9'. Filaments straight and equally wide throughout; plants 15–50 cm high 10
10. Leaves sword-shaped to lanceolate, sometimes falcate, mostly 8–20 mm wide; leaf sheaths brown .... *I. scillaris*
10'. Leaves falcate-arcuate, 2–4 mm wide; leaf sheaths orange-brown .... *I. curvata*
11. Flowers deep yellow to orange with a dark center 12
11'. Flowers pink to mauve, green, blue, red or white, to pale yellow, with or without a dark center 14
12. Bracts pellucid, whitish or pink, lightly striate and fairly short, 5–9 mm; filaments usually free, rarely united at base ... *I. dubia*
12'. Bracts ferruginous, or pale but then streaked above with brown or red; filaments partly to completely united 13
13. Perianth tube 10–15 mm long, filaments usually fully united ... *I. curta*
13'. Perianth tube 5–8 mm long; filaments united at the base or to the middle, rarely fully united .... *I. maculata*
14. Perianth tube short compared with the tepals 2–4(–6) mm long, less than a third as long as the tepals 15
14'. Perianth tube 4–15 mm long, half as long to about as long as the tepals 21
15. Bracts with 3 long, setaceous cusps .... *I. stolonifera*
15'. Bracts tridentate to tricuspidate or lacerate, but not with long setaceous cusps 16
16. Leaves linear, firm and erect, the lower 1–2 exceeding the spike .... *I. vinacea*
16'. Leaves linear to lanceolate, rarely reaching the base of the spike, usually much shorter 17
17. Flowering spike lax, the bracts not or only very slightly overlapping; stem base without a neck of fibers 18
17'. Flowering spike densely flowered, often more or less capitate, bracts distinctly overlapping; stem base with a prominent neck of fibers 19
18. Flowers with a conspicuous central, shiny blackish mark .... *I. gloriosa*
18'. Flowers concolorous or with an insignificant greenish or white circle in the center .... *I. patens*
19. Flowers uniformly crimson-red or white; stem usually unbranched .... *I. campanulata*
19'. Flowers pink, white or mauve, always with contrasting markings in the center; stem often branched 20
20. Stem usually subdivaricately 1- to 3-branched; bracts pellucid; flowers pale pink to lilac with a small purple center outlined with white; perianth tube 3–5 mm long ...... *I. metelerkampiae*
20'. Stem almost always unbranched; bracts pale or pinkish; flowers pink, mauve or white with a dark center; perianth tube 4–7 mm long .... *I. mostertii*
21. Leaves twisted with crisped margins; flowers rusty red to deep pink .... *I. vanzijliae*

5'. Leaves shorter or about as long as the inflorescence, persistently hairy when mature 6
6. Leaves with only the margins hairy .... *H. setosa*
6'. Leaves with both surfaces hairy .... *H. villosa*

21' Leaf margins not undulate 22
22 Flowers green to turquoise with a darker center; spike lax and many-flowered .... *I. viridiflora*
22' Flowers not colored green to turquoise; spike lax or congested, few- to many-flowered 23
23 Anthers as long as the filaments; perianth tube 4–6 mm long; flowers usually with radiating purplish lines in the center .... *I. flexuosa*
23' Anthers distinctly longer than the filaments, rarely as long but then perianth tube 6–12 mm long 24
24 Stem always simple; perianth tube slightly wider above .... *I. purpureorosea*
24' Stem simple or branched; perianth tube filiform throughout 25
25 Filaments usually united basally or above the middle; style branching at or above the base of the anthers; bracts spotted or flecked with brown toward the tips .... *I. monadelpha*
25' Filaments free or joined only at the base 26
26 Leaf margins thickened, cartilaginous, more or less crenulate; anthers connivent at the apex .... *I. versicolor*
26' Leaf margins hardly to moderately thickened but not crenulate; anthers divergent 27
27 Anther connective broadened, the pollen sacs separated before dehiscence 28
27' Anther connective not broadened, the pollen sacs touching throughout before dehiscence 29
28 Leaves 4–6, narrow, 2–6 mm wide; stem with one or more stiffly spreading branches .... *I. rouxii*
28' Leaves 3–4, broader, 6–10 mm wide; stem simple or with suberect branches .... *I. atrandra*
29 Tepals narrowed near the base and almost clawed, adjacent tepals usually gaping below; flowers yellow or purplish to red with a blackish mark in the center .... *I. lutea*
29' Tepals not as above, overlapping one another at the base; flowers mostly pink, mauve, white, or yellow with a darker but seldom blackish center especially when yellow .... *I. polystachya*

Ixia Subgenus *Morphixia*

1 Perianth tube cylindrical or barely widening upward, 10–70 mm long 2
1' Perianth tube narrowly to widely funnel-shaped, sometimes almost cylindrical but the mouth not closed by contiguous to united filaments, to 20 mm long but mostly less than 10 mm ...7
2 Perianth tube 10–16 mm long; leaves 1.5–4 mm wide 3
2' Perianth tube 18–70 mm long; leaves (3–)5–15 mm wide ... 4
3 Leaves mostly 2–4 mm wide; filaments and sometimes the anthers included in the tube; anthers 2–3 mm long ... *I. stohriae*
3' Leaves 1.5–3 mm wide; filaments exserted from the tube; anthers 4–5 mm long .... *I. fucata*
4 Stamens included in the perianth tube 5
4' At least the anthers exserted from the tube 6
5 Perianth tube (35–)40–50(–70) mm long; stem mostly 1- to 3-branched .... *I. paniculata*
5' Perianth tube 22–28 mm long; stem usually unbranched .... *I. splendida*
6 Leaves 2–3; filaments 2–4 mm long, partly or entirely included in the tube .... *I. paucifolia*
6' Leaves 4–6; filaments 5–8 mm long, partly exserted from the tube .... *I. longituba*
7 Bracts dark or rusty brown above or throughout, mostly with inconspicuous veins 8
7' Bracts translucent or whitish, or light brown but with darker veins 9
8 Bracts dark brown throughout; flowers pale pink or whitish .... *I. brunneobractea*
8' Bracts rusty brown in the upper half .... *I. tenuifolia*
9 Perianth tube short, no more than half as long as the tepals and 4–8 mm long 10
9' Perianth tube two-thirds as long to slightly longer than the tepals and 5–18 mm long 12
10 Leaves linear to linear-filiform, to 2 mm wide .... *I. capillaris*
10' Leaves sword-shaped to lanceolate, 4–18 mm wide 11
11 Plants usually more than 25 cm high with 4–7 branchlets; leaves with prominently thickened margins ...... *I. marginifolia*
11' Plants usually less than 20 cm high with 1–2 branchlets; leaf margins not usually noticeably thickened .... *I. latifolia*
12 Flowers white with large, dark purple blotches in the lower third of the tepals .... *I. leipoldtii*
12' Flowers variously colored but without conspicuous purple blotches 13
13 Leaves linear-filiform, to 1 mm wide; flowers 1–2(3) per spike; stamens declinate .... *I. pauciflora*
13' Leaves linear to lanceolate or falcate, at least 3 mm wide; stamens central 14
14 Stamens or at least the filaments included in the perianth tube 15
14' Stamens with the filaments at least partly exserted from the perianth tube 16
15 Perianth tube narrow, only slightly and gradually dilated and not more than 3 mm wide at the mouth; anthers sometimes included .... *I. stohriae*
15' Perianth tube widely funnel-shaped, fairly abruptly dilated and 5–10 mm wide at the mouth; anthers at least partly exserted .... *I. rapunculoides*
16 Flowers pale to deep pink or mauve or whitish 17
16' Flowers yellow or orange to brick red 20
17 Leaf linear, mostly 2–3 mm wide, with the margins raised into broad wings, thus H-shaped in cross section; spike wand-like and flowers partly nodding .... *I. thomasiae*

17′ Leaf linear to lanceolate, often fairly broad, 1.5–20 mm wide, with the margins not or only moderately thickened but not raised into broad wings, thus more or less plane 18
18 Perianth tube broadly funnel-shaped, 4–7 mm wide at the throat; leaves sword-shaped, to 20 mm wide . . . . *I. latifolia*
18′ Perianth tube narrowly funnel-shaped, 2–3 mm wide at the throat; leaves linear to narrowly sword-shaped, mostly 1–5 mm wide 19
19 Flowers rose to salmon pink; perianth tube 10–18 mm long; filaments distinctly longer than the anthers . . . . . . *I. cochlearis*
19′ Flowers cream to pale mauve or pinkish; perianth tube mostly 7–10 mm long; filaments usually shorter than to about as long as the anthers . . . . *I. orientalis*
20 Perianth tube widely funnel-shaped, at least 5 mm wide at the mouth; perianth brick red . . . . *I. pumilio*
20′ Perianth tube narrowly funnel-shaped, 2–3 mm wide at the mouth; perianth cream to yellow 21
21 Flowers relatively large, bright orange and unscented, tepals 16–23 mm long . . . . *I. aurea*
21′ Flowers relatively small, yellow to cream and usually fragrant, tepals 10–12 mm long 22
22 Plants 30–60 cm high; flowers 5–12 per spike; perianth tube 5–11 mm long; tepals usually without red reverse . . . . *I. odorata*
22′ Plants 10–15 cm high; flowers 1–6 per spike; perianth tube 4–5 mm long; tepals with deep red reverse . . . *I. esterhuyseniae*

Kniphofia

1 Bracts broader, ovate to oblong, rarely lanceolate, rounded to acute, 3–9 mm long 2
1′ Bracts narrow and tapering, lanceolate to linear-lanceolate, acute to acuminate, 7–12 mm long 3
2 Flowers 20–28 mm long with well-exserted stamens, yellow; smaller plants with globose inflorescences . . . . *K. citrina*
2′ Flowers 28–38 mm long with the stamens scarcely exserted, orange to greenish yellow; medium plants with oblong to globose racemes . . . . *K. uvaria*
3 Peduncles 1–2 m tall; flowers densely arranged in cylindrical racemes, reddish in bud, opening yellow or yellowish green . . . . *K. praecox*
3′ Peduncles rarely to 1 m tall; flowers mostly more laxly arranged at the base of the raceme 4
4 Plants erect or hanging from cliff faces; leaves 60–150 cm long, bright green; pedicels 5–7 mm long; flowers in a lax cylindrical raceme, red to orange with blackish tips in bud . . . . . *K. tabularis*
4′ Plants erect; leaves 30–60 cm long, grayish; pedicels 1–3 mm long; flowers more closely arranged in ovoid to cylindrical racemes, reddish in bud, opening buff . . . . *K. sarmentosa*

Lachenalia

Groups of *Lachenalia*

1 Leaves 3 to many, oblong or linear to subterete; flowers pedicellate, white or brownish blue, tepals subequal and similar, anthers usually exserted . . . . group 1
1′ Leaves 1–2 2
2 Flowers, at least the lowermost, sessile or subsessile with pedicels to 1 mm long, exceptionally longer but then bracts conspicuously developed or leaf with star-shaped hairs, and anthers included . . . . group 2
2′ Flowers pedicellate with pedicels at least 2 mm long or if sessile then anthers more or less exserted 3
3 Flowers (15–)20–35 mm long, either suberect or nodding; anthers included or shortly exserted . . . . group 3
3′ Flowers 5–18 mm long 4
4 Anthers well exserted, stamens more than 2 mm longer than the tepals . . . . group 4
4′ Anthers included or shortly exserted, stamens to 2 mm longer than the tepals . . . . group 5

Lachenalia Group 1

1 Peduncle subterranean at flowering; flowers strongly scented; flowering Apr.–May 2
1′ Peduncle well developed above ground at flowering; flowers usually unscented; flowering July–Oct. 3
2 Leaves linear-canaliculate, 1–5 mm wide, unmarked; peduncle club-shaped; filaments swollen above . . . . *L. barkeriana*
2′ Leaves oblong-lanceolate, plane, 4–15 mm wide, spotted; peduncle cylindrical; filaments not swollen above . . . . . *L. pusilla*
3 Flowers narrowly bell-shaped, the tepals scarcely spreading; filaments declinate, well exserted and about twice as long as the tepals 4
3′ Flowers widely bell-shaped, the tepals conspicuously spreading above; filaments straight or weakly declinate, less than twice as long as the tepals 5
4 Leaves with dark, raised banding in the lower part; inflorescence elongate, laxly several-flowered . . . . *L. moniliformis*
4′ Leaves unmarked, swollen and pubescent at the base; inflorescence congested, few-flowered . . . . *L. polyphylla*
5 Pedicels 2–7 mm long; anthers yellow; leaves glaucous . . . . *L. multifolia*
5′ Pedicels to 2 mm long; anthers maroon; leaves usually green . . . 6
6 Leaves conspicuously channeled, falcate; inflorescence cylindrical, (40–)50–100 × 20–25 mm; flowers suberect, 10–15 mm long . . . . *L. orthopetala*
6′ Leaves terete or subterete, erect; inflorescence conical, 30–40(–60) × 12–18 mm; flowers spreading, 6–9 mm long . . . . *L. contaminata*

Lachenalia Group 2

1. Leaf ovate and heart-shaped, prostrate, with star-shaped hairs on the upper surface, the hairs short or long .... *L. trichophylla*
1'. Leaf or leaves ovate-lanceolate, usually spreading or erect, hairless or with simple hairs 2
2. Flowers urn-shaped, the inner tepals scarcely longer than the outer and recurved only at the tips .... *L. elegans*
2'. Flowers narrowly bell-shaped or weakly urn-shaped, the inner tepals usually distinctly longer than the outer 3
3. Lower inner tepal distinctly longer than the upper inner tepals, scarcely spreading 4
3'. Lower and upper inner tepals subequal 6
4. Flowers spreading or nodding, 8–10 mm long, in an elongate, bicolored spike, the upper florets reduced, sterile and bluish .... *L. mutabilis*
4'. Flowers suberect, 12–18 mm long, in a shorter spike 5
5. Leaf 1, ovate, the margins thickened .... *L. marginata*
5'. Leaves (1)2, lanceolate, the margins unthickened .... *L. orchioides*
6. Inner tepals 1.5 times as long as the outer, strongly recurved, with conspicuous brown marks at the tips; leaves narrowly lanceolate, dry at flowering .... *L. muirii*
6'. Inner tepals less than 1.5 times as long as the outer; leaves green at flowering 7
7. Leaves papillate-hairy or with bristle-like hairs; flowers urn- to bell-shaped, the inner tepals conspicuously recurved above .... *L. ameliae*
7'. Leaves hairless 8
8. Outer bulb scales dark brown or black and cartilaginous 9
8'. Outer bulb scales pale and membranous 12
9. Leaves heavily barred on the sheath; inner tepals with purple tips .... *L. obscura*
9'. Leaves unmarked 10
10. Flowers suberect; plants producing numerous bulblets on short stolons from the base of the main bulb, the bulblets minute with hard, dark tunics .... *L. maximiliani*
10'. Flowers spreading 11
11. Leaves 2, suberect, ovate-lanceolate .... *L. undulata*
11'. Leaf 1(2), erect, oblong-lanceolate .... *L. bowkeri*
12. Flowers cylindrical, the inner tepals not flaring above, 11–15 mm long, white or cream .... *L. capensis*
12'. Flowers narrowly bell-shaped, the inner tepals more or less flaring above, 8–11 mm long 13
13. Leaf margins thickened and often undulate; flowers conspicuously speckled .... *L. variegata*
13'. Leaf margins not thickened 14
14. Leaf 1, ovate-lanceolate, tightly clasping and heavily banded for some distance below .... *L. marlothii*
14'. Leaves (1)2, lanceolate, somewhat loosely clasping below and not barred 15
15. Leaves prostrate, maroon beneath .... *L. congesta*
15'. Leaves suberect; upper bracts well developed 16
16. Inner tepals recurved above; flowers strongly scented .... *L. fistulosa*
16'. Inner tepals lightly flared above 17
17. Flowers bright yellow, strongly scented .... *L. arbuthnotiae*
17'. Flowers pale yellow and blue, weakly scented .... *L. longibracteata*

Lachenalia Group 3

1. Flowers suberect 2
1'. Flowers nodding 4
2. Flowers green or turquoise, not appressed to the peduncle; upper inner tepals symmetrical at the tips .... *L. viridiflora*
2'. Flowers yellow or greenish yellow, often appressed to the peduncle; upper inner tepals oblique at the tips 3
3. Peduncle exserted; flowers greenish yellow .... *L. algoensis*
3'. Peduncle suppressed; flowers bright yellow .... *L. reflexa*
4. Inflorescence subcorymbose; pedicels magenta, uppermost usually longest, 5–17 mm long .... *L. sargeantii*
4'. Inflorescence cylindrical or conical; pedicels usually green, uppermost usually slightly shorter than the lower, 2–7 mm long ... 5
5. Inner tepals as long as or slightly longer than the outer, usually purplish and green at the tips .... *L. bulbifera*
5'. Inner tepals conspicuously longer than the outer 6
6. Flowers yellow to orange or greenish or varicolored but never pink; outer tepals half to two-thirds as long as the inner; pedicels 2–7 mm long; leaves fully developed at flowering ..... *L. aloides*
6'. Flowers pink, often mottled; outer tepals about three-quarters as long as the inner; pedicels usually to 2 mm long; leaves not fully developed at flowering .... *L. rubida*

Lachenalia Group 4

1. Flowers sessile or subsessile 2
1'. Flowers pedicellate 4
2. Leaves spotted on the upper surface; peduncle never swollen above .... *L. karooica*
2'. Leaves unmarked or barred on the undersurface; peduncle more or less swollen above 3
3. Leaves (1)2, unmarked, plane; peduncle not or weakly swollen above; tepals spreading, the inner at least purple ... *L. splendida*
3'. Leaf 1, glaucous and more or less barred below, the margins crisped; peduncle club-shaped or swollen above; tepals connivent or scarcely spreading above, yellowish ... *L. ventricosa*
4. Leaves heavily barred beneath 5
4'. Leaves plain or mottled but never heavily banded 8
5. Leaves 2; filaments mauve .... *L. haarlemensis*
5'. Leaf 1; filaments pale 6
6. Flowers spreading, white with green marks at the tips .... *L. anguinea*

6′ Flowers nodding, bluish or gray to brown with darker marks at the tips 7
7 Leaves channeled or folded; flowers narrowly urn-shaped; capsule 3-winged, c. 10 mm diam. .... *L. zebrina*
7′ Leaves longitudinally rolled; flowers narrowly bell-shaped; capsule ovoid, 3-angled, to 7 mm long .... *L. whitehillensis*
8 Pedicels less than half as long as the tepals 9
8′ Pedicels about as long as the tepals or longer 15
9 Leaves conspicuously hairy above .... *L. comptonii*
9′ Leaves hairless 10
10 Leaf 1; peduncle more or less inflated above 11
10′ Leaves 2, rarely 1 but then peduncle not inflated above 12
11 Leaf base tightly clasping above the ground, spotted .... *L. leipoldtii*
11′ Leaf base subterranean, unmarked .... *L. physocaulos*
12 Leaves suberect, unmarked and without pustules; filaments strongly declinate .... *L. gillettii*
12′ Leaves suberect or prostrate, usually pustulate; filaments more or less spreading 13
13 Leaves ovate, striate, smooth, or irregularly pustulate; filaments widely spreading .... *L. nervosa*
13′ Leaves oblong to lanceolate; filaments weakly spreading ...14
14 Leaves densely pustulate, in the wild withered at flowering; filaments reddish near the tips; flowers strongly fragrant .... *L. purpureocaerulea*
14′ Leaves smooth, always green at flowering; filaments whitish; flowers weakly scented or unscented .... *L. salteri*
15 Flowers urn-shaped, the tepals converging above, in dense racemes .... *L. montana*
15′ Flowers more or less bell-shaped, the tepals flaring above ... 16
16 Leaves withering at flowering; flowers widely bell-shaped with the stamens spreading, maroon to magenta .... *L. macgregoriorum*
16′ Leaves green at flowering; flowers oblong or weakly bell-shaped, more or less nodding, white or blue to purple 17
17 Leaves linear-lanceolate to terete 18
17′ Leaves ovate to lanceolate 19
18 Leaves shorter than the inflorescence, terete above .... *L. juncifolia*
18′ Leaves longer than the inflorescence, channeled throughout ... *L. latimerae*
19 Leaves prostrate with few, scattered, large pustules .... *L. stayneri*
19′ Leaves mostly spreading or suberect, smooth or with numerous small pustules 20
20 Flowers white with large brown or green marks at the tips; pedicels white; leaves 2, smooth, the sheath magenta .... *L. thomasiae*
20′ Flowers cream or blue to purple with darker marks at the tips; pedicels brownish or green 21
21 Leaves 2, often pustulate; peduncle usually slender; inner tepals longer, flaring; flowers sweetly scented ...... *L. unicolor*
21′ Leaf usually 1, smooth; peduncle inflated above; tepals subequal, scarcely flaring; flowers coconut scented .... *L. violacea*

Lachenalia Group 5

1 Leaf 1, rarely 2, heavily banded below; flowers oblong or narrowly bell-shaped, green or bluish; anthers included 2
1′ Characters not combined as above 8
2 Leaves usually 2, with a distinct channeled midrib; flowers narrowly urn-shaped .... *L. aurioliae*
2′ Leaf usually single, without a distinct channeled midrib; flowers narrowly bell-shaped 3
3 Leaf ovate 4
3′ Leaf linear-lanceolate 5
4 Flowers nodding, bell-shaped; pedicels 2–5 mm long .... *L. bolusii*
4′ Flowers spreading, narrowly bell-shaped; pedicels 1–2 mm long .... *L. martinae*
5 Leaf blade abruptly widened at the base above the sheath; pedicels 3–12 mm long 6
5′ Leaf blade widening gradually into the sheath; pedicels to 3 mm long 7
6 Leaf hairy on the margins and beneath .... *L. hirta*
6′ Leaf hairless .... *L. unifolia*
7 Leaf involute .... *L. attenuata*
7′ Leaf channeled .... *L. perryae*
8 Flowers cylindrical, brownish yellow; leaf bases persisting in a straw-like neck .... *L. isopetala*
8′ Flowers bell- or urn-shaped; leaf bases not persisting in a neck 9
9 Leaves linear or terete above 10
9′ Leaves lanceolate 14
10 Leaves terete above, widening below, glaucous; flowers yellow .... *L. mathewsii*
10′ Leaves channeled throughout; flowers whitish or gray 11
11 Leaves narrow throughout, not widening into the sheath ... 12
11′ Leaves widening abruptly below into the sheath 13
12 Flowers nodding, pinkish gray .... *L. youngii*
12′ Flowers suberect, white with maroon keels ..... *L. bachmannii*
13 Flowers narrowly bell-shaped; inner tepals twice as long as the outer .... *L. dehoopensis*
13′ Flowers widely bell-shaped; inner tepals at most slightly longer than the outer .... *L. zeyheri*
14 Flowers urn-shaped, narrowed at the mouth 15
14′ Flowers shortly cylindrical to bell-shaped 17
15 Inner tepals abruptly recurved at the tips; anthers included; flowers carnation scented .... *L. peersii*
15′ Inner tepals not recurved; anthers slightly exserted; flowers unscented 16

16 Flowers pinkish or with pink tinge; peduncle at most lightly spotted .... *L. rosea*
16′ Flowers white or greenish; peduncle heavily spotted ... *L. lactosa*
17 Flowers suberect, widely bell-shaped, white, sometimes with purple tips, 15–20 mm long .... *L. liliiflora*
17′ Flowers spreading, narrowly bell-shaped, 5–12 mm long ... 18
18 Leaf base heavily banded with purple, the blade blotched with dark green; flowers cylindrical, the stamens spreading .... *L. schelpei*
18′ Leaf base not or lightly banded, the blade unmarked or purple spotted; flowers narrowly bell-shaped, the stamens more or less declinate 19
19 Plants dwarf; flowers c. 5 mm long, somewhat bell-shaped, white with conspicuous dark brown marks at the tips; stamens weakly declinate .... *L. margaretae*
19′ Plants not dwarf; flowers 7–12 mm long, narrowly bell-shaped, never with conspicuous dark brown marks at the tips; stamens conspicuously declinate 20
20 Flowers white with pale green marks at the tips 21
20′ Flowers usually yellow, blue, green, or gray 22
21 Leaves spreading, heavily spotted; flowers somewhat nodding .... *L. leomontana*
21′ Leaves suberect, unmarked; flowers suberect .... *L. alba*
22 Leaves ovate, spreading with the tips decurved and touching the soil surface, the veins on the upper surface conspicuously depressed .... *L. doleritica*
22′ Leaves suberect or spreading but the tips not decurved and touching the soil surface 23
23 Plants producing numerous bulblets on short stolons from the base of the main bulb, the bulblets minute with hard, dark tunics .... *L. neilii*
23′ Plants producing bulblets but the bulblets not minute and with membranous tunics 24
24 Upper bracts conspicuously developed, attenuate, spreading; flowers oblong .... *L. longibracteata*
24′ Upper bracts not conspicuous; flowers narrowly bell-shaped 25
25 Flowers yellow, fading dull red .... *L. pallida*
25′ Flowers cream or gray to green or blue 26
26 Leaves usually pustulate; anthers usually well exserted .... *L. pustulata*
26′ Leaves never pustulate; anthers included or exserted 27
27 Anthers shortly exserted .... *L. bowkeri*
27′ Anthers included .... *L. mediana*

Lapeirousia

Subgenera of *Lapeirousia*

1 Leaves plane; floral bracts subequal; flowers mostly in flat-topped panicles, sometimes in a spike .... Subgenus *Paniculata*
1′ Leaves ribbed; inner floral bracts small and 2-keeled; flowers in short to elongate spikes or in compact rosettes .... Subgenus *Lapeirousia*

Lapeirousia Subgenus *Lapeirousia*

1 Plants in a basal rosette with bracts and leaves crowded at ground level; flowers blue to violet, rarely cream 2
1′ Plants not forming rosettes, unless extremely depauperate; flowers various colors and zygomorphic with unilateral stamens ... 4
2 Perianth tube mostly 12–25 mm long; tepals mostly 5–10 mm long .... *L. plicata*
2′ Perianth tube mostly 40–60 mm long, tepals mostly 12–14 mm long 3
3 Flowers pale blue to whitish with darker blue markings, sweetly scented; perianth tube to 40 mm long .... *L. montana*
3′ Flowers dark blue-violet marked with white and darker blue, unscented; perianth tube to 60 mm long .... *L. oreogena*
4 Perianth tube fairly short, 5–12 mm long; dorsal tepal arising first, remaining 5 tepals united for a short distance . *L. divaricata*
4′ Perianth tube 25–60(–80) mm long; tepals mostly arising at the same level 5
5 Bracts folded on the midline and smooth along the fold, the apex retuse, thus bilobed .... *L. pyramidalis*
5′ Bracts keeled and minutely toothed or crisped along the keels, acute 6
6 Flowers purple usually with white markings on the lower tepals; plants branching from the base 7
6′ Flowers white to cream with red markings; branching above ... 8
7 Floral bracts 2-keeled below; flowers usually with linear white streaks on the lower tepals .... *L. jacquinii*
7′ Floral bracts weakly keeled, somewhat inflated; tepals with at most a small white spot on the lower tepals .... *L. violacea*
8 Perianth tube slender and cylindrical throughout; tepals narrow, lanceolate, 9–12 mm long .... *L. anceps*
8′ Perianth tube slender below, widening above; tepals spreading and ovate or clawed below and forming a cup, the limbs spreading .... *L. fabricii*

Lapeirousia Subgenus *Paniculata*

1 Flowers a spike; perianth pink to lilac .... *L. falcata*
1′ Flowers in rounded to flat-topped panicles, blue or white to yellow 2
2 Panicles open, rounded; flowers white or blue; corm surrounded by numerous cormels; leaves linear-falcate to lanceolate .... *L. neglecta*
2′ Panicles crowded, more or less flat-topped; flowers blue, yellow, or reddish; corm without cormels; leaves falcate, margins undulate to crisped 3
3 Flowers zygomorphic; perianth dark blue, the lower tepals with dark markings; stamens unilateral .... *L. azurea*

3' Flowers actinomorphic; perianth pale to middle blue with a central white star or yellow to maroon; stamens symmetrically arranged 4
4 Flower larger, tepals 11–15 mm long; perianth pale yellow, the tepals often with dark brownish markings .... *L. fastigiata*
4' Flower small, tepals 3–10 mm long; perianth pale to middle blue with a central white star or dull yellow to maroon 5
5 Perianth tube widely funnel-shaped, 4–7 mm long; tepals somewhat cupped, 7–10 mm long, blue with a central white star .... *L. corymbosa*
5' Perianth tube cylindrical, 8–10 mm long; tepals spreading, 3–5 mm long, dull yellow to maroon .... *L. micrantha*

Ledebouria

1 Ovary subglobose, broadly 3-lobed; leaves ascending, usually emergent or dry at flowering 2
1' Ovary top-shaped, 6-lobed; leaves ascending or more or less spreading, fully developed at flowering 3
2 Leaves dry at flowering, narrowly lanceolate and distinctly undulate; inflorescence dense, the flowers spreading .... *L. undulata*
2' Leaves emergent or green at flowering, oblanceolate or lanceolate; inflorescence lax, the flowers nodding ..... *L. ovalifolia*
3 Bulb scales and leaves not producing threads when torn; pedicels 3–4 mm long; tepals 3 mm long; ovary top-shaped with the apex tapering .... *L.* sp. 1
3' Bulb scales and sometimes leaves producing threads when torn; pedicels 7–12 mm long; tepals 5 mm long; ovary depressed and top-shaped with the apex rounded 4
4 Bulb scales loosely arranged and fleshy, producing copious threads when torn .... *L. ovatifolia*
4' Bulb scales tightly arranged, membranous or thinly fleshy, producing sparse threads when torn .... *L. revoluta*

Massonia

1 Anthers 2–3.5 mm long; perianth tube (3–)4–8 mm diam. at the mouth, open and not occluded by the filaments .... *M. depressa*
1' Anthers 1–2 mm long; perianth tube 1.5–2.5 mm diam. at the mouth, more or less occluded by the filaments 2
2 Filaments of two lengths, the inner shorter than the outer; leaves to 4 cm long .... *M. pygmaea*
2' Filaments of uniform length; leaves usually larger 3
3 Filaments (10–)16–24 mm long .... *M. pustulata*
3' Filaments to 10 mm long .... *M. echinata*

Micranthus

1 Leaves plane with a distinct midvein .... *M. alopecuroides*
1' Leaves terete or cylindrical without a distinct midvein 2
2 Leaves terete and needle-like, mostly 3–6 mm diam., gradually tapering at the tip .... *M. junceus*
2' Leaves cylindrical and swollen, mostly 8–14 mm diam., abruptly narrowed at the tip .... *M. tubulosus*

Moraea

Groups of Moraea

1 Flowers with a perianth tube; style lobed apically, the lobes entire or fringed .... *Galaxia* group
1' Flowers usually without a perianth tube; style dividing below or opposite the anthers, branches filiform, or flattened, appressed to the anthers, terminating in paired erect crests 2
2 Style branches filiform, simple or each divided to the base, thus with 6 branches, the branches extending between the stamens .... *Hexaglottis* group
2' Style branches flattened tangentially, as wide or much wider than the anthers, the branches ascending to upright and opposite the anthers, sometimes concealed by them 3
3 Plants stemless with the flowers crowded basally; flowers either with the ovary borne below or close to ground level or raised above ground on contractile pedicels ..... *Moraea* group
3' Plants with aerial stems; flowers with the ovary borne well above ground level 4
4 Ovary more or less sessile and extended distally in an elongate tubular sterile beak .... *Gynandriris* group
4' Ovary borne on long pedicels or occasionally subsessile but then the tepals united in a tube, without an elongate sterile beak 5
5 Flowers with prominent style branches wider than the anthers and terminating in paired erect crests; outer tepals mostly larger than the inner and often with long ascending claws .... *Moraea* group
5' Flowers with the style branches as wide or narrower than the anthers, often hidden by them, with a short bilobed apex opposite the stigmatic lobe(s); outer tepals only slightly larger than the inner, with long or short claws 6
6 Flowers yellow or salmon to pink, the stems never sticky .... *Homeria* group
6' Flowers either blue to purple or yellow but then the stems sticky .... *Moraea* group

Moraea Group Galaxia

1 Style lobes lobed or entire; flowers usually pink to reddish, sometimes white or yellow 2
1' Style lobes deeply fringed; flowers yellow or white with yellow

center 7
2　Flowers yellow or white 3
2'　Flowers pink to reddish 4
3　Flower yellow; tepals 18–30 mm long .... *M. citrina*
3'　Flower white; tepals 9–12 mm long .... *M. minima*
4　Style not reaching the anther apices; tepals spreading from the base .... *M. barnardiella*
4'　Style reaching or exceeding the anther apices 5
5　Tepals widely cupped to more or less laxly spreading; filaments free in the upper half .... *M. melanops*
5'　Tepals cupped; filaments united or free only near the tips 6
6　Filaments united completely; leaves more or less oblong with straight margins .... *M. variabilis*
6'　Filaments free in the upper 1 mm; leaves ovate-lanceolate with margins undulate .... *M. versicolor*
7　Leaves broad, ovate to oblong, spreading to prostrate 8
7'　Leaves narrow, linear or terete 11
8　Flowers white with yellow center; style shorter than the anthers .... *M. albiflora*
8'　Flowers yellow or fading to white toward the tips; style as long as or longer than the anthers 9
9　Filaments free in the upper two-thirds; tepals fading to paler yellow or white toward the tips .... *M. luteoalba*
9'　Filaments united entirely or free in the upper 1 mm; tepals uniformly yellow 10
10　Leaf margins smooth or minutely pilose, the hairs shorter than the width of the thickened margins .... *M. galaxia*
10'　Leave margins markedly pilose, the hairs longer than the width of the thickened margins .... *M. pilifolia*
11　Leaves terete, arching outward; corm with corky vertical flanges .... *M. angulata*
11'　Leaves linear or channeled, erect to spreading 12
12　Style exceeding the anthers .... *M. fugacissima*
12'　Style reaching the anther tips, the lobes curving over the anthers .... *M. stagnalis*

Moraea Group *Gynandriris*
1　Plants with suberect inner tepals 2
1'　Plants with weakly reflexed inner and outer tepals 3
2　Flowers white, fragrant .... *M. cedarmontana*
2'　Flower blue, faintly scented .... *M. australis*
3　Leaves tightly coiled, the blades with a pale median streak .... *M. pritzeliana*
3'　Leaves channeled and more or less straight, without a central pale band 4
4　Outer tepals 12–18 mm long, pale blue-mauve; style crests 4–7 mm long .... *M. setifolia*
4'　Outer tepals 21–30 mm long, deep blue to violet; style crests 7–10 mm long 5
5　Leaves 2; flowers opening in the evening .... *M. hesperantha*
5'　Leaf 1; flowers opening in the day and fading in the late afternoon .... *M. contorta*

Moraea Group *Hexaglottis*
1　Flowers blue or white; style branches simple, filiform, extending between the stamens 2
1'　Flowers yellow; style branches divided to the base, the arms extending between the stamens 3
2　Leaf hollow .... *M. fistulosa*
2'　Leaf solid .... *M. monticola*
3　Lower internode of the stem elongate and leaves clustered at the first node; branches all short, crowded above the leaves in a small fascicle; spathes more or less truncate or acute ... *M. nana*
3'　Lower internode not elongate and leaves not clustered; stem with sessile lateral flower clusters on the main and lateral branches; spathes attenuate 4
4　Tepals united below in a filiform tube; ovary sessile, enclosed by the spathes .... *M. virgata*
4'　Tepals free to the base; ovary exserted or held just below the spathe tips 5
5　Capsules narrowly ellipsoidal to cylindrical-trigonous, rarely more than 3 mm diam.; plants of open, fairly dry habitats .... *M. lewisiae*
5'　Capsules ovoid to club-shaped, 4–8 mm at the widest point; plants of moist habitats, stream banks, and shady slopes 6
6　Capsules 12–16(–23) × 6–8 mm; tepals 20–28 mm long .... *M. longifolia*
6'　Capsules 6–10(–12) × c. 4 mm; tepals 16–21 mm long .... *M. riparia*

Moraea Group *Homeria*
1　Basal internode elongate and leaves and branches clustered above the ground in a fascicle; corm tunics brown, of woody or fibrous layers 2
1'　Basal internode not unusually elongate and leaves and branches evenly dispersed along the stem 3
2　Tepals with short, diverging claws; anthers parallel and coherent, concealing the short style branches .... *M. maximiliani*
2'　Tepals with long, ascending claws forming a narrow cup enclosing the filaments; anthers appressed to narrow, diverging style branches .... *M. umbellata*
3　Plants with 2 or more fully developed foliage leaves 4
3'　Plants with a single foliage leaf 8
4　Stem finely velvety; leaves more or less flat and loosely coiled in corkscrew fashion distally .... *M. aspera*
4'　Stem smooth; leaves usually channeled, not coiled distally .. 5
5　Tepals with short, clasping claws; filament column swollen and bulbous below but pinched at the base .... *M. miniata*
5'　Tepals short to long but not clasping the filament column; filament column usually slender or slightly wider below 6

6 Tepal claws short, less than half as long as the tepal limbs, forming a wide cup including the lower part of the filament column; tepal claws abruptly narrowed at the base, the floral cup thus windowed .... *M. fenestrata*
6′ Tepal claws about as long as the limbs, forming a narrow or wide cup including the filament column; the floral cup not windowed below 7
7 Tepal claws diverging, forming a wide cup; style branches widely diverging, as long as or longer than the anthers .... *M. ochroleuca*
7′ Tepal claws ascending-erect, forming a narrow cup; style branches weakly diverging, shorter than the anthers .... *M. cedarmonticola*
8 Anthers short, 1.5-3 mm long, parallel and coherent, concealing the style branches and usually exceeding them; style crests not visibly developed 9
8′ Anthers (1.5-)4-12 mm long, appressed to the narrowly or broadly diverging style branches, mostly shorter, but sometimes longer than the style branches; style crests developed, short and erect 13
9 Leaf clasping the lower half of the stem; stem straight and erect 10
9′ Leaf diverging from the stem above the sheath; stem usually flexed outward above the leaf sheaths 12
10 Filament column bulbous below and pinched at the base; tepal claw c. 2 mm long, clasping the filament column ..... *M. bifida*
10′ Filament column slender, or slightly thickened below; tepal claws 3-5 mm long, diverging to form a cup including the filament column 11
11 Filaments 7-9 mm long; flowers not noticeably fragrant; tepal claws yellow edged with purple, the limbs salmon .... *M. karooica*
11′ Filaments 4-5 mm long; flowers sweetly fragrant; tepals pale yellow, the limbs with a yellow nectar guide edged in gray-green .... *M. fragrans*
12 Tepals salmon pink, darkly speckled in the center; filament column 6-8 mm long, sparsely hairy throughout .... *M. brachygyne*
12′ Tepals pale yellow, the nectar guides outlined in green; filament column c. 6 mm long, lightly pubescent below .... *M. fuscomontana*
13 Leaf clasping the stem below, not diverging from the stem above the sheath 14
13′ Leaf diverging from the stem above the sheath, the stem often sharply flexed outward above the leaf sheath 22
14 Tepal claws short, clasping the base of the filament column ... 15
14′ Tepal claws at least half as long as the limb and widely diverging or suberect and forming a narrow tube or cup including at least part of the filament column 17
15 Flowers nodding and tepal limbs reflexed when fully open; filament column bulbous below .... *M. reflexa*
15′ Flowers held erect or facing to the side and tepal limbs spreading; filament column more or less cylindrical or slightly thickened below 16
16 Flowers usually facing to the side; anthers usually exceeding the stigma lobes; tepals ovate .... *M. marlothii*
16′ Flowers held erect; anthers reaching to the base of the stigma lobes; tepals oblong to lanceolate .... *M. cookii*
17 Tepal claws widely diverging 18
17′ Tepal claws suberect and forming a narrow tube or cup including at least part of the filament column 19
18 Outer tepals pandurate-spathulate, widest in the upper third; anthers usually 10-13 mm long, not reaching the top of the style branches; ovary c. 18 mm long .... *M. comptonii*
18′ Outer tepals oblong-obovate, widest in the lower third; anthers 8-10 mm long, exceeding the style branches; ovary 12-15 mm long .... *M. elegans*
19 Ovary elongate, 16-24 mm long and capsules 20-45 mm long; filaments usually free in the upper 1-1.5 mm .... *M. britteniae*
19′ Ovary club-shaped, 2-12 mm long and capsules 4-22 mm long; filaments entirely united or free in the upper 1 mm ... 20
20 Spathes enclosing the flowers 5-10 mm long; flowers small, the tepals c. 14 mm long .... *M. vlokii*
20′ Spathes enclosing the flowers 40-80 mm long; flowers large, the tepals 22-40 mm long 21
21 Stem with several cormels at each node; style crests 1-2 mm long, horizontal and directed inward; leaf long and trailing above .... *M. bulbillifera*
21′ Stem not bearing cormels at the nodes; style crests erect, c. 2 mm long; leaf usually fairly short, and erect .. *M. autumnalis*
22 Filaments free; style vestigial, style branches virtually sessile, shorter than the stamens .... *M. radians*
22′ Filaments united in a column enclosing the style, style branches usually exceeding the anthers 23
23 Tepal claws 1-2 mm long clasping the filament column; style branches diverging, shorter than the anthers .... *M. louisabolusiae*
23′ Tepal claws short to long but not clasping the base of the filament column; style branches usually shorter than the anthers 24
24 Flowers small, tepals less than 25 mm long; staminal column (filaments plus anthers) less than 10 mm long 25
24′ Flowers medium to large, tepals mostly 25-40 mm long; staminal column more than 10 mm long 26
25 Outer tepals 10-12 mm long; anthers c. 2 mm long .. *M. demissa*
25′ Outer tepals 16-24 mm long; anthers 5-6 mm long .... *M. flavescens*
26 Tepal claws widely diverging, forming a wide or obscure cup; anthers not included in the floral cup 27

26' Tepal claws suberect, forming a narrow cup; anthers partly to completely included in the floral cup 29
27 Ovary 9-10 mm long; outer tepals to 27 mm long ... *M. patens*
27' Ovary 13-20 mm long; outer tepals 30-40 mm long 28
28 Ovary 13-16 mm long and capsules 20-30 mm long; nectaries diffuse with nectar exuded from the larger veins all along the tepal surface .... *M. ochroleuca*
28' Ovary 17-20 mm long and capsules 30-55 mm long; nectary a discrete area at the base of each tepal .... *M. flaccida*
29 Style dividing at or above the middle of the anthers or not divided at all; style branches erect, not diverging 30
29' Style dividing at or just above top of the filament column, always below the middle of the anthers; style branches usually slightly diverging when flower fully open 31
30 Ovary usually included in the spathes; style branches 1-2 mm long or not developed .... *M. longistyla*
30' Ovary usually exserted from the spathes; style branches well developed, 2-3 mm long .... *M. minor*
31 Ovary elongate, mostly 12-19 mm long and capsules mostly 25-40 mm long .... *M. collina*
31' Ovary club-shaped, mostly 6-12 mm long and capsules 12-16(-20) mm long 32
32 Plants flowering only after fire and usually May-July; foliage leaf seldom exceeding 20 cm, the apex prominently thickened and unifacial .... *M. pyrophila*
32' Plants not flowering only after fire and usually Aug.-Sept.; foliage leaf long and trailing, usually exceeding 30 cm, the apex not noticeably thickened .... *M. vallisbelli*

Moraea Group *Moraea*
1 Plants 3- to more-branched and stems conspicuously sticky ... 2
1' Plants branched or not but stems rarely sticky and if so always unbranched and ovary 3-angled 7
2 Style branches poorly developed, concealed by the anthers, bilobed and obtuse apically and without crests; anthers exceeding the style branches .... *M. elsiae*
2' Style branches well developed with prominent, linear to lanceolate crests; anthers shorter than the style branches ... 3
3 Flowers fairly small, the outer tepals less than 24 mm long; spathes 18-24 mm long 4
3' Flower medium to large, the outer tepals more than 23 mm long; spathes 25-40 mm long 5
4 Flowers white, the tepals brownish on the outside; sweetly scented when opening in the mid- to late afternoon; tepal limbs spreading to weakly reflexed .... *M. viscaria*
4' Flowers pale to deep yellow or buff to dark brown with yellow nectar guides; not noticeably scented when opening after midday; tepal limbs weakly to strongly reflexed .... *M. inconspicua*
5 Flowers white and opening in the late afternoon; outer tepals 40-43 mm long; foliage leaves 4-6 ...... *M. vespertina*
5' Flowers yellow or predominantly brown, rarely pale mauve; outer tepals 22-33 mm long; foliage leaves 2-3 6
6 Flowers bright yellow, rarely pale mauve; spathes subequal, the inner not much longer than the outer .... *M. bituminosa*
6' Flowers brown with yellow nectar guides on the inner and outer tepals; spathes unequal, the inner 1.5 times longer than the outer .... *M. bubalina*
7 Plants stemless or nearly so, the stem not or barely produced above the ground at flowering although often elongating in fruit; immature capsule borne at or close to ground level, within the spathes 8
7' Plants with an aerial stem and flowers and capsules borne well above the ground 12
8 Ovary borne at or close to ground level at flowering 9
8' Ovary borne above the ground on a long, contractile pedicel at flowering, later withdrawn into the base of the spathes; leaves often lightly to densely hairy 10
9 Spathes closely enveloping the flowers clusters; flowers deep blue-violet; ovary cylindrical, 17-21 mm long, with a marked beak; leaf or leaves linear, erect below, often trailing above .... *M. macrocarpa*
9' Spathes loosely enveloping the flowers and not clearly distinct from the leaves; flowers white with yellow nectar guides and a purple blotch on the inner tepals; ovary club-shaped, 4-5 mm long; leaves channeled, spreading .... *M. falcifolia*
10 Claw of the outer tepal 25-40 mm long, about twice as long as the limb; filaments (including column) 12-18 mm long .... *M. macronyx*
10' Claw of the outer tepal 10-18 mm long, shorter to about as long as the limb; filaments (including column) 3-10 mm long 11
11 Style crests broadly triangular; filaments 3-4 mm long; style branches c. 5 mm long .... *M. tricolor*
11' Style crests linear-lanceolate; filaments (3-)5-10 mm long; style branches 7-15 mm long .... *M. ciliata*
12 Plants with 2 produced leaves or more, not including the remaining entirely sheathing leafy organs that resemble bracts or the inflorescence spathes 13
12' Plants with a single produced leaf, remaining leafy organs entirely sheathing and resembling bracts or the inflorescence spathes 27
13 Leaves 2, subopposite and inserted well above the ground; ovary and capsules beaked .... *M. fugax*
13' Leaves few to several or if only 2 then the lowermost inserted close to the ground; ovary and capsule not beaked 14
14 Stem lightly hairy to velvety 15
14' Stem smooth 16

15 Leaves and spathes often hairy or at least leaf margins minutely hairy; capsules erect; leaf base and spathe margins united around the stem .... *M. papilionacea*
15' Leaves and spathes smooth, glaucous; capsules usually nodding; leaves and spathe margins free virtually to the base .... *M. vegeta*
16 Leaf margins undulate to crisped 17
16' Leaf margins straight 19
17 Ovary and capsules included in the spathes .... *M. serpentina*
17' Ovary and capsules exserted from the spathes 18
18 Flowers with the inner tepals erect, lanceolate to tricuspidate; leaves several .... *M. fergusoniae*
18' Flowers with the inner tepal limbs spreading, entire, lanceolate; leaves 2–3 .... *M. gawleri*
19 Style crests (tips of the style branches) feathery ... *M. lugubris*
19' Style crests flat, paired and usually erect, sometimes much reduced but never feathery 20
20 Style branches narrow, about as wide as the anthers; crests short or absent; nectar guides often on the limbs of both inner and outer tepals 21
20' Style branches fairly broad, mostly about as twice as wide as the anthers; crests usually well developed; nectar guides only on the limbs of the outer tepals 22
21 Anthers appressed to style branches diverging from the base, about as long as the style branches .... *M. polyanthos*
21' Anthers erect and contiguous, style dividing opposite the anther apices and the style branches shorter than the anthers .... *M. speciosa*
22 Flowers with only 3 tepals, those of the inner whorl lacking; tepals united in a tube .... *M. cooperi*
22' Flowers with 6 tepals; tepals free to the base 23
23 Flowers blue to violet 24
23' Flowers yellow to brick red, sometimes partly white 25
24 Tepals 20–30 mm long .... *M. bipartita*
24' Tepals 36–50 mm long .... *M. polystachya*
25 Plants tall, often to 1 m or more, and repeatedly branched; leaves several, arranged in 2 ranks, 15–30 mm wide and broadly channeled; roots forming a spiny network around the corm .... *M. ramosissima*
25' Plants not reaching 50 cm, often branched but seldom extensively; leaves 2–4, to 10 mm wide, narrowly channeled; roots not spiny 26
26 Plants with 2 more or less basal leaves, the margins often undulate or crisped; outer tepals mostly 15–25 mm long; anthers short, c. 3 mm .... *M. gawleri*
26' Plants with one basal leaf, remaining leaves inserted well above the ground, the margins straight; outer tepals c. 35 mm long; anthers c. 6 mm long .... *M. linderi*
27 Inner tepals with an expanded, more or less entire limb, narrowly lanceolate to ovate or triangular; leaves hairless ... 28
27' Inner tepals with a reduced limb, either tricuspidate, trilobed, filiform, threadlike, or absent, rarely the limb lanceolate but then the leaves hairy 51
28 Style branches narrower than to about as wide as the anthers; crests short or absent; tepals with nectar guides often on the limbs of both inner and outer tepals 29
28' Style branches fairly broad, mostly about twice as wide as the anthers; crests usually well developed; flowers various colors but with nectar guides only on the limbs of the outer tepals 33
29 Lateral flower clusters on main branches sessile 30
29' All flower clusters stalked 31
30 Ovary and capsule globose; plants flowering Dec.–Mar. .... *M. pseudospicata*
30' Ovary and capsule more or less fusiform; plants flowering Oct.–Nov. .... *M. verecunda*
31 Flowers cream to yellow; inner tepal limbs more or less triangular .... *M. deltoidea*
31' Flowers blue to violet; inner tepals limbs oblong to ovate ... 32
32 Tepals with short suberect claws forming a narrow cup including the lower half of the filament column ...... *M. crispa*
32' Tepals spreading from the base .... *M. worcesterensis*
33 Leaf inserted well above ground level, the lowermost internode elongate; ovary and capsule with a short beak ... 34
33' Leaf inserted near the base, often below the ground, lowermost internode not markedly longer than others; ovary and capsule without a beak 35
34 Leaf linear, mostly 2–3 mm wide; flowers relatively small, blue-violet, opening in the later afternoon; outer tepals 20–26 mm long .... *M. gracilenta*
34' Leaf linear to filiform, 0.5–4 mm wide; flowers small to large, blue, yellow, or white, opening shortly after midday; tepals 20–40 mm long, if blue then usually at least 30 mm long .... *M. fugax*
35 Leaf terete in the upper half, narrowly channeled in the lower half; ovary strongly 3-angled; nodes often sticky 36
35' Leaf channeled virtually throughout; ovary mostly terete but sometimes 3-lobed to 3-angled 39
36 Flowers small, the outer tepals 20–24 mm long ... *M. vallisavium*
36' Flowers fairly large, outer tepals mostly 30–45 mm long, sometimes longer 37
37 Filaments united in the lower 2–3 mm; sheathing leaves mostly 2 .... *M. anomala*
37' Filaments united in the lower 0.5–2 mm; sheathing leaves usually 1, rarely 2 38
38 Style branches about as long to shorter than the crests; nectar guide clear yellow, edged in darker color .... *M. angusta*
38' Style branches somewhat longer than the crests; nectar guide yellow with minutely dotted longitudinal streaks and not edged in darker color .... *M. neglecta*

39 Plants tiny, 3–5 cm high; outer tepals 10–14 mm long; flowers blue-purple .... *M. nubigena*
39′ Plants at least 10 cm high and to 1 m; outer tepals more than 10 mm long, variously colored 40
40 Anthers exceeding the style branches, usually overtopping the crests; flowers orange or sometimes cream to white ... *M. insolens*
40′ Anthers not reaching the top of the style branches; flowers mostly yellow or blue to mauve, sometimes other colors but never orange 41
41 Filaments united only at the base; style branches diverging almost at the top of the ovary; flowers pale yellow with darker veins .... *M. thomasiae*
41′ Filaments united at least in the lower third and often for half their length or more; style diverging well above the top of the ovary; flowers mostly blue to mauve, sometimes cream, maroon, or pink 42
42 Filaments more than 10 mm long 43
42′ Filaments 3–6 mm long 46
43 Flowers pale pink with dark purple markings or yellow with darker yellow markings; filaments free in the upper third 44
43′ Flowers blue (to violet); filaments united in the lower half to almost entirely 45
44 Flowers pale pink with dark purple markings; leaf mostly 3–5 mm at the widest .... *M. barkerae*
44′ Flowers yellow with darker yellow markings; leaf mostly 10–15 mm at the widest .... *M. spathulata*
45 Ovary exserted from the spathes; inner tepals erect; filaments united almost entirely .... *M. incurva*
45′ Ovary included in the spathes; inner tepals spreading when flower fully open; anthers free in the upper half ... *M. macgregorii*
46 Outer tepal limbs shorter than the claws; style crests short, c. 2.5 mm long; flowers usually dark maroon-red, sometimes the tepals edged in cream or entirely white to cream 47
46′ Outer tepal limbs about as long as or longer than the claws; style crests usually well developed, mostly 5–9 mm long; flowers blue to mauve 48
47 Tepal claws shorter than the limbs, 10 mm long, forming a cup c. 12 mm diam. at the mouth, enclosing the filaments and the base of the anthers only; flowers white to cream with the inner tepal claws darkly colored in the center ...... *M. cantharophila*
47′ Tepal claws longer than the limbs, 13–17 mm long, forming a cup c. 15 mm diam. at the mouth, enclosing the filaments and the anthers entirely; inner tepal claws uniformly colored, either dark or paler .... *M. lurida*
48 Filaments united almost entirely .... *M. amissa*
48′ Filaments free in the upper half 49
49 Flowers lasting 2–3 days; inner tepals erect, spathulate, broadest above the middle .... *M. algoensis*
49′ Flowers lasting a day; inner tepals spreading when flower fully open, lanceolate 50

50 Outer tepals 19–30 mm long; spathes 40–60 mm long .... *M. elliotii*
50′ Outer tepals c. 15 mm long; spathes 22–26 mm long .... *M. exiliflora*
51 Inner tepals lacking, not even represented by short cilia .... *M. barnardii*
51′ Inner tepals represented at least by short cilia 52
52 Filaments free almost to the base; style branches diverging just above the ovary base .... *M. tripetala*
52′ Filaments united at least in the lower half or entirely; style branches diverging above the top of the filament column and well above the ovary base 53
53 Inner tepals linear-filiform, reaching above the limbs of the outer tepals 54
53′ Inner tepal limbs divided into 3 equal or unequal lobes 55
54 Flowers white .... *M. longiaristata*
54′ Flowers dark violet .... *M. regalis*
55 Anthers exceeding the style branches, usually exceeding the style crests 56
55′ Anthers not reaching further than the base of the style crests, usually not reaching the stigma lobes 57
56 Flowers usually deep blue to mauve with iridescent blue nectar guides on the outer tepals; anthers 13–16 mm long; style crests obscure, not exceeding the stigma lobes ... *M. gigandra*
56′ Flowers orange to reddish, often with iridescent green or navy blue nectar guides; anthers 7–12 mm long; style crests short, 1–2 mm, erect and exceeding the stigma lobes .... *M. tulbaghensis*
57 Stem and leaves minutely to prominently hairy or at least the leaves long-hairy on the margins 58
57′ Stem and leaves smooth 63
58 Stem smooth 59
58′ Stem velvety hairy 60
59 Flowers light blue-purple fading to mauve and tepals becoming lightly mottled; leaf mostly 3–5 mm wide ... *M. debilis*
59′ Flowers dull cream, reddish brown on the outside; leaf 4–8 mm wide at the widest .... *M. atropunctata*
60 Outer tepal claws with a dense, blackish beard and without a pale nectar guide at the base of the limb 61
60′ Outer tepal claws with a dense, yellow to orange pubescence and sometimes with a conspicuous dark nectar guide at the base of the limb 62
61 Filaments 2–3 mm long; style branches ascending and with crests 3–4 mm long .... *M. calcicola*
61′ Filaments c. 4 mm long; style branches arching over the outer tepal claws and with short crests 1–2 mm long .... *M. loubseri*
62 Nectar guide not conspicuous, a small black or yellow mark edged in black; filaments 2–3 mm long .... *M. caeca*
62′ Nectar guide a conspicuous dark crescent, sometimes edged in pale color; filaments 4–5 mm long .... *M. villosa*

63 Central cusp of the inner tepals spreading at least 3 times as long as the outer lobes 64
63' Central cusp of the inner tepals erect or incurved, often less than twice as long as the lateral lobes 65
64 Outer tepals white with prominent violet to iridescent green nectar guides; outer tepals 30–35 mm long .... *M. aristata*
64' Outer tepals blue-mauve with small black or yellow nectar guides; outer tepals 23–28 mm long .... *M. caeca*
65 Tepal claws forming a wide, deep cup and claws longer than the limbs .... *M. lurida*
65' Tepal claws not obviously forming a cup and claws shorter than the limbs 66
66 Outer tepal limbs cupped to spreading; central cusp of the inner tepals usually obliquely twisted inward and less than twice as long as the lateral lobes 67
66' Outer tepal limbs laxly to strongly reflexed; central cusp of the inner tepals erect or symmetrically curved inward and more than twice as long as the lateral lobes 68
67 Flowers yellow; outer tepal limbs ascending and broadly cupped; filaments 3–5 mm long .... *M. bellendenii*
67' Flowers white to cream, rarely pale yellowish; outer tepal limbs spreading; filaments 5–6 mm long ...... *M. tricuspidata*
68 Flowers relatively small, the outer tepals mostly 12–16 mm long, rarely slightly longer; central lobe of the inner tepals curved inward .... *M. unguiculata*
68' Flowers medium to large, the outer tepals 24–40 mm long; central lobe of the inner tepals more or less straight and erect 69
69 Filaments c. 7 mm long; flowers pink with outer tepal claws 10–12 mm long .... *M. lilacina*
69' Filaments 12–15 mm long; flowers dark violet with outer tepal claws 12–16 mm long...................... *M. regalis*

Nerine

1 Tepals arranged regularly; stamens and style clustered centrally, filaments and style almost straight, only slightly curved toward the apex; flowers usually red or reddish pink, rarely white .... *N. sarniensis*
1' Tepals arranged irregularly to somewhat regularly; stamens and style clustered horizontally in the lower half of the flower, filaments and style distinctly upturned toward the apex; flowers pink or white 2
2 Flowers trumpet-shaped, tepals more or less overlapping, not undulate .... *N. pudica*
2' Flowers with all the tepals curved upward, only the stamens and style remaining in the lower half; tepals usually undulate 3
3 Plants robust; leaves 15–25 mm wide; tepals 5–7 mm wide, equally broad to the base .... *N. ridleyi*
3' Plants less robust; leaves at most 15 mm wide; tepals 3–5 mm wide, distinctly tapered toward the base .... *N. humilis*

Onixotis

1 Leaves all alike, lanceolate, more or less evenly scattered along the stem; styles free .... *O. punctata*
1' Leaves dissimilar, the lower 2 with slender terete blades and the uppermost entirely clasping, the upper 2 well separated from the lowermost and set just below the inflorescence; styles shortly united below .... *O. stricta*

Ornithogalum

Subgenera of *Ornithogalum*

1 Style longer than the ovary and stamens, usually deflexed; stigma globose or subglobose with long or hair-like papillae; tepals firm textured, white or yellow with a broad green keel; capsule subglobose to ovoid; seeds flattened and D-shaped, 2–4 mm long .... subgenus *Osmyne*
1' Style very short to about as long as the ovary and stamens, erect or rarely deflexed; stigma small, without long papillae; tepals various 2
2 Capsule fusiform to ellipsoidal, transparent, partially or completely concealed in the dry, closed perianth; tepals with or without a dark keel, white to orange; seeds angular or rounded, 0.5–3 mm long .... subgenus *Aspasia*
2' Capsule 3-angled or 3-winged, oblong-globose, leathery, partially or fully exposed by the withered perianth; tepals always with a dark midrib, whitish to green; seeds usually flattened, 3–12 mm long .... subgenus *Urophyllon*

Ornithogalum Subgenus *Aspasia*

1 Bracts boat-shaped, firm, entire; flowers bowl-shaped, often with a dark center; tepals 10–24 mm long, without a dark midrib; filaments sometimes markedly dimorphic 2
1' Bracts small, deltoid-aristate, auriculate or lobed at the base, minutely toothed or fringed, membranous; flowers star-shaped or tepals reflexed, never with a dark center; tepals 5–10(–18) mm long, usually with a dark midrib on drying ... 12
2 Stamens dimorphic, the three outer shorter than the inner and with larger anthers, the inner filaments with broad, scalloped or toothed wings in the upper part 3
2' Stamens monomorphic or dimorphic but then not as above, the stamens subequal and the inner tapering above 4
3 Flowers in lax, usually long racemes on pedicels 8–22 mm long; leaves in a basal rosette, absent at flowering .... *O. constrictum*
3' Flowers in compact subspicate racemes on pedicels 2–8 mm long; leaves superposed, usually still present at flowering .... *O. inclusum*
4 Style absent or very short and stout, the ovary usually attenuated into the style, which forms the beak of the

capsule; flowers white, cream, buff, yellow, or orange 5
4' Style about as long as the ovary; flowers white 8
5 Leaves oblong to lanceolate, flat or channeled 6
5' Leaves terete or narrowly linear with margins rolled inward ... 7
6 Filaments somewhat fleshy, ovate or with broad pointed incurved wings, dark above; flowers white or yellow to red with a dark center .... *O. dubium*
6' Filaments awl-shaped, the inner sometimes wider; flowers buff or orange to red, the outer tepals with a black or transparent apical spot .... *O. maculatum*
7 Flowers yellow to orange; leaves (2)3–12 ...... *O. multifolium*
7' Flowers white to buff; leaves 1–3 .... *O. rupestre*
8 Stamens strongly dimorphic, the inner with winged expansions in the lower half that are strongly eared above and curved inward over the ovary; ovary obtuse and sharply differentiated from the style .... *O. thyrsoides*
8' Stamens weakly or more strongly dimorphic, the inner ovate or expanded below but then with the lower expansion squared above and not curved inward over the ovary 9
9 Bulbs with soft whitish or grayish outer tunics ..... *O. conicum*
9' Bulbs with hard, dark outer tunics 10
10 Plants 5–10 cm high, dwarf, usually with 3–4 leaves contemporary with the flowers; peduncle short .. *O. subcoriaceum*
10' Plants 15–25 cm high 11
11 Leaves present at flowering, grayish, leathery with smooth margins .... *O. pruinosum*
11' Leaves usually withering at flowering, dark green, soft with fimbriate margins .... *O. fimbrimarginatum*
12 Leaves 3–5, at first in a basal rosette but later the sheaths lengthening with the developing peduncle to form a pseudostem with the blades diverging successively from their sheaths and apparently cauline and scattered along the pseudostem, ovate to narrowly lanceolate, usually withered at flowering ... 13
12' Leaves one to many, the sheaths never lengthening to form a pseudostem although the leaves may be surrounded by a short or long cataphyll but then emerging together from the top of the cataphyll and not apparently scattered along a pseudostem, linear to lanceolate, usually green at flowering ... 18
13 Bulb with hard, shiny black outer tunics; peduncles and pedicels minutely warty; leaf blades hairless but the margins thickened and hairy 14
13' Bulb with soft whitish or pale brown outer tunics; peduncle and pedicels smooth; leaves various 16
14 Bracts small, 2–6 mm long, at least the lower ones with hairy margins .... *O. ciliiferum*
14' Bracts larger, (5–)9–14 mm long, the margins never hairy but the tip sometimes aristate 15
15 Leaf cilia stiff and short, 0.5–3 mm, smooth, evenly spaced in a single row; style straight and erect, shorter than the ovary .... *O. pilosum*
15' Leaf cilia soft and long, 3–5.5 mm, rough, unevenly and untidily spaced in 2 rows; style sharply deflexed at the base then erect, longer than the ovary .... *O. pullulatum*
16 Flowers nocturnal; filaments with the basal appendages forming 2 curved lateral horns .... *O. bicornutum*
16' Flowers diurnal; filaments filiform or ovate with rounded or shortly toothed appendages; leaf sheaths green or white, often spotted 17
17 Tepals narrowly elliptical to oblong, 8–18 mm long; pedicels erect or spreading, 10–20 mm long .... *O. hispidum*
17' Tepals linear, 6–8 mm long; pedicels erect, 5–10 mm long .....
.... *O. thermophilum*
18 Leaves surrounded at the base by an elongate sheathing cataphyll and emerging together from the top some distance above the ground 19
18' Leaves not evidently surrounded by an elongate sheathing cataphyll although the leaf sheaths may form a neck but this finely fibrous 21
19 Sheath uniformly colored, hairless, often grayish or purple; leaves linear to lanceolate; raceme dense, spike-like ....
.... *O. graminifolium*
19' Sheath horizontally banded or hairy; leaves filiform; raceme lax 20
20 Sheath horizontally banded .... *O. zebrinellum*
20' Sheath hairy, the hairs often tufted .... *O.* sp. 1
21 Bulbs borne above ground; plants evergreen; leaves 20–50, incurved and triangular in cross section with as many as 6 rows of short stiff cilia, 15–25 mm long; plant resembling a small *Haworthia* .... *O. sardienii*
21' Bulbs largely subterranean; plants not evidently evergreen; leaves fewer and longer 22
22 Filaments united into a staminal cup c. 2 mm long ....
.... *O. synadelphicum*
22' Filaments free 23
23 Leaves narrowly oblong, curved, channeled and distinctly keeled with the tip blunt and boat-shaped, the margins with stiff backward-pointing hairs; inflorescence a short, dense, subcorymbose raceme .... *O. comptonii*
23' Leaves linear to filiform, at most grooved above, smooth or ribbed but not distinctly keeled; inflorescence either a dense spike-like raceme or a lax corymbose raceme 24
24 Leaf bases persisting as a finely fibrous neck, the blades more or less fibrotic; raceme dense and spike-like ..... *O. juncifolium*
24' Leaf bases not forming a neck or the neck not fibrous; raceme lax, usually subcorymbose 25
25 Leaves hairless or the margin hairy, linear to narrowly lanceolate, soft; inflorescence somewhat flexuous ....
.... *O. schlechterianum*
25' Leaves usually with minute cilia in longitudinal rows, subterete or filiform, hard; inflorescence wiry, straight 26

26 Leaves distinctly sinuate or tortuous; bulb neck shiny . . . .
. . . . O. tortuosum
26' Leaves straight; bulb neck dull . . . . O. nannodes

Ornithogalum Subgenus Osmyne

1 Leaf 1, oblong, channeled to boat-shaped, leathery with thickened, horny margin . . . . O. diluculum
1' Leaves 2 to many 2
2 Leaves more than 7, flat and loosely arranged at the base, not clasping the peduncle 3
2' Leaves 2–7, channeled below and clasping the peduncle 5
3 Leaves oblong, flat, the margins hyaline and smooth or fringed . .
. . . . O. secundum
3' Leaves narrowly oblong to terete, coiled or twisted 4
4 Leaves linear, flat, spirally coiled throughout . . O. concordianum
4' Leaves semiterete and channeled, erect but coiling loosely above on drying . . . . O. polyphyllum
5 Leaves not glandular . . . . O. suaveolens
5' Leaves glandular 6
6 Leaves and inflorescence glandular hairy, the leaves not noticeably ribbed . . . . O. pentheri
6' Leaves conspicuously ribbed, glandular-papillate and covered with adhering sand . . . . O. sabulosum

Ornithogalum Subgenus Urophyllon

1 Flowers cup-shaped with a distinct tube about as long as the tepals; filaments shortly joined at the base . . . . O. rotatum
1' Flowers star-shaped without a distinct tube; filaments free 2
2 Leaf 1, rarely 2–3 in older plants, spreading, oblong-lanceolate, c. 5 cm long, dry at flowering . . . . O. unifolium
2' Leaves 2–12, erect, linear to ovate-lanceolate, mostly more than 10 cm long, usually green at flowering 3
3 Plants of marshy places with the bulbs usually poorly developed; tepals white without a dark midrib; ovary stalked or narrowed below 4
3' Plants of drier places with the bulbs well developed; tepals white or greenish with a dark midrib 6
4 Inflorescence subspicate, the pedicels 2–4 mm long . . . .
. . . . O. paludosum
4' Inflorescence racemose or corymbose, the pedicels (2–)4–50 mm long 5
5 Tepals 10–14 mm long, united below into a tube 3–4 mm long; raceme subcorymbose with pedicels 5–50 mm long . . . .
. . . . O. esterhuyseniae
5' Tepals 6–7 mm long, scarcely united below; raceme cylindrical with pedicels (2–)5–25 mm long . . . . O. flexuosum
6 Leaves spreading in a basal rosette, 9–12, oblanceolate, often dry at flowering; inflorescence cylindrical, racemose with pedicels to 30 mm long . . . . O. xanthochlorum
6' Leaves suberect, green at flowering; inflorescence subspicate with pedicels to 10 mm long 7
7 Leaves wiry, with long basal, often faintly orange-spotted sheaths that break up into long, often netted strips . . . . O. dregeanum
7' Leaves various but without such sheaths 8
8 Plants 10–75 cm high; leaves linear, 2–8 mm wide; bracts short; capsule 5 mm long . . . . O. tenuifolium
8' Plants usually larger, with exposed bulbs that form bulblets; leaves lanceolate, 20–50 mm wide; bracts usually overtopping the flowers; capsule 10 mm long . . . . O. longibracteatum

Ornithoglossum

1 Perianth zygomorphic with most of the tepals held comb-like above the flower, cream and purple, pink, or maroon; filaments slender, uniformly pale . . . . O. undulatum
1' Perianth actinomorphic with all the tepals similarly orientated, dull greenish; filaments and style usually much shorter than the tepals, the filaments usually distinctly swollen near the middle and bicolored 2
2 Flowers larger, tepals 10–30 mm long, filaments 5–25 mm long and anthers 2.2–6 mm long 3
2' Flowers smaller, tepals 5–15 mm long, filaments 2–5 mm long and anthers 0.8–2 mm long 4
3 Leaves short, 3–10 cm, the margins conspicuously crisped; filaments usually with a distinct bulge in the middle; upper margin of the nectary with a tongue-like flap . . . . O. gracile
3' Leaves longer, (6–)10–30 cm, the margins straight or lightly undulate; filaments slender or only slightly swollen in the middle; upper margin of the nectary straight or notched . . . . O. vulgare
4 Nectary a small pocket- or mouth-like structure distinctly narrower than the tepal claw . . . . O. viride
4' Nectary pouch-like, formed by the hollow claw and as wide as long, with a straight upper margin . . . . O. parviflorum

Pauridia

1 Pedicel 2–30 mm long; perianth tube 2–4 mm long, shorter than the tepals . . . . P. minuta
1' Pedicel 0–2 mm long; perianth tube 8–30 mm long, at least twice as long as the tepals . . . . P. longituba

Polyxena

1 Perianth tube shorter than the tepals or as long, 3.5–6 mm long; ovary subglobose 2
1' Perianth tube longer than the tepals, 12–30 mm long; ovary ellipsoidal 3
2 Leaves linear, 1–5 mm wide; filaments 4–5 mm long; style longer than the ovary and 7–8 mm long . . . . P. corymbosa
2' Leaves narrowly lanceolate, 5–10 mm wide; filaments 1–2 mm

long; style shorter than the ovary and 1–2.5 mm long . . . . *P. paucifolia*

3 Stamen filaments 1.5–2 mm long, both series inserted within the tube; style about half as long as the tube and 10–15 mm long . . . . *P. maughanii*

3′ Stamen filaments 4–5 mm long, one or both series inserted on the tepals above the mouth of the tube; style longer than the tube and 15–27 mm long 4

4 Leaves broadly lanceolate to ovate, 10–30 mm wide; both stamen series inserted on the tepals above the tube . . . . *P. ensifolia*

4′ Leaves linear to narrowly lanceolate, 2–10 mm wide; outer stamens inserted within the tube . . . . *P. longituba*

Romulea

Groups of *Romulea*

1 Corms rounded or pointed at the base, the tunics split into coarse bent or straight acuminate teeth without fibrous tips; stems always short and subterranean 2

1′ Corms bell-shaped with a circular basal rim or obliquely flattened toward the base with a crescent-shaped basal ridge or compressed with a fan-shaped basal ridge, the tunics fringed or split into fibers at the tips; stems short or well developed 3

2 Corms pointed at the base, the teeth straight . . . . *Cruciata* group

2′ Corms rounded at the base, the teeth curved to one side . . . . *Rosea* group

3 Basal fibers aggregated into distinct rounded clusters often with a deeper fissure or line of weakness extending from the center of each cluster, the fibrils in each cluster converging and pointed . . . . *Aggregata* group

3′ Basal fibers not aggregated into clusters of converging fibrils, sometimes the basal ridge more deeply incised between groups of parallel fibers but without a deeper fissure extending from the center of each cluster, the fibrils more or less blunt . . . 4

4 Corms symmetrical and bell-shaped with a circular basal rim . . . . *Hirsuta* group

4′ Corms obliquely flattened with a crescent-shaped basal ridge or compressed with a fan-shaped basal ridge . . . . . *Ciliata* group

Romulea Group *Aggregata*

1 Flowers deep rosy red or scarlet; anthers longer than filaments . . . 2

1′ Flowers pink to yellow or greenish; anthers shorter than filaments 3

2 Corm with a circular basal ridge; flowers with a white or yellow cup . . . . *R. amoena*

2′ Corm with a horseshoe-shaped basal ridge; flowers uniformly red . . . . *R. sanguinalis*

3 Inner bracts with membranous margins unmarked; stem usually short 4

3′ Inner bracts with membranous margins brown-flecked or edged, at least in the upper part; stem usually well developed 5

4 Flowers white to pink . . . . *R. albomarginata*

4′ Flowers yellow to apricot . . . . *R. setifolia*

5 Basal foliage leaf 1, rarely 2 but then the lower leaf shorter 6

5′ Basal foliage leaves 2 7

6 Flowers yellow to orange; leaves 4-grooved and X-shaped in section . . . . *R. jugicola*

6′ Flowers pink or salmon pink; leaves with the lateral ridges reduced and I-shaped in section . . . . *R. dichotoma*

7 Flowers pink to magenta with violet blotches in the throat; corm usually with a fibrous neck . . . . *R. fibrosa*

7′ Flowers pale greenish, cream, yellow, or apricot, often with dark apricot-colored veins; corm without a fibrous neck . . . . *R. longipes*

Romulea Group *Ciliata*

1 Flowers salverform with a cylindrical perianth tube 11–17 mm long, white to purple; leaf 1(2) . . . . *R. stellata*

1′ Flowers funnel- or bell-shaped 2

2 Basal foliage leaves 4-winged, X-shaped in cross section and usually conspicuously hairy on the margins; peduncles hairy . . . . *R. tetragona*

2′ Basal foliage leaves 2- to 8-grooved, not X-shaped in cross section; peduncles hairless 3

3 Upper part of the basal foliage leaves 5- to 8-grooved; plants aquatic with the corms submerged 4

3′ Upper part of the basal foliage leaves 1- to 4-grooved; plants not aquatic although sometimes growing in marshy ground . . . 5

4 Basal foliage leaves 2; style 12–15 mm long; fruiting peduncles long and widely spreading . . . . *R. multisulcata*

4′ Basal foliage leaf 1; style 4–8 mm long; fruiting peduncles short and erect . . . . *R. aquatica*

5 Inner bracts wholly papery or submembranous, differing markedly from the green outer bracts; basal foliage leaf one when the stem is elongated 6

5′ Inner bracts usually with a green median zone and wide membranous margins, rarely both outer and inner bracts membranous; basal leaves 1–2 when the stem is elongated 8

6 Flowers white with large black blotches usually bordered by a yellow margin in the throat; leaves widely 2-grooved and T-shaped in cross section . . . . *R. barkerae*

6′ Flowers without dark blotches; leaves 4-grooved 7

7 Flowers pale or sulfur yellow, white, or blue; inner bracts usually papery . . . . *R. flava*

7′ Flowers golden yellow or orange-yellow; inner bracts often greenish in the upper half . . . . *R. saldanhensis*

8 Flowers yellow, with or without dark marks 9

8′ Flowers white, pink, or blue, with yellow cup 14

9 Corm more or less flattened with the basal ridge almost vertical, fan-shaped, wider than the corm or the leaves bifacial most of

their length (i.e., with a dorsal groove almost to the tip) 10
9' Corm not flattened, the basal ridge rarely wider than the corm and the leaves not bifacial most of their length 12
10 Foliage leaf 1(2), usually suberect, with adhering sand particles .... *R. sphaerocarpa*
10' Foliage leaves several, usually flexuous, without adhering sand particles 11
11 Basal ridge vertical, fan-shaped, much wider than the corm; bracts largely membranous or submembranous ... *R. tortuosa*
11' Basal ridge oblique, not much wider than the corm; bracts green or submembranous in the lower half .... *R. austinii*
12 Filaments at least twice as long as the anthers; flowers golden yellow or orange-yellow .... *R. sulphurea*
12' Filaments less than twice as long as the anthers; flowers bright or pale yellow 13
13 Inner bracts with brownish or brown-flecked margins; basal ridge of the corm often wider than the corm .... *R. montana*
13' Inner bracts with colorless margins; basal ridge of the corm narrower than the corm .... *R. elliptica*
14 Corm tunics with the basal row of parallel fibrils or small teeth sharply bent over a rather high ridge 15
14' Corm tunics with the basal row of fibrils not sharply bent over at the tips 16
15 Corm tunics with the basal fibrils aggregated into regular clusters of converging fibrils, each cluster bisected by a deeper cleft; outer bract submembranous in lower half ... *R. pratensis*
15' Corm tunics with the basal fibrils parallel and not clustered; outer bract green throughout .... *R. gigantea*
16 Corm higher than wide with a high, chisel-shaped basal ridge; flowers to 20 mm long; inner bracts usually with conspicuously brown-spotted membranous margins 17
16' Corm about as wide as high or wider; flowers to 35 mm long; inner bracts with unspotted or spotted membranous margins ... .18
17 Flowers 7–15 mm long, often with a mauve throat, the tepals less than 3 mm wide; stamens 3.5–6 mm long ... *R. minutiflora*
17' Flowers 15–20 mm long, the tepals 3–4 mm wide; stamens 6.5–8 mm long .... *R. sinispinosensis*
18 Flowers rose or pink with large violet blotches in the throat .... *R. biflora*
18' Flowers without blotches in the throat 19
19 Corm obliquely flattened with a wide fan-like basal ridge; flowers white .... *R. toximontana*
19' Corm not flattened, with a narrow crescent-shaped basal ridge 20
20 Anther connectives attenuate and produced 2.5–6 mm above the thecae; flowers white .... *R. flexuosa*
20' Anther connectives not attenuate 21
21 Tepals usually bicolored above the cup, the lower third or half yellow, the upper part white to blue or lilac; fruiting peduncles at first sharply recurved, later suberect; membranous margins of the inner bracts flecked with brown 22
21' Tepals uniformly colored above the cup; fruiting peduncles straight; membranous margins of the inner bracts plain or flecked with brown 23
22 Upper part of the tepals cream or white, 5–8 mm wide; outer tepals not blotched on the reverse .... *R. leipoldtii*
22' Upper part of the tepals bluish, rarely white, to 5 mm wide; outer tepals often irregularly blotched on the reverse .... *R. tabularis*
23 Tepals obtuse; outer tepals shiny and wine colored on the reverse, inner pale .... *R. vinacea*
23' Tepals acute to subobtuse; outer tepals not shiny and wine colored 24
24 Stem rigid; flowers cream, white, or lilac to pale mauve; filaments hairy near their bases; anthers 4–9 mm long .... *R. schlechteri*
24' Stem slender and wiry; flowers magenta; filaments minutely hairy almost to the top; anthers 3–4 mm long ..... *R. saxatilis*

Romulea Group *Cruciata*

1 Flowers salverform with a cylindrical perianth tube 35–70 mm long .... *R. hantamensis*
1' Flowers funnel- or bell-shaped with a cup-shaped perianth tube to 10 mm long 2
2 Flowers yellow; outer and inner bracts similar, both with broad membranous margins and apices .... *R. membranacea*
2' Flowers pink to magenta with a yellow cup; outer bracts with membranous margins narrower than the inner 3
3 Bracts with distinct brown-spotted membranous margins and conspicuous membranous apices and strong, closely spaced veins; flowers without dark blotches in the throat .... *R. vlokii*
3' Bracts with narrow, scarcely visible membranous margins and apices and usually more distantly spaced veins; flowers with dark blotches in the throat 4
4 Flowers (35–)40–60 mm long, old rose or red, with dark red blotches in the throat, the cup pale yellow or greenish yellow; filaments 9–12 mm long .... *R. eximia*
4' Flowers 25–35(–40) mm long, magenta to lilac, often with purple or blue blotches in the throat, the cup golden yellow or orange-yellow; filaments 3–6 mm long .... *R. cruciata*

Romulea Group *Hirsuta*

1 Flowers yellow or cream with a yellow cup 2
1' Flowers apricot or pink to magenta with a yellow cup; basal rim of the corm not scalloped 4
2 Corm strongly flattened, disk-shaped; flowers yellow with dark blotches in the throat .... *R. discifera*
2' Corm bell-shaped; flowers cream or yellow without yellow blotches in the throat 3

3   Flowers yellow to white, the outer tepals greenish or cream on the reverse; basal rim of the corm narrow; fruiting peduncles suberect or lightly spreading . . . . *R. triflora*
3' Flowers white, the outer tepals purplish or green on the reverse; basal rim of the corm wide and scalloped; fruiting peduncles abruptly spreading . . . . *R. sladenii*
4   Leaves tightly sinuous . . . . *R. tortilis*
4' Leaves straight 5
5   Tepals more than 6 mm wide . . . . *R. hirsuta*
5' Tepals 5–6 mm wide . . . . *R. gracillima*

Romulea Group *Rosea*

1   Flowers salverform with a cylindrical perianth tube 15–30 mm long 2
1' Flowers funnel- or bell-shaped with a cup-shaped perianth tube to 6 mm long 3
2   Flowers white, perianth tube 20–33 mm long; leaves suberect, conspicuously hairy; corm with a fibrous neck . . . . . *R. albiflora*
2' Flowers pink to purple, perianth tube 15–20 mm long; leaves curved, sparsely hairy; corm without a conspicuous fibrous neck . . . . *R. syringodeoflora*
3   Inner bract 2-keeled and with 2 stronger veins, especially in the upper half; bract often distinctly keeled in the upper half . . . 4
3' Inner bract not 2-keeled and without 2 stronger veins; bract not keeled 8
4   Flowers yellow . . . . *R. viridibracteata*
4' Flowers red, orange, or pink, with pale cup 5
5   Filaments oblong, black, united or closely pressed together into a stout column, smooth and hairless . . . . . *R. monadelpha*
5' Filaments tapering, pale or dark, free, usually hairy at the base 6
6   Leaves c. 1 mm diam., filiform, with 4 narrow grooves . . . . *R. sabulosa*
6' Leaves 2–5 mm diam., somewhat swollen, with 4 wide grooves 7
7   Produced leaves 4–9; flowers pinkish red . . . . . . *R. subfistulosa*
7' Produced leaf 1(2); flowers orange-red . . . . *R. unifolia*
8   Bracts usually with narrow, hardly visible membranous margins and the tip only minutely or hardly membranous 9
8' Bracts with narrow or pronounced membranous margins but always with a large membranous tip 14
9   Basal leaves 4-winged and H-shaped in cross section with 2 wide lateral grooves and a strong vein up the middle of each groove; flowers pale yellow . . . . *R. hirta*
9' Basal leaves narrowly 4-grooved without an evident vein up the middle of the grooves 10
10 Flowers bright yellow with darker veins in the throat; fruiting peduncles suberect or curved . . . . *R. monticola*
10' Flowers lilac or pink to apricot, rarely yellow but then fruiting peduncles widely spreading 11

11 Leaves 3–6, 0.5–1.5 mm diam.; flowers 2 or more; anthers about as long as or longer than the filaments 12
11' Leaves 1–2, rarely 3, c. 0.5–1 mm diam.; flower 1, rarely 2; anthers half as long as the filaments or less 13
12 Flowers apricot, terra-cotta, deep old rose or yellow; fruiting peduncles widely spreading from the base . . . . *R. obscura*
12' Flowers magenta, lilac-pink or rosy pink to white; fruiting peduncles straightening and suberect . . . . *R. rosea*
13 Leaves usually 2, not sticky; flowers with a distinct yellow cup; stamens yellow, the filaments 5–6 mm long . . . . *R. cedarbergensis*
13' Leaf 1, sticky; flowers with yellow at the base of the tepals but without a distinct yellow cup; stamens lilac, the filaments 9–10 mm long . . . . *R. lilacina*
14 Flowers yellow 15
14' Flowers white or lilac to magenta, with pale cup 17
15 Tepals unequal, the inner 2–3 mm wider than the outer; stigmas overtopping the anthers; flowers uniformly golden yellow . . . . *R. diversiformis*
15' Tepals equal; stigmas not overtopping the anthers 16
16 Flowers to 25 mm long, pale yellow; bract and inner bracts largely membranous or green in the center in the upper half . . . . *R. malaniae*
16' Flowers more than 25 mm long, bright yellow with or without dark blotches in the throat; bract and inner bracts firm and green . . . . *R. luteoflora*
17 Style branches much divided, stigmas usually more than 12 . . . . *R. multifida*
17' Style branches bifid, stigmas usually 6 18
18 Perianth cup brown at the base when fresh, not longitudinally striped; anthers usually coiled, the pollen usually brown or rust colored; membranous margins of inner bracts as wide as the green median zone throughout . . . . *R. komsbergensis*
18' Perianth cup yellow at the base, often longitudinally striped; anthers erect, the pollen yellow or orange; membranous margins of inner bracts narrower than the green median zone, at least below 19
19 Bracts with an ovate or oblong green median zone; flowers white or lilac to magenta . . . . *R. atrandra*
19' Bracts with a triangular green median zone; flowers pale wisteria blue . . . . *R. hallii*

Scadoxus

1   Leaves not sheathing; flowers surrounded by 4–5 uniform spathe bracts; pedicels 3–5 mm long . . . . *S. membranaceus*
1' Leaves sheathing to form a false stem 5 cm or more long; flowers surrounded by 5 spathe bracts or more, of variable shape; pedicels longer than 10 mm . . . . *S. puniceus*

Sparaxis

Sections of *Sparaxis*

1 Perianth actinomorphic; stamens either symmetrically disposed or the anterior stamen lying opposite the posterior tepal but the anthers held apart from one another .... section *Sparaxis*
1' Perianth zygomorphic and stamens unilateral and arcuate with the anthers parallel and more or less contiguous .... section *Synnotia*

Sparaxis Section *Sparaxis*

1 Stamens unilateral, the filaments diverging; anthers facing inward 2
1' Stamens central, the filaments contiguous; anthers facing outward 3
2 Stems often branched or at least with a node above the ground; bearing cormels at basal and aerial nodes .... *S. bulbifera*
2' Stems branching only below ground level, with no or few cormels at nodes .... *S. grandiflora*
3 Style branches filiform; flowers yellow to buff, rarely with black central markings 4
3' Style branches broad and flat; flowers copper to orange or red, rarely white, with dark central markings 5
4 Flowers plain yellow, 30–35 mm diam. .... *S. fragrans*
4' Flowers with a large central black mark, 50–65 mm diam. .... *S. maculosa*
5 Anthers straight, flowers scarlet to orange with yellow and black center .... *S. tricolor*
5' Anthers weakly to strongly twisted 6
6 Anthers strongly twisted; tepals spreading, salmon, rarely white, with purple and yellow center .... *S. elegans*
6' Anthers weakly twisted; tepals cupped, deep pink with blackish, and yellow center .... *S. pillansii*

Sparaxis Section *Synnotia*

1 Perianth tube more than 25 mm long, well exserted from the bracts; tube bent abruptly at the apex of the slender part 2
1' Perianth tube less than 24 mm long, not or only shortly exserted from the bracts 3
2 Flowers violet with white to pale yellow markings on the lower 3 tepals; upper tepal 14–17 mm long; anthers 3–4 mm long and purple .... *S. metelerkampiae*
2' Flowers with the upper tepal violet and the others pale yellow with purple markings at the tips or margins; upper tepal 25–30 mm long; anthers 5–6 mm long, whitish .... *S. variegata*
3 Flowers small, the tepals less than 10 mm long .... *S. parviflora*
3' Flowers larger, at least the upper tepals at least 15 mm long ... 4
4 Corm tunics of hard netted fibers not extending upward in a neck; upper tepal directed forward and somewhat hooded over the stamens 5
4' Corm tunics of fine fibers usually extending upward in a neck; upper tepal erect or directed backward 6
5 Upper tepal c. 16 mm long; bases of the leaves uniformly colored; style dividing opposite the lower half of the anthers, the style branches c. 2 mm long .... *S. villosa*
5' Upper tepal 22–24 mm long; bases of the leaves lightly speckled with purple; style dividing near anther apices, the style branches c. 5 mm long .... *S. caryophyllacea*
6 Cylindrical part of the perianth tube less than 8 mm long; upper tepal more than twice as long as wide .... *S. galeata*
6' Cylindrical part of the perianth tube at least 10 mm long; upper tepal less than to about twice as long as wide 7
7 Perianth tube 20–30 mm long, obliquely funnel-shaped, the lower cylindrical part 13–25 mm long; dorsal tepal 22–28 × 10–12 mm .... *S. roxburghii*
7' Perianth tube c. 18 mm long, obliquely funnel-shaped; dorsal tepal c. 25 × 18–20 mm .... *S. auriculata*

Spiloxene

1 Flowers sessile; tepals inserted on a gradually expanding neck extending as much as 70 mm above the ovary; ovary subterranean .... *S.* sp. 2
1' Flowers pedicellate; tepals inserted on the ovary or on a cylindrical neck extending as much as 35 mm above the ovary; ovary exserted above ground 2
2 Bracts lanceolate to linear-lanceolate, leaf-like, pale to dark green, sometimes with translucent margins, sheathing or clasping each pedicel at the base or for some distance above the base 3
2' Bracts linear, setaceous, translucent to pale brown, attached dorsally to each pedicel without sheathing or clasping the base 14
3 Corm largely naked with occasional untidy fibers around the neck, growing obliquely; mature ovary usually longer than the tepals 4
3' Corm covered with persistent tunics, growing vertically; tunics firm and netted, either cap-like or continuous from the base to the apex; mature ovary mostly shorter than the tepals 7
4 Tepals inserted on the ovary 5
4' Tepals inserted on a short to long neck above the ovary 6
5 Leaves firm, more or less triangular in cross section; flowers often more than 2 per scape, white .... *S. aquatica*
5' Leaves thin textured, bifacial with a prominent midrib; flowers 2 per scape, yellow, rarely white .... *S. umbraticola*
6 Leaves firm, somewhat triangular in cross section; tepals consistently 6, 10–20 mm long, white, rarely cream or yellow .... *S. alba*
6' Leaves soft, bifacial; tepals 4, rarely as many as 6, 2–6 mm long, yellow, cream, or white .... *S.* sp. 1

7 Bracts 2, sometimes 1, clasping each pedicel basally, the edges not convolute 8
7′ Bract 1, tightly sheathing the pedicel for more than half its length, the edges convolute 12
8 Corm broadest and distinctly flattened at the base with a prominent circular basal ridge .... *S. minuta*
8′ Corms narrowed and somewhat rounded toward the base, without a broad basal ridge 9
9 Leaf absent, solitary at flowering, rarely 2; scape subterranean or exserted by less than 10 mm at flowering .... *S. monophylla*
9′ Leaves 3 or more at flowering; scape exserted above ground at flowering, mostly by 10 mm or more 10
10 Leaves almost round to U-shaped in cross section; bracts firm, dark green, with irregularly shaped multicellular teeth on the apex; flowers with reddish brown backs .... *S. schlechteri*
10′ Leaves V-shaped in cross section; bracts soft textured, pale green, with translucent margins, apex smooth; flowers usually green-backed 11
11 Bracts lanceolate, 3- to 5-veined, pale green with translucent margins, often drying pale brown; tepals 5–20 mm long .... *S. flaccida*
11′ Bracts linear-lanceolate, 1- to 3-veined, translucent; tepals 5–7 mm long .... *S. trifurcillata*
12 Corm with a prominent neck of tightly clustered straight woody fibers; leaves surrounded by a long, bladeless sheath ... . *S. curculigoides*
12′ Corm with a detachable cap of short, branched fibers; leaves without a long, bladeless sheath 13
13 Leaves U-shaped without a midrib; seeds J-shaped .... *S. canaliculata*
13′ Leaves V-shaped with a prominent midrib, margins often raised; seeds ovoid .... *S. capensis*
14 Leaf margin with minute recurved teeth, at least in the new growth; scape with 2 bracts and a single flower, rarely 2 .... *S. serrata*
14′ Leaf margin often raised and papillate, without minute recurved teeth; scape with one bract and one flower 15
15 Corm covered with hard twisted roots; leaves narrow to broad, V-shaped with a prominent midrib .... *S. ovata*
15′ Corm covered with hard fibers; roots not twisted; leaves narrow, U-shaped without a prominent midrib .... *S. sp. 3*

Strumaria

1 Leaves linear, at most 1 mm wide, usually green at flowering ... 2
1′ Leaves strap-shaped to elliptical, at least 2.5 mm wide, dry or emerging at flowering 3
2 Scape more or less straight; flowers star-shaped; tepals free .. .. *S. tenella*
2′ Scape wiry and twisted at the base; flowers funnel-shaped; tepals united into a perianth tube 3–4 mm long ..... *S. spiralis*

3 Leaves 2–6, spreading into a fan, usually twisted, entirely smooth at all stages; flowers usually on lax nodding pedicels .. .. *S. truncata*
3′ Leaves 2(3), opposite, plane, hairy, pustulate or minutely fringed, sometimes only in juveniles; flowers on rigid, spreading or ascending pedicels 4
4 Flowers bell-shaped, white with broad reddish brown dorsal bands; filaments broad about half their length .... *S. picta*
4′ Flowers star- to funnel-shaped, white or pink with pink or red dorsal stripes or bands; filaments slender throughout or bulbous at their base 5
5 Flowers star shaped; pedicels at least twice as long as the flowers; style conspicuously broadened at the base 6
5′ Flowers funnel-shaped; pedicels slightly longer or shorter than the flowers; style slightly thickened in the lower half ... 12
6 Flowers large with tepals longer than 10 mm, if less then tepals distinctly clawed 7
6′ Flowers small with tepals less than 10 mm long, if 10 mm then tepals not clawed 8
7 Bulb whitish inside; tepals clawed, with conspicuous windows 1.5 mm wide between the tepal bases; flowers translucent when old .... *S. unguiculata*
7′ Bulb yellowish inside; tepals with small windows 0.5 mm wide between the tepal bases; flowers dark when old .... *S. karoopoortensis*
8 Flowers lemon yellow; tepals crisped, upper surface with a translucent swelling at the base .... *S. gemmata*
8′ Flowers white or pink; tepals sometimes more or less undulate but not crisped, upper surface not swollen at the base 9
9 Flowers delicate pink .... *S. karooica*
9′ Flowers white with pink dorsal stripes 10
10 Leaves densely fringed with long, soft, white hairs, both surfaces smooth .... *S. leipoldtii*
10′ Leaves with the upper surface and occasionally the lower surface hairy 11
11 Tepals flat; style tapering uniformly to the broadest point at the base .... *S. chaplinii*
11′ Tepals channeled; style abruptly swollen in the basal third .... *S. discifera*
12 Leaves pressed to the ground, the upper surface pustulate or minutely fringed, otherwise smooth 13
12′ Leaves spreading, both surfaces or only the upper covered with long, soft hairs 14
13 Upper surface of leaves with pustulate edges, the margin cartilaginous; tepals less than 3.5 mm wide ... *S. watermeyeri*
13′ Upper surface of leaves smooth, the margin minutely fringed; tepals more than 4 mm wide .... *S. salteri*
14 Bulbs whitish inside; leaves at most 5 mm wide; stamens slightly longer than the tepals .... *S. perryae*
14′ Bulbs yellowish inside; leaves at least 10 mm wide; stamens approximately half as long as the tepals .... *S. pubescens*

Syringodea

1 Leaves several, mostly or entirely bifacial, flat or channeled above 2
1' Leaf single, terete and unifacial in the distal half 3
2 Leaves linear-filiform, 0.5–1.5(–2) mm wide, often flexuous or twisted; perianth tube 20–33 mm long and tepals 10–15 mm long .... S. longituba
2' Leaves oblong-lanceolate, 3–6 mm wide, sharply spreading; perianth tube 25–35 mm long and tepals 15–20 mm long .... S. derustensis
3 Corm top-shaped with a short basal ridge; perianth tube 15–20 mm long and tepals 10–20 mm long; stigmas spathulate .... S. saxatilis
3' Corm flattened and almost lens-shaped with a wide, almost fan-shaped basal ridge; perianth tube 30–40 mm long and tepals 20–30 mm long; stigmas lacerate .... S. unifolia

Thereianthus

1 Perianth tube extremely short, 1–2 mm long, included in the bracts; bracts mostly 3–4 mm long .... T. racemosus
1' Perianth tube well developed, at least 5 mm long and usually longer than the bracts; bracts 3–18 mm long 2
2 Leaves mostly fairly broad, the lowermost falcate, with a prominent midrib and lightly thickened margins ...... T. minutus
2' Leaves linear, flat or oval to round in cross section, without a single prominent midrib and margins usually not much thickened 3
3 Inflorescence lax, the bracts not overlapping; bracts 3–4 mm long; perianth tube cylindrical, 12–20 mm long .... T. juncifolius
3' Inflorescence crowded with the bracts overlapping; bracts 7–18 mm long; perianth tube 8–33 mm long 4
4 Perianth tube filiform; style dividing opposite the base of the anthers; flowers white, sometimes with purple spot at the base of each lower tepal .... T. ixioides
4' Perianth tube cylindrical, widening slightly at the throat; style reaching at least to the middle of the anthers; flowers purple, blue, or sometimes white, then with prominent purple mark at the base of each lower tepal 5
5 Perianth tube elongate, mostly 25–45 mm long, at least 1.5 times as long as the tepals 6
5' Perianth tube 10–15(–20) mm long, mostly about as long to slightly longer or shorter than the tepals 7
6 Anthers c. 6 mm long; flowers lilac to whitish ...... T. longicollis
6' Anthers c. 3 mm long; flowers dark violet .... T. sp. 1
7 Flowers pale to deep blue or mauve, or almost whitish, the lower tepals more prominently marked than the upper; veins on the tepals never prominent; filaments mostly 4–6 mm long, unilateral with the anthers dehiscing toward the lower tepals .... T. spicatus
7' Flowers dark purple, all the tepals equally marked; tepals always prominently veined; filaments 8–10 mm long, well exserted, erect with the anthers dehiscing inward or toward the upper tepal .... T. bracteolatus

Tritonia

1 Flowers or at least the perianth actinomorphic with spreading tepals and a short funnel-shaped tube; stamens either erect and surrounding the erect style or unilateral and somewhat randomly spreading 2
1' Flowers zygomorphic, the dorsal tepal usually largest and often erect or hooded; stamens unilateral and arcuate with the anthers parallel 5
2 Style erect, central, surrounded by the stamens ...... T. dubia
2' Style unilateral, the stamens spreading, not closely applied to the style 3
3 Tepal margins not transparent in the lower half but outer tepals often with a dark median blotch or uniformly colored; perianth with a yellow star-shaped center .... T. deusta
3' Tepals margins transparent in the lower half but tepals otherwise uniformly colored; perianth tube not or hardly yellow within 4
4 Perianth bright orange, salmon, or pinkish orange, usually not darker in the center; tepals without conspicuous dark veins .... T. crocata
4' Perianth pink or mauve, darker in the center; tepals with conspicuous dark veins .... T. squalida
5 Spike fairly dense, flexed at the base and more or less horizontal; bracts usually green at least below, firm to leathery, obtuse to truncate and dark brown along the upper margins ... 6
5' Spike more or less lax, sometimes dense, erect; bracts membranous to dry and papery, often acute to attenuate, never dark brown along the upper margins 8
6 Leaf margins undulate and crisped .... T. crispa
6' Leaf margins smooth 7
7 Leaf margins raised into wings held at right angles to the blade, thus H-shaped in cross section .... T. cooperi
7' Leaf linear-lanceolate, the margins curving inward on the same side, one surface convex, the other concave ... T. lancea
8 Lower tepals of uniform texture or with a thickened median ridge but lacking a tooth-like callus 9
8' Lower tepals each with a prominent, median, tooth-like callus, sometimes only on the lower median tepal 12
9 Leaves linear and compressed-cylindrical or subterete, fleshy in texture, without a visible midrib but striate when dry .. .. T. bakeri
9' Leaves sword-shaped to lanceolate, with a visible midrib ... 10
10 Perianth tube slightly shorter to slightly longer than the tepals; leaves with a prominent vein along each margin .... T. lineata
10' Perianth tube 1.5–3 times as long as the dorsal tepal 11

11 Outer bract, especially of the lower flowers, acuminate or trifid with 3 acuminate tips; tepals with conspicuous dark venation . . . . *T. flabellifolia*
11' Outer bract with 2-3 short teeth; veins of the tepals not normally visible . . . . *T. pallida*
12 Leaf margins undulate and crisped . . . . *T. watermeyeri*
12' Leaf margins straight or lightly undulate 13
13 Perianth tube 1.5-3 times as long as the dorsal tepal 14
13' Perianth tube slightly shorter to about as long as the dorsal tepal 15
14 Perianth bright yellow without dark veins; dorsal tepal erect, the other tepals spreading; flower not scented; leaves straight, in a loose fan . . . . *T. chrysantha*
14' Perianth cream to dull yellow, often flushed with orange or pink, the tepals with conspicuous dark veins; flower strongly scented, especially at night; leaves falcate, in a tight fan . . . . *T. karooica*
15 Stem subterranean or not extending above the leaf bases; flowers crowded; leaves falcate . . . . *T. florentiae*
15' Stem produced well above the ground; flowers in fairly lax spikes; leaves usually straight, or weakly falcate 16
16 Leaves linear, flaccid, 1-4 mm wide . . . . *T. parvula*
16' Leaves sword-shaped to lanceolate, firm, at least the largest more than 3 mm wide 17
17 Plants flowering in the autumn, Mar.-May; capsules 10-15 mm long . . . . *T. laxifolia*
17' Plants flowering in the spring, Sept.-Nov.; capsules 7-10 mm long . . . . *T. securigera*

Tritoniopsis

1 Flowers red to salmon, rarely yellowish but then perianth with a slender lower part abruptly expanded into an upper tubular part and filaments more than 30 mm long 2
1' Flowers pink, cream, white, or yellow 9
2 Perianth actinomorphic; perianth tube erect and tepals spreading . . . . *T. lesliei*
2' Perianth zygomorphic and bilabiate; perianth tube horizontal, the dorsal tepal horizontal and largest 3
3 Basal leaves with long slender petioles extending 20 cm or more above the ground; cauline leaves long, brown, needle-like, with the margins rolled inward 4
3' Basal leaves slender or flattened below, seldom petiole-like and extending shortly above the ground; cauline leaves reduced, not conspicuous, the upper ones short and scale-like . . . 5
4 Perianth tube 25-30 mm long; filaments 20-25 mm long; dorsal tepal c. 15 mm long, the others slightly shorter, to 12 mm . . . . *T. triticea*
4' Perianth tube 30-40 mm long; filaments 30-37 mm long; dorsal tepal usually 20-25 mm long, the upper lateral tepals c. 20 mm long and 2-3 mm longer than the lower 3 . . . *T. burchellii*

5 Filaments 20-23 mm long; tepals subequal, not arising obliquely from the tube . . . . *T. pulchra*
5' Filaments 25-40 mm long; tepals usually unequal, usually arising obliquely from the tube 6
6 Lowermost tepals arising 3-8 mm beyond the dorsal . . . . *T. antholyza*
6' Dorsal tepal arising 3-8 mm beyond the lowermost 7
7 Tepals subequal, the dorsal 16-18 mm long, arising 2-3 mm beyond lower; capsules 3-lobed, densely rough-warty, to 10 mm long . . . . *T. williamsiana*
7' Tepals unequal, the dorsal 25-33 mm long, arising 3-8 mm beyond lower; capsules oblong to ellipsoidal, nearly smooth, 15-30 mm long 8
8 Lower tepals marked with dark purple; dorsal tepal arising 3-5 mm beyond the lowermost; leaves lanceolate, about half as long as the stem . . . . *T. intermedia*
8' Lower tepals uniformly colored; dorsal tepal arising 6-8 mm beyond the lowermost; leaves sword-shaped to linear, reaching at least to the base of the spike . . . . *T. caffra*
9 Basal leaves 1-2, abruptly narrowed below into a terete false petiole; perianth tube 20-40 mm long 10
9' Basal leaves more than 2, gradually tapering to a narrow base, rarely more abruptly narrowed into a flattened false petiole 11
10 Plants 50-65 cm high with a fairly lax spike; blade of the basal leaves sword-shaped and plane; perianth tube c. 20 mm long; . . . . *T. toximontana*
10' Plants 15-30 cm high with a dense spike; blade of the basal leaves oblong-ovate with undulate margins; perianth tube 35-40 mm long . . . . *T. flexuosa*
11 Perianth tube (20-)30-70 mm long 12
11' Perianth tube 4-15(-20) mm long 13
12 Flowers uniformly white, sweetly fragrant; perianth tube 30-40 mm long . . . . *T. nervosa*
12' Flowers pink with darker markings on the lower tepals, unscented; perianth tube (20-)40-70 mm long . . . . . . *T. revoluta*
13 Flowers whitish or cream to yellow 14
13' Flowers pink 19
14 Flowers small, 12-15 mm long; filaments 3-7 mm long 15
14' Flowers larger, at least 18 mm long; filaments 12-15 mm long 16
15 Flowers yellow; filaments 3-5 mm long; lower tepals not narrowed at the base into claws . . . . *T. caledonensis*
15' Flowers white to cream; filaments 6-7 mm long; lower tepals narrowed at the base into well-developed claws . . . *T. unguicularis*
16 Plants 60-150 cm high, usually branched, with a lax spike 20-35 cm long; leaves 10-25 mm wide with 5-7 main veins; flowers unscented, the lower tepals yellow with a median maroon streak; perianth tube 7-8 mm long . . . . . . *T. nemorosa*
16' Plants to 60 cm high, unbranched, with a dense spike 3-18 cm long; leaves 2-10 mm wide with 1-3 main veins;

flowers usually strongly scented, the lower tepals often mostly or completely maroon; perianth tube 2-5 mm long 17

17 Leaves 2-5 mm wide with one main vein; flowers strongly 2-lipped, the lower tepals joined to one another 3-4 mm; filaments 12-14 mm long .... *T. parviflora*

17' Leaves 5-10 mm wide with 1-3 main veins; flowers not strongly 2-lipped, the lower tepals joined to one another 1-2.5 mm; filaments 6-10 mm long 18

18 Leaves abruptly narrowed below into a semiterete false petiole, the blade with 1-2(3) main veins; flowers distinctly bicolored with the lower tepals mostly purple; filaments 6-7 mm long .... *T. bicolor*

18' Leaves gradually narrowed below into a flattened false petiole, the blade with 2-3 main veins; flowers mostly yellow with minute purple streaks at the base of the lower tepals; filaments 10 mm long .... *T. flava*

19 Stem almost always unbranched 20

19' Stem nearly always branched 21

20 Dorsal tepal 7-9 mm wide and at least 5 mm longer than the upper lateral tepals; perianth tube 7-10 mm long ... *T. lata*

20' Dorsal tepal 3-5 mm wide and as much as 4 mm longer than the upper lateral tepals; perianth tube 5-8 mm long ... *T. dodii*

21 Tepals truncate, the 3 upper tepals nearly equal in width and distinctly wider than the lower; perianth tube 15-20 mm long .... *T. pulchella*

21' Tepals not as above, the upper lateral and lower tepals nearly equal in width; perianth tube 6-20 mm long 22

22 Spike very long, as long as or longer than the nonflowering part of the stem; bracts conspicuously apiculate ... *T. elongata*

22' Spike shorter than the rest of the stem; bracts acute to shortly apiculate 23

23 Leaves (8-)15-40 mm wide; perianth tube 8-10 mm long .... *T. latifolia*

23' Leaves mostly 3-6 mm wide and perianth tube 8-20 mm long, or if wider (6-12 mm) then perianth tube 12-15 mm long .... *T. ramosa*

Tulbaghia

1 Corona scales united into a fleshy collar, sometimes deeply toothed 2

1' Corona scales free 3

2 Corona 6-8 mm deep, the upper whorl of anthers inserted on the corona; leaves dry or emergent at flowering; flowers brown or green with an orange corona .... *T. alliacea*

2' Corona 2 mm deep, the upper whorl of anthers inserted at the base of the corona; leaves well developed at flowering; flowers cream to greenish yellow with a cream or brown corona .... *T. dregeana*

3 Corona scales 6; flowers brownish to green with an orange corona .... *T. capensis*

3' Corona scales 3; flowers mauve .... *T. violacea*

Veltheimia

1 Leaves glossy dark green, seldom all deciduous; bulb tunics fleshy; bracts 10-30 mm long; spring flowering .... *V. bracteata*

1' Leaves glaucous or grayish, deciduous; outer bulb tunics papery; bracts 10-15 mm long; autumn and winter flowering ... . *V. capensis*

Wachendorfia

1 Tepals narrow, 3-6 mm wide; bracts herbaceous, erect; leaves usually as long as or longer than the flowering stem .... *W. multiflora*

1' Tepals broader, 5-18 mm wide; bracts papery or submembranous, the upper usually recurved; leaves usually shorter than the flowering stem 2

2 Plants tall, usually more than 100 cm high, evergreen; inflorescence dense, cylindrical; leaves 15-80 mm wide, hairless .... *W. thyrsiflora*

2' Plants shorter, usually shorter than 60 cm high, deciduous; inflorescence variable, lax to dense; leaves 5-35 mm wide, hairless or hairy 3

3 Stamens and style clustered together, to half as long as the tepals; flowers withering shortly after midday ... *W. brachyandra*

3' Stamens and style spreading, two-thirds to three-quarters as long as the tepals; flowers withering in the late afternoon .... *W. paniculata*

Watsonia

1 Flower tube short or long but gradually flaring above; perianth usually shades or purple to pink, rarely orange or white 2

1' Flower tube long, slender below but widening abruptly into a broadly cylindrical upper part; perianth usually shades or red to orange, occasionally purple, pinkish, or white 12

2 Flowers actinomorphic with stamens symmetrically arranged around the central style .... *W. marginata*

2' Flowers zygomorphic with perianth tube curved and stamens and style arcuate or declinate 3

3 Stamens and style declinate 4

3' Stamens and style arcuate 9

4 Outer floral bracts 20-60 mm long; perianth tube 25-46 mm long 5

4' Outer floral bracts 6-20 mm long; perianth tube 15-20 mm long 6

5 Bracts mostly 30-45 mm long; perianth tube mostly included in the bracts, nearly uniformly pink; bracts dry and becoming

lacerated .... *W. dubia*

5′ Bracts mostly 20–30 mm long; perianth tube partly exserted from the bracts, deep pink with darker markings in the throat; bracts becoming dry, remaining intact .... *W. strictiflora*

6 Basal leaves longer, reaching at least to the flowering spike; anthers 9–13 mm long 7

6′ Basal leaves relatively short, rarely more than half as long as the stem; anthers 4–8 mm long 8

7 Plants 20–50 cm high; leaves dull green, linear-lanceolate, usually 5–10 mm wide; tepals narrowly elliptical, 9–11 mm wide; upper part of the perianth tube 8–10 mm long .... *W. rogersii*

7′ Plants 1–2 m high; leaves glossy apple green, lanceolate, rarely less than 20 mm wide; tepals ovate, 13–18 mm wide; upper part of the perianth tube 8–20 mm long ... *W. borbonica*

8 Floral bracts broad below and clasping the stem; perianth pink, mauve, orange, reddish, or cream .... *W. laccata*

8′ Floral bracts narrow and not clasping the stem; perianth always pink .... *W. amabilis*

9 Plants robust with leaves mostly 10–40 mm wide 10

9′ Plants fairly slender with leaves rarely exceeding 6 mm wide 11

10 Upper part of the perianth tube 8–12 mm long; bracts 10–18 mm long .... *W. borbonica*

10′ Upper part of the perianth tube 15–26 mm long; bracts 16–26 mm long .... *W. versfeldii*

11 Anthers 10–13 mm long; Langeberg and Swartberg Mountains .... *W. emiliae*

11′ Anthers 5–6 mm long; Franschhoek Mountains .... *W. distans*

12 Tepals less than to about half as long as the upper (wide) part of the tube; tube usually recurved and facing the ground .. .. *W. aletroides*

12′ Tepals about as long as the upper (wide) part of the tube; tube usually horizontal or slightly drooping 13

13 Bracts fairly short, 5–14 mm (ignore the lowermost 2–3) ... 14

13′ Bracts fairly long, mostly more than 15 mm and as much as 45 mm 21

14 Anthers and style branches included in the perianth tube .... *W. elsiae*

14′ Anthers and style exserted from the perianth tube 15

15 Filaments 14–16 mm long 16

15′ Filaments (16–)18–45 mm long 18

16 Flowers pink .... *W. paucifolia*

16′ Flowers orange-red 17

17 Plants 10–45 cm high; plants with 2–4 leaves, often unbranched .... *W. minima*

17′ Plants 120–200 cm high; plants with 5–7 leaves and with several branches .... *W. galpinii*

18 Tepals 12–16 mm long 19

18′ Tepals 18–33 mm long 20

19 Bracts 5–8 mm long; leaf margins hardly thickened; marshes in the Western Cape mountains .... *W. stokoei*

19′ Bracts 9–12 mm long; leaf margins heavily thickened; well-drained stony slopes in the Swartberg Mountains . *W. marlothii*

20 Sheathing leaves of the stem inflated .... *W. tabularis*

20′ Sheathing leaves of the stem clasping .... *W. wilmaniae*

21 Capsules spindle-shaped, widest about the middle and strongly tapering toward the tip 22

21′ Capsules more or less obovoid, to 15 mm long 24

22 Inner floral bracts undivided or forked less than 2 mm; tepals 19–25 × 4–10 mm .... *W. angusta*

22′ Inner floral bracts deeply divided apically; tepals 20–33 × 8–13 mm 23

23 Tepals 20–22 × 8–11 mm; anthers c. 7 mm long; flowers bright orange to salmon .... *W. zeyheri*

23′ Tepals 24–33 × 9–13 mm; anthers 9–12 mm long; flowers scarlet to dull red or purple .... *W. fourcadei*

24 Plants flowering Apr.–July; leaves narrow, 4–10 mm wide and more or less dry or emergent at flowering and on separate shoots .... *W. hysterantha*

24′ Plants flowering mainly Oct.–Feb. and if at other times always borne with the leaves; leaves narrow to broad, 5–85 mm ... 25

25 Bracts mostly 18–40 mm long; inner bracts about as long to slightly longer than the outer 26

25′ Inner bracts consistently shorter than the outer (disregard flowers at the top of the spike) 29

26 Tepals mostly 33–35 mm long; flowers scarlet, the lowermost tepal separating from the others and curving backward ... . *W. spectabilis*

26′ Tepals 21–26 mm long; flowers red, purple, or pinkish, the lower 3 tepals held more or less together 27

27 Plants 50–200 cm high; stems usually branched; filaments 35–45 mm long .... *W. meriana*

27′ Plants 15–110 cm high; stems unbranched and mostly less than 40 cm high; filaments 25–35 mm long 28

28 Plants mostly 15–40 mm long; leaves 4–6; flowers scarlet, purple, or pink .... *W. coccinea*

28′ Plants mostly 40–80 cm high; leaves 2–4; flowers scarlet .... *W. fergusoniae*

29 Leaves 50–85 mm wide, margins heavily thickened; flowers 75–85 mm long .... *W. vanderspuyiae*

29′ Leaves to 25 mm wide, margins moderately or not noticeably thickened 30

30 Bracts with a ridged keel and curving outward near the tip; flowers whitish, flushed mauve, or more or less entirely mauve .... *W. humilis*

30′ Bracts rounded or folded on the midline but never with a ridged keel, the tip directed upward; flowers shades of red, orange, or purple 31

31 Flowers mauve-pink, the tepals all similarly oriented ....

.... *W. versfeldii*
31′ Flowers orange, red, or purple to mauve 32
32 Upper part of the floral tube fairly slender, 13–16 × 4 mm; flowers salmon-orange with a darker streak in the midline of each tepal .... *W. stenosiphon*
32′ Upper part of the floral tube 18–25 × 5–6 mm; flowers red, purple, or pink 33
33 Flowers pink to purple; filaments 16–25(–30) mm long .... *W. knysnana*
33′ Flowers orange to scarlet; filaments (25–)30–45 mm long ... 34
34 Leaf margins and midrib strongly thickened; floral tube without ridges between the lower part of the filaments; leaves 3–4; plants of open sandstone slopes, flowering mostly after fire ... . *W. schlechteri*
34′ Leaf margins and midrib moderately thickened; floral tube with ridges between the lower part of the filaments; leaves 4–6; plants mostly of damp or marshy sites .... *W. pillansii*

Wurmbea

1 Stamens nearly as long as the tepals 2
1′ Stamens much shorter than the tepals 3
2 Tepals 2.4–4 mm long, pink with slightly darker margins .... *W. compacta*
2′ Tepals 4.5–7.5 mm long, cream with thickened purple-brown margins .... *W. robusta*
3 Perianth tube indistinct, to 1 mm long; dwarf plants to 5 cm high, 1- to 7-flowered .... *W. minima*
3′ Perianth tube distinct, 2–17 mm long 4
4 Flowers red or dark purple to brown 5
4′ Flowers white or cream to yellowish, often with dark margins or spots 6
5 Tepals lanceolate, 6–11 mm long, spreading; spike 1.2–2.5 cm diam. .... *W. marginata*
5′ Tepals ovate-lanceolate, 3–4 mm long, recurved; spike to 1 cm diam. .... *W. recurva*
6 Perianth tube distinctly longer than the tepals 7
6′ Perianth tube shorter than the tepals or almost as long 9
7 Perianth tube 8–17 mm long, uniformly pale; tepals with a conspicuous dark blotch .... *W. dolichantha*
7′ Perianth tube 4–7 mm long, speckled; tepals with a dark or pale blotch 8
8 Spike to 1 cm diam.; tepals erect to slightly spreading, 2–3.5 mm long; styles hooked .... *W. capensis*
8′ Spike c. 1.5 cm or more diam.; tepals spreading, 4–7 mm long; styles not hooked .... *W. inusta*
9 Tepals with a conspicuous dark blotch; leaves often ovate .... *W. variabilis*
9′ Tepals without a distinct dark blotch, sometimes with two faint spots 10
10 Tepals about as long as the tube .... *W. hiemalis*
10′ Tepals longer than the tube 11
11 Spike lax; perianth tube wider than long, the tepals well separated at the base; filaments 0.5–0.8 mm long ... *W. monopetala*
11′ Spike relatively dense; perianth tube longer than wide, the tepals close together at the base; filaments 1.3–3.5 mm long 12
12 Spike c. 1 cm diam.; tepals 0.7–1 mm wide ...... *W. elongata*
12′ Spike 1.5–2.5 mm diam.; tepals 1.5–2.5 mm wide ... *W. spicata*

Zantedeschia

1 Spathe widely flaring; spadix 50–75 mm long; weakly scented; fruiting peduncle remaining erect .... *Z. aethiopica*
1′ Spathe scarcely flaring; spadix 25–35 mm long; highly fragrant; fruiting peduncle bending over .... *Z. odorata*

CONVERSION TABLE

CM	CM OR INCHES	INCHES	METERS	METERS OR FEET	FEET
0.3	0.1	0.04	0.3	1	3.3
0.5	0.2	0.08	0.6	2	6.6
0.8	0.3	0.12	0.9	3	9.8
1.0	0.4	0.16	1.2	4	13.1
1.3	0.5	0.20	1.5	5	16.4
1.5	0.6	0.24	1.8	6	19.7
1.8	0.7	0.28	2.1	7	23.0
2.0	0.8	0.31	2.4	8	26.2
2.3	0.9	0.35	2.7	9	29.5
2.5	1	0.4	3	10	33
5	2	0.8	6	20	66
8	3	1.2	9	30	98
10	4	1.6	12	40	131
13	5	2.0	15	50	164
15	6	2.4	18	60	197
18	7	2.8	21	70	230
20	8	3.1	24	80	262
23	9	3.5	27	90	295
25	10	4	30	100	328
51	20	8	61	200	656
76	30	12	91	300	984
102	40	16	122	400	1312
127	50	20	152	500	1640
152	60	24	183	600	1969
178	70	28	213	700	2297
203	80	31	244	800	2625
229	90	35	274	900	2953
254	100	39	305	1000	3281

SPECIALIST SUPPLIERS

Bloemendal Nursery, P.O. Box 14839, Kenwyn 7790, South Africa. Seeds and bulbs mainly of winter-rainfall species.

Botanical Society, Private Bag X10, Claremont 7735, South Africa. Telephone (+21) 797 2090, fax (+21) 797 2376, e-mail info@botanicalsociety.org.za. Seeds of South African species to members.

Bulbs d'Argence, MAS d'Argence, 30300 Fourques, France. Bulbs of winter-rainfall species.

Cape Flora Nursery, P.O. Box 10556, Linton Grange 6015, Port Elizabeth, South Africa. Telephone (+41) 379 2096, fax (+41) 379 3188, e-mail capeflor@iafrica.com. Seeds and bulbs mainly of Eastern Cape species.

Cape Seed and Bulbs, P.O. Box 23709, Claremont 7735, South Africa. Telephone (+21) 671 2005, fax (+21) 671 2005, e-mail capeseed@iafrica.com. Seeds and bulbs of winter- and summer-rainfall species, especially Amaryllidaceae, Iridaceae, and some Hyacinthaceae.

The Croft Wild Bulb Nursery, P.O. Box 1053, Stutterheim 4930, South Africa. Telephone and fax (+43) 683 2796, e-mail croft@eci.co.za. Seeds and bulbs mainly of Eastern Cape species.

Greenlady Gardens, 1415 Eucalyptus, San Francisco, California 94132, U.S.A. Telephone (415) 753-3332. Bulbs of South African species.

Indigenous Bulb Association of South Africa, P.O. Box 12265, N1 City 7463, South Africa. Seeds of mainly winter-rainfall species to members.

International Bulb Society, P.O. Box 92136, Pasadena, California 91109, U.S.A. Seeds to members.

Jim Duggen Flower Nursery, 1442 Santa Fe Drive, Encinitas, California 92024, U.S.A. Telephone (619) 943-1658. Bulbs mainly of Iridaceae, some lachenalias.

Monocot Nursery, Jacklands Bridge, Tickenham, Clevedon, Somerset BS21 6SG, England. Seeds mainly of North African and Mediterranean species but a few Western Cape species also.

New Plant Nursery, P.O. Box 4183, George East 6539, South Africa. Telephone (+44) 871 1806, fax (+44) 871 2732. Wholesale only; bulbs of some winter- and summer-rainfall species.

Rust-en-Vrede Nursery, P.O. Box 753, Brackenfell 7561, South Africa. Seeds and bulbs mainly of winter-rainfall species, especially Amaryllidaceae.

Silverhill Seeds, P.O. Box 53108, Kenilworth 7745, South Africa. Telephone (+21) 762 4245, fax (+21) 797 6609, e-mail rachel@silverhillseeds.co.za. Seeds of many winter- and summer-rainfall species.

Summerfield's Indigenous Bulbs and Seed, P.O. Box 5150, Helderberg 7135, South Africa. Telephone and fax (+21) 855 2442. Seeds and bulbs mainly of winter-rainfall species.

GLOSSARY

abaxial. Of the side or face of an organ facing away from the axis; usually the lower face

actinomorphic. Radially symmetrical

adaxial. Of the side or face of an organ facing toward the axis; usually the upper face

aneuploidy. Incremental increase or decrease in chromosome number

anthesis. Time of opening of the flower

aperturate. Of pollen with the indicated number of germination grooves

apiculate. With a short point

appressed. Lying flat against

arcuate. Curved upward like a bow

aril (adjective, **arillate**). Structure derived from the funicle and partially or wholly covering the seed, usually fleshy or waxy

arillode. Aril-like structure

aristate. Having a stiff, bristle-like awn or tip

auricle (adjective, **auriculate**). Ear-shaped appendage

awn. Bristle-like appendage

axil (adjective, **axillary**). Angle formed between a leaf or bract and the stem bearing it

axile. Of placentation in which the ovules are borne along the axis in the center of a compound ovary

basifixed. Attached at or by the base

bifacial. Of leaves, either flat or channeled, that have two anatomically distinct faces, typically flattened at right angles to the stem axis

bilabiate. Two-lipped

bract (adjective, **bracteate**). Leaf-like structure lacking an axillary bud and often subtending a flower or inflorescence, usually differing from foliage leaves in form or size

bulb. Specialized storage structure in which the storage function has been transferred from the stem to the leaves; the stem is reduced to a small disk of tissue bearing apical and axillary buds, all closely wrapped by enlarged, persistent leaves or leaf bases (tunics) that comprise the main storage tissues

bulblet. Small or secondary bulb; also called a bulbil

c. Circa, approximately

caducous. Soon falling

calyx. Sepals or outer sterile whorl of a flower

canaliculate. Longitudinally grooved or channeled

capitate. Globose or head-shaped

capsule. Dry fruit formed from two or more united carpels (i.e., with two or more locules) and dehiscing at maturity to release the seeds

cataphyll. Scale-like leaf lacking a blade, usually associated with a vegetatively propagating organ such as a corm or perennating bud

caudex. Thick, erect trunk

caulescent. Forming a stem or trunk

cauline. Borne along the stem or trunk

centrifixed. Of an anther appearing basifixed but filament attached to the center of the anther through a sheath or collar

chalazal. Toward the basal part of an ovule where it is attached to the funicle

cilia (adjective, **ciliate**). Minute hairs, more or less confined to the margins of an organ

ciliolate. Minutely ciliate

circumscissile. Breaking open along a transverse line around the circumference

claw. A narrow, stalk-like basal portion, usually of a tepal

columellate. Of pollen with an exine composed of small columns (columellae)

coma. Tuft or crown

concolorous. Of the same color throughout

connivent. Converging

corm. Shortened rhizome with relatively few nodes and usually replaced annually, comprising a fairly dry, starchy nugget of stem tissue topped by a small, fleshy apical bud

cormel. Small or secondary corm

corolla. Petals or inner sterile whorl of a flower

corona. Fleshy or petal-like appendages attached to the perianth

corymb (adjective, **corymbose**). Racemose inflorescence in which the pedicels of the lower flowers are longer than those of the upper flowers, bringing all flowers to about the same level and resulting in a more or less flat-topped inflorescence

cowled. Of tepals with a lobe of tissue at the top

crenulate. Minutely scalloped

cucullate. Hooded or hood-shaped

cuneate. Wedge-shaped

cuspidate. Tapering into a sharp, rigid point

cyme. Inflorescence in which each flower, in turn, is formed at the tip of the growing axis, and further flowers are formed on branches arising below it

declinate. Curved downward

decurrent. Extending downward below the point of insertion

decurved. Curved downward

deflexed. Bent abruptly downward

dehiscent. Breaking open at maturity to release the contents

depauperate. Abnormally small or less well developed

depressed. Flattened as if pressed down from the top or end

diam. Diameter

dichotomous. Forked in equal pairs

discolorous. Of different colors

divaricate (adjective, **divaricately**). Widely spreading, often almost horizontally

dorsifixed. Attached at or by the back

eccentric. Of a style that is off-centered

emarginate. With a notch at the apex

enantiomorphy. Having two forms that are mirror images of one another

enantiostylous. Enantiomorphic forms differing in the displacement of the style

exine. Outer layer of the wall of a pollen grain

exserted. Protruding

extrorse. Of anthers opening away from the center of the flower

fibrotic. Tough and full of fibers

-fid. Divided, usually about a third of the length

filament. Stalk of a stamen

filiform. Thread-like

fimbriate. Of a margin fringed with slender hair-like processes called fimbriae

flexuous. Bent from side to side in a zigzag form

foraminate. Of pollen with the indicated number of circular germination pores

foveolate. With small pits

fugacious. Fleeting, lasting only a few hours

funicle. Stalk of an ovule

fusiform. Spindle-shaped, swollen in the middle and tapering to both ends

fynbos. Heathy shrubland vegetation characteristic of sandy soils in the Cape Floristic Region, dominated by small to large evergreen shrubs with tough, often small and needle-like leaves

geophyte (adjective, **geophytic**). Plant whose perennating buds are buried underground

glabrous. Without hairs

glaucous. Bluish green in color with a whitish bloom

globose. Nearly spherical

helicoid. Coiled, branching repeatedly on the same side

hilum. Scar on a seed coat at the place where it was attached to the funicle

hirsute. Bearing coarse, relatively long hairs

hispid. Bearing stiff, bristly hairs

hysteranthus. Of leaves that appear after the flowers

immaculate. Without spots or marks

inaperturate. Of pollen without germination pores

incurved. Curved inward

indehiscent. Not opening at maturity

inferior. Of an ovary that is below the level of attachment of the other floral parts

inflexed. Bent abruptly upward or forward

inflorescence. Group or arrangement in which flowers are borne on the plant

infructescence. Group or arrangement in which fruits are borne on the plant

intectate. Of pollen without a layer of exine borne above the columellae

integument. Outer layer of an ovule

internode. Portion of stem between two adjacent leaf attachments (nodes)

introrse. Of anthers opening toward the center of the flower

involute. Rolled inward

isodiametric. With vertical and horizontal diameters equal

Karoo. Semiarid central plateau of South Africa

karroid. Adjective applied to the grassy, dwarf shrubland characteristic of the Karoo

kloof. Narrow valley or canyon

lanceolate. Broadest in the lower half and tapering toward the tip, about four times as long as broad

latrorse. Of anthers opening laterally (i.e., toward adjacent anthers)

limb. Blade-like portion of a tepal

locule (adjective, **locular**). Enclosed compartment within an organ, usually the ovary

loculicidal. Of the dehiscence of a fruit along lines coinciding with the center of the locules

medifixed. Attached at the center

multifid. Cleft into many parts

nectary. Multicellular gland secreting nectar

ob-. Prefix denoting reversed or inverted

oblong. Longer than broad with the sides parallel most of their length

obtuse. Blunt, not acute

operculum (adjective, **operculate**). Lid or cover

ovate. Oval in shape and attached at the broader end

ovoid. Egg-shaped in three dimensions and attached at the broader end

ovule. Structure inside the ovary that becomes the seed following fertilization and development

pandurate. Fiddle- or violin-shaped

panicle (adjective, **paniculate**). Branched or compound raceme

papilla (adjective, **papillate**). Small elongate projection on the surface of an organ

para-. Prefix denoting alongside, near

parietal. Of placentation in which the ovules are borne on the walls of an ovary

pedicel (adjective, **pedicellate**). Stalk of a flower

peduncle. Stalk of an inflorescence

perianth. Calyx and corolla of a flower, particularly when the two are similar

perigonal. Of the perianth

petaloid. Petal-like in texture and color

petiole (adjective, **petiolate**). Stalk of a leaf

phlobaphene. Brown pigment derived from tannins found in the seed coat

phytomelan. Brittle, black pigment found in the outer layer of the seed coat

pilose. Softly hairy

placenta. Region within an ovary to which the ovules are attached

placentation. Arrangement of placentas, hence ovules, within an ovary

plane. Of a leaf blade that is flat, that is, without ridges, grooves, raised veins, undulations, etc.

polyploidy. Increase in an entire set or sets of chromosomes

poricidal. Of the dehiscence of anthers or fruit by pores

puberulous. Minutely hairy

punctate. Conspicuously dotted

pustule (adjective, **pustulate**). Blister-like elevation

raceme (adjective, **racemose**). Indeterminate inflorescence in which the main axis produces a series of flowers on lateral stalks, the oldest at the base and the youngest at the top

radical. Of leaves clustered at the base of the stem

raphe (adjective, **raphal**). Portion of the funicle joined to the integument of the ovule

recurved. Curved or curled downward or backward

reflexed. Bent abruptly downward or backward

renosterveld. Low heathy shrubland dominated by the small-leaved evergreen shrub *Elytropappus rhinocerotis* (Asteraceae), characteristic of clay soils in the Cape Floral Region

reticulate. Of pollen with an exine surface that resembles a network

retuse. With a very blunt and slightly notched apex

rhipidium. Compound cyme with the lateral branches developed alternately on one side, then the other

rhizome (adjective, **rhizomatous**). More or less horizontal stem that is fleshy, filled with stored food (often starch), and produces roots from the underside and leaves at the apex

rufous. Rust colored

rugose. Deeply wrinkled

rugulose. Minutely wrinkled

sagittate. Arrowhead-shaped

salverform. With a long, narrow tube abruptly expanded into a flat or spreading limb

sandveld. Terrain of deep coarse sand

saponins. Heterogeneous group of slimy or slippery terpenoids characterized by their ability to foam in water

scabrid, scabrous (**scabrate** when applied to pollen sculpturing). Rough to the touch

scale. Of a bulb covering that is narrower than a tunic and not completely sheathing

scape. Stem-like flowering stalk of a plant with radical leaves or leaves in a rosette

scarious. Dry and membranous

scorpioid. Of a cyme with the main axis coiled like the tail of a scorpion

secund. With all the parts grouped on one side or turned to one side

semi-. Prefix denoting half

sepal. Member of the outer whorl of nonfertile floral parts, often green

septal. Originating from the walls between the locules of an ovary

septicidal. Of the dehiscence of a fruit along lines coinciding with the septa or partitions between the locules

septifragal. Of the dehiscence of a fruit through the valves or backs of the carpels, breaking away and leaving the septa intact

septum (adjective, **septal**). Partition, particularly between the locules of the ovary

serrate. Toothed, with asymmetrical teeth pointing forward

sessile. Not stalked

setose. With bristles

sp. (plural, **spp.**). Species

spadix. Spicate inflorescence with a stout, often succulent axis

spathe. Large bract enclosing the inflorescence

spathulate. Spoon-shaped

spike (adjective, **spicate**). Unbranched indeterminate inflorescence in which the flowers are sessile or without stalks on the axis

spinulose. Of pollen that has small spines on the surface

stamen (adjective, **staminal**). Member of the fertile whorl of floral parts, containing pollen in the anther, which is borne on the filament

staminode. Sterile stamen, often rudimentary or variously modified

stellate. Star-shaped

stolon. Prostrate or trailing stem, usually underground, producing roots or corms at the nodes

strandveld. Terrain and vegetation found along the coast and a short distance inland

strophiole (adjective, **strophiolate**). Outgrowth of the seed coat near the hilum

style (adjective, **stylar**). Stalk of the ovary bearing the pollen-receptive stigma; may be divided into styules, lobes, or branches

styloid. Of crystals that resemble a style in shape

sub-. Prefix denoting approximately, more or less

subulate. Narrow and tapering gradually to a fine point

sulcate. Of pollen with the indicated number of elongate germination pores located at the pole

superior. Of an ovary borne above the level of attachment of the other floral parts

tectate. Of pollen with a layer of exine borne above the columellae

tepal. Member of the nonfertile whorls of floral parts when both whorls (sepals and petals) are similar

terete. Cylindrical or nearly so

terminal. Borne at the tip

testa. Seed coat

thyrse. Branched inflorescence in which the main axis is indeterminate and the lateral branches determinate in their growth

trichotomosulcate. Of pollen with a single, three-branched germination pore located at the pole

trigonous, triquetrous. Three-angled

tuber. Swollen storage stem but typically not covered by tunics and having initiation buds scattered over the surface and not confined to the nodes, often developing from the tips of rhizomes and not as discrete as corms nor as upright

tubercle. Small wart-like outgrowth

tuberculate. Covered with tubercles

tunic. Bulb or corm covering that is wider than a scale and wrapping entirely around the stem portion in concentric layers, the outer layers often dry

umbel (adjective, **umbellate**). Inflorescence in which all the individual flower stalks arise at the same point in a cluster from the top of the peduncle and are of about equal length

umbonate. Having a rounded projection in the middle

unifacial. Of leaves with both faces anatomically identical, typically flattened parallel to the stem axis

valve. One of the separating parts of a capsule

veld. Vegetation other than forest in southern Africa

verrucate. Covered with wart-like outgrowths

versatile. Of an anther attached near its center to the filament and moving freely

villous. Bearing soft, relatively long hairs

vlei. Seasonally inundated grassland in South Africa

zonisulculate. Of pollen encircled with a ring-like germination pore passing through the poles

zygomorphic. Bilaterally symmetrical

REFERENCES

Adamson, R. 1950. *Baeometra,* page 202 in Flora of the Cape Peninsula. Juta & Co., Cape Town.

Archer, R. H., D. A. Snijman, and R. K. Brummitt. 2001. Proposal to conserve the name *Boophone* Herbert with that spelling (Amaryllidaceae). Taxon 50: 569-571.

Archibald, E. E. A. 1956. *Neopatersonia uitenhagensis.* Flowering Plants of Africa 31: pl. 1204.

Baker, J. G. 1896. *Hypoxis.* Flora capensis 6: 174-189.

Barker, W. F. 1940. The genus *Dilatris* Berg. with the description of a new species. Journal of South African Botany 6: 147-164.

Barker, W. F. 1963. Two new species of Amaryllidaceae. Journal of South African Botany 29: 163-166.

Barker, W. F. 1989. New taxa and nomenclatural changes in *Lachenalia* (Liliaceae-Hyacinthaceae) from the Cape Province. South African Journal of Botany 55: 630-646.

Batten, A. 1986. Flowers of Southern Africa. Frandsen, Sandton.

Bjørnstad, I. N., and I. Friis. 1974. Studies on the genus *Haemanthus* (Amaryllidaceae) 3. A revision of the sections *Gyaxis* and *Nerissa*. Norwegian Journal of Botany 21: 243-275.

Brandham, P. E. 1989. *Amphisiphon stylosa.* Kew Magazine 6: 58-61.

Brandham, P. E. 1990. *Androsiphon capense.* Kew Magazine 7: 124-128.

Brown, N. R., R. K. Crowden, J. R. Gorst, and A. Koutoulis. 1999a. Reproductive biology of *Nerine* (Amaryllidaceae) I: the annual growth cycle, floral development and gamete production. Herbertia 54: 139-152.

Brown, N. R., R. K. Crowden, J. R. Gorst, and A. Koutoulis. 1999b. Reproductive biology of *Nerine* (Amaryllidaceae) II: embryo development and seed germination. Herbertia 54: 153-170.

Bruyns, P. V., and C. G. Vosa. 1987. Taxonomic and cytological notes on *Bowiea* Hook. f. and allied genera (Liliaceae). Caryologia 40: 287-297.

Bryan, J., and M. Griffiths (editors). 1995. Manual of Bulbs. Timber Press, Portland, Oregon.

Burbidge, R. B. 1978. A revision of the genus *Tulbaghia* (Liliaceae). Notes from the Royal Botanic Garden Edinburgh 36: 77-103.

Burtt, B. L. 1970. The evolution and taxonomic significance of a subterranean ovary in certain monocotyledons. Israel Journal of Botany 19: 77-90.

Carter, S. 1962. Revision of *Walleria* and *Cyanastrum* (Tecophilaeaceae). Kew Bulletin 16: 185-195.

Codd, L. E. 1968. The South African species of *Kniphofia*. Bothalia 9: 363-513.

Cowling, R. (editor). 1992. The Ecology of Fynbos. Oxford University Press, Cape Town.

Cowling, R., and D. Richardson. 1995. Fynbos. Fernwood Press, Cape Town.

De Vos, M. P. 1972. The genus *Romulea* in South Africa. Journal of South African Botany, Suppl., 9: 1-307.

De Vos, M. P. 1974. Die Suid-Afrikaanse genus *Syringodea.* Journal of South African Botany 40: 201-254.

De Vos, M. P. 1979. The African genus *Ferraria.* Journal of South African Botany 45: 295-375.

De Vos, M. P. 1982. The African genus *Tritonia* Ker-Gawler 1. Journal of South African Botany 48: 105-163.

De Vos, M. P. 1983a. The African genus *Tritonia* Ker-Gawler 2. Journal of South African Botany 49: 347-422.

De Vos, M. P. 1983b. *Syringodea* and *Romulea* (Iridaceae). Flora of Southern Africa 7(2(2)): 1-76.

De Vos, M. P. 1985. Revision of the South African genus *Chasmanthe* (Iridaceae). South African Journal of Botany 51: 253-261.

De Vos, M. P. 1999a. *Ixia* (Iridaceae). Flora of Southern Africa 7(2(1)): 3-87.

De Vos, M. P. 1999b. *Tritonia* (Iridaceae). Flora of Southern Africa 7(2(1)): 89-128.

De Vos, M. P. 1999c. *Chasmanthe* (Iridaceae). Flora of Southern Africa 7(2(1)): 143–147.

Dewilde-Duyfjes, B. E. E. 1976. A revision of the genus *Allium* in Africa. Belmontia 7: 75–78.

Drewes, F. E., and J. van Staden. 1994. In vitro propagation of *Gethyllis linearis* L. Bol., a rare indigenous bulb. South African Journal of Botany 60: 295–296.

Duncan, G. D. 1988. The *Lachenalia* Handbook. Annals of Kirstenbosch Botanic Gardens 17.

Duncan, G. D. 1990a. *Cyrtanthus*—its horticultural potential—part 1. Veld & Flora 76: 18–21.

Duncan, G. D. 1990b. *Cyrtanthus*—its horticultural potential—part 2. Veld & Flora 76: 54–56.

Duncan, G. D. 1990c. *Cyrtanthus*—its horticultural potential—part 3. Veld & Flora 76: 72–73.

Duncan, G. D. 1993. *Lachenalia thomasiae*. Flowering Plants of Africa 52: pl. 2061.

Duncan, G. D. 1996. Four new species and one new subspecies of *Lachenalia* (Hyacinthaceae) from arid areas of South Africa. Bothalia 26: 1–9.

Duncan, G. D. 1998a. Grow *Agapanthus*. National Botanical Institute, Cape Town.

Duncan, G. D. 1998b. Five new species of *Lachenalia* (Hyacinthaceae) from arid areas of Namibia and South Africa. Bothalia 28: 131–139.

Duncan, G. D. 1999. Grow Clivias. National Botanical Institute, Cape Town.

Duncan, G. D. 2000. Growing South African Bulbous Plants. National Botanical Institute, Cape Town.

Duncan, G. D. 2001. *Lachenalia elegans* var. *flava*. Curtis's Botanical Magazine 18: 18–22.

Duncan, G. D. 2002. Grow Nerines. National Botanical Institute, Cape Town.

Duncan, G. D., and F. Anderson. 1997. *Lachenalia rosea*. Flowering Plants of Africa 55: pl. 2126.

Duncan, G. D., and F. Anderson. 1999. *Lachenalia convallarioides*. Flowering Plants of Africa 56: pl. 2145.

Duncan, G. D., and C. Linder Smith. 1999a. *Lachenalia duncanii*. Flowering Plants of Africa 56: pl. 2143.

Duncan, G. D., and C. Linder Smith. 1999b. *Lachenalia nervosa*. Flowering Plants of Africa 56: pl. 2144.

Du Plessis, N., and G. Duncan. 1989. Bulbous Plants of Southern Africa, a Guide to Their Cultivation and Propagation. Tafelberg, Cape Town.

Dyer, R. A. 1941. *Bowiea volubilis*. Flowering Plants of South Africa 21: pl. 815.

Dyer, R. A. 1946. *Cybistetes longifolia*. Flowering Plants of Africa 25: pl. 1000.

Dyer, R. A. 1950–1951. A review of the genus *Brunsvigia*. Plant Life 6: 63–83, 7: 45–64.

Dyer, R. A. 1953. *Boophone disticha*. Flowering Plants of Africa 29: pl. 1141.

Dyer, R. A. 1955. *Amaryllis belladonna*. Flowering Plants of Africa 30: pl. 1200.

Dyer, R. A. 1960. *Walleria nutans*. Flowering Plants of Africa 34: 1321.

Esler, K., P. Rundel, and P. Vorster. 1999. Biogeography of prostrate-leaved geophytes in semi-arid South Africa. Plant Ecology 142: 105–120.

Fennell, C. W., N. R. Crouch, and J. van Staden. 2001. Micropropagation of the river lily, *Crinum variabile* (Amaryllidaceae). South African Journal of Botany 67: 74–77.

Friis, I., and I. Nordal. 1976. Studies on the genus *Haemanthus* (Amaryllidaceae) 4. Division of the genus into *Haemanthus* s. str. and *Scadoxus* s. str. Norwegian Journal of Botany 23: 63–77.

Garside, S. A. 1935. A revision of the characters of *Neodregea*. Kew Bulletin 1935: 292–298.

Garside, S. 1936. The South African species of *Spiloxene* Salisb. Journal of Botany 74: 267–269.

Geerinck, D. 1973. Amaryllidaceae. Flore d'Afrique Centrale. Jardin Botanique National de Belgique, Bruxelles.

Goldblatt, P. 1969. The genus *Sparaxis*. Journal of South African Botany 35: 219–252.

Goldblatt, P. 1972a. Chromosome cytology in relation to classification in *Nerine* and *Brunsvigia* (Amaryllidaceae). Journal of South African Botany 38: 261–275.

Goldblatt, P. 1972b. A revision of the genera *Lapeirousia* Pourret and *Anomatheca* Ker in the winter-rainfall region of South Africa. Contributions from the Bolus Herbarium 4: 1–111.

Goldblatt, P. 1979. Biology and systematics of *Galaxia* (Iridaceae). Journal of South African Botany 45: 385–423.

Goldblatt, P. 1980. Systematics of *Gynandriris* (Iridaceae), a Mediterranean–southern African disjunct. Botaniska Notiser 133: 239–260.

Goldblatt, P. 1981a. Systematics, phylogeny and evolution of *Dietes* (Iridaceae). Annals of the Missouri Botanical Garden 68: 132–153.

Goldblatt, P. 1981b. Systematics of the southern African genus *Geissorhiza* (Iridaceae–Ixioideae). Annals of the Missouri Botanical Garden 72: 277–447.

Goldblatt, P. 1981c. Systematics and biology of *Homeria* (Iridaceae). Annals of the Missouri Botanical Garden 68: 413–503.

Goldblatt, P. 1982a. Systematics of *Freesia* Klatt (Iridaceae). Journal of South African Botany 48: 39–91.

Goldblatt, P. 1982b. Corm morphology in *Hesperantha* (Iridaceae, Ixioideae) and a proposed infrageneric taxonomy. Annals of the Missouri Botanical Garden 69: 370–378.

Goldblatt, P. 1984a. A revision of *Hesperantha* (Iridaceae) in the winter rainfall area of southern Africa. Journal of South African Botany 50: 15–141.

Goldblatt, P. 1984b. New species of *Galaxia* (Iridaceae) and notes on cytology and evolution in the genus. Annals of the Missouri Botanical Garden 71: 1082–1087.

Goldblatt, P. 1986. The Moraeas of Southern Africa. Annals of Kirstenbosch Botanic Gardens 14.

Goldblatt, P. 1987a. New species and notes on southern African *Hesperantha* (Iridaceae). South African Journal of Botany 53: 459–463.

Goldblatt, P. 1987b. Systematics of the southern African genus *Hexaglottis* (Iridaceae–Iridoideae). Annals of the Missouri Botanical Garden 74: 542–569.

Goldblatt, P. 1989a. *Geissorhiza callista* (Iridaceae). Flowering Plants of Africa 50: 49–52, pl. 1996.

Goldblatt, P. 1989b. The Genus *Watsonia*. Annals of Kirstenbosch Botanic Gardens 19.

Goldblatt, P. 1990. Status of the southern African *Anapalina* and *Antholyza* (Iridaceae), genera based solely on characters for bird pollination, and a new species of *Tritoniopsis*. South African Journal of Botany 56: 577–582.

Goldblatt, P. 1992. Phylogenetic analysis of the South African genus *Sparaxis* (including *Synnotia*) (Iridaceae: Ixoideae), with two new species and a review of the genus. Annals of the Missouri Botanical Garden 79: 143–159.

Goldblatt, P. 1998. Reduction of *Barnardiella, Galaxia, Gynandriris, Hexaglottis, Homeria,* and *Roggeveldia* in *Moraea* (Iridaceae: Irideae). Novon 8: 371–377.

Goldblatt, P. 1999. *Devia* and *Sparaxis* (Iridaceae). Flora of Southern Africa 7(2(1)): 148–168.

Goldblatt, P. 2002. A synoptic review of the African genus *Hesperantha* (Iridaceae: Crocoideae) with keys, miscellaneous notes, range extensions, and new species. Annals of the Missouri Botanical Garden 89.

Goldblatt, P., and A. Le Thomas. 1997. Palynology, phylogenetic reconstruction and the classification of the Afro-Madagascan genus *Aristea* Aiton (Iridaceae). Annals of the Missouri Botanical Garden 84: 263–284.

Goldblatt, P., and J. C. Manning. 1990. *Devia xeromorpha*, a new genus and species of Iridaceae–Ixoideae from the Cape Province, South Africa. Annals of the Missouri Botanical Garden 77: 359–364.

Goldblatt, P., and J. C. Manning. 1992. Systematics of the southern African *Lapeirousia corymbosa* (Iridaceae–Ixoideae) complex (sect. *Fastigiata*) and a new species of sect. *Paniculata*. South African Journal of Botany 58: 326–336.

Goldblatt, P., and J. C. Manning. 1994. New taxa and revisions to the taxonomy of southern African *Lapeirousia* subgenus *Lapeirousia* (Iridaceae subfamily Ixioideae). Novon 4: 339–346.

Goldblatt, P., and J. C. Manning. 1995a. New species of the southern African genus *Geissorhiza* (Iridaceae: Ixoideae). Novon 5: 156–161.

Goldblatt, P., and J. C. Manning. 1995b. New species of southern African *Moraea* (Iridaceae: Iridoideae), and the reduction of *Rheome*. Novon 5: 262–269.

Goldblatt, P., and J. C. Manning. 1995c. Phylogeny of the African genera *Anomatheca* and *Freesia* (Iridaceae–Ixioideae), and a new genus *Xenoscapa*. Systematic Botany 20: 161–178.

Goldblatt, P., and J. C. Manning. 1996a. Reduction of *Schizostylis* (Iridaceae: Ixioideae) in *Hesperantha*. Novon 6: 262–264.

Goldblatt, P., and J. C. Manning. 1996b. Phylogeny and speciation in *Lapeirousia* subgenus *Lapeirousia* (Iridaceae: Ixioideae). Annals of the Missouri Botanical Garden 83: 346–361.

Goldblatt, P., and J. C. Manning. 1997a. New species of *Aristea* section *Pseudaristea* (Iridaceae) from South Africa and notes on the taxonomy and pollination biology of the section. Novon 7: 137–144.

Goldblatt, P., and J. C. Manning. 1997b. New species of *Aristea* section *Racemosae* (Iridaceae) from the Cape Flora, South Africa. Novon 7: 357–365.

Goldblatt, P., and J. C. Manning. 1998. *Gladiolus* in Southern Africa. Fernwood Press, Cape Town; distributed by Timber Press, Portland, Oregon.

Goldblatt, P., and J. C. Manning. 1999. New species of *Sparaxis* and *Ixia* (Iridaceae: Ixioideae) from Western Cape, South Africa, and taxonomic notes on *Gladiolus*. Bothalia 29: 59–63.

Goldblatt, P., and J. Manning. 2000a. Cape Plants, a Conspectus of the Cape Flora of South Africa. Strelitzia 9. National Botanical Institute, Cape Town, and Missouri Botanical Garden, St. Louis.

Goldblatt, P., and J. C. Manning. 2000b. New species of *Moraea* (Iridaceae: Iridoideae) from southern Africa. Novon 10: 14–21.

Goldblatt, P., J. C. Manning, and P. Bernhardt. 1995. Pollination biology of *Lapeirousia* subgenus *Lapeirousia* (Iridaceae) in southern Africa: floral divergence and adaptation for long-tongued fly-pollination. Annals of the Missouri Botanical Garden 82: 517–534.

Goldblatt, P., J. C. Manning, and P. Bernhardt. 2000. Adaptive radiation of pollination mechanisms in *Sparaxis* (Iridaceae: Ixioideae). Adansonia, Sér. 3, 22: 57–70.

Goldblatt, P., P. Bernhardt, and J. C. Manning. 2001. Adaptive radiation of pollination mechanisms in *Ixia* (Iridaceae: Crocoideae). Annals of the Missouri Botanical Garden 87: 564–577.

Hammerton, R. D., and J. van Staden. 1988. Seed germination of *Hypoxis hemerocallidea*. South African Journal of Botany 54: 277–280.

Helme, N. A., and H. P. Linder. 1992. Morphology, evolution and taxonomy of *Wachendorfia* (Haemodoraceae). Bothalia 22: 59–75.

Henderson, R. J. F. 1987. *Hypoxis*. Flora of Australia 45: 178–190.

Hepper, F. N. 1968. Amaryllidaceae. Flora of Tropical West Africa. Crown Agent for Overseas Government and Administration, London.

Hilliard, O. M., and B. L. Burtt. 1973. Notes on some plants of Southern Africa chiefly from Natal: III. Notes from the Royal Botanic Garden Edinburgh 32: 303–387.

Hilliard, O. M., B. L. Burtt, and A. Batten. 1991. *Dierama*, Hairbells of Africa. Acorn Press, Johannesburg.

Holford, F. 1989. *Cyrtanthus* in the cool greenhouse. Plantsman 11: 170–175.

Holford, F. 1998. Breeding *Cyrtanthus* for cut flowers. Herbertia 53: 179–185.

Ising, G. 1997. Hybridization in *Cyrtanthus*. Herbertia 52: 153–165.

Jessop, J. P. 1970. Studies in the bulbous Liliaceae 1. *Scilla, Schizocarpus* and *Ledebouria*. Journal of South African Botany 36: 233–266.

Jessop, J. P. 1976. Studies in the bulbous Liliaceae in South Africa 6. The taxonomy of *Massonia* and allied genera. Journal of South African Botany 42: 401–437.

Jessop, J. P. 1977. Studies in the bulbous Liliaceae in South Africa 7: The taxonomy of *Drimia* and certain allied genera. Journal of South African Botany 43: 265–319.

Johnson, S. D., and D. A. Snijman. 1996. *Amaryllis belladonna*. Veld & Flora 82: 70–71.

Judd, W. S. 2000. The Hypoxidaceae in the southeastern United States. Harvard Papers in Botany 5: 79–98.

Knippels, P. J. M. 1999. Growing Bulbs Indoors. A. A. Balkema, Rotterdam.

Koopowitz, H. 1986. Horticultural potential of *Cyrtanthus* (Amaryllidaceae). Herbertia 42: 75–81.

Koshimizu, T. 1930. Carpobiological studies of *Crinum asiaticum* L. var. *japonicum* Bak. Memoirs of the College of Science, Kyoto Imperial University, Series B, Biology 5: 18–227.

Lehmiller, D. J. 1996. Cultivation of African *Crinum* in pots and tubs. Herbertia 51: 33–37.

Leighton, F. M. 1947. *Boophone haemanthoides*. Journal of South African Botany 13: 59–61.

Leighton, F. M. 1965. The genus *Agapanthus* L'Héritier. Journal of South African Botany, Suppl., 4: 1–50.

Letty, C. 1973. The genus *Zantedeschia*. Bothalia 11: 5–26.

Lewis, G. J. 1941. New genera and species and miscellaneous notes. Journal of South African Botany 7: 33–43.

Lewis, G. J. 1947. *Scilla plumbea*. Flowering Plants of Africa 26: pl. 1006.

Lewis, G. J. 1952. Plantae novae Africanae. Annals of the South African Museum 40: 6–9.

Lewis, G. J. 1956. A revision of the genus *Synnotia*. Annals of the South African Museum 40: 137–151.

Lewis, G. J. 1959a. The genus *Babiana*. Journal of South African Botany, Suppl., 3: 1–149.

Lewis, G. J. 1959b. South African Iridaceae. The genus *Tritoniopsis*. Journal of South African Botany 25: 319–355.

Lewis, G. J. 1960. South African Iridaceae. The genus *Anapalina*. Journal of South African Botany 26: 51–72.

Lewis, G. J. 1962. South African Iridaceae. The genus *Ixia*. Journal of South African Botany 28: 45–195.

Liltved, W. 1992. Kukumakranka past and present. Veld & Flora 78: 104–106.

McAlister, B. G., A. Strydom, and J. van Staden. 1998. In vitro propagation of some *Cyrtanthus* species. South African Journal of Botany 64: 229–231.

Manning, J. C., and P. Goldblatt. 2001a. Two new renosterveld species of Iridaceae: Crocoideae from South Africa. Bothalia 31: 189–192.

Manning, J. C., and P. Goldblatt. 2001b. Three new species of *Tritoniopsis* (Iridaceae: Crocoideae) from the Cape Region. Bothalia 31: 175–181.

Manning, J. C., and P. Goldblatt. 2001c. A synoptic review of *Romulea* (Iridaceae: Ixioideae) in sub-Saharan Africa, Arabia, and Socotra, including new species, biological notes, and a new infrageneric classification. Adansonia, Sér. 3, 23: 1–50.

Manning, J. C., P. Goldblatt, and F. Anderson. 1999a. *Albuca clanwilliamigloria*. Flowering Plants of Africa 56: pl. 2142.

Manning, J. C., P. Goldblatt, and P. D. J. Winter. 1999b. Two new species of *Gladiolus* (Iridaceae: Ixioideae) from southern Africa and notes on long-proboscid fly pollination in the genus. Bothalia 29: 217–223.

Manning, J. C., P. Goldblatt, and A. Batten. 2001. *Walleria gracilis*. Flowering Plants of Africa 57: 44–47.

Marais, W. 1972. The correct names for veltheimias, the winter red hot pokers. Journal of the Royal Horticultural Society 47: 483–484.

Mathew, B. 1998. Growing Bulbs. Timber Press, Portland, Oregon.

Milne-Redhead, E., and H. G. Schweickerdt. 1939. A new conception of the genus *Ammocharis* Herb. Botanical Journal of the Linnean Society 52: 159–197.

Müller-Doblies, D. 1986. De liliifloris notulae 3. Enumeratio specierum generum *Gethyllis* et *Apodolirion* (Amaryllidaceae). Willdenowia 15: 465–471.

Müller-Doblies, U. 1994. Enumeratio albucarum (Hyacinthaceae) Austro-Africanarum adhuc cognitarum. 1. Subgenus *Albuca*. Feddes Repertorium 105: 365–368.

Müller-Doblies, U. 1995. Enumeratio albucarum (Hyacinthaceae) Austro-Africanarum adhuc cognitarum. 2. Subgenus *Falconera*. Feddes Repertorium 106: 353–370.

Müller-Doblies, U., and D. Müller-Doblies. 1984. Zur Kenntnis der Gattung *Androcymbium* (Colchicaceae) im südlichen Afrika. Willdenowia 14: 179–197.

Müller-Doblies, D., and U. Müller-Doblies. 1985. De liliifloris notulae 2. De taxonomia subtribus Strumariinae (Amaryllidaceae). Botanische Jahrbücher für Systematik 107: 17–47.

Müller-Doblies, D., and U. Müller-Doblies. 1991. *Bowiea gariepensis*. Flowering Plants of Africa 51: pl. 2007.

Müller-Doblies, D., and U. Müller-Doblies. 1994. De liliifloris notulae 5. Some new taxa and combinations in the Amaryllidaceae tribe Amaryllideae from arid southern Africa. Feddes Repertorium 105: 331–363.

Müller-Doblies, U., and D. Müller-Doblies. 1996. Revisionula incompleta ornithogalorum Austro-Africanarum (Hyacinthaceae). Feddes Repertorium 107: 361–548.

Müller-Doblies, U., and D. Müller-Doblies. 1997. A partial revision of the tribe Massonieae (Hyacinthaceae). Feddes Repertorium 108: 49–96.

Müller-Doblies, U., and D. Müller-Doblies. 1998. De liliifloris notulae 6. De decuria prima specierum novarum generis *Androcymbium* sect. *Androcymbium* (Colchicaceae) in Africa Australe. Feddes Repertorium 109: 551–572.

Nordal, I. 1979. Revision of the genus *Cyrtanthus* (Amaryllidaceae) in East Africa. Norwegian Journal of Botany 26: 183–192.

Nordal, I. 1982. Amaryllidaceae. Flora of Tropical East Africa. A. A. Balkema, Rotterdam.

Nordenstam, B. 1970. Studies in South African Liliaceae III. The genus *Rhadamanthus*. Botaniska Notiser 123: 155–182.

Nordenstam, B. 1982. A monograph of the genus *Ornithoglossum* (Liliaceae). Opera Botanica 64: 1–51.

Nordenstam, B. 1986. The genus *Wurmbea* (Colchicaceae) in the Cape region. Opera Botanica 87: 1–41.

Norris, C. A. 1974. The genus *Nerine* part 2. Nerine Society Bulletin 6: 7–31.

Obermeyer, A. A. 1961. *Veltheimia capensis*. Flowering Plants of Africa 34: pl. 1356.

Obermeyer, A. A. 1962. *Pillansia templemannii*. Flowering Plants of Africa 35: pl. 1381.

Obermeyer, A. A. 1963. The South African species of *Dipcadi*. Bothalia 8: 117–137.

Obermeyer, A. A. 1965. *Whiteheadia bifolia*. Flowering Plants of Africa 35: pl. 1450.

Obermeyer, A. A. 1978. *Ornithogalum*: a revision of the southern African species. Bothalia 12: 323–376.

Obermeyer, A. A. 1980a. The genus *Sypharissa* (Liliaceae). Bothalia 13: 111–114.

Obermeyer, A. A. 1980b. A new subgenus *Rhadamanthopsis* and two new species of *Rhadamanthus*. Bothalia 13: 137–139.

O'Neill, C. 1991. The genus *Haemanthus*. Herbertia 47: 137.

Perry, P. L. 1987. A synoptic review of the genus *Bulbinella* (Asphodelaceae) in South Africa. South African Journal of Botany 53: 431–444.

Perry, P. L. 1989. A new species of *Zantedeschia* (Araceae) from the Western Cape. South African Journal of Botany 55: 447–451.

Perry, P. L. 1994. A revision of the genus *Eriospermum* (Eriospermaceae). Contributions from the Bolus Herbarium 17: 1–320.

Perry, P. L. 1999. A revision of *Bulbinella* (Asphodelaceae) in South Africa. Strelitzia 8: 1–78.

Pettit, G. 1999. The seven species of KwaZulu-Natal *Crinum*: a horticultural review. Herbertia 54: 119–123.

Phillips, E. P. 1922a. *Polyxena haemanthoides*. Flowering Plants of South Africa 2: pl. 56.

Phillips, E. P. 1922b. *Daubenya aurea*. Flowering Plants of South Africa 2: pl. 71.

Pole Evans, I. B. 1938. *Ammocharis coranica*. Flowering Plants of South Africa 18: pl. 712.

Rabe, T., and J. van Staden. 1999. In vitro propagation of three *Haemanthus* species. South African Journal of Botany 65: 438–440.

Rand, M. 1980. A shower of brilliant little stars. Veld & Flora 66: 81–82.

Reid, C., and R. A. Dyer. 1984. A review of the Southern African Species of *Cyrtanthus*. American Plant Life Society, La Jolla, California.

Reyneke, W. F. 1972. 'n Morphologiese Studie van die Genus *Eucomis* L'Hér. in Suid-Afrika. Unpublished M.Sc. thesis, University of Pretoria.

Rourke, J. P. 2002. *Clivia mirabilis* (Amaryllidaceae: Haemantheae), a new species from Northern Cape, South Africa. Bothalia 32: 1–7.

Schönland, S. 1912. *Neopatersonia*, a new genus of Liliaceae. Records of the Albany Museum 2: 250–253.

Scott, G. A. 1991. A revision of *Cyanella* (Tecophilaeaceae) excluding *C. amboensis*. South African Journal of Botany 57: 34–54.

Singh, Y. 1999. *Hypoxis*. Veld & Flora 85: 123–125.

Singh, Y., A. E. Van Wyk, and H. Baijnath. 1995. Know your arums: an easy guide to identify members of the genus *Zantedeschia*. Veld & Flora 81: 54–55.

Smee, S. 1984. Growing and breeding nerines. Journal of the Royal Horticultural Society 109: 408–413.

Snijman, D. A. 1984. A revision of the genus *Haemanthus* (Amaryllidaceae). Journal of South African Botany, Suppl., 12: 1–139.

Snijman, D. A. 1994. Systematics of *Hessea*, *Strumaria* and *Carpolyza* (Amaryllidaceae: Amaryllideae). Contributions from the Bolus Herbarium 16: 1–162.

Snijman, D. A. 1995. A new *Nerine* species (Amaryllidaceae tribe Amaryllideae) from the Koup Karoo, South Africa. Novon 5: 103–105.

Snijman, D. A. 1999a. New species and notes on *Cyrtanthus* in the southern Cape, South Africa. Bothalia 29: 258–263.

Snijman, D. A. 1999b. A new species, notes on subgeneric taxa, and new synonyms in *Hessea* (Amaryllidaceae: Amaryllideae). Novon 9: 107–110.

Snijman, D. A. 2001a. A new species of *Brunsvigia* (Amaryllidaceae: Amarylllideae) from Western Cape, South Africa. Bothalia 31: 34–37.

Snijman, D. A. 2001b. A new species of *Cyrtanthus* (Amaryllidaceae: Cyrtantheae) from the southern Cape, South Africa. Bothalia 31: 31–34.

Snijman, D. A., and H. P. Linder. 1996. Phylogenetic relationships, seed characters, and dispersal system evolution in Amaryllideae (Amaryllidaceae). Annals of the Missouri Botanical Garden 83: 362–386.

Snijman, D. A., and E. J. van Jaarsveld. 1995. *Cyrtanthus flammosus*. Flowering Plants of Africa 54: 100–103.

Snijman, D. A., and A. E. van Wyk. 1993. A new species of *Haemanthus* (Amaryllidaceae) from the eastern Transvaal Escarpment, South Africa. South African Journal of Botany 59: 247–250.

Snijman, D. A., and G. Williamson. 1994. A taxonomic re-assessment of *Ammocharis herrei* and *Cybistetes longifolia* (Amaryllidaceae: Amaryllideae). Bothalia 24: 127–132.

Snijman, D. A., and G. Williamson. 1998. A new species of *Amaryllis* from the Richtersveld, South Africa. Bothalia 28: 192–196.

Snijman, D. A., J. C. Manning, and P. Goldblatt. 1999. A new *Rhadamanthus* species (Hyacinthaceae) from the northwestern Cape, South Africa. Novon 9: 111–113.

Strid, A. 1974. A taxonomic revision of *Bobartia* L. (Iridaceae). Opera Botanica 37: 1–45.

Thompson, M. F. 1979. Studies in the Hypoxidaceae. 3. The genus *Pauridia*. Bothalia 12: 621–625.

Tjaden, W. 1989. The fair *Amaryllis*. Garden 114: 345–348.

Toogood, A., and D. Hide. 1996. Autumn sparklers. Garden 121: 646–649.

Traub, H. P. 1967. Review of the Genus *Nerine* Herb. American Plant Life Society, La Jolla, California.

Van Der Merwe, A. M., and E. M. Marais. 2001. A new species of *Polyxena* (Hyacinthaceae, tribe Massonieae) from Komsberg, Northern Cape Province. South African Journal of Botany 67: 44–46.

Van Jaarsveld, E. J. 1983. *Bowiea gariepensis:* a new *Bowiea* species (Liliaceae) from the north western Cape. Journal of South African Botany 49: 343–346.

Venter, S. 1993. A Revision of the Genus *Ledebouria* Roth (Hyacinthaceae) in South Africa. Unpublished M.Sc. thesis, University of Natal, Pietermaritzburg.

Verdoorn, I. C. 1973. The genus *Crinum* in southern Africa. Bothalia 11: 27–52.

Vorster, P. and C. Smith. 1994. *Clivia nobilis*. Flowering Plants of Africa 53: 70–74.

Vosa, C. G. 1975. The cytotaxonomy of the genus *Tulbaghia*. Annali di Botanica 34: 47–121.

Vosa, C. G. 2000. A revised cytotaxonomy of the genus *Tulbaghia* (Alliaceae). Caryologia 53: 83–112.

Vosa, C. G., and D. A. Snijman. 1984. The cytology of the genus *Haemanthus* L. (Amaryllidaceae). Journal of South African Botany 50: 237–259.

Weimarck, H. 1940. Monograph of the genus *Aristea*. Acta Universitatis Lundensis, Nova Series, Sectio 2 (Lunds Universitets Årsskrift, Ny Följd, Andra Afdelningen) 36(1): 1–140.

INDEX OF SYNONYMS

This index contains cross-references to those synonyms most likely to be encountered in the more popular literature as well as the names of plants that have been relatively recently described but for which the identity or status is uncertain. All currently accepted species are listed alphabetically in the chapter, Bulbs of the Cape. This index also includes names given to plants whose identity we have been unable to verify because of the lack of authentic material. We have elected to relegate these names of potentially dubious validity to the index rather than burden the text with them. This rather unusual situation has arisen because several species described more recently are known only from type specimens that have not been distributed to the South African herbaria designated to receive them; genera affected by this are *Albuca*, *Androcymbium*, *Gethyllis*, *Ornithogalum*, and *Polyxena*.

Albuca
 altissima Dryander, see *A. maxima*
 aspera U. Müller-Doblies, see *A. viscosa*
 bontebokensis U. Müller-Doblies, see *A. viscosa*
 brucebayeri U. Müller-Doblies, see *A. hallii*
 canadensis (Linnaeus) F. M. Leighton, see *A. flaccida*
 convoluta E. Phillips, see *A. acuminata*
 imbricata F. M. Leighton, see *A. juncifolia*
 jacquinii U. Müller-Doblies, see *A. viscosa*
 karooica U. Müller-Doblies, see *A. cooperi*
 materfamilias U. Müller-Doblies, see *A. flaccida*
 viscosella U. Müller-Doblies, see *A. viscosa*
Amphisiphon, see *Daubenya*
 stylosum W. F. Barker, see *Daubenya stylosa*
Anapalina, see *Tritoniopsis*
 burchellii N. E. Brown, see *Tritoniopsis burchellii*
 caffra (Ker Gawler ex Baker) G. J. Lewis, see *Tritoniopsis caffra*
 intermedia (Baker) G. J. Lewis, see *Tritoniopsis intermedia*
 longituba Fourcade, see *Tritoniopsis antholyza*
 nervosa (Thunberg) G. J. Lewis, see *Tritoniopsis antholyza*
 pulchra (Baker) N. E. Brown, see *Tritoniopsis pulchra*
 triticea (Burman fil.) N. E. Brown, see *Tritoniopsis triticea*
Androcymbium
 austrocapense U. & D. Müller-Doblies, see *A. eucomoides*
 ciliolatum Schlechter & Krause, see *A. capense*
 eghimocymbion U. & D. Müller-Doblies, see *A. eucomoides*

 fenestratum Schlechter & Krause, see *A. capense*
 hantamense Engler, see *A. capense*
 irroratum Schlechter & Krause, see *A. capense*
 kunkelianum U. Müller-Doblies et al., see *A. cuspidatum*
 pritzelianum Diels, see *A. crispum*
 pulchrum Schlechter & Krause, see *A. latifolium*
 undulatum U. & D. Müller-Doblies, see *A. eucomoides*
 worsonense U. & D. Müller-Doblies, uncertain species
Androsiphon, see *Daubenya*
 capense Schlechter, see *Daubenya capensis*
Anomalesia, see *Gladiolus*
 cunonia (Linnaeus) N. E. Brown, see *Gladiolus cunonius*
 saccata (Klatt) Goldblatt, see *Gladiolus saccatus*
 splendens (Sweet) N. E. Brown, see *Gladiolus splendens*
Anomatheca, see *Freesia*
 fistulosa (Sprengel ex Klatt) Goldblatt, see *Xenoscapa fistulosa*
 verrucosa (Vogel) Goldblatt, see *Freesia verrucosa*
 viridis (Aiton) Goldblatt, see *Freesia viridis*
Antholyza, see *Babiana*
 plicata (Linnaeus fil.) Goldblatt, see *Babiana thunbergii*
 ringens Linnaeus, see *Babiana ringens*
Aristea
 coerulea (Thunberg) Vahl, see *A. bracteata*
 cognata N. E. Brown ex Weimarck, see *A. abyssinica*
 confusa Goldblatt, see *A. bakeri*
 cuspidata Schinz, see *A. bakeri*

Aristea continued
   macrocarpa G. J. Lewis, see *A. bakeri*
   major Andrews, see *A. capitata*
   monticola Goldblatt, see *A. bracteata*
   thyrsiflora D. Delaroche, see *A. capitata*
Babiana
   plicata Ker Gawler, see *B. disticha*
   pulchra (Salisbury) G. J. Lewis, see *B. angustifolia*
Boophone
   flava W. F. Barker ex Snijman, see *Crossyne flava*
   guttata (Linnaeus) Herbert, see *Crossyne guttata*
Brunsvigia
   appendiculata F. M. Leighton, see *B. bosmaniae*
   gydobergensis D. & U. Müller-Doblies, see *B. josephinae*
   minor Lindley, see *B. striata*
Carpolyza, see *Strumaria*
   spiralis (L'Héritier) Salisbury, see *Strumaria spiralis*
Convallariaceae, see Ruscaceae
Cybistetes herrei (F. M. Leighton) D. & U. Müller-Doblies, see *C. longifolia*
Cyrtanthus
   pallidus Sims, see *C. ventricosus*
   purpureus (Aiton) Traub, see *C. elatus*
   speciosus R. A. Dyer, see *C. loddigesianus*
Daubenya
   angustifolia of authors, see *D. zeyheri*
   angustifolia (Linnaeus fil.) A. M. van der Merwe & J. C. Manning, see *Massonia echinata*
Dewinterella
   mathewsii (W. F. Barker) D. &. U. Müller-Doblies, see *Hessea mathewsii*
   pulcherrima (D. &. U. Müller-Doblies) D. &. U. Müller-Doblies, see *Hessea pulcherrima*
Dietes vegeta of authors, see *D. iridioides*
Dilatris paniculata Linnaeus fil., see *D. viscosa*
Dipidax
   punctata (Linnaeus) Hutchinson, see *Onixotis punctata*
   triquetra (Linnaeus fil.) Baker, see *Onixotis stricta*
Drimia
   altissima (Linnaeus fil.) Ker Gawler, see *D. capensis*
   forsteri (Baker) Obermeyer, see *D. capensis*
Empodium occidentale (Nel) B. L. Burtt, see *Spiloxene* sp. 2
Eriospermaceae, see Ruscaceae
Forbesia flexilis Nel, see *Empodium flexile* (Nel) M. F. Thompson ex Snijman
Galaxia, see *Moraea* (*Galaxia* group)
   alata Goldblatt, see *Moraea angulata*
   albiflora G. J. Lewis, see *Moraea albiflora*
   barnardii Goldblatt, see *Moraea barnardiella*
   ciliata Persoon, see *Moraea pilifolia*

   citrina G. J. Lewis, see *Moraea citrina*
   fugacissima (Linnaeus fil.) Druce, see *Moraea fugacissima*
   luteoalba Goldblatt, see *Moraea luteoalba*
   ovata Thunberg, see *Moraea galaxia*
   parva Goldblatt, see *Moraea minima*
   stagnalis Goldblatt, see *Moraea stagnalis*
   variabilis G. J. Lewis, see *Moraea variabilis*
   versicolor Salisbury ex Klatt, see *Moraea versicolor*
Geissorhiza
   erosa (Salisbury) R. C. Foster, see *G. inflexa*
   rochensis Ker Gawler, see *G. tulbaghensis*
Gethyllis
   multifolia L. Bolus, see *G. campanulata*
   undulata Herbert, see *G. ciliaris*
   uteana D. Müller-Doblies, see *G. roggeveldensis*
Gladiolus
   blandus Aiton, see *G. carneus*
   citrinus Klatt, see *G. trichonemifolius*
   floribundus subsp. *fasciatus* (Roemer & Schultes) Obermeyer, see *G. grandiflorus*
   floribundus subsp. *milleri* (Ker Gawler) Obermeyer, see *G. grandiflorus*
   floribundus subsp. *miniatus* (Ecklon) Obermeyer, see *G. miniatus*
   floribundus subsp. *rudis* (Lichtenstein ex Roemer & Schultes) Obermeyer, see *G. rudis*
   odoratus L. Bolus, see *G. guthriei*
   pillansii G. J. Lewis, see *G. martleyi*
   punctulatus Schrank, see *G. hirsutus*
   robustus Goldblatt, see *G. geardii*
   tenellus of authors, see *G. trichonemifolius*
Gynandriris, see *Moraea* (*Gynandriris* group)
   anomala Goldblatt, see *Moraea contorta*
   australis Goldblatt, see *Moraea australis*
   cedarmontana Goldblatt, see *Moraea cedarmontana*
   hesperantha Goldblatt, see *Moraea hesperantha*
   pritzeliana (Diels) Goldblatt, see *Moraea pritzeliana*
   setifolia (Linnaeus fil.) R. C. Foster, see *Moraea setifolia*
Haemanthus undulatus Herbert, see *H. crispus*
Hexaglottis, see *Moraea* (*Hexaglottis* group)
   lewisiae Goldblatt, see *Moraea lewisiae*
   longifolia (Jacquin) Salisbury, see *Moraea longifolia*
   nana L. Bolus, see *Moraea nana*
   riparia Goldblatt, see *Moraea riparia*
   virgata (Jacquin) Sweet, see *Moraea virgata*
Homeria, see *Moraea* (*Homeria* group)
   autumnalis Goldblatt, see *Moraea autumnalis*
   bifida L. Bolus, see *Moraea bifida*
   bolusiae Goldblatt, see *Moraea louisabolusiae*
   brachygyne Schlechter, see *Moraea brachygyne*
   britteniae L. Bolus, see *Moraea britteniae*

bulbillifera G. J. Lewis, see *Moraea bulbillifera*
cedarmontana Goldblatt, see *Moraea cedarmonticola*
collina (Thunberg) Salisbury, see *Moraea collina*
comptonii L. Bolus, see *Moraea comptonii*
cookii L. Bolus, see *Moraea cookii*
elegans (Jacquin) Sweet, see *Moraea elegans*
fenestrata Goldblatt, see *Moraea fenestrata*
flaccida (Sweet) Steudel, see *Moraea flaccida*
flavescens Goldblatt, see *Moraea flavescens*
fuscomontana Goldblatt, see *Moraea fuscomontana*
galpinii L. Bolus, see *Moraea pyrophila*
hantamensis Goldblatt & J. C. Manning, see *Moraea reflexa*
longistyla Goldblatt, see *Moraea longistyla*
marlothii L. Bolus, see *Moraea marlothii*
miniata (Andrews) Sweet, see *Moraea miniata*
minor (Ecklon) Goldblatt, see *Moraea minor*
ochroleuca Salisbury, see *Moraea ochroleuca*
odorata L. Bolus, see *Moraea odorata*
patens Goldblatt, see *Moraea patens*
spiralis L. Bolus, see *Moraea aspera*
tenuis Schlechter, see *Moraea demissa*
tricolor G. J. Lewis, see *Moraea karooica*
vallisbelli Goldblatt, see *Moraea vallisbelli*

Homoglossum, see *Gladiolus*
abbreviatum (Andrews) Goldblatt, see *Gladiolus abbreviatus*
fourcadei (L. Bolus) N. E. Brown, see *Gladiolus fourcadei*
guthriei (L. Bolus) L. Bolus, see *Gladiolus overbergensis*
merianellum (Thunberg) Baker, see *Gladiolus bonaspei*
muirii (L. Bolus) L. Bolus, see *Gladiolus teretifolius*
priorii (N. E. Brown) N. E. Brown, see *Gladiolus priorii*
quadrangulare (Burman fil.) N. E. Brown, see *Gladiolus quadrangularis*
watsonium (Thunberg) N. E. Brown, see *Gladiolus watsonius*

Hypoxis sobolifera Jacquin, see *H. villosa*

Ixia
bellendenii R. C. Foster, see *I. longituba*
conferta R. C. Foster, see *I. lutea*
framesii L. Bolus, see *I. tenuifolia*
frederickii M. P. de Vos, see *I. dubia*

Lachenalia
convallariodora Stapf, see *L. fistulosa*
esterhuysenae W. F. Barker, see *L. juncifolia*
latifolia Trattinick, see *L. nervosa*
pendula Aiton, see *L. bulbifera*
roodiae E. Phillips, see *L. splendida*
subspicata Fourcade, see *L. bowkeri*
tricolor Thunberg, see *L. aloides*

Litanthus, see *Drimia* (*Litanthus* group)
pusillus Harvey, see *Drimia uniflora*

Massonia
angustifolia of authors, see *Daubenya zeyheri*
angustifolia Linnaeus fil., see *M. echinata*
grandiflora Lindley, see *M. depressa*
heterandra (Isaac) Jessop, see *M. pygmaea*
zeyheri Kunth, see *Daubenya zeyheri*

Moraea
glaucopis (De Candolle) Drapiez, see *M. aristata*
neopavonia R. C. Foster, see *M. tulbaghensis*

Nerine
breachiae W. F. Barker, see *N. humilis*
marginata (Jacquin) Herbert, see *Brunsvigia marginata*
peersii W. F. Barker, see *N. humilis*
tulbaghensis W. F. Barker, see *N. humilis*

Onixotis triquetra (Linnaeus fil.) Mabberley, see *O. stricta*

Ornithogalum
adseptentrionesvergentulum U. & D. Müller-Doblies, uncertain species
albucoides (Aiton) Thunberg, see *O. suaveolens*
apertum (I. Verdcourt) Obermeyer, see *O. concordianum*
citrinum Schlechter ex Poellnitz, see *O. dubium*
comptum Baker, see *O. juncifolium*
gethylloides U. & D. Müller-Doblies, uncertain species
gifbergense U. & D. Müller-Doblies, see *O. ciliiferum*
hesperanthum U. & D. Müller-Doblies, see *O. nannodes*
namaquanum U. & D. Müller-Doblies, see *O. suaveolens*
nathoanum U. & D. Müller-Doblies, uncertain species
niveum of authors, see *O. schlechterianum*
oreogenes Poellnitz, see *O. schlechterianum*
ornithogaloides (Kunth) Obermeyer, see *O. flexuosum*
ovatum Thunberg, see *O. unifolium*
paucifolium U. & D. Müller-Doblies, uncertain species
perparvum Poellnitz, see *O. pilosum*
rogersii Baker, see *O. schlechterianum*
rossouwii U. & D. Müller-Doblies, uncertain species
semipedale (Baker) U. & D. Müller-Doblies, see *O. polyphyllum*
thunbergianulum U. & D. Müller-Doblies, see *O. tortuosum*
vallisgratae Schlechter ex Poellnitz, see *O. schlechterianum*
verae U. & D. Müller-Doblies, uncertain species
vittatum (Ker Gawler) Kunth., see *O. suaveolens*

Periboea, see *Polyxena*
oliveri U. & D. Müller-Doblies, see *Polyxena paucifolia*

Polyxena
calcicola U. & D. Müller-Doblies, uncertain species
odorata (Hooker fil.) Baker, see *P. ensifolia*
pygmaea (Jacquin) Kunth, see *P. ensifolia*

Rhadamanthus, see *Drimia* (*Rhadamanthus* group)
albiflorus B. Nordenstam, see *Drimia albiflora*
arenicola B. Nordenstam, see *Drimia arenicola*

Rhadamanthus continued
    convallarioides (Linnaeus fil.) Baker, see *Drimia convallarioides*
    involutus J. C. Manning & Snijman, see *Drimia involuta*
    karooicus Obermeyer, see *Drimia karooica*
    montanus B. Nordenstam, see *Drimia convallarioides*
    platyphyllus B. Nordenstam, see *Drimia platyphylla*
    urantherus R. A. Dyer, see *Drimia uranthera*
    vanzyliae M. P. de Vos, see *R. subfistulosa*
Rheome, see *Moraea* (*Hexaglottis* group)
    maximiliani (Schlechter) Goldblatt, see *Moraea maximiliani*
    umbellata (Thunberg) Goldblatt, see *Moraea umbellata*
Roggeveldia, see *Moraea* (*Hexaglottis* group)
    fistulosa Goldblatt, see *Moraea fistulosa*
    montana Goldblatt, see *Moraea monticola*
Romulea papyracea Wolley-Dod, see *R. schlechteri*
Schizobasis, see *Drimia* (*Schizobasis* group)
    intricata (Baker) Baker, see *Drimia intricata*
Schizostylis coccinea Backhouse fil. & Harvey, see *Hesperantha coccinea*
Scilla ensifolia (Ecklon) Britten, see *Ledebouria* sp. 1
Sessilistigma radians Goldblatt, see *Moraea radians*
Spiloxene
    cuspidata (Nel) Garside, see *S. ovata*
    declinata (Nel) Garside, see *S. curculigoides*
    dielsiana (Nel) Garside, see *S. serrata*
    gracilipes (Schlechter) Garside, see *S. ovata*
    linearis (Andrews) Garside, see *S. serrata*
    maximiliani (Schlechter) Garside, see *S. umbraticola*
Synnotia, see *Sparaxis*
    galeata (Ker Gawler) Sweet, see *Sparaxis galeata*
    metelerkampiae L. Bolus, see *Sparaxis metelerkampiae*
    parviflora G. J. Lewis, see *Sparaxis parviflora*
    roxburghii (Baker) G. Lewis, see *Sparaxis roxburghii*
    variegata Sweet, see *Sparaxis variegata*
    villosa (Burman fil.) N. E. Brown, see *Sparaxis villosa*
Sypharissa, see *Drimia* (*Tenicroa* group)
Tenicroa, see *Drimia* (*Tenicroa* group)
    exuviata (Jacquin) Speta, see *Drimia exuviata*
    filifolia (Jacquin) Obermeyer, see *Drimia filifolia*
    fragrans (Jacquin) Rafinesque, see *Drimia fragrans*
    multifolia (G. J. Lewis) Obermeyer, see *Drimia multifolia*
Thereianthus lapeyrousioides (Baker) G. J. Lewis, see *T. minutus*
Urginea, see *Drimia* (*Urginea* group)
    rigidifolia Baker, see *Drimia sclerophylla*
Veltheimia
    deasii Barnes, see *V. capensis*
    glauca (Aiton) Jacquin, see *V. capensis*
    viridifolia Jacquin, see *V. bracteata*
Wachendorfia parviflora W. F. Barker, see *W. multiflora*
Watsonia
    beatricis J. W. Matthews & L. Bolus, see *W. pillansii*
    bulbillifera J. W. Matthews & L. Bolus, see *W. meriana*
    roseoalba Ker Gawler, see *W. humilis*
Wurmbea ustulata B. Nordenstam, see *W. spicata*

INDEX OF COMMON NAMES

Although some Cape bulbs do have popular names, either in English or Afrikaans, the majority do not. *The Color Encyclopedia of Cape Bulbs* aims to stabilize the use of popular names at the level of genus, and this index contains essentially only those names. Genera and species are listed alphabetically in the chapter, Bulbs of the Cape.

African snowdrop, see *Drimia* (*Rhadamanthus* group)
African squill, see *Ledebouria*
Afrikaner, see *Gladiolus*
agapanthus, see *Agapanthus*
ammocharis, see *Ammocharis*
aristea, see *Aristea*
arum lily, see *Zantedeschia*
autumn star, see *Empodium*
babiana, see *Babiana*
beetle lily, see *Baeometra*
belladonna lily, see *Amaryllis*
blood lily, see *Scadoxus*
bloodroot, see *Dilatris*
bluebonnets, see *Sparaxis*
blue lily, see *Agapanthus*
blue scepter, *Aristea capitata*
bulbinella, see *Bulbinella*
buttercup, Cape, see *Sparaxis*
butterfly lily, see *Wachendorfia*
cabong, see *Lapeirousia*
calla lily, see *Zantedeschia*
candelabra lily, see *Brunsvigia*
Cape buttercup, see *Sparaxis*
Cape cowslip, see *Lachenalia*
Cape crocus, see *Syringodea*
Cape hyacinth, see *Polyxena*
Cape snowflake, see *Strumaria*
Cape star, see *Spiloxene*

Cape tulip, see *Moraea* (*Homeria* group)
chincherinchee, see *Ornithogalum*
climbing onion, see *Bowiea*
clivia, see *Clivia*
clockflower, see *Moraea* (*Galaxia* group)
cobra lily, see *Chasmanthe*
combflower, see *Micranthus*
cottonseed, see *Eriospermum*
cowslip, Cape, see *Lachenalia*
crocus, Cape, see *Syringodea*
cup-and-saucer, see *Androcymbium*
devia, see *Devia*
dietes, see *Dietes*
fairy bells, see *Melasphaerula*
fairy pipes, see *Xenoscapa*
fairy snowdrop, see *Drimia uniflora* (*Drimia* group *Litanthus*)
fire lily, see *Cyrtanthus*
fly lily, see *Neopatersonia*
freesia, see *Freesia*
garlic, wild, see *Tulbaghia*
gladiolus, see *Gladiolus*
golden scepter, *Wachendorfia thyrsiflora*
grass, star, see *Hypoxis*
ground lily, see *Apodolirion*
hairbell, see *Dierama*
harlequin flower, see *Sparaxis*
hedgehog lily, see *Massonia*
hesperantha, see *Hesperantha*

hyacinth, Cape, see *Polyxena*
iris, peacock, see *Moraea*
iris, rush, see *Bobartia*
iris, spider, see *Ferraria*
iris, wood, see *Dietes*
ixia, see *Ixia*
kapok lily, see *Lanaria*
kukumakranka, see *Gethyllis*
lady's-hand, see *Cyanella*
lapeirousia, see *Lapeirousia*
lily, arum, see *Zantedeschia*
lily, beetle, see *Baeometra*
lily, belladonna, see *Amaryllis*
lily, blood, see *Scadoxus*
lily, blue, see *Agapanthus*
lily, butterfly, see *Wachendorfia*
lily, calla, see *Zantedeschia*
lily, candelabra, see *Brunsvigia*
lily, cobra, see *Chasmanthe*
lily, fire, see *Cyrtanthus*
lily, fly, see *Neopatersonia*
lily, ground, see *Apodolirion*
lily, hedgehog, see *Massonia*
lily, kapok, see *Lanaria*
lily, Malgas, see *Cybistetes*
lily, marsh, see *Crinum*
lily, mosquito, see *Neodregea*
lily, pagoda, see *Whiteheadia*
lily, paintbrush, see *Haemanthus*

lily, parasol, see *Crossyne*
lily, pig, see *Zantedeschia*
lily, pincushion, see *Daubenya*
lily, pineapple, see *Eucomis*
lily, poison, see *Drimia* (*Tenicroa* group)
lily, potato, see *Walleria*
lily, powderpuff, see *Haemanthus*
lily, sand, see *Veltheimia*
lily, slime, see *Albuca*
lily, snake, see *Ornithoglossum*
lily, spider, see *Wurmbea*
lily, umbrella, see *Hessea*
little star, see *Pauridia*
Malgas lily, see *Cybistetes*
marsh lily, see *Crinum*
men-in-a-boat, see *Androcymbium*
moraea, see *Moraea* (*Moraea* group)
moraea, paper, see *Moraea* (*Gynandriris* group)
mosquito lily, see *Neodregea*
mountain pipes, see *Tritoniopsis*
nerine, see *Nerine*
onion, climbing, see *Bowiea*
onion, wild, see *Allium*
onion, wire, see *Drimia intricata* (*Drimia* group *Schizobasis*)
oxbane, see *Boophone*

pagoda lily, see *Whiteheadia*
paintbrush lily, see *Haemanthus*
painted petals, see *Lapeirousia*
paper moraea, see *Moraea* (*Gynandriris* group)
parasol lily, see *Crossyne*
peacock iris, see *Moraea*
phlox, water, see *Onixotis*
pig lily, see *Zantedeschia*
pillansia, see *Pillansia*
pincushion lily, see *Daubenya*
pineapple lily, see *Eucomis*
poison lily, see *Drimia* (*Tenicroa* group)
poison squill, see *Drimia*
potato lily, see *Walleria*
powderpuff lily, see *Haemanthus*
red-hot poker, see *Kniphofia*
romulea, see *Romulea*
rush iris, see *Bobartia*
sand lily, see *Veltheimia*
satinflower, see *Geissorhiza*
slime lily, see *Albuca*
snake lily, see *Ornithoglossum*
snakeroot, see *Dipcadi*
snowdrop, African, see *Drimia* (*Rhadamanthus* group)
snowdrop, fairy, see *Drimia uniflora* (*Drimia* group *Litanthus*)

spider iris, see *Ferraria*
spider lily, see *Wurmbea*
squill, see *Scilla*
squill, African, see *Ledebouria*
squill, poison, see *Drimia*
star, autumn, see *Empodium*
star, Cape, see *Spiloxene*
star, little, see *Pauridia*
star, thread, see *Moraea* (*Hexaglottis* group)
star grass, see *Hypoxis*
summer pipes, see *Thereianthus*
tallboy, see *Drimia*
thread star, see *Moraea* (*Hexaglottis* group)
tritonia, see *Tritonia*
tulip, Cape, see *Moraea* (*Homeria* group)
umbrella lily, see *Hessea*
water phlox, see *Onixotis*
watsonia, see *Watsonia*
wild garlic, see *Tulbaghia*
wild onion, see *Allium*
wine cup, see *Geissorhiza*; see also *Babiana rubrocyanea*
wire onion, see *Drimia intricata* (*Drimia* group *Schizobasis*)
wood iris, see *Dietes*